When should I travel to get the best airfare?
Where do I go for answers to my travel questions?
What's the best and easiest way to plan and book my trip?

frommers.travelocity.com

Frommer's, the travel guide leader, has teamed up with **Travelocity.com**, the leader in online travel, to bring you an in-depth, easy-to-use resource designed to help you plan and book your trip online.

At **frommers.travelocity.com**, you'll find free online updates about your destination from the experts at Frommer's plus the outstanding travel planning and purchasing features of Travelocity.com. Travelocity.com provides reservations capabilities for 95 percent of all airline seats sold, more than 47,000 hotels, and over 50 car rental companies. In addition, Travelocity.com offers more than 2,000 exciting vacation and cruise packages. Travelocity.com puts you in complete control of your travel planning with these and other great features:

Expert travel guidance from Frommer's - over 150 writers reporting from around the world!

Best Fare Finder - an interactive calendar tells you when to travel to get the best airfare

Fare Watcher - we'll track airfare changes to your favorite destinations

Dream Maps - a mapping feature that suggests travel opportunities based on your budget

Shop Safe Guarantee - 24 hours a day / 7 days a week live customer service, and more!

Whether traveling on a tight budget, looking for a quick weekend getaway, or planning the trip of a lifetime, Frommer's guides and Travelocity.com will make your travel dreams a reality. You've bought the book, now book the trip!

 Travelocity.com
A Sabre Company

Frommer's

Also available from Hungry Minds

the Unofficial Guide® to

San Francisco

3rd Edition

Joe Surkiewicz and Michelle Fama
with Richard Sterling

Hungry Minds™

Best-Selling Books • Digital Downloads • e-Books • Answer Networks • e-Newsletters
Branded Web Sites • e-Learning

New York, NY • Indianapolis, IN • Cleveland, OH

Please note that prices fluctuate in the course of time, and travel information changes under the impact of many factors that influence the travel industry. We therefore suggest that you write or call ahead for confirmation when making your travel plans. Every effort has been made to ensure the accuracy of information throughout this book, and the contents of this publication are believed correct at the time of printing. Nevertheless, the publishers cannot accept responsibility for errors or omissions or for changes in details given in this guide or for the consequences of any reliance on the information provided by the same. Assessments of attractions and so forth are based upon the author's own experience and, therefore, descriptions given in this guide necessarily contain an element of subjective opinion, which may not reflect the publisher's opinion or dictate a reader's own experience on another occasion. Readers are invited to write to the publisher with ideas, comments, and suggestions for future editions.

Your safety is important to us, so we encourage you to stay alert and be aware of your surroundings. Keep a close eye on cameras, purses, and wallets, all favorite targets of thieves and pickpockets.

Published by Hungry Minds, Inc.
909 Third Avenue
New York, NY 10022

Produced by Menasha Ridge Press
Cover design by Michael J. Freeland
Interior design by Michele Laseau

ISBN 0-7645-6578-8
ISSN 1096-522X

Manufactured in the United States of America

10 9 8 7 6 5 4 3 2

Contents

List of Maps

About the Authors and Contributors

JOE SURKIEWICZ has co-authored five titles in the *Unofficial Guides* series and written two guides to the best places to ride a mountain bike in the Mid-Atlantic states. Between book assignments, Joe is a legal affairs writer at *The Daily Record* in Baltimore, where he translates appellate court opinions into plain English and generally does his best to irritate the local legal establishment. He lives in Baltimore with his best friend and counselor, Ann Lembo. When not traveling or bicycling, they enjoy evenings curled up on the sofa with their black-and-white feline companion, Molly, to watch black-and-white movies starring 1930s film divas Barbara Stanwyck, Norma Shearer, and Jean Harlow.

MICHELLE FAMA, who headed up the extensive revision of this third edition, has globetrotted across East Africa and Asia, and is the author of two other guidebooks on the Philippines. She is currently a freelance travel writer based in New York City, but hopes some day soon to collect the heart she left in San Francisco while writing this book.

RICHARD STERLING wrote our sections on dining and night life. He is an author of and contributor to numerous cookbooks and guidebooks covering California, Latin America, and Asia. He is is well known in the Bay Area for his varied and eclectic accomplishments.

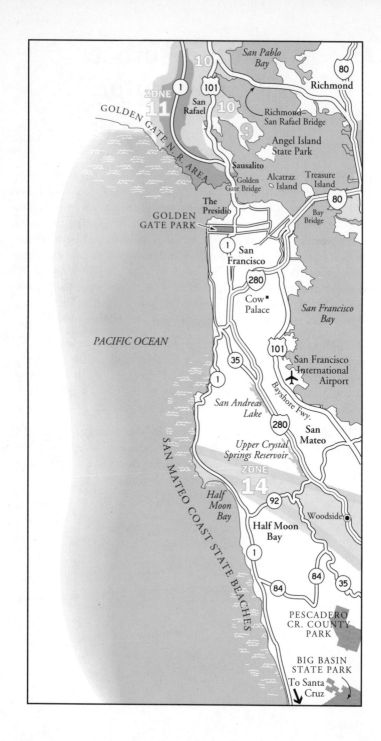

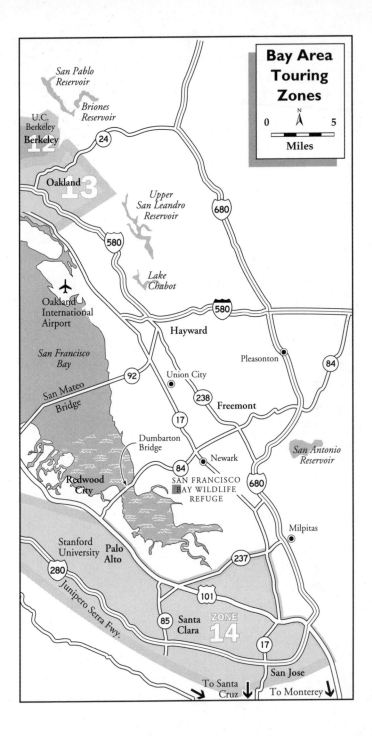

Bay Area Touring Zones

0 ⎪ N ⎪ 5
Miles

San Pablo Reservoir

Briones Reservoir

U.C. Berkeley
Berkeley *12*

Oakland *13*

24

Upper San Leandro Reservoir

680

580

Lake Chabot

Oakland International Airport

580

Hayward

San Francisco Bay

Pleasonton

84

San Mateo Bridge

92

Union City

238

Freemont

17

San Antonio Reservoir

Dumbarton Bridge

84

Newark

Redwood City

SAN FRANCISCO BAY WILDLIFE REFUGE

680

Milpitas

Stanford University

Palo Alto

280

Junipero Serra Fwy.

237

ZONE *14*

85 **Santa Clara**

101

17

San Jose

To Santa Cruz   To Monterey

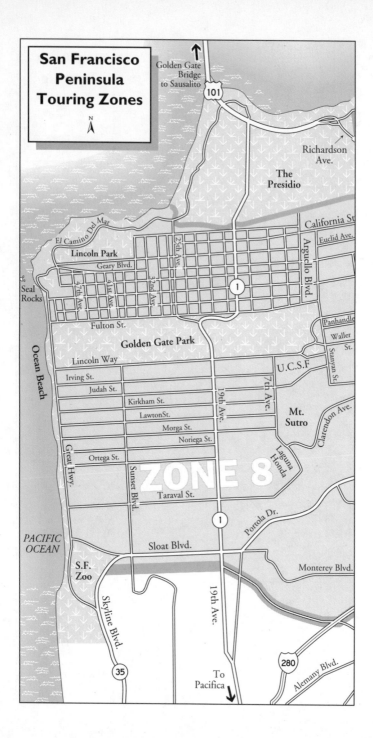

San Francisco Peninsula Touring Zones

N

Golden Gate Bridge to Sausalito

101

The Presidio

Richardson Ave.

California St.

El Camino Del Mar

Lincoln Park

Geary Blvd.

25th Ave.

Euclid Ave.

Arguello Blvd.

Seal Rocks

47th Ave.

41st Ave.

32nd Ave.

1

Fulton St.

Panhandle

Golden Gate Park

Waller St.

Stanyan St.

Lincoln Way

U.C.S.F

Irving St.

Judah St.

Kirkham St.

Lawton St.

Morga St.

Noriega St.

19th Ave.

7th Ave.

Mt. Sutro

Clarendon Ave.

Ocean Beach

Great Hwy.

Ortega St.

Sunset Blvd.

Laguna Honda

ZONE 8

Taraval St.

1

Portola Dr.

PACIFIC OCEAN

Sloat Blvd.

S.F. Zoo

Monterey Blvd.

Skyline Blvd.

19th Ave.

35

280

Alemany Blvd.

To Pacifica

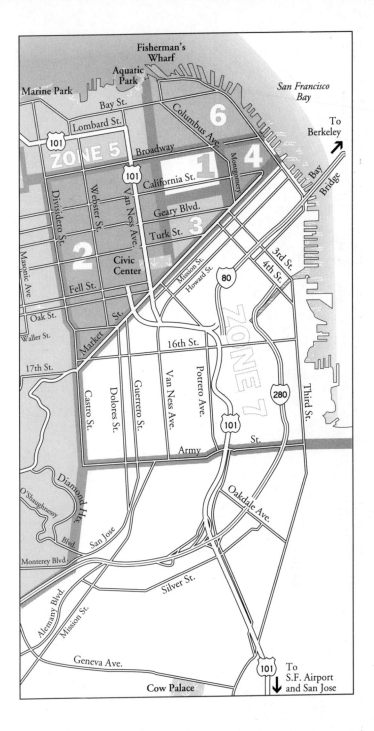

Zone 1 — Chinatown

ATTRACTIONS
1 Cable Car Museum

HOTELS
2 Fairmont Hotel
3 Holiday Inn Financial District
4 Huntington Hotel
5 Mark Hopkins Inter-Continental
6 Renaissance Stanford Court Hotel
7 Ritz-Carlton

RESTAURANTS
8 Carnelian Room
9 Palio D'Asti
10 Sam Who
11 Yuet Lee

NIGHTCLUBS
12 Li Po
13 Occidental Grill
14 Tonga Room
15 Top O' The Mark

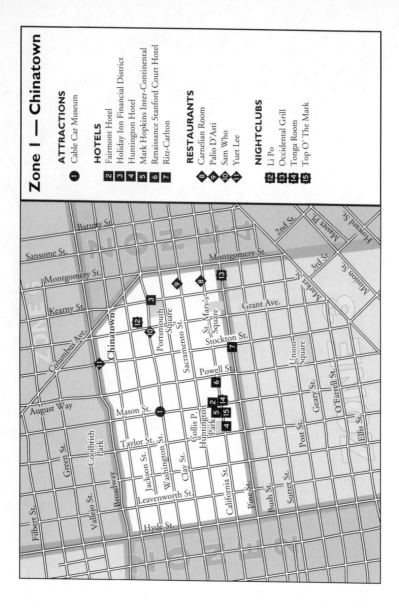

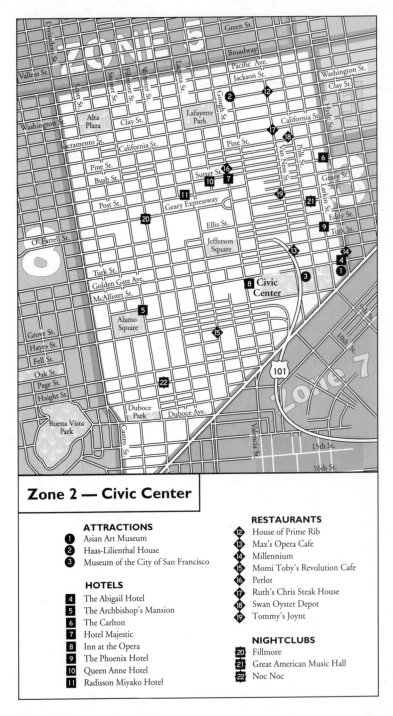

Zone 2 — Civic Center

ATTRACTIONS
1. Asian Art Museum
2. Haas-Lilienthal House
3. Museum of the City of San Francisco

HOTELS
4. The Abigail Hotel
5. The Archbishop's Mansion
6. The Carlton
7. Hotel Majestic
8. Inn at the Opera
9. The Phoenix Hotel
10. Queen Anne Hotel
11. Radisson Miyako Hotel

RESTAURANTS
12. House of Prime Rib
13. Max's Opera Cafe
14. Millennium
15. Momi Toby's Revolution Cafe
16. Perlot
17. Ruth's Chris Steak House
18. Swan Oyster Depot
19. Tommy's Joynt

NIGHTCLUBS
20. Fillmore
21. Great American Music Hall
22. Noc Noc

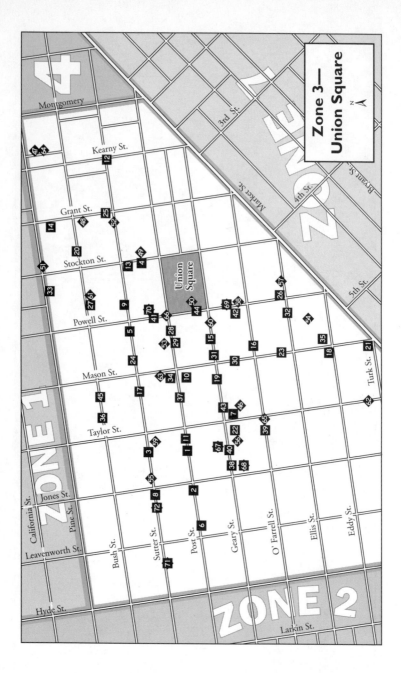

Zone 3—
Union Square

Zone 3 — Union Square

HOTELS

1. Andrews Hotel
2. Beresford Arms
3. Best Western Canterbury Hotel
4. Campton Place Hotel
5. Cartwright Hotel
6. Clarion Bedford Hotel
7. Clift Hotel
8. Commodore International Hotel
9. Crowne Plaza Union Square
10. The Donatello
11. The Fitzgerald
12. Galleria Park Hotel
13. Grand Hyatt San Francisco
14. Grant Plaza
15. Handlery Union Square Hotel
16. Hilton San Francisco
17. Hotel Beresford
18. Hotel Bijou
19. Hotel Diva
20. Hotel Juliana
21. Hotel Metropolis
22. Hotel Monaco
23. Hotel Nikko
24. Hotel Rex
25. Hotel Triton
26. Hotel Union Square
27. Hotel Vintage Court
28. Inn at Union Square
29. Kensington Park Hotel
30. King George Hotel
31. Maxwell Hotel
32. Monticello Inn
33. Nob Hill Lambourne
34. Pan Pacific Hotel
35. Parc Fifty Five
36. Petite Auberge
37. Prescott Hotel
38. Savoy Hotel
39. Serrano Hotel
40. Shannon Court Hotel
41. Sir Francis Drake Hotel
42. Villa Florence
43. Warwick Regis Hotel
44. Westin St. Francis
45. White Swan Inn

RESTAURANTS

46. Asia de Cuba
47. B-44
48. Cafe de la Presse
49. Campton Place
50. Compass Rose
51. Dining Room at the Ritz-Carlton
52. E&O Trading Company
53. Farallon
54. First Crush
55. Fleur de Lys
56. Grand Café
57. John's Grill
58. Kuleto's
59. Le Colonial
60. Lefty O'Doul's
61. Masa's
62. Original Joe's
63. Pacific Restaurant
64. Plouf
65. Ponzu
66. Scala's Bistro

NIGHTCLUBS

67. Biscuits & Blues
68. Blue Lamp
69. Gold Dust Lounge
70. Harry Denton's Starlight Room
71. The Plush Room
72. The Red Room

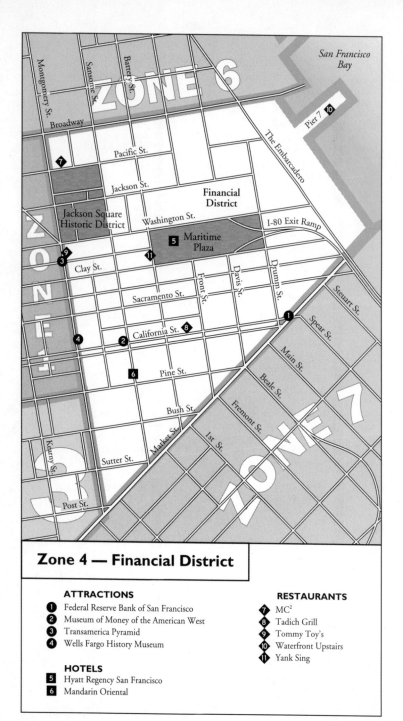

Zone 4 — Financial District

ATTRACTIONS
1. Federal Reserve Bank of San Francisco
2. Museum of Money of the American West
3. Transamerica Pyramid
4. Wells Fargo History Museum

HOTELS
5. Hyatt Regency San Francisco
6. Mandarin Oriental

RESTAURANTS
7. MC²
8. Tadich Grill
9. Tommy Toy's
10. Waterfront Upstairs
11. Yank Sing

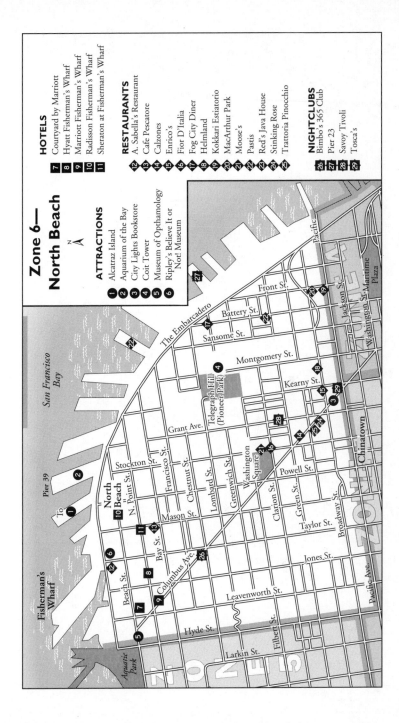

Zone 6—
North Beach

N

ATTRACTIONS

1. Alcatraz Island
2. Aquarium of the Bay
3. City Lights Bookstore
4. Coit Tower
5. Museum of Opthamology
6. Ripley's Believe It or Not! Museum

HOTELS

7. Courtyard by Marriott
8. Hyatt Fisherman's Wharf
9. Marriott Fisherman's Wharf
10. Radisson Fisherman's Wharf
11. Sheraton at Fisherman's Wharf

RESTAURANTS

12. A. Sabella's Restaurant
13. Cafe Pescatore
14. Calzones
15. Enrico's
16. Fior D'Italia
17. Fog City Diner
18. Helmland
19. Kokkari Estiatorio
20. MacArthur Park
21. Moose's
22. Pastis
23. Red's Java House
24. Stinking Rose
25. Trattoria Pinocchio

NIGHTCLUBS

26. Bimbo's 365 Club
27. Pier 23
28. Savoy Tivoli
29. Tosca's

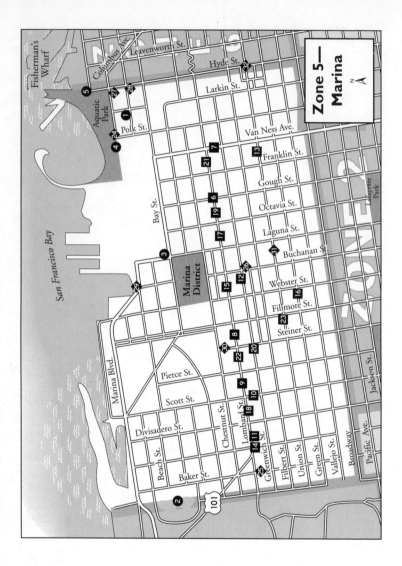

Zone 5—
Marina

N

Zone 5 — Marina

ATTRACTIONS

1. Ghirardelli Chocolate Manufacturoy and Soda Fountain
2. Palace of Fine Arts
3. San Francisco Craft and Folk Art Museum
4. San Francisco Maritime Museum
5. San Francisco Maritime National Historical Park—Hyde Street Pier

HOTELS

6. Buena Vista Motor Inn
7. Comfort Inn by the Bay
8. Cow Hollow Motor Inn and Suites
9. Days Inn Fisherman's Wharf
10. Edward II Inn
11. Marina Motel
12. Motel Capri
13. Pacific Heights Inn
14. Pacific Motor Inn
15. Ramada Limited Golden Gate
16. Sherman House
17. Star Motel
18. Super 8 Motel
19. Town House Motel
20. Travelodge Bel Aire
21. Travelodge by the Bay
22. Travelodge Golden Gate
23. Union Street Inn

RESTAURANTS

24. Ana Mandara
25. Baker Street Bistro
26. Brazen Head
27. Buena Vista Cafe
28. Gary Danko
29. Greens
30. Izzy's Steak and Chop House
31. Perry's
32. Zarzuela

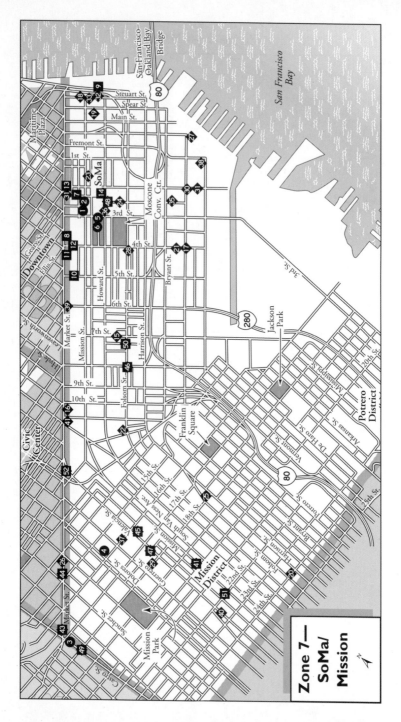

Zone 7—
SoMa/
Mission

Zone 7 — SoMa/Mission

ATTRACTIONS
1. California Historical Society
2. Cartoon Art Museum
3. Castro Theater
4. Mission Dolores
5. San Francisco Museum of Modern Art
6. Yerba Beuna Gardens/Center for the Arts

HOTELS
7. Argent Hotel San Francisco
8. Four Seasons Hotel and Residences
9. Harbor Court Hotel
10. Hotel Milano
11. Hotel Palomar
12. San Francisco Marriott
13. Sheraton Palace Hotel
14. W Hotel San Francisco

RESTAURANTS
15. Basque
16. Bistro Clovis
17. Bizou
18. Boulevard
19. Cosmopolitan Cafe
20. El Nuevo Fruitlandia
21. Fringale
22. Hamburger Mary's
23. Harpoon Loui's
24. Hawthorne Lane
25. Hung Yen
26. Johnfrank
27. LiveFire
28. Lulu
29. Luna Park Kitchen and Cocktails
30. Momo's
31. Paragon
32. Red Herring
33. Shanghai 1930
34. Sheraton Palace Garden Court
35. South Park Cafe
36. Thirstybear
37. Ti Couz
38. Town's End Restaurant and Bakery
39. Tu Lan
40. Watergate
41. Zuni Cafe and Grill

NIGHTCLUBS
42. Bruno's
43. The Café
44. Cafe du Nord
45. Cafe Istanbul
46. Cat Club
47. The Elbo Room
48. Gold Club
49. Harvey's
50. Julie's Supper Club
51. Make-Out Room
52. Martunis

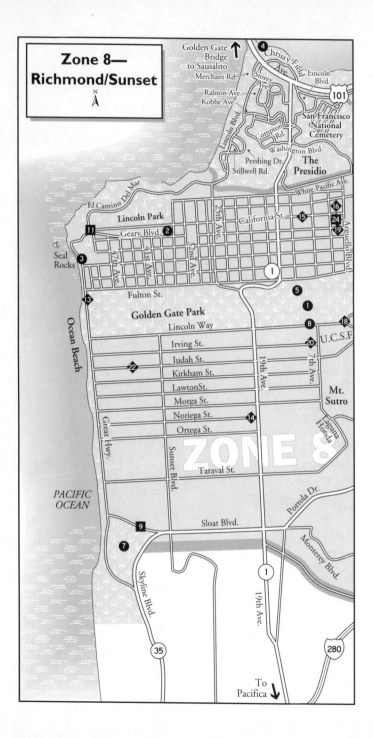

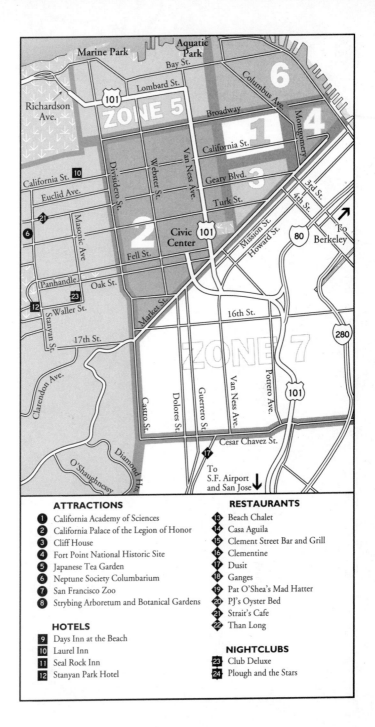

ATTRACTIONS

1. California Academy of Sciences
2. California Palace of the Legion of Honor
3. Cliff House
4. Fort Point National Historic Site
5. Japanese Tea Garden
6. Neptune Society Columbarium
7. San Francisco Zoo
8. Strybing Arboretum and Botanical Gardens

HOTELS

9. Days Inn at the Beach
10. Laurel Inn
11. Seal Rock Inn
12. Stanyan Park Hotel

RESTAURANTS

13. Beach Chalet
14. Casa Aguila
15. Clement Street Bar and Grill
16. Clementine
17. Dusit
18. Ganges
19. Pat O'Shea's Mad Hatter
20. PJ's Oyster Bed
21. Strait's Cafe
22. Than Long

NIGHTCLUBS

23. Club Deluxe
24. Plough and the Stars

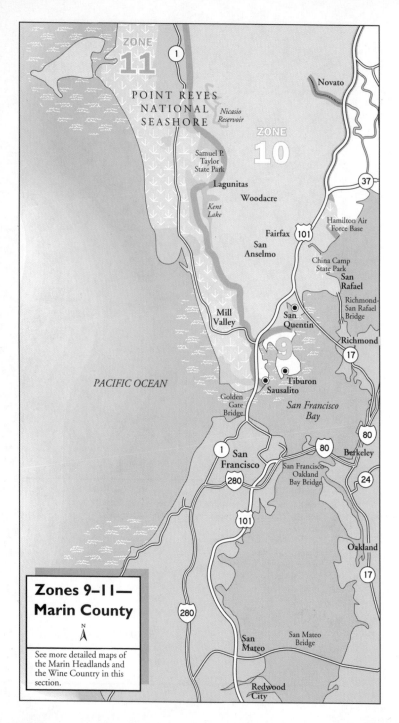

ZONE
11

1

POINT REYES
NATIONAL
SEASHORE

Nicasio
Reservoir

ZONE
10

Novato

37

Samuel P.
Taylor
State Park

Lagunitas

Woodacre

Kent
Lake

Fairfax

San
Anselmo

101

Hamilton Air
Force Base

China Camp
State Park

**San
Rafael**

Richmond-
San Rafael
Bridge

**Mill
Valley**

San
Quentin

9

Richmond

17

PACIFIC OCEAN

Tiburon
Sausalito

*San Francisco
Bay*

Golden
Gate
Bridge

80

1

**San
Francisco**

280

80

Berkeley

San Francisco
Oakland
Bay Bridge

24

Oakland

101

17

Zones 9–11—
Marin County

N

See more detailed maps of
the Marin Headlands and
the Wine Country in this
section.

280

San
Mateo

San Mateo
Bridge

Redwood
City

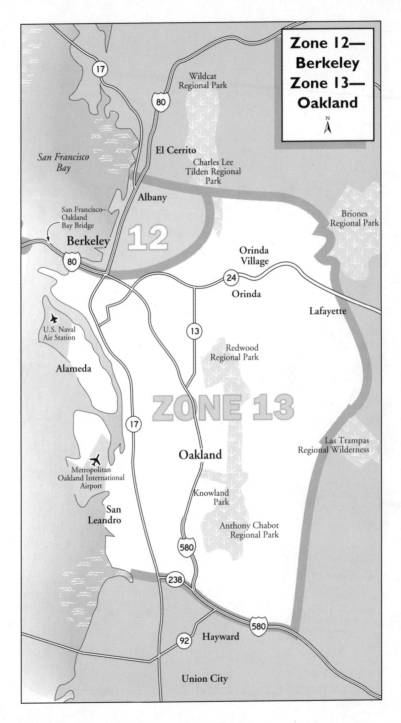

Zone 12—
Berkeley
Zone 13—
Oakland

N

17

Wildcat
Regional Park

80

El Cerrito

San Francisco
Bay

Charles Lee
Tilden Regional
Park

Albany

Briones
Regional Park

San Francisco–
Oakland
Bay Bridge

Berkeley

12

80

Orinda
Village

24

Orinda

Lafayette

U.S. Naval
Air Station

13

Redwood
Regional Park

Alameda

ZONE 13

Metropolitan
Oakland International
Airport

17

Oakland

Las Trampas
Regional Wilderness

San
Leandro

Knowland
Park

Anthony Chabot
Regional Park

580

238

92

Hayward

580

Union City

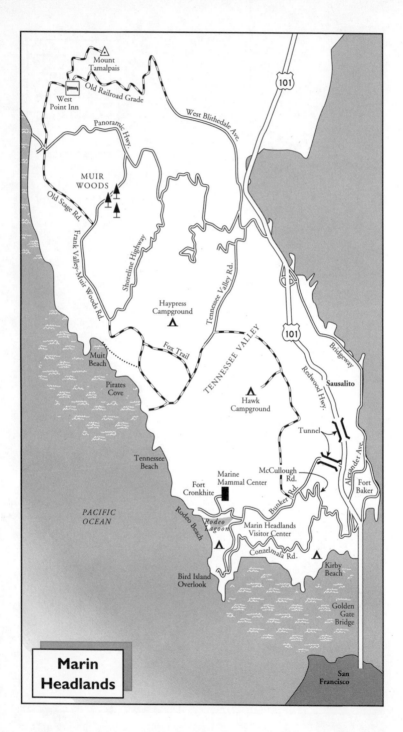

Mount Tamalpais

West Point Inn

Old Railroad Grade

West Blithedale Ave.

Panoramic Hwy.

MUIR WOODS

Old Stage Rd.

Frank Valley-Muir Woods Rd.

Shoreline Highway

Tennessee Valley Rd.

101

Haypress Campground

Fox Trail

TENNESSEE VALLEY

Bridgeway

101

Redwood Hwy.

Sausalito

Muir Beach

Pirates Cove

Hawk Campground

Tunnel

Alexander Ave.

Tennessee Beach

Marine Mammal Center

McCullough Rd.

Fort Baker

Fort Cronkhite

Bunker Rd.

PACIFIC OCEAN

Rodeo Beach

Rodeo Lagoon

Marin Headlands Visitor Center

Conzelmala Rd.

Bird Island Overlook

Kirby Beach

Golden Gate Bridge

Marin Headlands

San Francisco

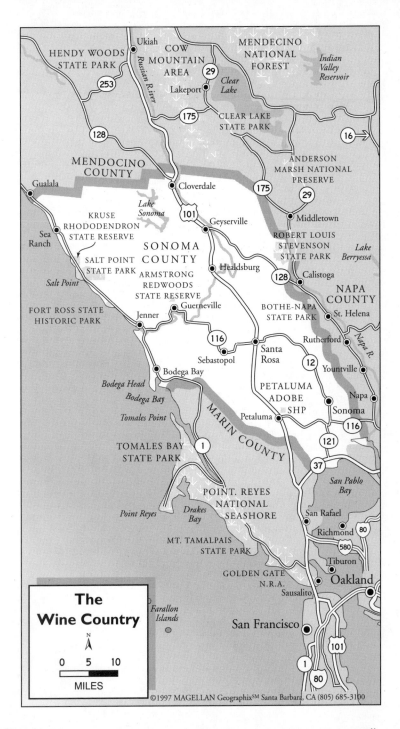

The Wine Country

N

0 5 10

MILES

©1997 MAGELLAN Geographix℠ Santa Barbara, CA (805) 685-3100

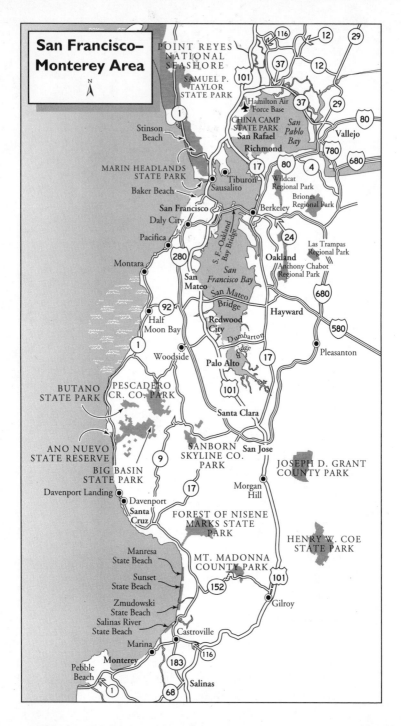

San Francisco–Monterey Area

POINT REYES NATIONAL SEASHORE
SAMUEL P. TAYLOR STATE PARK
Hamilton Air Force Base
CHINA CAMP STATE PARK
San Rafael
Richmond
San Pablo Bay
Vallejo
Stinson Beach
MARIN HEADLANDS STATE PARK
Tiburon
Sausalito
Baker Beach
Wildcat Regional Park
Briones Regional Park
San Francisco
Daly City
Berkeley
S. F.–Oakland Bay Bridge
Oakland
Anthony Chabot Regional Park
Las Trampas Regional Park
Pacifica
Montara
San Francisco Bay
San Mateo
San Mateo Bridge
Hayward
Redwood City
Half Moon Bay
Woodside
Dumbarton Bridge
Palo Alto
Pleasanton
PESCADERO CR. CO. PARK
Santa Clara
BUTANO STATE PARK
ANO NUEVO STATE RESERVE
BIG BASIN STATE PARK
SANBORN SKYLINE CO. PARK
San Jose
JOSEPH D. GRANT COUNTY PARK
Davenport Landing
Davenport
Santa Cruz
Morgan Hill
FOREST OF NISENE MARKS STATE PARK
HENRY W. COE STATE PARK
Manresa State Beach
MT. MADONNA COUNTY PARK
Sunset State Beach
Zmudowski State Beach
Salinas River State Beach
Castroville
Gilroy
Marina
Monterey
Pebble Beach
Salinas

Introduction

The City by the Bay: A Metropolitan Mecca

Face west. Yes, west—toward that revered and endeared bay city we call San Francisco. Gold diggers armed with little more than a pan and a dream pointed their wagons west to brave the new frontier. Westbound beatniks hitched rides with pockets full of poems, prepared for philosophical face-offs. Hippies happily hitched carrying all they could possibly want: a joint and a cause. Ivy League graduates hungry for opportunity headed west with an idea and a business plan—and made millions incidentally. East coasters with a desire for "more" (and better weather) packed up and settled here. And visitors looking for active or relaxing vacations have found everything they are looking for in one city—San Francisco, the Mecca of the West.

You won't find a single bit of bad press on San Francisco (San Fran for short, *never* Frisco). Sure, the boom fizzled and the lights may go dim from time to time, but this Paris of the Pacific, Athens of the West, Baghdad by the Bay, continues to leave the welcome mat out and the door unlocked for anyone desiring to experience its magical spirit and breath of opportunity.

The city never fails to live up to expectations. If thick afternoon fog has put a damper on your day, sunny skies await across any bridge. Not used to the towering buildings of downtown? Less than 20 minutes away, across the Golden Gate, are fat-tire trails, blazed hiking trails, cycling paths, romantic hideaways, and some of the best views in the country. There are certain things you can always count on in San Francisco—civil and cultural pride, cool summers, fog horns, hilly streets, mountain vista and ocean views, and sunny skies across both bridges (the Golden Gate and the Bay Bridge). You will put on and take off a sweater at least three times on any walk, so count on carrying one, as there are distinct pockets of climate in different areas. Maybe that's why visitors come year after year: San Francisco is different, diverse, and easy to love. Even its parameters are easy: 7 by 7 miles, which includes 43 steep hills! A simple formula for a simply enchanting place.

In spite of the gentrification that swept many of San Francisco's neighborhoods during the late 1990s, there still remains a strong mix of culture and cultural identity. The gateway to Asia, San Francisco supports a multicultural population of Chinese, Japanese, and Filipinos. And, lucky you, such cultural diversity brings an amazing assortment of culinary delights. For Dim Sum or the latest in Chinese herbal medicine, a stroll in Chinatown will cure any craving or cramp. Homemade ravioli is redolent through the streets of North Beach, the city's little Italy. For great Hispanic food, head on over to Cha Cha Cha's after perusing the vibrant art at the Mexican Museum. And what good is a city by a bay if it doesn't boast seafood? Alioto's and Scoma's at Fisherman's Wharf are musts for newbies! Adding to this cosmopolitan bouillabaisse is a gay population that may constitute as much as 25% of the city's total population. The neighborhoods of San Francisco overlap and interrelate, but they maintain distinct identities.

As a result of such strong cultural influences, the arts flourish here. The Mission District is a melting pot of public murals (more than 60 in an 8-block area). More organized venues exist as well: Fort Mason, where you can touch down artistically on three continents; museums showcasing Mexican, Italian American, and African-American culture; and a world-class opera house, symphony, and ballet company. Contemporary-art lovers will enjoy the Renaissance of SoMa, the Soho of San Francisco. The opening of the Museum of Modern Art and the Center for the Arts sparked a gallery boom South of Market (SoMa). Whether you like independent theater, poetry readings, or grand ole opera, it is all represented here. And no exploration of the city's arts would be complete without a perusal of Victorians. The houses line the steep hills of the city like trim on a wedding cake. A must do—to really take in the beauty of the homes, hills, and views that the city offers—is a drive down (and I mean down) Divisadero Street. This is just one of a bunch of vantage points that allow you, in one glance, to capture the beauty and enchantment of the city on film and on the spirit.

Europeans love San Francisco because it's the most European of American cities, and Hispanics gravitate to its Spanish-speaking community. San Francisco is home to one of the largest Chinese populations in the United States. Even tough-skinned and proud New Yorkers adore San Francisco, comparing it favorably with the Big Apple.

This book is designed for folks planning a solo getaway, a romantic escape, a visit to a friend or family member, or a family trip. It's for anyone who wants to see San Francisco's famous vistas, distinct neighborhoods, excellent museums, theater companies, and fabled night life; and it is also for business travelers who want to avoid its worst hassles. We show you the best times to visit San Francisco's best-known sights, how to get off the beaten path, and how to avoid the worst crowds and traffic. We suggest the best seasons to visit and offer detailed itineraries and touring strategies for seeing some spectacular destinations beyond the city limits.

In spite of the challenges it presents to first-time visitors, San Francisco never fails to charm. Like the joke says, San Francisco is everyone's favorite city—even to people who have never been there. Locals love their city and most enjoy sharing its attractions. With their help, and armed with this book, you're ready to discover the incomparable City by the Bay.

About This Guide

How Come "Unofficial"?

Just as the city of San Francisco inspires unconventional ideals and promotes individuality, so does the goal of the "Unofficial" series. Most "official" guides to San Francisco tout the well-known sights, promote the local restaurants and hotels indiscriminately, and leave out the nitty-gritty. This one is different. We'll be up-front with you. There is more than Fisherman's Wharf, after all. Instead of nabbing you by the ankles in a tourist trap, we'll tell you if it's not worth the wait for the mediocre food served at a well-known restaurant. We'll complain loudly about overpriced hotel rooms that aren't convenient to downtown or the Moscone Convention Center, and we'll guide you away from the crowds and congestion for a break now and then. We'll direct you to little known local joints and other unique experiences so you can earn bragging rights and satisfy your adrenaline craving.

We sent in a team of evaluators who toured downtown, its outlying neighborhoods and popular attractions, ate in the Bay Area's best and most unique restaurants, performed critical evaluations of the hotels, and visited San Francisco's best and most offbeat nightclubs. If a museum is boring or a major attraction is overrated, we say so—and, in the process, make your visit exactly that: *your* visit. We got into the guidebook business because we were unhappy with the way travel guides make the reader work to get any usable information. Wouldn't it be nice, we thought, if we made guides that were easy to use?

Other Guidebooks

Most guidebooks are compilations of lists. This is true regardless of whether the information is presented in list form or artfully distributed through pages of prose. There is insufficient detail in a list, and with prose the presentation can be tedious and contain large helpings of nonessential or marginally useful information. Not enough wheat, so to speak, for nourishment in one instance, and too much chaff in the other. Either way, other guides provide little more than departure points from which readers initiate their own quests.

Sure, many guides are readable and well researched, but they tend to be difficult to use. To select a hotel, for example, a reader must study several pages of descriptions with only the names of the hotels in bold type breaking up the text. Because each description essentially deals with the same variables, it is difficult to recall what was said concerning a particular hotel. Readers generally have no alternative but to work through all the write-ups before beginning to narrow their choices. The presentation of restaurants, clubs, and attractions is similar except that even more reading is usually required. To use such a guide is to undertake an exhaustive research process that requires examining nearly as many options and possibilities as starting from scratch. Recommendations, if any, lack depth and conviction. By failing to narrow travelers' choices down to a thoughtfully considered, well-distilled, and manageable few, these guides compound rather than solve problems.

How *Unofficial Guides* Are Different

While a lot of guidebooks have been written about San Francisco, very little has been evaluative. Most guides come close to regurgitating the hotels' and tourist offices' own promotional material. In preparing this work, however, nothing was taken for granted. Each museum, monument, art gallery, hotel, restaurant, shop, and attraction was visited by a team of trained observers who conducted detailed evaluations and rated each place according to formal criteria. Interviews were conducted to determine what tourists of all ages enjoyed most and least during their visit to San Francisco.

Readers care about the author's opinion. The author, after all, is supposed to know what he is talking about. This, coupled with the fact that the traveler wants quick answers (as opposed to endless alternatives), dictates that authors should be explicit, prescriptive, and, above all, direct. The *Unofficial Guide* tries to do just that. It spells out alternatives and recommends specific courses of action. It simplifies complicated destinations and attractions and allows the traveler to feel in control in the most unfamiliar environments. The objective of the *Unofficial Guide* is not to have the most information or all of the information; it aims to have the most accessible, useful information, unbiased by affiliation with any organization or industry.

An *Unofficial Guide* is a critical reference work that focuses on a travel destination that appears especially complex. Our authors and research team are completely independent from the attractions, restaurants, and hotels we describe. The *Unofficial Guide to San Francisco* is designed for everyone—couples, women, groups, or individuals traveling for fun, as well as for business travelers and convention-goers, especially those visiting the city for the first time. The guide is directed at value-conscious, consumer-oriented adults who seek a cost-effective, though not Spartan, travel style.

In compiling this guide, we recognize that tourists' age, background, and interests will strongly influence their taste in San Francisco's wide array of activities and attractions and will account for a preference of one over another. Our sole objective is to provide the reader with sufficient description, critical evaluation, and pertinent data to make knowledgeable decisions according to individual tastes.

Special Features

The *Unofficial Guide* incorporates the following special features:

- Friendly introductions to San Francisco's vast array of fascinating neighborhoods.

- "Best of" listings giving our qualified opinion on things ranging from bagels to baguettes, five-star hotels to the best views of San Francisco and the Bay Area by night.

- Listings keyed to your interests, so you can pick and choose.

- Advice to sightseers on how to avoid crowds; advice to business travelers on how to avoid traffic and excessive cost.

- A zone system and maps to find places you want to and avoid places you don't want to visit. The zones also make planning a day of touring easy on the legs and mind, as you can easily organize the city's sights.

- A hotel chart that helps narrow your choices fast, according to your needs.

- Shorter listings that include only those restaurants, clubs, and hotels we think are worth considering.

- A detailed index and table of contents to help you find things quickly.

How This Guide Was Researched and Written

While our observers are independent and impartial, they do not claim to have special expertise. Like you, they visited San Francisco as tourists or business travelers, noting their satisfaction or dissatisfaction.

The primary difference between the average tourist and the trained evaluator is the evaluator's skills in organization, preparation, and observation. The trained evaluator is responsible for much more than simply observing and cataloging. While the average tourist is engrossed when touring Alcatraz, for instance, the professional is rating the attraction in terms of pace, how quickly crowds move, the location of rest rooms, and how well children can see through the cellhouse windows to the San Francisco skyline across the bay. The evaluator also checks out other nearby attractions, alternatives places to go if the line at a main attraction is too long, and the best local lunch options. Observer teams used detailed checklists to analyze hotel rooms, restaurants, nightclubs, and attractions. Finally, evaluator ratings and observations were integrated with tourist reactions and the opinions of patrons for a comprehensive profile of each feature and service.

How Information Is Organized:
By Subject and by Geographic Zones

To give you fast access to information about the best of San Francisco, we've organized material in several formats.

Hotels   Because most people visiting San Francisco stay in one hotel for the duration of their trip, we have summarized our coverage of hotels in charts, maps, ratings, and rankings that allow you to quickly focus your decision-making process. We do not go on for page after page describing lobbies and rooms that, in the final analysis, sound much the same. Instead we concentrate on the variables that differentiate one hotel from another: location, size, room quality, services, amenities, and cost.

Restaurants   We provide a lot of detail when it comes to restaurants. Because you will probably eat a dozen or more restaurant meals during your stay, and because not even you can predict what you might be in the mood for on Saturday night, we provide detailed profiles of the best restaurants in and around San Francisco.

Attractions   There are those of you who love taking in all the sights and attractions, and those of you who are offended at the thought of taking a cable car to Fisherman's Wharf or Coit tower. OK, OK. We understand the needs of all our selective readers and, as such, have organized much of the city's sites into a handy time-saving chart divided by geographic zone. Gonna be in the Marina for dinner? Well, see what's in the area and organize your day accordingly. Saves you time, money, and foot ache!

Entertainment and Nightlife   Visitors frequently try several different clubs or nightspots during their stay. Because clubs and nightspots, like restaurants, are usually selected spontaneously after arriving in San Francisco, we believe detailed descriptions are warranted. The best nightspots and lounges in San Francisco are profiled by category under nightlife in the same section.

Geographic Zone   Once you've decided where you're going, getting there becomes the issue. To help you do that, we have divided the San Francisco Bay Area into geographic zones.

Zone 1	Chinatown
Zone 2	Civic Center
Zone 3	Union Square
Zone 4	Financial District
Zone 5	Marina
Zone 6	North Beach
Zone 7	SoMa/Mission, including Noe Valley and Potrero Hill
Zone 8	Richmond/Sunset
Zone 9	Tiburon/Sausalito
Zone 10	Suburban Marin
Zone 11	Marin Headlands to Point Reyes
Zone 12	Berkeley
Zone 13	Oakland
Zone 14	South Bay
	The Wine Country
	Oakland International Airport
	San Francisco International Airport

All profiles of hotels, restaurants, and nightspots include zone numbers. If you are staying at the Maxwell Hotel near San Francisco's Union Square, for example, and are interested in a steak dinner, scanning the restaurant profiles for restaurants in Zone 3 (Union Square) will provide you with the best choices.

Letters, Comments, and Questions from Readers

Do you have some issues with our suggestion for the best place to find a scoop of ice cream or cup of Joe to go, or did we overlook a well-known San Francisco institution? We want to hear from you! We expect to learn from our mistakes, as well as from the input of our readers, and to improve with each book and edition. Many of those who use the *Unofficial Guide* write to us asking questions, making comments, or sharing their own discoveries and lessons learned in San Francisco. We appreciate your input, both positive and critical, and encourage our readers to continue writing. Readers' comments and observations will be frequently incorporated into revised editions of the *Unofficial Guide* and will contribute immeasurably to its improvement.

How to Write the Authors

Joe and Michelle
The Unofficial Guide to San Francisco
P.O. Box 43673

Birmingham, AL 35243

UnofficialGuides@menasharidge.com

When you write by mail, be sure to put your return address on your letter as well as on the envelope—sometimes envelopes and letters get separated. And remember, our work takes us out of the office for long periods of time, so please forgive us if our response is delayed.

Our warmest welcome to San Francisco, the City by the Bay,

—Joe and Michelle

Part One

Planning Your Visit to San Francisco

Understanding the City: A Brief History of San Francisco

After New York City, San Francisco is the most densely populated city in the United States, with more than 720,000 people crowded on a 49-square-mile peninsula. Understanding why so many people choose to live here is easy: you never need a down-filled coat or shorts really, and the city serves as a backdrop to some of the most beautiful natural landscape on the planet! The Golden Gate Bridge is the Cindy Crawford of bridges, photographed widely for its red towering features above the misty fog that engulfs the city predictably every summer and early mornings. Make a turn down Marina Boulevard toward the bridge and you will certainly feel a sense of wonderment and peace at the surreal beauty that surrounds the city within and across the bridge. Mountains abound, scenic drives straight out of a video game with hairy cliff-side drops are everywhere, palm trees and parks punctuate the city . . . it is one of the most beautiful and interesting cities you will ever experience.

The Original Natives

The first Spanish settlers arrived just over 200 years ago. But for thousands of years before that, the Bay Area was occupied by Miwok, Ohlone, and Wituk Native American people, who lived across much of Northern California. They formed small villages and survived mainly by hunting and fishing. Not much is known about the earliest San Francisco natives, and the ecologically conscious can only imagine the kinds of lives these Native Americans enjoyed in this beautiful landscape.

One of the first colonists characterized the Indians as "constant in their good friendship and gentle in their manners." But without any political or social organization beyond the tribal level, it didn't take long after the first Spanish settlement was built for the local tribes to be wiped out, probably through epidemics rather than outright genocide. Today, no Bay Area Native Americans survive on their original homelands.

Early Explorers

As you drink in the view from Fort Point or the visitor center at the southern end of the Golden Gate Bridge, it's hard to imagine that ships cruising up or down the California coast could miss such an impressive sight. But they did. Dozens of European explorers, including heavy hitters such as Juan Cabrillo, Sir Francis Drake, and Sebastian Vizcaino, sailed past for centuries, oblivious of the great harbor beyond. Why? The opening is cloaked in fog for much of the year; even on clear days the East Bay hills rise behind the opening and disguise the entrance to the point of invisibility.

Sir Francis Drake may have come close. In 1579, while on a mission from Queen Elizabeth I to "annoy" the Spanish provinces, he passed by the bay's entrance. Like so many other explorers, he never saw it. Drake anchored his ship, the *Golden Hind,* just to the north and sent several landing parties ashore. He was met by a band of Miwoks who greeted him with food and drink; in return, Drake claimed their lands for Queen Elizabeth and named them Nova Albion (New England).

The first Europeans to cast their eyes on the Bay Area and the site of the future San Francisco were in a company of 60 Spanish soldiers, mule skinners, priests, and Indians led by Gaspar de Portola. The small contingent was the advance party of 300 soldiers and clergy on an overland mission from Mexico in 1769 to secure lands north of the colony for Spain and convert the heathens. Somewhere around Half Moon Bay, south of San Francisco, Portola sent out two scouting parties, one north up the coast and the other east into the mountains. Both groups returned with extraordinary descriptions of the Golden Gate—the entrance from the Pacific into the safe waters of the harbor—and the huge bay. On November 4 the entire party gathered on an exposed ridge, overwhelmed by the incredible view. Father Crespi, the priest, wrote that the bay "could hold not only all the armadas of our Catholic Monarch, but also all those of Europe."

First Settlement

It was another six years before the Spanish sent an expedition to explore the bay Portola had discovered. Juan Manuel de Ayala became the first European to sail into San Francisco Bay, in May 1775, when he piloted the *San Carlos* through the Golden Gate. A year later Captain Juan Bautista de Anza came back with 200 soldiers and settlers to establish the Presidio of San Francisco overlooking the Golden Gate. He also established a mission three miles to the southeast along a creek he named Nuestra Señora de Dolores—"Our Lady of Sorrows"—from which comes the mission's name, Mission Dolores. (It's the oldest building in San Francisco.)

Four more missions were established in the Bay Area in the following years. Each was similar, with a church and cloistered residence surrounded by irrigated fields, vineyards, and ranch lands. A contingent of soldiers protected the missions, many of which were attacked by Native Americans. To resist fire, the ubiquitous red-tiled roof replaced the thatched roof. By the end of the eighteenth century, the Bay Area settlements' population remained less than 1,000. Northern California was still a remote outpost and held little appeal for foreign adventurers. While the garrison was strong enough to resist Indian attacks, it would have easily fallen to attacks from the sea, had there been any.

Small towns, called "pueblos," were established to grow food for the missions and to attract settlers. The first, San Jose, was built in a broad, fertile valley south of Mission Santa Clara. Though considered successful, less than 100 inhabitants lived there until well into the 1800s. Another small village, not sanctioned by Spanish authorities, emerged between Mission Dolores and the Presidio around a deep-water landing spot southeast of Telegraph Hill. Called Yerba Buena, or "good grass" (after the sweet-smelling minty herb that grew wild on the nearby hills), it was little more than a collection of shanties and ramshackle jetties. Although not called San Francisco until the late 1840s, this was the beginning of the city.

Mexican Independence and American Settlers

In the 1820s, the Bay Area was still a remote backwater. The mission era ended with the independence of Mexico in 1821; in a few years the missions were secularized, and their lands were handed over to Californios—mostly former soldiers who had settled there after completing their service. The Mexican government hardly exercised any control over distant Yerba Buena and was more willing than the Spanish to let foreigners settle and remain.

In the early part of the decade, a number of Americans and Brits started to arrive in the Bay Area. Many were sailors who jumped ship—even in its toddler years, San Francisco attracted those souls seeking a better life! Other settlers came, started businesses and influenced the development of San Francisco into a major port town. William Richardson, for example, arrived on a whaling ship in 1822 and stayed for the rest of his life. He married the daughter of the Presidio commander, eventually owned most of southern Marin County, started a profitable shipping company, and ran the only ferry service across the treacherous bay waters.

While the locals were doing well by the 1840s, the Bay Area wasn't viewed as being rich in natural resources, and as a result it wasn't a major factor in international relations. In the 1830s the U.S. government decided to buy all of Mexico north of the Rio Grande, but nothing happened until June 1846, when the Mexican-American War broke out in Texas. U.S. naval forces quickly took over the West Coast—the fulfillment of the United States' "manifest destiny" to cover the continent from coast to coast—and captured San Francisco's Presidio on July 9.

At about the same time an interesting—although historically insignificant—event occurred north of San Francisco. An ambitious U.S. army captain, John C. Fremont, had been encouraging unhappy settlers to declare independence from Mexico and set him up as their leader. He assembled an unofficial force of about 60 sharpshooting ex-soldiers, spread rumors that war with Mexico was imminent, and persuaded settlers to join him. The result was the Bear Flag Revolt. On June 14, 1846, a force descended on the abandoned Presidio in Sonoma, took the retired commander captive, raised a makeshift flag over the plaza, and declared California independent. The flag, featuring a grizzly bear above the words "California Republic," was eventually adopted as the California state flag.

But the republic was short-lived. Three weeks after the disgruntled settlers hoisted the flag, it was replaced by the Stars and Stripes. California was now U.S. territory. Ironically, on January 24, 1848, just nine days before the U.S. government took formal control at the signing of the Treaty of Guadalupe (which ended the war with Mexico and ceded California to the United States), gold was discovered in the Sierra Nevada foothills 100 miles east of San Francisco. It changed the face of the city—and California—forever.

Sutter's Sawmill and the Gleam of Gold!

It all started with a sawmill. Contractor James Marshall and a work crew were commissioned to construct a sawmill for John Sutter, a Swiss immigrant whose Sacramento Valley ranch had been granted to him by the Mexican governor of California. On January 24, 1848, along the American River near Sacramento Marshall uncovered a few tiny gold nuggets. Sutter tried to keep the find under his cap, but word got out. Aided by a notice printed in *The Californian* in San Francisco, as well as more discoveries of gold by General John Bidwell, the great human migration west began. More than a half-million pioneering spirits from around the world descended upon California in search of instant wealth. By the end of May the editor of *The Californian* announced the suspension of his newspaper because the entire staff had quit. "The whole country from San Francisco to Los Angeles and from the sea shore to the base of the Sierra Nevada," he wrote, "resounds with the sordid cry of gold! GOLD! GOLD!—while the field is left half-planted, the house half-built and everything neglected but the manufacture of shovels and pickaxes." Before the year was over, more prospectors arrived from neighboring territories, Mexico, and South America.

At the time gold was discovered, the total population of the Bay Area was around 2,000, about a quarter of whom lived in tiny San Francisco (changed from Yerba Buena the year before). Within a year, 100,000 men, known collectively as Forty-Niners (now you'll have one correct answer to a sports trivia question—that's the origin of the modern-day football team's name) had arrived in California; it was one of the most madcap migrations in history. While many of the prospectors passed through San Francisco, few stayed long before moving on to the gold fields. About half made a three-month slog across the continent to get there. And once there, as reflected in an essay written by a gold-hopeful Mr. Chandler, they were "bound to stick awhile longer." The lure of fortune was irresistable. Others arrived by ship in San Francisco, which at that time consisted of a few shoddily constructed buildings, abandoned hulks in the harbor, and rats overrunning filthy streets; there was also a shortage of drinking water. But by the winter of 1850, the shanty-town settlement began to evolve into a proper city. Former miners set up foundries and sawmills to supply prospectors, while traders arrived to cash in on miners' success, selling them clothing, food, drink, and entertainment.

The city where successful miners came to blow their hard-earned cash now boasted luxury hotels and burlesque theaters, some of which featured the semiclad "spider dance" of Lola Montez—the famous femme fatale of the gold rush. Throughout the 1850s immigrants continued to pour into San Francisco. While many headed on to the mines, enough stuck around, to increase the city's population to about 35,000 by the end of 1853. More than half were foreigners, chiefly Mexicans, Germans, Chinese, and Italians.

Early comers to the gold fields made instant fortunes by merely washing nuggets out of streams or scraping gold dust from easily accessible veins in the rock, but it was much more difficult for later arrivals. The real money was being made by merchants, many of whom charged outrageous prices for essentials: $50 for a dozen eggs, $100 for a shovel or pickax. There were reports of exuberant miners trading a shot glass full of gold dust for an equal amount of whiskey—something like $1,000 a shot.

But the real necessities were buckets, shovels, dippers, and pans. Before long, those who supplied everyday items to prospectors were richer than the miners themselves. Levi Strauss, for instance, arrived from Germany to sell tents but ended up converting his supply of canvas into durable pants. Women, too, were in short supply. Hundreds of prostitutes boarded ships in Mexico and South America, knowing their fares would be paid on arrival by captains selling them to the highest bidder.

LOLALAND

She may have been a bad dancer—booed and hissed off stage most of her performing life—but she made history with her vicious temper, whip snapping, and bedroom antics. The infamous femme fatale of the Victorian age, Lola Montez stormed the gold rush in California for a fresh start after many marriages and a decade of seducing kings and czars across Europe in order to pursue her dream of becoming a respected performer and actress.

She opened a frontier saloon in a boisterous mining town called Grass Valley. Her act included Louis XVI cabinets, ormolu mirrors, priceless jewels from her ex-husbands, a pet bear, a swan bed, gold leaf, and one extra-large deep-red-top billiard table with dragons carved on its legs. With a bosom worth as much as the nuggets of gold and her crazy delusions of capturing California from the USA and becoming the Queen of "Lolaland," she attracted governors, senators, and millionaires.

The Gold Bust

Five years after the discovery of gold, the easy pickings were gone and the freewheeling mining camps evolved into corporate operations. San Francisco swelled from a frontier outpost to a bustling city with growing industry, a branch of the U.S. Mint, and a few newspapers. But when revenues from the gold fields leveled out in the late 1850s, the speculative base that had made so many fortunes dried up. Building lots that had been advertised at premium rates couldn't be given away, banks went belly-up, and San Francisco declared bankruptcy, following years of political corruption. The freewheeling city descended into near anarchy, and mobs roamed the streets. By the summer of 1856 the Committee of Vigilance was the city's de facto government and hanged petty criminals in front of enthusiastic mobs. Soon, though, cooler heads prevailed and the city was restored to legitimate governance. The rest of the 1850s was relatively uneventful.

Boom . . .

But whatever chance San Francisco had of becoming placid ended in 1859, when another torrent of riches flowed down the slopes of the Sierras. This time it was silver, not gold. The Comstock Lode, one of the most fantastic deposits ever discovered, was a solid vein of silver mixed with gold, ranging from 10 to more than 100 feet wide and stretching to more than 2 miles long. It would be an even bigger boom than the gold rush of a decade before.

Most of the silver, however, was buried several hundred feet underground, and mining it would be nothing like the freelance prospecting of the early gold rush. Many of San Francisco's great engineers, including George Hearst, Andrew Hallidie, and Adolf Sutro, put their talents to the formidable task. As the mines went deeper to get at the valuable ore, the mining companies needed larger infusions of capital, which they attracted by issuing shares dealt on the San Francisco Stock Exchange. Speculation was rampant, and the value of shares vacillated wildly, depending on daily rumors and forecasts. Fortunes were made and lost in a day's trading; cagier speculators made millions. By 1863 $40 million in silver had been wrenched from the tunnels around the boomtown of Virginia City, 105 miles from San Francisco, and 2,000 mining companies had traded shares on the city's mining exchange, further pumping up the city's economy.

. . . And Bust

While San Francisco enjoyed unsurpassed prosperity in the 1860s, another major development was taking place: the construction of a transcontinental railroad, completed in 1869. Although the trains opened up California, they also brought problems. The Southern Pacific ensnared San Francisco in its web, creating a monopoly over transportation in the Bay Area. Besides controlling long-distance railroads, the firm also owned the city's streetcar system, the network of ferry boats that crisscrossed the bay, and even the cable-car line that lifted rich San Franciscans up California Street to their Nob Hill palaces.

The coming of the railroad usurped San Francisco's role as the West Coast's primary supply point, and products began to flood in from the East well under prices that local industry could meet. At about the time the Comstock mines began to taper off, a depression set in. A series of droughts wiped out agricultural harvests, followed by the arrival of thousands of now unwanted Chinese workers who had built the railroads. As unemployment rose through the late 1870s, frustrated workers took out their aggression on the city's substantial Chinese population. At mass demonstrations, thousands rallied behind the slogan, "The Chinese Must Go!" For much of the late nineteenth century, San Francisco wrestled with problems of racism; the need to build a varied, stable economy; and corruption in city politics.

A Golden Age

At the beginning of the early twentieth century San Francisco was entering a golden age. The city now boasted a population of some 400,000 inhabitants—about 45% of the population of California (today it's about 4%). Political corruption was still a problem, but the economy was expanding—due in equal parts to the Spanish-American War and the Klondike Gold Rush in Alaska. Both events increased ship traffic in the port, where dockworkers were beginning to organize themselves into unions on an unprecedented scale.

The Great Earthquake

Civic reformers' efforts to reverse municipal abuses were well under way when one of San Francisco's most defining events occurred: the Great Earthquake of 1906. On April 18 the city was awakened by violent earth tremors. At 8.1 on the Richter scale, it was the worst earthquake to hit the U.S. before or since (over ten times as strong as the 1989 quake). While the earthquake, which lasted 48 seconds, destroyed hundreds of buildings, the postquake conflagration caused the most damage. Ruptured natural gas mains exploded and chimneys toppled, starting fires across the city that destroyed 28,000 buildings. Looting was rampant forcing the mayor to post his "Shoot to Kill" order. The fire raged for three days and all but leveled the entire area from the waterfront north and south of Market Street and west to Van Ness Avenue (where mansions were dynamited to form a fire break). Five hundred people were killed in the immense disaster and 100,000 were left homeless. Those who didn't flee the city made camp in what is now Golden Gate Park, where soldiers from the Presidio set up a tent city for about 20,000 displaced San Franciscans. Today you can pay tribute to one of the allies of the fight against total devastation—one fire hydrant that saved the Mission District from burning to the ground. The 1906 earthquake fire hydrant is on the corner of 20th and Church streets.

Recovery

Restoration of the ruined city began almost immediately. Financial assistance flooded in from around the world, $8 million in a few weeks. Even the hated Southern Pacific railroad pitched in, freighting in supplies without charge, offering free passage out of the city, and putting heavy equipment and cranes to work on clearing up rubble.

Much of the reconstruction was completed by 1912, and an era of political reform and economic restructuring was ushered in when James Rolph was elected mayor. The opening of the Panama Canal in 1914, which made the long sea journey around Cape Horn obsolete, and the first transcontinental phone call later that year (from Alexander Graham Bell himself), held great significance for San Francisco. The completion of the Civic Center and the opening of the Panama Pacific International Exhibition (which attracted 19 million visitors) were icing on the cake. The distant war in Europe had few repercussions in San Francisco beyond boosting the economy.

The Roaring Twenties and the Depression

Like most American cities, San Francisco prospered through the 1920s after recovering from a steep drop in employment after World War I. Financiers and industrialists erected the city's first skyscrapers, and the jazz clubs and speakeasies of the Barbary Coast District were in full swing. San Francisco, now completely recovered from the 1906 quake, was the West Coast's premier art and culture center—a role that it passed to Los Angeles in the next decade. It was also a major banking center; the Bank of America, headquartered here, became the largest bank in the world.

After the stock-market crash of 1929, San Francisco bore the full brunt of a recession that hit its port activities particularly hard. In 1934 one of the most severe strikes in its history broke out. On July 5—Bloody Thursday—police protecting strike-breakers from angry picketers fired into the crowd, wounding 30 and killing 2. The army was sent in to restore order; in retaliation, unions called a general strike, and 125,000 workers put down their tools, halting San Francisco's economy for 4 days.

It was also an era that saw some of the city's finest monuments take form—for example, Coit Tower. In 1933 Alcatraz Island became the site of America's notorious federal prison. But most importantly, two great structures over San Francisco Bay, the Golden Gate Bridge and the San Francisco–Oakland Bay Bridge, were built. Before the bridges opened, the Bay Area was served by an impressive number of ferry boats; in 1935, their peak year, 100,000 commuters crossed San Francisco Bay by boat each day. Just five years later, the last of the ferries was withdrawn from service, unable to compete with the new bridges.

World War II

Following Japan's attack on Pearl Harbor and the advent of World War II, San Francisco became the main military port on the Pacific; more than 1.5 million servicemen were shipped to the South Pacific from Fort Mason. New shipyards sprang up within months, the number of factories tripled, and the Bay Area was transformed into a massive war machine. The Kaiser Shipyards in Richmond, the largest shipbuilding facility, employed more than 100,000 workers on round-the-clock shifts.

Men and women poured into the region from all over the country for jobs in the plants. Today Hunters Point, one of the most economically distressed neighborhoods in San Francisco, and Marin City, one of its most affluent suburbs, are remnants of cities built to house the influx of workers who moved to the Bay Area during the war.

The 1950s: Emergence of a Beat Generation

Following the war, thousands of GIs returning from the South Pacific passed through San Francisco and many decided to stay. New neighborhoods such as Sunset, with massive tracts of look-alike housing, were formed, and huge highways were built. The postwar years broughtprosperity but also created a backlash. As the middle class moved out of the inner city, many of their offspring moved back in. North Beach bars and cafés incubated a wellspring of iconoclastic, anti-establishment youth in what was to become the Greenwich Village of the West Coast. Leading this movement was writer Jack Kerouac who, after the publication of the movement-defining book "On the Road," was asked by reporters to define the term "beat." He first heard the term a decade before his writing, from a rough-and-tumble 42nd Street–hustler who used the term to describe a state of exalted exhaustion. The novel was a classic story that broke open conformist 1950's America. The Beat Generation was news, and Kerouac had been officially dubbed its chief incarnation in human form. Beat with conventional America, this tribe was searching—on a quest for spiritual identity and vision—and many of them found clarity in San Francisco.

The Beat Generation rebelled against the empty materialism of the 1950s; many lost themselves in orgies of jazz, drugs, and Buddhism. The new counterculture also fostered a highly personal, expressive blend of prose and poetry. City Lights Bookstore in North Beach became the focal point for the new literary movement, which included poets Lawrence Ferlinghetti (the shop's owner who you can still spot in between book shelves—usually the poetry section) and the late Allen Ginsberg.

Psychedelic 1960s

By the early 1960s the steam was gone from the Beat movement. Shortly thereafter, though, an offshoot of the anti-establishment trend surfaced—the hippies. Originally the term was a Beat putdown for the inexperienced, enthusiastic young people following in the footsteps of their countercultural elders; the first hippies appeared on college campuses around San Francisco.

There was a difference, though. Hippies were experimenting with a new hallucinogenic drug called LSD (better known by its street name, acid). Around 1965, hippies began moving into communes in low-rent Victorian houses in the Haight-Ashbury District, west of the city's center. It was the beginning of flower power and would culminate in 1967's "Summer of Love," when 100,000 young people converged on the area.

Revolutionary Politics

While hippies tuned into psychedelic music by bands such as Jefferson Airplane, Big Brother and the Holding Company, and the Grateful Dead, across the bay, in Berkeley and Oakland, it was politics, not acid and acid rock, that topped the agenda. The Free Speech Movement began at the University of California, Berkeley campus, in 1964 and laid the ground for passionate protests against the Vietnam War in the Bay Area and around the country later in the decade.

The most famous protest took place in Berkeley's People's Park, a plot of university-owned land that local activists took over as a community open space. Four days later, an army of police under the command of Edwin Meese (later attorney general under U.S. President Ronald Reagan) tear-gassed demonstrators and stormed the park, accidentally killing one bystander and seriously injuring more than a hundred others.

In a response to the era's overt racism, in the impoverished flatlands of Oakland the Black Panthers emerged. Formed in 1966 by Bobby Seale, Huey Newton, and Eldridge Cleaver, the Panthers were a heavily armed but outnumbered band of activists who wanted self-determination for blacks. A nationwide organization sprung from the Oakland headquarters; 30 members across the country died in gun battles with police and the FBI.

Making Headlines: The 1970s and 1980s

Student unrest, antiwar protests, and flower power spilled over into the early 1970s, though at a less fevered pitch. One headline-grabbing event was the 1974 kidnapping of Patty Hearst, who was snatched from her Berkeley apartment by the Symbionese Liberation Army, a small, hard-core group of revolutionaries demanding free food for Oakland's poor in exchange for the rich heiress. Later on, during her captivity, Hearst helped the SLA and was photographed wielding a submachine gun in the robbery of a San Francisco bank.

Compared to the 1960s, most of the decade was quiet. The Bay Area Rapid Transit (BART) finally opened, and the Golden Gate National Recreation Area was established to protect 75,000 acres of incredibly scenic open areas on both ends of the Golden Gate Bridge. In 1973 the Transamerica Pyramid was completed, receiving mixed reviews from San Francisco critics; today it's a beloved piece of the city's skyline.

New battle lines were being drawn. The city's homosexuals, inspired by the 1969 Stonewall Riots in New York City, began to organize, demanding equal status with heterosexuals. Just as important, gays and lesbians "came out," refusing to hide their sexuality and giving rise to the gay liberation movement. One leader, Harvey Milk, won a seat on the city Board of Supervisors, becoming the first openly gay man to win public office in San Francisco. When he was assassinated in 1978 along with Mayor George Moscone, the entire city was shaken. A riot ensued when Milk's killer, former Supervisor Dan White, was found guilty of manslaughter and not murder.

In the 1980s, San Francisco's gay community retreated somewhat, hit by a staggering AIDS epidemic that toned down a notoriously promiscuous scene. The gay community, in conjunction with City Hall, continues to fight the disease.

During Mayor (now Senator) Diane Feinstein's term, San Francisco added millions of square feet of office towers to downtown's Financial District as some bemoaned the Manhattanization of the city.

There were also setbacks. A hundred million people watched on national TV as a 7.1 magnitude earthquake shook San Francisco during the third game of the 1989 World Series game between Bay Area rivals, the San Francisco Giants and the Oakland As; freeways collapsed, power was out for three days, and dozens were killed. Two years later a horrific fire in the Oakland hills killed 26 people and destroyed 3,000 homes. In the early 1990s, most of the problems San Francisco faced were similar to those in other American cities: urban poverty, drug abuse, homelessness, and AIDS. An ongoing economic turndown in California was amplified by post–cold war military cutbacks, which saw the closure of military bases in the Bay Area and the loss of 35,000 civilian jobs. But things were brewing about 30 miles south of San Francisco that would send the city into a mass of hysterics reminiscent of the flash and fortune during the gold rush era.

The Dot: RIP

Nothing defines the economic and social climate in San Francisco in the mid-1990s more than a dot. The "dot com," as the Internet industry became known, redefined the global economy and sent investors running like dogs to a bone. In this case, an apparent billion-dollar bone that in the end would prove to be bare for most investors and entrepreneurs alike.

The Nasdaq was at an all-time high, jobs were plentiful, and San Francisco more than any other city was riding high on the dot com coattails thanks to the technological revolution pouring out of neighboring Silicon Valley. Industrial Soma District became the hub of Internet companies, trendy bars, and elaborate bashes. Rents soared, neighborhoods became gentrified, and stock options landed in the laps of everyone from landlords to graduating nieces. It seemed that retiring at the ripe old age of 30 wasn't just a pipe dream, and a million dollars could be earned by anyone from the mail clerk to the janitor. Hopes were high, bank accounts overflowing, and Mercedes and BMW dealerships quite busy.

Then in April 2000 there was a crash that sent heads spinning, horses galloping, and doors slamming in the Internet industry. As hard as it tried, the dot com empire couldn't keep out impending profit loss, market devaluation, and ultimate downsizing. Pioneering fortune seekers were left in the rubble, sharing casualty stories at pink slip parties. Their inflated titles and salaries faced judgment day in front of a more frugal post–dot com market. Jobs were hard to come by, and as a result most returned from where they came, with their tails between their legs.

Today, with the drop of the dot bomb, the city is in a state of transition. The transition comes with mixed feelings, however. Some native

San Franciscans are happy to see the hype and prices fall, while others mourn the loss of the boom. In any case, vacancy signs in a once impossible real-estate market are swinging on chains outside buildings, rents are lowering, and the artistic community is seeing a revival. The face of technology is changing also and it is a matter of time before recovery comes full circle and a new trend surfaces.

When to Go: The Sweater Season and the . . . Well, Sweater (Wetter) Season

Maybe you haven't heard, but San Francisco isn't very warm—and summer is its coolest time. Yes, it's true. So right now you are probably staring stunned at your suitcase packed with tanks, sundresses, and (g-strings) thinking, "What the heck do I pack?" The answer is simple. Pack the fleece, *and* the tank. The City by the Bay is in fact just that—a city by a bay—and it is regularly swept by winds from the water that surrounds it on three sides. Yet it boasts one of the most stable climates in the world. Daytime temperatures rarely venture more than 5° from the average 60°. Night temperatures rarely drop lower than 40°, and snow is virtually unheard of. This stable weather, however, can be quite frustrating. It is impossible to predict. With sunny rays beaming through your window you'll wake up like a cat that just had kittens and by the time you've showered and tied your shoes, the fog is thick enough to cut a door into and the temperature has turned chilly. We don't mean to sound like a nagging old grandmother, but dress in layers!

Now for the tank. Take a drive across any bridge and you'll feel a heat resurrection. The toes will start to uncurl and the hairs will flatten as all things simmer under the sun and heat that await in the East Bay, South Bay, and Marin County. Almost everywhere else in the Bay Area is warmer than San Francisco, especially in the summer, when Berkeley and Oakland bask in sunshine, and the wine country and surrounding valleys shrivel like prunes under the intense heat.

The Dry Season

Sorry-I'm-not-that-warm San Francisco has two kinds of weather: wet and dry. The dry season starts in April and usually lasts through October (and sometimes a week or two into November). If the virtually rainless months of July and August sound too good to be true, you're right. It is too good to be true. There's a catch—the city's fabled fog envelopes the city mornings and evenings during much of the summer, hovering over the Golden Gate and obscuring the bridge. But the fog usually burns off by noon or early afternoon—just in time for you to burn off that burrito by jogging, biking, or kayaking.

Summer is also the most crowded. If you're visiting in the summer don't be like the rest of the shivering shorts-clad tourists at Fisherman's Wharf—bring the sweater! The city can be decidedly unsummerlike, even in July and August, especially at waterside locales such as the Wharf, Fort Point, the ocean beaches, and the Golden Gate Bridge. A final note: when dense afternoon fogs roll in during the summer months, the temperature can drop as much as 20° in a matter of hours.

The Wet Season

Winter brings most of San Francisco's rainfall, usually starting sometime in November and continuing through March. Often the rain is quite torrential, especially in December and January. Yet daytime highs rarely plunge far below 60° and the lows hover in the mid-40s. Two days in a row without rain are rare on a winter trip to the city, but crowds are nonexistent and finding a convenient and reasonably priced hotel room is less of a hassle. And again, bring the sweaters.

The Shoulder Seasons

If you want to enjoy San Francisco when the weather is on its best behavior and want to avoid large crowds, you have two options: spring and fall. These are the favorite seasons of *Unofficial Guide* researchers. In May and June the hills are at their greenest and are covered with wildflowers. Yet rainfall is nearly nil and daytime highs average in the mid-60s. Crowds at major tourist attractions usually don't pick up until later in the summer, when families with children begin to arrive. September and October are San Francisco's warmest months. They're popular months with visitors, but they lack the big crowds that pack the city's attractions during the height of the summer season. Warm, cloudless days are the norm. As an added bonus, it's grape-harvesting season in the wine country, making a one- or two-day excursion to Napa or Sonoma imperative. These are the city's least foggy months (although many visitors don't seem to mind the fog).

Avoiding Crowds

In general, popular tourist sites are busier on weekends, and Saturdays are busier than Sundays. The summer season by far is the busiest time of year at most attractions. If Alcatraz is on your itinerary (and if you're a first-time visitor to San Francisco, it should be), call in advance for tickets on a weekday, and hit attractions at Fisherman's Wharf on the same day. On summer weekends the wharf is jammed with visitors.

Driving in San Francisco's rush-hour traffic is a true bang-your-head, bite-your-nails experience. The major arteries and bridges are very congested during rush hour. If you're driving to the city on a weekday, avoid hitting town between 7 a.m. and 9 a.m., and between 4 p.m. and 6 p.m. If you're driving in on a weekend, you're still not off the hook. Traffic in and around San Francisco on Saturday and Sunday afternoons sometimes exceeds weekday rush-hour intensity. One theory is that frisky San Franciscan's like to play and head to playgrounds outside of the city. Evidence of this is seen as cars toting surfboards, snowboards, bikes, kayaks, and ropes venture across the bridges. Another theory is that the region around the city, the fifth-largest in the country, registers a population of 6 million. On weekends many residents of San Jose, Berkeley, Oakland, and other towns nearby do what you would if you lived here. They drive to San Francisco. Try to arrive before noon on weekends and you'll miss the worst of the weekend crush.

How to Get More Information on San Francisco before Your Visit

For additional information on entertainment, sightseeing, maps, shopping, dining, and lodging in San Francisco, call or write:

San Francisco Convention and Visitors Bureau
Hallidie Plaza, 900 Market Street (Powell and Market Streets)
P.O. Box 429097, San Francisco, CA 94142
(415) 283-0177 or fax (415) 362-7323; www.sfvisitor.org

The Convention and Visitors Bureau's Visitor Information Center is in the Benjamin Swig Pavilion on the lower level of Hallidie Plaza at Market and Powell Streets. It's easy to find, and the center's multilingual staff can help answer any questions you may have. Hours are 8:30 a.m. to 5 p.m. The center is closed Easter, Thanksgiving, Christmas, and New Year's Day.

There are great websites that can help in your preparation. A few to check out include:

- www.sfstation.com for up-to-the-minute events and insider information.

- www.sfarts.org will give you the scoop on everything indy, contraversial, and artistic that's happening in all forms of art.

- www.sfchamber.com is your run-of-the-mill tourist information put out by the Chamber of Commerce. It's handy for maps and mainstream attractions.

- www.sfgate.com is a branch of the newspaper, the *Chronicle*. Great place for current events and activities, as well as jobs (if the city inspires you enough to move!).

- www.sfvisitor.org is valuable for a rundown of neighborhoods and maps.

- http://bayarea.citysearch.com is the San Francisco leg of the popular "what to do and where to go" nationwide city guide.

- www.sonoma.com is your guide to everything wine in Sonoma County. Current info on Napa lodgings, dining, and tours.

Gays and Lesbians

In San Francisco, "the love that dare not speak its name" is expressed more freely than in any other U.S. city. San Francisco boasts the largest gay and lesbian population of any city in America, with some reports estimating that one quarter of its total population of 723,000 is gay. Hundreds of restaurants, hotels, shops, and other businesses and services are owned and operated by gays, who enjoy a high level of visibility, acceptance, and political clout in the community at large.

History

The roots of the city's large gay population and its live-and-let-live ambiance go back to the waning days of World War II, when the U.S. military began purging its ranks of homosexuals and suspected homosexuals, booting them out at the point of embarkation. This was often San Francisco, the major military stepping-off point. Many of the men, officially stigmatized, stayed in the Bay Area. Another migration occurred in the McCarthy era of the early 1950s, when the federal government dismissed thousands of homosexuals from their jobs. Persecution by the U.S. military and local police was common in the postwar years; in the early 1960s gays began organizing for their civil rights.

By the 1970s, an estimated one in four San Francisco voters was gay, and homosexuals were an influential minority group. It didn't hurt that gays tended to vote in larger numbers and contributed to political candidates who supported issues important to gays. As gays of the flower-power generation began moving in and restoring Victorian townhouses, Castro Street (formerly an Irish American neighborhood going to seed) became a flourishing enclave and the embodiment of the gay drive for acceptance.

In 1977 the Castro District elected Harvey Milk to the city Board of Supervisors. Milk, a gay activist who organized the district's merchants group, became the first openly gay city official elected in the United States. The drama of gay liberation heightened when former Supervisor Dan White, a former cop and the city's most anti-gay politician, assassinated Milk and pro-gay mayor George Moscone in City Hall in 1978. Six months later, after White was sentenced to only five years for the double murder, a mob marched on City Hall, drawing worldwide attention and headlines. (White, paroled in 1985, eventually committed suicide.)

In the 1970s San Francisco became notorious for its bar and bathhouse culture and the anonymous promiscuity that went along with it. But the reputation toned down after the AIDS tragedy struck early in the 1980s, causing more than 11,000 deaths in San Francisco. Socially, the city's gay scene mellowed in the 1990s, although gay bars, parades, and street fairs swing better than most.

The 1980s also saw a flowering of the city's lesbian culture that parallels the male upswing of the 1970s. Today, as in most American cities, the lesbian community is more subtle and less visible than the gay scene (but it's just as powerful politically). Much smaller than the Castro, the main lesbian community is concentrated around 16th and Valencia Streets in the Mission District, while larger lesbian communities are across the bay in Oakland and Berkeley.

In the late 1990s, the city's gays and lesbians have escaped the moral backlash provoked by AIDS in other parts of the country, thanks to San Francisco's tolerance and the gay community's support of people with AIDS and their survivors. Gays have, by and large, melded into the mainstream. Gay life is less ghettoized, and gay bars and clubs are scattered all over town. For years the city has had gay and lesbian political leaders, police officers, bureaucrats, and judges. It can be argued that one of the major aims of the gay liberation movement has been met—the acceptance of people regardless of whether they're gay or straight.

Gay Visitors

What does all this mean for gay and lesbian visitors to the city? By and large, you needn't concern yourself with fitting in during a visit to gay-friendly San Francisco. Take, for example, getting a room. While many hotels are gay-owned and cater to a gay clientele, the Bay Area's high level of tolerance just about guarantees that a visitor's sexual orientation—and the gender of his or her roommate—isn't going to be an issue at any hotel in or around San Francisco.

Before You Go

For up-to-the-minute information on the city's gay scene, check out www.timeout.com/sanfrancisco/gay/index.html. A good site for tours is www.sfgaytours.com

Gay and Lesbian Publications and Community Bulletin Boards

Numerous local newspapers and magazines in San Francisco cater to the gay and lesbian community. The largest and best-known are the *San Francisco Bay Times* (distributed every other Thursday; (415) 626-0260), *San Francisco Frontiers* (distributed every other Thursday; (415) 487-6000; www.frontiersweb.com) and the weekly *Bay Area Reporter* (distributed on Thursdays; (415) 861-5019; www.ebar.com); all are free and are distributed to bookstores, bars, and street vending boxes. The newspapers provide complete event calendars and resource listings for gays and lesbians.

Other publications include *Anything That Moves* (a quarterly magazine for bisexuals; (415) 626-5069; www.anythingthatmoves.com), *Drummer* (a gay leather and S/M webzine; www.drummer.com), *Girlfriends* (a monthly magazine for lesbians; (415) 648-9464; www.girlfriendsmag.com), *Odyssey* (a gay nightclub and listing guide published every other Friday; (415) 621-6514), and *Q San Francisco* (a "best of" guide for gays and lesbians; (415) 764-0324; www.qsanfrancisco.com). The *Gay Guide,* and *Betty and Pansy's Severe Queer Review* are more underground papers found at cafes throughout the Castro and the Mission. An excellent place to find these publications and others under one roof is at the bookstore **A Different Light** (489 Castro Street; (415) 431-0891).

The San Francisco gay and lesbian community has several information resources by phone. One of the more popular is the **Women's Building of the Bay Area** in the Mission District (phone (415) 431-1180). It's a clearinghouse for feminist and lesbian art, entertainment, and resource information; call from 9 a.m. to 5 p.m. weekdays.

Celebrate Gay Times: Top Gay Attractions

- AIDS Memorial Chapel and the Keith Haring Altarpiece in Grace Cathedral off of California Street, (415) 749-6300.

- The Names Project Visitor Center on Market Street is perhaps the most well known of all AIDS memorials. You can watch the panels being created and there are tons of informational videos on the making of the quilt and the meaning of the project. The local number is (415) 863-1966, and the national headquarters number in Atlanta is (404) 688-5500.

- Gay, Lesbian, and Transgender Pride Parade every June following Market Steet from the Civic Center to the Embarcadero is for the flamboyant, shy, family, couple … anybody wanting to express themselves for a day! Dykes on Bikes kicks off the celebration.

- Castro Street Fair in October is a scaled-down version of the Pride Parade. Costumes, shopping, and munching are all part of the festivities.

- A Different Light Bookshop (489 Castro Street, (415) 431-0891) stocks its shelves with mostly gay and lesbian literature by gay and lesbian authors.

- Hello Gorgeous! is a store that dedicates itself to the Diva of Divas: Barbara Streisand. Browse or undergo a makeover resembling her in any one of her movies.

- Theatre Rhinoceros (2926 16th Street, in the Mission at South Van Ness, (415) 861-5079) is the place to come for gay performance art.

- Bay to Breakers Race held in May is not just the largest foot race in the world, it's also the most fun you'll ever have on a Sunday afternoon! Come dressed up, although clothes are optional, bring the beer or margarita and race your way from Fremont Street to Ocean Beach.

- Cruisin' the Castro Tour with Trevor Hailey on Tuesdays through Saturdays (phone (415) 550-8110) takes you on a walking tour to all the sights of the Castro, highlighting history along the way.

Gay Neighborhoods

The traditional neighborhood for gay men has been the sprawling Castro, now more typified by prepped-up, well-heeled yuppies than the disheveled leftists and ex-hippies that symbolized the early days of the gay liberation movement. SoMa, the city's emerging art and nightlife district, features a gay enclave around Folsom Street; the look tends toward black leather and chains. Polk Street and the edges of the Tenderloin District is the tight-blue-jeans-and-pimps zone of young gay transients; it's not the safest part of town at 2 a.m. (or anytime—see below). An enclave of successful gay business executives resides in posh and proper Pacific Heights. Noe's 24th street, Bernal Heights, and Hayes Valley are San Francisco's newest lesbian/gay oriented neighborhoods. Just take a look inside Bernal's dyke bar Wild Side West—the oldest women's bar in the city.

While San Francisco is hands-down the most tolerant city in the country, gay bashing is still alive. Avoid open displays of affection in the Mission District, the largely Hispanic neighborhood where street gangs have attacked gay men. While the Polk Street area has a long gay history, it's now primarily a hustling scene with many bars and porn shops; it's a dangerous area, and more gay bashing is reported here than in any other part of the city.

Calendar of Special Events

San Francisco hosts a variety of annual special events throughout the year, including film, jazz and blues festivals, craft fairs, art festivals, street fairs, and ethnic festivals. Exact dates are subject to change, so be sure to call the number indicated if you are interested in attending. We've highlighted some not-to-be missed events that are true showcases of the cities vibrant arts, funk, and soul (look for the ★).

January

San Francisco Independent Film Festival Showcases the best of indy films and videos from the Bay Area and beyond. Various locations. (415) 931-3456.

MacWorld Expo Moscone Center Where better to see the latest in chips, bytes, and megahertz than San Francisco! (415) 974-4000.

Grand National Roadster Show San Mateo County Exposition Center. The show celebrates one of the biggest gatherings of roadsters and includes a NASCAR virtual-reality ride and vintage hot rods. (503) 236-0632.

San Francisco Sports and Boat Show Cow Palace Boats, fishing tackle, camping gear, and hunting equipment on display. (415) 931-2500.

Martin Luther King Jr.'s Birthday Celebration Yerba Buena Center for the Arts. A host of festivities highlight the city's commemoration of Dr. King's life. (510) 268-3777.

Chinese New Year Celebration The city's largest festival ends with a grand parade from Market and Second Streets to Columbus Avenue. (415) 391-9680.

February

San Francisco Tribal, Folk, and Textile Arts Show Fort Mason More than 100 folk and ethnic art dealers sell North American pottery, basketry, textiles, and jewelry. (310) 455-2886.

San Francisco Arts of Pacific Asia Show Fort Mason Exhibitors from around the world offer antiques and art from the Pacific-Asia region. (310) 455-2886.

San Francisco Orchid Society's Pacific Orchid Exposition Fort Mason An annual expo featuring dozens of floral collections. (415) 546-9608.

Sex Tour San Francisco Zoo. The zoo hosts its world-renowned Valentine's Day Sex Tour. The tours showcase the mating and courtship rituals of animals. Saturdays only. (415) 753-7165.

★ **California International Antiquarian Book Fair** Concourse Exhibition Center. World's largest rare book fair. (415) 551-5190.

March

★ **St. Patrick's Day Parade Downtown** The Irish have their day on this annual march from Fifth and Market to the Embarcadero. (415) 731-0924.

San Francisco International Asian-American Film Festival AMC Kabuki Theaters. The biggest ever in North America dedicated to the exhibition of Asian-American and Asian cinema. (415) 863-0814.

Bouquets to Art California Palace of the Legion of Honor Works by 100 floral designers, lectures by horticultural experts, luncheons, and tea service. (415) 750-3504.

★ **TulipMania** Pier 39, Fisherman's Wharf. View more than 40,000 brilliantly colored tulips from around the world. (415) 705-5500.

San Francisco Flower and Garden Show Cow Palace. 27 gardens, 300 market booths, orchid show, and 75 free seminars. (800) 829-9751.

KFRC Houlihan's 12K Race Sausalito to Fisherman's Wharf, is the largest run ever to cross the Golden Gate Bridge. It ends with a bang, at the post-race party at Fisherman's Wharf. 9 a.m. to noon. (415) 759-2690.

Whole Life Expo Concourse Exhibition Center. Nutrition, personal growth, alternative healing methods, and environmental issues fill the agenda. (415) 721-2484.

April

Street Performers Festival   Pier 39. All those eccentric, strange, and freaky street performers including comedians, jugglers, unicyclists, slack ropewalkers, and many more come in full force. (415) 705-5500.

Cherry Blossom Festival   Japantown. Taiko drumming, martial arts, Japanese food, and music highlight a parade from Civic Center to Japantown. (415) 563-2313.

★ **San Francisco International Film Festival**   (April through May) Various locations but mostly at the Kabuki and Castro Theaters. More than 100 films and videos from around the world. (415) 831-2783.

May

San Francisco Decorator Showcase   Pacific Heights. Top Bay-Area designers display the latest design innovations at luxurious San Francisco homes. (415) 447-3115.

Cinco de Mayo Celebration   Mission District. Arts, crafts, and food, as well as a parade to celebrate Mexican independence. (415) 826-1401.

San Francisco Youth Arts Festival   Golden Gate Park. Area students display their works. (415) 759-2916.

★ *San Francisco Examiner* **Bay to Breakers Footrace**   The Embarcadero to the Great Highway. Come sporting your birthday suit or whatever other costume you can muster up and take part in the world's largest footrace. Clothes optional, beer mandatory. (415) 808-5000.

Carnaval   Mission District. San Francisco's Mardi Gras with a parade, street festival, and costume contest. (415) 826-1401.

A Fair to Remember   Some big Hollywood names serve as honorary co-chairs of this upscale event, which features a bazaar, auction, and great food in Golden Gate Park. (415) 750-8340.

June

Art Deco Weekend by the Bay   Concourse Exhibition Center. The largest Art Deco–1960's sale in the country. (650) 590-DECO.

★ **Union Street Spring Festival Arts & Crafts Fair**   Union Street. Arts and crafts, wine, food, a waiter's race, tea dancing, a fashion show, street performers and a swing dance contest. (415) 441-7055.

Ethnic Dance Festival   Palace of Fine Arts Theater. Performances by 900 dancers and musicians showcase traditional dance and music from around the world. (415) 474-3914.

San Francisco International Lesbian and Gay Film Festival   Castro Theatre and other locations. The second-largest film festival in California showcases more than 100 films and videos from around the world. (415) 703-8650.

North Beach Festival   Grant Avenue and Green Street. San Francisco's oldest street fair offers arts, crafts, and live entertainment. (415) 989-6426.

Juneteenth Festival   Fillmore Street. An annual outdoor event celebrating African-American culture. (415) 229-1220.

Make a Circus   Parks throughout the city. Features a professional musical circus theater show, a circus skills workshop, and a performance by workshop participants. Shows begin at noon and last about three hours. Opening ceremonies are in Golden Gate Park. (415) 242-1414.

★ **Haight Street Fair**   Haight Street. Bring out the tie-dye and lava lamps—the Haight celebrates its roots with arts, crafts, and entertainment. (415) 661-8025.

★ **Lesbian, Gay, Bisexual, Transgender Pride Celebration Festival and Parade**   Castro District. San Francisco's celebration of lesbian and gay pride. (415) 864-FREE.

July

Fourth of July Waterfront Festival   Fisherman's Wharf. Snap, crackle, pop—it's not Rice Crispies but that childhood favorite—fireworks! Live entertainment, food, arts, and crafts. (415) 705-5500.

The Webby Awards   Hailed as the Oscars of the Internet, the presentations are made by the International Academy of Digital Arts and Sciences. It's the premier honor for websites—the ones that are still around that is! (415) 964-7400.

Cable Car Bell-Ringing Competition   Fisherman's Wharf. Where the cars come to belt out their favorite tune—operators clang out melodies on the car's bells and compete for top bell-ringer. (415) 923-6217.

Books by the Bay   The Embarcadero. Forty bookstore booths, author readings and signings, live music, and children's activities. (415) 927-3937.

Jewish Film Festival   Castro. Films from American and international filmmakers showcase Jewish culture. (415) 621-0556.

August

Afro Solo Arts Festiva   Yerba Center of Arts and other locations. Festival commemorating the African-American experience through solo performances. (415) 771-AFRO.

Nihonmachi Street Fair   Japantown and Japan Center. Lion dancers, taiko drummers, Japanese arts and crafts, music, food, and children's events. (415) 771-9861.

Golden Gateway to Gems   San Francisco County Fair Building. Minerals, crystals, and jewelry from all over the world. (415) 564-4230.

ACC Craft Fair   Fort Mason. The largest juried craft fair on the West Coast features necklaces, stoneware, silk scarves, quilts, and more. (800) 836-3470.

Comedy Celebration Day   Sharon Meadow, Golden Gate Park. It's a free funny-bone frenzy as comedians from Northern California's entertain for four hours; food, drink, and souvenirs. (415) 386-5035.

Renaissance Pleasure Faire   Blackpoint Forest, Novato. A trip back to Merry Olde England with 1,500 costumed performers, jousting knights, crafts, theater, dance, food, and drinks. (800) 523-2473.

September

Sausalito Art Festival   Sausalito. A top-rated fine arts festival with more than 20,000 original works of art from around the world. (415) 332-3555.

Blues Festival   Great Meadow, Fort Mason. The oldest blues festival in America presents some of the best blues musicians in the world. (415) 979-5588.

San Francisco Fringe Festival   Downtown. Marathon of 260 performances by 50 theater companies in various venues. (415) 931-1094.

★ **Absolut à la Carte**   A la Park, Golden Gate Park. Bring an empty stomach and an adventurous gastronomic appetite for this outdoor smorgasbord. Outdoor dining with 40 restaurants and chefs, 40 wineries and microbreweries, celebrity chefs, and music. (415) 478-BASS.

San Francisco Shakespeare Festival   Golden Gate Park. All of Shakespeare's classics. Pack a picnic lunch and those *Cliffs Notes* and enjoy during weekends at 1:30 p.m.; locals arrive by noon for a seat. (415) 422-2222.

Festival of the Culinary Arts   Polk and Turk Streets. Foodie block party outside the California Culinary Academy with chef demonstrations and yummies from all over the world. (415) 252-3640.

Autumn Moon Festival   Grant Avenue between California and Pacific Streets. Multicultural entertainment, traditional lion and dragon dances, Chinese costumes, and children's activities. (415) 982-6306.

★ **San Francisco Blues Festival**   Great Meadow, Fort Mason. The oldest blues festival in the country. (415) 979-5588.

Folsom Street Fair   Folsom Street. A popular fair with arts and crafts, kinky collectables, entertainment, and food. For obvious reasons it's for adults only! (415) 861-3247.

Ghirardelli Square Chocolate Festival   Ghirardelli Square. A chocolate lover's dream! Sample chocolate treats and more. (415) 775-5500.

San Francisco International Art Exposition   Fort Mason. Tons of galleries exhibit their collections, representing the world of over 1,500 artists, ranging from painting to drawing to sculpture to prints and video. (312) 587-3300.

October

Italian Heritage Parade and Festival   North Beach, Fisherman's Wharf. A commemoration of the city's Italian heritage with a parade through North Beach. (415) 989-2220.

Halloween   San Francisco Civic Center. Largest Halloween party in San Francisco featuring a laser show, a variety of music, dancing, and food. (415) 826-1401.

International Vintage Poster Fair   Fort Mason Center. The oldest and largest vintage poster fair in the world. (415) 546-9608.

November/December

Ghirardelli Square Annual Tree Lighting Ceremony   Ghirardelli Square. Deck the 35-foot Christmas tree with cheer and good tidings. (415) 775-5500.

Harvest Festival and Christmas Crafts Market   Concourse Exhibition Center. An arts and crafts fair for the holiday season. (707) 778-6300.

San Francisco International Auto Show   Moscone Center. The latest and greatest in automobiles. (415) 331-4406.

Christmas at Sea   Hyde Street Pier. Caroling, storytelling, hot cider, cookies, children's crafts, and Santa. (415) 561-6662.

San Francisco Ballet's *Nutcracker*   War Memorial Opera House. America's oldest ballet company, regarded as one of its finest, presents Tchaikovsky's beloved family classic every December. (415) 861-5600.

Hotels

Deciding Where to Stay

San Francisco hotels generally offer good values, interesting Pacific urban architecture and decor, and remarkably diverse amenities. As a generalization, service at San Francisco hotels, if not quirky, is somewhat differently defined. At the bar your drinks may not come any faster than they would at home, and your room-service breakfast may arrive cold. But ask the bartender or food server, "What should I do next?" and you're in for a spirited and opinionated discourse on the city.

The idea that information is the most valuable service a hotel can offer is novel in most cities. In San Francisco, however, hotels that don't even have room service or a bar may publish their own guidebooks and pamphlets on attractions, or they may have 24-hour concierge service. With 32% of San Francisco guest rooms scoring four stars or higher, the quality of guest rooms is exceptionally high. Plus, guest rooms in the Bay Area are reasonably priced. On average, rooms here are less expensive than rooms in New York City, Washington, D.C., Chicago, and other comparable destinations. This combination of high-quality rooms and reasonable rates makes San Francisco attractive for both leisure and business travelers.

Hotels dot the San Francisco peninsula and Bay Area suburbs, so you need not be more than ten minutes from tourist attractions or businesses. As in most cities, guest-room rates are higher in more desirable areas. The steepest rates are generally found within walking distance of Union Square, and some of the best hotel bargains are located in less fashionable neighborhoods. Of these, many have excellent on-premises security and may be of particular interest to those who plan to tour by car.

A distinctive characteristic of San Francisco's hotel scene is an artful marriage of historic architecture with modern interior design. Some of the city's hotels are modern, but the vast majority are housed in older buildings. Historic hotel buildings include some of the world's oldest skyscrapers and quaint Victorian and Edwardian mansions.

Step inside the nicer San Francisco hotels and you'll find some of the more inventive interior design you'll encounter in this country. Though palatial room size is not characteristic of San Francisco hotels, utilizing square footage wisely is. In both common areas and guest rooms, the *Unofficial Guide* hotel inspectors were impressed by how creatively form and function are blended. Several of San Francisco's nicest hotels have such ergonomically exact guest rooms that we were reminded of Tokyo. The comfortable integration of modern technology such as in-room fax machines, microwaves, and coffeemakers is noteworthy in guest rooms that are sometimes smaller than 200 square feet.

In San Francisco, you are more likely to find a guest room suited to your individual needs than in destinations where hotel homogeneity rules. The **Nob Hill Lambourne,** for example, offers a state-of-the-art, in-room treadmill and an honor bar with healthy foods for quite reasonable rates. Similarly, the **Hotel Triton** boasts 24 environmentally-sensitive guest rooms and suites designed by Jerry Garcia and nature artist Wyland.

The decor runs the gamut of historical and modern styles. Classic opulence, signaled by airplane hangar–sized lobbies, chandeliers the size of canoes, and richly textured upholstery can be found at hotels such as the **Fairmont** and the **Westin Saint Francis.** There is also an emphasis on modern interior decorating. Using elements of art deco, art nouveau, and modern art, the finished interior in the modern design style contains whimsically curved lines, bold patterns, and metallic and bright colors. You can see one of the best examples of this style at the **Hotel Diva,** where black and primary colors accent the theme of brushed chrome. Another is the newly renovated **Hotel Monaco,** which uses lush textures such as velvet and deep colors, including eggplant and ruby, to create a look of futuristic affluence.

San Francisco hotels market and cater to diverse groups, and hotel amenities and their ambience reflect this trend. While some properties target business or leisure travelers, others have more specific target markets. These include rock 'n' rollers—both professionals and fans—at the **Phoenix Inn,** opera fans at the **Inn at the Opera,** wine lovers at many Bay Area hotels, and spa junkies at others. Aspiring actors and film buffs will want to check out the **Hotel Bijoux,** which offers a small movie theater and a 24-hour hotline to current San Francisco film shoots and casting-call opportunities.

A Few Noteworthy Properties

San Francisco is home to a few noteworthy properties that we have not ranked and rated because their clientele is so narrowly defined.

Those wishing to relive the Summer of Love may want to stay at the **Red Victorian Bed, Breakfast, and Art Center.** Owned and run by veteran flower child Sami Sunchild, the bed-and-breakfast is in the heart of the historic Haight-Ashbury neighborhood. Each of its 18 rooms is decorated with a different theme, ranging from the Summer of Love room and the Rainbow room to the Japanese Tea Garden room and the Teddy Bear room, replete with 50 or so stuffed bears.

Guests of the "Red Vic" are encouraged to socialize at the breakfast table, and reclusive types may find this aspect of the bed-and-breakfast overwhelming if not downright annoying. Outgoing folks will probably have a lot of fun, as Ms. Sunchild conducts breakfast like a love-in; each guest is encouraged to tell the others where they are from and what they do for a living. Tip: if you make your living working for a right-wing political organization, conducting experiments that include vivisection, or designing weapons, you'll want to lie. When one guest told the group he was a social worker from New Zealand, Ms. Sunchild almost squealed with delight as she exclaimed, "See, we take care of the people who take care of the world!" Room rates at the Red Victorian Bed, Breakfast, and Art Center range from $96 to $200. For more information, call (415) 864-1978.

If you are looking for a bed-and-breakfast that touts itself as "welcoming diversity," you might try the **Hayes Valley Inn,** located in the Civic Center area at Gough and Hayes Streets. The owners pride themselves on catering to alternative lifestyles and making gay travelers feel at ease. Special rooms are provided for guests traveling with pets. Rates range from $68 to $114, with all rooms having shared baths in the hall. Call (415) 431-9131 for information and reservations.

House O' Chicks is a women's bed-and-breakfast in the Castro District. Two guest rooms share a bathroom; one guest room has a TV and VCR, the other has a stereo, and both have a homey atmosphere. Innkeeper Dorie Lane tells prospective guests that "it's like coming to a friend's house and she has a room all made up for you." Common areas include the living room, dining room, library, and kitchen, and all rooms contain original women's artwork. The innkeeper prefers to set room rates at the time of booking. Call (415) 861-9849 for information and reservations.

Most of the other hotels and bed-and-breakfasts in the Castro District are places where everyone will feel comfortable, though they are particularly convenient for gay travelers wishing to explore shops and clubs in the Castro area.

Edward II Bed and Breakfast offers three guest rooms with private entrances in a 1906 Edwardian mansion and has a strict nonsmoking policy. Call (415) 922-3000.

The **Delores Park Inn** has received various awards, offers four antique-furnished guest rooms and one suite, and is a favorite stay-over for visiting celebrities. It also has a strict nonsmoking policy. Call (415) 621-0482.

The **Castillo Inn** has four guest rooms that share one bathroom, and a two-bedroom suite at another location. This bed-and-breakfast on Henry Street in the heart of the Castro District is also strictly nonsmoking. Call (800) 865-5112.

By now you may be wondering, "Can't I just get a normal room in San Francisco?" The answer, of course, is yes. For those whose tastes tend to be more conservative, traditional hotel rooms are not hard to come by. But you will need to ask for what you want. In San Francisco, the difference between name-brand corporate hotels and freestanding, proprietary, or "boutique" hotels is not clearly delineated. This is because many of the corporate hotels in San Francisco occupy older buildings that once housed freestanding and family-owned hotels. Don't expect cookie-cutter guest rooms just because you're staying at your favorite name-brand hotel. If you prefer to stay in a rectangular room with the bathroom adjacent to the front door, two double beds, and a picture window opposite the front door, be sure to shop around.

Getting a Good Deal on a Room

Money-Saving Tips

To say that you receive good value for your lodging dollar in San Francisco doesn't mean that San Francisco is cheap. If you are looking for ways to save money beyond getting a discount on the price of a room, consider the following.

1. Stay in a less-than-fashionable neighborhood. San Francisco is made up of many distinct neighborhoods, and this emphasis on address reflects itself in pricing. Unless you need to be there for convenience, it may not be worth it to stay on Nob Hill when the same level of room in North Beach may be half the cost. The most expensive areas are Union Square and Nob Hill.

2. Seek a suite that includes a kitchen. Several hotels offer this option; suites can accommodate four or more people and help save on restaurant bills.

3. Stay at the worst room at a good hotel instead of the best one at a lesser hotel. Ask for the smallest room, lowest floor, worst view. The cost differential can be considerable, although the rest of the hotel services, amenities, and public rooms remain the same. You're getting the biggest bang for your buck.

4. Avoid room service and minibars. Bring food up from groceries, delis, or convenience stores. Or make like a resident and have a restaurant deliver (allowed at some hotels, frowned on at others—check first). Neighborhood restaurants, especially the "ethnics," are good and reasonable. If you eat like a local rather than a tourist, you will save money.

5. Skip the in-house movies. Bring a book. Better yet, walk down the street to see dramatic stories and sights beyond fiction.

6. Try a bed-and-breakfast. They are plentiful in the Bay Area and range from accommodations in houseboats and Victorian mansions to Junior's room when he's away at college. For information and options call Bed & Breakfast California at (800) 872-4500, or look up www.bbintl.com.

Getting a Discounted Rate

Because San Francisco is popular year-round, room rates tend not to fluctuate much. Even so, the market is highly competitive and there are deals for the smart shopper. Check out deals through ads, agents, special events, and openings. These include weekend and convention deals, frequent-mileage clubs, automobile or other travel clubs, senior rates (some with age requirements as low as 50 years), military or government discounts, corporate or shareholder rates, packages, long-stay rates (usually at least five nights), and travel industry rates. Some hotels might even give lower rates if you are visiting because of bereavement or medical problems. You can also try some of the following.

Surf the Net

Check out the Internet. Last-minute bargains are now available online. You can judge comparative value by seeing a listing of hotels—what they offer, where they are located, and what they charge.

Special Weekend Rates

Most hotels that cater to business, government, and convention travelers offer special weekend discount rates that range from 15% to 40% below normal weekday rates. Find out about weekend specials by calling individual hotels or consulting your travel agent.

Getting Corporate Rates

Many hotels offer discounted corporate rates (5–20% off rack rate). Usually you do not need to work for a large company or have a special relationship with the hotel to obtain these rates. Simply call the hotel of your choice and ask for their corporate rates. Many hotels will guarantee you the discounted rate on the phone when you make your reservation.

Others may make the rate conditional on your providing some sort of verification, for instance a fax on your company's letterhead requesting the rate, or a company credit card or business card upon check-in. Generally the screening is not rigorous.

Preferred Rates

If you cannot book the hotel of your choice through a half-price program (see below), you and your travel agent may have to search for a smaller discount, often called a preferred rate. A preferred rate might be a discount available to travel agents to stimulate their booking activity or a discount initiated to attract a certain class of traveler. Most preferred rates are promoted through travel industry publications and are accessible only through an agent.

We recommend sounding out your travel agent about possible deals. Be aware, however, that the rates shown on agents' computerized reservations systems are not always the lowest rates obtainable. Zero in on a couple of hotels that fill your needs in terms of location and quality of accommodations, and then have your agent call the hotel for the latest rates and specials. Hotel reps are almost always more responsive to travel agents because agents represent a source of additional business. Again, there are certain specials that hotel reps will disclose only to agents. Travel agents also come in handy when the hotel you want is supposedly booked. A personal appeal from your agent to the hotel's director of sales and marketing will get you a room more than half the time.

Half-Price Programs

Larger discounts on rooms (35–60%) in San Francisco or anywhere else are available through half-price hotel programs, often called travel clubs. Program operators contract with an individual hotel to provide rooms at deep discounts, usually 50% off, on a "space available" basis. Space available in practice means that you can reserve a room at the discounted rate whenever the hotel expects to be at less than 80% occupancy. A little calendar sleuthing to help you avoid special events and citywide conventions will increase your chances of choosing a time when these discounts are available.

Most half-price programs charge an annual membership fee or directory subscription rate of $25–$125. Once you're enrolled, you'll receive a membership card and a directory listing participating hotels. You will notice immediately that there are many restrictions and exceptions. Some hotels, for instance, "black out" certain dates or times of year. Others may offer the discount only on certain days of the week or require you to stay a certain number of nights. Still others may offer a much smaller discount than 50% off the rack rate.

Programs specialize in domestic travel, international travel, or both. More established operators offer members between 1,000 and 4,000 hotels in the United States to choose from. All of the programs have a heavy concentration of hotels in California and Florida, and most have a very limited selection of participating properties in New York or Boston. Offerings in other cities and regions of the United States vary considerably. The programs with the largest selections of San Francisco hotels are Encore, ITC-50, Great American Traveler, Quest, Privilege International, and Entertainment Publications. Each of these programs lists between 25 (Great American Traveler) and over 60 (Encore) hotels in the greater San Francisco area.

Encore	(800) 444-9800
Entertainment Publications	(800) 445-4137
ITC-50	(800) 987-6216
Great American Traveler	(800) 548-2812
Privilege International	(800) 236-9732
Quest	(800) 742-3543

One problem with half-price programs is that not all hotels offer a full 50% discount. Another slippery problem is the base rate against which the discount is applied. Some hotels figure the discount on an exaggerated rack rate that nobody would ever have to pay. A few participating hotels may deduct the discount from a supposed "superior" or "upgraded" room rate, even though the room you get is the hotel's standard accommodation. Though hard to pin down, the majority of participating properties base discounts on the rate published in the *Hotel & Travel Index* (a quarterly reference work used by travel agents) and work within the spirit of their agreement with the program operator. As a rule, if you travel several times a year, your room-rate savings will easily compensate you for program membership fees.

A noteworthy addendum: deeply discounted rooms through half-price programs are not commissionable to travel agents. In practical terms this means that you must ordinarily make your own inquiry calls and reservations. If you travel frequently, however, and run a lot of business through your agent, he or she will probably do your legwork, lack of commission notwithstanding.

Wholesalers, Consolidators, and Reservation Services

If you do not want to join a program or buy a discount directory, you can take advantage of the services of a wholesaler or consolidator. Wholesalers and consolidators buy rooms or options on rooms (room blocks) from hotels at a low, negotiated rate. Then they resell the rooms at a profit through travel agents or tour operators, or directly to the public.

Most wholesalers and consolidators have a provision for returning unsold rooms to participating hotels, but they are not inclined to do so. The wholesaler's or consolidator's relationship with any hotel is predicated on volume. If they return rooms unsold, the hotel may not make as many rooms available to them the next time around. Thus wholesalers and consolidators often offer rooms at bargain rates, anywhere from 15–50% off rack, occasionally sacrificing their profit margins in the process, to avoid returning the rooms to the hotel unsold.

When wholesalers and consolidators deal directly with the public, they frequently represent themselves as "reservation services." When you call, you can ask for a rate quote for a particular hotel or ask for their best available deal in the area you prefer. If there is a maximum amount you are willing to pay, say so. Chances are the service will find something that will work for you, even if they have to shave a dollar or two off their own profit. A list of services that sell rooms in San Francisco follows.

Accommodations Express	(800) 444-7666
Hotel Locators	(800) 576-0003
Central Reservations Service	(800) 548-3311
Hotel Reservations Network	(800) 964-6835
Travel Shop	(800) 458-6161
Quikbook	(800) 789-9887
RMC Travel	(800) 245-5738
San Francisco Reservations	(800) 677-1550

The discount available (if any) from a reservation service depends on whether the service functions as a consolidator or a wholesaler. Consolidators are strictly sales agents who do not own or control the room inventory they are trying to sell. Their discounts are determined by the hotels with rooms to fill and vary enormously, depending on how desperate the hotel is to unload the rooms. When you deal with a room reservation service that operates as a consolidator, you pay for your room as usual when you check out of the hotel.

Wholesalers have longstanding contracts with hotels; this allows the wholesaler to purchase rooms at an established deep discount. Some wholesalers hold purchase options on blocks of rooms, while others actually pay for rooms and own the inventory. Because a wholesaler controls the room inventory, it can offer whatever discount it pleases consistent with current demand. In practice, most wholesaler reservice discounts fall in the 10–40% range. When you reserve a room with a reservation service that operates as a wholesaler, you must usually pay for your entire stay in advance with your credit card. The service then sends you a written confirmation and usually a voucher (indicating prepayment) for you to present at the hotel.

Our experience has been that the reservation services are more useful for finding rooms when availability is scarce than for obtaining deep discounts. When we called the hotels ourselves, we were often able to beat the reservation services' rates when rooms were generally available. When the city was booked, however, and we could not find a room by calling the hotels ourselves, the reservation services could almost always get us a room at a fair price.

How to Evaluate a Travel Package

Hundreds of San Francisco package vacations are offered to the public each year. Packages should be a win-win proposition for both the buyer and the seller. The buyer has to make only one phone call and deal with a single salesperson to set up the whole vacation—transportation, rental car, lodging, meals, attraction admissions, and even golf and tennis. The seller, likewise, has to deal with the buyer only once, eliminating the need for separate sales, confirmations, and billing. In addition to streamlining sales, processing, and administration, some packagers also buy airfares in bulk on contract like a broker playing the commodities market. Buying a large number of airfares in advance allows the packager to buy them at a significant savings from posted fares. The same practice is applied to hotel rooms. Because selling vacation packages is an efficient way of doing business, and because the packager can often buy individual package components (airfare, lodging, etc.) in bulk at a discount, savings in operating expenses realized by the seller are sometimes passed on to the buyer. This means that, in addition to convenience, the package is an exceptional value. In any event, that's the way it is supposed to work.

In practice, all too often the seller cashes in on discounts and passes none on to the buyer. In some instances, packages are loaded with extras that cost the packager next to nothing but inflate the retail price sky-high. As you would expect, the savings to be passed along to customers do not materialize.

When considering a package, you should choose one that includes features you are sure to use; whether you use all the features or not, you will most certainly pay for them. Second, if cost is of greater concern than convenience, make a few phone calls and see what the package would cost if you booked its individual components (airfare, rental car, lodging, etc.) on your own. If the package price is less than the à la carte cost, the package is a good deal. If the costs are about the same, the package is probably worth buying just for the convenience.

If your package includes a choice of rental car or airport transfers (transportation to and from the airport), take the car if your hotel offers free (or at least affordable) parking. Take the transfers if you plan to spend your time in the area from Nob Hill and Union Square down to the San Francisco Bay. If you want to run around town or go on excursions outside the city, take the car. And if you take the car, be sure to ask if the package includes free parking at your hotel.

Tour operators, of course, prefer to sell you a whole vacation package. When business is slow, however, they will often agree to sell you just the lodging component of the package, usually at a nicely discounted rate.

Hotel-Sponsored Packages

In addition to tour operators, packages are frequently offered by hotels. Usually "land only" (i.e., no airfare included), the hotel packages are sometimes exceptional deals. Promotion of hotel specials tends to be limited to the hotel's primary markets, which for most properties is California, Washington, Oregon, Arizona, Hawaii, Nevada, Texas, Illinois, and New York. If you live in other parts of the country, you can take advantage of the packages but probably will not see them advertised in your local newspaper. An important point regarding hotel specials is that the hotel reservationists do not usually inform you of existing specials or offer them to you. In other words, you have to ask.

Helping Your Travel Agent Help You

When you call your travel agent, ask if he or she has been to San Francisco. If the answer is no, be prepared to give your travel agent some direction. Do not accept any recommendations at face value. Check out the location and rates of each suggested hotel and make sure the hotel is suited to your itinerary.

Because some travel agents are unfamiliar with San Francisco, your agent may try to plug you into a tour operator's preset package. This essentially allows the travel agent to set up your whole trip with a single phone call and still collect an 8–10% commission. The problem with this scenario is that most agents will place 90% of their San Francisco business with only one or two wholesalers or tour operators. In other words, it's the line of least resistance for them and leaves you with very little choice.

Travel agents will often use wholesalers who run packages in conjunction with airlines, such as Delta Vacations or American Airlines' Fly-Away Vacations. Because of the wholesaler's exclusive relationship with the carrier, these trips are easy for travel agents to book. However, they will probably be more expensive than a package offered by a high-volume wholesaler who works with a number of airlines in a primary San Francisco market.

To help your travel agent get you the best possible deal, do the following:

1. Determine where you want to stay in San Francisco, and if possible choose a specific hotel. This can be accomplished by reviewing

the hotel information in this guide and by writing or calling hotels that interest you.

2. Check out the hotel deals and package vacations advertised in the Sunday travel sections of the *Los Angeles Times, San Francisco Examiner,* or *Dallas Morning News* newspapers. Often you will be able to find deals that beat the socks off anything offered in your local paper. See if you can find specials that fit your plans and include a hotel you like.

3. Call the hotels or tour operators whose ads you have collected. Ask any questions you have about their packages, but do not book your trip with them directly.

4. Tell your travel agent about the deals you find and ask if he or she can get you something better. The deals in the paper will serve as a benchmark against which to compare alternatives your agent proposes.

5. Choose from the options that you and your travel agent uncover. No matter which option you select, have your agent book it. Even if you go with one of the packages in the newspaper, it will probably be commissionable (at no additional cost to you) and will provide the agent some return on the time invested on your behalf. Also, as a travel professional, your agent should be able to verify the quality and integrity of the deal.

If You Make Your Own Reservation

As you poke around trying to find a good deal, there are several things you should know. First, always call the specific hotel rather than the hotel chain's national, toll-free number. Quite often, the reservationists at the national number are unaware of local specials. Always ask about specials before you inquire about corporate rates. Do not be reluctant to bargain. If you are buying a hotel's weekend package, for example, and want to extend your stay into the following week, you can often obtain at least the corporate rate for the extra days. Do your bargaining, however, before you check in, preferably when you make your reservations.

HOTEL AND MOTEL TOLL-FREE NUMBERS

Best Western	(800) 528-1234 U.S. and Canada
	(800) 528-2222 TDD
Comfort Inn	(800) 228-5150 U.S. and Canada
	(800) 228-3323 TDD
Courtyard by Marriott	(800) 321-2211 U.S.
	(800) 228-7014 TDD
Days Inn	(800) 325-2525 U.S.
	(800) 329-7155 TDD

HOTEL AND MOTEL TOLL-FREE NUMBERS (continued)

Doubletree Hotels	(800) 222-8733 U.S. and Canada
	(800) 451-4833 TDD
Econo Lodge	(800) 424-4777 U.S.
Embassy Suites	(800) 362-2779 U.S. and Canada
	(800) 528-9898 TDD
Hampton Inn	(800) 426-7866 U.S. and Canada
	(800) 451-4833 TDD
Hilton	(800) 445-8667 U.S. and Canada
	(800) 368-1133 TDD
Holiday Inn	(800) 465-4329 U.S. and Canada
	(800) 238-5544 TDD
Howard Johnson	(800) 654-2000 U.S. and Canada
	(800) 654-8786 TDD
Hyatt	(800) 233-1234 U.S. and Canada
	(800) 228-9548 TDD
Marriott	(800) 228-9290 U.S. and Canada
	(800) 228-7014 TDD
Quality Inn	(800) 228-5151 U.S. and Canada
	(800) 228-3323 TDD
Radisson	(800) 333-3333 U.S. and Canada
	(800) 906-2200 TDD
Ramada Inn	(800) 228-3838 U.S.
	(800) 228-3232 TDD
Renaissance Hotels and Resorts	(800) 468-3571 U.S. and Canada
Ritz-Carlton	(800) 241-3333 U.S.
Sheraton	(800) 325-3535 U.S. and Canada
	(800) 329-7155 TDD
Wyndham	(800) 822-4200 U.S.

Hotels and Motels: Rated and Ranked

What's in a Room?

Except for cleanliness, state of repair, and decor, most travelers do not pay much attention to hotel rooms. There is, of course, a discernible standard of quality and luxury that differentiates Motel 6 from Holiday Inn, Holiday Inn from Marriott, and so on. In general, however, hotel guests fail to appreciate the fact that some rooms are better engineered than others.

Contrary to what you might suppose, designing a hotel room is (or should be) more complex than picking a bedspread to match the carpet and drapes. Making the room usable to its occupants is an art, a planning discipline that combines form and function.

Decor and taste are important, certainly. No one wants to spend several days in a room with a decor that is dated, garish, or even ugly. But beyond the decor, several variables determine how livable a hotel room is. In San Francisco, for example, we have seen some beautifully appointed rooms that are simply not well designed for human habitation. The next time you stay in a hotel, pay attention to the details and design elements of your room. Even more than decor, these will make you feel comfortable and at home.

It takes the *Unofficial Guide* researchers quite a while to inspect a hotel room. Here are a few of the things we check and suggest you check, too.

Room Size   While some smaller rooms are cozy and well designed, a large and uncluttered room is generally preferable, especially for a stay of more than three days.

Temperature Control, Ventilation, and Odor   The guest should be able to control the temperature of the room. The best system, because it's so quiet, is central heating and air-conditioning controlled by the room's own thermostat. The next best system is a room module heater and air-conditioner, preferably controlled by an automatic thermostat but usually by manually operated button controls. The worst system is central heating and air without any sort of room thermostat or guest control.

The vast majority of hotel rooms have windows or balcony doors that have been permanently sealed. Though there are some legitimate safety and liability issues involved, we prefer windows and balcony doors that can be opened to admit fresh air. Hotel rooms should be odor free and smoke free, and they should not feel stuffy or damp.

Room Security   Better rooms have locks that require a plastic card instead of the traditional lock and key. Card and slot systems allow the hotel to change the combination or entry code of the lock with each new guest. A burglar who has somehow acquired a conventional room key can afford to wait until the situation is right before using the key to gain access. Not so with a card-and-slot system. Though larger hotels and hotel chains with lock-and-key systems usually rotate their locks once each year, they remain vulnerable to hotel thieves much of the time. Many smaller or independent properties rarely rotate their locks.

In addition to the entry lock system, the door should have a deadbolt and preferably a chain that can be locked from the inside as well. A chain by itself is not sufficient. Doors should also have a peephole. Windows and balcony doors should have secure locks.

Safety   Every room should have a fire or smoke alarm, clear fire instructions, and preferably a sprinkler system. Bathtubs should have a nonskid surface, and shower stalls should have doors that open outward or slide side to side. Bathroom electrical outlets should be high on the wall and not too close to the sink. Balconies should have sturdy, high rails.

Noise   Most travelers have been kept awake by the television, partying, or amorous activities of people in the next room, or by traffic on the street outside. Better hotels are designed with noise control in mind. Wall and ceiling constructions are substantial, effectively screening routine noise. Carpets and drapes, in addition to being decorative, also absorb and muffle sounds. Mattresses mounted on stable platforms or sturdy bed frames do not squeak even when challenged by the most acrobatic lovers. Televisions are enclosed in cabinets and have volume governors so that they rarely disturb guests in adjacent rooms.

In better hotels, the air-conditioning and heating system is well maintained and operates without noise or vibration. Likewise, plumbing is quiet and positioned away from the sleeping area. Doors to the hall and adjoining rooms are thick and well fitted to better block out noise.

If you are easily disturbed by noise, ask for a room on a higher floor, off main thoroughfares, and away from elevators and vending machines.

Darkness Control   Ever been in a hotel room where the curtains would not quite meet in the middle? Thick, lined curtains that close completely in the center and extend beyond the edges of the window or door frame are required. In a well-planned room, the curtains, shades, or blinds should almost totally block light at any time of day.

Lighting   Poor lighting is a common problem in American hotel rooms. The lighting is usually adequate for dressing, relaxing, or watching television, but not for reading or working. Lighting needs to be bright over tables and desks, and beside couches and easy chairs. Since so many people read in bed, there should be a separate light for each person. A room with two queen beds should have individual lights for four people. Better bedside reading lights illuminate a small area, so if one person wants to sleep and another wants to read, the sleeper will not be bothered by the light. The worst situation by far is a single lamp on a table between beds. In each bed, only the person next to the lamp has sufficient light to read. This deficiency is often compounded by weak light bulbs.

In addition, closet areas should be well lit, and there should be a switch near the door that turns on room lights when you enter. A desirable but seldom seen feature is a bedside console that allows a guest to control all or most lights in the room from bed.

Furnishings   At a bare minimum, the bed(s) should be firm. Pillows should be made with nonallergenic fillers, and a blanket should be provided in addition to the sheets and a spread. Bedclothes should be laundered with fabric softener and changed daily. Better hotels usually provide extra blankets and pillows in the room or on request, and they sometimes place a second top sheet between the blanket and spread.

There should be a dresser large enough to hold clothes for two people during a five-day stay. A small table with two chairs, or a desk with a chair, should be provided. The room should be equipped with a luggage rack and a three-quarter- to full-length mirror.

The television should be color and cable-connected; ideally, it should have a volume governor and a remote control. It should be mounted on a swivel base and preferably enclosed in a cabinet. Local channels should be posted on the set, and a local TV program guide should be supplied. The telephone should be touch-tone and conveniently situated for bedside use, and it should have on or near it clear dialing instructions and a rate card. Local white and Yellow Pages should be provided. Better hotels install phones in the bathroom and equip room phones with long cords.

Well-designed hotel rooms usually have a plush armchair or a sleeper sofa for lounging and reading. Better headboards are padded for comfortable reading in bed, and there should be a nightstand or table on each side of the bed(s). Nice extras in any hotel room include a small refrigerator, a digital alarm clock, and a coffeemaker.

Bathroom   Two sinks are better than one, and you cannot have too much counter space. A sink outside the bath is a great convenience when one person bathes as another dresses. Sinks should have drains with plugs.

Better bathrooms have a tub and shower with a nonslip bottom. Tub and shower controls should be easy to operate. Adjustable shower heads are preferred. The bath needs to be well lit and should have an exhaust fan and a guest-controlled bathroom heater. Towels and washcloths should be large, soft, fluffy, and generously supplied. There should be an electrical outlet for each sink, conveniently and safely placed.

Complimentary shampoo, conditioner, and lotion are a plus, as are robes and bathmats. Better hotels supply tissues and extra toilet paper in the bathrooms. Luxurious baths feature a phone, a hair dryer, and sometimes a small television or even a Jacuzzi.

Vending   Complimentary ice and a drink machine should be located on each floor. Welcome additions include a snack machine and a sundries (combs, toothpaste) machine. The latter are seldom found in large hotels that have restaurants and shops.

Room Ratings

To distinguish properties according to quality, tastefulness, state of repair, cleanliness, and size of standard rooms, we have grouped the hotels and motels into classifications denoted by stars. Star ratings in this guide apply to San Francisco–area properties only and do not necessarily correspond to ratings awarded by Mobil, AAA, or other travel critics. Because stars carry little weight when awarded in the absence of commonly recognized standards of comparison, we have linked our ratings to expected levels of quality established by specific American hotel corporations.

★★★★★	Superior	Tasteful and luxurious by any standard
★★★★	Extremely Nice	What you would expect at a Hyatt Regency or Marriott
★★★	Nice	Holiday Inn or comparable quality
★★	Adequate	Clean, comfortable, and functional without frills (like a Motel 6)
★	Budget	Spartan, not aesthetically pleasing, but clean

Star ratings apply to room quality only and describe the property's standard accommodations. For most hotels and motels, a "standard accommodation" is a hotel room with either one king bed or two queen beds. In an all-suite property, the standard accommodation is either a one- or two-room suite. In addition to standard accommodations, many hotels offer luxury rooms and special suites that are not rated in this guide. Star ratings for rooms are assigned without regard to whether a property has restaurant(s), recreational facilities, entertainment, or other extras.

In addition to stars (which delineate broad categories), we also employ a numerical rating system. Our rating scale is 0–100, with 100 as the best possible rating, and zero (0) as the worst. Numerical ratings are presented to show the difference we perceive between one property and another. For instance, rooms at the **Fairmont Hotel,** the **Hotel Monaco,** and the **Westin Saint Francis** are all rated as four and a half stars (★★★★½). In the supplemental numerical ratings, the Fairmont Hotel is rated a 95, the Hotel Monaco is rated a 94, and the Westin Saint Francis is a 91. This means that within the four-and-a-half-star category, the Fairmont Hotel and Hotel Monaco are comparable, and both have slightly nicer rooms than the Westin Saint Francis.

The location column identifies the greater San Francisco area where you will find a particular property.

How the Hotels Compare

Cost estimates are based on the hotel's published rack rates for standard rooms. Each "$" represents $50. Thus a cost symbol of "$$$" means that a room (or suite) at that hotel will cost about $150 a night.

Below is a hit parade of the nicest rooms in town. We've focused strictly on room quality and have excluded any consideration of location, services, recreation, or amenities. In some instances, a one- or two-room suite can be had for the same price or less than that of a hotel room.

If you use subsequent editions of this guide, you will notice that many of the ratings and rankings change. In addition to the inclusion of new properties, these changes also consider guest-room renovations or improved maintenance and housekeeping. A failure to properly maintain guest rooms or a lapse in housekeeping standards can affect negatively the ratings.

Finally, before you begin to shop for a hotel, take a hard look at this letter we received from a couple in Hot Springs, Arkansas:

> We cancelled our room reservations to follow the advice in your book [and reserved a hotel room highly ranked by the Unofficial Guide. We wanted inexpensive, but clean and cheerful. We got inexpensive, but [also] dirty, grim, and depressing. I really felt disappointed in your advice and the room. It was the pits. That was the one real piece of information I needed from your book! The room spoiled the holiday for me aside from our touring.

Needless to say, this letter was as unsettling to us as the bad room was to our reader. Our integrity as travel journalists, after all, is based on the quality of the information we give our readers. Even with the best of intentions and the most conscientious research, however, we cannot inspect every room in every hotel. What we do, in statistical terms, is take a sample. We check out several rooms selected at random in each hotel and base our ratings and rankings on those rooms. The inspections are conducted anonymously and without the knowledge of the management. Although unusual, it is certainly possible that the rooms we randomly inspect are not representative of the majority of rooms at a particular hotel. Another possibility is that the rooms we inspect in a given hotel are representative, but that by bad luck a reader is assigned a room that is inferior. When we rechecked the hotel our reader disliked, we discovered our rating was correctly representative, but that he and his wife had unfortunately been assigned to one of a small number of threadbare rooms scheduled for renovation.

The key to avoiding disappointment is to snoop around in advance. We recommend that you ask for a photo of a hotel's standard guest room before you book, or at least get a copy of the hotel's promotional brochure. Be forewarned, however, that some hotel chains use the same guest-room photo in their promotional literature for all hotels in the chain; a specific guest room may not resemble the brochure photo. When you or your travel agent call, ask how old the property is and when your guest room was last renovated. If you arrive and are assigned a room inferior to that which you had been led to expect, demand to be moved to another room.

HOW THE HOTELS COMPARE IN SAN FRANCISCO

Hotel	Zone	Overall Quality	Room Quality	Cost ($=$50)
Four Seasons Hotel and Residences	7	★★★★★	98	$$$$$$$$$+
Mandarin Oriental	4	★★★★★	98	$$$$$$$$$$$$+
Pan Pacific Hotel	3	★★★★★	98	$$$$$$+
W Hotel San Francisco	7	★★★★★	98	$$$$$$$+
Campton Place Hotel	3	★★★★★	97	$$$$$$$+
Ritz-Carlton Half Moon Bay	14	★★★★★	97	$$$$$$$$–
Hotel Nikko	3	★★★★★	96	$$$$$$$–
Ritz-Carlton	1	★★★★★	96	$$$$$$$$
The Sherman House	5	★★★★★	96	$$$$$$$–
Fairmont Hotel	1	★★★★½	95	$$$$$$$
Argent Hotel San Francisco	7	★★★★½	94	$$$$$–
Hotel Monaco	3	★★★★½	94	$$$$$$
Archbishop's Mansion	2	★★★★½	93	$$$$$$–
Inn Above the Tide	9	★★★★½	93	$$$$$$$$$$–
Claremont Resort	12	★★★★½	92	$$$$$$$–
Nob Hill Lambourne	3	★★★★½	92	$$$$$$$
Prescott Hotel	3	★★★★½	92	$$$$$$
Clift Hotel	3	★★★★½	91	$$$$$
Westin St. Francis	3	★★★★½	91	$$$$$$
Casa Madrona	9	★★★★½	90	$$$$+
Huntington Hotel	1	★★★★½	90	$$$$$$–
Inn at the Opera	2	★★★★½	90	$$$$$–
White Swan Inn	3	★★★★½	90	$$$$$
Hotel Majestic	2	★★★★	89	$$$$$$–
Hotel Palomar	7	★★★★	89	$$$$$$
Renaissance Stanford Court Hotel	1	★★★★	89	$$$$$
Sheraton Palace Hotel	7	★★★★	89	$$$$$$$+
Hyatt Regency San Francisco	4	★★★★	88	$$$$$$$$–
Grand Hyatt San Francisco	3	★★★★	87	$$$$$$
The Donatello	3	★★★★	86	$$$$$+
Hilton San Francisco	3	★★★★	86	$$$$$$–
Hotel Triton	3	★★★★	86	$$$$$$
Hyatt Regency San Francisco Airport	SFIA	★★★★	86	$$$$+
San Francisco Marriott	7	★★★★	86	$$$$$$+
Embassy Suites SFO	SFIA	★★★★	85	$$$$$–
Hotel Milano	7	★★★★	85	$$$$$–
Wyndham Garden Hotel	10	★★★★	85	$$$$$–

HOW THE HOTELS COMPARE IN SAN FRANCISCO *(continued)*

Hotel	Zone	Overall Quality	Room Quality	Cost ($=$50)
Galleria Park Hotel	3	★★★★	84	$$$$+
Hotel Union Square	3	★★★★	84	$$$−
Mark Hopkins Inter-Continental	1	★★★★	84	$$$$$$$$−
Parc Fifty Five	3	★★★★	84	$$$$$−
Westin Hotel San Francisco Airport	SFIA	4.0	84	$$$$$$−
Berkeley Marina Radisson	12	★★★★	83	$$$$
Embassy Suites Hotel	10	★★★★	83	$$$$−
Hotel Diva	3	★★★★	83	$$$$$−
Hotel Juliana	3	★★★★	83	$$$$$−
Kensington Park Hotel	3	★★★★	83	$$$$
San Francisco Airport Marriott	SFIA	★★★★	83	$$$$$−
Serrano Hotel	3	★★★★	83	$$$$$−
Warwick Regis Hotel	3	★★★★	83	$$$+
Commodore International Hotel	3	★★★½	82	$$$
Hotel Bijou	3	★★★½	82	$$$+
Hotel Metropolis	3	★★★½	82	$$$+
Hyatt Fisherman's Wharf	6	★★★½	82	$$$$$$$
Sheraton at Fisherman's Wharf	6	★★★½	82	$$$$$$
Sheraton Gateway Hotel	SFIA	★★★½	82	$$$$$+
Sir Francis Drake Hotel	3	★★★½	82	$$$$$+
Union Street Inn	5	★★★½	82	$$$+
Waterfront Plaza Hotel	13	★★★½	82	$$$$
Holiday Inn Financial District	1	★★★½	81	$$$$$
Hotel Rex	3	★★★½	81	$$$$
Acqua Hotel	11	★★★½	80	$$$$
Doubletree Hotel San Francisco Airport	SFIA	★★★½	80	$$$$$−
Harbor Court Hotel	7	★★★½	80	$$$$
Marriott Fisherman's Wharf	6	★★★½	80	$$$$$$−
Oakland Airport Hilton	OIA	★★★½	80	$$$$$$$−
Ramada San Francisco Airport	SFIA	★★★½	77	$$$$−
Crowne Plaza Union Square	3	★★★½	76	$$$$$$−
Radisson Miyako Hotel	2	★★★½	76	$$$$$$
The Carlton	2	★★★½	75	$$$+

HOW THE HOTELS COMPARE IN SAN FRANCISCO *(continued)*

Hotel	Zone	Overall Quality	Room Quality	Cost ($=$50)
Inn at Union Square	3	★★★½	75	$$$$+
Phoenix Hotel	2	★★★½	75	$$$+
Savoy Hotel	3	★★★½	75	$$$+
Shannon Court Hotel	3	★★★½	75	$$$$–
Best Western Canterbury Hotel	3	★★★	74	$$$+
Edward II Inn	5	★★★	74	$$
Monticello Inn	3	★★★	74	$$$$$–
Oakland Marriott City Center	13	★★★	74	$$$
Howard Johnson Hotel Fisherman's Wharf	6	★★★	73	$$$+
Villa Florence	3	★★★	73	$$$$$–
Andrews Hotel	3	★★★	72	$$+
Beresford Arms	3	★★★	72	$$$$–
Handley Union Square Hotel	3	★★★	72	$$$$$–
Maxwell Hotel	3	★★★	72	$$$$
Hotel Durant	12	★★★	70	$$$
Stanyan Park Hotel	8	★★★	70	$$$+
Cartwright Hotel	3	★★★	69	$$$+
Petite Auberge	3	★★★	69	$$$$$
Best Western Grosvenor Hotel	SFIA	★★★	68	$$$+
Hotel Vintage Court	3	★★★	68	$$$$$$
Queen Anne Hotel	2	★★★	67	$$$$$$
Cow Hollow Motor Inn and Suites	5	★★★	65	$$
Grant Plaza	3	★★★	65	$$–
King George Hotel	3	★★★	65	$$$+
Laurel Inn	8	★★★	65	$$$
Park Plaza	SFIA	★★★	65	$$$$–
Park Plaza Hotel	OIA	★★★	65	$$$+
Radisson Fisherman's Wharf	6	★★★	65	$$$$$–
Ramada Limited Golden Gate	5	★★★	65	$$$–
Abigail Hotel	2	★★½	64	$$$–
Days Inn at the Beach	8	★★½	64	$$
The Fitzgerald	3	★★½	64	$$$–
Hampton Inn Oakland Airport	OIA	★★½	64	$$$–

HOW THE HOTELS COMPARE IN SAN FRANCISCO *(continued)*

Hotel	Zone	Overall Quality	Room Quality	Cost ($=$50)
Travelodge San Francisco Airport North	SFIA	★★½	64	$$+
Clarion Bedford Hotel	3	★★½	62	$$$$–
Super 8 Motel	5	★★½	62	$$$
Travelodge Bel Aire	5	★★½	62	$$$–
Travelodge by the Bay	5	★★½	62	$$$
Buena Vista Motor Inn	5	★★½	61	$$+
Comfort Inn by the Bay	5	★★½	60	$$$$–
Town House Motel	5	★★½	60	$$+
Pacific Heights Inn	5	★★½	59	$$$$
Pacific Motor Inn	5	★★½	59	$$$$
Seal Rock Inn	8	★★½	59	$$$–
Vagabond Inn Airport	SFIA	★★½	58	$$+
Marina Motel	5	★★½	56	$$$
Red Roof Inn	SFIA	★★½	56	$$$
Villa Inn	10	★★½	56	$$+
Days Inn Fisherman's Wharf	5	★★	55	$$+
Hotel Beresford	3	★★	55	$$$
Travelodge Golden Gate	5	★★	55	$$$$–
Star Motel	5	★★	53	$$$–
Motel Capri	5	★★	47	$$–

HOW THE HOTELS COMPARE IN THE WINE COUNTRY

Hotel	Room Rating	Quality Rating	Cost ($=$50)
Auberge du Soleil	★★★★★	99	$$$$$$$
Vintner's Inn	★★★★½	94	$$$$$+
Inn at Southbridge	★★★★½	92	$$$$$$$$$$–
Napa Valley Lodge	★★★★½	92	$$$$$$$
Vintage Inn	★★★★½	91	$$$$$$$+
Sonoma Mission Inn and Spa	★★★★½	90	$$$$$$$$–
Cedar Gables Inn	★★★★	89	$$$$–
Rancho Caymus	★★★★	87	$$$$$$$–
Silverado Country Club and Resort	★★★★	85	$$$$$$+
Harvest Inn	★★★★	84	$$$$+
Marriott Hotel Napa Valley	★★★★	84	$$$$$+
El Dorado Hotel	★★★★	83	$$$$
Sonoma County Hilton Santa Rosa	★★★★	83	$$$$+

HOW THE HOTELS COMPARE IN THE WINE COUNTRY (continued)

Hotel	Room Rating	Quality Rating	Cost ($=$50)
Fountaingrove Inn	★★★½	82	$$$$$–
Mount View Hotel	★★★½	81	$$$$$
Napa Valley Railway Inn	★★★½	75	$$$–
Sonoma Hotel	★★★½	75	$$$$–
Best Western Sonoma Valley Inn	★★★	74	$$$$$$–
Hotel St. Helena	★★★	74	$$$$$$$–
Chateau Hotel	★★★	68	$$$–
El Pueblo Inn	★★★	66	$$+
Dr. Wilkinson's Hot Springs	★★★	65	$$$+
El Bonita Motel	★★★	65	$$$$+
John Muir Inn	★★★	65	$$$$–

THE TOP 30 BEST DEALS IN SAN FRANCISCO

Hotel	Zone	Room Rating	Quality Rating	Cost ($=$50)
1. Hotel Union Square	3	★★★★	84	$$$–
2. Grant Plaza	3	★★★	65	$$–
3. Edward II Inn	5	★★★	74	$$
4. Cow Hollow Motor Inn and Suites	5	★★★	65	$$
5. Warwick Regis Hotel	3	★★★★	83	$$$+
6. Commodore International Hotel	3	★★★½	82	$$$
7. Argent Hotel San Francisco	7	★★★★½	94	$$$$$–
8. Casa Madrona	9	★★★★½	90	$$$$+
9. Inn at the Opera	2	★★★★½	90	$$$$$–
10. Hotel Bijou	3	★★★½	82	$$$+
11. Andrews Hotel	3	★★★	72	$$+
12. Embassy Suites Hotel	10	★★★★	83	$$$$–
13. Hotel Metropolis	3	★★★½	82	$$$+
14. Union Street Inn	5	★★★½	82	$$$+
15. Days Inn at the Beach	8	★★½	64	$$
16. Hyatt Regency San Francisco Airport	SFIA	★★★★	86	$$$$+
17. Berkeley Marina Radisson	12	★★★★	83	$$$$
18. The Carlton	2	★★★½	75	$$$+
19. Phoenix Hotel	2	★★★½	75	$$$+
20. White Swan Inn	3	★★★★½	90	$$$$$

THE TOP 30 BEST DEALS IN SAN FRANCISCO (continued)

Hotel	Zone	Room Rating	Quality Rating	Cost ($=$50)
21. Kensington Park Hotel	3	★★★★	83	$$$$
22. Clift Hotel	3	★★★★½	91	$$$$$
23. Ramada Limited Golden Gate	5	★★★	65	$$$–
24. Pan Pacific Hotel	3	★★★★★	98	$$$$$$+
25. Galleria Park Hotel	3	★★★★	84	$$$$+
26. Savoy Hotel	3	★★★½	75	$$$+
27. Archbishop's Mansion	2	★★★★½	93	$$$$$$–
28. Hotel Milano	7	★★★★	85	$$$$$–
29. Hotel Juliana	3	★★★★	83	$$$$$–
30. Oakland Marriott City Center	13	★★★	74	$$$

THE TOP 10 BEST DEALS IN THE WINE COUNTRY

Hotel	Room Rating	Quality Rating	Cost ($=$50)
1. Napa Valley Railway Inn	★★★½	75	$$$–
2. Cedar Gables Inn	★★★★	89	$$$$–
3. El Dorado Hotel	★★★★	83	$$$$
4. El Pueblo Inn	★★★	66	$$+
5. Vintner's Inn	★★★★½	94	$$$$$+
6. Sonoma County Hilton Santa Rosa	★★★★	83	$$$$+
7. Harvest Inn	★★★★	84	$$$$+
8. Sonoma Hotel	★★★½	75	$$$$–
9. Chateau Hotel	★★★	68	$$$–
10. Auberge du Soleil	★★★★★	99	$$$$$$$

SAN FRANCISCO HOTELS BY ZONE

Zone 1: Chinatown

Fairmont Hotel
Holiday Inn Financial District
Huntington Hotel
Mark Hopkins Inter-Continental
Renaissance Stanford Court Hotel
Ritz-Carlton

Zone 2: Civic Center

Abigail Hotel
Archbishop's Mansion
The Carlton
Hotel Majestic
Inn at the Opera
Phoenix Hotel

SAN FRANCISCO HOTELS BY ZONE *(continued)*

Zone 2: Civic Center *(continued)*
Queen Anne Hotel
Radisson Miyako Hotel

Zone 3: Union Square
Andrews Hotel
Beresford Arms
Best Western Canterbury Hotel
Campton Place Hotel
Cartwright Hotel
Clarion Bedford Hotel
Clift Hotel
Commodore International Hotel
Crowne Plaza Union Square
The Donatello
The Fitzgerald
Galleria Park Hotel
Grand Hyatt San Francisco
Grant Plaza
Handlery Union Square Hotel
Hilton San Francisco
Hotel Beresford
Hotel Bijou
Hotel Diva
Hotel Juliana
Hotel Metropolis
Hotel Monaco
Hotel Nikko
Hotel Rex
Hotel Triton
Hotel Union Square
Hotel Vintage Court
Inn at Union Square
Kensington Park Hotel
King George Hotel
Maxwell Hotel
Monticello Inn
Nob Hill Lambourne
Pan Pacific Hotel
Parc Fifty Five
Petite Auberge
Prescott Hotel
Savoy Hotel

Serrano Hotel
Shannon Court Hotel
Sir Francis Drake Hotel
Villa Florence
Warwick Regis Hotel
Westin St. Francis
White Swan Inn

Zone 4: Financial District
Hyatt Regency San Francisco
Mandarin Oriental

Zone 5: Marina
Buena Vista Motor Inn
Comfort Inn by the Bay
Cow Hollow Motor Inn and Suites
Days Inn Fisherman's Wharf
Edward II Inn
Marina Motel
Motel Capri
Pacific Heights Inn
Pacific Motor Inn
Ramada Limited Golden Gate
Sherman House
Star Motel
Super 8 Motel
Town House Motel
Travelodge Bel Aire
Travelodge by the Bay
Travelodge Golden Gate
Union Street Inn

Zone 6: North Beach
Howard Johnson Hotel Fisherman's
   Wharf
Hyatt Fisherman's Wharf
Marriott Fisherman's Wharf
Radisson Fisherman's Wharf
Sheraton at Fisherman's Wharf

Zone 7: SoMa/Mission
Argent Hotel San Francisco
Four Seasons Hotel and Residences
Harbor Court Hotel

SAN FRANCISCO HOTELS BY ZONE *(continued)*

Zone 7: SoMa/Mission *(continued)*
Hotel Milano
Hotel Palomar
San Francisco Marriott
Sheraton Palace Hotel
W Hotel San Francisco

Zone 8: Richmond/Sunset
Days Inn at the Beach
Laurel Inn
Seal Rock Inn
Stanyan Park Hotel

Zone 9: Tiburon/Sausalito
Casa Madrona
Inn Above the Tide

Zone 10: Suburban Marin
Embassy Suites Hotel
Villa Inn
Wyndham Garden Hotel

Zone 11: Marin Headlands to Point Reyes
Acqua Hotel

Zone 12: Berkeley
Berkeley Marina Radisson
Claremont Resort
Hotel Durant

Zone 13: Oakland
Oakland Marriott City Center
Waterfront Plaza Hotel

Zone 14: South Bay
The Ritz-Carlton Half Moon Bay

Oakland International Airport
Hampton Inn Oakland Airport
Oakland Airport Hilton
Park Plaza Hotel

San Francisco International Airport
Best Western Grosvenor Hotel
Doubletree Hotel San Francisco Airport
Embassy Suites SFO
Hyatt Regency San Francisco Airport
Park Plaza
Ramada San Francisco Airport
Red Roof Inn
San Francisco Airport Marriott
Sheraton Gateway Hotel
Travelodge San Francisco Airport North
Vagabond Inn Airport
Westin Hotel San Francisco Airport

The Wine Country
Auberge du Soleil
Best Western Sonoma Valley Inn
Cedar Gables Inn
Chateau Hotel
Dr. Wilkinson's Hot Springs
El Bonita Motel
El Dorado Hotel
El Pueblo Inn
Fountaingrove Inn
Harvest Inn
Hotel St. Helena
Inn at Southbridge
John Muir Inn
Marriott Hotel Napa Valley
Mount View Hotel
Napa Valley Lodge
Napa Valley Railway Inn
Rancho Caymus
Silverado Country Club and Resort
Sonoma County Hilton Santa Rosa
Sonoma Hotel
Sonoma Mission Inn and Spa
Vintage Inn
Vintner's Inn

Hotel/website	Room Rating	Zone	Street Address
The Abigail Hotel	★★½	2	246 McAllister Street SanFrancisco,CA 94102
Acqua Hotel www.acquahotel.com	★★★½	11	555 Redwood Highway Mil Valley, CA 94941
Andrews Hotel www.andrewshotel.com	★★★	3	624 Post Street San Francisco, CA 94109
The Archbishop's Mansion www.archibishopsmansion.com	★★★★½	2	1000 Fulton Street San Francisco, CA 94117
Argent Hotel San Francisco www.argenthotel.com	★★★★½	7	50 Third Street San Francisco, CA 94103
Auberge du Soleil www.aubergedusoleil.com	★★★★★	WC	180 Rutherford Hill Road Rutherford, CA 94573
Beresford Arms www.beresford.com	★★★	3	701 Post Street San Francisco, CA 94109
Berkeley Marina Radisson www.radisson.com	★★★★	12	200 Marina Boulevard Berkeley, CA 94710
Best Western Canterbury Hotel & White Hall Inn	★★★	3	750 Sutter Street San Francisco, CA 94109
Best Western Grosvenor Hotel	★★★	SFIA	380 S. Airport Boulevard So. San Francisco, CA 94080
Best Western Miyako Inn	★★★	2	1800 Sutter Street San Francisco, CA 94115
Best Western Sonoma Valley Inn www.sonomavalleyinn.com	★★★	WC	550 Second Street West Sonoma, CA 95476
Buena Vista Motor Inn www.ernestallen.com	★★½	5	1599 Lombard Street San Francisco, CA 94123
Campton Place Hotel www.camptonplace.com	★★★★★	3	340 Stockton Street San Francisco, CA 94108
The Carlton www.carltonhotel.com	★★★½	2	1075 Sutter Street San Francisco, CA 94109
Cartwright Hotel	★★★	3	524 Sutter Street San Francisco, CA 94103
Casa Madrona www.casamadronahotel.com	★★★★½	9	801 Bridgeway Sausalito, CA 94965
Cedar Gables Inn www.cedargablesinn.com	★★★★	WC	486 Coombs Street Napa, CA 94559
Château Hotel www.napavalleycateauhotel.com	★★★	WC	4195 Solano Avenue Napa, CA 94558
Claremont Resort and Spa www.claremontresort.com	★★★★½	12	41 Tunnel Road Berkeley, CA 94705

Local Phone	Guest Fax	Toll-Free Res. Line	Cost ($=$50)	Discounts Available	No. of Rooms
(415) 861-9728	(415) 861-5848	(800) 243-6510	$$$–	Government	61
(415) 380-0400	(415) 380-9696	(888) 662-9555	$$$$	AAA, AARP, Senior, Govt.	75
(415) 563-6877	(415) 928-6919	(800) 926-3739	$$+	AAA, senior, Government	48
(415) 563-7872	(415) 885-3193	(800) 543-5820	$$$$$$–		15
(415) 974-6400	(415) 543-8268	(877) 222-6699	$$$$$–	AAA	693
(707) 963-1211	(707) 963-8764	(800) 348-5406	$$$$$$$		52
(415) 673-2600	(415) 929-1535	(800) 533-6533	$$$$–	AAA, AARP	102
(510) 548-7920	(510) 548-7944	(800) 333-3333	$$$+	AAA, AARP	375
(415) 474-6464	(415) 474-5856	(800) 227-4788	$$$+	AAA, AARP	254
(650) 873-3200	(650) 589-3945	(800) 722-7141	$$$+	Government AAA, AARP	207
(415) 921-4000	(415) 923-1064	(800) 528-1234	$$$–	Senior, AAA, AARP	125
(707) 938-9200	(707) 938-0935	(800) 334-5784	$$$$$$–	AAA, AARP	78
(415) 923-9600	(415) 441-4775	(800) 835-4980	$$+	AAA, AARP	50
(415) 781-5555	(415) 955-5536	(800) 235-4300	$$$$$$$+	AAA	127
(415) 673-0242	(415) 673-4904	(800) 227-4496	$$$+	AAA, AARP	165
(415) 421-2865	(415) 983-6244	(800) 794-7661	$$$+	AAA, AARP	114
(415) 332-0502	(415) 332-2537	(800) 567-9524	$$$$+		35
(707) 224-7969	(707) 224-4838	(800) 309-7969	$$$$–	AAA, AARP	6
(707) 253-9300	(707) 253-0906	NA	$$$–	AAA, AARP, Govt., Military	115
(510) 843-3000	(510) 848-6208	(800) 551-7266	$$$$$$$–	AAA, AARP	279

Hotel	On-site Dining	Room Service	Bar	Parking per Day	Meeting Facilities
The Abigail Hotel	✔			$20	
Acqua Hotel	✔	✔	✔	Free	✔
Andrews Hotel	✔	✔	✔	$15	Conference facilities
The Archbishop's Mansion				Free	
Argent Hotel San Francisco	✔	✔	✔	$32	✔
Auberge du Soleil	✔	✔	✔	Free	✔
Beresford Arms	✔		✔	$20	
Berkeley Marina Radisson	✔	✔	✔	Free	✔
Best Western Canterbury Hotel	✔	✔	✔	$25	✔
Best Western Grosvenor Hotel	✔	✔	✔	Free	✔
Best Western Miyako Inn	✔	Limited	✔	$12	✔
Best Western Sonoma Valley Inn				Free	✔
Buena Vista Motor Inn				Free	
Campton Place Hotel	✔	✔	✔	$35	✔
The Carlton	✔	✔		$16-self $21-valet	✔
Cartwright Hotel				$20-self $$26-valet	✔
Casa Madrona	✔	✔		$7	✔
Cedar Gables Inn				Free	
Château Hotel	✔	✔	✔	Free	✔
Claremont Resort and Spa	✔	✔	✔	$12	✔

Extra Amenities	Business Amenities	Decor	Pool/ Sauna	Exercise Facilities
Free breakfast, massage avail.	Dataport	European boutique		
Breakfast, afternoon tea	✔	Pacific Rim		Access to health club
Free breakfast, free wine	Dataport, 2-line phone	Queen Anne/ Victorian		
Free breakfast, free wine hour		French chateau		
Gift shop	Dataport, Internet	Art deco	Sauna	✔
Spa services avail. for fee	Dataport	Southwestern	Pool, steam room, whirlpool	✔
Free breakfast, satellite TV	Dataport, 2-line phone	European	Whirlpool	
Marina	Dataport, 2-line phone	Nautical	Pool, sauna, whirlpool	✔
$12 shuttle service, gift shop	Dataport, 2-line phone	Old English		✔
Free breakfast, airport shuttle	Dataport	European	Pool	
Asian-style guest rooms	Dataport	Western		
Free breakfast, wine in room	Dataport	Modern/ Calif.	Pool, whirlpool	✔
Rooftop sun deck	Dataport			
	Dataport, 2-line phone	European		Privileges
Wine bar evenings	Dataport	Early San Francisco Estate		
Free breakfast, wine/tea hour	Dataport, 2-line phone	European Boutique	Privileges	Privileges
Free breakfast, wine/cheese hour		Each room different	Hot tub by reservation	
Breakfast, wine, hors d'oeuvres		English country manor		
	Dataport	American	Pool, whirlpool	
Full spa, tennis courts	Dataport, 2-line phone	Traditional	Pool, sauna, whirlpool	✔

Hotel/website	Room Rating	Zone	Street Address
Clarion Bedford Hotel www.bedfordhotel.com	★★½	3	761 Post Street San Francisco, CA 94109
Clift Hotel	★★★★½	3	495 Geary Street San Francisco, CA 94102
Comfort Inn by the Bay	★★½	5	2775 Van Ness Avenue San Francisco, CA 94109
Commodore International Hotel	★★★½	3	825 Sutter Street San Francisco, CA 94109
Courtyard by Marriott Fisherman's Wharf	★★★	6	580 Beach Street San Francisco, CA 94133
Cow Hollow Motor Inn and Suites	★★★	5	2190 Lombard Street San Francisco, CA 94123
Crowne Plaza Union Square	★★★½	3	480 Sutter Street San Francisco, CA 94108
Days Inn at the Beach	★★½	8	2600 Sloat Boulevard San Francisco, CA 94116
Days Inn Fisherman's Wharf	★★	5	2358 Lombard Street San Francisco, CA 94123
The Donatello	★★★★	3	501 Post Street San Francisco, CA 94102
Doubletree Hotel San Francisco Airport	★★★½	SFIA	835 Airport Boulevard Burlingame, CA 94010
Dr. Wilkinson's Hot Springs www.drwilkinson.com	★★★	WC	1507 Lincoln Avenue Calistoga, CA 94515
Edward II Inn	★★★	5	3155 Scott Street San Francisco, CA 94123
El Bonita Motel www.elbonita.com	★★★	WC	195 Main Street St. Helena, CA 94574
El Dorado Hotel www.hoteleldorado.com	★★★★	WC	405 First Street West Sonoma, CA 95476
El Pueblo Inn www.elpuebloinn.com	★★★	WC	896 W. Napa Sonoma, CA 95476
Embassy Suites Hotel www.embassymarin.com	★★★★	10	101 McInnis Parkway San Rafael, CA 94903
Embassy Suites SFO	★★★★	SFIA	150 Anza Boulevard Burlingame, CA 94010
Fairmont Hotel www.fairmonthotel.com	★★★★½	1	950 Mason Street San Francisco, CA 94108
The Fitzgerald www.fitzgeraldhotel.com	★★½	3	620 Post Street San Francisco, CA 94109

```
        WH SMITH GIFT SHOP # 713
    320 BOOKS                16.99 T


        SUBTOTAL            16.99
        TAX                  1.44
        TOTAL               18.43
        CASH               (20.00)
        CHANGE               1.57


Cshr 2222: GURVITS,BIANA.    878  # 26
Register: REG1 Apr 15 2003  9:22 AM
              Thank You
```

Local Phone	Guest Fax	Toll-Free Res. Line	Cost ($=$50)	Discounts Available	No. of Rooms
(415) 673-6040	(415) 563-6739	(800) 252-7466	$$$$–	AAA, AARP, Government	144
(415) 775-4700	(415) 441-4621	(800) 65-CLIFT	$$$$$	AAA	375
(415) 928-5000	(415) 441-3990	(800) 228-5150	$$$$–	AAA, AARP, Military	138
(415) 923-6800	(415) 923-6804	(800) 338-6848	$$$	AAA, AARP, Government	110
(415) 775-3800	(415) 441-7307	(800) 654-2000	$$$+	AAA, AARP, Government	132
(415) 921-5800	(415) 922-8515	NA	$$		129
(415) 398-8900	(415) 989-8823	(800) 243-1135	$$$$$$–	AAA, AARP, Government	401
(415) 665-9000	(415) 665-5440	(800) 325-2525	$$	AAA, AARP, Government	33
(415) 922-2010	(415) 931-0603	(800) DAYS-INN	$$+	AAA, AARP, Government	22
(415) 441-7100	(415) 885-8842	(800) 227-3184	$$$$$+	AAA, AARP Government	943
(650) 344-5500	(650) 340-8851	(800) 222-TREE	$$$$$–	AAA, AARP, Government	400
(707) 942-4102	NA	NA	$$$+	AAA	42
(415) 922-3000	(415) 931-5784	(800) 473-2846	$$	AAA	32
(707) 963-3216	(707) 963-8838	(800) 541-3284	$$$$+	AAA, AARP	41
(707) 996-3030	(707) 996-3148	(800) 289-3031	$$$$		26
(707) 996-3651	(707) 935-5988	NA	$$+	AAA, AARP	38
(415) 499-9222	(415) 499-9268	(800) EMBASSY	$$$$–	AAA, AARP, Government	235
(650) 342-4600	(650) 343-8137	(800) EMBASSY	$$$$$–	AAA, AARP, Government	344
(415) 772-5000	(415) 837-0587	(800) 527-4727	$$$$$$$	AAA, AARP, Government	596
(415) 775-8100	N/A	(800) 334-6835	$$$–	AAA, AARP, Government	47

Hotel	On-site Dining	Room Service	Bar	Parking per Day	Meeting Facilities
Clarion Bedford Hotel				$25	✔
The Clift Hotel	✔	✔	✔	$35	✔
Comfort Inn by the Bay				$18	
Commodore International Hotel	✔		✔	$20	✔
Courtyard by Marriott Fisherman's Wharf	✔			$5	
Cow Hollow Motor Inn and Suites	✔			Free	
Crowne Plaza Union Square	✔	✔	✔	$29	✔
Days Inn at the Beach				Free	
Days Inn Fisherman's Wharf				Free	
The Donatello	✔	✔	✔	$26	✔
Doubletree Hotel San Francisco Airport	✔	✔	✔	$12	✔
Dr. Wilkinson's Hot Springs				Free	✔
Edward II Inn			✔	$11	
El Bonita Motel				Free	
El Dorado Hotel	✔		✔	Free	
El Pueblo Inn				Free	
Embassy Suites Hotel	✔	✔	✔	Free	✔
Embassy Suites SFO	✔	✔	✔	Free	✔
Fairmont Hotel	✔	✔	✔	$32 $4 each 20 min.	✔
The Fitzgerald				$14	

Extra Amenities	Business Amenities	Decor	Pool/ Sauna	Exercise Facilities
Free wine evenings	Dataport	Boutique		
Babysit, pet care	Dataport, fax, 2-line phone	European		✔
Free breakfast, tennis court	Dataport			
	Dataport	Neo-Deco		
Breakfast	Dataport			✔
Flower shop, newspaper stand	Dataport, 2-line phone			✔
Free breakfast, playground			Sauna privileges	Privileges
Free breakfast				
Music in lounge, spa services	Dataport, 2-line phone	European boutique	Sauna, whirlpool	✔
Free airport shuttle	Dataport			✔
Spa	Dataport	Victorian, Neo-Deco	Pool, whirlpool	
Evening sherry, free breakfast		English country		
Free breakfast		1950s	Whirlpool, pool, sauna	
Free breakfast, wine on arrival	Dataport	Old World	Pool	Privileges
Coffee and biscotti		Early California	Pool, whirlpool	
Free breakfast, p.m. reception	Dataport, 2-line phone		Pool, whirlpool	✔
Free breakfast, p.m. reception	Dataport, 2-line phone	Atrium hotel	Pool, sauna, steam room	✔
Massage available	Dataport, 2-line phone	Grand hotel	Sauna, whirlpool	✔
Free breakfast	Dataport, 2-line phone	European	Privileges	Privileges

Hotel/website	Room Rating	Zone	Street Address
Fountaingrove Inn www.fountiangroveinn.com	★★★½	WC	101 Fountaingrove Parkway Santa Rosa, CA 95403
Four Season Hotel www.fourseasons.com	★★★★★	7	757 Market Street San Francisco, CA 94103
Galleria Park Hotel www.galleriapark.com	★★★★	3	191 Sutter Street San Francisco, CA 94104
Grand Hyatt San Francisco www.hyatt.com	★★★★	3	345 Stockton Street San Francisco, CA 94108
Grant Plaza www.grantplaza.com	★★★	3	465 Grant Avenue San Francisco, CA 94108
Hampton Inn Oakland Airport www.hamptoninn.com	★★½	OIA	8465 Enterprise Way Oakland, CA 94621
The Handlery Union Square Hotel www.handlery.com	★★★	3	351 Geary Street San Francisco, CA 94102
Harbor Court Hotel	★★★½	7	165 Steuart Street San Francisco, CA 94105
Harvest Inn	★★★★	WC	1 Main Street St. Helena, CA 94574
Hilton San Francisco www.hilton.com	★★★★	3	333 O'Farrell Street San Francisco, CA 94102
Holiday Inn Financial District www.basshotels.com	★★★½	1	750 Kearny Street San Francisco, CA 94108
Hotel Beresford www.beresford.com	★★	3	635 Sutter Street San Francisco, CA 94102
Hotel Bijou www.hotelbijou.com	★★★½	3	111 Mason Street San Francisco, CA 94102
Hotel Diva www.hoteldiva.com	★★★★	3	440 Geary Street San Francisco, CA 94102
Hotel Durant www.hoteldurant.com	★★★	12	2600 Durant Avenue Berkeley, CA 94704
Hotel Juliana www.julianahotel.com	★★★★	3	590 Bush Street San Francisco, CA 94108
Hotel Majestic www.thehotelmajestic.com	★★★★	2	1500 Sutter Street San Francisco, CA 94109
Hotel Metropolis www.hotelmetropolis.com	★★★½	3	24 Mason Street San Francisco, CA 94102
Hotel Milano	★★★★	7	55 Fifth Street San Francisco, CA 94103
Hotel Monaco	★★★★½	3	501 Geary Street San Francisco, CA 94102

Local Phone	Guest Fax	Toll-Free Res. Line	Cost ($=$50)	Discounts Available	No. of Rooms
(707) 578-6101	(707) 544-3126	(800) 222-6101	$$$$$$–	AAA, AARP, Govt., seniors	126
(415) 633-3000	(415) 633-3009	(800) 332-3442	$$$$$$$$$+		323
(415) 781-3060	(415) 433-4409	(800) 792-9639	$$$$+	AAA, AARP, Government	177
(415) 398-1234	(415) 391-1780	(800) 233-1234	$$$$$$	AAA, senior, Government	685
(415) 434-3883	(415) 434-3886	(800) 472-6899	$$–	AAA, AARP, Government	72
(510) 632-8900	(510) 632-4713	(800) HAMPTON	$$$–	AAA, AARP, Government	152
(415) 781-7800	(415) 781-0216	(800) 843-4343	$$$$$–	AAA, AARP	377
(415) 882-1300	(415) 882-1313	(800) 346-0555	$$$$	AAA, AARP, Government	131
(707) 963-9463	(707) 963-4402	(800) 950-8466	$$$$+	AAA, AARP	54
(415) 771-1400	(415) 771-6807	(800) 695-8284	$$$$$$–	AAA, AARP, Government	1,896
(415) 433-6600	(415) 765-7891	(800) 424-8292	$$$$$	AAA, AARP, Government	571
(415) 673-9900	(415) 474-0449	(800) 533-6533	$$$	AAA, AARP, Government	114
(415) 771-1200	(415) 346-3196	(800) 771-1022	$$$+	AAA, AARP, Govt., seniors	65
(415) 885-0200	(415) 346-6613	(800) 553-1900	$$$$$–		1102
(510) 845-8981	(510) 486-8336	(800) 2-DURANT	$$$	AAA, AARP, Government	140
(415) 392-2540	(415) 391-8447	(800) 328-3880	$$$$$–	AAA, AARP, Government	107
(415) 441-1100	(415) 673-7331	(800) 869-8966	$$$$$$–	AAA, AARP, Government	57
(415) 775-4600	(415) 775-4606	(800) 553-1900	$$$+	Corporate, Govt., Military	105
(415) 543-8555	(415) 543-5885	(800) 398-7555	$$$$$–	AAA, AARP, Government	116
(415) 292-0100	(415) 292-0111	(888) 852-3551	$$$$$$	AAA, AARP	201

Hotel	On-site Dining	Room Service	Bar	Parking per Day	Meeting Facilities
Fountaingrove Inn	✔	✔	✔	Free	
Four Seasons Hotel	✔	✔	✔	$35	✔
Galleria Park Hotel	✔	✔	✔	$27	✔
Grand Hyatt San Francisco	✔	✔	✔	$38	✔
Grant Plaza				$17.50	
Hampton Inn Oakland Airport				Free	
The Handlery Union Square Hotel	✔	✔	✔	$25	✔
Harbor Court Hotel	✔	✔	✔	$28	
Harvest Inn			✔	Free	✔
Hilton San Francisco	✔	✔	✔	$30	✔
Holiday Inn Financial District	✔	✔	✔	$27.50	✔
Hotel Beresford	✔		✔	$18	
Hotel Bijou				$19	
Hotel Diva	✔	✔		$22	✔
Hotel Durant	✔	Limited hours	✔	$7	✔
Hotel Juliana	✔	✔	✔	$30-valet $22-self	✔
Hotel Majestic	✔	✔	✔	$23	✔
Hotel Metropolis				$19	✔
Hotel Milano	✔	✔	✔	$28	
Hotel Monaco	✔	✔	✔	$28	✔

Extra Amenities	Business Amenities	Decor	Pool/ Sauna	Exercise Facilities
Piano bar, free breakfast	Dataport, 2-line phone	Equestrian	Pool, whirlpool	Privileges
Technology ctr., babysitting	✔		✔	✔
Wine tastings rooftop track/park	Dataports, 2-line phone	Art nouveau		✔
Babysittings	Dataport, 2-line phone	European with Oriental accents		✔
Free b'fast, free airport shuttle			Pool, whirlpool	Privileges
Hair salon, video games	Dataport	Traditional European	Pool, sauna	Privileges (fee)
Wine tasting, video games	Dataport, 2-line phone	1907 landmark bldg.	Privileges	Health facility
VCR rental, free breakfast	Dataport, 2-line phone	English Tudor	Pool, whirlpool	
Gift shop	Dataport, 2-line phone	Modern	Pool, sauna, whirlpool	Fitness room
Email, Internet PC facility	2-line phone	Chinese	Pool	Fitness room
Free breakfast, satellite TV	Dataport	Victorian		Privileges
B'fast, theater, film tours, casting calls	Dataport	San Francisco cinema	Privileges	Privileges
Free breakfast, wine reception	Dataport	Modern Italian	Privileges	Cardio workout rm
	Dataport	Old Europe		Privileges
Wine reception, breakfast	Dataport, fax	European boutique		Privileges
Afternoon sherry	Dataport, 2-line phone	Victorian boutique	Privileges	Privileges
Breakfast, wine reception	Dataport, 2-line phone	Colorful eclectic		✔
Video games	Dataport	Modern Italian	Sauna, steam room, whirlpool	✔
Massage	Dataport modern eclectic	Beaux arts/	Whirlpool	✔

Hotel/website	Room Rating	Zone	Street Address
Hotel Nikko San Francisco www.nikkohotels.com	★★★★★	3	222 Mason Street San Francisco, CA 94102
Hotel Palomar	★★★★	3	12 Fourth Street San Francisco, CA 94103
Hotel Rex www.thehotelrex.com	★★★½	3	562 Sutter Street San Francisco, CA 94102
Hotel St. Helena www.hotelsthelena.com	★★★	WC	1309 Main Street St. Helena, CA 94574
Hotel Triton www.hotel-tritonsf.com	★★★★	3	342 Grant Avenue San Francisco, CA 94108
Hotel Union Square www.hotelunionsquare.com	★★★★	3	114 Powell Street San Francisco, CA 94102
Hotel Vintage Court www.vintage.court.com	★★★	3	650 Bush Street San Francisco, CA 94108
The Huntington Hotel www.huntingtonhotel.com	★★★★½	1	1075 California Street San Francisco, CA 94108
Hyatt Fisherman's Wharf www.hyatt.com	★★★½	6	555 North Point Street San Francisco, CA 94133
Hyatt Regency San Francisco www.hyatt.com	★★★★	4	5 Embarcadero Center San Francisco, CA 94111
Hyatt Regency San Francisco Airport www.sanfranciscohyatt.com	★★★★	SFIA	1333 Bayshore Highway Burlingame, CA 94010
Inn Above the Tide www.innabovetide.com	★★★★½	9	30 El Portal Sausalito, CA 94965
The Inn at Southbridge	★★★★½	WC	1020 Main Street St. Helena, CA 95474
Inn at the Opera	★★★★½	2	333 Fulton Street San Francisco, CA 94102
The Inn at Union Square	★★★½	3	440 Post Street San Francisco, CA 94102
John Muir Inn	★★★	WC	1998 Trower Avenue Napa, CA 94558
Kensington Park Hotel www.kensingtonparkhotel.com	★★★★	3	450 Post Street San Francisco, CA 94102
King George Hotel www.kinggeorge.com	★★★	3	334 Mason Street San Francisco, CA 94102
The Laurel Inn www.thelaurelinn.com	★★★	8	444 Presidio Avenue San Francisco, CA 94115
Mandarin Oriental www.mandarinoriental.com	★★★★★	4	222 Sansome Street San Francisco, CA 94104

Local Phone	Guest Fax	Toll-Free Res. Line	Cost ($=$50)	Discounts Available	No. of Rooms
(415) 394-1111	(415) 394-1106	(800) NIKKO-US	$$$$$$$–	AAA, Government	554
(415) 348-1111	(415) 348-0302	(800) 695-8284	$$$$$$	AAA, AARP, Corp., Govt., Mil.	198
(415) 433-4434	(415) 433-3695	(800) 433-4434	$$$$	AAA, AARP, Government	94
(707) 963-4388	(707) 963-5402	(888) 478-4355	$$$$$$$–	Mid-week	18
(415) 394-0500	(415) 394-0555	(800) 433-6611	$$$$$$	AAA, AARP, Government	140
(415) 397-3000	(415) 398-1874	(800) 553-1900	$$$–	Corporate, Govt., Military	131
(415) 392-4666	(415) 433-4065	(800) 853-1750	$$$$$$	AAA, AARP, Government	107
(415) 474-5400	(415) 474-6227	(800) 227-4683	$$$$$$–	Government	132
(415) 563-1234	(415) 749-6122	(800) 233-1234	$$$$$$$	AAA, Government	313
(415) 788-1234	(415) 398-2567	(800) 233-1234	$$$$$$$$$–	AAA, Government	805
(650) 347-1234	(650) 696-2669	(800) 233-1234	$$$$+	AAA, AARP, Government	793
(415) 332-9535	(415) 332-6714	(800) 893-8433	$$$$$ $$$$$–		30
(707) 967-9400	(707) 967-9486	(800) 520-6800	$$$$$ $$$$$–	AARP	21
(415) 863-8400	(415) 861-0821	(800) 325-2708	$$$$$–	AAA, Govt.	48
(415) 397-3510	(415) 989-0529	(800) 288-4346	$$$$+	Senior	30
(707) 257-7220	(707) 258-0943	(800) 522-8999	$$$$–	AAA, AARP, Govt., senior	60
(415) 788-6400	(415) 399-9484	(800) 553-1900	$$$$	AAA, AARP, Government	88
(415) 781-5050	(415) 391-6976	(800) 288-6005	$$$+	AAA, AARP, Government	142
(415) 567-8467	(415) 928-1866	(800) 552-8735	$$$	AAA, senior, Government	49
(415) 885-0999	(415) 433-0289	(800) 622-0404	$$$$$$ $$$$$$+	Government	158

Hotel	On-site Dining	Room Service	Bar	Parking per Day	Meeting Facilities
Hotel Nikko San Francisco	✔	✔	✔	$30	✔
Hotel Palomar	✔			$32	✔
Hotel Rex	✔	✔	✔	$28-valet $22-self	✔
Hotel St. Helena			✔	Free	
Hotel Triton	✔	✔	✔	$28	✔
Hotel Union Square				$19 reception	✔
Hotel Vintage Court	✔	On request	✔	$28-valet $20-self	✔
The Huntington Hotel	✔	✔	✔	$1950	✔
Hyatt Fisherman's Wharf	✔	✔	✔	$30	✔
Hyatt Regency San Francisco	✔	✔	✔	$38	✔
Hyatt Regency San Francisco Airport	✔	✔	✔	$17-valet $13-self	✔
Inn Above the Tide				$12	
The Inn at Southbridge	✔	✔		Free	✔
Inn at the Opera	✔	✔	✔	$22	
The Inn at Union Square		✔	✔	$23	
John Muir Inn				Free	✔
Kensington Park Hotel	✔			$22	✔
King George Hotel	✔	✔		$18	✔
Laurel Inn		On request		Free	
Mandarin Oriental	✔	✔	✔	$34	✔

Extra Amenities	Business Amenities	Decor	Pool/ Sauna	Exercise Facilities
Hair salon	Dataport, 2-line phone	Modern	Pool, whirlpool	✔
Wine reception, stereo	Dataport, fax, 2-line phone	Modern	Whirlpool in some rooms	
Free wine bar	Dataport, 2-line phone	1920's–1940's literary salon		Privileges
Free breakfast		Victorian		
Wine reception, Tarot card reader	Dataport	Ultra modern		✔
Breakfast, wine boutique	Dataport	Contemporary	Privileges	
Wine reception	Dataport	European boutique		Privileges
Chauffered limo, sherry	Dataport, 2-line phone	European	Privileges	Privileges
Video games		Wharf/ Victorian	Pool, sauna, whirlpool	✔
Complimentary wine, newspaper		Modern atrium high-rise		✔
Newspaper	Dataport, 2-line phone	Modern	Pool, whirlpool	✔
Free breakfast, wine/cheese	Dataport 2-line phone	Nautical	Spa services	
Full spa, wine bar, free breakfast	Dataport, 2-line phone	European	Pool, steam room, whirlpool	✔
Free breakfast, Sat. wine hour	Dataport	Classic European		
Cont'l breakfast, wine afternoons	Dataport, 2-line phone	Boutique	Privileges	Privileges
VCR rental, cont'l breakfast	Dataport		Pool, whirlpool	
Free breakfast, afternoon sherry	Dataport	Queen Anne	Privileges	✔
	Dataport	English boutique	Privileges	Privileges
Free breakfast, kitchenettes	Dataport	Modern		Privileges
Many in-room	Dataport, 2-line phone	Modern		✔

Hotel/website	Room Rating	Zone	Street Address
Marina Motel www.marinamotel.com	★★½	5	2576 Lombard San Francisco, CA 94123
Mark Hopkins Inter-Continental	★★★★	1	1 Nob Hill San Francisco, CA 94108
Marriott Fisherman's Wharf	★★★½	6	1250 Columbus Avenue San Francisco, CA 94133
Marriott Hotel Napa Valley www.hotels.com	★★★★	WC	3425 Solano Avenue Napa, CA 94558
Maxwell Hotel www.maxwellhotel.com	★★★	3	386 Geary Street San Francisco, CA 94102
Monticello Inn www.monticelloinn.com	★★★	3	127 Ellis Street San Francisco, CA 94102
Motel Capri	★★	5	2015 Greenwich Street San Francisco, CA 94123
Mount View Hotel	★★★½	WC	1457 Lincoln Avenue Calistoga, CA 94515
Napa Valley Lodge www.woodsidehotels.com	★★★★½	WC	2230 Madison Street Yountville, CA 94599
Napa Valley Railway Inn	★★★½	WC	6503 Washington Street Yountville, CA 94599
Nob Hill Lambourne www.nobhilllambourne.com	★★★★½	3	725 Pine Street San Francisco, CA 94108
Oakland Airport Hilton	★★★½	OIA	1 Hegenberger Road Oakland, CA 94621
Oakland Marriott City Center www.marriott.com	★★★	13	1001 Broadway Oakland, CA 94607
Pacific Heights Inn www.pacificheightsinn.com	★★½	5	1555 Union Street San Francisco, CA 94123
Pacific Motor Inn	★★½	5	2599 Lombard Street San Francisco, CA 94123
The Pan Pacific Hotel www.panpac.com	★★★★★	3	500 Post Street San Francisco, CA 94102
Parc Fifty Five www.renaissancehotels.com	★★★★	3	55 Cyril Magnin Street San Francisco, CA 94102
Park Plaza www.parkhtls.com	★★★	3	1177 Airport Boulevard Burlingame, CA 94010
Park Plaza Hotel	★★★	OIA	150 Hegenberger Road Oakland, CA 94621
Petite Auberge www.foursisters.com	★★★	3	863 Bush Street San Francisco, CA 94108

Local Phone	Guest Fax	Toll-Free Res. Line	Cost ($=$50)	Discounts Available	No. of Rooms
(415) 921-9406	(415) 921-0364	(800) 346-6118	$$$		38
(415) 392-3434	(415) 421-3302	(800) 327-0200	$$$$$$$$–		380
(415) 775-7555	(415) 474-2099	(800) 525-0956	$$$$$$–	AARP, Govt.	285
(707) 253-7433	(707) 258-1320	(800) 228-9290	$$$$$+	AAA, AARP, Government	191
(415) 986-2000	(415) 397-2447	(888) 734-6299	$$$$	AAA, AARP	153
(415) 392-8800	(415) 398-2650	(800) 669-7777	$$$$$–	AAA, AARP, Government	91
(415) 346-4667	(415) 346-3256	NA	$$–	AAA	46
(707) 942-6877	(707) 942-6904	(800) 816-6877	$$$$$	AAA	32
(707) 944-2468	(707) 944-9362	(800) 368-2468	$$$$$$$	AAA, AARP	55
(707) 944-2000	NA	NA	$$$–	AAA, AARP, Military	9
(415) 433-2287	(415) 433-0975	(800) 274-8466	$$$$$$$	AAA, AARP	20
(510) 635-5000	(510) 383-4062	(800) HILTONS	$$$$$$$$–	AAA, AARP	365
(510) 451-4000	(510) 835-3466	(800) 228-9290	$$$	AAA, AARP, Government	494
(415) 776-3310	(415) 776-8176	(800) 523-1801	$$$$	AAA, AARP, Government	40
(415) 346-4664	(415) 346-4665	(800) 536-8446	$$$$		42
(415) 771-8600	(415) 398-0267	(800) 533-6465	$$$$$$+	AAA, AARP, Government	329
(415) 392-8000	(415) 403-6602	(800) 650-7272	$$$$$–	AAA, AARP, Government	1,028
(650) 342-9200	(650) 342-1655	(800) 437-7275	$$$$–	AAA, AARP, Government	302
(510) 635-5300	(510) 635-9661	(800) 635-5301	$$$+	AAA, Government	190
(415) 928-6000	(415) 673-7214	(800) 365-3004	$$$$$		26

Hotel	On-site Dining	Room Service	Bar	Parking per Day	Meeting Facilities
Marina Motel				Free	
Mark Hopkins Inter-Continental	✔	✔	✔	$35	✔
Marriott Fisherman's Wharf	✔	✔	✔	$20	✔
Marriott Hotel Napa Valley	✔	✔	✔	Free	✔
Maxwell Hotel	✔	✔	✔	$19	✔
Monticello Inn				$25	
Motel Capri				Free	
Mount View Hotel				Free	
Napa Valley Lodge				Free	✔
Napa Valley Railway Inn				Free	
Nob Hill Lambourne				$24	
Oakland Airport Hilton	✔	✔	✔	Free	✔
Oakland Marriott City Center	✔	✔	✔	$19	✔
Pacific Heights Inn				Free	
Pacific Motor Inn				Free	
The Pan Pacific Hotel	✔	✔	✔	$27	✔
Parc Fifty Five	✔	✔	✔	$27	✔
Park Plaza	✔	✔	✔	Free	✔
Park Plaza Hotel	✔	✔	✔	Free	✔
Petite Auberge				$19	

Extra Amenities	Business Amenities	Decor	Pool/ Sauna	Exercise Facilities
Kitchenettes, breakfast coupons				
Live music/ lounge, car rental	Dataport, 2-line phone	Grand hotel		✔
Mini-bars (some)	Dataport, 2-line phone	Modern	Sauna, whirlpool	✔
Basketball & tennis courts	Dataport	Modern	Pool, whirlpool	✔
	Dataport, 2-line phone	Art deco		
Free breakfast, wine tasting	Dataport, fax, 2-line phone	Contemporary Colonial	Privileges	Privileges
Free cont'l brkfst, full spa		California spa	Whirlpool, pool	
Free champagne breakfast, wine tasting	Dataports	California hacienda	Pool, sauna, whirlpool	✔
No telephones		Rooms in antique train cars		
B'fast, wine bar, kitchenettes, spa	Dataport, fax, 2-line phone	Business & wellness boutique		
Airport shuttle	Dataport 2-line phone	Modern	Pool	✔
Massage	Dataport, service	Modern 2-line phone	Pool, sauna	✔
Free breakfast				
Free breakfast				
Limo service, pillow preference	Dataport, fax	Modern		✔
VCR in room, bay windows	Dataport, 2-line phone	Modern	Sauna, steam rm., whirlpool	✔
24-hour airport shuttle, piano bar		Modern	Pool, whirlpool	✔
Airport shuttle, park, stay, & fly	Dataport		Pool, sauna, whirlpool	✔
Free breakfast, afternoon tea	Dataport	French country inn	Privileges	

Hotel/website	Room Rating	Zone	Street Address
The Phoenix Hotel	★★★½	2	601 Eddy Street San Francisco, CA 94109
The Prescott Hotel www.prescotthotel.com	★★★★½	3	545 Post Street San Francisco, CA 94102
Queen Anne Hotel www.queenanne.com	★★★	2	1590 Sutter Street San Francisco, CA 94109
Radisson Hotel at Fisherman's Wharf www.radisson.com	★★★	6	250 Beach Street San Francisco, CA 94133
Radisson Miyako Hotel www.radisson.com	★★★½	2	1625 Post Street San Francisco, CA 94115
Ramada Limited Golden Gate www.ramada.com	★★★	5	1940 Lombard Street San Francisco, CA 94123
Ramada San Francisco Airport www.ramada.com	★★★½	SFIA	1250 Old Bayshore Highway Burlingame, CA 94010
Rancho Caymus www.ranchocaymus.com	★★★★	WC	1140 Rutherford Road Rutherford, CA 94573
Red Roof Inn www.redroofinn.com	★★½	SFIA	777 Airport Boulevard Burlingame, CA 94010
Renaissance Stanford Court Hotel www.renaissancehotels.com	★★★★	1	905 California Street San Francisco, CA 94108
The Ritz-Carlton www.ritzcarlton.com	★★★★★	1	600 Stockton Street San Francisco, CA 94108
The Ritz-Carlton Half Moon Bay www.ritzcarlton.com	★★★★★	1	1 Miramontes Point Road Half Moon Bay, CA 94019
San Francisco Airport Marriott www.marriotthotels.com	★★★★	SFIA	1800 Old Bayshore Highway Burlingame, CA 94010
San Francisco Marriott www.marriotthotels.com	★★★★	7	55 Fourth Street San Francisco, CA 94103
Savoy Hotel www.savoyhotel.com	★★★½	3	580 Geary Street San Francisco, 94102
Seal Rock Inn www.sealrockinn.com	★★½	8	545 Point Lobos Avenue San Francisco, CA 94121
Serrano Hotel www.serranohotel.citysearch.com	★★★★	3	405 Taylor Street San Francisco, CA 94102
Shannon Court Hotel www.shannoncourthotel.com	★★★½	3	550 Geary Street San Francisco, CA 94102
Sheraton at Fisherman's Wharf	★★★½	6	2500 Mason Street San Francisco, CA 94133
Sheraton Gateway Hotel	★★★½	SFIA	600 Airport Boulevard Burlingame, CA 94010

Local Phone	Guest Fax	Toll-Free Res. Line	Cost ($=$50)	Discounts Available	No. of Rooms
(415) 776-1380	(415) 885-3109	(800) 248-9466	$$$+	AAA, Government	44
(415) 563-0303	(415) 563-6831	(800) 283-7322	$$$$$$	AAA, AARP	164
(415) 441-2828	(415) 775-5212	(800) 227-3970	$$$$$$	AAA, AARP, Government	49
(415) 392-6700	(415) 986-7853	(800) 578-7878	$$$$$–	AAA, AARP, Government	355
(415) 922-3200	(415) 921-0417	(800) 333-3333	$$$$$$	AAA, AARP, Government	218
(415) 775-8116	(415) 775-9937	(800) 2-RAMADA	$$$–	AAA, AARP, Government	37
(650) 347-2381	(650) 348-8838	(800) 2-RAMADA	$$$$–	AAA, AARP, Government	144
(707) 963-1777	(707) 963-5387	(800) 845-1777	$$$$$$$–	AAA, AARP	26
(650) 342-7772	(650) 342-2635	(800) RED-ROOF	$$$	AAA, senior	200
(415) 989-3500	(415) 391-0513	(800) 468-3571	$$$$$	AAA, AARP, Government	415
(415) 296-7465	(415) 291-0288	(800) 241-3333	$$$$$$$$		380
(650) 712-7000	(650) 712-7070	(800) 241-3333	$$$$$$$$–		261
(650) 692-9100	(650) 692-8016	(800) 228-9290	$$$$$–	AAA, AARP, Government	705
(415) 896-1600	(415) 777-2799	(800) 228-9290	$$$$$$+	AAA, AARP, Government	1,500
(415) 441-2700	(415) 441-0124	(800) 227-4223	$$$+	Government	83
(415) 752-8000	(415) 752-6034	(888) 732-5762	$$$–		27
(415) 885-2500	(415) 474-4879	(877) 294-9709	$$$$$–	AAA, Corp., Govt., Military	236
(415) 775-5000	(415) 775-9388	(800) 228-8830	$$$$–	AAA, AARP, Government	172
(415) 362-5500	(415) 956-5275	(800) 325-3535	$$$$$$	AAA, Government	529
(650) 340-8500	(650) 343-1546	(800) 827-0880	$$$$$+	AAA, AARP, Government	404

Hotel	On-site Dining	Room Service	Bar	Parking per Day	Meeting Facilities
The Phoenix Hotel	✔		✔	Free	
The Prescott Hotel	✔	✔	✔	$30	✔
Queen Anne Hotel				$14	✔
Radisson Hotel at Fisherman's Wharf	✔	✔	✔	$22	
Radisson Miyako Hotel	✔	✔	✔	$20	✔
Ramada Limited Golden Gate				Free	
Ramada San Francisco Airport	✔	✔	✔	Free	✔
Rancho Caymus	✔	✔	✔	Free	
Red Roof Inn	✔			Free	
Renaissance Stanford Court Hotel	✔	✔	✔	$32 1 block away	✔
The Ritz-Carlton	✔	✔	✔	$45	✔
The Ritz-Carlton Half Moon Bay	✔	✔	✔	$25	✔
San Francisco Airport Marriott	✔	✔	✔	$17-valet $13-self	✔
San Francisco Marriott	✔	✔	✔	$27	✔
Savoy Hotel	✔	Breakfast only		$18	✔
Seal Rock Inn	✔			Free	
Serrano Hotel		✔		$27	✔
Shannon Court Hotel	✔		✔	$25	✔
Sheraton at Fisherman's Wharf	✔	✔	✔	$30	✔
Sheraton Gateway Hotel	✔	✔	✔	Free	✔

Extra Amenities	Business Amenities	Decor	Pool/ Sauna	Exercise Facilities
Massage, free breakfast		Artsy 1950s courtyard hotel	Pool	
Wine reception, video games	Dataport, fax, 2-line phone	Early California	Privileges	✔
Free breakfast, afternoon tea & sherry		Victorian	Privileges	Privileges
Bay views	Dataport, 2-line phone	Contemporary	Pool	
Japanese rooms available	Dataport, 2-line phone	Contemporary Japanese	Privileges	✔
Free breakfast	Dataport			Privileges
Free airport shuttle	Dataport		Pool	✔
Free breakfast		California mission		
Free shuttle, park, stay, & fly	Dataport		Pool	Privileges
Child-care services	Dataport, 2-line phone			✔
Massage for a fee	Dataport, 2-line phone	Traditional	Pool, sauna, whirlpool	✔
Childcare, golf spa, shuttle	✔	Modern		✔
Video games, running path	Dataport, 2-line phone	Traditional	Pool, sauna, whirlpool	✔
Hydrotherapy	Dataport, 2-line phone	Modern	Pool, sauna, whirlpool	✔
Sherry, video games	Dataport, 2-line phone	European boutique		Discounted privileges
Kitchenettes, fireplace	Dataport		Pool	
Wine reception	Dataport, fax, 2-line phone	Eclectic Californian	Sauna	✔
Cookies, video games	Dataport	Traditional European		
Video games	Dataport	Contemporary	Pool	✔
	Dataport, 2-line phone	Traditional	Pool, sauna, whirlpool	✔

Hotel/website	Room Rating	Zone	Street Address
Sheraton Palace Hotel	★★★★	7	2 New Montgomery Street San Francisco, CA 94105
The Sherman House	★★★★★	5	2160 Green Street San Francisco, CA 94123
Silverado Country Club and Resort www.silveradoresort.com	★★★★	WC	1600 Atlas Peak Road Napa, CA 94558
Sir Francis Drake Hotel www.SirFrancisdrake.com	★★★½	3	450 Powell Street San Francisco, CA 94102
Sonoma County Hilton Santa Rosa www.hilton.com	★★★★	WC	3555 Round Barn Boulevard Santa Rosa, CA 95403
Sonoma Hotel www.sonomahotel.com	★★★½	WC	110 W. Spain Street Sonoma, CA 95476
Sonoma Mission Inn and Spa	★★★★½	WC	18300 Highway 12 Sonoma, CA 95476
Stanyan Park Hotel www.stanyanpark.com	★★★	8	750 Stanyon Street San Francisco, CA 94117
Star Motel	★★	5	1727 Lombard Street San Francisco, CA 94123
Super 8 Motel	★★½	5	2440 Lombard Street San Francisco, CA 94123
Town House Motel	★★½	5	1650 Lombard Street San Francisco, CA 94123
Travelodge Bel Aire www.travelodge.com	★★½	5	3201 Steiner San Francisco, CA 94123
Travelodge by the Bay www.travelodge.com	★★½	5	1450 Lombard Street San Francisco, CA 94123
Travelodge Golden Gate www.travelodge.com	★★	5	2230 Lombard Street San Francisco, CA 94123
Travelodge San Francisco Airport North	★★½	SFIA	326 S. Airport Boulevard South San Francisco, CA 94080
Union Street Inn www.unionstreetinn.com	★★★½	5	2229 Union Street San Francisco, CA 94123
Vagabond Inn Airport www.vagabondinn.com	★★½	SFIA	1640 Bayshore Highway Burlingame, CA 94010
Villa Florence	★★★	3	225 Powell Street San Francisco, CA 94102
Villa Inn	★★½	10	1600 Lincoln Avenue San Rafael, CA 94901
Vintage Inn www.vintageinn.com	★★★★½	WC	6541 Washington Street Yountville, CA 94599

Local Phone	Guest Fax	Toll-Free Res. Line	Cost ($=$50)	Discounts Available	No. of Rooms
(415) 512-1111	(415) 543-0671	(800) 325-3535	$$$$$$$+	AAA, Government	550
(415) 563-3600	(415) 563-1882	(800) 424-5777	$$$$$$$$−		14
(707) 257-0200	(707) 257-2867	(800) 532-0500	$$$$$$+	AAA, AARP	281
(415) 392-7755	(415) 391-8719	(800) 795-7129	$$$$$+	AAA, AARP, Government	417
(707) 523-7555	(707) 569-5550	(800) HILTONS	$$$$+	AAA, AARP, Government	246
(707) 996-2996	(707) 996-7014	(800) 468-6016	$$$$−	Group	16
(707) 938-9000	(707) 938-42501	(800) 862-4945	$$$$$$$$−	AARP	228
(415) 751-1000	(415) 668-5454	NA	$$$+	AAA	36
(415) 346-8250	(415) 441-4469	(800) 835-8143	$$$−	AAA, AARP, Government	52
(415) 922-0244	(415) 922-8887	(800) 800-8000	$$$	AAA, AARP, Government	32
(415) 885-5163	(415) 771-9889	(800) 255-1516	$$+	AARP, Government	24
(415) 921-5162	(415) 921-3602	(800) 578-7878	$$$−	AAA, AARP, Government	32
(415) 673-0691	(415) 673-3232	(800) 578-7878	$$$	AAA, AARP, Government	72
(415) 922-3900	(415) 921-4795	(800) 578-7878	$$$$−	AAA, AARP, Government	29
(650) 583-9600	(650) 873-9392	(800) 578-7878	$$+	AAA, AARP, Government	197
(415) 346-0424	(415) 922-8046	NA	$$$+		6
(650) 692-4040	(650) 692-5314	(800) 522-1555	$$+	AAA, AARP, Government	91
(415) 397-7700	(415) 397-1006	(800) 553-4411	$$$$$−	AAA, AARP, Government	183
(415) 456-4975	(415) 456-1520	(888) 845-5246	$$+	AAA, AARP, Government	60
(707) 944-1112	(707) 944-1617	(800) 351-1133	$$$$$$$+	AAA, AARP	80

Hotel	On-site Dining	Room Service	Bar	Parking per Day	Meeting Facilities
Sheraton Palace Hotel	✔	✔	✔	$30	✔
The Sherman House	✔	✔		Free valet included in rate	
Silverado Country Club and Resort	✔	✔	✔	Free	✔
Sir Francis Drake Hotel	✔	✔	✔	$31	✔
Sonoma County Hilton Santa Rosa	✔	✔	✔	Free	✔
Sonoma Hotel	✔		✔	Free	✔
Sonoma Mission Inn and Spa	✔	✔	✔	Free	✔
Stanyan Park Hotel				$12	
Star Motel				Free	
Super 8 Motel				Free	
Town House Motel				Free	
Travelodge Bel Aire				Free	
Travelodge by the Bay				$10	
Travelodge Golden Gate				Free	
Travelodge San Francisco Airport North	✔			Free	✔
Union Street Inn				$15	
Vagabond Inn Airport				Free	
Villa Florence	✔		✔	$28	✔
Villa Inn				Free	
Vintage Inn			✔	Free	✔

Extra Amenities	Business Amenities	Decor	Pool/ Sauna	Exercise Facilities
Massage available	Dataport, 2-line phone	Grand hotel	Pool, sauna, whirlpool	✔
Full breakfast, champagne		French and English	Privileges	Privileges
Golf courses, spa, tennis	Dataport, 2-line phone	Contemporary	Pool, sauna, whirlpool	✔
	2-line phone	California Colonial		✔
	Dataport	Wine Country	Pool, whirlpool	✔
No TV		French Provençal		
Full spa, massage, golf course	Dataport	Variety	Pool, sauna, steam room	✔
Free breakfast, afternoon tea	Dataport	Victorian		
Free breakfast				
Free breakfast, children's rates		Modern		
				Nearby
	Modem lines			
Airport shuttle	Dataport	Modern Tropical	Pool	
Full breakfast, wine hour		Victorian		
Free breakfast	✔			
Wine evenings, Nintendo	Dataport	Italian Renaissance		
Free breakfast	2-line phone		Pool, whirlpool	
Wine, spa, free breakfast	Dataport, 2-line phone	California	Pool, sauna, whirlpool	✔

Hotel/website	Room Rating	Zone	Street Address
Vintner's Inn	★★★★½	WC	4350 Barnes Road Santa Rosa, CA 95403
W Hotel San Francisco www.whotel.com	★★★★★	7	181 Third Street San Francisco, CA 94103
Warwick Regis Hotel www.warwickhotels.com	★★★★	3	490 Geary Street San Francisco, CA 94102
Waterfront Plaza Hotel www.waterfrontplaza.com	★★★½	13	10 Washington Street Oakland, CA 94607
Westin Hotel San Francisco Airport	★★★★	SFIA	1 Old Bayshore Highway Millbrae, CA 94030
The Westin St. Francis	★★★★½	3	335 Powell Street San Francisco, CA 94102
White Swan Inn www.foursisters.com	★★★★½	3	845 Bush Street San Francisco, CA 94108
Wyndham Garden Hotel www.wyndham.com	★★★★	10	1010 Northgate Drive San Rafael, CA 94903

Hotel	On-site Dining	Room Service	Bar	Parking per Day	Meeting Facilities
Vintner's Inn	✔	✔	✔	Free	✔
W Hotel San Francisco	✔	✔	✔	$36	✔
Warwick Regis Hotel	✔	✔	✔	$23	✔
Waterfront Plaza Hotel	✔	✔	✔	$15	✔
Westin Hotel San Francisco Airport	✔	✔	✔	$14-valet $12-self	✔
The Westin St. Francis	✔	✔	✔	$35	✔
White Swan Inn				$25	✔
Wyndham Garden Hotel	✔	✔	✔	Free	✔

Local Phone	Guest Fax	Toll-Free Res. Line	Cost ($=$50)	Discounts Available	No. of Rooms
(707) 575-7350	(707) 575-1426	(800) 421-2584	$$$$$+	AARP	44
(415) 777-5300	(415) 817-7800	(877) WHOTELS	$$$$$$$+		423
(415) 928-7900	(415) 441-8788	(800) 827-3447	$$$+	AAA, AARP, Government	80
(510) 836-3800	(510) 832-5695	(800) 729-3638	$$$$	AAA, AARP	144
(650) 692-3500	(650) 872-8111	(800) 228-3000	$$$$$$−	AAA, senior, Government	396
(415) 397-7000	(415) 774-0124	(800) 695-8284	$$$$$$	AAA, AARP, Government	1,189
(415) 775-1755	(415) 775-5717	(800) 999-9570	$$$$$		26
(415) 479-8800	(415) 479-2342	(800) 996-3426	$$$$$−	AAA, AARP, Government	235

Extra Amenities	Business Amenities	Decor	Pool/ Sauna	Exercise Facilities
Free breakfast	Dataport, 2-line phone	European	Whirlpool	Privileges
Stereo, videos, Internet	Dataport, fax, 2-line phone	Ultra-modern	Pool, steam, whirlpool	✔
	Dataport	European boutique	Privileges	Privileges
Ferry to San Francisco	Dataport	Nautical	Pool, sauna	✔
Airport shuttle, jogging trail	Dataport		Pool, whirlpool	✔
	Dataport, cordless phone	Grand Hotel		✔
Free breakfast, tea	Dataport	English garden inn	Privileges	✔
	Dataport, 2-line phone	Contemporary	Pool, whirlpool	✔

Part Three

Visiting San Francisco on Business

Not All Visitors Are Headed for Fisherman's Wharf

While some people make it their business to vacation in San Francisco, others have no choice. Whether or not those lucky few who are getting forced to this wonderful city know it or not, San Francisco is a business traveler's dream. The city is compact enough to allow you to make deals in the afternoon and by evening go to dinner and catch some of the city's natural wonders as the sun is setting.

In case you haven't noticed, Silicon Valley, located about 50 miles south of San Francisco, is a global center for high-technology business and manufacturing. Headquarters of major corporations that make their home here: Chevron, Hewlett-Packard, Bank America, Intel, Apple Computer, Sun Microsystems, Wells Fargo, Seagate Technology, and Gap.

The city is also a major center for higher education. It's the home of San Francisco State University, the University of San Francisco, Hastings College of Law (University of California), the University of California Medical Center, the San Francisco Art Institute, and other public and private colleges. Across the bay is the University of California, Berkeley, one of the world's great research institutions. As a result, San Francisco hosts many visiting academics, college administrators, and students and their families.

In many ways, the problems facing business visitors on their first trip to San Francisco don't differ much from the problems of folks in town intent on seeing its best-known tourist attractions and breathtaking scenery. Business visitors need to be in a hotel that's convenient; they want to avoid the worst of the city's traffic, they face the same problems getting around an unfamiliar city, and they want to know the locations of San Francisco's best restaurants. For the most part, though, business visitors aren't nearly as flexible about the timing of their visit as folks who pick San Francisco as a vacation destination. While we advise that the best times to visit are the shoulder seasons between winter and summer, the necessities of business may dictate that August, when the city is often shrouded in fog, or January, the rainiest month, is when you pull into town. No matter the time of year, though, you should certainly find the time to squeeze a morning or afternoon out of your busy schedule, grab this book, and spend a few hours exploring some of the places that draw millions of visitors to San Francisco each year.

The Moscone Center

San Francisco is home to one major convention center, the 1.3-million-square-foot **Moscone Center** (747 Howard Street, San Francisco, CA 94103; (415) 974-4000; www.moscone.com). The facility is actually two convention venues (Moscone North and Moscone South) on adjacent 11-acre blocks bounded by Mission, Folsom, Third, and Fourth Streets near the heart of downtown. Named for San Francisco Mayor George R. Moscone (murdered in 1978 along with Supervisor Harvey Milk), this modern, $330-million convention center is located in the booming SoMa District (South of Market) four blocks south of Union Square.

Within walking distance are 20,000 hotel rooms, the city's major shopping district, the Powell Street cable cars to **Chinatown, Nob Hill,** and **Fisherman's Wharf,** and many of San Francisco's best restaurants. Next door is the **San Francisco Museum of Modern Art (SFMOMA),** and across the street is the **Yerba Buena Center,** with a park, art gallery, theaters, cafés, public ice skating and bowling, and **The Rooftop** children's area. Nearby is **Metreon,** the Sony entertainment center with 4 stories and 350,000 square feet offering 15 movie theaters, an IMAX theater, 8 restaurants and shopping. Without a doubt, San Francisco and the Moscone Center add up to one of the best convention destinations in the world.

But there's more to come. Already home to the **San Francisco Museum of Modern Art,** the **California Historical Society,** the **Cartoon Art Museum,** and several art galleries, SoMa will also become home to two other established San Francisco museums—the **Mexican Museum** and the **Jewish Museum;** both should be in new digs near the Moscone Center in the next few years. Plus, the convention center is expanding. Moscone West, a 300,000-square-foot addition, will be located on the northwest corner of Fourth and Howard Streets, facing Moscone South. The $191-million building is scheduled for completion in early 2003 and will increase the size of the convention center to 900,000 square feet.

The Layout

Moscone South, which opened in 1981, offers 260,560 square feet of primary exhibit area in a column-free space that can be divided into three halls. (The distinctive arches that make the hall column-free also reduce usable floor space by about 40%.) Forty-one flexible meeting rooms provide more than 60,000 square feet of meeting space. The lobby-level, 42,675-square-foot Esplanade Ballroom (a newer facility added in 1991) accommodates more than 5,000 delegates and is surrounded by terraced patios.

Across the street and connected to Moscone South by an underground concourse and a pedestrian sky bridge is the smaller Moscone North, which opened in 1992 and contains 181,440 square feet of exhibit space in 2 halls and up to 53,410 square feet of flexible meeting space in 17 rooms. The lobby provides a striking entrance to the exhibit level; delegates descend on escalators and stairs illuminated by skylights.

Both buildings are modern, bright, and airy, featuring extensive use of skylights and large expanses of glass that admit ample light to the mostly underground site. Outside, the two buildings are enhanced by landscaped walkways, gardens, patios, sculptures, and a walk-through fountain. The meeting rooms on the mezzanine level in Moscone South have windows that overlook the main hall.

All major exhibit areas and most meeting rooms are on one underground level linked by the underground concourse; additional meeting rooms are located on Moscone South's mezzanine level. Twenty completely enclosed loading docks are located on the same level as the main halls, providing direct drive-in access to both exhibit halls.

A note to exhibitors: All installation and dismantling of exhibits, and all handling of materials require union labor, including signs and carpet laying. But union labor isn't required for the unpacking and placement of exhibitors' merchandise in the booth, or if the display is installed by one person in less than 30 minutes without the use of tools.

Services

Two business centers, one each in the lower lobbies of Moscone North and Moscone South, provide access to photocopying services, transparencies, fax, overnight mail, UPS, office supplies, and cellular phone rental. The centers are open during event hours, and major credit cards are accepted for purchases and services.

Nursing services are on site during events at first-aid stations in Moscone North, Moscone South, and the esplanade level. A gift shop in the Moscone South lower lobby sells souvenirs. Hungry? Each convention group works with the Moscone Center to set up food service, so food availability differs with each convention. However, the neighborhood is full of places to eat, ranging from fast food and cafés to gourmet fare. The closest places to grab a quick bite to eat are the two cafés located in **Yerba Buena Center** (Mission at Third Street; (415) 978-2787) and the **Museum of Modern Art Café** (151 Third Street; (415) 357-4000), which offers reasonably priced sandwiches, salads, desserts, beer, and wine (closed Wednesdays).

Parking and Public Transportation

The Moscone Center has no on-site parking. But 5,000 parking spaces can be found within walking distance in garages and parking lots and on the street. Still, dealing with a car in this dense city scene is a hassle. With so many hotels, restaurants, museums, art galleries, and public transportation within walking distance of the convention center, why bother with a car?

Consider using San Francisco's public transportation systems instead. Powell Street Station, only two blocks from the convention center, provides access to BART (Bay Area Rapid Transit) and Muni Metro (streetcars); adjacent are the Powell Street cable-car lines to Nob Hill and Fisherman's Wharf (although the wait in line to get aboard a cable car can be lengthy during peak tourist seasons).

Muni Metro will get you to the Financial District and the city's outlying neighborhoods, while BART can whisk you beyond the city to Oakland and Berkeley. Muni buses and cable cars will get you just about everywhere else. Plus, there are cabs.

Lodging within Walking Distance of the Moscone Center

A couple of hotels are within an easy stroll of the Moscone Center: the **San Francisco Marriott** (55 Fourth Street; (415) 896-1600) offers 1,500 rooms; the **Sheraton Palace** (2 New Montgomery Street; (415) 512-1111) has 550 rooms; the **Argent Hotel San Francisco** (50 Third Street; (415) 974-6400) has 693 rooms; and the **Galleria Park Hotel** (191 Sutter Street; (415) 781-3060) offers 177 rooms.

Convention Rates: How They Work and How to Do Better

If you're attending a major convention or trade show, the meeting's sponsoring organization has probably negotiated "convention rates" with a number of hotels. Under this arrangement, hotels agree to "block" a certain number of rooms at an agreed upon price for conventioneers. In the case of a small meeting, only one hotel may be involved; but city-wide conventions may involve almost all downtown and airport hotels.

Because the convention sponsor brings big business to San Francisco and reserves many rooms, often annually, it usually can negotiate volume discounts substantially below rack rate. But some conventions and trade shows have more bargaining clout and negotiating skill than others, and your convention sponsor may not be one of them.

Once a convention or trade show sponsor completes negotiations with participating hotels, it sends its attendees a housing list that includes all the hotels serving the convention, along with the special convention rate for each. Using the strategies covered in the previous section, you then can compare these convention rates with the rack rates.

If the negotiated convention rate doesn't sound like a good deal, try to reserve a room using a half-price club, a consolidator, or a tour operator. Remember, however, that many of the deep discounts are available only when the hotel expects to be at less than 80% occupancy, a rarity when a big convention is in town.

Strategies for Beating Convention Rates

1. Reserve early. Most big conventions and trade shows announce meeting sites one to three years in advance. Get your reservation booked as far in advance as possible using a half-price club. If you book well ahead of the time the convention sponsor sends out the housing list, chances are good that the hotel will accept your discounted reservation.

2. Compare your convention's housing list with the list of hotels presented in this guide. You may be able to find a suitable hotel not on the housing list.

3. Use a local reservations agency or consolidator. This is also a good strategy if you need to make reservations at the last minute. Local reservations agencies and consolidators almost always control some rooms, even in the midst of a huge convention or trade show.

The Moscone Center can have a considerable impact on San Francisco when, say, 65,000 exhibitors and trade-show attendees come into town and snatch up almost every hotel room in the city. Luckily, though, the large conventions and trade shows register no discernible effect on the availability of restaurant tables or traffic congestion; it's just hotel rooms that get scarce. Check the Moscone Center's website at www.moscone. com for a complete and up-to-date list of 2002 and 2003 conventions and trade shows scheduled. It can help when planning your trip if you are crowd weary.

EXECUTIVE AMUSEMENT

Best Hotel for Fitness Freaks Nob Hill Lambourne (725 Pine Street; (415) 433-2287). Each room comes with stationary bike and treadmill, or rowing machine and private yoga classes.

Climbing the Ladder If you are feeling stuck at the mid-management level, consider climbing to new heights at the world's largest indoor climbing gym, **Mission Cliffs** (2295 Harrison Street; (415) 550-0515). You'll find that clinging onto that left handhold is about as tricky as holding onto a dot com position.

Savvy Spin Doctors Looking for the best in dry cleaning? If it's the top choice for fashion designers, celebrities, and models it's good enough for you. **Buchanan Cleaners** (2137 Buchanan Street; (415) 923-9251).

Presidential Putting Greens Lincoln Park (34th Avenue and Clement Street) has one of the most amazing panoramic vistas of downtown San Francisco anywhere. And it's close to home!

Best Tour Temptation Feeling trapped by the confines of corporate America? Head to Alcatraz—not just the run-of-the-mill tour—but the **Alcatraz After Dark Tour** (Thursday to Sunday only). It's amazing what is revealed when the lights go out in "The Rock." For information on this tour, call (415) 705-5555 or look online at www.nps.gov/alcatraz.

Better than a Punching Bag Feeling the urge to stalk and shoot after a rather stressful day of meetings? Instead head to **Pacific Rod and Gun** (520 Muir Drive; (415) 586-8349). You know the cue "pull," and BAM!– shoot that skeet!

Ma and Pa Car Rental If you are tired of dealing with big rental car agencies that simply ask for a corporate number, head to **City Rent-A-Car** (1748 Folsom Street; (415) 359-1331). You get small-town service by the two brothers that own it, and the rates are cheaper than those of the big guns.

Floppy Got the Flu? If you are in need of a computer doctor to get that Power-point sharpened for your presentation, **Tech Bench** at the Robert Austin Computer Show meets at the Cow Palace or Oakland Convention Center most weekends. Call (650) 692-1448 or check out www.robertaustin.com.

Part Four

Arriving and Getting Oriented

Coming into the City

By Car

San Francisco is located on the tip of a peninsula linked to the mainland by two bridges. As a result, visitors arriving by car enter the city by one of three routes: from the south on US 101, from the east on I-80 (via the San Francisco–Oakland Bay Bridge), or from the north on US 101 (on the Golden Gate Bridge).

US 101 and a parallel highway, I-280, link the city to the rest of the peninsula to the south, including Palo Alto, Santa Clara, and San Jose, located at the southern end of San Francisco Bay. US 101 is also the coastal highway that continues farther south to Gilroy, Salinas, San Luis Obispo, Santa Barbara, and Los Angeles, 400 miles away. A more scenic— and significantly slower—option that hugs the coast is California Route 1, which leads directly to Santa Cruz, Carmel, Big Sur, and Morro Bay.

Travelers coming from the east on I-80 (which goes through Sacramento, Reno, Salt Lake City, Omaha, Chicago, and other points east before reaching New York City) pass through Oakland before crossing San Francisco Bay on the Bay Bridge and entering downtown San Francisco. It's also the route for people coming to the Bay Area on Interstate 5, the north-south interstate through California's Central Valley (and the fastest driving route from Los Angeles).

Drivers coming through Oakland are confronted with a maze of interstate highways that link together to form a kind of beltway around San Francisco. In addition to the San Francisco–Oakland Bay Bridge, San Francisco Bay is crossed by two more bridges to the south (these connect with the San Francisco peninsula well south of the city). I-580 crosses San Pablo Bay north of San Francisco, where it connects the East Bay city of Richmond with San Rafael. US 101 to the north, via the Golden Gate Bridge, links San Francisco to Marin County and the rest of

Northern California, including San Rafael, Petaluma, Healdsburg, and Eureka. Again, California Route 1 is the slow and scenic option; the two-lane road follows the coast north.

By Plane

Most domestic and foreign visitors who fly to San Francisco land at the San Francisco International Airport, 14 miles south of downtown directly on US 101. It's the fifth-busiest airport in the United States, and it's undergoing a major expansion. Luckily, many domestic flyers have a choice: Oakland International Airport, a smaller, more distant facility is worth considering, especially if you can get a direct flight from your hometown. Oakland International is located 5 miles south of downtown Oakland, across San Francisco Bay (about 24 miles from downtown San Francisco.)

San Francisco International Airport (SFO)

Seventy-four percent of visitors arrive by air, most of them through the San Francisco International Airport (SFO); www.san-francisco-sfo.com. A $2.4-billion construction project is well under way to ready the airport for a projected volume of 51 million passengers in 2006. Plans include a new international terminal, an airport rail-transit system, a BART (Bay Area Rapid Transit) station, and elevated roadways. The centerpiece of the program is a 2-million-square-foot international terminal that was completed in the spring of 2000. Because of the huge project, navigating the roadways surrounding the airport will be a real headache for the next couple of years, especially for first-time visitors.

The Layout   SFO handles an average of 109,000 passengers a day on 50 passenger airlines. It's a horseshoe-shaped facility with three major terminals: the South Terminal, the International Terminal, and the North Terminal. The terminals surround a parking garage and are linked by indoor corridors featuring changing art exhibits (nice to know if you've got time to kill). Each terminal features shops, restaurants, and newsstands, and the International Terminal has a small boutique shopping mall. Five airport information booths, open from 8 a.m. to midnight, are located in the baggage-claim areas; multilingual agents can provide information on ground transportation, Bay Area lodging, and cultural events.

Arriving   From your gate, follow the signs down to the baggage area on the lower level. Then for most folks it's back to the main level to reach the bus to the central rental-car facility, door-to-door vans, public transportation, and hotel shuttles . . . a major inconvenience only slightly mitigated by nearby elevators. Cabs and limos, however, are outside the lower-level doors. Short-term parking is across the street from the terminals in the parking garage; from the North Terminal take the escalator up to reach the garage. From the International and South Terminals, take a shuttle van (available at the curb outside on the arrival level) to the garage.

Airport Security   Airport security at SFO has been upgraded since the terrorst attacks on the United States of September 11, 2001. Passengers are advised:

- That all carry-on and checked luggage will be screened;
- To arrive two hours prior to departure for domestic flights and three hours prior to departure for international flights;
- That all unattended vehicles left in front of the terminal building will be ticketed and towed;
- That a government-issued ID is required for identification. You will be asked to show your ID at check-in, prior to boarding, and possibly at other points in the pre-flight/boarding process.
- That only passengers with airline tickets are allowed beyond screening check-points;
- That all electronic devices are subject to screening at checkpoints;
- That passengers are limited to one carry-on bag plus one personal carry-on item;
- That knives of any length must be placed in checked baggage;
- That all cutting and puncturing instruments and athletic equipment that can be used as a weapon must be placed in checked baggage.

For the latest information on security procedures at SFO, visit their website at www.flysfo.com.

Getting Downtown

Driving   If you're renting a car, you'll find rental agency counters on the lower baggage level. Next, haul your luggage up to the arrival level, walk outside to the outer curb, and board the bus which takes you through the confusion of new construction to the central car-rental building. A suggestion: If you've got lots of baggage and you're with someone else, leave the luggage and one person at the curb while you fetch the rental car. After picking up your car keys, get explicit directions to US 101, which goes to downtown San Francisco. (It's a good idea to call ahead to your hotel for turn-by-turn driving directions.)

To reach Market Street near Union Square (the main downtown hotel district), take US 101 to I-280 north; then take the Sixth Street exit. Market Street is about six blocks from the end of the exit; across Market Street, Sixth Street becomes Taylor Street, a one-way street heading north toward Fisherman's Wharf. It's about a 25-minute drive to downtown from the airport (longer during rush hour).

Cabs and Shuttles   Cabs are available outside the baggage area near the yellow column at all terminals. Typical fares to downtown San Francisco are about $35–40; up to five riders can split the cost. Door-to-door shared van service to downtown San Francisco, available outside the doors of the arrival level on the center island, is priced at around $12–20 per person ($5–10 for children). The vans leave every 15 to 20 minutes between 6 a.m. and 11 p.m. and every 30 minutes during late night hours.

SHUTTLE SAVVY: TIPS FOR A SMOOTH RIDE

1. Generally shuttles to and from both SFO and Oakland are equal in service and price—you can expect to pay around $30 per person from Oakland and about $20 from SFO.
2. The trip to downtown from SFO generally takes about 30 minutes, although traffic can sometimes make it up to an hour. Oakland is further away and the Bay Bridge traffic can be relentless; expect about an hour commute into downtown.
3. If there are three or more in your party it might be cheaper to split the cost of a taxi. With taxis you don't have to wait. Be sure to check with the shuttle as to when they will be leaving. More often than not, the shuttle waits for a few flights to land in the hopes of filling up before heading out. So if you are the first one be prepared for a wait. There seems to be a rule, however, that the ground transportation center enforces that states shuttles must leave within ten minutes of its first customer.
4. If there are numerous people in the shuttle, check to see where on the drop-off list you fit. If you are last to be dropped off it could make your trip torturously long.

Major shuttle van services include **Bay Shuttle** (phone (415) 564-3400) and **Supershuttle** (phone (800) BLUEVAN). Supershuttle allows you to make back-to-the-airport reservations on their website (www.supershuttle.com). You can also make reservations by phone for your return trip with any of the shuttle services. For more information, contact one of the van services or the SFO ground transportation hotline (call (800) SFO-2008 between 7:30 a.m. and 5 p.m. weekdays) or visit www.san-francisco-sfo.com/transportation.html.

Public Transportation   Travelers on a budget with only one bag (but no luggage) and plenty of time can take a **SamTrans** bus to the Transbay Terminal at First and Mission Streets in downtown San Francisco; the KX Express leaves from the upper level about every 30 minutes. The one-way fare is $3, and the trip downtown takes about 35 minutes. The slower, cheaper 292 Local is another option, and you can bring luggage; the fare is $1.10 from the airport in and $2.20 from downtown out, and the trip takes about an hour. Both buses require exact change, and reservations are not accepted. Call (650) 508-6200 for more information.

A free **CalTrain-SFO** Shuttle (upper level) provides a 10-minute bus ride to a commuter train station at nearby Millbrae, where you can catch the next train to downtown San Francisco; a one-way fare is about $3, and you purchase tickets from the conductor after you board. On weekdays, trains run about every 10 minutes during rush hour and about every 30 minutes the rest of the day and on weekdays and holidays. The commuter trains arrive at Third and Townsend Streets in the SoMa District, where you can grab a cab or bus to downtown. And it's okay to carry luggage. For more information, call (800) 720-6661 or visit www.caltrain.com.

Oakland International Airport (OAK)

Smaller is better at Oakland International Airport (www.oaklandairport.com), across the bay from San Francisco and five miles south of downtown Oakland. With only two terminals and everything on one level, Oakland is a lot less confusing to weary travelers. It's also new, bright, and attractive. While Oakland is the obvious airport choice if your destination is in the East Bay area, it's also the hassle-free alternative to SFO for San Francisco–bound travelers—at least, the ones who can book a direct flight from their hometowns.

The Layout   Terminal 1 handles all domestic and international airlines, with the exception of Southwest Airlines, which claims all of Terminal 2. From your gate, follow signs to the baggage area near the entrance and to the right. Ground transportation is outside the door, including shuttle vans to downtown San Francisco (to the left of Terminal 1 under the covered walkway). Most rental-car agencies are across the street; no need to take a shuttle bus to a remote lot. Shuttles to the BART station in Oakland and bus service are located outside the terminals.

Getting Downtown

Driving   To reach downtown San Francisco from Oakland International, exit the airport and take Hegenberger Road to I-880 north. Follow signs for I-80, which takes you across the double-decker San Francisco–Oakland Bay Bridge where the toll costs $2 westbound at Oakland. The first two exits after the bridge take you downtown. It's about a 30-minute drive (longer during rush hour).

Cabs and Shuttles   Cabs are usually available outside the baggage areas between Terminal 1 and Terminal 2; a typical fare to downtown San Francisco is $40 and can be split among riders. Door-to-door, shared-ride shuttle services to downtown San Francisco (usually $30) include **City Express** (phone (888) 874-8885 or (510) 638-8830), **Air Transit Shuttle** (phone (510) 568-3434), and **Citywide Shuttle Service** (phone (510) 336-0090).

Public Transportation   Shuttle service via AirBART to the BART Oakland Coliseum station is $2 one way (50 cents for children, disabled, and seniors). Ticket machines for AirBART are in Terminal 1 and Terminal 2 in the airport. The machines don't give change for bills larger than $1. The ride should take about 15 minutes. Once you arrive at Coliseum station, take a BART train to one of four downtown San Francisco stations on Market Street ($2.80 one way). For BART info, call (510) 465-2278 or visit www.bart.gov. **AC Transit's Line 58** bus connects the airport with the Alameda/Oakland Ferry and downtown Oakland's Jack London Square. One-way fare is $1.35; exact fare is required. The ferry also provides a scenic trip across San Francisco Bay to the city's Ferry Terminal and Pier 39 in Fisherman's Wharf. One-way fares are $5 for adults, $2.25 for children ages 5–12, and $3 for seniors, disabled, and active military personnel. For ferry schedules, call (510) 522-3300 or look up www.east bayferry.com.

By Train

Amtrak's staffed ticket office, waiting room, and baggage check is located in the Ferry Building at the foot of Market Street. Motor coaches transport departing and arriving passengers to the Amtrak train station in Emeryville, near Oakland, and to three other downtown San Francisco points: Pier 39 in Fisherman's Wharf, the Hyatt Regency in the Financial District, and Macy's near Union Square.

The motor-coach trip from Emeryville takes about ten minutes; your luggage is checked through to your final stop downtown (or, for departing passengers, to your train). Cities with daily round-trip service to San Francisco are Los Angeles and San Diego (five trips a day), Sacramento (four trips a day), Seattle and Portland (one trip a day), and Chicago (one trip a day). For exact schedule and fare information check www.amtrak.com or call (800) USA-RAIL.

Where to Find Tourist Information in San Francisco

If you're short on maps or need more information on sight-seeing, restaurants, hotels, shopping, or things to do in San Francisco and the Bay Area, there are several places to stop and pick up maps and brochures.

- In downtown San Francisco: **San Francisco Convention and Visitors Bureau,** Hallidie Plaza at Powell and Market Streets (lower level). Phone (415) 283-0177, Fax (415) 362-7323, or visit www.sfvisitor.org. Open weekdays 9 a.m. to 5 p.m. and weekends 9 a.m. to 3 p.m.; closed Easter, Thanksgiving, Christmas, and New Year's Day.

- In Marin County: **Marin County Convention and Visitors Bureau,** 103 Larkspur Landing Circle, Larkspur. Phone (415) 499-5000, or visit www.visitmarin.org. Open weekdays 9 a.m. to 5 p.m.; closed Thanksgiving, Christmas, and New Year's Day.

- In Napa Valley wine country: **Napa Valley Conference and Visitors Bureau,** 1310 Napa Town Center, Napa. Phone (707) 226-7459, Fax (707) 255-2066, or visit www.napavalley.com. Open daily 9 a.m. to 5 p.m.; closed Thanksgiving, Christmas, and New Year's Day.

■ In Sonoma wine country: **Sonoma Valley Visitors Bureau,** 453 First Street East, Sonoma. Phone (707) 996-1090, or visit www.sonomavalley.com. Open daily 9 a.m. to 5 p.m.

A Geographic Overview of San Francisco and the Bay Area

San Francisco, with more than 750,000 residents, is the second most densely populated city in the country (after New York). The city, on the West Coast of the United States about halfway between the northern and southern ends of California, is situated on the tip of a hilly peninsula jutting into San Francisco Bay and, to the west, overlooking the Pacific Ocean. San Francisco is the epicenter of a larger metropolitan area with a total population of about 6 million, making it the fifth-largest urban area in the United States.

California, the most populous state in the Union (and its third largest), is bordered to the east by Arizona and Nevada. To the north is Oregon and the Pacific Northwest; to the south is the international border with Mexico. Along California's nearly 800-mile coastline, which forms the western edge of the state, is the Pacific Ocean. The largest city in California is Los Angeles, 400 miles to the south; the state capital is Sacramento, about 90 miles northeast of San Francisco.

The Big One!

We've all heard stories as kids that "the Big One" is going to rock California and forever knock it off our map where it will find restful solitude in the Pacific Ocean. And the culprit of such a sinking fate? The San Andreas Fault, of course. The San Andreas Fault, the active frontier between the Pacific and North American tectonic plates, runs vertically through California. And like a nose on a dangerous face, San Francisco is smack dab in the center, which allows the fault to create violent tremors and devastating earthquakes as it readjusts itself in the earth below. She is temperamental to a fault, as evidenced by the quake of 1906, 1989, and the impending granddaddy of them all predicted for sometime in the future.

Seismologists are unable to predict when tremors or earthquakes will occur or how severe they'll be. The actual shifting of the plates isn't what causes the damage but instead the resulting collapses, fires, and landslides that kill hundreds. Since the 1989 quake, many buildings in San Francisco have been strengthened to withstand tremors, and shelters (such as the one at the Moscone Convention Center) are stocked as emergency relief sites. In addition, most hotels have their own evacuation procedures. For more detailed information on what to do in the event of a tremor while you're in San Francisco, check the local phone directory, which has pages full of detailed advice.

You Oughtta Be in Pictures!

Visitors might hate the United States, but love San Francisco. It's because of its breathtaking beauty and sense of care and compassion over its inhabitants. It is an easy place to live, visit, navigate, and easy to fall in love with. If you are not convinced at first glimpse of the Golden Gate Bridge, just look beyond at the Marin Headlands, the carpet of mountains that in the spring become covered with flowers and chaparral (dense, scrubby brushland). Year-round the Headlands harbor secret playgrounds for adrenaline junkies of all ages. Further away from the Headlands is Mount Tamalpais, or Mount Tam as it is affectionately called. Hike, bike, drive . . . you name it and the Mountain will provide it. It also has one of the best views of the city and the surrounding Bay area—on a clear day you can see across to the Sierra Nevada. If you survive the hike or winding drive involved in getting to the top, you can head south to Stinson Beach or toward Muir Woods where you can drive your car through one of the giant redwoods that tower in the forest. Both ends of the Golden Gate Bridge are anchored in the Golden Gate National Recreation Area, more than 75,000 acres of parkland managed by the National Park Service; it's a recreational Mecca to San Franciscans.

North of the Marin Headlands is Point Reyes National Seashore, a windswept peninsula on the Pacific coast covered with woodlands, prairies, and marshes. A geologic "island" cut off from the mainland by the San Andreas fault, Point Reyes was discovered by Sir Francis Drake in 1579. Today it is a carefully preserved sanctuary for more than 350 species of birds and a paradise for botanists and nature lovers in general, who with a little luck can spot elk, lynx, coyotes, and falcons. In the winter, visitors can watch migrating whales at an overlook near the 1870 Point Reyes Lighthouse.

Closer to home within the bay (one of the greatest natural harbors in the world) is Angel Island, only reachable by ferry from Tiburon, Oakland, and San Francisco. No vehicles exist in this state park which is chock full of trails for hiking or biking. Throughout the island are picnic tables, and there is even spooky ruins of a military garrison that served as a quarantine station for Asian immigrants until November 1940 (it was known as the "Ellis Island of the West"). And nearby Alcatraz is becoming a place that you don't want to escape from—it's now making a comeback as a nature and wildlife habitat.

Heaven exists South also. Just follow the number 1—Route 1 that is. It's narrow road winds along the crashing waves of the Pacific Ocean.

You'll be so close to the edge and the water that you may even feel the salty spray from below! It's a high like no other. Along the way are villages and towns like Half Moon Bay, and the occasional nude beach. The Santa Cruz Mountains, running down the spine of the San Francisco peninsula, provide a dramatic backdrop to crashing ocean waves and offer fantastic views of the ocean and bay along Skyline Boulevard, which follows the mountain ridges.

San Francisco Neighborhoods

Hills or no hills, the first developers of the city decided on a grid system. A convenient way of organizing neighborhoods and streets but they did not have to consider the stick shift vehicle back then! San Francisco's hills, more than anything else, thrill visitors with astounding vistas. Surrounded by the shimmering waters of the bay and the Pacific Ocean, the city's land mass is packed on and around nearly four dozen hills—steep markers that delineate San Francisco's shifting moods and economic prosperity—the higher you get the higher the real estate! The Financial District is the granddaddy of commercial square footage while the rest of the city remains charming in its residential—almost suburban—nature. "It's a city you can actually live in," is the catch phrase most use when explaining the benefits of this urban bliss.

Armed with a good map, comfortable walking shoes, and ankle weights (if you are so inclined) to take advantage of the quad workout while pounding the hills, the best way to absorb the city's aura is to walk. You can hit most of downtown San Francisco's major sights and neighborhoods in a day. The city is compact and thanks to that grid layout, well organized. It's easy to foot the city and the bus maps are free and easy to read. Nowhere else can you take in the smell of a corner *taqueria* and within the same block the aroma of a flower garden! You'll be amazed at the cleanliness as well as the differing architecture and personality that each neighborhood boasts.

Chinatown (Zone 1)

North along Grant Avenue and through the flamboyant, green-and-ocher imperial Dragon Gate is bustling Chinatown, a dense warren of restaurants and tacky tourist shops that's the second-largest Chinese community outside of Asia (New York's is number one). Since gold rush days, 24-square-block Chinatown has served as the hub for San Francisco's Chinese population. It's a city within a city, crowded with retail outlets and sidewalk displays jammed with silk, porcelain, teak furniture, handmade jewelry, and the usual tourist gewgaws (the farther you walk up Grant Avenue, the cheaper the postcards get). Walk a little farther to Chinatown's open-air markets, glitzy emporiums, and herbalists' shops filled with exotic herbs and spices. At Grant Avenue and Stockton Street is the main Chinese food-shopping district, crowded with displays of unfamiliar fruits (you have to try the infamous Durian fruit—"smells like hell but tastes like heaven") and fish stores with tanks of live eels, fish, frogs, and turtles waiting to be killed on the spot for customers.

If you have only one experience in Chinatown, make it dim sum. The delicious tidbits, generally served for brunch, are a local institution. Most dim sum houses open at 10 a.m. and close by mid- or late afternoon. Typically, waiters circle the restaurant's dining room, pushing carts stacked with covered bamboo or stainless-steel containers filled with steamed or fried dumplings, shrimp balls, spring rolls, steamed buns, and Chinese pastries. Just point to what looks appealing; the waiters usually don't speak English and ordering is done by gestures. It's cheap, too—you have to order an awful lot of food to spend more than $10 a person. One of the oldest dim-sum institutions in Chinatown is Hang Ah Tea Room on Pagoda Place, off Sacramento and Stockton Streets. Keeping in tune with 24-hour breakfasts, they are open until 9 p.m. Dim sum at dusk? Why not!

For a feel of the real, nontouristy Chinatown, duck into a side alley (such as Waverly Street, which parallels Grant Avenue between Clay and Washington Streets), where you'll see stores that sell lychee wine, Chinese newspapers, dried lotus, and powdered antlers (reputed to restore male virility). Ross Alley, which runs above Grant Avenue between Washington and Jackson Streets, houses small garment shops, laundries, florists, and one-chair barber shops. At the Golden Gate Fortune Cookie Company at 56 Ross Alley, visitors can watch little old women fold bits of wisdom into that oh so familiar shape. Early morning, when shopkeepers are busy setting out their wares, is a good time to get a feel for the real Chinatown. Late January is the Chinese New Year's fest and parade. Slithering giant snakes and dragons, lanterns, and floats march down Grant Avenue in celebration. It is definitely a sight to see, especially if you are traveling with children. For an abbreviated version of the Chinese New Year celebrations, the weekly Lion Dance, held every Sunday, snaps, crackles, and pops its way down Grant Avenue.

Civic Center and the Tenderloin (Zone 2)

Eight blocks west of Union Square on Geary Boulevard is Van Ness Avenue, a broad north-south boulevard and the main thoroughfare of the Civic Center District, acclaimed by critics as one of the finest collections of beaux arts buildings in the country. **City Hall,** built in 1914, is widely considered one of the most beautiful public buildings in America; on a historical note, it's the building in which Dan White shot Mayor George Moscone and Supervisor Harvey Milk in 1978.

Across the plaza from City Hall is the stately former public library, slated to become in spring 2003 the new home of the **Asian Art Museum,** the largest collection of Asian art in the West. The south end of the plaza contains the **Civic Auditorium** (built in 1913), and on the north side is the **State Office Building** (1926). Also in the neighborhood are a few other distinguished buildings, including the **Veterans Auditorium Building** (1932), the **Opera House,** and the **Louise M. Davies Symphony Hall.** Two blocks away is the contemporary **San Francisco Public Library** (1996), a modern interpretation of the classic beaux arts style.

Surrounding the area is a diverse collection of restaurants, antique shops, and galleries. But Civic Center and its fine collection of buildings (and the adjacent Tenderloin, on the north side of Market Street between the theater district and Civic Center) have become the focal point for San Francisco's most glaring problem, the homeless. Periodically police evict hundreds of street people who converge on the plaza opposite City Hall and its lawns. With suited and gowned San Franciscans heading in and out of the ballet, opera, and symphony, it's not a problem easily disguised. Civic Center and the Tenderloin remain one of the last down-and-out sections of town.

Nob Hill/Russian Hill (Zones 1, 2, 3, and 6)

In a city renowned for its hills, Nob Hill heads the list. As California novelist and journalist Joan Didion wrote, Nob Hill is "the symbolic nexus of all old California money and power." Its mansions, exclusive hotels, and posh restaurants tower over the rest of the city. While early San Franciscans of wealth preferred lower sections of town, the installation of cable cars in the 1870s turned Nob Hill into a valuable piece of real estate. The generally accepted borders of Nob Hill are Bush Street and Pacific Avenue, and Stockton and Larkin Streets.

For visitors, however, Nob Hill doesn't offer much in the way of sights—unless it's the fantastic views from the top of the hill 376 feet above sea level. Your best bet is to wander, gaze at the exteriors of exclusive clubs (such as the Pacific Union Club at 1000 California Street), stop at a hotel bar for a drink, and bask in the aura of privilege and luxury that distinguishes this most famous of San Francisco locales.

Speaking of hotel bars, you won't find better than one of the grande dames of Nob Hill—the **Mark Hopkins,** the **Fairmont,** or the **Huntington.** Perhaps Nob Hill's most famous landmark is the Mark Hopkins Inter-Continental San Francisco, a 392-room hotel at California and Mason Streets; great views open at the **Top O' the Mark** lounge, which dates from 1939 and is a charming place to watch the setting sun. You may recognize the Fairmont from its TV stint as the hotel in the show *Hotel* (its penthouse suite goes for $6,000 a day, butler, maid, and limo included).

More Nob Hill treasures include Huntington Park, a flowered square where visitors can see nannies pushing trendy baby joggers and walking well-groomed poodles. The great, gray eminence atop Nob Hill on California Street is **Grace Cathedral,** the largest Gothic structure in the West. Among its many splendors is the cast of the gilded bronze doors created by Lorenzo Ghiberti for the Baptistry in Florence; their ten rectangular reliefs depict scenes from the Old Testament. They stand at the top of the steps to the cathedral's east entrance.

Russian Hill, next door, manages to be both expensive and Bohemian. Home to many rich and famous people, it also has a fair share of artists, struggling writers, and students from the nearby **San Francisco Art Institute.** Again, there's not much here in the way of sights—except for great views, wooded open spaces, picturesque cul-de-sacs, and "the crookedest street in the world" (Lombard Street, with eight turns in one block at its eastern end). Russian Hill, named for a graveyard (long since removed) for Russian seamen, is also where Armistead Maupin's fictional crew in *Tales of the City* made their home. Russian Hill, within walking distance of Union Square, is bordered by Broadway and Chestnut, Taylor, and Larkin Streets.

Union Square (Zone 3)

Perhaps the nearest thing to a city center in San Francisco is Union Square, its liveliest urban space. A few acres of concrete and greenery surrounded by huge department stores, swank hotels, and expensive shops, its adjacent streets are jammed with cars and tour buses, upscale shoppers, befuddled tourists, street musicians, beggars and street people bumming quarters, and businesspeople late for appointments. It's all here, from the sleazy to the sublime. Union Square is safe during the day, but it's best to avoid the area after dark.

In addition to giving credit cards a workout at Neiman-Marcus, Saks Fifth Avenue, or Macy's, you can catch a cable car on Powell Street for a ride up Nob Hill or board a motorized trolley for a city tour. Maiden Lane, an elegant, tree-lined alley that extends two blocks east of Union Square from Stockton to Kearny Streets, features exclusive shops and restaurants. Union Square is also the focal point for the city's main hotel district, so for a lot of visitors it's the obvious place to start a walking tour.

Union Square is also San Francisco's primary theater district. **The American Conservatory Theater** (ACT) at the Geary Theater (415 Geary Boulevard) offers both classic and contemporary works (and a penchant for Moliere) in a restored landmark theater that reopened in 1996. The city's premier African-American theater company calls the **Lorraine Hansberry Theater** (500 Sutter Street) home, while the **Curran Theatre** (445 Geary Boulevard) and the **Marine's Memorial** (609 Sutter Street) present Broadway musicals from New York.

The Financial District (Zone 4)

Frequently called "the Wall Street of the West," the Financial District lies northeast of Union Square in an area bordered by Embarcadero and Market, Third, Kearny, and Washington Streets. Among the towering skyscrapers are several corporate headquarters and the Pacific Coast Stock Exchange, along with lots of elaborate corporate architecture (including the city's tallest landmark, the Transamerica Pyramid).

Brokers, bankers, and insurance agents pursue wealth during the week on several acres of landfill on and around Montgomery Street; unlike most cities' financial areas, the Financial District remains lively on evenings and weekends, thanks to its many restaurants and nightclubs. What motivates these financial movers and shakers can be studied at several museums that attempt to explain the mysteries of the financial world. The lobby of the **Federal Reserve Bank** (101 Market Street) and the **Wells Fargo History Museum** (420 Montgomery Street) offer insights into the city's rich history. All the museums, by the way, keep bankers' hours.

The Marina District and Pacific Heights (Zone 5)

So what if the Marina district is snubbed by many anti-yuppies as the Mecca for all things moneyed? And so what if it is built on earthquake friendly landfill? Filled with Mediterranean-style houses painted in lollipop colors, the Marina District is one of the most beautiful districts in the city, which is why most of its inhabitants are young 20- and 30-something professionals or families. Prices are high and some would argue—so are the egos. With the Presidio to the west and Fort Mason to the east, the Marina is also one of the city's greenest neighborhoods. Yacht clubs, kite flyers, and joggers, make the district feel somewhat like a resort. Ironically, the Marina, built to celebrate the rebirth of the city after the 1906 quake, was the city's worst casualty in the 1989 disaster. Tremors tore through the unstable landfill on which the district is built, and many homes collapsed into smoldering ruins. Rebuilding occurred almost immediately, though, and many of the shimmering new homes are just that—new houses built after the last major earthquake. Nor was the disaster enough to bring rents down; the Marina continues to attract a very well-heeled and smart set.

The Marina's main commercial drag is Chestnut Street, an urban thoroughfare with a swinging-singles reputation; the local Safeway has been dubbed "the Body Shop" for the inordinate amount of cruising that goes on there. A long stretch of turf at Marina Green is popular with the fit, the Lycra-clad, and Frisbee-catching dogs.

A bit east of the Marina is Fort Mason, located on the other side of Aquatic Park and the 1,800-foot curving Municipal Pier (great spots, by the way, to escape the congestion of nearby Fisherman's Wharf). Millions of GIs shipped out to the South Pacific in World War II from Fort Mason, but today it's a public park. Some locals call it "Fort Culture"; here you'll find in its old, shed-like buildings a variety of nonprofit arts organizations, museums, and galleries.

Although mainly a daytime destination, Fort Mason attracts crowds at night for performances of its acclaimed Magic Theatre, one of the oldest and largest theater companies on the West Coast. At night, the fort's pretty bluff is one of the most romantic spots in the city. Fort Mason is also the start of the Golden Gate Promenade, a three-and-a-half-mile paved walkway along San Francisco Bay that ends at Fort Point National Historical Site, directly under the Golden Gate Bridge. A new park along this promenade introduced in 2001 is Crissy Field. The park is the result of restoring approximately 100 acres of the neglected "back yard" of the Presidio. It was transformed from asphalt, chain-link fences, and deteriorating buildings to a vibrant new park that follows along the sands of the bay.

At the westernmost edge of the Marina is its most notable landmark, the **Palace of Fine Arts** (at Baker and Beach Streets). An interpretation of a classical ruin complete with manicured lawns, ponds, and ducks, it's all that's left of the 1915 Panama Pacific Exhibition. Next door is the **Exploratorium,** a unique science museum with more than 700 hands-on science exhibits for youngsters and adults.

When a cable-car line opened in the Pacific Heights District in 1878, this neighborhood south of Fort Mason and west of Van Ness Avenue quickly evolved into an enclave for San Francisco's nouveaux riche. Attempting to outdo the wooden castles on Nob Hill with mansions featuring Gothic arches, Byzantine domes, and stained-glass windows, the denizens of Pacific Heights created monuments to the bonanza era of the late nineteenth century. But the opulence and magnificence was short-lived. The earthquake of 1906 reduced the exquisite homes to shambles and the district never fully recovered. Much of the area was rebuilt with luxury apartment houses, but many original Victorian houses remain, including the city's most photographed group of dainty "painted ladies."

Today, Pacific Heights, along with the adjacent Cow Hollow and Presidio Heights Districts, are home to more college graduates, professionals, and high-income families than any other city district. A fine collection of Victorian houses on Union Street has evolved into a premiere shopping area with more than 300 boutiques, restaurants, antique shops, and coffeehouses.

Fisherman's Wharf (Zone 5)

Although visitors are hard pressed to find vestiges of its once busy shipbuilding, fishing, and industrial might, Fisherman's Wharf was once a busy fishing port. Then, about 30 years ago, the area was transformed into a tourist circus, and that's what it remains today. Here your tourist dollar is pursued with a vengeance at T-shirt shops, fast-food joints, stalls selling sweatshirts and baseball caps, and piers transformed into souvenir complexes, overpriced restaurants, and places to take a cruise on the bay.

In spite of the lamentable statistic that more than 10 million visitors a year come to Fisherman's Wharf, it's tempting to say that, unless you've got restless children in tow, stay away. And while by and large that's good advice, there remain a few good reasons to come (aside from the view, which is great).

Probably the best is **Alcatraz,** 12 minutes away by ferry in San Francisco Bay; it's one of the best places to go in San Francisco and shouldn't be missed. (The ferry leaves from Pier 41; advance reservations are a good idea.) Other worthwhile activities at the wharf include taking a cruise on the bay, renting a bike, or strolling down the **Golden Gate Promenade,** a three-and-a-half-mile paved path by the bay leading to the bridge of the same name. Last but not least, walk out on Pier 41 and wave at the collection of barking sea lions just offshore.

For those restless kids, a cluster of pricey attractions should do the trick. **Aquarium of the Bay** is a commercial aquarium where visitors walk through a submerged transparent tunnel and view Pacific Coast marine creatures. Along Jefferson Street are two rainy-day places: the **Wax Museum** and **Ripley's Believe It or Not.** Things get better at the **Hyde Street Pier,** where the National Park Service has berthed a collection of real nineteenth-century ships open to the public. Another block west is the **Maritime Museum,** a gorgeous art deco building full of nautical treasures.

The wharf also has two refurbished shopping complexes. **The Cannery,** a former fruit-packing factory on Jefferson Street at Leavenworth Street, has three levels of shops and restaurants. **Ghirardelli Square** at 900 North Point Street (at the western end of Fisherman's Wharf) is a boutique mall that's come a long way since its days as a chocolate factory. Its handsome red-brick facade and red neon sign are San Francisco landmarks.

North Beach (Zone 6)

The Italians moved the Irish out in the late nineteenth century causing quite a fury. In the 1960s, the beatniks stomped the area causing everyone to complain. And now that the neighborhood is becoming increasingly Chinese thanks to its Chinatown borders, the Italians are ready to fling fettuccini. But despite such change of the guard over the decades, North Beach remains one of the most interesting districts—thanks to the diverse cultural invades. It was once San Francisco's original waterfront and years later landfill extended the waterfront farther north. One of the city's oldest neighborhoods, North Beach still has the well-worn feel of a pair of old, comfortable shoes. It's a great place for lounging around in cafés and bars, casual shopping and browsing, and exploring side streets on foot.

To get a feel for the neighborhood's melting-pot ethnic mix, stop by **Washington Square,** where you'll see elderly Italians playing bocci ball and Chinese gracefully slicing through the air in the early morning doing their Tai Chi routines. Kick off the shoes, lay in the park and gaze up at spires of the Church of St. Peter and Paul, where Joe DiMaggio married Marilyn Monroe. Or get up early one morning and head to Molinari's Deli, opened in 1896. Leave through the swinging salami and pick up a cannoli and cappuccino at Liguria bakery on the northeast corner of the park. When the caffeine kicks in, consider walking up **Telegraph Hill** to **Coit Tower** for a great vista of San Francisco (see below).

The corner of Grant and Columbus Avenues in North Beach was the crossroads of the Beat world of the 1950s. "It was a good time to be in San Francisco," wrote journalist Hunter S. Thompson. "Anybody with half a talent could wander around North Beach and pass himself off as a 'comer' in the new era. I know, because I was doing it. . . It was a time for breaking loose from the old codes, for digging new sounds and new ideas, and for doing everything possible to unnerve the Establishment."

For a taste of North Beach's literary and Beatnik past, stop in **City Lights Bookstore** (at Columbus Avenue and Broadway), ground zero for the Beat Generation; the small alley that runs down the side of the shop is now called Jack Kerouac Street after the most famous of the beat writers. Also at Columbus and Broadway poetry meets porn on a block of declining strip joints and rock clubs; the most famous is the Condor Club, former home of Carol Doda and her silicone-enhanced breasts.

Telegraph Hill (Zone 6)

Bordering North Beach is Telegraph Hill, noted for its great views of the bay, vine-covered lanes, quaint cottages, pastel clapboard homes, and lousy parking. Once the home of struggling writers and artists, Telegraph Hill is now occupied by a wealthier class of people. At the top is **Coit Tower,** named for Lillie Hitchcock Coit, who bequeathed the funds to build this popular tourist landmark.

Getting there, though, can be a chore. Many of the houses dangle precipitously over the steep inclines, and the sidewalks turn to steps as you near the top. An easier option is to take the No. 39 bus to the tower and then walk down the Greenwich Steps, a brick staircase lined with ivy and roses that descends steeply to Montgomery Street. Near the base of the steps is an all-glass-brick art-deco apartment house used in the Humphrey Bogart film *Dark Passage*.

The Castro District (Zone 7)

One of the most fascinating, social, and educational gay-oriented parts of the city is the Castro District. The lesbian and gay community that makes its home in the Castro has contributed significantly to every aspect of the city's life, from economics and the arts to politics. (It's said that no San Francisco politician can win citywide election without the backing of the gay community.)

Some say that the Castro is still the wildest neighborhood in town, and others say that in the late 1990s it's merely a shadow of its former self. It's a good guess that much of the Castro's energy and unabashed hedonism has been channeled into AIDS support groups, care for the sick, and city politics. In the 1970s the gay community transformed the neighborhood into a fashionable, upscale enclave of shops, restaurants, bars, and restored homes.

Probably the best way to explore the Castro is by taking a walking tour. One of the best we have found is Trevor Hailey's Cruisin' the Castro Tour, which meets most mornings at the corner of Castro and Market at around 10 a.m. On this retired army nurse's tour you will learn about gay history in the district, about the lavender Cowboys, an all-male square-dance troop of the gold rush era, about the pre-Castro gay ghettos such as North Beach and Polk Street, and about the Castro Theater, one of San Francisco's better movie houses, specializing in foreign, repertory, and art films. If you get hungry, you must visit a few Castro institutions like Café Flore, or Red Dora's Bearded Lady Dyke Café.

The Mission District (Zone 7)

For culture vultures craving salsa or an authentic taqueria, the Mission is the place to come. This mostly Latino neighborhood is hip, happening, and historical, made up of Mexican, Central American and, increasingly, a wave of New Bohemia. Named for Mission Dolores, San Francisco's oldest building and the sixth in a chain of Spanish settlements that stretched for 650 miles, the district is one of the cheaper districts to live in, which explains the Bohemian appeal.

Positioned way south of downtown, the Mission, as it is simply called, is blanketed in sun and warmth most of the summer while the rest of the city suffocates in the rolling afternoon fog. The district is large also and is serviced by two BART stations, one at each end.

The Mission is an international hodgepodge, with large numbers of South Americans, Samoans, Vietnamese, Koreans, and Native Americans moving in; it's considered San Francisco's most transitional neighborhood. Check out Valencia Street and its active community of lesbians and feminists if you want to see how transitional it truly is!

The district's main drag, Mission Street, is a bustling commercial avenue filled with discount shops, used-clothing stores, pawn brokers, cafés, cheap ethnic restaurants, bars, clubs, produce stands, and pool rooms. Salsa and Mexican music blast from bars, and the air is redolent with the aroma of Hispanic cooking.

Mission Street is also a good place to start a tour of the Mission's 200-odd murals, painted as a result of a City Hall scheme to channel the energy of the district's poor youth; the biggest concentration is along 24th Street between Mission Street and South Van Ness Avenue. More Latino culture is on display at the **Mission Cultural Center** (2868 Mission Street), where visitors can enjoy temporary art exhibits, theatrical productions, and poetry readings. While the neighborhood is safe during the day, visitors should use extra caution at night when visiting clubs and restaurants in the district.

Noe Valley (Zone 7)

One of the newer, more hip neighborhoods bordering along the Mission is Noe Valley. This is *the* place to live these days. A walk up Valencia Street to 24th Street will take you to the heart of this beloved and sunny neighborhood. It is the land of organic produce, smoothies, new age music, and paint-it-yourself pottery stores. Trendy cafés and bookstores and funky boutiques are everywhere and it seems that many Mission weary have migrated here for its quaint village feel. The neighborhood has a large lesbian population but more noticeably are the new moms, dads, and babies that crawl, stroll, and toddle the streets in Noe. It is safer and quieter than nearby Mission, and up until recently quite cheap to rent. **Dolores Park** is nearby and is one of the best features of Noe, with views of downtown that will knock your socks off! The sprawling greenery lined with palm trees, friendly frolicking dogs, and pairs of lounging lovers make the park one of the best vantage points near the Mission.

Potrero Hill (Zone 7)

Tucked away from the hustle and bustle of city life, Potrero Hill is probably San Francisco's newest trend in neighborhood. Quiet streets, funky houses that seem right out of the movie **Edward Scissorhands,** and unobstructed views of downtown from every vantage point, qualify Potrero as a fortified funky hood. Even though it might not seem like there's much going on, you'll be surprised to find some very popular cafés, bars, and restaurants located on Potrero Hill's 17th and 18th Streets, like **Bottom of Hill, Farley's, Lilo Lounge,** and **Thanya & Salee.** Everything has a homegrown feel to it—you won't find any Barnes and Noble or Starbucks here. Its recent revitalization in art, theater, healing arts, and loft and warehouse spaces makes Potrero prime real estate.

And for those in the know, the crookedest street doesn't reside on Lombard but at Vermont and 20th Street. The end of Vermont Street packs more thrilling twists and turns into its eight switchbacks than Lombard; plus, the views are almost as good, and you get the added bonus of landing in the Mission district, home of the best burritos this side of Tijuana!

South of Market (SoMa) (Zone 7)

Over the last 15 years or so, this dreary area of old factory spaces has been spruced up into galleries, a convention center, trendy restaurants, museums, gay bars, and nightclubs. SoMa is becoming the West Coast version of SoHo in a big way. A new building housing the **San Francisco Museum of Modern Art** (151 Third Street) has popped up; some critics carp that the $62 million structure is more beautiful than any of the art inside.

Whether you are purveying Picasso or pump-up-the-music VIP clubs, SoMa is where it's happening. The district can be divided roughly into four regions: the increasingly developed area around the art museum, the Moscone Convention Center and the futuristic Metreon entertainment center; the nightclub region around 11th and Folsom Streets; the blocks between Third and Fourth Streets, where you'll find the new Yerba Buena Center; and the still undeveloped dock areas of Mission Rock and China Basin. Artists, dancers, and musicians like SoMa for the relatively low rents (by San Francisco standards) for huge spaces they can convert into studios and living quarters.

By day, SoMa remains an oddly colorless and semi-industrial neighborhood of warehouses and factory outlets. That's no surprise, considering that the area has always been home to industry. Several foundries were located in SoMa in the 1850s, along with rows of prefabricated housing imported from the East, making the neighborhood San Francisco's first industrial population. But in the late 1990s, the city's denizens, including artists, trendsetters, and hipsters of all kinds, descended on a formerly gray landscape lit up by the neon facades of bars and clubs.

If you've already hit the Top O' the Mark (see Nob Hill, above), you can continue your high-altitude buzz at the Saul Steinberg-esque **San Francisco Marriott Hotel** and its 39th-floor bar, the **View Lounge.** Located near Fourth and Market Streets south of Union Square near the edge of SoMa, the bar features concentric parabolic windows that slope backward to form a kind of half dome, creating the illusion that you're floating over the city in the nose of a helicopter. Drink prices surpass the bar's altitude but absorbing the cool attitude of the place is an experience worth the price. On your way out pay tribute to the sole surviving martini glass forever enshrined in the bar—it stood the test of the 1989 earthquake that rocked the hotels' walls on opening night!

The Presidio, Fort Point, and the Golden Gate Bridge (Zone 8)

After hundreds of years of sporadic military occupation by Spain, Mexico, and the United States, this northwestern tip of the San Francisco peninsula was handed over to the National Park Service in 1994. Now the former army base is in the slow process of evolving into a national park. Blissfully free of developed attractions, the **Presidio** offers miles of eucalyptus-scented roadways, trails, ancient gun fortifications, and incredible views from its sandy buffs. Almost 30 of its 1,500 acres are part of the **San Francisco National Military Cemetery.**

The Presidio's main entrance is on Lombard Street, west of Pacific Heights and the Marina District. Small military buildings remain scattered across the former army post. The Presidio's dramatic location (and maybe the most impressive view in the city) is **Fort Point,** the ruins of an old brick fortress overlooking the impossibly scenic Golden Gate, with breathtaking vistas that include the San Francisco skyline on one side and the Marin Headlands across the straight.

Overhead at Fort Point, traffic roars on the **Golden Gate Bridge,** probably the most famous bridge in the world. Formerly thought unbridgeable, the mile-wide Golden Gate between the tip of the San Francisco peninsula and Marin County was finally spanned in 1937, and until 1959 it ranked as the world's longest suspension bridge (4,200 feet). Visitors should consider both driving and walking across the bridge; the drive is thrilling as you pass under the huge towers, and the half-hour walk allows the bridge's enormous size and spectacular views to sink in. A sobering note: about seven people a month commit suicide by jumping off the bridge to the water 260 feet below.

There's a viewing area off the northbound lanes of US 101, with parking and access to trails and the bridge's walkways. (There's no need to cross the bridge by car to return to US 101 southbound.) If you drive across to Marin County, a $3 toll for cars is collected at the southern end of the bridge.

The Beaches, Lands End, the Palace of the Legion of Honor, and Cliff House (Zone 8)

South of the Golden Gate Bridge along the Pacific coastline are some of the city's finest beaches. Former military installations hidden among trees and behind sand dunes provide protection from the wind for picnickers. The sandy shoreline of **Baker Beach** faces the entrance of Golden Gate, a scenic backdrop for hiking, fishing, and sunbathing; swimming in these treacherous waters, alas, is dangerous. Behind Baker Beach, **Battery Chamberlain** points a 95,000-pound cannon ominously to sea.

A bit farther south, **China Beach** provides an intimate atmosphere on a small beach nestled on a steep shoreline—perfect for family outings and picnics. It's also San Francisco's safest swimming beach (although not as popular as the more accessible Baker Beach).

Hikers are attracted to **Lands End,** a shoreline noted for its absence of cars and abundance of birds, trees, and scenic vistas. Hallmarks are the sound of the ocean, the smell of pine and cypress, and views of coastal scenery. At low tide the wrecks of ships that fell victims to the treacherous water are visible. You can also follow the route of an abandoned turn-of-the-nineteenth-century railroad that once led to Cliff House; stay on the main trail because the cliffs are steep and dangerous. Visitors can also explore defense batteries at **West Fort Miley.**

At the south end of Lands End is the **Palace of the Legion of Honor,** a white-pillared twin of the famous Legion d'Honneur in Paris. Some say it's the city's best art museum, but there's no argument about its spectacularly scenic setting overlooking the Pacific Ocean. And with Rodin's "Thinker" in the courtyard, this art museum makes an elegant impression.

Cliff House, a mainstay of San Francisco tourism for more than a century, still attracts plenty of visitors, sometimes by the busload. Just offshore from the restaurant and visitor center are **Seal Rocks,** home base for sea lions and marine birds. Next door are the ruins of the once-elaborate **Sutro Baths,** a turn-of-the-nineteenth-century swimming emporium that could hold 24,000 people in its heyday; it burned to the ground in the 1960s. Come just before sunset for cocktails and a view of Seal Rocks and the setting sun from the restaurant; it's a San Francisco tradition.

Cliff House also marks the northern terminus of **Ocean Beach,** a four-mile stretch of sand and crashing surf that's always windy and wavy. You won't find much in the way of frills or stunning scenery, but the beach is a great place for jogging, walking, and people-watching. Don't go in the water, though. The ocean is always dangerous, even when it looks calm.

Farther down the coast are two more notable San Francisco locales. The **San Francisco Zoo** (at Great Highway and Sloat Boulevard) is Northern California's largest animal emporium and features animals in grassy enclosures behind moats, not pacing in cages. Next is **Fort Funston,** with easy hiking trails, great views of the ocean and coastal scenery, and hang gliders floating overhead. Locals call this place Fort Fun.

Golden Gate Park (Zone 8)

In a city awash in greenery, Golden Gate Park is San Francisco's biggest open space; in fact, it's the largest man-made urban park in the world. The park dazzles visitors with a nearly endless succession of sandy beaches, urban vistas, and rolling coastal hills, and the wide expanse of the Pacific Ocean. Exploration of the 1,040-acre park, which stretches from Haight-

Ashbury in the east for 52 blocks to the Pacific coast in the west, could take days. Ideally, the best way to discover Golden Gate Park is to wander aimlessly. That, unfortunately, isn't an option for most visitors. The park slopes gently from east to west and is roughly divided into two parts. The easternmost part contains all the main attractions—art and science museums, horticultural gardens, bandstands, and the Japanese Tea Garden. The western end is less developed, contains more open space and trails, and has a less-sculpted look. It's also where you'll find a herd of buffalo and a Dutch windmill. Overall the park is safe, but it's a good idea to stay on well-populated paths and avoid the park entirely on foot after dark.

Golden Gate Park's major attraction is the **de Young Memorial Museum,** a gallery of mostly American art, which happens to be closed for renovation until 2005. Across the Music Concourse is the **California Academy of Sciences,** a popular destination for families that includes a planetarium and an aquarium; kids love the place.

The **Japanese Tea Garden** shows how trees, landscape, rocks, and buildings can be arranged into a work of art; you can also get tea and cookies served by kimono-clad waitresses. The **Strybing Arboretum** is 70 gorgeous acres of lawns and trees illustrating the diversity of plant life that thrives in San Francisco's Mediterranean-style climate.

While most people head to the western end of the park to do nothing whatsoever, **Stow Lake** can also feed the urge to loaf. Boats of all types—including the nonrowing kind—are available for rent by the hour, as are bicycles for riding on the nearly flat paths that honeycomb the park. You'll also find rest rooms, drinking water, and a snack bar.

A herd of buffalo roam inside the **Bison Paddock** off JFK Drive at 38th Avenue. You can get close to the shaggy (and once nearly extinct) beasts at their feeding area near the western end. At the edge of the park near the ocean is a tulip garden and a Dutch windmill (a can't-be-missed landmark).

Haight-Ashbury (Zone 8)

Hippies and the Haight. You can't have one without the other. The Haight was once the free-love zone and although the era of free sex, love, drugs, and the Grateful Dead has found restful solitude in the hearts of its followers and present-day wannabes, the Haight remains true to its tie-dye roots. Just take a stroll and you'll see for yourself—from Mama's tattoo parlor, leather and vintage shops, to the flowers and candles left at 710 Ashbury Street, the one-time home of the Grateful Dead. The biggest flashback of the year occurs during the Haight Street Fair in June. A must-see for all!

About eight blocks long, the area is surrounded by gorgeous restored Edwardian and Victorian houses. Today, though, there are more homeless than hippies on the blocks around the district's epicenter at Haight and Ashbury Streets. A neighborhood of more than a thousand Victorian houses in decline in the 1950s, the Haight was reborn with the hippie movement of the late 1960s. The big houses were subdivided into flats, and the flower children disseminated the values of the counterculture all around Haight Street. But idealism mixed with drugs and unemployment didn't prove to be an effective formula for social improvement. In the 1970s and 1980s the neighborhood devolved into a place only street-wise natives could navigate safely. With the rise of real estate prices around the city, gentrification has set in—although the drug-dazed, backpack-toting drifters asking for change are still common. Today young execs and upper-middle-class professionals rub shoulders with the homeless remnants of the hippie era. The result is a tense bustle of eclectic eccentrics, perfect for people-watchers.

Japantown (Zone 8)

Bounded by Geary Boulevard and California Street, Octavia, and Fillmore Streets, Japantown is called home by only about 4% of San Francisco's Japanese-American residents. Most, though, return regularly for shopping and social and religious activities. The construction of Japan Center in 1968 was the inspiration for a community-renewal effort, with residents and merchants pitching in to beautify the surrounding blocks. The block-long Buchanan Mall, landscaped with flowering trees and fountains, marks the center's northern entrance.

Full of restaurants and stores, **Japan Center** is also the home of the **Japanese Consulate** and the **Kabuki Complex,** an eight-screen, ultra-modern movie complex that hosts the Independent Film Festival annually. The other highlight at Japan Center is the **Kabuki Hot Springs,** genuine Japanese baths that offer shiatsu massage, steam baths, and other luxuriating facilities.

Compared to Chinatown, Japantown looks bland, well tended, and new. For a taste of ethnicity, visit on weekends, especially in spring and summer, when many Japanese cultural events, from tea ceremonies to martial arts demonstrations and musical performances, take place. Other places of interest include the **Buddhist Church of San Francisco** (Pine Street and Octavia Street), a sumptuous temple filled with what are claimed to be relics of Buddha, and **St. Mary's Cathedral** (where Geary Boulevard meets Gough Street), the city's newest Roman Catholic cathedral (1971); walk inside and gaze at its 190-foot dome.

Twin Peaks (Zone 8)

Ah yes, the Jekyll and Hyde temperament of Twin Peaks. At once the granddaddy of inspiration points and one of San Francisco's most distinctive landmarks and at the same time, the foggiest, most mist-filled part of town. You love it for the views but hate it for the behind-a-water-fall, bring-the-raincoat, and Prozac kinda weather.

Why is the district called Twin Peaks? There are two hills that make up the area, and Spanish explorers first called them "breasts of the Indian girl," but prudish Americans settled on the less-descriptive Twin Peaks. The peaks' slopes contain curving roads that feature some of the most expensive homes in San Francisco, a testament to the theory that the better the view, the higher the price of real estate. And what a view! The 360 degree overlook, on a clear evening, is magical. Both the Golden Gate and Bay Bridges are visible as is all of downtown and its surrounding districts. A hot date spot for sure!

Luckily, Twin Peaks is one of a few hills in the city spared from development, making a walk, bike ride, or drive to the top doable. (It's also on the itinerary of almost every tour bus in town, so keep that in mind.)

Richmond and the Sunset (Zone 8)

Don't let the name fool you. The Sunset is not very sunny. Due to the heavy fog which blankets the area through most of the year, much of the Sunset District has developed a distinctly quiet and residential character. The vast size of the district, however, has fostered the development of several varied and vibrant neighborhoods. The west end of the Sunset (abutting the Pacific Ocean) bears a closer resemblance to a beach town than a suburb; surfers and nature lovers brave the cool sea spray to combine the convenience of city living with a raw outdoor lifestyle. The San Francisco Zoo borders the Sunset to the south, as does the Stonestown Galleria, a large mall complex. Along the northeastern border, the Upper Haight meets the Sunset to produce a quieter and more upscale neighborhood with a 1960s influenced mindset, including the requisite cafés and poetry readings. The southeastern corner runs up to the western side of Twin Peaks and the neighborhoods of Forest Hill and West Portal. This area around 8th Avenue and Irving Street is filled with local but city-wide favorite food stops as The House (Asian fusion) and Café For All Seasons (French Bistro), in addition to a wide array of Chinese restaurants and Japanese noodle parlors and sushi bars.

Across Two Bridges: The Bay Area and Nearby Cities

The East Bay, as you will hear it referred, consists of Berkeley and Oakland and is connected to San Francisco via the double-decker Bay Bridge. The red pillars of the Golden Gate Bridge connect the city to points north, including Marin County, Sausalito, Tiburon, Marin City, and Mill Valley. North of these points on US 101 above Marin County is Petaluma and Santa Rosa (57 miles away), and, slightly to the east, country valleys, Napa and Sonoma (about 60 miles away). About 125 miles north along the rugged coastline is Mendocino, a small picturesque town that was once a logging village, then a haven for artists in the 1950s. The Oregon State line is almost 400 miles to the north.

The Sierra Nevada Mountains and the Nevada state line are about 200 miles east of the city. Yosemite National Park, southeast of San Francisco in the Sierra Nevada range, is 184 miles away. Fifty miles south along the peninsula (below the southern end of San Francisco Bay) are San Jose and Silicon Valley. South along the coast are the cities of Santa Cruz (80 miles), Monterey (115 miles), Santa Barbara (320 miles), Los Angeles (400 miles), and San Diego (550 miles).

The Major Highways

San Francisco's major highway, US 101, links Seattle and San Diego along the California coast. The freeway threads its way through the city on Van Ness Avenue after crossing the Golden Gate Bridge at the northwestern tip of the city and continues south along the peninsula to San Jose and beyond.

I-80 crosses the San Francisco–Oakland Bay Bridge and continues northeasterly to Sacramento. I-80 also intersects with I-580 and I-880 in Oakland. I-580 (the Eastshore Freeway) heads north toward Richmond and then swings west across San Pablo Bay to San Rafael and US 101, north of San Francisco. To the south, I-880 follows the eastern shore of San Francisco Bay south toward San Jose, while I-580 swings east toward Stockton and an intersection with I-5, the inland interstate link that runs from Vancouver to San Diego.

Below San Francisco, I-280 begins south of the city and parallels US 101 toward Redwood City, Stanford, and Sunnyvale; its northern end is one of the most beautiful stretches of interstate highway in the country. US 101 (here called the Bayshore Freeway) follows the western shore of San Francisco Bay on a more direct route to the cities of Palo Alto, Santa Clara, and San Jose.

The Layout

Someone back in the day had the idea to lay the city out on a grid. A nice concept when considering flat terrain like New York City, but when you are negotiating a stick shift up steep Divisidero, Lombard, or Filbert Streets, you'll be sweating bricks and cursing the wise guy! Admittedly the city is easy to navigate as a result of this checkerboard pattern. The city's 42 hills, like stones beneath a checked tablecloth, divide the city into areas that are the foundation for distinctive neighborhoods. If you know the cross street when searching for an address, the task is fairly simple. The major east/west axis is Geary Boulevard which runs from downtown to the Pacific Ocean. The major north/south streets are Van Ness Avenue, Divisadero

Street, and Park Presidio Boulevard. The exception is Market Street, which cuts diagonally across the city from the Embarcadero to the Castro.

Most of San Francisco's streets are very long, with numbers typically ranging from 1 to 4000. Street numbers get higher going from east to west and from south to north. Distances are measured in blocks, with numbers rising by 100 from block to block. South of Market Street the streets are numbered (beginning with 1st Street and continuing through 30th Street). Do not confuse these streets with the numbered avenues that begin three miles west of downtown and run from 2nd Avenue to 48th Avenue at the ocean.

It would be nice if street addresses along Market, Mission, and other streets in the SoMa District had street numbers that corresponded with the intersecting numerical streets, but they don't.

Throughout the northwest sector of the city (downtown to Fisherman's Wharf) and in the cookie-cutter neighborhood of Sunset, streets are one way, with the exceptions of Columbus Avenue, Market Street, and Van Ness Avenue. When traffic on a street goes only one way, the traffic in the two streets on either side of it move in the opposite direction.

Major Arteries and Streets

Market Street is San Francisco's main drag. Many of the city's buses and streetcars follow this route from the outlying suburbs past the Castro and Mission Districts, Civic Center, SoMa, and Union Square to the downtown Financial District. Underground subways operated by BART and light-rail trains operated by Muni Metro load and disgorge passengers at seven underground stations located along Market Street.

The tall office buildings clustered downtown are at the northeast end of Market Street; one block beyond lie the Embarcadero and the bay. The building with the tall tower at the end of the street is the Ferry Building, one of a few major structures to survive the 1906 earthquake and fire. The Embarcadero curves along San Francisco Bay from south of the Bay Bridge to the northeast perimeter of the city and ends at Fisherman's Wharf, San Francisco's famous cluster of piers and tourist attractions. (The elevated freeway used to continue along the bay west of the wharf but was almost completely removed after the 1989 earthquake, much to the relief of many San Franciscans, who can now enjoy unimpeded views of the bay.) Beyond Fisherman's Wharf are Aquatic Park, Fort Mason, the Presidio, and Golden Gate National Recreation Area, all linked by the Golden Gate Promenade, a three-and-a-half-mile pedestrian walkway.

From the eastern perimeter of Fort Mason, Van Ness Avenue runs due south back to Market Street; it's also US 101 south of the Golden Gate Bridge. The rough triangle formed by these three major thoroughfares—Market Street to the southeast, the Embarcadero and the waterfront to the north, and Van Ness Avenue to the west—contains most of the city's major tourist attractions and neighborhoods of interest to visitors.

Other Major Streets

A few other major thoroughfares that visitors are bound to encounter include Mission Street, which parallels Market Street to the south in SoMa; it's also the main street in the Mission District south of downtown. Montgomery Street in the Financial District links to Columbus Avenue in North Beach, while Bay, Jefferson, and Beach Streets are major east-west arteries in and around Fisherman's Wharf.

Grant Avenue is Chinatown's touristy main street, while Powell Street runs north-south from Market Street to the bay past Union Square; it's also a major cable-car route, as the street climbs Nob Hill. Lincoln Boulevard is the major road through the Presidio, a former army base at the northwest corner of the city that's now part of Golden Gate National Recreation Area.

Geary Boulevard, California Street, and Broadway are major east-west streets downtown; Geary goes the distance to the Pacific Ocean, where it merges with Point Lobos Avenue just before reaching Cliff House, a major tourist landmark. Visitors following signs for US 101 on Van Ness Avenue to reach the Golden Gate Bridge will make a left onto Lombard Street, then zoom past the Palace of Fine Arts as they approach the famous span.

At the southern end of Market Street (just past Twin Peaks) the name changes to Portola Drive; turn right on Sloat Boulevard to reach the San Francisco Zoo and Ocean Beach. There you'll find Great Highway, which parallels the ocean. Turn right on Great Highway and head north to reach the western end of Golden Gate Park (look for the Dutch windmill). The park's main drag is John F. Kennedy Drive, which is closed to traffic on Sundays. At the eastern end of Golden Gate Park are Fell and Oak Streets, which head east to Van Ness Avenue and Market Street.

Things the Natives Already Know

Tipping

Everybody needs a refresher course on the tipping protocol. To start, tipping is not a question. Do tip, it's as simple as that. You'll find service to be outstanding at restaurants, hotels, and even in taxis. Here are some guidelines for those sticky moments when you are left wondering if the hotel or restaurant is spitting in your food or naming their first born after you.

Porters and Skycaps $1–1.50 a bag.

Cab Drivers   A lot depends on service and courtesy. If the fare is less than $8, give the driver the change and $1. Example: If the fare is $4.50, give the cabbie fifty cents and a buck for tip. If the fare is more than $8, give the driver the change and $2. If you ask the cabbie to take you only a block or two, the fare will be small, but your tip should be large ($2–3) to make up for his or her wait in line and to partially compensate him or her for missing a better-paying fare. Add an extra dollar to your tip if the driver handles a lot of luggage. You'll find the cab drivers in San Francisco the most amusing and interesting of most major cities. Strike up a conversation and learn what makes them tick!

Parking Valets $2 is correct if the valet is courteous and demonstrates some hustle. $1 will do if the service is just okay. Pay only when you check your car out, not when you leave it.

Bellmen and Doormen When a bellman greets you at your car with a rolling luggage cart and handles all of your bags, $5 is about right. The more luggage you carry yourself, of course, the less you should tip. Add another $1 or $2 if the bellman opens your room. For calling a taxi, tip the doorman $1.

Waiters Whether in a coffee shop or an upscale eatery, or ordering room service from the hotel kitchen, the standard gratuity range is 15–20% of the tab, before sales tax. At a buffet or brunch where you serve yourself, leave a dollar or two for the person who brings your drinks. Some restaurants, however, are adopting the European custom of automatically adding a 15% gratuity to the bill, so check before leaving a cash tip.

Cocktail Waiters and Bartenders Here you tip by the round. For two people, $1 a round; for more than two people, $2 a round. For a large group, use your judgment: is everyone drinking beer, or is the order long and complicated? Tip accordingly.

Hotel Maids When you check out, leave $1–2 per day for each day of your stay, provided service was good.

How to Look and Sound Like a Native

You may feel the pressure to polish up on beatnik literature, pull out those old bell-bottoms, or read the latest version of Windows in order to fit in San Francisco. Home to artists, performers, intellectuals, and folks of every describable (and sometimes indescribable) sexual bent, the city is where most of America's new personal, technical, and social trends materialize. If it's important to you not to look like a visitor on holiday, disguise the camera and adhere to the following advice.

1. Don't go to Fisherman's Wharf and if you do, be in the know about the guy who stands behind handheld branches scaring unsuspecting tourists! It's a hoot to watch.

2. If you do the Wharf thing, don't wear shorts and a T-shirt; freezing, underdressed tourists huddling for warmth at the wharf is an enduring San Francisco cliché.

3. Don't call cable cars "trolleys."

4. Don't pronounce Ghirardelli with a soft "g"; the square's name is pronounced "GEAR-ar-delly."

5. Never utter the two syllable "Frisco." We are not responsible for what could happen should you get caught saying this.

6. Wear a sweater when it's 75° outside 'cause chances are the temp will drop.

7. Don't talk about stock options. It's like rubbing salt into an open wound in this town!

8. Rice-A-Roni originated on Madison Avenue.

Local Publications

San Francisco has two daily newspapers, the *San Francisco Chronicle*, www.sfgate.com, published in the morning, and the *San Francisco Examiner*, www.examiner.com, which comes out in the afternoon; the publications combine on Sundays for one big edition. Both newspapers cover local, national, and international news, and Friday editions feature up-to-the-minute information on weekend entertainment.

Free weekly tabloid papers include the *San Francisco Bay Guardian*, www.sfbg.com, and the *SF Weekly*, www.sfweekly.com. Both offer coverage on everything from art to politics and generally provide more detailed information on local night life and entertainment than the dailies. *Where San Francisco* is a free monthly magazine for tourists, offering information on shopping, dining, and entertainment, as well as maps and listings of things to do while in town; look for a copy in your hotel room. *Bay City Guide*, www.baycityguide.com, found in many museums and shops, is a free monthly magazine; it provides maps and listings of things to do for visitors.

San Francisco Magazine, www.sanfran.com, is the city's leading glossy magazine, and it focuses on dining, the arts, entertainment, and ten-best lists. A newly launched city magazine in direct competition with *San Francisco Magazine* is *7 x 7*, www.7x7mag.com—named for the city's square area. It aims to provide more in-depth, investigative pieces as opposed to the cookie-cutter top-ten lists and such that *San Francisco Magazine* produces. *San Francisco Arts Monthly*, www.artsmonthlysf.org, is a tabloid listing the city's visual and performing arts calendars. *Street Sheet*, sold by homeless and formerly homeless people on the city's streets for a buck, provides a street-level view of homelessness and helps the homeless earn money. The *Bay Area Reporter*, www.ebar.com, distributed free on Thursdays, covers the gay community, including in-depth news, information, and a weekly calendar of goings-on for gays and lesbians.

Live from WKR—San Francisco

Aside from the usual babble of format rock, easy listening, and country music stations, San Francisco is home to a few radio stations that really stand out for high-quality broadcasting. Tune in to what hip San Franciscans listen to:

San Francisco's High-Quality Radio Stations

Format	Frequency	Station
Jazz	91.1 FM	KCSM
NPR	91.7 FM	KQED
Talk, classical, community affairs	94.1 FM	KPFA
Classical	102.1 FM	KDFC
Rock	104.5 FM	KFOG
Rock	105.3 FM	KTIS

A good Saturday-morning outing is to NPR's taping of West Coast Live radio show hosted by Sedge Thomson at Fort Mason. For $10 you can be part of the audience of fascinating interviews with musicians, authors, poets, comics, etc . . . Bring your best sound effects as the audience is usually called upon to create some together.

Access for the Disabled

Steep hills aside, travelers with mobility problems are likely to find San Francisco more in tune with their needs than other U.S. cities; it's considered one of the most barrier-free towns around. Nearly all buildings and public transportation are equipped for easy access. In compliance with the American Disabilities Act, direction signs, toilets, and entrances are adapted for blind and disabled visitors. In addition, many theaters (both movie and stage) offer special audio equipment for hearing-impaired people.

Parking spaces reserved for handicapped people with disabled permits are marked by a blue-and-white sign and a blue curb; frequently a wheelchair outline is painted on the pavement. Disabled persons may pay a $6 fee and present a state-of-origin permit or plaque with photo I.D. to get a temporary permit at the Department of Motor Vehicles (1377 Fell Street); there's a service window reserved for the disabled.

Most street corners downtown have dropped curbs and most city buses have wheelchair lifts. Major museums throughout the Bay Area are fitted with wheelchair ramps, and many hotels offer special accommodations and services for wheelchair-bound visitors.

All Muni Metro and BART stations are wheelchair accessible. Wheelchair-boarding platforms are located at many stops, including some islands on Market Street. In addition, Muni operates more than 30 accessible bus lines. For a complete listing of transit lines, including a chart indicating which lines offer disabled access, pick up a copy of the *Official San Francisco Street and Transit Map,* available at most newsstands for $2. Call (415) 923-6336 (touch-tone only) to get recorded schedule information. For more information on disabled access to public transportation or a *Muni Access Guide,* write to the Accessible Services Program, 949 Presidio, San Francisco, CA 94115, call (415) 673-6864 or (415) 923-6366 (TDD), or visit www.sfmuni.com/rider.

A Paratransit Taxi Service provides discount taxi service to qualified disabled persons unable to use fixed Muni lines; to get a certificate, call the San Francisco Paratransit Broker at (415) 351-7000. Golden Gate Transit, which operates buses between the city and Marin County, publishes a handbook on accessible equipment and procedures; to get a copy of *Welcome Aboard,* call (415) 923-2000 or (415) 257-4554 (TDD).

Time Zone

San Francisco is in the Pacific time zone, which puts it three hours behind New York, two hours behind Chicago, one hour behind the Rocky Mountains, and eight hours behind Greenwich Mean Time.

Phones

The San Francisco area is served by three area codes: (415) inside the city and Marin County, (510) in Alameda and Contra Costa Counties in the East Bay (including Oakland and Berkeley), and (650) to the south in San Mateo County and around San Francisco International Airport. Calls from pay phones range from 25 to 35 cents (depending on which carrier owns the pay phone); if you talk for more than three minutes, additional payments may be requested. To call outside the (415) area code, dial 1 plus the appropriate area code and the seven-digit number.

Liquor, Taxes, and Smoking

Liquor and grocery stores and some drug stores sell packaged alcohol from 6 to 2 a.m. daily. Most restaurants, bars, and nightclubs are licensed to serve a full line of alcoholic beverages during these hours, although some have permits to sell beer and wine only. The legal drinking age is 21.

An 8.5% sales tax is added to purchases in San Francisco. If your purchases are shipped to a destination outside of California, they're exempt from the sales tax. An 8% tax is added to restaurant bills, and most hotels tack on a 14% room tax to the bill.

Before you light up, think twice in San Francisco. The city has stiff anti-smoking laws, making it illegal to light up in offices, public buildings, banks, lobbies, stores, sports arenas, stadiums, public transportation, and theaters. And shockingly, this extends into bars and restaurants. The no-smoking-in-bars law gets cheers and jeers. Non-smokers, you won't come home smelling like the Marlboro man, but you may find yourself solo at the bar while your compadres escape to the front for a drag every 15 minutes.

How to Avoid Crime and Keep Safe in Public Places

Crime in San Francisco

San Francisco, like any large city, has its share of violent crime, drug abuse, and poverty. But the good news for visitors is that by and large the city is safe. San Francisco ranks low among U.S. cities for serious crime.

Downtown San Francisco, where tourists and business visitors spend most of their time, is unusually safe for a large city. "One good thing is that we've got a very lively downtown with lots of different things going on at all hours of the day. It's never completely dead," notes Dewayne Tully, a police service aid with the San Francisco Police Department. "Even the Financial District, an area usually dead at night in most cities, has lots of clubs and restaurants." Because of crowds and 24-hour foot, horse, motorcycle, and car patrols by San Francisco's finest, few visitors to San Francisco are victims of street crime.

Exercising Caution: Some Hot Spots

Certain neighborhoods require different behaviors. The Tenderloin area, on the downtown side of the Civic Center, is a rather seedy part of town. Interesting culturally, this area, as well as the Mission District, houses most of the cities diminishing minorities. Both districts have resisted the gentrification that has swept most of the cities neighborhoods. But after dark the Tenderloin and the Mission get suspect. There are usually always people hanging around—and if you come from other big cities, like New York, Miami, or Chicago, it will be nothing you aren't used to. Just take a few precautions. Girls leave purses at home. Put money in the bras, and noticeable sparkling carats leave in the jewelry box at home. Just be cautious and you should be fine. Checking over your shoulder constantly will only bring attention to your wary wonderings. Look confident and secure and you should be fine. South of downtown, Market Street gets seedy also and is a haven for vagrants from about Fifth Street west to Gough Street. If you will be heading out to any of these areas at night, simply take a taxi to your destination. If you have to walk a few blocks you will most likely be fine. Some of San Francisco's hottest neighborhoods for nightlife, including Mission, SoMa, and Haight-Ashbury, also require some extra caution at night.

If you are the victim of a crime or witness one, you can get immediate police, fire, or medical assistance by dialing 911 from any pay phone without inserting money. For nonemergency help (for instance, to report a car break-in), dial the San Francisco Police Department at (415) 553-0123. For more information on personal safety in San Francisco, call San Francisco SAFE, Inc. (SAFE stands for Safety Awareness for Everyone) at (415) 673-SAFE; www.sfsafe.org.

The Dos and Don'ts

1. Have a plan: random violence and street crime are facts of life in any large city. You've got to be cautious and alert, and you've got to plan ahead. When you're out and about, remember to know your route, and have your agenda somewhat outlined; that way you appear to know what you are doing and where you are going.

2. Confirm your route or transportation with your hotel.

3. Leave all valuables in a safe deposit box in your hotel or leave them at home.

4. Leave identification on your children indicating a phone number or hotel where you are staying in case they become lost or separated from you.

5. Write down all traveler's cheque numbers and leave them at home or at the hotel.

6. Girls, the bra is still a viable option for money! Guys, a money belt below the pants is a convenient way to carry wallet and money.

7. At night—women, keep your purses tucked under your arm; if you're wearing a coat, put it on over your shoulder-bag strap. If you're wearing rings, turn the setting palm-in.

8. Don't wave money around. Be discreet when dealing with money.

Tip: Men can carry two wallets. Carry an inexpensive wallet in your hip pocket with about $20 in cash and some expired credit cards. This is the one you hand over if you're accosted. Your real credit cards and the bulk of whatever cash you have should be in a money clip or a second wallet hidden elsewhere on your person. Women can carry a fake wallet in their purse and keep the real one in a pocket or money belt.

If You're Approached or Accosted

In Public Transport　Transportation in the city is quite organized and generally safe. It becomes questionable late at night when riders are few.

If you find yourself riding the bus or train at night it is best to take a seat close to the conductor or bus driver. These people have a phone and can summon help in the event of trouble.

In Cabs   At night, it's best to go to one of the hotel stands or call for a cab on the phone. Once you have secured a cab, and if you suspect foul play on the cab driver's part check the driver's certificate, which by law must be posted on the dashboard. Address the cabbie by his last name (Mr. Jones or whatever) or mention the number of his cab. This alerts the driver to the fact that you are going to remember him and/or his cab. Not only will this contribute to your safety, it will keep your cabbie from trying to run up the fare. Generally, though, the cabs in the city are safe and the drivers can be quite interesting to talk to!

If you need to catch a cab at the train stations, bus terminals, or airports, always use the taxi queue. Taxis in the official queue are properly licensed and regulated. Never accept an offer for a cab or limo made by a stranger in the terminal or baggage claim. At best, you will be significantly overcharged for the ride. At worst, you may be abducted.

Self-Defense

In a situation where it is impossible to run, you'll need to be prepared to defend yourself. Most police insist that a gun or knife is not much use to the average person. More often than not, they say, the weapon will be turned against the victim. The best self-defense device for the average person is Mace. Not only is it legal in most states, it's nonlethal and easy to use.

When you shop for Mace, look for two things. The dispenser should be able to fire about eight feet, and it should have a protector cap so it won't go off by mistake in your purse or pocket. Carefully read the directions that come with your device, paying particular attention to how it should be carried and stored and how long the active ingredients will remain potent. Wear a rubber glove and test-fire your Mace, making sure you fire downwind.

When you are out about town, make sure your Mace is easily accessible, say, attached to your keychain. If you are a woman and you keep your Mace on a keychain, avoid the habit of dropping your keys (and the Mace) into the depths of your purse when you leave your hotel room or car. The Mace will not do you any good if you have to dig through your purse for it. Keep your keys and your Mace in your hand until you safely reach your destination.

Carjackings and Highway Robbery

With the recent surge in carjackings, drivers also need to take special precautions. "Keep alert when you're driving in traffic," one police official warns. "Keep your doors locked, with the windows rolled up and the air-conditioning or heat on. In traffic, leave enough space in front of you so that you can make a U-turn and aren't blocked in. That way, if someone approaches your car and starts beating on your windshield, you can drive off." Store your purse or briefcase under your knees when you are driving, not on the seat beside you.

Also be aware of other drivers bumping you from the rear or driving alongside you and gesturing that something is wrong with your car. In either case, do not stop or get out of your car. Continue until you reach a very public and well-lit place where you can check things out and, if necessary, get help.

Ripoffs and Scams

A lively street scene is an incubator for ripoffs and scams. Although pickpockets, scam artists, and tricksters work throughout San Francisco, they are particularly thick in Union Square, along the Embarcadero and Fisherman's Wharf, and at BART stations. While some scams are relatively harmless, others can be costly and dangerous.

Pickpockets work in teams, sometimes using children. One person creates a diversion, such as dropping coins, spilling ice cream on you, or trying to sell you something, and a second person deftly picks your pocket. In most cases your stolen wallet is almost instantaneously passed to a third team member walking by. Even if you realize immediately that your wallet has been lifted, the pickpocket will have unburdened the evidence.

Because pickpockets come in all sizes and shapes, be especially wary of any encounter with a stranger. Anyone from a man in a nice suit asking directions to a six-year-old wobbling toward you on in-line skates could be creating a diversion for a pickpocket. The primary tip-off to a con or scam is someone approaching you. If you ask help of somebody in a store or restaurant, you are doing the approaching and the chances of being the victim of a scam are quite small. When a stranger approaches you, however, regardless of the reason, beware.

Most travelers carry a lot more cash, credit cards, and other stuff in their wallet than they need. If you plan to walk in San Francisco or anywhere else, transfer exactly what you think you will need to a very small, low-profile wallet or pouch. When the *Unofficial Guide* authors are on the street, they carry one American Express card, one VISA card, and a minimum amount of cash. Think about it. You do not need your gas credit cards if you're walking, and you don't need all those hometown department store credit cards if you're away from home.

Don't carry your wallet and valuables in a fanny pack. Thieves and pickpockets can easily snip the belt and disappear into the crowd with the pack before you realize what's happened. As far as pockets are concerned, front pockets are safer than back pockets or suitcoat pockets, though pickpockets (with a little extra effort) can get at front pockets, too. The safest place to carry valuables is under your arm in a holster-style shoulder pouch. Lightweight, comfortable, and especially accessible when worn under a coat or vest, shoulder pouches are available from catalogs and most good travel stores. Incidentally, avoid pouches that are worn on your chest and suspended by a cord around your neck. Like the fanny pack, they can be easily cut off or removed by pickpockets.

The Homeless

If you're not from a big city or haven't visited one in a while, you're in for a shock when you come to San Francisco, where there is a large homeless population. The homeless are more evident in some areas than others, but you're likely to bump into them just about anywhere. Take a drive down Van Ness Avenue and you will see one perched at almost every street corner with the most amusing signs. "No lies. It's for beer," reads one. They definitely are the most creative in their approach.

Most of them are harmless and are simply looking for a little help here and there. Don't be afraid of them. And if you feel the urge to give, keep a little pocket change handy. If you are approached for money and don't want to or can't give anything the best method is to say, "Sorry, I don't have anything." A simple acknowledgment goes a long way and they most likely will part your company with a "Have a nice day," or "God bless you." There is a notion, perhaps valid in some instances, that money given to a homeless person generally goes toward the purchase of alcohol or drugs. If this bothers you, carry granola bars for distribution or buy some inexpensive gift coupons that can be redeemed at a McDonald's or other fast-food restaurant for coffee or a sandwich.

Those moved to get more involved in the nationwide problem of homelessness can send inquiries—or a check—to the National Coalition for the Homeless, 1612 K Street, NW, Suite 1004, Washington, D.C. 20006; www.nationalhomeless.org.

Part Five

Getting around San Francisco

Driving Your Car

You'll have a love/hate relationship with driving in San Francisco. In one sense, the city's best sites and scenery are most easily explored in a car (mix one convertible and a sunny day for an unforgettable experience). From Route 1 along the Pacific Coast, driving across the Golden Gate Bridge to the Headlands or Mount Tamalpais, to driving through rolling vineyards of Napa or Sonoma, the bay area offers the best of scenic drives. And the hills . . . Filbert between Hyde and Leavenworth, Hill Street at Twenty Second, or Divisidero from Broadway to the Marina . . . white knuckled and gasping, you'll plunge over the edge maniacally laughing, yoddeling, screaming . . . whatever inspires you! Stick-shift novices need not apply. The city is compact enough to get in a good bit of sites on your own time, too. Here's where the hate parts come in. Finding parking, legal parking that is (many innovative parking-blazers have initiated rather creative solutions to the crunch), is about as frustrating as Christmas at the in-laws. And to add insult to injury, traffic is a nightmare. There are even websites devoted to the highway horror (check out the "I Hate Bay Area Traffic Homepage": www.geocities.com/MotorCity/Speedway/2004/traffic.html). Downtown, near the financial center, is usually crowded throughout the day, but during peak rush hours of about 8 a.m. to 10 a.m. and 4:30 p.m. to 6:30 p.m. you'll feel about as slow moving and cramped as the Tin Man without a lube job. Most of the traffic frustration comes into play when approaching either of the two bridges. The same goes for North Beach, Chinatown, and Telegraph Hill, areas infamous for traffic congestion and scarce parking. Our advice is to keep your car in your hotel's garage and use it sparingly for excursions away from downtown and beyond the city or in the evenings after rush hour. If you are planning to go outside of the city, especially during winter months, it is best to call California Road Conditions before heading out. They can inform you of any mudslides, construction, or weather conditions. Call (800) 427-ROAD (7623) if calling from within California or (916) 445-ROAD (7623) if calling from outside California.

Rental Cars

All the major car-rental agencies operate in the city and have desks at the airports. Take your pick from the national agencies of **Alamo, Avis, Budget, Dollar, Hertz, National,** and **Thrifty.** There are also some homegrown places to rent a car, like **City Rent-A-Car** (call (415) 861-1312), **Fox Rent-A-Car** (call (800) 225-4369), or **Specialty Car Rental** (call (800) 400-8412), for your chance at that convertible or dream BMW 323i.

All car rental agencies require a minimum age of 25 usually, and fares range depending on class of car, length of rental, where and when you pick up and drop off, and mileage plans. Usually you can find good deals online. Check out expedia.com, or travelocity.com. If you are an uninsured driver, you may want to buy an insurance plan for the duration of your rental. The city is notorious for fender benders, and knicks and scrapes on vehicles, so to protect yourself it is advisable to purchase the insurance. Keep in mind also that some credit cards offer protection as well. Inquire with the credit card company, or if you do have car insurance, call to verify your plan.

Time of Day

San Francisco's weekday rush hour starts before 8 a.m. and lasts until around 10 a.m.; it picks up again around 4 p.m. and goes to about 6 p.m. In between, traffic is congested but usually flows—at least beyond downtown and Fisherman's Wharf.

Weekends, on the other hand, can be just as bad as weekday rush hours—and often worse. While traffic on Saturday and Sunday mornings is usually light, it picks up around noon and doesn't let up until well into the evening. Remember, about 6 million people live in the Bay Area, and on weekends many of them jump in their cars and head to San Francisco or to surrounding playgrounds across either bridge.

A Prayer before Parking

Parking is one of the main reasons to *not* explore San Francisco by car. The task is arduous and in some areas you will drive around blocks for more than an hour finding a vacant parking spot. When you do find a spot, the meter is often timed to allow only a half hour of parking (not a lot of time to go sight-seeing or attend a business meeting) or if it's a non-metered street you have only two hours without a color-coded neighborhood permit. Rules, rules, rules. Traffic cops and meter maids on their mini mobiles uphold those rules diligently, and the meters, unless posted otherwise, are in effect Monday through Saturday, usually from 8 a.m. to 6 p.m. (Meter rates are as follows: Downtown, 75 cents for 30 minutes; Fisherman's Wharf, $1 for one hour; rest of the city, 50 cents for one hour.)

Colored curbs in San Francisco indicate reserved parking zones. Red means no stopping or parking; yellow indicates a half-hour loading limit for vehicles with commercial plates, yellow and black means a half-hour loading limit for trucks with commercial plates; green, yellow, and black indicates a taxi zone; and blue is reserved for vehicles marked with a California-issued disabled placard or plate. Green is a ten-minute parking zone for all vehicles, and white is a five-minute limit for all vehicles.

San Francisco cops don't take parking regulations lightly, and any improperly used spot can become a tow-away zone. The number one source of citations in the city is failing to recognize street cleaning, which requires one side of the street to be vacated on particular days, usually during morning hours. Be aware of street-cleaning signs and stay out of parking lanes opened up for rush-hour traffic. Many residential neighborhoods have permit parking, and a parking ticket can cost you more than $30, plus $100 for towing and additional charges for storage. Parking in a bus zone or wheelchair-access space can set you back $250, while parking in a space marked handicapped or blocking access to a wheelchair ramp costs $275. If you get towed, go to the nearest district police department for a release and then pick up your car at the towing company.

From meters, color-coded permits and curbs, to the task of constantly parallel parking—and, let's face it, there are some of you who haven't done it since driver's ed—you may wonder how to survive your trip without parking citations taking up half your scrapbook. You can opt for one of many city parking garages throughout the city's neighborhoods. They cost anywhere from $10 to $25 a day. If you are staying at a hotel, check with your hotel to see if you can get a reduced rate at a nearby garage that allows unlimited access to your car. Or, take advantage of the city's convenient and reliable public transportation, or our favorite, foot it.

When you're parking on San Francisco's steep hills, there is only one way to rest easy: curb your wheels. Turn the front tires away from the curb when your car is facing uphill so that if the brake fails the car rolls back into the curb. If facing downhill turn your wheels toward the curb so that the car can roll forward into the curb, effectively using it as a block. Because even the best brakes can fail, curbing your wheels is the law in San Francisco (and you'll see plenty of street signs to remind you).

The "You Didn't Know to Ask" Q & A:

- **Should I park in the middle turning lane when I see others doing it?**
  What you'll see sometimes in and around the Mission and SoMa, especially on busy weekend evenings, is that middle turning lanes become a row of parked cars.

Do not follow the leader here, the city will dispatch tow trucks faster than you can say "Hold the anchovies."

- **Where can I leave the car for a few days if I don't want to pay for a parking garage?** This is just between you and us—one of the best-kept secrets of the Bay Area—the Presidio! Enter from Lombard Street in the Marina, or Park Presidio in the Richmond and you'll enter parking paradise. No meters, and no permits necessary! The only threats to this parking nirvana are the leaves, pollen, and bird poop that come from tree-lined streets.

- **What time in the morning should I move my car if it's parked in a two-hour permit zone?** Usually the permit zones are enforced from 8 a.m. to 6 p.m. If you have left your car overnight you have until 10 a.m. (two hours past 8 a.m.). So go ahead, set that snooze.

- **How do the traffic cops know that my car has exceeded the meter or permit limit?** Everything you needed to know you learned in kindergarten— chalk! They chalk tires and check back to see if the car has or hasn't moved. One way around this is to check for chalk marks on your tires and if there are none, you might be good for another two hours. Or simply roll your car back and forth to get rid of it.

- **What areas are easiest for parking?** The Marina is fairly easy but *do not* even come an inch over someone's driveway. They are sticklers about that sort of thing. Bernal Heights, Potrero Hill, and parts of Noe Valley are all pretty stress-free. What constitutes stress free, you might ask? Less than a 15-minute search.

- **Where should I worry about theft or vandalism?** The Mission, Chinatown, the financial center, and the Tenderloin Districts are hot spots for broken windows, car break-ins, and keying. Never leave purses or CDs where they are visible from the window. Store them in the trunk.

- **Why do I sometimes see cars parked on the sidewalks outside a house or apartment building?** There is something fun about pulling up the curb onto the sidewalk and parking your vehicle! The thrill of trespassing is sweet indeed. There is a level of understanding between parking officials and residents. Usually it is tolerated during late hours (after midnight). But be ready for an early morning wake-up call to move it before anybody complains, or worse, you get busted!

Public Transportation

San Francisco Municipal Railway, www.sfmuni.com, commonly called Muni, is a citywide transportation system that consists of all cable cars, streetcars (called Muni Metro), conventional buses, and electric buses. All fares are $1 for adults and 35 cents for seniors, disabled passengers (with a valid Regional Transit Connection Discount Card), and children ages 5–17; children ages 4 and under ride free. Cable-car fare is $2 per person (kids ages 4 and under ride free). One-dollar bills are accepted on most buses, but the drivers don't give change. If you need a transfer, ask for one when you board; it's free and valid for two hours and a maximum of two rides in any direction.

Many San Franciscans feel a fierce devotion to the system; some affectionately call it "Joe Muni." No wonder; it's a European-style transportation system that gets people around the city cheaply and efficiently. You're never more than a couple of blocks from a bus stop or train station. Not that it's without some drawbacks—buses can be jam packed, especially at rush hour and on weekends, and occasionally you may have to wait for a bus while fully loaded buses pass you by. Yet despite its problems, riding Muni is interesting. You can learn more about the city from the friendly bus drivers and helpful passengers than from any guidebook.

Passport to Savings

Muni passports allow unlimited use of all buses, cable cars, and Muni Metro streetcars in San Francisco. It's a great money-saving deal that makes it even easier and more convenient to use San Francisco's public transportation. In addition, Muni passports provide discounts at dozens of city attractions, including museums, theaters, and bay tours.

Muni passports come in three versions: one-day ($6), three-day ($10), and seven-day ($15). Pocket-sized and easy to use, the passports are available at locations throughout the city, including the **San Francisco Convention and Visitors Bureau Visitor Information Center** (in Hallidie Plaza at Powell and Mason Streets), **TIX Bay Area** (Stockton Street on Union Square), and **Muni** (949 Presidio, room 239). Be sure to pick up a copy of the *Official San Francisco Street and Transit Map* for $2. To use a passport, scratch off the dates of the day (or days) you're using the pass and simply show it to the driver, who will wave you aboard.

Buses

You'll never see a more clean, quiet, and pollutant-free (thanks to some of the electric buses) or friendly bus service in any other city besides San Francisco. Bus service in San Francisco reaches into all parts of the city and beyond. Numbers are placed smack dab on the top of the bus with their destinations on the front. Along the streets, bus stops are indicated by signs displaying the Muni logo; the route numbers of the buses serving the stop are listed below the sign. Some stops are merely marked on light posts with a yellow sign and the bus number spray painted in black. Usually stops along a route are every three or four blocks. Some bus stops have three-sided glass shelters, with route numbers painted on the exterior and route maps posted inside. Along Market Street, some buses stop at the curb while others stop at islands in the street.

When you board, give the driver $1 or flash your Muni passport; if you need a transfer, get it as soon as you board. The driver will rip off a transfer ticket and it is good for two hours usually. You are really only supposed to use the transfer for one other bus ride, but if the bus driver doesn't take it or you don't throw it away, you can keep using it! It's one of those little treasures of public transportation. If you're not sure about where to get off, ask the driver to let you know when you're near your destination. Drivers are usually considerate and glad to help. The buses get very crowded at times. Often you will be standing in the aisle and you may not be aware that your stop has arrived. Fellow passengers are quite cordial and helpful and you'll be pleased when "back door please" is yelled out in your favor, or "wait" as the driver pulls away to soon. Another FYI? Using a cell phone on the bus is totally asking for it. San Franciscans have no patience with such selfish, un-PC behavior and they will not hesitate to say something. Rush hour is obviously busy but also consider the after-school rush between 2 and 3 p.m. Kids talking Britney, boys, and basketball snap their gum and fling their backpacks as they load onto the buses on their way home.

Most bus lines operate from 6 a.m. to midnight, after which there is an infrequent Night Owl service; for safety's sake, take a cab at those late hours. Popular tourist bus routes include numbers 5, 7, and 71, which go to Golden Gate Park; numbers 41 and 45, which go up and down Union Street; and number 30, which runs through Union Square, Ghirardelli Square, and the Marina. If you need help figuring out which bus or buses to take to reach a specific destination, call Muni at (415) 673-MUNI (6864). The large maps are very helpful, as all routes are marked and it is easy to plan your path and see where different routes intersect.

Muni Metro Streetcars

Muni Metro streetcars operate underground downtown and on the streets in the outer neighborhoods. At four underground stations along Market Street downtown, Muni shares quarters with BART, the Bay Area's commuter train system. Orange, yellow, and white illuminated signs mark the station entrances; when you get inside the terminal, look for the separate Muni entrance.

Pay or show your Muni passport and go down to the platform. To go west, choose the outbound side of the platform; to go east, choose the downtown side. Electronic signs with the name of the next train begin to flash as it approaches. The doors open automatically; stand aside to let arriving passengers depart before you step aboard. To open the doors and exit at your stop, push on the low bar next to the door.

Five of Muni Metro's six streetcar lines are designated J, K, L, M, and N, and these share tracks downtown beneath Market Street but diverge below the Civic Center into the outer neighborhoods. The J line goes to Mission Dolores; the K, L, and M lines go to Castro Street; and the N line parallels Golden Gate Park. The sleek trains run about every 15 minutes and more frequently during rush hours. Service is offered daily from

5 a.m. to 12:30 a.m., Saturday from 6 a.m. to 12:30 a.m., and Sunday from 8 a.m. to 12:20 a.m.

A new addition to the streetcar system (and its sixth route) is the F-Market line, beautiful green- and cream-colored, 1930s-era streetcars that run along Market Street from downtown to the Castro District and back. The historic cars are charming, and they're a hassle-free alternative to crowded buses and underground terminals.

BART

BART (www.bart.gov), an acronym for Bay Area Rapid Transit, is a 71-mile system of high-speed trains that connects San Francisco with the East Bay cities of Berkeley, Oakland, Richmond, Concord, and Fremont, and to the south, with Daly City. Four stations are located underground along Market Street (these also provide access to Muni Metro streetcars). Fares vary depending on distance; tickets are dispensed from self-service machines in the station lobbies. The trains run every 15 to 20 minutes on weekdays from 4 a.m. to midnight, on Saturday from 6 a.m. to midnight, and on Sunday from 8 a.m. to midnight.

BART is mostly used by commuters from the East Bay and is not a very useful means of traveling in the city for visitors. The stop in Berkeley, however, is close enough to the campus and other sites of interest. Part of the renovations of San Francisco Airport is to extend BART to the airport. This will be a dream-come-true for wary travelers who are tired of pouring their cash into taxis or shuttle services. The dream should become a reality in the next few years.

Cable Cars

After the red crown of the Golden Gate Bridge atop fluffy clouds, cable cars are probably San Francisco's most famous symbol. They should be ridden at least once just to say you've hung off one as it rung its bells up Powell Street. Cynical natives will snub their noses at such a thing—it's as if they are being asked to eat a bowl full of Rice-A-Roni. Generally the only ones hanging off and freezing their buns are tourists. That's OK though. It's a fun thing to bring the kids to do—and anybody can appreciate the Willy Wonka-esque Cable Car Barn and Museum on Mason Street (415) 474-1887; there you can stand at an observation platform and watch the cable wind around the giant wheels. The cars, pulled by cables buried underneath the streets, operate on three lines from 6:30 a.m. to 12:30 a.m. daily at about 15-minute intervals.

The first San Francisco cable car made its maiden voyage in 1873. By 1906, just before the earthquake, the system hit its peak, with 600 cars on a 110-mile route. But the system was heavily damaged by the quake and

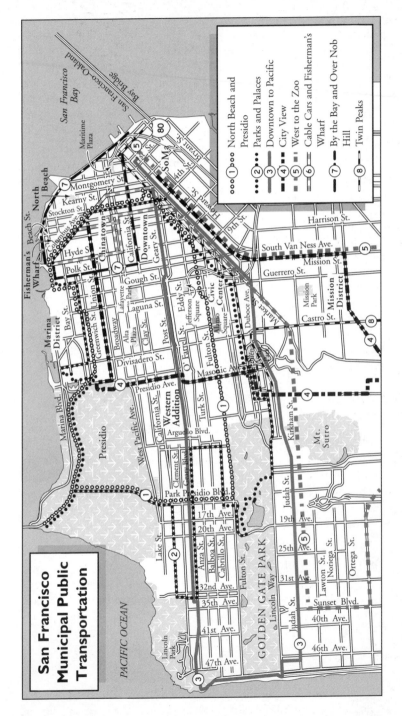

San Francisco
Municipal Public
Transportation

fire, and many lines weren't rebuilt. Electric trolleys took over some routes, and the number of cable cars dwindled over the years. In 1955 the city voted to save the famous hill climbers, and in 1984 it spent more than $60 million on a two-year renovation of the system, including new track and cable vaults, renovation of the Cable Car Barn, and restoration of the cars, which were given a new coat of shiny maroon, blue, and gold paint, as well as new brakes, seats, and wheels. Today there are 44 cable cars in all, with 27 in use at peak times. An average of 13 million people travel on the 17 miles of tracks each year—more than 35,000 people a day.

Three Lines

There are three cable-car lines in San Francisco. The most popular route for tourists is the Powell-Hyde line, which starts at the Powell and Market Street turntable south of Union Square. The line skirts Union Square, climbs Nob Hill (with good views of Chinatown), goes past the Cable Car Barn, crosses Lombard Street, and descends to Hyde Street to the turntable near Aquatic Park and Fisherman's Wharf. The Powell-Mason line starts at the same place, but after the Cable Car Barn it passes by North Beach and ends at Bay Street. For the best views on either line, try to face east.

The California line runs from California and Market Streets to Van Ness Avenue, passing through the Financial District and Chinatown; it's used more by commuters than tourists (a tourist attraction in itself). At Nob Hill the Powell lines cross over the California line, so passengers can transfer between lines (but they have to pay again). At the end of all lines, all passengers must get off.

For each of the three lines, the return journey follows the outward route, so riders can catch different views from the other side of the car. If you'd rather sit than stand, you're more likely to be successful if you board at the end of the line. During peak tourist seasons and on weekends, lines are long to board the cars at the turntables where the cars get turned around, and boarding at cable-car stops along the routes can be impossible as the cars rumble by, full of smiling, camera-toting tourists.

Safety Tips

As much fun as the cable cars are to ride, it's important to keep safety in mind when you're on one. If it's not crowded—not likely in the summer or fall after 9 a.m. or so—you can choose to sit or stand inside, sit outside on a bench, or stand at the end of the car. Adventurous types and some cable-car purists prefer hanging on to a pole while standing on a side running board. But wherever you decide to ride, hang on tight.

Try not to get in the way of the gripman, who operates the grip lever that holds and releases the cable pulling the car; he needs a lot of room. A yellow stripe on the floor marks an off-limits area, and passengers should stay out of it. Be extra cautious while the car is moving. Passing other cable cars is exciting because they pass so close, but be careful not to lean out too far. And be careful getting on and off. Often cable cars stop in the middle of busy intersections; you don't want to step in front of a moving car or truck.

Ferries

In the days before the Golden Gate and Bay Bridges were built, Bay Area commuters relied on hundreds of ferries to transport them to and from the northern counties and the East Bay. Although no longer a necessity, ferries continue to operate in smaller numbers, transporting suburban commuters who prefer a tension-free boat ride across the bay to the headache of rush-hour traffic. The ferries are also favorite ways for local residents and visitors to enjoy San Francisco's incredible scenery. On weekends, many suburban families leave their cars at home and take the ferries for fun and relaxation.

One person's commute can be another's excursion. Although the ferries don't offer the narrated audio tours of the commercial sight-seeing cruises offered at Fisherman's Wharf, they're less expensive. Food and bar service are offered on board, but the modern ferries only transport foot traffic and bicycles, not cars.

The Ferry Building at the foot of Market Street is the terminus for ferries to Sausalito and Larkspur. For prices and schedules, call Golden Gate Transit at (415) 923-2000. Private ferry service to Sausalito, Tiburon, and Angel Island operates from Pier 41 at Fisherman's Wharf. For more information, call the **Blue & Gold Fleet** at (415) 705-5555, or visit www.blueandgoldfleet.com.

Taxis

Unlike New York and Chicago, cabs in San Francisco tend to be expensive and scarce. You may be able to hail a moving taxi downtown, but in general it's better to call and make arrangements for pickup. The dispatch will call your number to alert you of the taxi's arrival. Another option is to head toward a cab stand at a major hotel, but the wait can be long during rush hour and in bad weather.

San Francisco taxis have rooftop signs that are illuminated when the cab is empty. Rates are $2.50 for the first mile and increase 40 cents each fifth of a mile. Major cab companies include **Veteran's Cab,** (415) 552-1300; **Yellow Cab,** (415) 626-2345; **DeSoto Cab,** (415) 970-1300; and **Luxor Cab,** (415) 282-4141.

Walking

Forfeit the gym. You have a leg press on almost every street in San Francisco. The quads will get pumped as you tread the hills—some so steep that stairs have been cut to make the trek easier, and your spirit will be fed dessert as the brightly-colored Victorians, and backdrop of blue ocean surprise at every corner. It's a walking nirvana. What separates this city from the others is the respect for pedestrians paid by vehicles and buses, and its compact size. Major tourist areas are within a half hour or less of one another. Another nice feature to footing the city is the surprising green spaces still firmly rooted within the city. Duck under a tree or sit in one of the many parks for a picnic as you glare at the glass-covered skyscrapers of downtown.

You don't have to ask the Scarecrow for directions here—most street intersections are marked with green-and-white signs bearing the name of the cross street; this can get confusing along Market Street, where street names are different on each side of the thoroughfare. Street names are also frequently imprinted in the pavement at corners. Often, electronic "walk" signs indicate when it's safe (and legal) to cross the street.

TO CROSS OR NOT TO CROSS?

San Francisco ranks among the top pedestrian fatality rates in the country. In 1999, there were 834 injuries and 25 deaths. In a city that seems so careful and organized, this comes as quite a surprise. One thing to be aware of when crossing the street or aggressively pursuing a yellow light in a car: the traffic lights in San Francisco, unlike pedestrian-heavy cities like New York, or D.C., don't have delayed timing. As soon as one side turns red, the other instantly turns green.

A Walk for Any Mood

If you've never made it a point to take walks you will find much inspiration in San Francisco to lace up and put feet to the path. One of the most active and exhilerating walks is **The Golden Gate Promenade**'s 3.5 mile path. Along its trail are joggers, and views of Alcatraz and those cold-blooded souls braving the frigid Pacific as they windsurf or kite-surf. All along the way are pit stops—Aquatic Park, Fort Mason, Marina Green, to the newly renovated Crissy Field. For a more romantic stroll, the **Presidio** is one of the most valued green spaces in the city. And the fact that there is a spot called **Lover's Lane** should be indicative enough. The whole trail takes only about 15 minutes. Another killer spot within the Presidio to walk is **Inspiration Point,** which looks out toward the Palace of Fine Arts and the Golden Gate. A mandatory walk that would fit in nicely if you are already strolling The Golden Gate Promenade is to walk across the **Golden Gate Bridge.** You'll be humming Tony Bennett's classic in no time! If you are a foodie and love to walk, stop, eat, walk, stop, eat, then a stroll down **Union Street** or **Chestnut** in the Marina, or almost any street in the **Mission** will satisfy your craving. **Bernal Heights** is one neighborhood being resurrected with community gardens and green spaces and an all out funky vibe. A walk down Cortland Avenue, the main drag here, will take you to **Good Prospect Community Garden,** and further along on Eugenia Street, you climb hidden stairways, past bizarre and brightly colored Victorians and bungalows to **Bernal Community Gardens.** The cherry on top of this walk is the short hike to the bald top of **Bernal Hill,** which offers views of Mount Diablo and the Golden Gate. It's really one of the best vantage points to watch the foggy fingers move in and choke the bridge and surrounding neighborhoods. There are great walks even for bargain shoppers. The secondhand stores on **Upper Fillmore Street** are chock full of great deals on hot brand-name items.

Part Six

Sightseeing, Tours, and Attractions

Touring San Francisco

As the old saying goes, what's good for the grandma isn't good for the grad. Or something like that. The beauty of touring San Francisco is that grandma can feel right at home sitting on a bench next to Dolores Park in the Mission while the college grad can sit on the grass in the same park and feel a compatible vibe. It's a friendly city for anybody who wants to experience its spectrum of offerings. There is much to see, yet the city is manageable when taken in neighborhood by neighborhood. San Francisco is remarkably compact, too. And like the consummate Californian, San Francisco is continually reinventing itself, working on self-improvement, getting in shape. The Marina District, devastated by the 1989 earthquake, is thriving with new and rebuilt Mediterranean-style houses in lollipop colors. The waterfront is reawakening; the Presidio is being transformed into a national park; and major projects such as the Yerba Buena Gardens are changing the face of the city.

Half the fun of discovering this town is simply wandering around and stumbling on great views, interesting shops, a location used in a favorite movie, and things that even the locals may not be aware of. While metropolitan, San Francisco is small; if you get disoriented, just remember that downtown is east, and the Golden Gate Bridge is north. And if you do get lost, you can't go too far because the city is surrounded by water on three sides. Here are some hints for first-time visitors.

Taking an Orientation Tour

Visitors to San Francisco can't help but notice the regular procession of open-air tour buses—"motorized cable cars" is probably a more accurate term—that prowl Union Square, Fisherman's Wharf, North Beach, and major tourist spots such as Fort Point. Not to be confused with real cable cars (the rubber tires are a dead giveaway), the trolleys operated by

Gray Lines offer regularly scheduled shuttle buses along regular routes that include the city's top attractions. Between stops, a tour guide discusses the city's cataclysmic fire of 1906, Barbary Coast days during the gold rush, and the flower-power era of the 1960s.

The guides also suggest good places to eat and drop tidbits of interesting and often funny San Francisco trivia. Our advice: If this is your first visit, take one of the tours early in your trip, even on the first day. The narrated tours are a no-brainer for jet-lagged or otherwise exhausted visitors who want spoon-fed details of San Francisco's major sights while learning the lay of the land. Think of the tours as an educational system that not only gets you to the most well-known attractions, but provides a timely education on the city's history and scope. On Gray Line motorized "cable cars," your ticket allows unlimited reboarding privileges for that day, so you can get off at any scheduled stop to tour, eat, shop, or explore, and you can reboard on a later bus. That way you can determine which sights warrant another day of exploration. Tour buses run about every 30 minutes (every hour in the winter), and boarding locations include some of the city's most popular attractions.

Gray Line

Both of the guided tours that operate a regular route in and around downtown San Francisco are good values. **Gray Line** features San Francisco–style motorized cable cars and a tour guide for trips lasting two-and-a-half hours and trips with unlimited on/off privileges. On the two-and-a-half-hour tour, passengers board at Union Square or Pier 39 in Fisherman's Wharf. On the on/off tour, visitors can get off and reboard at Pier 39, the Palace of Fine Arts, Fort Point, the Golden Gate Bridge, the Presidio, and Union Square. If it rains, tours may be canceled or an enclosed vehicle may be substituted.

Reservations aren't required for either tour. The cost for the two-and-a half-hour tour is $30 for adults and $15 for children ages 5–11. For the on/off tour, the price is $24 for adults and $12 for children ages 5–11. Departures begin at 10 a.m. daily and continue about every half hour until 4 p.m.; during the winter, the tours depart hourly. Passengers can pay an additional $12 and go on a bay cruise departing from Fisherman's Wharf. Tickets for both tours can be purchased at booths in Union Square or at Pier 39 in Fisherman's Wharf. For more information, call (800) 826-0202, or visit www.gray.linesanfrancisco.com

Specialized Tours

Gray Line offers several general-interest tours around the city and special tours to destinations beyond San Francisco. A four-hour deluxe city tour via motor coach takes visitors to the city's major attractions, including the Civic Center, Mission Dolores, Twin Peaks, Golden Gate Park, and Cliff House. Reservations are required for the tour, which departs daily at 9 a.m., 10 a.m., 11 a.m., and 2 p.m. (with an additional 3:30 p.m. departure June through September). The price is $37 for adults and $18.50 for children ages 5–11.

Gray Line offers tours to Muir Woods and Sausalito daily; they leave at 9 a.m. and 11 a.m. and last four hours. The cost is $37 for adults and $18.50 for children ages 5–11. Gray Line also offers day tours to Yosemite, the wine country, and Monterey, as well as airplane and helicopter tours. Coach tours from San Francisco include pick-up and drop-off at your hotel. For more information or reservations, call (800) 826-0202 or (415) 558-9400, or visit www.graylinesanfrancisco.com.

Tower Tours leads a deluxe city tour to Chinatown, North Beach, Telegraph Hill and Coit Tower, the Marina District, the Presidio, Cliff House and Seal Rocks, and Golden Gate Park. Scheduled stops on the tour (which uses minibuses with large windows, not motor coaches) are Vista Point at the Golden Gate Bridge, Cliff House above Seal Rocks, the Japanese Tea Garden in Golden Gate Park (small admission fee not included), and Twin Peaks (weather permitting).

Trips depart daily at 9:15 a.m., 11:15 a.m., and 2:15 p.m. The cost of the three-and-a-half-hour tour is $34 for adults and $17 for children ages 5–11. Tower Tours also offers day trips to Muir Woods and Sausalito, the wine country, Yosemite, Alcatraz, and Monterey and Carmel. All tours include pick-up and return to your hotel; meals aren't included. For more information, call (415) 434-8687.

Off-the-beaten-track tours of San Francisco architecture and the city's best sights are offered by **Quality Tours.** A customized, seven-passenger Chevy Suburban provides more comfort and greater visibility than a bus, and it can handle Lombard Street, "the crookedest street in the world." Rates are $80 an hour and the tour guide is a former UC Berkeley architecture professor. Pick-up and drop-off at your hotel is included. In addition, custom tours are available. For more information and reservations (required), call (650) 994-5054.

Bay Cruises

Visitors can enjoy spectacular views of the city skyline, the Golden Gate and Bay Bridges, and Alcatraz Island on narrated cruises around San Francisco Bay. **Red & White Fleet** offers a Golden Gate Bridge cruise that passes Fort Mason, the Presidio, and Fort Point before going under the famous bridge. The cruises, which last an hour, depart from Pier 43 in Fisherman's Wharf every 45 minutes, from 10 a.m. to 6 p.m. in the summer and from 10 a.m. to 4:45 p.m. in the winter. The price is $18 for adults, $14 for seniors and children ages 12–18, and $10 for children ages 5–11. For more information, call (415) 673-2900; or visit www.red andwhite.com

Blue & Gold Fleet offers one-hour cruises in San Francisco Bay departing from Pier 39 in Fisherman's Wharf every day except Christmas. The boats leave every half hour from 10 a.m. to 6:45 p.m. spring through fall, and every 45 minutes from 10 a.m. to 4 p.m. in the winter. The price is $18 for adults, $14 for seniors and children ages 12–18, and $10 for children ages 5–11. Blue & Gold also offers ferry service to Sausalito and Tiburon from Pier 41, a Muir Woods tour, and a Napa-Sonoma wine-country tour. For more information, call (415) 773-1188; to make advance reservations, call (415) 705-5555; or visit www.blue andgoldfleet.com.

For an elegant introduction to the San Francisco Bay, enjoy a champagne brunch aboard the *San Francisco Spirit,* a 3-deck, 150-foot charter vessel that can accommodate up to 700 passengers. The two-hour cruise departs every Sunday at 11:30 a.m. from Pier 39 in Fisherman's Wharf. The cost is $59 a person; the children's rate is $25, free for kids ages 4 and under. For reservations, call (415) 788-9100.

Air Tours

For 50 years **San Francisco Seaplane Tours** has whisked visitors aloft from the waters of the San Francisco Bay on flights over the city and its famous landmarks. Thirty-minute sight-seeing rides from Pier 39 in Fisherman's Wharf leave daily from 9 a.m. to sunset; the price is $119 for adults and $99 for children (minimum of two passengers). Flights are also offered from Sausalito, including a 30-minute city and bay tour ($119 for adults, $99 for children). Champagne sunset tours leave 30 minutes before sundown and take passengers over San Francisco at dusk; the ride lasts 35–40 minutes and costs $139 a person. Reservations are recommended for all tours and required for the sunset tour; call toll-free (888) SEA-PLANE or look up www.seaplane.com for more information.

San Francisco Helicopter Tours and Charters offers jet helicopter flights daily from San Francisco International Airport, about a half-hour south of downtown. Fifteen-minute flights ($95 for adults, $85 for children ages 11 and under) provide spectacular views of downtown and Fisherman's Wharf. Twenty-minute flights ($110 for adults, $90 for children) add the Golden Gate Bridge to the itinerary, while 30-minute tours ($150 for adults, $115 for children) include all of the above plus the California coast around Cliff House and Seal Rocks. Hotel pick-up and return is included in the price; the maximum number of passengers is between four and six. For more information and reservations (required), call (800) 400-2404, or visit www.sfhelicoptertours.com.

Walking Tours

San Francisco is best seen up close, and the best way to do that is on a walking tour. **City Guides Walking Tours,** presented by the San Francisco Friends of the Library, provides more than 200 trained volunteers who conduct about 20 different history walks each month. The one- to two-hour tours are led daily year-round, rain or shine. And here's the good part: the guided walks are free. An expanded schedule, offered in May and October, provides more than 40 different walks, with more than 125 free tours available. Walking tours are offered of San Francisco's most famous (and, in some cases, infamous) districts, as well as hidden neighborhoods most tourists miss.

No reservations are required; just meet at the place and time designated in the current tour schedule. Wear comfortable shoes (although tours are not strenuous unless so listed) and look for the City Guide, who should be wearing a badge. For a recorded schedule of walks, call (415) 557-4266 or visit www.sfcityguides.org. You can pick up a printed walk schedule at the San Francisco Convention and Visitors Bureau, Hallidie Plaza at Powell and Market Streets, or at any city library.

Victorian Home Walk takes visitors on tours of the city's famed Victorian houses, with an emphasis on exploring neighborhoods off the beaten tourist path. Tours depart daily at 11 a.m. from the lobby of the Westin St. Francis Hotel at 335 Powell Street; rates are $20 a person. The walk lasts about two and a half hours, and transportation is included. For more information or to make reservations (required), call (415) 252-9485, or visit www.victorianwalk.com.

Feel like a native on **Helen's Walk Tour,** a three-and-a-half-hour exploration of Union Square, Chinatown, and North Beach offered Monday through Thursday. The walk begins at 9 a.m. "under the clock" in the lobby of the Westin St. Francis Hotel on Union Square. The cost is $40 per person; family and group rates are available. For more information and to make reservations, call (510) 524-4544, or visit www. ollin.com/walk.html.

Learn about San Francisco's history on the **San Francisco Then . . . and Now,** a two-and-a-half-hour walking tour, which takes visitors through Union Square, Chinatown, North Beach, and the former Barbary Coast. The tours depart from the Flood Building, 870 Market Street, at 11 a.m. on weekends and holidays (and in evenings during the summer). The cost is $25 a person (free for children ages 17 and under, with some exceptions), and no steep hills are encountered on the 3-hour walk. For more information or to make reservations, call (415) 317-8687, or visit www.sfhistorytour.com.

Roger's Custom Tours offers a variety of ways to explore the city on foot, including a 3-hour San Francisco High Points tour ($40 for adults,

$20 for children ages 11 and under), a 90-minute Golden Gate Bridge tour ($30 for adults, $15 for children), and a 2-hour Chinatown tour ($30 for adults, $15 for children). Foreign language and custom tours are also available; the $40-an-hour custom tour includes transportation in a luxury car (maximum four people). For more information, call (650) 742-9611.

Relive the 1960s on the two-hour **Haight-Ashbury Flower Power** walking tour. Learn about the Summer of Love and the Diggers and see shrines to the late Jerry Garcia (of the Grateful Dead). The tours depart at 9:30 a.m. on Tuesdays and Saturdays at the corner of Stanyan and Waller Streets in the Haight; the cost is $15 per person. Reservations are required; call (415) 863-1621.

For free, in-depth walking tours of Golden Gate Park, call **Friends of Recreation & Parks** at (415) 263-0991, or visit www.frp.org/events/ walkingtours.html. A variety of guided walks are offered throughout the week, including tours of the Japanese Tea Garden and Stern Grove. **Cruisin' the Castro** is an award-winning tour with an emphasis on the neighborhood's history; sights include Harvey Milk's camera shop and the AIDS quilt museum. The walk, offered daily, starts at 10 a.m. and lasts four hours; lunch is included. The cost is $40 a person. For reservations, call (415) 550-8110.

All About Chinatown takes visitors on a behind-the-scenes walk of this colorful neighborhood, covering its history, culture, and traditions. Tours leave daily at 10 a.m. from 812 Clay Street. The two-hour walk finishes with a dim sum lunch. The cost is $39 a person with lunch, $25 without lunch; children ages 6–11, $24 with lunch, $10 without; youth ages 12–17, $29 with lunch, $15 without. For more information and reservations, call (415) 982-8839, or visit www.allaboutchinatown.com.

Touring on Your Own: Our Favorite Itineraries

If your time is limited and you want to experience the best of San Francisco in a day or two, here are some suggested itineraries. The schedules assume you're staying at a downtown hotel, have already eaten breakfast, and are ready to go around 9 a.m. If you've got two days, make reservations for a morning ferry ride to Alcatraz Island and for *Beach Blanket Babylon* (Wednesday through Sunday evenings) before you hit town.

Day One

1. Walk to Union Square or Fisherman's Wharf and tour San Francisco's major sights on one of the open-air, motorized "cable car" services; Gray Line offers unlimited reboarding privileges for the day. You can also pay an additional $10 for a one-hour narrated cruise of San Francisco Bay.

2. At Fisherman's Wharf, skip touristy Pier 39 and walk west to the Hyde Street Pier, where you can explore real nineteenth-century ships; or walk another block or two to the National Maritime Museum, which is free and chock-full of nautical goodies. Or, if it's a nice day, take a bay cruise.

3. For lunch, try the clam chowder served in a bowl of sourdough bread at Boudin's Bakery in Fisherman's Wharf; it's fast and cheap ($5).

4. On the "cable car" tour, stop at the Golden Gate Bridge. Don't just gaze at the scenery from the overlook near the visitor center; walk onto the bridge for even better views. Take a jacket (it gets very windy).

5. Back at Union Square after your circuit on the "cable car," walk up Grant Avenue to Chinatown; to get the real flavor of this exotic neighborhood, walk a block west to Stockton Street, which is less touristy.

6. Continue walking north through Chinatown to Columbus Avenue; now you're in North Beach. Settle in at a nice sidewalk café for a latte and primo people-watching; then browse at City Lights Bookstore, a North Beach landmark.

7. For a spectacular view of San Francisco, hike up Telegraph Hill to Coit Tower; if your legs and feet aren't up for the steep walk, take the No. 39 bus (board near Washington Square). After savoring the view (at its best around sunset), walk down the Greenwich Steps, a brick staircase lined with ivy and roses that descends steeply to Montgomery Street. Near the base of the steps is a glass-brick, art-deco apartment house used in the Humphrey Bogart film *Dark Passage*.

8. Have dinner at The Stinking Rose (825 Columbus Avenue in North Beach), which features "garlic seasoned with food." This fun restaurant is popular with locals as well as tourists.

Day Two

1. Get to Fisherman's Wharf for a morning ferry ride to Alcatraz. Allow at least two hours to explore the prison ruins and island.

2. Have lunch at Greens (in Building A at Fort Mason), with a full view of the Golden Gate Bridge and the Marin Headlands. It's an outstanding vegetarian restaurant (not sprouts and tofu) in a former enclosed pier with polished wood floors and a serene atmosphere. Call ahead for reservations: (415) 771-6222.

3. Take a stroll along the Marina Green where kite flyers, happy joggers, and prancing dogs converge. You can continue toward Crissy

Field (closer to the Golden Gate Bridge) or turn on Broderick or Divisidero, and then explore the Marina District and its beautiful waterside houses. If you've got time, stroll the park-like grounds of the Palace of Fine Arts. Right off of the Marina Green is a simple snack stand that serves hot chili (great on cool afternoons), hot dogs, veggie sandwiches, ice cream, Gatorade, and other hunger-curbing snacks. It's convenient if you want to picnic near the Palace of Fine Arts.

4. Take the cable car from the Beach and Hyde Streets turnaround (Powell-Mason line) or the turnaround near Taylor and Bay Streets (Powell-Hyde line); both head toward Union Square as they pass through Nob Hill. If it's a nice day, hop off and explore Nob Hill and Russian Hill. At sunset, order cocktails at the Top O' the Mark lounge in the Mark Hopkins Inter-Continental San Francisco, a 392-room hotel at California and Mason Streets.

5. Have dinner at John's Grill (63 Ellis Street near Union Square), where you can pay homage to Dashiell Hammett and Sam Spade while enjoying 1930s dining at its best.

6. Enjoy an evening of zany entertainment at *Beach Blanket Babylon* (at Club Fugazi in North Beach), San Francisco's long-running musical revue famous for its excellent singers, enormous hats, and stunning costumes; advance reservations are required.

If You've Got More Time

If you're spending more than two days in town or if this is not your first visit, consider some of these options.

1. Drive or take a bus up Van Ness Avenue to Union Street and Pacific Heights, where you'll find some of the best examples of San Francisco's famed Victorian houses. The Union Street shops are an upscale retail experience, with more than 300 boutiques, restaurants, antique shops, and coffeehouses.

2. Visit the California Palace of the Legion of Honor, a world-class European art museum in Lincoln Park with a spectacular view of the Pacific and the Marin Headlands. It's also a location used in Hitchcock's classic thriller *Vertigo*. Drive or take the No. 38 bus from Union Square.

3. Spend at least half a day in Golden Gate Park. The Japanese Tea Garden is a work of art; families should head to the California Academy of Sciences. Other options include renting a bike or rowboat.

4. Go to Sausalito or Tiburon for lunch and an afternoon. You can drive, but taking the ferry from Fisherman's Wharf is a better way

to reach these two upscale, bay-side communities across from San Francisco.

5. Serious shoppers will want to exercise their credit cards around Union Square, where they'll find the city's major department stores and many high-end specialty shops. Discount shoppers should head to SoMa, which is loaded with warehouse retail spaces. On-the-edge fashion victims and vintage-clothes browsers should head to Haight-Ashbury.

6. If you've got a car, make the trip across the Golden Gate Bridge to Muir Woods (giant redwoods) and Mount Tamalpais (a knock-your-socks-off view of San Francisco Bay and the Pacific). You can do both in half a day.

7. Drive up Twin Peaks for its stunning view of the city (from its highest location). *Hint:* go at night (and take a jacket or sweater).

8. The San Francisco Museum of Modern Art is the city's newest art emporium, and even if you're not a big fan of modern art, the building alone is worth the price of admission. It's a knockout.

9. Don't miss Fort Point. While the Civil War–era brick fortress isn't much to get excited about, the view, framed by the Golden Gate Bridge, is. It's got our vote as the most scenic spot in the city (and not just because it's the place where Jimmy Stewart pulls Kim Novak out of the water in Hitchcock's *Vertigo*).

10. Take a drive along the city's western edge south of the Golden Gate Bridge, and you'll see yet another reason why San Franciscans love living here. The views of the Pacific and the coast are spectacular. Good places to explore include Seal Rocks, Cliff House, Ocean Beach, and Fort Funston.

The Mangia! Tour

There are two things everyone raves about when referring to San Francisco—the weather and the food. Here's an agenda for you foodies out there who want to take in the diverse flavor of the city. A word on planning: definitely make a reservation for dinner. Eating is the main event for most on weekends and even weekdays for top restaurants. It's just the way—so call ahead.

Day 1

Breakfast We're going to start this day's gastronomic adventures in Berkeley. As the T-shirt boasts you get "friendly service and good food" at one of the most loved breakfast joints in the bay area, **Bette's Oceanview Diner** (1807 Fourth Street, Berkeley; (510) 644-3230). You'll come for the pancakes, as most people do, and want to endure the never-ending lines for the fat omelettes. Or are you a scrapple fan? They got that too!

The lines are extraordinarily long, as people come from all over, so be sure to get there early if you want to be seated in a timely manner. If you get there late, don't fret. Stroll along Fourth Street shops and you'll hear your name yelled over the loudspeaker.

Lunch   While you are in Berkeley, after shopping or taking in the hippies on Telegraph near campus, a must-stop is **Viks Distributors Inc.** (726 Allston Way, Berkeley; (510) 644-4412). International cuisine in San Francisco is fantastic, evidenced by the publicity their sushi and Chinese food get. But Viks is probably one of the best Indian food restaurants anywhere! Don't expect frills here. It resembles a warehouse with folding chairs and tables and you have to order at the counter and wait for your name to be announced when it is ready. What makes this place stand out from the rest is the freshness and hard-to-find Indian dishes you may never have tried before. Our recommendation is to order from the *chaat*—the snack bar. Portions are small so you can sample more of the menu (a billboard on the wall).

Dinner   After eating such a heavy Indian meal we're going to take it down a notch and direct you to **Millenium Restaurant** (246 McAllister Street; (415) 487-9800) for the most creative and innovative vegetarian meals. You can't leave San Francisco without trying things their way. It's probably the one place where vegetarians outnumber the carnivores. You'll be amazed at the many different uses for tofu. This restaurant is in constant competition with another top vegetarian haunt—Greens. But the atmosphere here is more hearty as is the food. It's not just salads.

After Dinner Café   So you had a long day touring Berkeley, survived the Bay Bridge traffic getting back into the city, settled your insides with some avocado and tomato salad, and now what? Head to North Beach to the popular Beat Generation watering hole, **Caffe Trieste** (609 Vallejo Street; (415) 392-6739) for the best coffee in town. Its imported Italian coffee is sold by the cup or by the bean. Snacks like pizza and sandwiches are available, and on Saturday afternoons musicians and opera singers take over the existential vibe and perform.

Or you'll scream for **Mitchell's Ice Cream** (688 San Jose Avenue; (415) 648-2300), unarguably the best ice cream in town as evidenced by the lines of people awaiting their number to be called. You'll be craving this family-owned treasure months after returning from San Francisco. The range of unique flavors—Chicago Cheesecake, Avocado, and Halo-Halo (a popular East Asian-style melange) to name a few, are true representations of the diverse cultural population and dining experiences in San Francisco. Unexplainably good.

Subdued Late Night   Unlike New York, San Francisco isn't open all night. It is hard to find a place open at midnight after that late movie to grab a bite to eat—not just a bite but a big slab of hearty meat if you are up for it! One neighborhood favorite that is open until 2 a.m. is **Brazen Head** (3166 Buchanan Street; (415) 921-7600) in Cow Hollow.) The atmosphere is mellow, pub-like but with a down-home, cozy feeling.

Pump Up the Volume Late Night   If you are just coming from a showing of *Beach Blanket Babylon,* or are heading to the latest top club in town, then **Steps of Rome Trattoria** in North Beach (362 Columbus Avenue; (415) 986-6480) is in order. The music is loud, waiters right out of the pages of the Italian *Vogue,* and they dance your food on over to you. If you aren't up for a bowl of pasta then try their hot chocolate, rumored to be the best in town.

Day 2

Breakfast   For over 90 years, **Sears Fine Foods Restaurant** in the heart of Union Square (439 Powell Street; (415) 986-1160) has been flipping over 16 varieties of pancakes for locals and tourists alike who have made this a city landmark. Resembling an old style diner from the 1940s, lines can form on weekends so be sure to get an early jump on the day. If flapjacks aren't your thing then try their hard-to-beat corned beef with hash, or varieties of eggs and omelettes.

Brunch   If you do get a late start to your day, you may want to consider participating in a citywide tradition—brunch. Fresh flowers at each table, thoughtful place settings, and the open kitchen are what attract locals to **Ella's Restaurant** (500 Presidio Avenue; (415) 441-5669). Every detail is thought of, down to the lemon and ginger oatmeal pancakes. Her menu's change weekly but expect eclectic lunches and creative soups! The restaurant also serves dinners, but it is an obligatory brunch destination on weekends. The pastries are also tops.

Option Two: Dim Sum! **Ton Kiang Restaurant** is one of San Francisco's best Chinese restaurants (5821 Geary Boulevard; (415) 386-8530). It is hectic and seems chaotic but they are used to it. The dishes get so so reviews, but people come for the fun of dim sum. Be sure to grab a table by the kitchen doors so you can be the first to take your pick off the dim sum trays as they come out fresh and hot.

Dinner   There are two things you can't leave the city without trying—sushi and burritos. We've got your bases covered. Decide on what you feel up for first. You can't go wrong with most of the sushi restaurants in town, but **Ebisu Sushi** in the Sunset (1283 Ninth Avenue; (415) 566-1770) is voted as one of the best. The sushi chefs at this lively place will become your closest friends after one sitting of their spicy tuna rolls. Don't be surprised with little freebies that the chefs will divvy up among guests. It's their way of turning you on to new sushi creations. The fish is the freshest, and rolls very creative. It's also along the main strip in the sunset, so an after meal stroll to see other restaurants or stores is possible.

Or if the idea of raw fish sends your stomach in an upchuck, **La Taque-ria** (2889 Mission Street; (415) 285-7117) will roll you the best burrito in town. It's a rather rundown place in the Mission, but looks are deceiving. It's fresh, cheap, and filling. There are tons of Mexican taco stands in this part of town so keep an eye out for the bright red electric sign.

The Adrenaline Tour

You'll never find a place so chock-full of outdoor activity as San Francisco. Its never-break-a-sweat weather and bay breezes, not to mention mountains, proximity to national parks, and ocean, make it a prime destination for outdoor enthusiasts.

Day 1: Close to Home

To Start Your Day   Pick up a smoothie with a wheat grass booster at **Jambo Juice** on Chestnut and Pierce Streets and take an early morning misty walk along the Marina Green. You have two choices—you can choose to walk along the water toward the bridge and then walk over the bridge toward the Marin Headlands, or you can choose to drive across the bridge. Either way hiking the **Headlands** is a must-do while in San Francisco. It's so close to the city, offers dramatic views, and it's a great way to get the heart rate and spirit escalated. Any hiker of any ability can do the Headlands. You can begin shortly after exiting the Golden Gate Bridge at the Bay Area Ridge Trail, a.k.a. the Coastal Trail. The trail can get narrow and steep but the effort is worthwhile. The trail loops around, and about mid-way don't forget to look back—you will see clear across the famous Golden Gate out to sea, and if it's a clear day you can see the jagged silhouette of the Farallon Islands only 22 miles away. You can obtain trail maps and more information on the Headlands by stopping at the **Visitor Center,** which is to the right off the exit ramp onto Alexander Avenue. Turn left on Bunker Road and you'll see signs. Their website is www.nps.gov/goga/mahe.

Or, a trek in the Headlands is completely self-led and vast—great for couples and power hikers. But if you want something a bit more confined and subdued, particularly if you have children with you, give **Angel Island** your full morning attention. Ferries leave from Fisherman's Wharf every half hour or so and deposit you at the carless island in the middle of the Bay. You will be dropped right at Perimeter Trailhead, which takes you around the island along well groomed and wide trails passing shops for bicycle rentals, tram tours, kayak rentals, and the Cove Café. For more information, call (415) 435-1915.

A Breather ...   Return from your hike and deposit yourself along the beach at Crissy Field near the Marina District. You can sit and watch the kite flyers and the wind or kite surfers in the water circle the pillars of the

Golden Gate Bridge. There is a snack bar nearby if you need to rehydrate yourself or get a sandwich.

Or Not . . . If you haven't had enough, you can rent a bike at **Blazing Saddles** (1095 Columbus Avenue; (415) 202-8888). The obligatory bike route for those who want the best scenery and burn for their body is the Great Highway bike path until it ends. The path leads you right into Fort Funston and Lake Merced—which takes you into late afternoon.

A Great Finish **Lake Merced** off the Great Highway to Skyline Boulevard offers you the chance to jog, rollerblade, bike, or hike. If you've never tried it before (and the wind is right), the lake offers windsurfing lessons, including all equipment. You can pick up a bite to eat and rehydrate yourself with a thick malt beer or the pure H_2O at the Boat House. On the drive or pedal back toward the city you can watch the sunset and decompress at **Fort Funston** off of the Great Highway. Pick a perch—benches conveniently offered—and watch the hangliders soar weightlessly off a cliff and over the crashing waves below. A great finish to the day.

Day 2: Further Afield

To Start the Day What rollerblading was in the 1990s, mountain biking is today. And **Mount Tamalpais,** or Mount Tam for those in the know, is supposedly the place where it originated. Tons of bike trails crisscross the mountain and most lead to the popular **Old Railroad Grade**—which portion to take depends on how far you want to go. You could choose to start your fat-tire tryst from quaint Mill Valley off West Blithedale Avenue, or you could drive up Summit Avenue if you are feeling less ambitious. If you need bike rentals, you can get them before taking off at Blazing Saddles (1095 Columbus Avenue; (415) 202-8888).

A Breather . . . Your butt will most definitely be in need of a break. There is no better place on that side of the bridge to take lunch or brunch than **Sam's** (27 Main Street; (415) 435-4527) in Tiburon. You could choose to bike it or drive, but it is one of the most popular brunch places in the city, because of its relaxed seaside mood and excellent views. Grab a cold one.

Or Not . . . Close to Tiburon is the savvy town of Sausalito. Here you will find **Sea Trek Ocean Kayaking Center,** an all-inclusive rental service. They offer classes, guided trips, and kayaks for newbies and pros alike. Their prices are reasonable and service top notch. You'll slice through the water starting out at Sausalito's Schoonmaker Point Marina and there's a good chance of meeting face to face with seals, pelicans, even the occasional whale in Richardson Bay. For more information, call (415) 488-1000, or check out www.seatrekkayak.com. The currents in the bay are very strong and with the occasional huge cargo ship coming through the Golden Gate from an overseas journey, expect to battle waves. You will sweat! Just remain calm and stick close to your party or a guide if that makes you more comfortable. Life jackets provided for everyone. You'll be too exhausted for anything else so spend the evening at a movie or soaking that bruised behind in a hot bath!

Or, if rumors of Great White Sharks lurking 22 miles away at the Farallon Islands deter you from sticking an inch of your toe in the bay (although according to locals, they *never* enter the bay), we have another plan. Instead of heading to Sausalito from Mount Tam, continue your adrenaline journey along Highway 1 down toward **Stinson Beach.** The drive is winding, twisting, and at some points nail biting but the heights of the pavement will prepare you for the heights of the cliff face that you can scale just south of Stinson Beach at **Red Rock Beach,** also known by locals as Mickey's. You'll climb your way up a cliff overlooking the Pacific below. The route is pretty challenging and only those who are seasoned in climbing should attempt it. For more information, call (415) 388-2070.

San Francisco for Children

Fitting any vacation and tour around diaper changes, feeding times, and cranky kids is about as challenging as getting a tan during San Francisco summers. So what do you do? San Francisco offers plenty of fun-filled places and things to do that will satisfy the most curious—and fidgety—kids. But the beauty is that you will love it too.

The *Unofficial Guide* rating system for attractions includes an "appeal to different age groups" category with a range of appeal from one star (★), don't bother, to five stars (★★★★), not to be missed. Before we get you started on specific attractions that will keep you and the little ones occupied, here are some tips to keep in mind to smooth over any sticky situations that may arise, and prevent further gray hairs.

There is a reason that the mats came out at noon during kindergarten. And there is a reason that parents are droopy-eyed at 6 a.m. while their kids are wide-eyed and bushy tailed. Kids are morning people—and it seems that energy fades around mid-afternoon. Try to plan the bulk of the activities in the early morning, when their attention is easily harnessed. There are plenty of mellow activities to plan after lunch—like sitting in a park, watching the boats in the bay . . .

If you have babies with you, make sure that you are allowed to bring them in to certain "grown up" places. Life would be much different for many if the final words of *Gone with the Wind* were intercepted by a howling screech.

Any parent-survival manual will tell you this, but it is our responsibility to remind you too: pack a bag of "goodies" for the kids. Buses can take longer than expected, and lines can be frustratingly long even for the grown-ups. Their favorite coloring book with some crayons, action figures, a portable radio, Teddy Grahams, crushed peaches … whatever it will take to make things less traumatic for you, them, and those around you.

Some Suggestions

San Francisco has more for kids to enjoy than museums, a zoo, and vistas of the bay. A **cable-car ride** never fails to delight—let's face it, even a ride on BART could be a fun experience for kids. The icing on the cake is a stop at the **Cable Car Museum** near Chinatown (it's free). And while you are near **Chinatown,** take a stroll. All the trinkets and barking toys that the shops have on display will amuse—and thankfully, if ripping out that fuzzy eraser from the hand causes a tantrum, almost everything here is cheap! Another kid pleaser raved about by native parents is the **Basic Brown Bear** (444 De Haro Street; (415) 626-0781). This is where teddy is conceived—albeit in a rated-G kinda way. Kids can select a teddy bear from among dozens of styles and then stuff it themselves. Tours of the factory are offered on Saturdays.

A Park for Every Sue, Sam, and Spot

So the Exploratorium sent the kids spinning in orbit. What to do with all that energy? A great cool-down option for you, and a place for them to release their energy in a vast open space, is to visit one of the many parks found within the city. **Golden Gate Park** is your best option. It is huge and has the **Children's Playground,** with a carousel that's fun for toddlers. You can also rent a boat on Stow Lake; bicycles, in-line skates, and roller skates are also available for rent. Another bizarre kid-pleasing attraction in the giant park is the **Bison Paddock** at the western end. You won't be able to get close enough to pet them but it is still an oddly amusing sight to see bisons roaming freely in the prairie of a city park. Near the paddock is **Spreckels Lake** where remote control boats cruise up and down. It's a fun place to sit and watch the miniboats go by. **The Presidio** is second runner up. It's big, green, has a children's playground, a pretty cheap and uncrowded bowling alley, cannons to climb on, and there is even a Burger King. There is plenty of free parking here too. Near the Presidio is the **Marina Green,** a strip of green that runs along the bay by the Marina. It is kite flying heaven—and a great place for a picnic. While you are in the Marina, be sure to visit the **wave organ**—a funky creation of granite pipes that are nestled at different depths within the breaking water. The "organ" creates different tones when the waves hit the pipes. Expect sounds of orchestral proportions at high tide. If you happen to catch a hot, sunny day in the city, a good idea might be to head to **China Beach,** one of the kid-friendliest beaches in our view. It's located in the posh Sea Cliff neighborhood and the beach is small enough to keep your eye on the kids as they run free. The facilities here are spotless and the surf is calm thanks to the protective cliffs and coves that surround the beach. Along the Great Highway 1, right after the San Francisco Zoo, is **Fort Funston.** This isn't so much a play park but rather a park for sitting and watching the humans with wings soar off cliffs. Fort Funston is one of the only places to watch hang gliders 1-2-3-jump off a cliff right next to your bench and soar above the crashing Pacific Ocean.

Most kids will like the view of the Pacific Ocean and the Golden Gate Bridge from atop 200-foot cliffs near the California Palace of the Legion of Honor in Lincoln Park. The kids might also enjoy taking a bay cruise and seeing San Francisco from the water. And don't forget another place popular with both children and adults: **Lombard Street,** "the crookedest street in the world," so steep that the road has to zigzag to make the descent (between Hyde and Leavenworth Streets).

Great places to walk include the **Golden Gate Promenade** (a three-and-a-half-mile, paved walkway that starts near Fisherman's Wharf and follows the bay shore west to the bridge of the same name) and Ocean Beach, a four-mile stretch of sand beginning just south of Cliff House.

Rainy Day Blues

Kids climbing the hotel walls? Let them work it off at **Mission Cliffs,** the world's largest indoor climbing gym (2295 Harrison Street at 19th Street; (415) 550-0515).

Another option to wipe the rainy day blahs away is to visit the kid classic shopping spot—**FAO Schwarz,** a 3-floor megastore packed with toys, dolls, games, books, and stuffed animals; the 25-foot-high singing clock is as impressive as it is annoying. The toy emporium is near Union Square at 48 Stockton Street (phone (415) 394-8700). And don't forget the other classic rainy-day option—a movie. The **AMC Kabuki 8** in Japantown is an eight-screen theater complex that's sure to be playing something the kids will enjoy. **Metreon Center** (101 Fourth Street at Mission Street; (415) 369-6000), featuring 15 movie theaters, a Sony IMAX theater, 8 restaurants, shopping, and interactive, Disneyland-style attractions geared to families, is located three blocks south of Union Square. Other shopping excursions could include a stop at Union Square where the **Disney Store** and **Virgin Records** sit practically right next to FAO Schwarz.

Kid-Friendly Menus

If you are tired of making stops at the golden arches or Pizza Hut there are several options that will please your palate as well as satisfy the picky eats of your little ones. **The Garden Terrace** in the Downtown Marriott has kids in mind for sure. They offer a half-price kids' buffet, and drinks are served with a straw straight from the crookedest street in San Fran. The menu was also designed by kids. The loud rock music and Britney paraphenalia might make you gag, but kids love **Planet Hollywood,** where the theme decor is better than the food. The restaurant is located at 2 Stockton Street, (415) 421-7827. Other dining spots children enjoy include the **Hard Rock Café,** featuring great burgers, rock memorabilia, and yet another deafening sound level (1699 Van Ness Avenue; (415) 885-1699); and **Mel's Drive-In,** straight out of *American Graffiti* and as American as it gets, with greasy fries, frothy milk shakes, and Patsy Cline crooning on the table-top jukeboxes (2165 Lombard Street, (415) 921-3039; or 3355 Geary Boulevard, (415) 387-2244). **Johnny Rockets** has burgers, fries, shakes, and it's open late. It's also a short walk from the Marina Green, located on Chestnut Street, (415) 931-6258) right next to **Mrs. Field's Cookies,** which is across the street from **Ben & Jerry's Ice Cream. Barney's Hamburgers** at Steiner Street (phone (415) 563-0307) or at 4138 24th Street (phone (415) 282-7770), has no relation to the purple beast that frolics on the boob tube. It has a wide selection of beef burgers but also could be the kids' first introduction to alternatives, like tofu burgers and garden burgers. One of our favorites is **In the Night Kitchen** (101 Fourth Street, 4th floor; (415) 369-6080) in the Metreon, which relives the adventures of the popular children's book *Where the Wild Things Are.* Kids love shapes, and what better than grilled cheese sandwiches not cut just diagonally but into star and moon shapes? Other kid pleasers include mac-and-cheese and PBJ. Don't think fast food here, as most of the ingredients are organically grown. Be sure to have a cupcake while you are here—they include a packet of squeeze-it-yourself icing and sprinkles. Best new experience for the kid's palate? **Sushi.** There is no better place to have your first chopstick-and-wasabi experience than San Francisco. Give it a go—if anything, it will be fun to see their face when you tell them it is raw fish.

Pro Sports and Other Amusements

Depending on the season and ticket availability, take the gang to a 49ers, Giants, Golden State Warriors, Oakland As, or Oakland Raiders game. If you are visiting in the sports off-season you might want to try visiting the **Potrero Hill Recreation Center** (Arkansas and 22nd Streets; (415) 695-5009) where, every summer, college basketball players and pros play in a Pro-Am League. Games are usually scheduled Monday through Thursday evenings at 8 p.m. And it's free!

The kids will enjoy sailing on **Lake Merritt** or taking a ride on the Merritt Queen, a miniature Mississippi sternwheeler that plies the lake on weekends. Youngsters enjoy **Children's Fairyland** on the north shore of Lake Merritt; it's one of the most imaginative children's parks in the country; call (510) 452-2259 for information.

Farther afield are some kid-pleasing attractions that are still near San Francisco. **Six Flags Marine World** is a 160-acre theme park with wildlife of all kinds, including elephants, seals, butterflies, and giraffes. Admission also includes a variety of shows. The park is a 45-minute drive northeast of the city in Vallejo and is open March through September. You can also take a ferry from Fisherman's Wharf. For more information, call (707) 643-6722.

Paramount's Great America is a giant amusement park filled with rides such as the *Top Gun* Jetcoaster and the *Days of Thunder* Racetrack, both based on Paramount movies; it's just the place for the roller-coaster crowd. The park is a one-hour drive south of San Francisco in Santa Clara; just drive south on US 101 until you see the signs. The park is open March through September. For more information, call (408) 988-1776. Something to combine with a scenic drive down Route 1 along the Pacific Coast is a stop at **Monterey Bay Aquarium** (886 Cannery Row, Monterey; (408) 648-4888.) The neon jellyfish tank and the walk-through tour of the Monterey Bay that starts underwater make this one of the best aquariums in the country. A little less ambitious than roller coasters and glow-in-the-dark fish is the age-old backup plan—bowling. How long has it been since you stuck your fingers in a black ball and kicked back the leg, sending pins crashing (or cleaning the gutter over and over)? **Japantown Bowl** (Post and Webster Streets; (415) 739-0724) offers glow-in-the-dark bowling on Tuesday, Saturday, and Sunday evenings. Keeping in tune with city weather, they turn on the fog machines and hand out glow-in-the-dark bowling balls. Laser lights add to the bowling mayhem.

Helpful Tips for Tourists

How to Get into Museums for Half Price

Save over $30 when you visit San Francisco's most popular museums and attractions with a **CityPass,** a book of tickets that cuts the price of admission in half. Participating attractions are the California Academy of Sciences, California Palace of the Legion of Honor, Exploratorium, San Francisco Bay Cruise, and the San Francisco Museum of Modern Art.

The passes cost $33.75 for adults, $26.75 for seniors ages 65 and older, and $24.75 for children ages 5–17. Children ages 4 and under pay the regular reduced fare at each attraction. Ticket books are sold at the participating attractions and are good for 9 days, beginning with the first day you use them. Don't remove the individual tickets from the booklet; just present the CityPass at each attraction, the clerk at the site removes the ticket, and you walk in.

When Admission Is Free

Many San Francisco museums that usually charge admission open their doors for free one day a month. If you'd like to save a few bucks during your visit, use the following list when planning your touring itinerary. And don't forget that summer is the season of free events and outdoor concerts.

- California Academy of Sciences (first Wednesday of the month)
- California Historical Society (first Tuesday of the month)
- California Palace of the Legion of Honor (second Wednesday of the month)
- Center for the Arts at Yerba Buena Gardens (first Thursday of the month)
- Exploratorium (first Wednesday of the month)
- Mexican Museum (first Wednesday of the month)
- San Francisco Craft and Folk Art Museum (first Wednesday of the month and every Saturday between 10 a.m. and noon)
- San Francisco Museum of Modern Art (first Tuesday of the month)
- San Francisco Zoo (first Wednesday of the month)

   In addition, a few worthy attractions around town are free to the public all the time. Here's the list.

- Cable Car Museum
- Federal Reserve Bank of California
- Fort Point National Historic Site
- Golden Gate Band Concerts (Sundays at 1 p.m., April–October)
- Golden Gate Bridge (pedestrians and bicyclists)
- Midsummer Music Festival (Stern Grove, Sloat Avenue at 19th Street, Sunday afternoon at 2 p.m., June–August)
- Museum of Money of the American West
- National Maritime Museum
- San Francisco Shakespeare Festival (Golden Gate Park, Sundays in September)
- Strybing Arboretum
- Wells Fargo History Museum

Breathtaking Views

We are all drawn to *the view*—a glimpse of something larger, majestic, something that can breathe new life in us or suck it out if it so chooses. Breathtaking. Whether it's nature at its most expansive, or the sparkling twilight of a sky filled with stars or a cityscape bright with energy—

everyone requests a view. You don't have to know the manager of the Fairmont Hotel to get compelling views in San Francisco. Simply take a stroll and use our list of some of the best views in the city as your guide.

1. **Fort Point.** Ideally, you should be blindfolded and brought to this Civil War–era fortress. You should remove the blind as you face the Marin Headlands across the Golden Gate. Overhead is the massive Golden Gate Bridge, perhaps the most beautiful suspension bridge in the world. It's a view to die for.

2. Although it's better at night, the view from **Twin Peaks** is good whenever the weather is clear. It's a stupendous, 360° view of San Francisco.

3. The best view of the city's skyline is from **Treasure Island.** To get there, take the Treasure Island Exit from the Bay Bridge and drive to the parking area just outside the naval station.

4. For the best view of the waterfront, hike up **Telegraph Hill** to Coit Tower. Don't drive, though; parking is scarce. Either walk or take the No. 39 bus.

5. Drive across the **Golden Gate Bridge,** get off in Sausalito and follow signs to Mount Tamalpais, where you can drive to the 2,800-foot summit (well, almost) for a heart-stopping view of San Francisco Bay, the city, the Golden Gate and Bay Bridges, and the Pacific Ocean.

6. For a view of the bay that's almost as good as the one from Mount Tam, drive to Berkeley, go through the University of California Berkeley campus and find Grizzly Peak Boulevard. Then drive up the winding road to the **Lawrence Hall of Science.** Park in the lot and enjoy the vista from the plaza of the Children's Science Museum.

7. The view from the **Golden Gate Bridge** is best at sunset, when the slanting sun casts shadowy patterns on the lofty bridge towers and on the sea below—and the tour buses have left for the day. The pedestrian walkway is open until 9 p.m.

8. For an even better view of **Seal Rocks** than the one you get at Cliff House, walk up to Sutro Heights Park, which overlooks the Pacific from a lofty vantage point. Park in the lot just north of Cliff House (on the other side of the Great Highway).

9. Drive across the Golden Gate Bridge to **Vista Point,** which offers superb views of the bridge and the San Francisco skyline. It's beautiful on a sunny day, but it might be even better when the fog rolls over the hills or at night when the city glimmers beyond the Golden Gate. **The Headlands** offer the postcard perfect views of the city and the approaching fog just knocking at the gate.

10. The neighborhood of Potrero Hill, at Nineteenth and Texas Streets, makes the city skyline appear like a pop-up book. Honorable mention goes to **Dolores Park.**

Secret Staircases

Scattered throughout San Francisco's many hills are pocket parks, restful benches, and many stairways—about 350 of them, mostly in residential neighborhoods and often adorned with flowers planted by neighbors. The stairways are used by residents to allow direct vertical access from one street to another; because most streets wind around the hills, people frequently use staircases as shortcuts.

A walk centered around an exploration of the city's staircases is cheaper than a fitness center and frequently offers views that rival what you'll find on the Golden Gate Bridge. Put on your walking shoes, grab your camera, and explore some of the city's oldest, most scenic hidden attractions—its stairways. For a comprehensive guide to the city's stairways, pick up a copy of *Stairway Walks in San Francisco, 4th ed.* by Adah Bakalinsky, available in bookstores or directly from the Wilderness Press (phone (510) 558-1666), or on Amazon.com. Here's a sampling of some of San Francisco's best stairways.

1. The carefully landscaped stairs found near the famous Lombard Street (between Hyde and Leavenworth Streets).

2. At Broadway and Lyon Street, more than ten flights of majestic stone steps surrounded by well-kept greenery and regal views of the Palace of Fine Arts, the bay, and the Marin Headlands.

3. The Greenwich Street Steps at the base of Coit Tower on Telegraph Hill; more than three separate flights of stairs that climb through tall trees and past hillside gardens and stunning views. (see Exercise and Recreation section for more specifics, page 363.)

4. The Fort Mason/Aquatic Park Steps overlooking Alcatraz; the small clearing at the top features tranquility and picnic tables.

5. Pemberton Stairway in the Twin Peaks neighborhood, newly renovated with terra-cotta concrete stairs and just-planted gardens.

6. Filbert Street Steps, between Sansome Street and Telegraph Hill, a 377-step climb through verdant flower gardens and charming nineteenth-century cottages.

San Francisco on Film

Some of you may remember that scene in the classic *It Came From Beneath the Sea* circa 1955, where a giant octopus attacks the Golden Gate Bridge and tears it in half. If you don't, it's a sure rental before you set out seeing the sights of the city. If you are a movie junkie and love to relive favorite scenes then San Francisco is just the fix. Before going out and renting any flicks pick up a copy of *The San Francisco Movie Map,* sold at the California Historical Society gift shop and other locations around town. Some other notable movies that feature San Francisco include:

Sweet November (2000), starring Keanu Reeves and Charlize Heron, was a flop at the box office, but it showcased the best of San Francisco as the goo-goo-eyed couple pranced around Potrero Hill and Noe Valley.

The Rock (1996), starring Sean Connery, Nicolas Cage, and Ed Harris, was another Alcatraz action adventure.

Interview with the Vampire (1994) The devilish leader of the vampires played by Tom Cruise offers Christian Slater "the choice" in a nighttime drive across the Golden Gate Bridge.

The Joy Luck Club (1993), noted for its realistic depiction of Chinese Americans, was made in Chinatown.

Basic Instinct (1992), you know the shot—that crossing the leg with no panties shot that made the movie famous. The entire movie was shot in San Fran, evidenced by the car-chase scenes through town.

Escape from Alcatraz (1979), a true story starring Clint Eastwood as the leader of a trio of escapees who actually made it off the Rock. *Birdman of Alcatraz* (1962) with Burt Lancaster.

What's Up, Doc? (1972), a screwball comedy starring Barbara Streisand and Ryan O'Neal, was filmed at the San Francisco Hilton (33 O'Farrell Street), called Hotel Bristol in the film. While we are on hotels: the lobby of the Fairmont Hotel on Nob Hill was featured in that 1980s television series *Hotel.*

Vertigo (1958) It's not a place, it's a classic thriller directed by Alfred Hitchcock. The British director loved San Francisco and he shows the town at its best in this 1958 film starring James Stewart and Kim Novak. Locations in the movie include Mission Dolores, the California Palace of the Legion of Honor (the movie's scenes were filmed in Gallery 6), the Palace of Fine Arts, and Fort Point (where Stewart dives into San Francisco Bay to save Novak).

Day Trips in and around the Bay Area

If you've got the time or if your visit to San Francisco is a repeat trip, consider exploring some places outside the city. Northern California is spectacularly scenic and a trip to the area really isn't complete unless you take at least one day to venture beyond town limits.

From Marin County, Point Reyes, and the wine country to the north; to the East Bay cities of Oakland and Berkeley; to the villages, mountains, and coastal scenery to the south, there's plenty to see and do. A trip beyond hectic San Francisco can be a welcome respite from the heavy traffic and round-the-clock activity in the city's livelier neighborhoods. Here are a few suggestions for day trips that get beyond the city's limits.

Marin County

Sausalito and Tiburon

For folks on a tight schedule or without a car, these two bay-side villages across from San Francisco are destinations well worth visiting. And with ferry service available from Fisherman's Wharf, it's a short trip that combines a refreshing boat ride with spectacular scenery. Neither destination requires a full day; a sunny afternoon is just about perfect.

Sausalito Sausalito was once a gritty little fishing village full of bars and bordellos, but today it's decidedly more upscale. Think French Riviera, not Barbary Coast. With approximately 7,500 residents (not all of them cash-flush yuppies), the town still manages to hang on to a faintly Bohemian air, although most of its attractions are upscale boutiques and restaurants. The main drag is Bridgeway, where sleek, Lycra-clad bicyclists, inline skaters, and joggers flash by along the waterfront.

Caledonia Street, one block inland, has a wider selection of cafés and shops. Half a mile north of town, the tourist onslaught is less evident and visitors can see the town's well-known ad-hoc community of houseboats and barges. But most folks come just to exercise their credit cards or hang out in a bar or waterfront restaurant. And that's not a bad idea: the views of the bay and the San Francisco skyline are great. Suggestions: **The No Name Bar** (757 Bridgeway; (415) 332–1392) is a no-frills Sausalito institution. It's smoky, small, and funky, with great Irish coffee and decent martinis.

The **Blue & Gold Fleet** provides ferry service to Sausalito, a 20-minute boat ride from Pier 41 in Fisherman's Wharf. The cost of a round-trip is $13.50 for adults and $6.50 for children ages 5–11. For departure times and information, call (415) 773-1188. **Golden Gate Ferries** depart from the Ferry Building at the foot of Market Street. One-way tickets are $5.30 for adults, $4 for seniors and the physically disabled, and $2.65 for children. For schedules, call (415) 923-2000. If you're driving, take US 101 north across the Golden Gate Bridge; then take the first right, the Alexander Avenue exit. Alexander becomes Bridgeway in Sausalito. For more information, visit www.blueandgoldfleet.com.

Tiburon Less touristy but more upscale is the best way to describe Tiburon, which is frequently compared to a New England fishing village. (Maybe so, if the New Englanders are wealthy and commute to high-rise offices by ferry every day.) Visitors can soak up this heady ambience in pricey waterfront restaurants and bars, then stroll the gorgeous promenade. Tiburon is also the most convenient stepping-off point to nearby Angel Island, where you can hike or bike on 12 miles of trails in the state park. A good lunch or dinner destination in Tiburon is **Guaymas** (5 Main Street; (415) 435-6300), with authentic Mexican cuisine and a panoramic view of San Francisco and the bay.

Ferry service to Tiburon is provided by the **Blue & Gold Fleet** from Pier 41 in Fisherman's Wharf; round-trip tickets are $13.50 for adults and $6.50 for children. For departure times and information, call (415) 773-1188. By car, take US 101 north across the Golden Gate Bridge to the Tiburon/Highway 131 Exit; then follow Tiburon Boulevard all the way to downtown. It's about a 40-minute drive from San Francisco. Our advice: take the ferry. For more information, visit www.blueandgoldfleet.com.

Angel Island

Over the years Angel Island has been a prison, a notorious quarantine station for immigrants, a missile base, and a favorite site for duels. Today the largest island in San Francisco Bay is a state park; it's a terrific desti-nation for a picnic, stroll, hike, or mountain-bike ride, or simply a place to get away from traffic, phones, and television.

Angel Island, located across Raccoon Straight from Tiburon, is accessi-ble only by ferry. Visitors arrive at a small marina abutting a huge lawn area equipped with picnic tables, benches, barbecue pits, and rest rooms. There's also a small store, café, gift shop, and mountain bike rental con-cession. (To save money, rent a bike in San Francisco and bring it on the ferry.) Tram tours highlight the island's history. You can also rent a stable, two-person sea kayak and see the island from the water. There are 12 miles of trails on the wooded island, and cyclists and hikers can explore the spooky ruins of the former immigration center (called the "Ellis Island of the West"). *Note:* Tram tours and bike and kayak rentals are closed from mid-November to mid-February.

Blue & Gold Fleet ferries to Angel Island depart from Pier 41 in Fish-erman's Wharf daily in the summer and on weekends in the winter. The round-trip fare is $10.50 for adults, $5.50 for children ages 6–12; chil-dren age 5 and under, free. For departure times and information, call (415) 773-1188. The **Angel Island–Tiburon Ferry** operates daily in summer and on weekends in winter. Round-trip fares are $5.50 for adults and $4.50 for children ages 5–11. A $1 fee is charged for bicycles. For schedule information and directions, call (415) 435-2131, or visit www.angelislandferry.com.

Marin Headlands

Aside from offering the postcard views of San Francisco, the **Headlands** as they are affectionately called, is *the* playground for restless San Franciscans.

It is closer than most grocery stores for many residents—particularly those who live in the Marina District, and the fact that it is anchored to the city by the walkable Golden Gate Bridge, makes it one of the most prized places to play on weekends. With minimal hassle—except bridge traffic— you can park for free and within ten minutes of leaving your hotel or home, you can put boot to the dirt on tons of hiking trails. Or if you pre- fer fat-tire skirmishes, there are plenty of mountain-biking opportunities also—you would expect nothing less from the place that is said to be the origination of mountain biking as we know it! The Headlands, largely undeveloped terrain, is dominated by 2,800-foot Mount Tamalpais. The coastline here is more rugged than on the San Francisco side of the bridge, and it's a Mecca for nature lovers. Visitors are treated to great views of the city, ocean, and bay; hiking trails and rugged beaches; and the concrete remains of old forts and gun emplacements standing guard over the Golden Gate (no shots were ever fired in anger).

While physically close to San Francisco, the headlands seem a world apart. Windswept ridges, protected valleys, and beaches offer the best of nature, but they're less than an hour's drive from the hectic city. The hill- sides near the Golden Gate provide magnificent views of the entrance of the bay. The Marin Headlands Visitor Center (phone (415) 331-1540) is open daily from 9:30 a.m. to 4:30 p.m. and offers detailed information on enjoying the rugged countryside.

The headlands offer a vast expanse of wild and open terrain; rolling hills covered with shrubs, grasses, and wildflowers; small coves, large beaches, and rocky coastal cliffs; and forested ridges and redwood valleys. The park, part of Golden Gate National Recreation Area, has abundant wildlife—hawks, deer, and seabirds are common, and bobcats and whales are sometimes sighted. Fog is heaviest in the summer in areas closer to the Golden Gate, and ocean swimming is always dangerous. Also, use caution when walking on the rocky coastline, where unwary hikers can be swept away by large waves or trapped by the incoming tide.

Major attractions include the Point Bonita Lighthouse (open spring through fall on weekends), Muir and Stinson Beaches, Muir Woods and Mount Tamalpais, and Olema Valley. Trails, many of them rugged and steep, crisscross the headlands; remember to bring drinking water and stay off the cliffs, which are prone to landslides and covered with poison oak. Hikers, cyclists, and equestrians can pick up detailed trail maps and information at the visitor center. And don't forget to bring your lunch: With the exceptions of cafés in Muir Woods and Stinson Beach, there are no places to eat in the headlands.

To reach the Marin Headlands and the visitor center, drive north on US 101 across the Golden Gate Bridge, take the first exit (Alexander Avenue), bear left, and follow the road up the hill. Go through the one-way tunnel (there's a traffic light), which puts you on Bunker Road and leads to the visitor center, Rodeo Beach, and the Point Bonita Lighthouse.

The East Bay

Across the Bay Bridge from San Francisco, two cities offer startling contrasts to the chic town on the peninsula. Oakland is a gritty, blue-collar city that earns its livelihood with shipping and transportation to and from the Port of Oakland, dominated by huge cranes. The city spreads north toward Berkeley, a college town that's home to a campus of the University of California and a fascinating cross-section of aging hippies and radicals, hustling young Republicans, students, and Nobel Prize laureates. The two towns blend together so that they're physically indistinguishable, although Oakland's lowbrow reputation stands in stark contrast to Berkeley, a self-consciously hip, intellectual hotbed. However, Oakland lays claim to some impressive historical and literary associations of its own. Gertrude Stein and Jack London both grew up in the city at about the same time, albeit at different ends of the social spectrum.

Oakland

Located just over the Bay Bridge, or via BART, Oakland is the workhorse of the Bay Area, with one of the busiest ports on the West Coast. Yet in spite of its blue-collar reputation and Ms. Stein's oft-quoted withering reference to her hometown ("There is no there there"), Oakland has a few tricks up its sleeve that make the town worth a visit. Not the least of its attributes is the weather, often mild and sunny while San Francisco is draped in chilly fog.

Leading the list is the **Oakland Museum,** really three museums in one, that focus on the history, geography, and culture of California. Other things to do in Oakland include sailing a boat on downtown **Lake Merritt,** taking the kids to **Children's Fairyland** (on the north shore of Lake Merritt), or ogling the restored art deco interior of the **Oakland Paramount Theater** (2025 Broadway; (510) 893-2300). Tours of the beautiful theater are offered on the first and third Saturdays of the month (excluding holidays), starting at 10 a.m. and lasting two hours. The cost is $1 a person and no reservations are necessary.

Jack London Square is Oakland's version of Fisherman's Wharf and shamelessly plays up the city's connection with the writer, who grew up along the city's waterfront. The complex of boutiques and eateries is just about as tacky as its cousin across the bay—and about as far from "the call of the wild" as you can get. A better eating option is **Bay Wolf** (3853 Piedmont Avenue; (510) 655-6004), the city's most venerable and revered restaurant.

To reach Oakland's Jack London Square by car, take the Bay Bridge to I-880 to Broadway, turn south, and go to the end. On BART, get off at the 12th Street station and walk south along Broadway about a half mile (or grab the No. 51a bus to the foot of Broadway). To get to Lake Merritt, cross the Bay Bridge and follow signs to downtown Oakland and exit at Grand Avenue South. To get to the Oakland Museum, take I-580 to I-980 and exit at Jackson Street. Via BART, get off at the Lake Merritt station, a block south of the museum.

Berkeley

Probably more than any other town in the country, Berkeley conjures up images of the rebellious 1960s when students of the University of California, Berkeley, led the protests against the Vietnam War. At times, virtual full-scale battles were fought almost daily between protestors and cops, both on campus and in the streets of the surrounding town (most notably in People's Park, off of Telegraph Avenue).

These days, things are more sedate in this college town, although admirers and detractors still refer to it as "Berserkley" and the "People's Republic of Berkeley." While student angst is down, the progressive impulse lingers and is best experienced on **Telegraph Avenue,** south of the campus. On the four blocks or so closest to the university, it's a regular street fair filled with vendors selling handmade jewelry, tie-dyed T-shirts, and bumper stickers promoting leftist causes and lifestyles. The sidewalks on both sides of Telegraph Avenue are usually jammed with students, tourists, bearded academics, homeless people, and gray-haired hippies.

Coffeehouses, restaurants, art and crafts boutiques, head shops, and excellent used-book-and-record stores line the street; order a latte and enjoy the endless procession of interesting people who throng the street most afternoons and evenings. A good lunch option on Telegraph Avenue is **Cafe Intermezzo** (2442 Telegraph Avenue; (510) 849-4592), a crowded self-serve sandwich, salad, and soup place that serves great over-sized sandwiches on homemade bread. Cheap, too. But the selection of restaurants is truly intimidating in Berkeley; every ethnic cuisine in the world, it seems, is represented.

The 31,000-student **University of California** campus is noted for its academic excellence and its 15 Nobel Prize winners. There are several museums on campus worth exploring, including the **Berkeley Art Museum** and, for kids, the **Lawrence Hall of Science** (easiest to reach if you've got a car; the view of San Francisco Bay from the science museum is stupendous).

To reach Berkeley, about ten miles northeast of San Francisco, take the Bay Bridge, follow I-80 east to the University Avenue exit, and follow the wide street until you hit the campus. Turn right to get to Telegraph

Avenue. Parking close to the campus is notoriously difficult, so try to arrive early on weekends and get a space in one of the many private parking lots located just off campus. Another option is BART, which has a Berkeley station two blocks from the campus.

Point Reyes National Seashore

This 85,000-acre park of sandy beach and scrubland is on a geologic "island" located about an hour's drive north of San Francisco. Windswept and ruggedly beautiful, Point Reyes is a wildlife paradise. Shorebirds, seabirds, invertebrates, and marine mammals thrive on this peninsula, which juts into the cold waters of the Pacific just west of the San Andreas fault. Folks who love scenic beauty and wildlife should put this scenic destination on their "A-list" of places to go on an excursion from San Francisco.

English explorer Sir Francis Drake is said to have anchored his ship, the *Golden Hind,* in Drakes Bay, on the southern coast of the wing-shaped peninsula, in 1579. There's evidence he careened his ship to make repairs and stayed about five weeks before sailing westward across the Pacific on his round-the-world voyage of discovery. Nearly 200 years passed before settlers arrived. After the U.S. conquest of California, the land was broken into dozens of dairy ranches, and beef and dairy cattle have roamed the brushy flatlands of Point Reyes ever since.

Touring Suggestions

The best place to begin a visit is the **Bear Valley Visitor Center** and its extensive collection of exhibits, specimens, and artifacts. The center is open from 9 a.m. to 5 p.m. on weekdays and 8 a.m. to 5 p.m. on weekends and holidays. You can pick up maps and tide tables and get advice from a ranger on places to hike, picnic, and view wildlife. Ranger-led tours are also offered on a varying schedule, and several hiking trails are accessible from the visitor center. For more information, call (415) 663-1092, or visit www.nps.gov/pore.

From December through March **gray whales** make their 10,000-mile migration between the Bering Sea and Baja California, swimming past Point Reyes. The best spot to view the whales is from **Point Reyes Light-house,** which has limited parking. Because of the popularity of whale-watching on weekends, the park provides shuttles to the lighthouse from Bear Valley. A better bet is to come early on a weekday to avoid the crowds. Dress warmly—it's usually cold and windy—and bring binoculars and a camera with a telephoto lens.

Nearly 500 tule elk roam Point Reyes (reintroduced following an absence of more than 100 years). The **Tule Elk Preserve** is at the northern tip of the park, and you're apt to spot some elk on a walk down the moderately difficult **Tomales Point Trail.** Other good places to view wildlife include **Fivebrooks Pond** (waterfowl), the wetlands of Limantour (ducks), and the promontory overlooking Chimney Rock (sea lions, harbor seals, and seabirds).

If you want to make a weekend of your visit to Point Reyes, consider camping. Backcountry camping is limited to four areas maintained by the park service: Coast, Sky, Glenn, and Wildcat Camps.

A Car Tour

Point Reyes is worth a full day or more of exploration. But if your time is limited, you can get a good sampling of what Point Reyes has to offer in about half a day—mostly through the windows of your car. From the visitor center, continue on Bear Valley Road to Sir Francis Drake Boulevard, pass through the village of Inverness and follow signs for the Point Reyes Lighthouse. For a spectacular view of the entire peninsula, turn right on Mount Vision Road, a steep and twisty paved lane that rises to almost 1,300 feet before it dead-ends.

Return to Sir Francis Drake Boulevard and turn left to continue toward the lighthouse. On the right are two beaches ripe for exploration (but not swimming; the waters are cold and dangerous) before you reach the **Lighthouse Visitor Center.** The lighthouse offers a spectacularly scenic view of the ocean and the tip of the peninsula; it's just under a half-mile walk from the parking area, followed by a 300-step descent down the cliff to the lighthouse. The visitor center is open Thursday through Monday from 10 a.m. to 5 p.m., closed Tuesday and Wednesday (call (415) 669-1534).

After you visit the lighthouse, backtrack by car to the turn to **Chimney Rock** (a good place to view wildlife) or continue driving to the mainland. To reach the elk reserve, turn left about two miles past Mount Vision Road, and then turn left on Pierce Point Road and drive to **Pierce Point Ranch,** a renovated dairy ranch with a self-guided trail through the historic complex. Then hike down the **Tomales Point Trail,** and you may spot some elk. Wear hiking boots and be prepared for changes in the weather.

Food, Lodging, and Directions

You'll find restaurants, cafés, delicatessens, general stores, and bakeries in the nearby villages of Olema, Point Reyes Station, Inverness, and Marshall; a café is located at Drakes Beach inside the park. Inns and bed-and-breakfasts are also nearby. For more information, call the **West Marin Visitor Bureau** at (415) 543-3035.

To reach Point Reyes from San Francisco, cross the Golden Gate Bridge and stay on US 101 north. Exit at Sir Francis Drake Boulevard and head west; it's about a 20-mile drive (much of it through congested Marin County, although the scenery improves dramatically around Taylor State Park) to Route 1 at Olema. From here it's about a one-minute drive to the Bear Valley Visitor Center. A longer and more scenic route is California Route 1, reached from US 101 in Sausalito.

The Wine Country

After a few days of touring hectic San Francisco, what could be better than relaxing in a setting of pastoral splendor only an hour from Union Square? The wine country is a region of wooded hills and luxuriant valleys where tilled fields create geometric patterns across the landscape and narrow lanes wind among the hills. Quaint country inns and designer restaurants with massive wine lists are abundant and pamper the well-heeled visitors who flock to these valleys, defined by low oak- and chaparral-covered ridges.

For most folks, the visual grandeur is secondary to the lure of the fruit of the land. The wines produced in the Napa and Sonoma Valleys rival the best vintages of France—and everybody wants to see where the magic is being made. Wineries are everywhere in the two neighboring valleys, located north of San Francisco and inland of the Pacific Coast. They are so numerous that it's easy think this is the wine-making capital of California. In fact, only about 5% of the state's total production comes from the region. But far and away the best wines produced in the country come from here. The reason is the region's Mediterranean climate: hot, dry summers and cool, wet winters result in stressed-out grapevines that produce small, thick-skinned fruit. Because most of a wine's flavor and character comes from the skin, not the pulp, the grapes that grow in these valleys result in premium vintages that impress wine snobs around the world.

Wine has been made in the valleys since the eighteenth century, when clerics in Spanish missions planted vineyards to produce black grapes for sacramental wines. After a series of ups and downs over the centuries, the wine business began booming in the 1960s. Wine has evolved into an increasingly popular national drink, and the valleys have recovered from the last slump caused by Prohibition, when many vineyards were converted into orchards.

Today's renaissance is extraordinary; acreage has expanded exponentially and big business has moved in, most notably Coca-Cola and Nestlé. Even the French, formerly aloof, have formed partnerships with local growers. Napa Valley boasts more than 250 wineries, while Sonoma Valley has about 35. Winemaking in the valleys is now a multibillion-dollar business, and millions of folks tour the wine country each year.

Which Valley?

Daytrippers on a self-guided day tour of the wine country are faced with a choice: **Napa** or **Sonoma**? Alas, touring both valleys in one day just isn't practical. Napa, the easternmost valley, is by far the best known of the two. It stretches for 35 miles from the town of Napa north to the resort town of Calistoga. In the long, narrow valley, grape arbors alternate with wild grasses, and the rich bottomland gives way to forested slopes of the surrounding ridges. Once past the congested and unexciting town of Napa, the beautiful valley looks more like southern France than Northern California.

Yet Napa is fashionable beyond belief and attracts millionaires the way a magnet draws iron filings. The valley also seems to draw more than its fair share of pinch-faced connoisseurs who mutter in mangled French as they swirl and sniff premium vintages in the tasting rooms of the wineries. Thankfully, the wine snobs are vastly outnumbered. Napa Valley has been discovered and hordes of tourists have made it one of California's most popular attractions. Many of the wineries along Route 29 are huge, with massive parking lots that contain special areas reserved for tour buses. While the countryside is pretty (increasingly so the farther north you go), very little in Napa Valley is small scale or intimate.

Sonoma Valley, on the other hand, has fewer wineries. Most are relatively small, still family-run, and tucked away on side roads. They don't line the highway like designer discount outlets (also found in Napa). There's also notably less pretension in the wine-tasting rooms. In addition, Sonoma has more to offer than wineries, including a Spanish mission and the former estate of Jack London, one of America's greatest writers. As you've probably guessed by now, *Unofficial Guide* researchers, who loathe crowds and tourist hype, give the edge to Sonoma over its eastern neighbor. Another plus: it's closer to San Francisco (though not by much).

We prefer less-touristy Sonoma, but that doesn't mean you should rule out Napa. If one of your favorite wines is produced by, say, the Robert Mondavi Winery, by all means head to Napa, where that well-known firm provides free tours and tastings. You'll have a great time. Plus, the crowds and oversized wineries decrease the farther north you go in Napa. Calistoga, at the top of the valley, offers a lot for visitors to see and do. Another solution to the "Which valley?" conundrum is to make your visit an overnight affair and tour both valleys. We suggest a two-day tour later in this chapter.

Touring Strategies

Visiting the wine country shouldn't be about following a strict itinerary and seeing how much you can do in one day of hectic touring. It's quite the opposite, a joie-de-vivre kind of thing: a celebration of the good things in life, such as wonderful scenery, great food, and good friends. These are all complimented by fine wine—thus the popularity of touring the wine country.

Don't schedule too rigidly your visit to Napa or Sonoma. Still, little judicious planning can go a long way to ensuring that a visit is pleasant, even memorable. Whether you decide to visit Napa, Sonoma, or both valleys, we'll provide you with specific advice that will allow you to get the most enjoyment from a one- or two-day excursion.

Planning

Although several tour companies in San Francisco provide bus tours to the wine country, we think the best way to enjoy a visit is to rent a car which gives you the flexibility to ensure a relaxing, fun-filled trip. If at all possible, don't go on a weekend; the best time to visit is early in the week. Plan on leaving San Francisco around 9 a.m. to get past the worst of morning rush-hour traffic and into the wine country by midmorning. Be sure to eat a good breakfast before leaving; you'll appreciate it later in the morning when you've sampled your first glass or two of wine.

You'll get more from a wine-country excursion if you can give it some focus. For example, plan on visiting one or two wineries that produce wines you enjoy at home. Or structure your day around a bike ride or something else not wine-related (we provide suggestions below). Then leave some time for a spontaneous stop at one or two other wineries, a picnic in a park, a museum visit, or shopping in one of the many towns.

Don't plan on visiting more than two or three wineries in a day. Otherwise the day becomes a blur of wine-tasting rooms that run together in your memory and your palate—not to mention the problem of too much alcohol consumption. One advantage of a two-day wine-country tour is that you can trade off driving; that way, there's always someone who can taste the wine and someone who can safely navigate the car.

Many folks pack a picnic lunch, visit a winery, buy a bottle of wine, and enjoy an outdoor meal in a picnic area provided at many wineries. (Most of the picnic areas are in fabulously beautiful settings surrounded by forests and vineyards.) You can buy sandwiches or fixings at delicatessens and groceries; don't forget to bring a corkscrew. Keep in mind that the whole point of visiting the wine country is to relax and have a good time.

Winery Tours

With something like 300 wineries in and around the Napa and Sonoma Valleys, picking a few to visit can be tough. You can just wander around and stop in wineries on a whim, but we think it pays to be selective. Visit a winery that makes a wine you like or, if you need some help, consult the list of wineries below (page 179).

Virtually all of the wineries are open to the public from about 10 a.m. to 4 p.m. daily (and an hour to two later in the summer). Most have only tasting rooms and maybe a picnic area outside. While many firms offer free wine tastings, increasingly some wineries (especially in Napa) are charging a few dollars for the opportunity to sample the fruits of their vineyards.

Larger winemaking concerns, for example Mondavi in Napa and Sebastiani in Sonoma, offer free guided tours of the premises. Visitors tour in groups of about 30; the tours last a half hour or so, ending with a visit to a tasting room. These are usually large, comfortable, and well-appointed rooms where visitors sample the wares; they can also purchase wine here or in a nearby sales room. Smaller wineries, by and large, require reservations at least a day in advance (even earlier in the summer and fall) for a tour with a smaller group that may last two hours.

So Which Tour Is Right for You?

Nonreservation Tours   If your interest in wine is casual, a nonreservation tour at one of the larger wineries should do the trick. You'll gain insight into the wine country's unusual climate, which is the main reason the area produces such good wine. You'll also get a glimpse of the wine-making process, from the huge stainless-steel vats where the grapes are fermented to the large warehouses where the new wine is stored as it ages in oak barrels. Tour guides provide a good overview of the fascinating and complex operation of a winery; tours usually depart on the hour or half-hour throughout the day. The icing on the cake, of course, is the end of the tour, when you arrive in the tasting room and sample different wines made on the premises; often you can help yourself to hors d'oeu-vres as you sample different vintages.

Reservation-Only Tours   Reservation-only guided tours, also free, are longer and best appreciated by wine-savvy folks who know the basics of winemaking and want to learn more. And they will as they're led around the winery by their tour guide, often an employee who really knows and appreciates good wine. On many tours, visitors spend a lot of time in the aging rooms, which are stacked to the ceiling with oak barrels. The guide may not only discuss, say, how American versus French oak barrels affect the tannin content in red wines; he or she will also tap barrels at various stages of aging and let you taste the difference. With the exception of the actual quaffing of the grape, this can be either utterly fascinating or excruciatingly boring, depending on your level of interest.

On a reservation-only tour, you'll also get from-the-hip insights into the winemaking business (such as how much of the winery's grape pro-duction comes from leased vineyards—and why). You may also pick up some valuable tips, such as which vintages are best for particular wines. *Here's one:* 1995 gets rave reviews for virtually all wines produced in the wine country; warm winds from the Central Valley swept through just before the harvest, making the grapes smaller and thickening their skins.

Wine Tasting: To Swirl or to Sniff?   The ancient Greeks had it wrong. The nectar of the gods isn't sweet ambrosia, it's wine. Yet deciding which wine is the best can be like trying to determine the one true religion. That's okay. A trip to the wine country can be the start of a lifetime enjoyment of the fermented grape as you begin an education on how to savor this mysterious beverage.

Keep in mind that there are two types of California wines: varietals, made primarily from a particular kind of grape, such as cabernet sauvignon or zinfandel, and the lower-quality generics, wines blended from several different grapes and often named for a European wine region such as Burgundy.

To learn more about wines, you need to taste them. Unfortunately, folks who are unversed in the liturgy of wine tasting can feel awfully uncomfortable as a nearby wine snob swirls and sniffs a glass of wine. Don't be intimidated. You're on vacation. Why let a self-styled connoisseur ruin your fun?

Here are some things that will provide the start to the education of your palate. First, the look or appearance is important. Wine should be clear and brilliant, not cloudy. Consider the smell, or "nose" of the vintage, which includes the aroma or scent of the grapes themselves, and the "bouquet," the smell from fermentation and aging. Finally, consider the taste. Let the wine wash around your mouth for a moment and determine if it's sweet or dry, light-bodied (watery) or full-bodied (like milk), rough or mellow. But mainly, enjoy. Chat it up with the winery employees behind the counter and you'll gain more insight (and maybe they'll pour some reserve vintages for your tasting enjoyment).

When to Go

The best time to visit the wine country is in the fall, when the harvest occurs and the air is redolent with the aroma of fermenting wine. Depending on the weather, this can be anytime in September or October. Street fairs and festivals are the norm, and it's the season of golf tournaments, wine auctions, and art and food fairs. The countryside is beautiful, with trees turning brilliant gold and red. And the weather usually cooperates, too. It can get hot, and there's not much chance of rain.

Yet there are drawbacks to visiting at harvest time: traffic clogging the major roads in both valleys and a decrease in attention from winery employees, who are justifiably consumed with getting the grapes in. If you do plan to visit the wine country in the fall, try to go during the week, not on weekends, to avoid the worst of the tourist crush. It's also a good idea to make lodging and dinner reservations weeks in advance.

Spring and summer are also prime times for visiting the wine country. And it shows—Route 29 in Napa Valley is often backed up on weekends.

(You'll encounter a bit less traffic in Sonoma on spring and summer weekends.) Summer in the wine country is notoriously hot and dry, so be sure to pack a sun hat and try to get an early start. Winter, the rainy season, is a good time to visit; although the landscape isn't as colorful, there's a stark beauty to the valleys and mountains and a more laid-back atmosphere in the wineries. And the crowds are minimal.

Purchasing Wine at a Winery

Question: Can you get great deals on wine sold at wineries? The answer, by and large, is no. The sales rooms in the wineries aren't there to compete with retail liquor outlets in your hometown. As a result, the prices are pretty much what you would pay at home, give or take a couple of bucks a bottle. Of course, the selection is usually a lot better, and you'll also find special vintages available only at the winery. So while the sales rooms do a brisk business, nobody is getting great bargains.

Wine is also sold by the case at the wineries. Depending on the state you live in, you can have your purchase shipped home (you pay the shipping cost). States that allow shipments from the wineries are California, Colorado, Idaho, Illinois, Iowa, Minnesota, Missouri, Nebraska, New Mexico, Oregon, Washington, West Virginia, and Wisconsin. If you don't live in one of these states, you're not completely out of luck. Make your purchase and ship it home yourself (tax laws limit shipments by wineries to the states listed above). The cost is about $40 a case, and the folks at the winery can suggest where to take your purchase and have it shipped.

Getting There

The wine country spreads north from the top of San Francisco Bay in two parallel valleys, Napa and Sonoma; in between are the oak-covered Mayacamas Mountains. To get there by car, cross the Golden Gate Bridge on US 101 to Route 37 east. Then bear left onto Route 121; next, turn left onto Route 12 for Sonoma Valley or drive a few miles more and turn left onto Route 29, Napa Valley's main drag. In nonrush-hour traffic, it's about an hour's drive from downtown San Francisco to the southern entrances of the valleys.

Napa Valley

The heart of America's wine culture is found in Napa Valley, a region with roots going back to the mid-nineteenth century. The valley is defined by two rough-hewn mountain ranges, and vestiges of its tumultuous geologic past still bubble to the surface of the earth at hot springs in Calistoga and at (the other) Old Faithful Geyser.

Compared to the natural features, the wineries in Napa Valley are recent interlopers. Virtually the entire California wine industry was killed by Prohibition; only a few wineries survived. This means most of the players in the valley today are relative newcomers—a diverse collection of wealthy doctors, lawyers, actors, filmmakers, artists, and business executives all motivated to outdo their neighbors in creating memorable vintages. The joke used to be that they were all going broke creating wine—and loving it. Today, not all of them are going broke.

Napa Valley is anchored in the south by the town of the same name, and visitors on a one-day outing should pass it by. Continue up Route 29 toward the villages of Yountville, Oakville, and Rutherford, where things start to get more interesting (and scenic). St. Helena, the next town, is considered the heart of Napa's wine-growing region, while Calistoga, a resort town for more than 100 years, is its northern anchor.

You can make a drive in the valley more interesting by heading south from Calistoga on the more scenic Silverado Trail, which creates a circuit instead of an out-and-back excursion. While not nearly as commercial, this pleasant two-lane highway passes plenty of wineries. The crossroads between the two parallel roads are also scenic and worth exploring.

Napa Valley Dining and Lodging

Whether you are planning a marriage proposal, a solo retreat, or a gathering of friends, there are top-rated dining and lodging options in all areas of wine country. Here are a few we recommend:

Rutherford

Dining

Auberge du Soleil Restaurant, (707) 963-1211. French cuisine at its best. You better know which fork is which at this restaurant.

Napa

Dining

Piccolino's Italian Café, (707) 251-0100. Authentic Northern Italian cuisine inspired by the Solerno family. Come with an empty stomach. On weekends they have live jazz.

Lodging

The **Napa Inn Bed and Breakfast,** (707) 257-1444. Candlight breakfasts and fireplaces make this a very romantic spot within the valley. About $150 per night.

Blue Violet Mansion, (707) 253- 2583. Won an award for best B&B in North America. About $200 per night.

Cedar Gables Inn, (707) 224-7969. A historic B&B centrally located within the heart of Napa. About $170 per night.

Yountville

Dining

The French Laundry, (707) 944-2380. Redolent of roses and pure culinary artistry atop the porcelain plate—your palate will experience its very first … well, you know.

Brix Restaurant, (707) 944-2749. Watch the renowned chef in the exhibition kitchen that is the centerpiece of the beautifully decorated space. The menu is cutting-edge.

Napa Valley Grille, (707) 944-8686. Best for warm-weather dining on garden patio. Excellent views, and excellent California cuisine.

Lodging

Castle in the Clouds, (707) 944-2785. High on the hill overlooking Napa, as the name suggests. Amazing views! About $250 per night.

Bordeaux House, (707) 944-2855. Centrally located B&B. Perfect for those who like to stroll around. About $135 per night.

Villagio Inn & Spa, (707) 944-8877. Tuscan-inspired countryside inn and spa. Gardens and trickling water outside ease any tension away. A great weekend getaway. About $175 per night.

St. Helena

Dining

Tra Vigne, (707) 963-4444. Operated by the Tra Vigne family, this romantic eatery located on picturesque Highway 29 is all about fine Italian dining. Visit the Cantinetta Delicatesse and stock your picnic basket with gourmet Italian groceries and wines.

Wine Spectator Greystone Restaurant, (707) 967-1010. Their "today's temptations," a selection of the chef's daily creations, is a big table pleaser. Fresh herbs from their garden accompany all French dishes.

Lodging

The Inn at Southbridge, (707) 967-9400. You'll feel like you're on a European holiday. One of the most coziest inns complete with down comforters, fireplaces, and private balconies overlooking Napa. More than $200 per night.

Harvest Inn, (707) 963-9463. Private terraces look out onto eight acres of beautiful landscape and vineyards. Jogging and biking trails are on the property as well. More than $200 per night.

La Fleur Bed and Breakfast Inn, (707) 963-0233. Charming 1882 Queen Anne Victorian introduces you to award-winning winemaker, Don McGrath. About $200 per night.

Calistoga

Lodging

Cottage Grove Inn, (707) 942-8400. Intimate B&B with private cottages complete with own Jacuzzi. Prices more than $200 per night.

Safari West Wildlife Preserve and Tent Camp, (707) 579-2551. Get up close and personal with African animals in this luxury safari tent camp. A unique experience. About $225 per night.

The Pink Mansion, (707) 942-0558. Elegance at its best. Built in 1875 this B&B is a historic landmark. In-room massages and facials and fireplaces create a relaxing ambience. About $200 per night.

Winery Lunches

Lunches, on the other hand, can be more spontaneous. Most visitors stop at wineries between meals. Some wineries, for example the Niebaum-Coppola (owned by Francis Ford Coppola of *The Godfather* fame), promote reserve tastings of their better wines. If the tasting-room staff doesn't mention anything about reserve wines, just ask. Usually the staff will pour the better stuff (and you'll pay a bit more).

Napa Valley, however, is about more than eating and drinking. The scenery is stunning, with a big blue sky from May through October (the dry season), gnarled oak trees, babbling brooks, and chaparral-covered mountain ridges. It's all enjoyable through the window of a car, on a bike, or on a stroll. Other diversions include a petrified forest, a mud bath in Calistoga, and shopping in trendy St. Helena.

Wineries

With something like 240 wineries in Napa Valley (most of which are open to the public), it's just not possible to provide a comprehensive listing. Plus, part of the fun is touring on your own without a rigid itinerary, and making your own discoveries. First-time visitors will have no trouble finding wineries; both of the valley's two major routes (Route 29 and, to the east, the Silverado Trail) pass dozens of estates. To get you on your way, here's a sampling of Napa wineries well worth a visit.

Robert Mondavi Winery, on Route 29 in Oakville, is wine central for the Napa wine industry. The winery was founded in 1966, when there were only about six wineries in the valley with national distribution. Today Mondavi offers one of the best tours in the valley, and its Spanish mission–style architecture is a knockout. A retail area sells wines, T-shirts, and books, and there is a tasting room where reserve wine is sold by the glass. Tours are offered on the hour, and it's a good idea to make reservations. Call (707) 226-1335.

Up the road in Rutherford is the **Niebaum-Coppola Estate,** a huge operation with a fountain-enhanced plaza and a small museum highlighting the career of its owner, film director Francis Ford Coppola. The entire place is unmatched for sheer panache. The museum is free and fun; on display are old movie projectors, film props from *The Godfather* movies, a real Tucker automobile (from *Tucker: A Man and His Dream*). Of course, you'll also find a tasting room and a retail sales room. Winery tours are by appointment only; call (707) 968-1100.

Frog's Leap, also in Rutherford, was once a deserted "ghost winery." But today it sits beside 40 acres of organically grown Merlot and Sauvignon Blanc vines. Originally built in 1884, the winery features a big red, wooden barn with period photos dotting the interior. Winery tours are by reservation only; call (800) 959-4704.

At the top of the valley in Calistoga, **Sterling Vineyards** was built with tourists in mind. An aerial tram leads to the a white cluster of Mediterranean monastic stucco buildings that rise from a bluff south of town. The 300-foot knoll features a visitor center, tasting room, self-guided winery tour, gift shop, and retail room. Call for information, (707) 942-3300.

Silverado Vineyards, on the Silverado Trail in Napa, has spectacular views across the valley and excellent wines. Owned by the family of the late Walt Disney, the winery has a stunning setting and an interior display of original art by American naturalist painters John James Audubon and Thomas Hill. Winery tours are by appointment only; call (707) 257-1770.

For a low-key, off-the-beaten-path and virtually non-commercial winery experience, stop by **Vincent Arroyo Winery,** just north of Calistoga off Route 29. Joy, the resident canine, has a wine named after her—and the Petite Sirah is superb. Call (707) 942-6995 for directions.

Attractions

Other things to do and see in Napa include **Bale Grist Mill State Historic Park** (north of St. Helena on Route 29), a flour mill operation that predates California statehood. Built in 1846 and restored to operating condition, the mill features a 36-foot wooden waterwheel and large millstones. On weekends, a miller grinds grain and visitors can see baking demonstrations. You can also purchase flour from the mill. For more information, call (707) 963-2236.

California's **Old Faithful Geyser,** outside of Calistoga (not to be confused with a similar geothermal phenomena at Yellowstone National Park in Wyoming), offers a spectacular show by nature as 350° water shoots 60 feet in the air for 3 or 4 minutes. The cycle repeats about every 17 to 40 minutes, and kids love it. The setting is breathtakingly scenic, with Mount Saint Helena and the craggy Palisades Mountains in the background. The cost is a pricey $6 a person ($2 for children ages 6–12, free for ages 6 and under; and 15% discount with AAA), and no, you can't see this natural performance from the parking lot—tall bamboo blocks the view. For more information, call (707) 942-6463.

The **Petrified Forest,** west of Calistoga, offers a pleasant walk in the woods past 3.5-million-year-old fallen giants—fossilized redwoods, some of them 8 feet in diameter. Alas, they're not upright and some of the specimens were buried and now lie in pits. It's a pleasant and scenic place to walk off that second (or third, or fourth) glass of wine. Admission is $5 a person. For more information, call (707) 942-6667.

In St. Helena there's more to do than shop. The **Silverado Museum** is dedicated to the life and works of Robert Louis Stevenson, author of classic works of literature such as *The Treasure Island* and *Dr. Jekyll and Mr. Hyde*. The Scottish writer lived in the area in 1880 with his bride and regained his health in the mountain air and sunshine. The two-room museum includes memorabilia, manuscripts, childhood letters, paintings, and the desk used by the writer. Located near the public library in St. Helena (from Route 29, go east on Adams Street to Library Lane), the museum is open from noon to 4 p.m. daily, except Monday and holidays; admission is free. Call (707) 963-3757 for more information.

Revisit the early days of Calistoga and Napa Valley at **The Sharpsteen Museum** in Calistoga. Built by a retired Walt Disney animator, this one-room museum highlights the resort's history with dioramas, old photographs, doll houses, recreations of Victorian interiors, gold-panning displays, and a horse carriage. It's an eclectic mix of historical items that's worth a peek. Admission is free; the museum is open daily (except Christmas and Thanksgiving) from 10 a.m. to 4 p.m. April through October, and from noon to 4 p.m. November through March. For more information, call (707) 942-5911.

Outdoor Fun

Napa Valley is famous for bicycling, with gentle hills, wide shoulders on the main roads, low traffic on the side roads, and great scenery. **St. Helena Cyclery** rents bikes, and the town is a good, centrally located starting point to enjoy a ride. The hourly rate is $7 for high-quality hybrid (city) bikes; included are a lock, water bottle, rear rack, and bag to carry your picnic supplies. The daily rate is $25. The shop, at 1156 Main Street in St. Helena, also provides maps and tour information. No reservations are accepted; the shop is open daily. Call (707) 963-7736 for more information.

Getaway Adventures in Calistoga has been leading bicycling, hiking, kayaking, and other outdoor tours since 1992. Offering both bike rentals and van-supported, single-day and multi-day trips in the wine country, Getaway specializes in what owner Randy Johnson calls a "stop and smell the Zinfandel pace." He also offers this advice to bicycle enthusiasts who want to explore the fabled back roads of Napa and nearby Sonoma on their own: ship your own bike to the wine country. "If you have a bike you're happy with, ship it out," he advises. "I don't recommend bringing it on the plane, because it's liable to get lost. Most shops will reassemble your bike for little or no cost. If you're in the wine country for more than a few days and cycling is your main focus, there's no way you'll duplicate the experience on a rental bike." For more information on tours, bike rentals and advice on shipping your bike safely and cheaply, call Getaway at (800) 499-2453

Horseback riding in Napa Valley is scenic and fun. **Napa Valley Trail Rides** provides horses and guides April through November at Bothe-Napa Valley State Park outside Calistoga. Rates start at $50 for a 90-minute ride; sunset and full-moon rides are also available. Reservations are required; call (707) 996-8566.

Napa's dry, southerly breezes create optimal conditions for all kinds of aerial sports. **Balloons Above the Valley,** at 5091 Solano Avenue in Napa, launches hot-air balloons with 8 to 16 passengers. Liftoff is around 6:30 a.m., when the cool morning air is best for ballooning (making a stay in the valley the night before almost mandatory). The flight lasts about an hour and ends with a champagne breakfast. Daily flights (weather permitting) cost $185 a person; reservations are required. Call (800) 464-6824.

Shopping

Napa Premium Outlets in Napa features 50 stores specializing in discounted designer fashions and name-brand merchandise, ranging from Brooks Brothers to Tommy Hilfiger. To reach the outlet mall, take Route 29 to the First Street Exit. St. Helena, generally recognized as Napa Valley's main hub, is also Grand Central for shoppers. Main Street, noted for its arching sycamore trees, is lined with upscale gift shops, boutiques, clothing stores, jewelers, and wine shops.

Outside of town, **Hurd's Beeswax Candles** elevates candlemaking to an art, with candles fashioned in a myriad of shapes. At **St. Helena Premium Outlets** two miles north of town on Route 29, bargain hunters can shop till they drop at ten factory outlet and specialty stores.

In Calistoga, general-interest shops mix with more specialized retailers, including antique stores, clothing shops, and a bookstore. The historic **Calistoga Depot,** a former railway station, has been converted into a mall; the **Calistoga Wine Stop** is housed in an antique railroad car. The wine shop at **All Seasons Cafe** (1400 Lincoln Avenue) offers a wide selection of hard-to-find Napa wines. For a $10 fee, you can sample your purchase with dinner.

Health Spas

For folks who prefer their entertainment closer to the ground, Calistoga is home to about a dozen health spas featuring hot mineral springs, heated pools, mud baths, steam baths, and massages. At **Calistoga Spa Hot Springs,** guests can steep in four different mineral pools (starting at $10) or indulge in a volcanic-ash mud bath with steam rinse ($46). The spa, at 1006 Washington Street, also has 57 rooms, ranging from $91 to $136 a night. For more information, call (707) 942-6269, or visit www.calistogaspa.com.

Dr. Wilkinson's Hot Springs Resort, at 1507 Lincoln Avenue in Calistoga, offers a full range of soothing, invigorating treatments, including mud baths, mineral whirlpool baths, blanket wraps, therapeutic massage, facials, acupressure face-lifts, and salt glow scrubs. The Works, a two-hour spa treatment, is $99; facials start at $49. The resort is open daily, and appointments are recommended; call (707) 942-4102 for more information, or visit www.drwilkinson.com.

Napa Valley Wine Train

Enjoy a relaxing gourmet dining excursion on one of several restored 1915 Pullman railroad cars that run between Napa and St. Helena year-round. The **Napa Valley Wine Train** offers a 3-hour, 36-mile excursion through Napa Valley. You won't stop at any wineries—in fact, you don't stop at all—but you can enjoy classic European cuisine with California overtones prepared on board. There are two seatings for lunch and dinner; passengers spend half the trip in a dining car and half in a lounge car.

Brunch ($59.50 a person) includes a glass of champagne and three courses; lunch ($79 a person) offers three courses; dinner ($79 a person) offers five courses. Train fare and tips are included; a trip without a meal in the Deli Car, where there's an à la carte menu, costs $35. Wine, liquor, and cocktails are extra. Reservations are required; call (800) 427-4124, (707) 253-2111, or visit www.winetrain.com.

Visitor Information

You can get more information on wineries, accommodation, dining, and attractions by contacting the **Napa Valley Conference and Visitors Bureau** (1310 Napa Town Center, Napa, CA 94559; (707) 226-7459; www.napavalley.com/nvcvb.html). Other visitor contacts in Napa Valley include the **Calistoga Chamber of Commerce** (phone (707) 942-6333; www.calistogafun.com) and the **St. Helena Chamber of Commerce** (phone (800) 799-6456, (707) 963-4456, or visit www.sthelena.com).

For help finding a room, especially in the harvest season when this can be challenging, try these free reservation services: **Napa Valley Reservations Unlimited** (call (800) 251-6272; www.napavalleyreservations.com)

and **Wine Country Concierge** (phone (888) 946-3289, (707) 252-4472; www.winecountryreservations.com). Both keep a list of available rooms at B&Bs and other lodging. A word of advice: If your visit to Napa Valley is in the spring, summer, or fall, remember that traffic along Route 29 is relentless. Make it a point to request sleeping quarters that face the vineyards, not the highway.

Sonoma Valley

While Napa Valley is upscale and elegant, its next-door neighbor, Sonoma Valley, is overalls and corduroy. Unlike of the eye-catching architecture in the wineries of Napa, the wineries here tend to be understated converted barns. Smaller producers whose families have grown grapes for generations still make wine in rustic buildings that are often beautiful in their simplicity. Here, family-run wineries are more apt to treat visitors like friends, and tastings are usually free.

Sonoma Valley is home to Northern California's earliest winemaking, with stunning old vineyards planted on rolling hills. The Spanish-era town of Sonoma is the cultural hub for Sonoma Valley, one of four major wine regions found in Sonoma County (the others are Alexander Valley, Russian River Valley, and Dry Creek Valley). A charming eight-acre plaza green in Sonoma built by General Mariano Guadalupe Vallejo in 1834 is a rural oasis surrounded by the area's best shops and restaurants.

Crescent-shaped Sonoma Valley curves between oak-covered mountain ranges and, most folks say, beats its neighbor hands-down on looks. (The scenery attracted writer Jack London, who owned a ranch in Glen Ellen; now it's a state park.) The valley presents a crisscross pattern of vineyards; unlike the nearly endless procession of mega wineries lining the highway at Napa, most wineries are tucked away on winding back roads.

Wineries

About a half-dozen wineries are located a mile east of Sonoma Plaza, down East Napa Street. You could combine a visit to a few of these wineries with a tour of the Sonoma Mission, lunch on the plaza, and a side trip to an attraction outside of town. The result would be a day with a minimum amount of driving and maximum time for fun.

Wineries outside town are often located on small back roads, so get a map from the tourist office on the plaza; also, keep your eyes peeled for signposts leading to the vineyards (otherwise it's easy to miss a turn). If you get tired of running around, visit the **Wine Exchange of Sonoma** (452 First Street; (707) 938-1794), a tasting bar open daily; you can sample wines and beers from Sonoma and the rest of California. To get you started, here's a short selection of wineries worth a visit. Another tasting bar is **Lo Spuntino** (400 First Street; (707) 935-5656), also on the plaza; it features live jazz on weekends, a deli, and prepared foods.

For sheer convenience, **Sebastiani Winery** (www.sebastiani.com) can't be beat. Free shuttle buses whisk visitors from Sonoma Plaza to the stone winery about a mile away. Professional guides lead tours throughout the day, and visitors learn about winemaking, see a large collection of hand-carved casks, and view a display of antique winemaking equipment.

Not as convenient to reach but a must-see is **Buena Vista Winery,** east of Sonoma. Set among towering trees and fountains, this is the birthplace of Sonoma Valley winemaking; founded in 1857, it's California's oldest premium winery. It's also drop-dead gorgeous, with huge stone buildings, a mezzanine art gallery, and historical exhibits. History tours are given at 2 p.m. daily; there's also a beautiful terraced picnic area. For more information, call (800) 926-1266 or visit www.buenavistawinery.com.

Almost as beautiful is **Bartholomew Park Winery,** not far from Buena Vista. Surrounded by vineyards, the winery features an attractive museum that highlights winemaking, the history of the area, and the winery's previous owners. In addition, there are hiking trails, a picnic area, and a "wine garden" (a picnic area with a pavilion). For more information, call (707) 935-9511 or visit www.bartpark.com.

Ravenswood Winery, also east of Sonoma, is a small winery in a gorgeous hillside setting. Best known for its hearty zinfandels and its anti wine-snob attitude, the winery offers reservation-only tours led by knowledgeable and enthusiastic employees. To make a reservation for a winery tour (offered daily at 10:30 a.m.), call (888) 669-4629 or visit www.ravenswood-wine.com.

Head up Route 12 a few miles to reach the **Benziger Family Winery** in Glen Ellen. The winery specializes in premium estate and Sonoma County wines; they're also well known for their labels designed by famous artists. Guided and self-guided tours are offered, and there's a picnic area where you can have lunch. For more information, call (707) 935-4046, (888) 490-2739, or visit www.benziger.com.

You can enjoy a tour of caves at **Kunde Estate Winery** in Kenwood, north of Glen Ellen. A new winery and visitor center is located at the foot of a stunning mountain of grapes. The family owns 2,000 acres, with 800 acres under vine. Rustic grounds at Kenwood Vineyards complement the attractive tasting room and the winery's artistic bottle labels. Tours are by appointment only; call (707) 833-5501 or visit www.kunde. com for more information.

Attractions

The town of Sonoma is the site of the last and the northernmost of the 21 missions established by Spain and Mexico, called El Camino Real ("the king's highway"). Popularly called **Sonoma Mission,** El Camino Real was founded in 1823 and features a stark white facade and, inside, a small museum. Across the street is the **Sonoma Barracks,** built with

Native American labor in the 1830s to house Mexican troops. It's a two-story adobe structure with sweeping balconies and a museum dedicated to California history.

Next door, the **Toscano Hotel** is furnished as it was in the nineteenth century, with wood-burning stoves, brocade armchairs, and gambling tables. These and other antique buildings around Sonoma Plaza are part of **Sonoma State Historic Park;** the $2 adults, $1 childern admission fee gets you into all the historic buildings. In the oak-studded plaza across the street is a monument to the Bear Flag Revolt, located on the spot where California was declared an independent republic in 1846 (and remained so for 25 days). For more information, visit www.napanet.net/~sshpa.

Another excellent pit stop before heading to sights further in Sonoma is the **Sonoma Cheese Factory** (2 Spain Street on Sonoma Plaza, Sonoma; (707) 996-1000.) You can choose to picnic here on the cute benches that are scattered nearby, or simply browse inside and watch them slap, drain, and drag clumps of Jack and Cheddar through cheese-cloth. There are plenty of samples on hand for you to try.

Traintown, a mile south of Sonoma Plaza, offers a 20-minute steam or diesel train ride through 10 acres of landscaped park; it's nirvana for children. There's also a petting zoo, an antique carousel, and cabooses. Train fare is $3.25 for youngsters and $3.75 for adults; open daily June through September, and Friday through Sunday the rest of the year. For more information, call (707) 938-3912 or visit www.traintown.com.

If Napa Valley is Robert Louis Stevenson country, then Sonoma belongs to Jack London. A world adventurer and the most famous American writer of his time (he died in 1916 at age 40), London bought a 1,400-acre ranch a few miles northwest of Glen Ellen; today it's **Jack London State Historic Park.** Attractions include a museum with memorabilia, a reconstruction of London's office, and exhibits on the fascinating life of the author of *The Call of the Wild.* There's also a continuously running video of a film made about the writer just days before his death; silent, grainy, and shaky, the short home movie is haunting.

Almost as spooky are the ruins of London's mansion, **Wolf House,** which mysteriously burned to the ground in 1913 before the author could move in. It's a half-mile stroll through gorgeous woods to the stone ruins; you can also detour to visit the writer's simple grave. For fans of American literature, the park is a real find. Admission is $6 a car. For more information, call (707) 938-5216 or visit www.parks.sonoma.net/JLPark.html.

Outdoor Fun

Sonoma Valley is 7 miles wide and 17 miles long, and with its rolling hills, 13,000 acres of vineyards, and forested mountains on either side, the valley offers much to do outdoors. **Goodtime Touring Company,** at 18503 Sonoma Highway in Sonoma, rents bikes for exploring the valley's miles of paved, low-traffic back roads. Rentals are $5 an hour and $25 a day, including a helmet, lock, cable, maps, and road service and repair during regular business hours. The shop also offers lunch rides, including food, for $65 a person (reservations required three days in advance). For more information, call (888) 525-0453 or visit www.goodtimetouring.com.

The **Sonoma Cattle Company** offers organized horse rides at Jack London State Historic Park and Sugarloaf Ridge State Park. The guided tours range from general 90-minute and 2-hour rides to a western barbecue ride, a sunset ride, a full-moon ride, and a gourmet boxed-lunch ride and winery tour. Reservations are required, and rates start at $45 per person for a 90-minute ride. For more information, call (707) 996-8566 or visit www.napasonomatrailrides.com.

See Sonoma Valley from a hot-air balloon. **Air Flambuoyant,** based in Santa Rosa, has offered lighter-than-air excursions since 1974. The trips last about an hour, and groups of two or more can be accommodated. The cost is $175 a person and includes a gourmet champagne breakfast (balloon rides typically start at 6 a.m. in the summer). For reservations and more information, call (800) 456-4711, (707) 838-8500, or visit www.airflambuoyant.com.

Combine a scenic view from the air, the nostalgia of a bygone era, and the excitement of a roller coaster at **Aeroschellville Biplane and Glider Rides.** The firm offers a variety of rides in its fleet of 1940 Boeing Stearman biplanes and a North American–built, World War II Navy, SNJ-4 pilot trainer. All pilots are certified by the FAA. Twenty-minute one-passenger rides are $120; two-passenger rides are $170. Aerobatic rides lasting 20 minutes are $130 for one passenger and $190 for two. Warplane rides start at $199 and glider rides begin at $139. For more information, call (707) 938-2444 or look up www.vintageaircraftco.com.

Shopping

The central plaza in the old Spanish town of Sonoma is where you'll find the best shops, including gourmet stores, boutiques, a designer lingerie shop, antique stores, poster galleries, and a brass shop. The **Sonoma Cheese Factory** (2 Spain Street; (707) 996-1931) on the square is the place to go for picnic supplies, a bottle of wine, or sandwiches for that winery picnic; you can also eat on the premises and watch cheese being made. The **Mercado,** a small shopping center just east of the plaza, houses several stores with unusual items. **Baksheesh** (14 West Spain Street) features handmade gifts crafted by third-world artisans. **Milagros** (414 First Street East) sells Mexican folk art, home furnishings, masks, and wood carvings.

Seven miles north of Sonoma off Route 12 in Glen Ellen is **Jack London Village** (14301 Arnold Drive), located on the banks of Sonoma Creek. It's a collection of shops, art studios, craft shops, cafés, a wine shop, and a music shop in a bucolic setting. There's also the **Glen Ellen Winery** (phone (707) 935-4046) and, across the street, the **Jack London Bookstore** (phone (707) 996-2888), an important resource center for the writer's fans.

Dining

As it is throughout the wine country, dining is serous business in Sonoma Valley. Dinner reservations should be made at least two weeks in advance in summer and fall. Top-rated dining establishments include:

Della Santina's (133 East Napa Street in Sonoma; (707) 935-0576)

Kenwood Restaurant and Bar (9900 Highway 12 in Kenwood; (707) 833-6326)

Mixx (135 Fourth Street in Santa Rosa; (707) 573-1344)

Willowside Café (3535 Guerneville Road in Santa Rosa; (707) 523-4814)

Café La Haye (140 East Napa Street in Sonoma; (707) 935-5994)

Glen Ellen Inn Restaurant (13670 Arnold Drive in Glen Ellen; (707) 996-6409)

Top-rated Accommodations

The Lodge at Sonoma (1325 Broadway in Sonoma; (707) 935-6600)

MacArthur Place, Historic Inn and Spa (29 East MacArthur Street in Sonoma; (707) 938-2929)

Bristol Manor (2413 Bristol Road in Kenwood; (707) 833-6335)

Visitor Information

For more information on wineries, attractions, restaurants, and lodging in Sonoma Valley, call the **Sonoma Valley Visitors Center** at (707) 996-1090; ask for a free visitors' guide. You can also stop at the small visitor center located on the north side of the plaza near the Sonoma Barracks and pick up maps and brochures. For help locating a room, especially in the busy summer and fall, contact **Wine Country Concierge** (phone (888) 946-3289 or (707) 252-4472; www.winecountryconcierge.com), which has a list of available rooms at B&Bs and other lodging.

A Two-Day Excursion in the Wine Country

With so much to do and see in the Napa and Sonoma Valleys—and because of their different characters—we think the ideal way for visitors to tour the wine country is to spend a night. That way you can visit both gorgeous locales, share the driving (you'll need a car), split wine-imbibing chores with a friend, and have a more relaxed trip. Here's our recommendation for an overnight trip to the wine country for first-time visitors.

If you've got a room in San Francisco and you're heading to the wine country before the end of your vacation, don't check out; the hassle of repeatedly packing and unpacking is too time consuming. (That is, unless you've scheduled your getaway at the end of your vacation and your night in the wine country is the last night.) Reserve a room at a hot-springs resort in Calistoga at the north end of the valley, grab your toothbrush and a change of underwear, and get out of town. Admittedly this is not cheap, but it's definitely hedonistic—and totally in character with this vacation within a vacation.

Here's the plan. After touring Napa Valley, head to Calistoga, where your room at one of the hot-springs resorts awaits you—say, Dr. Wilkinson's Hot Springs or Calistoga Spa Hot Springs (see Health Spas in Napa on page 183). Rooms range from basic motel-style and cheap (think Janet Leigh in *Psycho*) to Victorian and expensive (including **Hideaway Cottages,** all with kitchens and some with living rooms; (707) 942-4108). Then—here's the really decadent part—take a mud bath in a composition of local volcanic ash, imported peat, and naturally boiling mineral hot-springs water. Folks have been coming to Calistoga for about 150 years to experience this; now it's your turn. Your naked body will simmer at a temperature of about 104°. It's about a 90-minute experience, and your body will love you for it. A full treatment costs about $99.

The next day, drive to Sonoma Valley. Get there by either heading south through Napa Valley on the Silverado Trail to Route 121 and west to Route 12, or by taking a back road. If you go the back-road route, you can spend the second day of your wine-country visit driving south through the valley. When you get to the southern end of Sonoma Valley at the end of the day, you're less than an hour from San Francisco.

South of San Francisco

Coastal Highway 1 is a spectacularly scenic road that stretches south of San Francisco to Carmel, winding past cliffs and coves, pocket beaches, lighthouses, state parks, and old historic towns and villages. While that's too far for a day trip by car, visitors to San Francisco can still enjoy driving along the coast for about 75 miles to the resort town of Santa Cruz. From there, turn inland and north to return along the crest of the Santa Cruz Mountains for scenery from a higher perspective.

A Scenic Car Tour

Here's a suggested itinerary for a full day of scenic car touring. Get started around 9 a.m. and head to the Great Highway (south of Cliff

House and at the western end of Golden Gate Park) and drive south. Bring picnic supplies or plan on getting something to eat in one of the restaurants in the many towns and villages along the way. While you'll have time to get out and enjoy many of the attractions, don't linger too long if you want to get back before evening. And don't forget to bring a state highway map (in case of detours or in case you want to devise your own circuit route).

The coastline of the San Francisco peninsula south of the city is largely undeveloped. Bluffs protect the many nudist beaches from prying eyes and make excellent launching points for hang gliders, as you can see at Fort Funston, about a mile south of the San Francisco Zoo. Skyline Boulevard follows the coast here past Daly City, a community of ticky-tacky housing that's probably the ugliest thing most folks will see on a visit to San Francisco.

But things improve after you reach Highway 1. San Pedro Beach marks the end of San Francisco's suburban sprawl and is a popular surfing beach. Continually eroding cliffs offer great scenery from the road but don't handle the presence of the highway well, and the road is washed away regularly in winter storms. Gray Whale Cove State Beach is clothing-optional and, in spite of its name, isn't an especially good place for whale-watching.

Half Moon Bay and a Scenic Side Trip

Main Street in Half Moon Bay features a gentrified shopping area with gift shops, bookstores, a saddlery, jewelry stores, cafés, bars, restaurants, and art galleries. There's also a full-size grocery store that sells sandwiches and picnic supplies. For a view of the town's eponymous bay, go to **Half Moon Bay State Beach** (turn onto Kelly Avenue from Highway 1; (650) 726-8820). Parking is $2, but you can enter the park free for 15 minutes and watch the waves roll in.

For a contrast to the surf, continue south on Highway 1 and turn right onto Higgins-Purisima Creek Road. The narrow paved road winds and climbs for eight miles through ranch country before returning to Highway 1. Turn left to continue south. **Pigeon Point Lighthouse** (phone (650) 879-2120) is in a spectacular coastal setting, and guided lighthouse tours are offered; the half-hour tours are $2 for adults and $1 for children. Children under the age of 8 years must be chaparoned by an adult. Visit www.pigeonpointlighthouse.org for more information.

Elephant Seals

For sightings of some unusual wildlife, stop at **Año Nuevo State Reserve** just south of Pigeon Point. Huge northern elephant seals come ashore from early December through March to give birth and mate. Bull seals often engage in battles for breeding access to the females.

Popular guided walks to view the wildlife activity are offered by trained naturalists from December 15 through March 31 and last two hours. Advance reservations are recommended for the three-mile (round-trip) hike. The cost is $4 a person, plus $2 for parking. Call (800) 444-7275 daily between 8 a.m. and 5 p.m. to reserve a spot; for additional information, call (650) 879-2025. Juvenile seals are present year-round, and you can walk the trail unescorted to see them; in the winter, when 300 to 400 adults appear, visitors must be on guided tours.

Just north of Santa Cruz is **Wilder Ranch State Park,** a cultural preserve with adobe farm buildings from the Spanish Mission era and buildings from the late nineteenth century. Docent-led tours are offered on weekends; there are also 28 miles of trails for hiking.

Mountain Scenery and Giant Redwoods

In Santa Cruz you'll have time to grab something to eat, but on a one-day outing there isn't enough time to explore this resort city, famous for its boardwalk and roller coaster. It's a good turnaround point; you can head back to San Francisco through the mountains. Follow signs to Route 9 north, a scenic road that twists and turns through mountains, forests, and the towns of Felton and Boulder Creek, where you turn left onto Route 236.

At **Big Basin Redwoods State Park** you don't need to get out of the car to be overwhelmed by the huge trees. This forest of giant redwoods is more impressive than the stand at Muir Woods in Marin. But get out of the car anyway, even if it's just to take a few minutes to explore the park headquarters and a small museum. Then get back in the car and continue toward San Francisco, 67 miles away. Route 236 gets narrow and twisty before returning to Route 9; turn left to continue north.

Next, turn left on Route 35 (Skyline Drive) for more incredible scenery; after a while, views open up of the Pacific on the left and San Francisco Bay on the right. There are plenty of overlooks where you can stop and enjoy the vistas. Next, take Route 92/35 (a right turn) and then turn left onto Route 35, which leads to I-80, a 20-mile stretch of some of the most scenic interstate highway in the country—and, in a few minutes, San Francisco.

Beyond the Bay Area

Many outstanding destinations are too far from San Francisco for a day trip but close enough to consider for an overnight trek—or as separate destinations on a later trip. Leading the list is **Yosemite National Park,** a wilderness of evergreen forests, alpine meadows, and sheer walls of granite.

Spectacular Yosemite Valley features soaring cliffs, plunging waterfalls, gigantic trees, and rugged canyons. The park is about 200 miles from San Francisco, which works out to about a 5-hour drive. World-famous Yosemite attracts about 4 million visitors a year. Peak tourist season is June to August, and crowds diminish in the fall. Advance lodging reservations are essential year-round. For more information, call (209) 372-0299.

Lake Tahoe, about 200 miles from the city, is rated one of the most beautiful bodies of water in the world. It lies in an alpine bowl on the border between Nevada and California and is surrounded by forested peaks. Tahoe features resorts, gambling, hiking trails, lakeside cabins, historic architecture, and special events such as golf tournaments. For more information, call the **Lake Tahoe Visitors Authority,** (800) 288-2463 or (530) 544-5050.

South of the city down the Pacific coast is **Monterey Bay,** with Santa Cruz at its northern end and Monterey at its southern end. The first capital of California, Monterey was established by the Spanish in 1770; many Spanish, Mexican, and early American buildings still stand. South of Monterey is **Carmel-by-the-Sea,** a pretty hillside town founded as an artists' colony in the early twentieth century. The **Monterey Peninsula** is about a two-hour drive from San Francisco. For visitor information, call the **Monterey Peninsula Visitors and Convention Bureau** at (831) 649-1770.

North of San Francisco along the rugged coastline is **Mendocino,** a small picturesque town that was once a logging village. In the 1950s it became a haven for artists and was so well restored that the town was declared a historic monument. Inland from town are forests of giant redwood trees. The town itself is tucked away on a rocky promontory above the Pacific and retains the charm of its logging days; it's largely unspoiled by tourism. Mendocino is about 125 miles from San Francisco; a leisurely drive up the spectacular coast can take as long as 10 hours one way. For visitor information, call the **Mendocino Coast Chamber of Commerce** at (707) 961-6300.

Attraction Profiles

Fisherman's Wharf and Beyond

Let's face it, there are just some places that a visit to San Francisco wouldn't be complete without seeing. It would be like going to China and not seeing the Wall, going to New York and not running out of money, going to Italy and not eating pizza . . . you get the picture. There are certainly some sights that should be at the top of your checklist—those obligatory shots of you in the "I escaped Alcatraz" T-shirt, or standing next to the barking sea lions at Pier 39 near Fisherman's Wharf. But the beauty of this city is that the untourist track is just as interesting, and colors a vivid picture of San Francisco's creative, innovative, and quaint spirit. The streets of San Francisco offer even the cheapskate, satisfied with a brisk walk up a hill and a good view of the bridge, something for his money. And at the end of the day the tourist, the untourist, the cheapskate, and even the splurger will be smiling on the bus as the sun sets behind another San Francisco day.

Each neighborhood has its own cluster of attractions to see. And conveniently, this book separates them into zones, providing you with a comprehensive guide to San Francisco's top attractions, including some "coulda left San Fran without it" sights. We give you enough information so that you can choose the places you want to see based on your own interests. Each attraction is organized by zone so you can plan your visit logically, without spending valuable time crisscrossing the city.

A Time-Saving Chart

Because of the wide range of attractions in and around San Francisco— from a hall filled with sculptures by Rodin at the Legion of Honor, to historic ships that you can explore at Hyde Street Pier in Fisherman's Wharf—we've provided the following chart to help you prioritize your touring. In it, you'll find the zone, location, author's rating from one star (skip it) to five stars (not to be missed), and a brief description of the attraction. Some attractions, usually art galleries without permanent collections, aren't rated because exhibits change. Each attraction is individually profiled later in this section.

SAN FRANCISCO ATTRACTIONS

Name	Type	Author's Rating
Zone 1 Chinatown		
Cable Car Museum	History and real machinery	★★½
Zone 2 Civic Center		
Asian Art Museum	Largest collection in West	n/a
Haas-Lilienthal House	Furnished Victorian mansion	★★½
Museum of the City of San Francisco	Local history	★★½
Zone 4 Financial District		
Federal Reserve Bank	Currency exhibit	★
Museum of Money of the American West	History of the West	★★

SAN FRANCISCO ATTRACTIONS *(continued)*

Name	Type	Author's Rating
Zone 4 *Financial District* (continued)		
Transamerica Pyramid	Virtual observatory	★
Wells Fargo History Museum	Pony Express and more	★★½
Zone 5 *Marina*		
Ghirardelli Chocolate Manufacturoy and Soda Fountain	Demonstrates how chocolate is made	★★★
Palace of Fine Arts/Exploratorium	Classical Roman rotunda with hands-on museum	★★★½
San Francisco Craft and Folk Art Museum	Small gallery	n/a
San Francisco Maritime Museum	Seafaring exhibits	★★★½
San Francisco Maritime National Historical Park/Hyde Street Pier	19th-century ships that visitors can board	★★★★
Zone 6 *North Beach*		
Alcatraz Island	Island prison and wildlife destination	★★★★★
Aquarium of the Bay	Commercial aquarium	★★
City Lights Bookstore	Beat bookstore	★★★★
Coit Tower	View from Telegraph Hill	★★½
Museum of Ophthalmology	Museum of all things eyes	★★
Ripley's Believe It or Not! Museum	Museum of the odd and unusual	★
Zone 7 *SoMa/Mission*		
California Historical Society	History exhibits	★★
Cartoon Art Museum	Gallery of cartoons	★★★★
Castro Theater	Landmark	★★★★
Mission Dolores	City's oldest building	★★★
San Francisco Museum of Modern Art	Huge modern art gallery	★★★★½
Yerba Buena Gardens/ Center for the Arts	Art complex and gardens	★★
Zone 8 *Richmond/Sunset*		
California Academy of Science	Natural history museum, aquarium, and planetarium	★★★
California Palace of the Legion of Honor	Museum of ancient and European art in scenic setting	★★★★
Cliff House	Oceanside tourist landmark	★★½
Fort Point National Historic Site	Civil War–era fort, great views	★★★★★
Japanese Tea Garden	Stroll-style garden	★★★★
Neptune Society Columbarium	Cemetery housed in copper-domed neoclassical structure	★★★
San Francisco Zoo	Largest zoo in northern CA	★★★½
Strybing Arboretum and Botanical Gardens	70 acres of gardens	★★★

SAN FRANCISCO ATTRACTIONS (continued)

Name	Type	Author's Rating
Zone 11 Marin Headlands to Point Reyes		
Marine Mammal Center	Rehabilitation and education center	★★★★
Mount Tamalpais/East Peak	Scenic hike with stunning view of city	★★★½
Muir Woods National Monument	Grove of majestic, coastal redwoods	★★★★
Zone 12 Berkeley		
Berkeley Art Museum and Pacific Film Archive	Eclectic art on UC Berkeley campus	★★★
Berkeley Rose Gardens	Landmark with terraced gardens	★★★
Lawrence Hall of Science	Hands-on children's science museum	★
Phoebe Hearts Museum of Anthropology	Native American artifacts	★½
Zone 13 Oakland		
Oakland Museum of California	Museum of state's ecology	★★★½

Alcatraz Island
Zone 6 North Beach

Type of Attraction The island in San Francisco Bay best known for its maximum-security, minimum-privilege federal penitentiary: a cellhouse tour, trails, museum exhibits, wildflowers, wildlife, and spectacular views of the San Francisco skyline. Self-guided, audio, and guided tours.

Location In San Francisco Bay; to get there, take a 12-minute (one-way) ferry trip from Pier 41 (in Fisherman's Wharf, at the foot of Powell Street).

Admission With audio tour: $13.25 for adults and children ages 12–18; $11.50 for seniors (ages 62 and over); and $8 for children ages 5–11. Tickets can be purchased without the audio tour: subtract $4 from the adult and senior rates, and $2 from the children's rate. Self-guided tour maps and guides are available on the island in English, Spanish, German, and Japanese for $2. To purchase tickets in advance by phone, call (415) 705-5555; a $2.25 service charge per ticket is included in the above prices.

Hours Ferries leave about every half hour throughout the day, beginning at 9:30 a.m. Alcatraz closes at 6:30 p.m. in the summer and 4:30 p.m. the rest of the year. Closed on Christmas and New Year's Day. Special evening tours called "Alcatraz After Dark" are also available. Schedules and prices can be found at www.blueandgoldfleet.com.

Phone (415) 705-1042; Blue & Gold Fleet (415) 705-5555

Website www.nps.gov/alcatraz/; or for ticket and ferry information, www.blueand goldfleet.com.

When to Go Try to make the first ferry of the day; it's less crowded, and the weather is generally better and less windy.

Special Comments Weather in the middle of San Francisco Bay is unpredictable; it's also frequently different from mainland weather. The best advice is to be prepared and dress in layers; shorts and T-shirts are not a good idea. You have to hike steep grades to get to the cellhouse; wear sturdy shoes. There's no food service on the island, but you can buy a snack on the ferry. Rest rooms, telephones, drinking water, and soft-drink vending machines are available on the island.

Overall Appeal by Age Group

Pre-school ★★★★   Grade School ★★★★★   Teens ★★★★★

Young Adults ★★★★★ Over 30 ★★★★★   Seniors ★★★★★

Author's Rating A San Francisco and U.S. landmark that shouldn't be missed; the audio tour of the cellhouse is outstanding. ★★★★★

How Much Time to Allow At least two hours; bring a lunch and you can easily spend half a day on the Rock. You can catch any returning ferry back to Fisherman's Wharf; a schedule is posted at the dock.

Description and Comments One of Golden Gate National Recreation Area's most popular destinations, Alcatraz Island offers a close-up look at a federal prison long off limits to the public (and that has captured almost everyone's imagination). A couple of hours on the Rock is time well spent. Virtually no one is disappointed.

The island is best known for its sinister reputation. It was called the Rock, Hellcatraz, and Uncle Sam's Devil Island by the hardened criminals who lived there during its federal penitentiary years (1934–63). Most of the 1,545 men who did time were deemed to be escape risks and troublemakers. Only a handful were truly notorious; the list includes Al "Scarface" Capone, Doc Barker, Alvin "Creepy" Karpis, George "Machine Gun" Kelly, and Robert Stroud, the Birdman of Alcatraz (who actually conducted his famous bird studies as a prisoner in another federal pen, Leavenworth).

On the cellhouse tour you'll see why a sentence to Alcatraz was rated hard time by prisoners. The cells are tiny (inmates were confined 23 hours a day), and extreme precautions were taken to control the prisoners, prevent escapes, and quell riots. In the dining room, considered potentially the most dangerous place in the prison, tear-gas canisters are visible in the ceiling. Some cells are also furnished as they were when Alcatraz was a working prison, with cots, personal items (such as packets of Bugler cigarette tobacco, brushes, and books), and a few pictures. *A poignant note:* If the wind was right on New Year's Eve, some prisoners could hear voices and music from the annual party held at a yacht club on the mainland—excruciating to men who had years to countdown instead of minutes.

In stark contrast to the deteriorating prison, Alcatraz (Spanish for "pelican") is a place of natural beauty. On trails around the island visitors can see flowers such as fuchsias, geraniums, jade trees, agave, and periwinkles, as well as outstanding views of San Francisco and Oakland. Tide pools teem with marine life, including crabs and sea stars. Alcatraz, rich in history, American iconography, and natural beauty, is an outstanding tourist attraction.

Touring Tips Make advance reservations; Alcatraz is very popular. During peak summer and holiday periods ferry rides to the island are booked as much as a week in advance. The down side to advance reservations is that no refunds are given if the weather is lousy. But Alcatraz in bad weather is better than no Alcatraz at all.

After disembarking and listening to a park ranger's introductory remarks, go inside for the 13-minute video presentation that gives a good overview of the island's history (including the takeover by Native Americans that began on November 20, 1969, and lasted 19 months). Then make note of the schedule of outdoor ranger walks offered daily. The guided walks highlight a variety of topics, including the island's military history, famous inmates, escapes, natural history, and the Native American occupation. If you arrived on the first ferry of the day (strongly recommended), make a note of the time of any ranger walks that interest you. Then take the audio cellhouse tour while it's not too crowded; go on a ranger-led tour afterward. After the video ends, walk up to the cellhouse for the 35-minute audio tour narrated by guards and inmates. Their recounting of daily life is vivid, blunt, and often scary. It's not to be missed. After the tour, don't be in a hurry to leave. Take a ranger walk or hike some of the trails to discover the natural beauty and abundant wildlife (hawks, ravens, geese, finches, and hummingbirds) that thrive on this evolving ecological preserve.

Other Things to Do Nearby Fisherman's Wharf, where ferries to and from Alcatraz embark and arrive, is Tourist Central and has countless ways to separate you from your money. Major attractions worth your time include UnderWater World, the San Francisco Maritime Museum, and historic ships at Hyde Pier. You can also take ferries to Angel Island and Tiburon or a cruise on San Francisco Bay. Another option is to rent a bike and ride the Golden Gate Promenade to the famous bridge with the same name; it's three-and-a-half miles one way. Restaurants, most of them not that good, abound in Fisherman's Wharf. A good, less expensive option is clam chowder in a bowl of sourdough bread (about $5) from Boudin's Bakery.

Aquarium of the Bay *Zone 6 North Beach*

Type of Attraction An aquarium where visitors are transported on a moving walkway through a clear tunnel to view thousands of marine animals. A self-guided audio tour.

Location Pier 39, San Francisco 94133; in Fisherman's Wharf

Admission $12.95 for adults, $6.50 for seniors ages 65 and over and children ages 3–11. Free for kids age 2 and younger. Family rate for two adults and either one or two children is $29.95.

Hours Monday–Thursday, 10 a.m.–6 p.m.; Friday–Sunday, 10 a.m.–7 p.m. Closed on Christmas Day.

Phone (415) 623-5300

Website www.pier39.com

When to Go Anytime

Special Comments Don't refuse the audio-tour gizmo handed out before the tour begins; not much of what follows will make sense without it. Not for the claustrophobic or folks who get sweaty hands in highway tunnels.

Overall Appeal by Age Group

Pre-school ★★★★   Grade School ★★★★   Teens ★★★★

Young Adults ★★★★   Over 30 ★★★   Seniors ★★★

Author's Rating While it's neat to see a shark or ray glide overhead, this is a small attraction—and too expensive. ★★

How Much Time to Allow 40 minutes to an hour

Description and Comments Aquarium of the Bay offers a different take on the massive fish emporiums that are sprouting like mushrooms across America's urban landscape. Instead of walking past windows and peering into large tanks, you'll find yourself transported on a moving walkway through tanks in clear tunnels where you look at fish and other marine creatures on both sides and overhead. It's a treat to see a four-foot shark pass directly over you—only inches away. The emphasis is on the marine life of northern California; the CD player hanging around your neck provides an audio commentary as you're transported (or walk—you can step off the moving sidewalk at any time) through the aquarium. After the tank tour, visitors walk through a couple of small exhibits on California nonmarine habitats and a "touch tank" for the kids. But these pale in comparison to the underwater experience and inadvertently emphasize the brevity of the tour.

Touring Tips On weekends and holidays the line for the audio tour contraption and the elevator can get long. But once under way, the line moves briskly. If a tour bus pulls in front of you and disgorges 40 tourists, go window-shopping on Pier 39 to kill some time until the line goes down (it won't take long).

Other Things to Do Nearby Walk on Pier 41 (where the Alcatraz ferry departs) and wave at the barking sea lions that congregate just offshore. If you bought tickets in advance, take the ferry to Alcatraz. You can also shop for overpriced tourist gewgaws on Pier 39 or eat in one of many overpriced seafood restaurants. A better bet in this tourist-crazed section of town are the San Francisco Maritime Museum and the Museum of the City of San Francisco (in the Cannery); neither of these quality establishments are trying to get their hands in your wallet. For lunch, try the clam chowder served in a bowl of sourdough bread at Boudin's Bakery just past Pier 41; it's good and cheap.

Asian Art Museum *Zone 2 Civic Center*

Type of Attraction The largest museum in the western hemisphere devoted exclusively to Asian art. A self-guided tour.

Location Moved from its previous location in Golden Gate Park to Civic Center Plaza across from City Hall and bordering Larkin, McAllister, Hyde, and Fulton Streets. The new Asian Art Museum is slated to be completed and open to the public in early 2003.

Admission $7 for adults, $5 for seniors, $4 for children ages 12–17, free for children ages 11 and under. Free to everyone on the first Wednesday of the month.

Hours Wednesday–Sunday, 9:30 a.m.–4 p.m. Closed Mondays, Thanksgiving, Christmas, and New Year's Day.

Phone (415) 379-8801

Website www.asianart.org

When to Go Anytime

Special Comments John F. Kennedy Drive is closed to traffic on Sunday; walk, ride a bike, or take public transportation.

Overall Appeal by Age Group Not open at press time

How Much Time to Allow With expansion of exhibits into the new space, two to three hours should suffice to take in most of the sights.

Description and Comments   The new Asian Art Museum is carrying its fantastic holdings of over 12,000 art objects spanning 6,000 years to one of the most historic structures in the city—the city's former Main Library. The new space of more than 185,000 square feet will continue to display lavish paintings, sculptures, textiles, bronzes, jade from India, Korean ceramics, and more art from Japan, Persia, and Southeast Asia.

Other Things to Do Nearby   Across the street is the Museum of the City of San Francisco in City Hall. Haas-Lilienthal House on Franklin Street gives the public a glimpse of a fully furnished Victorian home. Two other impressive Victorian houses—the Edward Coleman House at Franklin and California Streets and the Bransten House at 1735 Franklin Street—are nearby. Pacific Heights is home to some of the city's most expensive and dramatic real estate, with some mansions and townhouses exceeding the $1-million mark.

Berkeley Art Museum/Pacific Film Archive   Zone 12 Berkeley

Type of Attraction   One of the largest university art museums in the world. A self-guided tour.

Location   2626 Bancroft Way, Berkeley 94720 (on the University of California at Berkeley campus)

Admission $6 for adults; $4 for seniors and children ages 12–17, non–UC Berkeley students, and disabled persons; free for children ages 11 and under. Free to everyone on Thursdays, 11 a.m.–noon, and 5–9 p.m.

Hours   Wednesday, Friday–Sunday, 11 a.m.–5 p.m; Thursday, 11 a.m.–9 p.m. Closed Monday, Tuesday, and major holidays.

Phone   (510) 642-0808

Website   www.bampfa.berkeley.edu

When to Go   Anytime

Special Comments   The museum's seven galleries are linked by carpeted ramps and stairs, and an elevator is available.

Overall Appeal by Age Group

Pre-school ★	Grade School ★★	Teens ★★★
Young Adults ★★★	Over 30 ★★★	Seniors ★★★

Author's Rating   Not on par with the Legion of Honor or the de Young Museum (which is closed for renovation until 2005) across the bay, but still a major collection in a visually striking building. ★★★

How Much Time to Allow   One to two hours

Description and Comments   In seven linked, spiraling galleries, the Berkeley Art Museum displays its collections of Asian art, Western art from the Renaissance to the present, and the work of twentieth-century painter Hans Hoffmann. The other four galleries are devoted to exhibitions that change about four times a year. The poured concrete walls, carpeted ramps, and unusual layout add to the enjoyment of the eclectic collection of art on display, although—as is the case with many state university buildings—it's a bit shabby around the edges.

Touring Tips   Parking in Berkeley is notoriously bad; if you decide to drive, arrive as early as possible to find a space in one of the many public lots in the vicinity of the campus. A better bet from San Francisco is BART; the Berkeley station is located at Center and Shattuck Streets, and it's a short walk east to the campus. The Museum Store, open during gallery hours, offers a wide range of books and periodicals on art and film, as well as posters, cards, and jewelry. Cafe Grace features better-than-average museum dining indoors or in the sculpture garden.

Other Things to Do Nearby   The Hearst Museum of Anthropology is across Bancroft Way on the ground floor of Kroeber Hall. Fossil hunters and Barney fans won't want to miss the Museum of Paleontology, which houses one of the largest and oldest collections of fossils in North America. It's open Monday through Friday, noon to 4 p.m., and it's located in the Valley Life Sciences Building on campus; admission is free. Youngsters will love the Lawrence Hall of Science, a hands-on science museum with an added bonus—a spectacular view of the Bay Area. Either drive or take a university Hill Service Shuttle to get there. Telegraph Avenue, located in the heart of the People's Republic of Berkeley, features an incredibly diverse selection of restaurants, gift shops, street vendors, street musicians, street people, and gray-haired hippies; it's as if the 1960s never ended.

Berkeley Rose Gardens   Zone 12 Berkeley

Type of Attraction   A 3.6-acre Berkeley landmark with terraces of various roses
Location   At Euclid and Eunice Streets, in Berkeley
Admission   Free
Hours   From dawn to dusk
Phone   None
Website   www.ci.berkeley.ca.us/news/99jun
When to Go   Late spring and early summer are the best times to go to catch the roses in full bloom.
Overall Appeal by Age Group

Pre-school ★★	Grade School ★★	Teens ★★★
Young Adults ★★★	Over 30 ★★★	Seniors ★★

Author's Rating   ★★★

How Much Time to Allow   A half of an hour would be sufficient, but longer if you are looking for a quiet place to relax.

Description and Comments   A terraced amphitheater redolent with the smell of roses—hundreds of different types of roses—color the terraces that overlook the San Francisco Bay and Skyline. The Garden was built between 1933 and 1937 and has been maintained by volunteers who, ever since, call themselves the Friends of the Berkeley Gardens. The gardens are clearly labeled with what breed of rose a particular bush is, and paths lead you through them. It is no wonder that couples get married here month after month—it is truly an inspiration and romantic stop. And if you aren't the type to stop and smell the roses, there is a tennis court right next door.

Touring Tips   Come when the sun is setting. The views of the city skyline and the sparkling bay are breathtaking. You can simply park your car along the side of the street and get out and walk. There is no formal place to park.

Other Things to Do Nearby   Had your fill of flowers? How about a bug show at the Essig Museum of Entomology? The museum is located on the Berkeley campus, in room 211 of Wellman Hall. For hours and parking information, contact the museum at (510) 643-0804.

Cable Car Museum *Zone 1 Chinatown*

Type of Attraction A building housing the machinery that moves the city's famed cable cars; museum features photographs, old cable cars, signposts, mechanical devices, and a video explaining the system. A self-guided tour.

Location 1201 Mason Street (at Washington Street), San Francisco 94108 (Nob Hill)

Admission Free

Hours April–October, daily, 10 a.m.–6 p.m.; rest of the year, daily, 10 a.m.–5 p.m. Closed on major holidays.

Phone (415) 474-1887

Website www.cablecarmuseum.com

When to Go Anytime

Special Comments One set of stairs leads up to the mezzanine viewing area, and another set heads down to an enclosed area where you can see the inside the system.

Overall Appeal by Age Group

Pre-school ★★½	Grade School ★★★	Teens ★★
Young Adults ★★½	Over 30 ★★½	Seniors ★★★

Author's Rating It's fun to watch the machinery that pulls San Francisco's famed cable cars, and the price is right. ★★½

How Much Time to Allow 30 minutes to an hour

Description and Comments When you try to envision what makes San Francisco's cable cars go, think horizontal elevator. Here you can see the machinery that moves the cables pulling the cars on the four lines of the only cable-car operation in the world. You'll also see nineteenth-century photos, an old cable car, some of the machinery that grip and release the cable running under the streets, and an informative video on the system. It's noisy and smells like a factory—which it is, in a way. A must for railroad buffs and most children, and a fun fill-in spot for everyone else.

Touring Tips If you're frustrated in your attempts to board the jam-packed cable cars, you can at least stop in to satisfy your curiosity about how it works. It's also a place to pick up a one-day or multiday Muni pass for unlimited rides on the city's buses, subways, and—if you're lucky or have the patience to wait in line—cable cars.

Other Things to Do Nearby Chinatown is only two blocks away. Three blocks south at California and Mason Streets is the Mark Hopkins Inter-Continental Hotel, famous for its Top O' the Mark lounge. Nob Hill, which overlooks Union Square, is home to many of the city's elite and some of its finest hotels.

California Academy of Sciences *Zone 8 Richmond/Sunset*

Type of Attraction A natural history museum, aquarium, and planetarium. A self-guided tour.

Location Music Concourse Drive, Golden Gate Park, San Francisco 94118

Admission $8.50 for adults, $5.50 for seniors and children ages 12–17, $2 for children ages 4–11. Free to all on the first Wednesday of the month. Tickets for 45-minute planetarium shows are an additional $2.50 for adults and $1.25 for seniors and children ages 6–17. $2.50 discount with a Muni bus transfer.

Hours Memorial Day to Labor Day, daily, 9 a.m.–6 p.m.; rest of the year, daily, 10 a.m.–5 p.m.

Phone (415) 750-7145

Website www.calacademy.org

When to Go To avoid boisterous school groups on school days, go in the afternoon. Penguins are fed at 11:30 a.m. and 4 p.m.; feeding in the Fish Roundabout is at 2 p.m.

Special Comments Free one-hour tours led by museum-trained guides are offered throughout the day; inquire at information desk near entrance.

Overall Appeal by Age Group

Pre-school ★★★★★   Grade School ★★★★★   Teens ★★★★★

Young Adults ★★★★   Over 30 ★★★★   Seniors ★★★★

Author's Rating Kids go nuts over this place. But other than the fish in the aquarium, it's a museum full of static displays and dioramas. ★★★

How Much Time to Allow Two hours

Description and Comments The lobby of the West's oldest scientific institution (founded in 1853) greets visitors with a huge fossil skeleton of a Tyrannosaurus rex; this sets the tone for this kid-friendly science museum. Major exhibits include African Safari, which is full of wildlife dioramas and an African water-hole display where families can pose for snapshots. The action picks up in the Steinhart Aquarium, a classic fish emporium that kids love. The aquarium features 14,000 species of fish, plus reptiles and amphibians. Especially creepy are the prehistoric-looking gar fish and tanks full of piranhas. At the Fish Roundabout, visitors stroll up a ramp and peer through windows into a 100,000-gallon tank to see rays and circling sharks. The very young will like the Touch Tidepool, where they can pick up and inspect live sea urchins, hermit crabs, and starfish. Wild California has more dioramas and displays that show off the state's scenery and varied wildlife. Downstairs is Academy Café, which features reasonably priced family fare. The Academy Store offers books, toys, posters, and gifts for naturalists of all ages.

Touring Tips From the main entrance, head left into African Safari and work your way counterclockwise past temporary exhibits to the aquarium (on the other side of the central courtyard). Then come back to the main entrance to view Wild California and an exhibit of gems and minerals. The Morrison Planetarium offers sky shows at 2 p.m. on weekdays and on the hour from 11 a.m. to 4 p.m. on weekends; tickets go on sale half an hour before show time at the box office in the Earth and Space Hall. Shows aren't offered on some days, so call ahead.

Other Things to Do Nearby The Japanese Tea Garden is across the Music Concourse. Behind the natural history museum is Shakespeare Garden, an oasis of quiet that could prove beneficial to adults after a hectic tour of the California Academy of Sciences. Gardeners—and just about everyone else—will enjoy Strybing Arboretum, 70 acres of plants and gardens; it's just past the Japanese Tea Garden. If it's a nice day, drive or walk to Stow Lake and rent a rowboat ($11 an hour), or a bike (starting at $5 an hour). You'll find a snack bar at Stow Lake.

California Historical Society   Zone 7 SoMa/Mission

Type of Attraction A gallery displaying temporary exhibitions from the society's collection of paintings, watercolors, drawings, lithographs, photographs, and artifacts. A self-guided tour.

Location 678 Mission Street, San Francisco 94103; in SoMa near Third Street

Admission $3 general admission, $1 for seniors and students, free for children ages 6 and under with an adult. Free to everyone on the first Tuesday of the month.
Hours Tuesday–Saturday, 11 a.m.–5 p.m. Closed Sunday, Monday, major holidays.
Phone (415) 357-1848
Website www.calhist.org
When to Go Anytime
Special Comments The gallery is all on one level.
Overall Appeal by Age Group

Pre-school ★	Grade School ★	Teens ★★
Young Adults ★★	Over 30 ★★	Seniors ★★★

Author's Rating The airy, sky-lit central gallery is beautiful, but its small size relegates this museum to the fill-in category. ★★

How Much Time to Allow One hour

Description and Comments Founded in 1871, the California Historical Society moved to this location, a block east of Yerba Buena Gardens, in 1995. Items from the society's vast collection rotate about four times a year, so what you see on your visit won't be what we saw on ours. But it's a very attractive gallery and worth a stop, especially for first-time visitors to California looking for insight into the state's fascinating history.

Touring Tips Don't miss the storefront book store, which features books by California authors ranging from Jack London to Joan Didion. You'll also find unusual postcards and a map showing places around San Francisco used as locations in Hollywood films.

Other Things to Do Nearby Yerba Buena Gardens is a block away, and just beyond that is the San Francisco Museum of Modern Art.

California Palace of the Legion of Honor
Zone 8 Richmond/Sunset

Type of Attraction A recently renovated museum of ancient and European art housed in a reproduction of an eighteenth-century French palace; a spectacularly scenic setting. A self-guided tour.
Location In the northwest corner of San Francisco at 34th Avenue and Clement Street, in Lincoln Park
Admission $8 for adults, $6 for seniors, and $5 for children ages 12–17; children ages 11 and under, free. A $2 discount is given to holders of Muni bus transfers. Admission is free to all every Tuesday.
Hours Tuesday–Sunday, 9:30 a.m.–5 p.m.; first Tuesday of the month, 9:30 a.m.–8:45 p.m. Closed Monday and Thanksgiving, Christmas, and New Year's Day.
Phone (415) 863-3330 (recorded information); (415) 750-3600 (main switchboard)
Website www.sfstation.com/museums
When to Go Anytime
Special Comments Admission to the Legion of Honor also gives you free, same-day admission to the de Young Museum in Golden Gate Park, but the museum is closed and won't be reopened until 2005 due to renovation.
Overall Appeal by Age Group

Pre-school ★★	Grade School ★★★	Teens ★★★
Young Adults ★★★★	Over 30 ★★★★	Seniors ★★★★

Author's Rating Rather highbrow in tone, but the building (reopened in 1995 after undergoing a $36 million seismic retrofitting and modernization) and much of the art and physical location are spectacular. ★★★★

How Much Time to Allow Two hours

Description and Comments Built in the 1920s and dedicated to the thousands of California servicemen who died in France in World War I, the California Palace of the Legion of Honor (most folks just say Legion of Honor) is visually stunning. Visitors enter through a magnificent courtyard dominated by an original cast of Auguste Rodin's "The Thinker." The building is in an eye-popping location overlooking the Golden Gate Bridge and the Marin Headlands; its design was inspired by the Palais de la Legio d'Honneur in Paris, built in 1786. If it all looks vaguely familiar, that's because you've watched *Vertigo* too many times on late-night TV; it's where Kim Novak went to gaze upon the portrait of Carlotta (a movie prop you won't find in the museum).

Inside is an impressive collection of ancient and European art covering 4,000 years. Heavy hitters include David, Monet, Manet, Degas, Gainsborough, Reynolds, Rubens, Rembrandt, Van Gogh, Dalí, Picasso, Renoir, and Seurat. But more than paintings and sculptures are on display in sumptuous galleries, which feature soaring ceilings, blond hardwood floors, and copious natural light. You'll also find extensive collections of furniture, silver, and ceramics.

Touring Tips Most of the art is on the main level, and ancient art and ceramics are on the lower-level terrace, where you'll also find an excellent, reasonably priced café, a gift shop, rest rooms, and phones. Probably the most popular galleries are the two dedicated to Rodin; these stunning rooms are just past the central rotunda on the main level. Galleries 1–9 (to the left as you face the entrance) feature medieval, Renaissance, and eighteenth-century art; galleries 11–19 (to the right) contain art from the eighteenth through the early twentieth centuries. Special exhibits, which sometimes charge an extra admission fee, are held in Rosekrans Court, housed under a glass structure that floods the galleries with natural light.

Although parking is abundant around the museum, the convenient lot across from the entrance is small and fills quickly; leaving your car parked on a nearby side street may result in a stiff, uphill hike to the museum entrance. A good option is public transportation; from Union Square, take the No. 38 bus to 33rd and Clement Streets; transfer to the No. 18 bus (and save $2 on admission) or walk uphill to the museum.

Other Things to Do Nearby Cliff House, a mile or so south on the coast, provides fantastic views of the Marin coast and Seal Rocks, home base for sea lions and a variety of marine birds; bring binoculars. There's also a restaurant and a visitor center. To the north are Fort Point and the Golden Gate Bridge; to the south are Ocean Beach (don't worry if you forget a swimsuit; the water is cold and dangerous) and Golden Gate Park. A couple of miles down the coast are the San Francisco Zoo and Fort Funston, with great views, easy trails, and hang gliders doing their thing on the strong ocean air currents.

Cartoon Art Museum   *Zone 7 SoMa/Mission*

Type of Attraction The only museum west of the Mississippi dedicated to the preservation, collection, and exhibition of original cartoon art. A self-guided tour.

Location 655 Mission Street, between New Montgomery and Third Street
Phone (415) CARTOON
Website www.cartoonart.org
When to Go Anytime
Special Comments While there's lots here to delight children, cartoons of an explicitly adult nature are placed in rooms restricted to ages 18 and older. Kids may need a lift to see most of the cartoons, which are displayed at adult eye level. If you're making a special trip, call ahead to make sure the museum isn't closed due to installation of a new exhibit.
Overall Appeal by Age Group

Pre-school ★★   Grade School ★★★   Teens ★★★
Young Adults ★★★   Over 30 ★★★★   Seniors ★★★

Author's Rating How can you resist a cartoon art museum? You'll have a blast. ★★★★

How Much Time to Allow One to two hours

Description and Comments From at least the turn of the century, the Bay Area has been home to a healthy population of professional cartoonists. (Maybe it's a combination of great vistas and San Francisco's relaxed atmosphere.) Well-known cartoonists spotlighted in this small museum over the years include Scott Adams ("Dilbert"), Bill Griffith ("Zippy the Pinhead"), Morrie Turner ("Wee Pals"), Phil Frank ("Farley"), and Paul Mavrides ("The Fabulous Furry Freak Brothers"). Many of the cartoons hail from San Francisco's underground "comix" movement of the late 1960s and early 1970s. Needless to say, most of the art is satirical, scathingly funny, and often risqué. Wonderful, in other words.

Touring Tips The new space is larger than the previous space so exhibits have been expanded to feature more. There are over three major shows a year.

Other Things to Do Nearby Yerba Buena Gardens and Center for the Arts is a block down Mission Street, and the Museum of Modern Art is on Third Street on the other side of Yerba Buena Gardens. The California Historical Society has a small gallery at 678 Mission Street.

Castro Theater   Zone 7 SoMa/Mission

Type of Attraction A city landmark that stands as an icon to one of the world's most prominent gay neighborhoods.
Location 429 Castro Street, San Francisco 94144
Admission Movie tickets unless otherwise noted are $7.50. Matinee tickets as well as tickets for senior citizens over 60 and children under 12 are $4.50.
Hours The box office opens an hour before the first movie of the day and only sells tickets for the current day.
Phone (415) 621-6120 is the information line with a recording of current movies; to reach the box office directly call (415) 621-6350.
Website www.thecastrotheatre.com
When to Go Anytime
Special Comments The theater is easily spotted, just look for the massive marquee on Castro Street—easily becoming as recognizable as the Transamerica Building.

Overall Appeal by Age Group

Pre-school ★	Grade School ★	Teens ★
Young Adults ★★	Over 30 ★★★★	Seniors ★★★★

Author's Rating From classic movies like *Funny Girl*, to its interesting architecture it's a nice way to either get in a neighborhood icon from the outside or step in for a night at the movies. ★★★★

How Much Time to Allow If you are stopping to glimpse at the exterior only allow a few minutes. Movies usually run about two hours.

Description and Comments The interior and exterior of this elaborate landmark on Castro Street can't make up its mind whether its motif is Roman, Asian or Arabic, or that Miami style—Art Deco. After a major renovation, the theater still boasts an interior and exterior that remains true to its 1920s and 1930s heyday and vision of designer Timothy Pflueger (the same guy who gave the city the Paramount Theater in Oakland, the former I. Magnin building on Union Square, 450 Sutter, and the Pacific Telephone Building on New Montgomery.)

The ceiling and and light fixtures are elaborate, as is most of the interior. Be sure to get to the theater early to take in the splendor of this classic space. The small theater feels a bit like an opera house, with the help of the huge Wurlitzer organ that begins each movie. It rises out of the theater pit just before showtime leading the audience in a series of classic show tunes followed by "San Francisco."

Touring Tips The hooting and hollering and sing alongs of the audience bring down the house! Loads of fun especially if they are showing such campy classics as *My Fair Lady* or *Return of the Body Snatchers*.

Other Things to Do Nearby If you are making it a movie night, why not include ice cream? Ben and Jerry's is down the street.

City Lights Bookstore   Zone 6 North Beach

Type of Attraction A Beat bookstore made famous by its Beat inhabitants such as Jack Kerouac, Allen Ginsberg, and owner/artist Lawrence Ferlinghetti

Location 261 Columbus Avenue (off of Broadway), San Francisco 94133

Admission Free (all new poetry welcome!)

Hours Everyday of the year from 10 a.m.–midnight

Phone (415) 362-8193

Website www.citylights.com

When to Go Anytime

Special Comments If you see a gray-haired and bearded man standing in the aisles chances are it is the Beat owner and poet laureate himself—Lawrence Ferlinghetti.

Overall Appeal by Age Group

Pre-school —	Grade School —	Teens —
Young Adults ★★	Over 30 ★★★★	Seniors ★★★

Author's Rating You'll feel a sudden creative surge of creative energy just by reading the titles of the new releases from independent literary forces. The Beat Generation held such a spell over the city, and this bookstore is one of the few landmarks left. A definite stop. ★★★★

How Much Time to Allow Anywhere from a few minutes to purchase a postcard to all day, browsing the poetry and literature stacked on the wooden shelves.

Description and Comments   Founded in 1953 by poet Lawrence Ferlinghetti and Peter D. Martin, City Lights is one of the few truly great independent bookstores or alternative literary scenes in the United States. Famed the world over for unique "finds" and rare first editions, it is made even more famous by the icons of a generation—those beatniks—who nurtured their creative restlessness here.

Touring Tips   Often the bookstore hosts readings and book signings. Contact them directly for a schedule of guest authors and poets. Also, aisles and shelves are often overflowing and crowded and it is difficult to find a specific title. If you are looking for a specific title, don't hesitate to ask for help.

Other Things to Do Nearby   Stop by Vesuvio Café across the street, the famous bar and literary hangout that was once the favorite watering hole of Jack Kerouac. Coit Tower is also in North Beach. Pick up a good read and head to the top!

Cliff House   Zone 8 Richmond/Sunset

Type of Attraction   A San Francisco oceanside tourist landmark with spectacular views, a restaurant, a small museum, a collection of antique mechanical amusement machines, shops and a deli, a cliffside park, the ruins of a Victorian-era resort, and a camera obscura. Self-guided tour.

Location   1090 Point Lobos Avenue (at the Great Highway), San Francisco 9412.

Admission   Free

Hours   Visitor center: daily, 10 a.m.–5 p.m.; restaurant: 9 a.m.–10:30 p.m. weekdays, 8:30 a.m.–11 p.m. weekends

Phone   (415) 386-3330 (Cliff House Restaurant); (415) 556-8642 (visitor center)

Website   www.cliffhouse.com

When to Go   When the coast isn't socked in by fog. Cocktails at sunset in the restaurant are a San Francisco tradition.

Special Comments   Lots of stairs and climbing if you opt to explore Sutro Heights Park and the ruins of Sutro Baths. There's also a steep set of stairs down to the visitor center.

Overall Appeal by Age Group

Pre-school ★★★★	Grade School ★★★★	Teens ★★★★
Young Adults ★★★	Over 30 ★★★	Seniors ★★★

Author's Rating   A bizarre blend of spectacular scenery, an overpriced seafood restaurant with a view, San Francisco history, and tourist schlock. Probably not to be missed, but it's no tragedy if you do. ★★★

How Much Time to Allow   30 minutes to an hour (longer if you dine)

Description and Comments   A San Francisco tourist landmark for more than 100 years, Cliff House still packs them in—often by the busload. The attraction? Dining with a magnificent view of the Pacific, with Seal Rocks in the foreground just off shore. (Seal Rocks is a haven for sea lions and marine birds.) But there's more here than the opportunity to drop big bucks for an expensive lunch or dinner while you watch waves crash against the rocks. The whole place is owned by the National Park Service (it's part of the Golden Gate National Recreation Area); at the visitor center next to the restaurant you can view vintage photographs of Cliff House through its various incarnations (it was destroyed by fire twice). Next door (so to speak) are the concrete ruins of Sutro Baths, a 3-acre swimming emporium that once held 1.6 million gallons of water and rented 20,000 bathing suits and 40,000 towels a day. Kids and adults will enjoy Musee Mechanique, an unworldly collection of antique penny arcade amusements that will still eat up your quarters; and the Giant Camera, a huge camera obscura you walk into to see an image of Seal Rocks magnified on a huge parabolic screen.

Touring Tips   Across the Great Highway and just up the hill is Sutro Heights Park, where you walk up a short, steep path to a great view overlooking Cliff House, Seal Rocks, the ruins, and the Pacific. It's worth the effort.

Other Things to Do Nearby   Drive a few miles south to Fort Funston and watch hang gliders calmly jump off cliffs and swoop and soar along the shore. You can take a walk along Ocean Beach, which starts just below Cliff House, and view actual native San Franciscans. Golden Gate Park, with museums and trails, and a lake that rents rowboats, is to the south. You can't miss the entrance; look for the Dutch windmill.

Coit Tower   Zone 6   North Beach

Type of Attraction   A landmark tower with an observation deck atop Telegraph Hill. A self-guided tour.

Location   At the top of Telegraph Hill Boulevard, near North Beach in San Francisco

Admission   The elevator ride to the top is $3.75 for adults, $2.50 for seniors, and $1.50 for children ages 6–12.

Hours   Daily, 10 a.m.–6 p.m.

Phone   (415) 362-0808

When to Go   Come in the evening for a great view of the setting sun and a great photo opportunity.

Special Comments   The elevator doesn't go all the way to the top; you must negotiate a set of steep, winding stairs to the observation deck. Small children will need a lift to see the outstanding 360° view. Skip it in lousy weather.

Overall Appeal by Age Group

Pre-school ★★★	Grade School ★★★	Teens ★★★
Young Adults ★★★	Over 30 ★★★	Seniors ★★★

Author's Rating   A great view, but it's almost as good from the parking lot at the base of the tower. ★★½

How Much Time to Allow   30 minutes to an hour

Description and Comments   Built as a monument to San Francisco's volunteer firefighters with funds left by renowned eccentric Lillie Hitchcock Coit, this landmark provides a breathtaking view of the city, San Francisco Bay, the Oakland and Golden Gate bridges—the works. Some say the tower is shaped to resemble a firehose nozzle, but others disagree. There's no doubt about Ms. Coit's dedication to firefighters. Early in the gold rush, she is said to have deserted a wedding party and chased after her favorite fire engine. Lillie died in 1929 at age 86, leaving the city $125,000 to "expend in an appropriate manner . . . to the beauty of San Francisco." Coit Tower is the result. In the lobby of the tower base are 19 WPA-era murals depicting labor-union workers; admission to the murals and the ground-floor gift shop is free.

Touring Tips   Don't drive; the parking lot at the base of Coit Tower is small, and the wait for a space can be long. Walk (though the hill is very steep) or take the No. 39 Coit bus at Washington Square Park (board at Columbus Avenue and Union Street), which will take you up Telegraph Hill. Hour-long tours of the murals in the lobby are offered on Tuesday and Thursday at 10:15 a.m. ($5) and on Saturday at 11 a.m. (free).

Other Things to Do Nearby Walk down steep Telegraph Hill to Washington Square and North Beach, the city's Bohemian district of bars, Italian restaurants, coffee houses, and City Lights Bookstore, the former hangout of Jack Kerouac, Allen Ginsberg, and other Beatnik greats.

Federal Reserve Bank of San Francisco *Zone 4 Financial District*

Type of Attraction The American Currency Exhibit and the World of Economics, two lobby attractions on the ground floor of the San Francisco office of America's central bank. Guided and self-guided tours.

Location 101 Market Street, San Francisco 94105

Admission Free

Hours Monday–Friday, 9 a.m.–4:30 p.m. Closed weekends and holidays. Guided tours: Monday–Thursday, 9:30 and 11 a.m.

Phone (415) 974-3252

Website www.frbsf.org

When to Go Anytime; reservations required for guided tours

Special Comments All on one level. Rest rooms, public phones, and drinking water are also in the lobby.

Overall Appeal by Age Group

Pre-school ★	Grade School ★★	Teens ★
Young Adults ★	Over 30 ★	Seniors ★

Author's Rating Some interesting things (such as a $10,000 bill), but overall dry and boring. ★

How Much Time to Allow 30 minutes to an hour

Description and Comments The lobby of the Federal Reserve Bank contains two exhibits of particular interest to serious collectors of paper currency (and we don't mean Silicon Valley fat cats) and budding capitalists. The American Currency Exhibit, a one-room display of paper money from colonial days to the present, is the most interesting. Notes from the original 13 colonies are displayed on a historical timeline with more than 400 selections from the bank's permanent collection, many of them rare and irreplaceable. Many of the designs are outstanding examples of engraving and feature images of historical events, Native American warriors, emblems, and monuments. Some of the more unusual items on display are specially marked currency printed for Hawaii (in case the Japanese invaded during World War II) and a $10,000 bill, no longer produced. The rest of the lobby is dedicated to the World of Economics, a group of elaborate displays (some interactive) that purport to explain the complexities of global currency exchange, inflation, stagflation, and supply and demand. Is this any way to spend a vacation? Especially when you are spending on your vacation!

Touring Tips Head straight for the American Currency Exhibit, located in a small room at the south end of the lobby. A few quick glances at the towering exhibits in the World of Economics and you'll soon know if it's for you. They offer guided tours by appointment only and the tour lasts 90 minutes from 9:30 a.m. to 11 a.m. Monday through Thursday.

Other Things to Do Nearby   The Ferry Building at the foot of Market Street (you can't miss it; it's the one with the tower) is one of the few buildings to survive the 1906 earthquake and fire. Here you can board a ferry to Sausalito, Angel Island, and other San Francisco Bay destinations.

Fort Point National Historic Site   *Zone 8 Richmond/Sunset*

Type of Attraction   A Civil War–era brick coastal fortification beneath Golden Gate Bridge; superb vistas of San Francisco's key topographical features. Guided and self-guided tours.

Location   In the Presidio at the end of Marine Drive (at the southern end of the Golden Gate Bridge), San Francisco.

Admission   Free; donation requested

Hours   Thursday–Monday, 10 a.m.–5 p.m. Closed Tuesday and Wednesday, Thanksgiving, Christmas, and New Year's Day.

Phone   (415) 556-1693

Website   www.nps.gov/fopo

When to Go   In July and August come before noon if you're driving; the small parking lot fills fast. A better option in these busy months (or whenever the weather is nice) is to ride a bike or walk along the Golden Gate Promenade to the fort and its dramatic setting.

Special Comments   Lots of steep, narrow stairs, tricky footing, and a scarcity of handrails in the fort. Portable rest rooms are located outside the entrance of the fort, and flush toilets are near the wharf on Marine Drive. Bring a jacket or sweater; Fort Point can be very windy and cool.

Overall Appeal by Age Group

Pre-school ★★★   Grade School ★★★★   Teens ★★★★
Young Adults ★★★★   Over 30 ★★★★★   Seniors ★★★★★

Author's Rating   Come just for the view; the old fort is neat, too. Put this on your "must see" list. ★★★★★

How Much Time to Allow   One hour; longer for a guided tour and a demonstration

Description and Comments   This fort, built between 1853 and 1861 by the U.S. Army Corps of Engineers, was designed to prevent the entrance of a foreign fleet into San Francisco Bay. The setting—the Golden Gate Bridge overhead, the San Francisco skyline to the east, the rugged Marin Headlands across the straight, and the Pacific Ocean stretching to the horizon—is breathtaking. Ideally, first-time visitors to San Francisco should be blindfolded and brought to Fort Point, where the blindfold should come off; the result would leave them gasping for breath. It's that spectacular.

History buffs will enjoy exploring the fort, which symbolizes the commercial and strategic military importance of San Francisco. But most visitors will simply want to hoof it to the fourth (and highest) level for an even better view of the dramatic panorama (with Golden Gate Bridge traffic pounding overhead). The interior of the fort is bare bones, but some of the rooms on upper levels contain photo exhibits about its past. Film buffs will recognize the spot where James Stewart fished Kim Novak out of San Francisco Bay in Alfred Hitchcock's classic thriller, *Vertigo*. A final note: the fort's impressive muzzle-loading cannons (rendered obsolete by rifled cannons during the Civil War and removed by 1900) were never fired in anger.

Touring Tips Go to the gift shop on the ground level to catch a free 17-minute video introduction to the fort. You can sign up here for a free guided tour, pick up a self-guided tour booklet, see a schedule of demonstrations (such as gun-loading by costumed personnel), and buy a postcard. You can also rent a 40-minute audio tour of the fort ($2.50 for adults, $1 for children). Be sure to walk around the sea wall to the chain-link fence for a full view of the Pacific Ocean. You may also see die-hard surfers and swimmers in wetsuits negotiating the surf and ships passing under the bridge.

Other Things to Do Nearby At the southern end of the Golden Gate Bridge on Lincoln Boulevard is a scenic overlook, visitor center, parking lot, and starting point for a walk on the bridge or along paths overlooking the Pacific. The best bet for getting there is to drive, although you can walk up the very steep path. The Presidio, a former U.S. Army base that's now part of Golden Gate National Recreation Area, is filled with old buildings, a museum, a military cemetery, a golf course, trails, and stands of eucalyptus trees planted with military precision.

Drive south along the Pacific for more great views, magnificent private residences, the California Palace of the Legion of Honor (a classy art museum also used in *Vertigo*), Cliff House, and Ocean Beach. On the way back downtown from Fort Point are the Palace of Fine Arts and the Exploratorium (a hands-on science museum) and Fort Mason (with museums, restaurants, fishing piers, marinas, and picnic areas).

Ghirardelli Chocolate Manufactory and Soda Fountain
Zone 5 Marina

Type of Attraction Come and see how the chocolate is made. An excellent excursion for the little ones.

Location Ghirardelli Square Clock Tower, 900 North Point Street, San Francisco 94109

Admission Free

Hours Weekdays from 9 a.m.–11:30 a.m.; weekends from 9 a.m.–midnight

Phone (415) 474-3938

Website www.ghirardelli.com

When to Go Anytime, but great for dessert

Special Comments The tour is self-guided. Start at the soda fountain.

Overall Appeal by Age Group

Pre-school ★★★   Grade School ★★★★   Teens ★★★★★
Young Adults ★★★★★   Over 30 ★★★★   Seniors ★★★

Author's Rating It's probably going to be a major hit with the kids. But who outgrows chocolate? ★★★

How Much Time to Allow One hour or more depending on cravings!

Description and Comments It's the garden of delectable chocolates. From truffles, to their world famous hot fudge sundaes, and the ever-popular Alcatraz Rock (rocky road ice cream in a shell of hard chocolate)—it's interactive tasting while you get to see the machinery that pumps out such delicious treats.

Touring Tips Foggy or rainy days and weekends create swamps of chocolate lovers. If you want to avoid crowds come on a weekday, preferably in the morning. That's when the goodies are fresh anyway.

Other Things to Do Nearby   Of course, Fisherman's Wharf is a hop, skip, and a jump away and Pier 39 is close also.

Haas-Lilienthal House   *Zone 2 Civic Center*

Type of Attraction The only fully furnished Victorian house in San Francisco open to the public. A guided tour.

Location 2007 Franklin Street, San Francisco 94109; near Washington Street in Pacific Heights

Admission $5 per person; $3 for seniors and under 12

Hours Wednesday, noon–3 p.m.; Sunday, 11 a.m.–4 p.m.

Phone (415) 441-3000

Website www.sfheritage.org

When to Go Anytime

Special Comments Two flights of stairs on the tour.

Overall Appeal by Age Group

Pre-school ★	Grade School ★★	Teens ★★
Young Adults ★★	Over 30 ★★★	Seniors ★★★

Author's Rating A fascinating glimpse into the life of an upper-middle-class San Francisco family of the late nineteenth century. ★★½

How Much Time to Allow One hour

Description and Comments This exquisite 1886 high Victorian mansion has been maintained in nearly original condition since the last descendant of the builders to live in the house died in 1972. The hour-long, docent-led tour reveals a wealth of details both on the house (one of a very few to survive the 1906 earthquake and fire) and the life of a rich (but not fabulously so) Jewish merchant family. The distinctive Queen Anne, third-floor tower is strictly decorative; the windows are nine feet above the floor, while the sliding doors on the recessed front entrance were only open when the family was receiving visitors.

Inside, the formal front parlor was used for receiving important guests, while the family parlor behind it was used for guests lower on the social scale. More fascinating details include the small dining room off the main dining room used by children and servants; what appears to be a window at the back is in fact a jib door that slides up and may have been built so that coffins could be passed in and out of the house when a family member died.

Touring Tips Don't walk up the stairs to the main entrance; you'll get to do this later. Instead, walk to the right (as you face the house) and down the sidewalk to the tour entrance. A two-hour walking tour of Pacific Heights is offered Sundays at 12:30 p.m.; $5 person.

Other Things to Do Nearby Two other impressive Victorian houses are nearby. You can't go in, but they're worth a look: the Edward Coleman House at Franklin and California Streets and the Bransten House at 1735 Franklin Street. Pacific Heights is home to some of the city's most expensive and dramatic real estate, with some mansions and townhouses selling for prices starting at $1 million.

It is a great neighborhood to walk around. Stroll down the hill toward the Marina and take lunch on either Union or Chestnut Streets.

Japanese Tea Garden   *Zone 8 Richmond/Sunset*

Type of Attraction A stroll-style garden with a harmonious blend of architecture, landscape, bridges, footpaths, shrines, and gates; tea house serves tea, soft drinks, juices, and cookies. A self-guided tour.

Location In Golden Gate Park

Admission $3.50 for adults and teenagers, $2.50 for seniors and children ages 6–12; children ages 5 and under, free. Admission is free to all daily from 8:30 to 9 a.m. and after 5 p.m. Scheduled events have a separate admission charge.

Hours Daily, 8:30 a.m.–6:30 p.m. Open every day of the year.

Phone (415) 752-4227

When to Go In nice weather. In April the cherry trees are in bloom.

Special Comments Some mild uphills and uneven footing.

Overall Appeal by Age Group

  Pre-school ★★   Grade School ★★   Teens ★★

  Young Adults ★★★★   Over 30 ★★★★   Seniors ★★★★

Author's Rating Beautiful and fascinating. ★★★★

How Much Time to Allow One to two hours

Description and Comments In Japan, a garden is considered one of the highest art forms, and after a visit to the Japanese Tea Garden you'll understand why. On winding paths visitors encounter carp pools, a pagoda, a bronze Buddha, dwarf trees, flowers, cherry trees, footbridges, and a Zen garden. Even when it's packed with hordes of visitors, this artfully designed garden imparts a sense of tranquility.

    The garden was part of the Japanese Village exhibit of the California Midwinter International Exposition of 1894, which was held in what is now the Music Concourse in Golden Gate Park. It was built by Japanese artisans, and in the decades after the exposition closed, the garden was expanded from one acre to five acres. In that limited amount of space the garden expresses the essence of nature by the use of specially selected plants and stones arranged in harmony with the landscape. Really.

Touring Tips Come in nice weather and take your time. The atmosphere in the garden is extremely soothing—a perfect stop on a harried touring schedule. Tea service by a kimono-clad waitress in the Tea House is $2.50. The fortune cookies were originally introduced here in 1914. (Ironically, they're called Chinese fortune cookies now.) Stop in the gift shop to see a wide array of Japanese gifts and toys, including kites and fans.

Other Things to Do Nearby The Asian Art Museum, where you can find more Japanese art, is next door. The California Academy of Sciences is on the south side of the Music Concourse and is a favorite with families. Inside the Academy of Sciences you'll find the Steinhart Aquarium (a must for children) and the Morrison Planetarium (a must for space cadets). Across Martin Luther King Jr. Drive is the Strybing Arboretum, 70 acres of gardens. If it's a nice day, drive or walk to Stow Lake and rent a rowboat ($11 an hour) or a bike (starting at $5 an hour).

Lawrence Hall of Science   *Zone 12 Berkeley*

Type of Attraction A hands-on science museum for youngsters. A self-guided tour.

Location Centennial Drive, Berkeley 94720 (below Grizzly Peak Boulevard, overlooking the University of California, Berkeley campus)

Admission $7 for adults; $5 for seniors, students, and children ages 5–18; $3 for children ages 3–4. Parking, 50 cents hourly, $4 daily.

Hours Daily, 10 a.m.–5 p.m. Closed on major holidays.

Phone (510) 642-5132 for 24-hour information

Website www.lhs.berkeley.edu; or www.lawrencehallofscience.org

When to Go When the weather is clear and you can enjoy the spectacular view.

Special Comments Parking is very tight on this hilltop setting, so try to arrive early. Visitors must pay 50 cents per half hour to park. If you're not driving, take BART to the downtown Berkeley station and catch the Local Shuttle at Center Street and Shattuck Avenue. Then transfer to the Hill Service Shuttle at the Hearst Mining Circle on campus. Call Transportation Services at (510) 643-5708 for info.

Overall Appeal by Age Group

Pre-school ★★★★★	Grade School ★★★★★	Teens ★★★
Young Adults ★★	Over 30 ★★	Seniors ★★

Author's Rating A great view of the bay but otherwise strictly for youngsters. ★

How Much Time to Allow At least half a day for kids; you'll have to drag them away.

Description and Comments Named after Ernest O. Lawrence, one of the University of California at Berkeley's best-known Nobel Prize laureates, this hands-on science museum enthralls tots through grade-schoolers. It's hard to list a sampling of the many activities available, but they include a gravity wall, earthquake exhibits, play areas, and math and chemistry exhibits (where kids play scientific sleuths and use real chemical and forensic tests to solve a whodunit). Hour-long planetarium shows are offered on weekend and holiday afternoons; tickets are $2, and children ages 8 and under aren't admitted. The Lawrence Memorial Room, probably the only exhibit in the museum that's not hands-on and geared toward children, features artifacts, an explanation of how a cyclotron works, and awards given to Ernest O. Lawrence (including his Nobel Prize in physics).

Touring Tips Outside, youngsters can clamber on Pheena—a 50-foot, 3,000-pound replica of a fin whale—and a 60-foot long, scientifically accurate model of a double-helix DNA molecule. Adults can keep one eye on the kids and the other on the drop-dead view. A cafeteria on the lower level offers school lunch–style fare and a panoramic view, while the museum store sells books, games, puzzles, and science-oriented gift items.

Other Things to Do Nearby The university's Botanical Garden is located in Strawberry Canyon, on the winding road below the Lawrence Hall of Science and above the campus stadium; it includes a redwood grove, a large selection of native plants, plant species from around the world, and picnic tables. Fossil hunters won't want to miss the Museum of Paleontology, which houses one of the largest and oldest collections of fossils in North America. It's open Monday through Friday, noon to 4 p.m.; it's located in the Valley Life Sciences Building on campus and admission is free. The Berkeley Art Museum, also on campus, is an excellent art museum. Telegraph Avenue is a hopping street scene with an incredibly diverse selection of restaurants, gift shops, street vendors, street musicians, street people, and gray-haired hippies.

Marine Mammal Center Zone 11 *Marin Headlands to Point Reyes*

Type of Attraction A rehabilitation and education center that nurtures orphaned or injured sea lions and seals and any other marine mammal.

Location Fort Cronkite near Rodeo Lagoon in the Marin Headlands

Admission Free, donations welcome however

Hours Everyday from 10 a.m.–4 p.m. except Thanksgiving and Christmas Day

Phone (415) 289-7325

Website www.tmmc.org

When to Go The best time of year to visit the center depends on the season really. Winter is usually inactive—they don't get many mammals in at that time. Spring, however is pupping season when young pups are abundant in the waters—thus making the center busy. Winter and Spring, there are more northern elephant seals and harbor seals. The summer and fall months see more California sea lions. You can call the center before your visit to check on the number of "residents" they have that particular day. Or you can check their web site under "current patients page" at www.tmmc.org/patients.html.

Special Comments The organization gets funding from grants and loans. Although it's free to get in, donations would be a nice gesture.

Overall Appeal by Age Group

Pre-school ★★★★ Grade School ★★★★ Teens ★★★★

Young Adults ★★★★ Over 30 ★★★ Seniors ★★★

Author's Rating When people have got you going in circles (especially after Fisherman's Wharf) this is a nice escape. You truly get an understanding of the marine life in and around the bay. ★★★★

How Much Time to Allow One to two hours

Description and Comments This hospital in the headlands is one of the main organizations devoted to the welfare of the seals and sea lion population off of the bay area. Every year they get orphaned or injured pups and adult seals or sea lions and open the facility to visitors to generate donations and educational awareness on the impact the environment and human handling can have on the populations. Volunteers are on hand at the center to answer any questions you might have regarding the patients currently at the center or involving marine life in the bay in general including whales. A great source of information. You can see the pups get bottle fed, and read about the successful release of past patients.

Touring Tips Call before you go to see just how many patients are available that day. The health of the animals comes first here, so sometimes the biologists keep many of the animals out of public viewing. Be respectful of the animals!

Other Things to Do Nearby The Headlands offer much in the way of outdoor recreation or scenic drives. Since you probably would drive to the center, consider driving to Mount Tamalpais for amazing views, or down along Highway 1 to Stinson Beach, for vertigo inducing cliffside roads, and R&R.

Mexican Museum   Zone 7 SoMa/Mission

The gallery is closed until 2004 for relocation. The new location will be at Mission Street between 3rd and 4th Streets. The information number is (415) 202-9700.

M. H. de Young Memorial Museum   Zone 8 Richmond/Sunset

San Francisco's oldest art museum in Golden Gate Park features American paintings, sculpture, and decorative arts from colonial times to the twentieth century. Closed for demolition and renovation until 2005.

Mission Dolores   *Zone 7 SoMa/Mission*

Type of Attraction San Francisco's oldest building (1791) and the sixth of 21 missions built by Franciscan priests along El Camino Real, the Spanish road linking the missions from Mexico to Sonoma. Self-guided and audio tours.

Location 3321 16th Street, in the Mission District, San Francisco 94114

Admission $3 for adults and teenagers, $2 for children ages 5–12. The 45-minute audio tour is $4 per person, or pay $5 for admission and audio tour combined.

Hours Summer, daily, 9 a.m.–4:30 p.m.; other times of year, 9 a.m.–4 p.m. Closes at noon on Good Friday and at 2 p.m. on Easter. Closed Thanksgiving and Christmas.

Phone (415) 621-8203

Website www.missiondolores.citysearch.com

When to Go Try to go when it's not raining; the cemetery, probably the most interesting part, is out in the open.

Special Comments Rest rooms are near the cemetery entrance.

Overall Appeal by Age Group

Pre-school ★	Grade School ★★	Teens ★★
Young Adults ★★	Over 30 ★★★	Seniors ★★★

Author's Rating Surprisingly small, but worth visiting for an authentic taste of San Francisco's Spanish heritage. ★★

How Much Time to Allow 30 minutes to an hour

Description and Comments With adobe walls four feet thick and the original redwood logs supporting the roof, Mission Dolores has survived four major earthquakes and is the only one of the original missions along the El Camino Real (the Royal Way) that has not been rebuilt. Mass is still celebrated in the building, which is 114 feet long and 22 feet wide. The repainted ceiling depicts original Ohlone Indian designs done with vegetable dyes. The decorative altar came from Mexico in 1796, as did the two side altars (in 1810).

Outside the mission, a diorama shows how it appeared in 1791. Peek inside the basilica, completed in 1918, to view beautiful stained-glass windows. The small museum displays artifacts such as lithographs of the California missions and a revolving tabernacle from the Philippines. You can also see the adobe walls, which were formed and sun-dried nearby. The highlight (for us anyway) is the cemetery—really a lush garden with headstones. Most of the markers are dated in the years following the California gold rush and many of the family names are Irish.

Touring Tips Film buffs won't find the headstone of Carlotta Valdes in the mission's cemetery. It was a prop in Alfred Hitchcock's *Vertigo,* part of which was filmed here.

Other Things to Do Nearby Walk a couple of blocks down 16th Street for a selection of ethnic restaurants. Dolores Street, with an aisle of palm trees up and down the center street is fun and funky. The Mission District is full of the good and the bad— homeless people, taquerias, a thriving alternative scene, organic cafés, hash houses . . . you name it and the Mission's got it. Both 16th Street and Mission Street show off the Mission District's diverse flavors, including offbeat bookstores, Asian restaurants, and interesting shops. (Good Vibrations, 1210 Valencia Street at 23rd Street, features everything you wanted to know about sex, and then some.) The Mission Cultural Center at 2868 Mission Street (Tuesday–Saturday, 10 a.m.–4 p.m.; (415) 821-1155) has a large second-floor gallery with changing art exhibitions, usually with a Hispanic flavor; it's free.

Mount Tamalpais—
East Peak
Zone 11 Marin Headlands to Point Reyes

Type of Attraction A half-mile hike to the summit of Mount Tamalpais and a stunning view of San Francisco, the bay, the Golden Gate Bridge, and the Pacific Ocean. A self-guided tour.

Location Mount Tamalpais State Park, 12 miles north of the Golden Gate Bridge in Marin County; exit US 101 at Sausalito and follow signs to the park

Admission Free. Parking in the lot below the summit is $5 per car; $4 for seniors.

Hours Daily, sunrise–sunset

Phone (415) 388-2070

Website www.parks.ca.gov

When to Go In clear weather

Special Comments Locals call it "Mount Tam." Wear sturdy shoes if you opt for the steep hike to the summit.

Overall Appeal by Age Group

Pre-school ★★　　　Grade School ★★★　　Teens ★★★

Young Adults ★★★　Over 30 ★★★　　　Seniors ★★

Author's Rating Yet another mind-boggling view of San Francisco; this one may be the best. ★★★½

How Much Time to Allow One hour

Description and Comments The incredible vistas you see on the drive up to the top of Tamalpais are a trip in themselves. *Warning:* Anyone afraid of heights and falling off narrow, cliff-clinging curved roads with a thousand foot drop should either pass on the drive up or go blindfolded. Until 1930, tourists rode the Mount Tamalpais and Muir Woods Railway to the top, where a tavern and dance pavilion were located near the present parking lot. From the summit, the view is spectacular—including 3,890-foot Mount Diablo to the east and, on a clear day, the snow-capped Sierras 140 miles to the east. Any soaring birds you see are probably turkey vultures. If you're not up for the half-mile, 220-foot-elevation-gain hike to the summit, you can opt for a self-guided tour around the peak or just enjoy the view from the overlook near the rest rooms.

Touring Tips Unless you're wearing hiking boots and are used to narrow foot trails, don't take the plank trail to the summit. Although it looks easy, it quickly turns very steep, with treacherous footing. Instead, take the Verna Dunshee Trail, a self-guided tour just over half a mile long that goes counterclockwise around the peak; pick up a brochure in the gift shop. The trail starts to the right of the rest rooms. A snack bar, phones, and drinking water are available near the parking lot.

Other Things to Do Nearby Hikers of all abilities will find plenty of scenic trails in the state park. Muir Woods National Monument is a grove of majestic coastal redwoods, the tallest trees in the world. Stinson Beach, located beneath steep hills rising to Mount Tam, offers vistas of the sea and hills, while Muir Beach, further south down Route 1, has a semicircular cove where you can relax and enjoy the scenery. To the north, Point Reyes National Seashore provides more stunning scenery, hiking trails, miles of undisturbed beaches, and, December through April, whale-watching. In Sausalito, you'll find restaurants, shopping, and yacht- and people-watching opportunities galore. Tiburon is where really wealthy San Franciscans live; stroll the path along the waterfront and shop in the town's upscale retail stores.

Muir Woods
National Monument   *Zone 11 Marin Headlands to Point Reyes*

Type of Attraction   A grove of majestic coastal redwoods, the tallest trees in the world. A self-guided tour.

Location   12 miles north of the Golden Gate Bridge in Marin County. Exit US 101 at Sausalito and follow the signs.

Admission $3 per person ages 17 and up

Hours   Daily, 8 a.m.–7 p.m.; visitor center is open daily, 9 a.m.–4:30 p.m.

Phone   (415) 388-2595

Website   www.visitmuirwoods.com or www.nps.gov/muwo

When to Go   When it's not raining. To avoid crowds, arrive before 10 a.m. or after 4 p.m.

Special Comments   Roads leading to the park are steep and winding; vehicles more than 35 feet long are prohibited. No picnicking is allowed in Muir Woods.

Overall Appeal by Age Group

  Pre-school ★★★   Grade School ★★★★   Teens ★★★★
  Young Adults ★★★★   Over 30 ★★★★   Seniors ★★★★★

Author's Rating   Go ahead and hug a tree—if you are the Jolly Green Giant! These huge trees are truly awesome. ★★★★

How Much Time to Allow   30 minutes to an hour to stroll the paved loops in Redwood Canyon; avid hikers can spend several hours or the entire day hiking unpaved trails leading to Mount Tamalpais State Park.

Description and Comments   No trip to Northern California would be complete without a glimpse of these world-famous giant redwood trees, which are much like the trees that covered much of the Northern hemisphere 140 million years ago. Today, redwoods are only found in a narrow, 500-mile discontinuous strip of Pacific coast from southern Oregon to below Monterey, California. The huge specimens in the Cathedral and Bohemian Groves are the largest redwoods in Muir Woods. The tallest is 252 feet; the thickest is 14 feet across. The oldest is at least 1,000 years old, but most of the mature trees here are 500 to 800 years old. The towering trees, the fallen giants, and the canyon ferns impart awe and tranquility—even when the paved paths are clogged with visitors.

Touring Tips   Take the time and the modest effort to walk the paved path to Cathedral Grove; you'll encounter fewer people, and there are more fallen trees. Try walking the paths in a figure 8 by crossing footbridges over Redwood Creek. Avoid visiting on weekends and holidays; parking is usually a real hassle. The best time to come is early or late in the day; you'll encounter fewer people, and there's a better chance of seeing wildlife. The park's 560 acres include 6 miles of walking trails; except for the mostly level and paved main trail, the footpaths are unpaved. Wear sturdy hiking boots. The park, located in a deep canyon, is cool and shaded, so wear a jacket. If you plan to venture beyond the main trail, bring rain gear. A gift shop, snack bar, rest rooms, drinking water, and telephones are located near the main entrance.

Other Things to Do Nearby   You can drive almost to the summit of Mount Tamalpais for yet another incredible view of San Francisco, the Golden Gate Bridge, and the Pacific Ocean. On a scenic drive through Marin County, stop at Stinson Beach (where you can relax and enjoy the coastal scenery) and take the white-knuckle curves along Route 1, which follows the Pacific coast. Drive north to Point Reyes National Seashore to enjoy windswept terrain, miles of undisturbed beaches, hiking trails, and whale-watching (December through April). Plenty of places to eat and drink in Mill Valley and Sausalito.

Museum of the City of San Francisco   Zone 2 Civic Center

Type of Attraction Permanent and rotating exhibits showcasing the history of San Francisco from its origins as a Spanish garrison to modern times; a resource center for visitors. A self-guided tour.

Location City Hall, San Francisco 94117

Admission Free

Hours The exhibit at the City Hall South Light Court at Grove and Van Ness is open to the public Monday–Friday, 8 a.m.–8 p.m.; City Hall is also open noon–4 p.m. on Saturday and is closed on Sunday.

Phone (415) 928-0289

Website www.sfmuseum.org

When to Go Anytime

Overall Appeal by Age Group

Pre-school ★★	Grade School ★★★	Teens ★★
Young Adults ★★★	Over 30 ★★★	Seniors ★★★

Author's Rating Attractive and informative. ★★½

How Much Time to Allow 30 minutes

Description and Comments This museum is chock-full of historical gems. Items on display during our visit included part of a thirteenth-century Spanish palace purchased by media baron William Randolph Hearst, the head of the Goddess of Progress (recovered from the statue that once stood atop the San Francisco City Hall, destroyed in the 1906 earthquake), and a small exhibit dedicated to beloved newspaper columnist Herb Caen. Other memorabilia include movie posters, an exhibit on the celebration of the end of World War II, memorabilia from the 1906 earthquake, and photos and exhibits from the 1989 earthquake that devastated the nearby Marina District.

Touring Tips Take advantage of the museum's large selection of free city maps, brochures, visitor guides, and discount coupon books.

Other Things to Do Nearby Across the plaza from City Hall is the stately former public library, which will house the new Asian Art Museum soon.

Museum of Money
of the American West   Zone 4 Financial District

Type of Attraction A small museum highlighting the gold rush, gold mining, and the development of money in California's history. A self-guided tour.

Location Basement of the Union Bank of California, 400 California Street, San Francisco 94111; in the Financial District

Admission Free

Hours Monday–Friday, 9 a.m.–5 p.m. Closed weekends and bank holidays.

Phone (415) 291-4653

When to Go Anytime

Special Comments One set of stairs to climb and descend; rest rooms are next to the museum entrance.

Overall Appeal by Age Group

Pre-school ★	Grade School ★★	Teens ★★
Young Adults ★★	Over 30 ★★	Seniors ★★

Author's Rating So that's what a gold nugget looks like. An interesting but narrow slice of California history that's worth a peek when you're in the neighborhood. ★★

How Much Time to Allow 30 minutes

Description and Comments California history and gold are the focus of this one-room museum in the basement of the huge Bank of California building. On display are gold nuggets, coins, old banknotes, diagrams of the Comstock mines (the source of the fortune that founded this bank and many civic projects in San Francisco), a set of dueling pistols, and plenty of nineteenth-century photos of the gold rush era that put California on the map. Some interesting items on display—and it's small enough that you're not overwhelmed.

Touring Tips Check out the huge vault at the bottom of the stairs outside the entrance to the museum. You can't miss the stunning bank lobby in this colonnaded building, which was completed in 1908.

Other Things to Do Nearby The Wells Fargo History Museum is around the corner on Montgomery Street. Although its 27th-floor observation deck is now closed, the Transamerica Pyramid on Montgomery Street has a lobby observatory that lets you control cameras on the roof for TV-monitor views of the city; not nearly as exciting as seeing it with your own eyes, but it's free. Transamerica Redwood Park is next to the distinctive landmark; its fountains, greenery, and whimsical sculptures make for a nice place for a brown-bag lunch.

Museum of Ophthalmology   *Zone 6 North Beach*

Type of Attraction A zany, off-beat stop after hitting the more conventional museums. It's a showcase of all things eyes.

Location 655 Beach Street, third floor (at Hayes Street), near Fisherman's Wharf

Admission Free

Hours Monday–Friday, 8 a.m.–5 p.m., by appointment only

Phone (415) 561-8500, ext. 297

When to Go Anytime. Fun close to Halloween.

Special Comments Some of the preserved eyes may make you want to take lunch a bit late. But the kids will certainly get a kick out of it.

Overall Appeal by Age Group

Pre-school ★★★	Grade School ★★★★	Teens ★★★
Young Adults ★★★	Over 30 ★★★	Seniors ★★★

Author's Rating ★★, a small but interesting stop if you are so inclined to watch what watches!

How Much Time to Allow An hour should suffice

Description and Comments From diseased eyeballs that have found rest in a jar of formaldahyde, as well as glass eyes, to old surgical instruments and rare books are on display. It's a historical medical museum, so lectures are often given.

Touring Tips Information tours can be given if you choose not to be self-guided.

Other Things to Do Nearby Fisherman's Wharf is around the corner.

Neptune Society Columbarium   Zone 8 Richmond/Sunset

Type of Attraction A cemetery of sorts—a beautiful copper-domed neoclassical work of Victorian architecture serves as a repository for the ashes of some of San Francisco's famed and upper crust deceased.

Location 1 Loraine Court, off Anza and Stanyan Streets

Admission Free

Hours Weekdays, 10 a.m.–4 p.m.; weekends 10 a.m.–2 p.m.

Phone (415) 752-7892

When to Go Anytime—especially when the tourists are flocking to other well-known sites in the city.

Special Comments Reading the gravestones is interesting, and if you are death-wary the gardens on the outside are beautiful to stroll through.

Overall Appeal by Age Group

Pre-school ★	Grade School ★	Teens ★★
Young Adults ★★	Over 30 ★★★	Seniors ★★★

Author's Rating The architecture is marvelous and the gardens are excellent to browse through and sit and relax. It's also a non-touristy and unique place. ★★★

How Much Time to Allow An hour should be fine

Description and Comments In the early twentieth century cemeteries were banned from San Francisco, so those wealthy few who were laid to rest in Odd Fellows' Cemetery in the Richmond had to be placed indoors. Thus the Columbarium. Those unlucky souls who didn't have the money to "move on up" still remain below. The Columbarium houses the ashes, tombstones, and family memorabilia of the deceased. Most of them are wealthy aristocrats who made their stamp on the city. Among them are the remains of the Folgers of coffee fame, the Magnins, Kaisers, Eddys, Shattucks, Hayeses, and Brannans. You'll see fancy urns of alabaster, copper, and some more offbeat ones as well. Even better are the letters, pictures, and artifacts left behind.

Touring Tips Emmit Smith, the eccentric caretaker, also leads guided tours. His storytelling is worth the visit!

Other Things to Do Nearby Across the street is a nice park and the Coronet Movie Theater is on Geary. There are also lots of shops to explore on Arguello and Clement Streets.

Oakland Museum of California   Zone 12 Oakland

Type of Attraction A museum showcasing California's ecology, history, and art. A self-guided tour.

Location 1000 Oak Street, Oakland 94607. The museum is one block from the Lake Merritt BART station. If you're driving from San Francisco, cross the Oakland Bridge and get on Interstate 880 south; exit at Jackson Street. The museum parking garage has entrances on Oak Street and 12th Street.

Admission $6 for adults, $4 for seniors and students, free to children ages 5 and under. Free on the second Sunday of the month

Hours Wednesday–Saturday, 10 a.m.–5 p.m.; Sunday, noon–5 p.m. Closed Mondays and Tuesdays, and July Fourth, Thanksgiving, Christmas, and New Year's Day. Open until 9 p.m. on the first Friday of the month.
Phone (510) 238-2200 or (888) OAK-MUSE
Website www.museumca.org
When to Go Anytime
Special Comments Free tours are available on request most weekdays and at 1:30 p.m. on weekends. Check with the information desk at the entrance of each gallery.
Overall Appeal by Age Group

Pre-school ★★★	Grade School ★★★★	Teens ★★★
Young Adults ★★★	Over 30 ★★★★	Seniors ★★★★

Author's Rating Everyone should find something to like in this large, attractive, and diversified museum. ★★★½

How Much Time to Allow Depending on your interests in things Californian, anywhere from two hours to half a day.

Description and Comments The Oakland Museum is actually three museums in one. The first level features beautiful displays and dioramas of California's various ecosystems, ranging from coastal to mountains to deserts. Level two focuses on history, culture, and technology from precolonial days through the twentieth century. In the exhibits focusing on modern life, you'll find displays and artifacts that touch on Hollywood, mountain bikes, Harley-Davidson choppers, the Beat movement, surfboards, political and labor strife, and most of the things we associate with the frenetic, hedonistic California lifestyle; a confusing jumble, but fascinating. Level three is a large art gallery highlighting California artists and art ranging from huge landscapes to off-the-wall modern work. It's a gorgeous, airy, and light-filled space.

Touring Tips Plan to linger on the second level's exhibits on history, technology, and culture. California's muticultural past is on display in all its diversity, with stories of Native American weavers and hunters, Spanish missionaries, vaqueros, gold miners, railroad builders, factory workers, union organizers, and immigrants—virtually everyone who sought the California dream. It's a big chunk of Americana. Outside—integrated with the graceful, three-tiered building erected in 1969—are seven and a half acres of gardens that give the museum the look of an old, overgrown villa. Evergreens around the perimeter provide a tall screen, while regular rows of small trees mark elevations inside the complex; flowers and fragrant plants line the walkways.

Other Things to Do Nearby The historic Paramount Theater (at 21st Street and Broadway) is a spectacular example of Art Deco architecture; the old movie palace has been converted to a general entertainment complex. Oakland's waterfront Jack London Square is the city's version of Fisherman's Wharf—and just as contrived. At Lake Merritt, a beautiful outdoor wildlife sanctuary, you can rent a boat, take a lakeside stroll, and view wildlife. Kids will enjoy Children's Fairyland on the north side of the lake. Fairy tales come alive at old Gepetto's workshop and other settings from children's stories. The Oakland Museum's café serves salads, sandwiches, snacks, and desserts; for more upscale dining, the Bay Wolf (3853 Piedmont Avenue) is known for its California and Mediterranean cuisine; it's open for lunch and dinner.

Palace of Fine Arts/Exploratorium *Zone 5 Marina*

Type of Attraction A landmark classical Roman rotunda originally built for the Panama-Pacific Exposition of 1915; a hands-on science museum for children and adults. A self-guided tour.

Location 3601 Lyon Street, San Francisco 94123; in the Marina District just off US 101 near the Golden Gate Bridge

Admission Palace of Fine Arts and grounds, free. Exploratorium, $9 for adults, $7.50 for seniors and students, $6 for people with disabilities and children ages 5–17, and $2.50 for children ages 4 and under. Free to all on the first Wednesday of the month. The Tactile Dome is $12 per person and includes admission to the museum; advance reservations are required.

Hours Palace: always open. Exploratorium: Memorial Day–Labor Day, daily, 10 a.m.–6 p.m.; Wednesday, 10 a.m.–9 p.m. Rest of the year, Tuesday–Sunday, 10 a.m.–5 p.m.; Wednesday, 10 a.m–9 p.m. Closed Mondays, except holidays.

Phone Exploratorium: (415) 561-0360 (recorded information), (415) 561-0399 (recorded directions), or (415) 563-7337 (further information)

Website www.exploratorium.edu/history/palace

When to Go Palace of Fine Arts: in nice weather, although the fake ruins are lovely in a light rain; just make sure you bring an umbrella. Exploratorium: avoid weekday mornings during the school year, when school field trips are scheduled. Weekends and holidays are almost always busy, but lines at exhibits are rare.

Special Comments The Palace of Fine Arts is outdoors; dress accordingly. Ample free parking is available for both attractions.

Overall Appeal by Age Group

Pre-school ★★★★   Grade School ★★★★★   Teens ★★★★
Young Adults ★★★★   Over 30 ★★★★   Seniors ★★★

Author's Rating A restored recreation of a Roman ruin and a hands-on science museum are an odd coupling, but both succeed in their own ways. ★★★½

How Much Time to Allow Two to 4 hours for the Exploratorium; 30 minutes for the Palace of Fine Arts, although it's a scenic and peaceful setting that will tempt most visitors to linger.

Description and Comments Originally built in 1915 and restored in the late 1960s, the Palace of Fine Arts is a colossal fake Roman ruin with beautifully manicured greenery, an artificial lake, and waterfowl. The gorgeous setting is a great place to stroll, eat a picnic lunch, or take a break from a hectic touring schedule. The palace was so popular that after the 1915 Panama-Pacific Exhibition (which drew more than 18 million visitors), it was retained and later completely rebuilt (after decaying into real ruins). It's a San Francisco landmark and a favorite stop for tour buses.

Inside the adjacent exhibition shed is the Exploratorium, a hands-on science museum with more than 600 exhibits dedicated to the principle that one learns by doing. Bring your thinking cap. Exhibits range from a protein production line (where you chain together metal "molecules" to form DNA in a kind of jigsaw puzzle) to gyroscopes, a pendulum, AIDS exhibits, optical illusions, and a video-enhanced bobsled run—not to be missed for the 6- to 12-year-old set. Another major attraction is the Tactile

Dome, a geodesic dome that visitors explore in the dark—crawling, climbing, sliding, and exploring different textures in 13 chambers. (Some reports say private groups have experienced it in the nude.) Advanced reservations are required, and an extra fee is charged; call (415) 561-0362 weekdays between 10 a.m. and 4 p.m. Not recommended for people in casts, women in the last trimester of pregnancy, or the claustrophobic.

Touring Tips   Neither attraction lends itself to strategic touring. The palace, with its towering, curved colonnades and rotunda, is stunningly gorgeous—and otherwise empty (a great place for a brown-bag lunch). The Exploratorium is best approached with an open mind and some strong preferences for specific branches of science and technology; otherwise you run the risk of wandering until something strikes your fancy. If, say, you've always been fascinated by magnetism or acoustics, keep that in mind as you explore. Many ground-floor exhibits inside the huge, hangar-like space will appeal more to children (or stoned adults), while the upper mezzanine level contains an array of hands-on science exhibits that will keep the curious occupied for hours.

Other Things to Do Nearby   The residences of the nearby Marina District reflect the Mediterranean-revival architecture popular in the 1920s, with lots of pastel town-houses on curving streets. If you're hungry, head toward Chestnut Street to find good neighborhood restaurants and shops. The Presidio, a former army base now managed by the National Park Service, has hiking and biking trails and hundreds of historical buildings. On the shores of San Francisco Bay, Marina Green is often full of kite fliers, sunbathers, joggers, and yachters. The Golden Gate Promenade, a three-and-a-half-mile path stretching between Fisherman's Wharf and the Golden Gate Bridge, offers fine views, and you're near the halfway point.

Phoebe A. Hearst Museum of Anthropology   *Zone 12 Berkeley*

Type of Attraction   A small museum highlighting California cultural anthropology, ethnography, and archaeology. A self-guided tour.

Location   University of California at Berkeley, 103 Kroeber Hall, Berkeley 94720 (Bancroft Way at College Avenue on the University of California Berkeley campus)

Admission $2 for adults, $1 for seniors, and 50 cents for children 16 and under. Free to everyone on Thursday.

Hours   Wednesday–Sunday, 10 a.m.–4:30 p.m. Closed Monday, Tuesday, and major holidays.

Phone   (510) 643-7648

Website   www.qal.berkeley.edu/~hearst

When to Go   Anytime

Special Comments   The gift shop offers a good selection of handmade crafts.

Overall Appeal by Age Group

Pre-school ★★	Grade School ★★	Teens ★★
Young Adults ★★	Over 30 ★★	Seniors ★★★

Author's Rating   Ho-hum. Unless you have a strong interest in anthropology, think of this small gallery of static exhibits as a fill-in spot. ★½

How Much Time to Allow   30 minutes

Description and Comments   In this one-room gallery you'll find tools and implements of California's Native Americans, including food preparation utensils, baskets, brushes, trays, paddles, bowls, fishing gear, and hunting tools such as slings, traps, and bows and arrows. Interesting, yes, but the exhibits don't get the adrenaline flowing.

Touring Tips   The most interesting display is about Ishi, the last Yahi Indian of Northern California who lived and worked in the museum from 1911 until his death in 1916. But it's a very small exhibit.

Other Things to Do Nearby   The Berkeley Art Museum is across the street. Fossil hunters will like the Museum of Paleontology, housing one of the largest and oldest collections of fossils in North America. It's open Monday through Friday, noon to 4 p.m.; it's located in the Valley Life Sciences Building on campus and admission is free. Youngsters will love the Lawrence Hall of Science, a hands-on science museum with a spectacular view of the Bay Area. Drive or take a university Hill Service Shuttle to get there. Telegraph Avenue features a lively street scene with an incredibly diverse selection of restaurants, gift shops, street vendors, street musicians, street people, and gray-haired hippies.

Ripley's Believe It or Not! Museum   Zone 6 North Beach

Type of Attraction   250 exhibits of the odd and unusual based on the comic strip by Robert Ripley, "the modern Marco Polo." A self-guided tour.

Location   175 Jefferson Street (at Taylor), San Francisco 94133; across from Fisherman's Wharf

Admission $9.95 for ages 13 and older, $7.50 for seniors, $6.95 for children ages 5–12.

Hours   Sunday–Thursday, 10 a.m.–10 p.m.; Friday and Saturday, 10 a.m.–midnight

Phone   (415) 771-6188

Website   www.ripleysf.com

When to Go   Anytime

Special Comments   Anyone nervous about earthquakes should skip the simulated event.

Overall Appeal by Age Group

Pre-school ★★★   Grade School ★★★★   Teens ★★★★

Young Adults ★★   Over 30 ★★   Seniors ★

Author's Rating   Silliness aimed at 11-year-old boys and not much on hand that has anything to do with San Francisco. ★

How Much Time to Allow   One hour

Description and Comments   Here's where you come to gawk at displays of human oddities such as Unicorn Man (with a 13-inch spike growing out of the back of his head), the world's tallest man, and grainy films of restless natives chowing down on baked crocodile. For minor titillation, a few sexy teasers are thrown in, such as the optical illusion of the naked lady on the beach who's not there when you walk back for a better look.

While the overwhelming majority of exhibits have nothing to do with San Francisco (and are repeated at other Ripley museums from Australia to Key West), there are a couple of exceptions: the scale model of a cable car made of matches and a simulated earthquake, along with pictures of the 1989 event. Neither is worth the price of admission.

Touring Tips   Only come in lousy weather and in the company of adolescents. Better yet, send the youngsters in while you check out better options around Fisherman's Wharf.

Other Things to Do Nearby   The San Francisco Maritime Museum is close, as is Aquarium of the Bay, a fish emporium that gives visitors a different perspective from the other large aquariums sprouting up around the nation. A good and relatively cheap lunch alternative is the clam chowder in a bowl of sourdough bread, served across the street at Boudin's Bakery.

San Francisco Craft and Folk Art Museum   *Zone 5 Marina*

Type of Attraction   Temporary exhibitions of contemporary crafts, American folk art, and traditional ethnic art. A self-guided tour.

Location   Landmark Building A North, Fort Mason Center (Laguna Street and Marina Boulevard), San Francisco 94123

Admission $3, $1 seniors and students. Free for children ages 12 and under. Admission is free on Saturday, 10 a.m.–noon, and on the first Wednesday of the month, 11 a.m.–7 p.m.

Hours   Tuesday–Friday and Sunday, 11 a.m.–5 p.m.; Saturday, 10 a.m.–5 p.m. Closed on Monday.

Phone   (415) 775-0990

Website   www.sfcraftandfolk.org

When to Go   Anytime

Special Comments   A steep, narrow spiral staircase leads to the upper gallery.

Overall Appeal by Age Group

   Because this small gallery features constantly changing exhibits, it's not possible to rate it by age group.

Author's Rating   The museum only features temporary shows, so it's not possible to give it a rating.

How Much Time to Allow   30 minutes to an hour

Description and Comments   This small museum in the Fort Mason Center features changing exhibits of crafts and folk art. On display during our visit were contemporary works of art in silver, hammered brass, found objects (such as manual can openers), and other media. Lots of nifty stuff, in other words, in a bright and cheery setting that's also very small.

Touring Tips   Because of its small size, visit the museum on a Saturday morning, when admission is free.

Other Things to Do Nearby   Fort Mason Center, part of the Golden Gate Recreation Area, houses theaters, restaurants, and art galleries. Aquatic Park provides plenty of open lawns, seating, a sandy shoreline, and the Hyde Street cable-car turnaround. The San Francisco Maritime Museum features a wide array of items from San Francisco's seafaring past. The three-and-a-half-mile Golden Gate Promenade is a broad footpath and bike trail that links Fisherman's Wharf and the Golden Gate Bridge; while usually windy, the scenery is great.

San Francisco Maritime Museum   *Zone 5 Marina*

Type of Attraction   Maritime art, ship figureheads, intricate models, and thematic exhibits echoing San Francisco's maritime past. A self-guided tour.

Location 900 Beach Street, San Francisco 94109; a few blocks west of Fisherman's Wharf
Admission Free
Hours Daily, 10 a.m.–5 p.m.
Phone (415) 556-3002
Website www.nps.gov/safr/local
When to Go Anytime
Special Comments One set of stairs; rest rooms, drinking water, and telephones are available.
Overall Appeal by Age Group

Pre-school ★★★	Grade School ★★★	Teens ★★★
Young Adults ★★★	Over 30 ★★★	Seniors ★★★★

Author's Rating After exploring real ships at Hyde Street Pier, this museum is icing on the cake for folks fascinated by San Francisco's colorful seafaring past; an excellent, nontouristy destination at Fisherman's Wharf. ★★★½

How Much Time to Allow One to two hours

Description and Comments Located in a gorgeous Art Deco building at the foot of Polk Street, this small museum is jam-packed with an amazing array of maritime arti-facts. While the exhibits are heavy on exquisitely detailed ship models (including the battleship *U.S.S. California* and a German five-masted schooner), also on hand are scrimshaw, carved nautilus shells, a ship's medicine box, a seagoing doll once owned by a sea captain's daughter (from the days when skippers took their families on long voy-ages), an exploding harpoon used to hunt whales, nineteenth-century photographs, and some small boats (not models). Not to be missed if you're fascinated by ships, nautical lore, and seafaring.

Touring Tips A great destination on a rainy day. If it's not foggy, the view of San Fran-cisco Bay from the second-floor balcony is terrific. If looking at all those models makes you yearn for the real thing, walk a few blocks east to the Hyde Street Pier, where you can board and explore ships built in the nineteenth century.

Other Things to Do Nearby Aquatic Park features plenty of greenery and seating, a sandy shoreline, and great views. The Golden Gate Promenade is a scenic, usually windy, three-and-a-half-mile path to the bridge of the same name; walk or rent a bike, pack a lunch, and have a picnic at a quiet spot along the way. Aquatic Park surrounds the Hyde Street cable-car turnaround; if the line's not too long, hop on board. Ghirardelli Square and the Cannery are both only a credit card's throw away and are loaded with restaurants and shops. Walk a few blocks east to Fisherman's Wharf and the heart of the tourist hubbub, where you can rent a bike, buy a T-shirt, eat clam chowder out of a bowl made of sourdough bread (at Boudin's Bakery), take a ferry to Alcatraz (with advance reservations), or walk across the bottom of a giant fish tank (at Aquarium of the Bay).

San Francisco Maritime National Historical Park— Hyde Street Pier
Zone 5 Marina

Type of Attraction A collection of real nineteenth-century ships that visitors can board. Self-guided and guided tours.

Location At the foot of Hyde Street in San Francisco near Fisherman's Wharf

Admission $6 for adults, $3 for children ages 12–17 and seniors over age 62; children ages 12 and under, free.

Hours Daily, 9:30 a.m.–5 p.m.

Phone (415) 556-0859 for tickets and info

Website www.nps.gov/safr

When to Go When the weather is good. Wind or rain can make for potentially perilous conditions on ship decks—and because the pier juts into San Francisco Bay, it can get cold.

Overall Appeal by Age Group

Pre-school ★★★★	Grade School ★★★	Teens ★★★
Young Adults ★★★½	Over 30 ★★★★	Seniors ★★★½

Author's Rating Step aboard one of these great old ships and enter the long-gone world of Cape Horn passages and coastal runs under sail. Fabulous. ★★★★

How Much Time to Allow One hour to half a day, depending on your interest

Description and Comments While you stroll the decks and explore the passageways in these old ships, it's easy to make a mental trip back in time. On the *C.A. Thayer*, a three-masted schooner that once carried lumber and fished for cod in the Bering Sea, you can peer inside the captain's cabin and, below deck, watch a video of the ship's final voyage in 1950 narrated by her last skipper. This is nirvana for anyone who has fantasized about a sea voyage under sail.

Other ships to explore include the *Eureka*, a sidewheel ferry built in 1890 and the world's largest passenger ferry in her day. The *Alma* is the last San Francisco Bay scow schooner still afloat, and the *Balclutha* is a square-rigged Cape Horn sailing vessel launched in 1886 in Scotland. Around the corner on Pier 45 you can take an audio tour of the *U.S.S. Pampanito*, a restored World War II long-range submarine.

There are more ships to explore and exhibits on boat building and tools, old photographs, and detailed displays. You may also see riggers working high aloft on the masts of ships and shipwrights using traditional skills and tools. For newcomers to San Francisco, it's a pleasant surprise to discover this fascinating, high-quality national park plunked down in the dross of touristy Fisherman's Wharf.

Touring Tips A guided tour of each ship is offered daily, based on ranger availability; stop by or call the day before for a schedule. If the weather turns bad or you get tired, come back; your ticket is good for five days.

Other Things to Do Nearby More naval history and lore is on display in the Art Deco building housing the San Francisco Maritime Museum (at the foot of Polk Street). Aquatic Park is the perfect place for a breather after the stresses of exploring Fisherman's Wharf. You can also follow the Golden Gate Promenade past the museum all the way to the Golden Gate Bridge. If the line isn't long at the cable-car stop, go for it. Almost directly across the street is Ghirardelli Square, a boutique mall where you can give your credit cards a workout. Boudin's Bakery a few blocks to the east serves clam chowder in a bowl made of sourdough bread; it's good and cheap.

San Francisco Museum of Modern Art   Zone 7 SoMa/Mission

Type of Attraction Modern and contemporary art from the museum's permanent collection of 15,000 works and temporary shows. Self-guided and guided tours.

Location 151 Third Street, San Francisco 94103; south of Market Street below Union Square, between Mission and Howard Streets (adjacent to Yerba Buena Gardens and across from Moscone Convention Center)

Admission $10 for adults, $7 for senior citizens, $6 for students, free for children ages 12 and under (with an adult); half-price admission on Thursday, 6–9 p.m.; free to all on the first Tuesday of the month

Hours Friday–Tuesday, 11 a.m.–6 p.m.; Thursday, 11 a.m.–8:45 p.m. Closed Wednesday and July Fourth, Thanksgiving, Christmas, and New Year's Day.

Phone (415) 357-4000

Website www.sfmoma.org

When to Go Anytime

Special Comments Free 45-minute gallery tours are offered daily, starting at 11:30 a.m. and about every 60 minutes thereafter.

Overall Appeal by Age Group

Pre-school ★	Grade School ★★	Teens ★★★
Young Adults ★★★	Over 30 ★★★★	Seniors ★★★★

Author's Rating World-class modern art in a magnificent gallery that's a work of art itself. ★★★★½

How Much Time to Allow Two hours to get the gist of the place, but art buffs should figure on half a day, easily.

Description and Comments This modern art emporium is just what you'd expect in San Francisco, an international center of the avant garde. Physically stunning and still new (it opened in 1995), the museum is designed to let the Bay Area's fabled light flood the four gallery levels. Even the floors are great; blond hardwood on a springy dance-floor base makes it easy on the feet. A central skylight bathes the piazza-inspired atrium in natural light; from above, you can watch other gallery visitors walk across a white metal bridge that spans the four levels below. Simply breathtaking.

Touring Tips Take a free 45-minute tour; the first is offered at 11:30 a.m. and skips around to various galleries, whetting your appetite and revealing the museum's layout. It usually starts on level two, where the permanent collection features works by Henri Matisse, one of the first modern artists to use color as an expression of emotion. In other rooms you'll see works by masters such as Pablo Picasso and Georges Braque, who relied on form more than color in their paintings. After viewing the art on level two, take the elevator to level five, which features changing exhibits from artists of the 1990s. Bring an open mind and be ready to have some fun. You'll find more outrageous art on level four (walk across the white bridge and down the stairs) and a small photo gallery on level three.

The museum shop on the ground level is huge and has a great selection of postcards (none, alas, of the Golden Gate Bridge or Chinatown) and art books, among other things. Caffe Museo opens an hour before the museum and offers a good selection of reasonably priced items ($7 to $10), including salads, sandwiches, pizza, beer, and wine.

Other Things to Do Nearby Yerba Buena Gardens, with an art gallery and attractive grounds, is across the street. Market Street, with a wide selection of restaurants, is a block and a half away. The Cartoon Art Museum is nearby on Mission Street. Metreon, an entertainment complex with theaters, shopping and more, is at Fourth and Howard Streets.

San Francisco Zoo   *Zone 8 Richmond/Sunset*

Type of Attraction At 66 acres and growing, the largest zoo in northern California. A self-guided tour.

Location Sloat Boulevard at 45th Street; in southwest San Francisco near Great Highway and the Pacific Coast

Admission For nonresidents of San Francisco: $10 adults, $7 children ages 12–17 and seniors, $4 children ages 3–11, free for children ages 2 and under. For residents of San Francisco: $8 adults, $3.50 children ages 12–17 and seniors, $1.50 children ages 3–11, free for children ages 2 and under. Free on the first Wednesday of the month. With Muni pass, $1 off original price.

Hours Daily, 10 a.m.–5 p.m. The Children's Zoo is open Monday–Friday, 11 a.m.–4 p.m.; Saturday and Sunday (and daily in the summer), 10:30 a.m.–4:30 p.m.

Phone (415) 753-7080

Website www.sfzoo.org

When to Go In nice weather. Also, animals are more active early in the day and late in the afternoon.

Special Comments Most animals are in unenclosed exhibits that are open to the elements; bring an umbrella if rain is expected.

Overall Appeal by Age Group

Pre-school ★★★★★   Grade School ★★★★★ Teens ★★★★
Young Adults ★★★★   Over 30 ★★★   Seniors ★★★

Author's Rating An older zoo that's nice but not spectacular. Most animals are in natural habitats behind moats, not pacing in fenced enclosures. ★★★½

How Much Time to Allow Two hours to half a day

Description and Comments   This venerable animal park, which opened in 1929, is making a comeback after the 1989 earthquake (it damaged a few exhibits). Millions of dollars have been spent on innovative exhibits such as the Primate Discovery Center; a recently passed San Francisco bond issue paves the way for more renovations and repairs—and ultimately, the management hopes, world-class status. Unlike most older zoos, the majority of the 1,000-plus animals are housed in naturalistic enclosures behind moats, and visitors can see the exotic wildlife hanging from trees, roaming through fields, and frequently snoozing in high grass.

The zoo's major exhibits include Gorilla World, one of the largest naturalistic gorilla habitats in the world; visitors can get close-up views of the huge primates from strategically placed viewing areas. This is also one of only a handful of zoos in the United States with koalas, the cuddly, eucalyptus-munching marsupials from Down Under. Penguin Island features a colony of more than 50 Magellanic penguins frolicking in a 200-foot pool (black tie required). Another recent addition is the Feline Conservation Center, a 20,000-square-foot sanctuary where rare and endangered cats such as snow, black, and Persian leopards are bred and studied. At the Children's Zoo youngsters can pet and feed barnyard animals such as goats, sheep, chickens, donkeys, and even a llama. Be careful, though: if this South American cousin of the camel starts to smile, he may be about to spit.

Touring Tips   The San Francisco Zoo Zebra Train no longer runs. The Little Puffer Steam Train (an actual steam locomotive built in 1904 and brought to the zoo in 1923)

has been reintroduced to the public. Boarding is located across from the Polar Bears, adjacent to the Zoo Terrace Café. The locomotive will take passengers along a one-third mile route past the blackbuck, sea lions, bears, and lower lake. Each ride lasts about 6 minutes and is $2. Children under age 3 get on for free.

The Panorama Café, slated for completion summer 2002, will most definitely be the best lunch spot. It will be found uphill from the Carousal. The place will be much larger than the current Terrace Café and will provide indoor seating for visitors to escape the ocean breezes and fog that come from being so close to the ocean.

Visitors can schedule their visits during animal-feeding times. The Lion House does feedings at 2 p.m., and the Penguins at 3 p.m. except Thursday, when they chow at 2:30 p.m. Summers at the zoo allow the opportunity to sit on the Meet the Keeper Talks. Please call ahead to get the updated seasonal schedule.

Other Things to Do Nearby   Breathe salt air and feel sand between your toes at nearby Ocean Beach, four miles long and always windy and wavy. But don't plan on a frolic in the surf; the water is always dangerous, even when it looks calm. To the south is Fort Funston ("Fort Fun" to the natives), where you'll find easy hiking trails, great views of the ocean and the seaside terrain, and hang gliders taking advantage of the area's high winds. To the north along Ocean Beach is Golden Gate Park, with some of San Francisco's best museums, trails, gardens, monuments, the Japanese Tea Garden, and a Dutch windmill. Across from the entrance to the San Francisco Zoo is the Carousel Diner, a hot-dog stand out of the 1950s; looming over the parking lot is an oversized representation of a dog clad in a chef's hat. Fans of Bill Griffith's "Zippy the Pinhead" comic strip will instantly recognize this fine example of suburban kitsch.

Strybing Arboretum and Botanical Gardens
Zone 8   Richmond/Sunset

Type of Attraction   A botanical garden featuring more than 7,500 plant species on 70 acres. Guided and self-guided tours.

Location   Ninth Avenue at Lincoln Way, Golden Gate Park, San Francisco 94122

Admission   Free

Hours   Monday–Thursday, 8 a.m.–4:30 p.m.; Saturday, Sunday, and holidays, 10 a.m.–5 p.m.

Phone   (415) 661-1316

Website   www.strybing.org

When to Go   When it's not raining or extremely windy. The California Native Garden is spectacular from late March to early April.

Special Comments   Free docent tours are offered Monday–Friday at 1:30 p.m., and Saturday and Sunday at 10:30 a.m. and 1:30 p.m.; no tours on major holidays. No bicycles, roller skates, skateboards, Frisbees, active sports, barbecues, or pets are allowed in the park.

Overall Appeal by Age Group

Pre-school ★★★	Grade School ★★	Teens ★★
Young Adults ★★★	Over 30 ★★★	Seniors ★★★★

Author's Rating   Blissfully peaceful and beautiful; a chance to further appreciate San Francisco's Mediterranean climate. ★★★

How Much Time to Allow One to two hours

Description and Comments Manicured grounds, paved paths, benches, ponds, and towering trees that absorb most of the nearby traffic sounds are the hallmarks of this world-class botanical garden in Golden Gate Park, which opened in 1940. San Francisco's unusual climate allows an astounding range of plant life to flourish in the gardens, including plants from Australia, South Africa, Chile, Mexico, Central America, New Zealand, and Asia. Seventeen gardens are grouped in three major collections: Mediterranean Climate, Temperate Climate, and Montane Tropic.

Touring Tips The garden has a north entrance near the Japanese Tea Garden and a main entrance on Martin Luther King, Jr. Drive near Lincoln Boulevard. Unless you have a specific interest in, say, the plant life found in New World cloud forests, just wander around in a clockwise or counterclockwise direction, and eventually you'll see everything. The Strybing Bookstore offers botany and horticulture books, cards, gift items, and maps for self-guided tours of the garden and other nearby attractions (such as the Marin Headlands). Hard-core gardeners may want to check out the Helen Crocker Russell Library of Horticulture, the largest of its kind in California; it's open daily (except major holidays), 10 a.m. to 4 p.m. The store and library are located near the main entrance.

Other Things to Do Nearby The Japanese Tea Garden is close to the north entrance of the garden. The California Academy of Sciences across the Music Concourse is very popular with families. If it's a nice day, drive or walk to Stow Lake and rent a rowboat ($11 an hour), or a bike (starting at $5 an hour). Hungry? You'll also find a snack bar at Stow Lake.

Transamerica Pyramid   *Zone 4 Financial District*

Type of Attraction San Francisco's tallest and most distinctive building; a virtual observatory and temporary art exhibits in the ground-floor lobby; half-acre Redwood Park, an oasis of green in the Financial District. Self-guided tour.

Location 600 Montgomery Street, San Francisco 94111

Admission Free

Hours Monday–Friday, 8 a.m.–5 p.m. Closed weekends and major holidays.

Phone (415) 983-4000

Website www.tapyramid.com

When to Go Anytime, but skip it if you can't see the top of the building.

Special Comments All on one level—ironically, the ground level of the highest building in San Francisco.

Overall Appeal by Age Group

Pre-school ★	Grade School ★★	Teens ★★
Young Adults ★★	Over 30 ★★	Seniors ★

Author's Rating Enjoy the building from the distance—say, from Alcatraz. Not worth going out of the way for. ★

How Much Time to Allow 10 to 30 minutes

Description and Comments At 48 floors and a total height of 848 feet, Transamerica Pyramid (headquarters to a huge financial services company) is the city's most distinctive high rise. The structure, completed in 1972, is topped by a spire covered with vertically louvered aluminum panels; at the tip is an aircraft warning light. Two windowless wings rise vertically from the 29th floor; the east wing contains elevators and a stairwell, and the west wing has a smoke tower. Alas, it's a shame you can't ascend San Francisco's highest building to catch the view. But all's not lost; in the lobby is the Virtual Observatory, with four stations (north, east, south, west), color TV monitors, and controls hooked to cameras on the top of the building that let you scan and zoom images of the city's skyline and environs. Is the Oakland Bay Bridge bumper to bumper? Will that bicycle messenger make it through the intersection? If it's not foggy, find out here. The lobby also features changing art exhibits.

Touring Tips Kids, who are the ones most likely to get a kick out of the remote-controlled cameras, will have trouble reaching the controls and may need a lift.

Other Things to Do Nearby Redwood Park, part of the Transamerica complex, features greenery, redwood trees, whimsical sculptures, a fountain and benches, and free concerts on Fridays at lunchtime during the summer.

Wells Fargo History Museum Zone 4 Financial District

Type of Attraction A museum displaying artifacts and memorabilia of the American West and Wells Fargo, the banking and express firm founded in San Francisco in 1852. A self-guided tour.
Location 420 Montgomery Street, San Francisco 94163
Admission Free
Hours Monday–Friday, 9 a.m.–5 p.m. Closed weekends and bank holidays.
Phone (415) 396-2619
Website www.wellsfargohistory.com/museums
When to Go Anytime
Special Comments One set of stairs up to the mezzanine.
Overall Appeal by Age Group

Pre-school ★★★	Grade School ★★★	Teens ★★★
Young Adults ★★	Over 30 ★★	Seniors ★★

Author's Rating Although small, this attractive museum is chock-full of authentic items that make the old West come alive. ★★½

How Much Time to Allow 30 minutes to an hour

Description and Comments A real, century-old stagecoach is the main attraction of this museum run by the Wells Fargo Bank, a firm famous for operating the Pony Express and a stagecoach empire throughout the western United States in the late nineteenth century. Other displays include mining tools, an incredibly complicated harness worn by the horses that pulled the stagecoaches, gold, money, treasure boxes, old postal envelopes, and photographs of the 1906 San Francisco earthquake and fire. It's a bright and attractive space. While not worth a special trip, it's a nice fill-in spot while you're exploring the Financial District, especially if you've got kids in tow.

Touring Tips Don't miss the mezzanine level, where you can climb inside a stagecoach compartment and listen to a taped presentation. The real thing, on the main level below, is strictly hands-off.

Yerba Buena Gardens/Center for the Arts Zone 7 SoMa/Mission

Type of Attraction A new cultural complex of green grass and public art, an art gallery, a theater, cafés, ice skating and bowling, and a gift shop. A self-guided tour.

Location 701 Mission Street, San Francisco 94103; at Third Street south of Union Square in the SoMa District

Admission Gallery: $6 for adults, $3 for students and seniors. Free for center members, Thursday, 11 a.m.–3 p.m.; free for everyone on the first Thursday of the month, 6–8 p.m. Gardens are free.

Hours Gallery and theater hours are Saturday–Wednesday, 11 a.m.–6 p.m.; Thursday and Friday, 11 a.m.–8 p.m. Gardens are open daily, sunrise–10 p.m.

Phone (415) 978-2700 (administration); (415) 978-ARTS (ticket office)

Website www.yerbabuenaarts.org

When to Go Anytime for the art gallery; in nice weather for the outdoor gardens.

Special Comments A nice side trip—and a place to relax—after a visit to the huge San Francisco Museum of Modern Art or the Moscone Convention Center.

Overall Appeal by Age Group

Pre-school ★★	Grade School ★★	Teens ★★
Young Adults ★★	Over 30 ★★	Seniors ★★★

Author's Rating Of more interest to San Franciscans than to most visitors, who must take potluck on Yerba Buena's constantly changing schedule of exhibitions, shows, concerts, lectures, films, and videos. ★★

How Much Time to Allow One hour for the gallery and as long as you care to linger in the five-and-a-half-acre gardens.

Description and Comments Yerba Buena is a nonprofit arts complex that opened in 1993 in the up-and-coming SoMa neighborhood. It features two buildings (a two-level art gallery and a theater) and a park with an outdoor stage, two cafés, the Butterfly Garden, a redwood grove, sculptures, a waterfall, and a memorial to Dr. Martin Luther King Jr. The small gallery features temporary art exhibits that change about every two and a half months; on our visit there was a display of modern and avant-garde paintings and multimedia art—very San Francisco and a lot of fun.

Touring Tips Stop in the gallery and pick up a current copy of the *Center for the Arts* newsletter, which gives a complete description of events at Yerba Buena. If the exhibit looks interesting, tour the gallery. Next, if it's a nice day, stroll the gardens; lunch or coffee at one of the cafés is another option. Free (with admission) walk-in gallery tours are offered on the second Saturday of the month at 1 p.m.

Other Things to Do Nearby The San Francisco Museum of Modern Art is across Third Street and the Cartoon Art Museum is nearby on Mission Street. Metreon, an entertainment complex featuring theaters, shopping and more, is at Fourth and Howard Streets. The area is surrounded by dozens of restaurants.

Part Seven

Dining and Restaurants

The voluptuous pleasures of San Francisco's table still ring with the echoes of the Barbary Coast and Baghdad by the Bay. People have been writing of memorable dining here since Mark Twain sojourned in the city and wrote of its charms in the 1860s. More than ever, people in San Francisco consider restaurants and the culinary arts one of the most important topics of discussion. And the chefs and their patrons concern themselves with both the end result and the entire process—from the origin and freshness of the ingredients, to the utensils with which they are prepared, to diners' and servers' states of mind. There's a personal quality to gastronomy in the city. Chefs adapt the lessons learned in European kitchens to the dictates of locally grown foodstuffs and further incorporate the diverse cultural influences of the region.

Perhaps unique to the city is the possibility of genuinely friendly service. The best San Francisco restaurants are not stuffy or formal and will not treat you with condescension. Most are happy to hear about unsatisfactory service or a dish that was improperly prepared. Unlike New York, San Francisco has few of the imposing, intimidating, ghastly expensive Taj Mahals whose raison d'être has been obscured by interests other than the table. And as for Los Angeles . . . well, San Francisco eats L.A.'s lunch!

This is the capital of the three-star restaurant. Diners want the best in food and service and the best in price. And they want no snooty waiters. Even the four- and five-star restaurants are short on pretense and long on service. The common person is king here; he (or she) just happens to have a discriminating palate.

Whence came this egalitarian attitude? The Old West—with its frontier meritocracy, lusty democracy, and demand for good vittles—is newest here. You still find the legacies of Spanish missionaries and ranchers, Chinese railroad workers, Italian vintners, and nouveau riche gold miners seeking to mirror European splendor. Mix in Japanese, Vietnamese, and Russian immigration. Add the organic and sustainable agriculture movement, local growers' experimentation with artisan crops such as Japanese persimmons, kiwis, habanero peppers, and heirloom varieties of fruits and vegetables; and the blossoming of boutique wineries, cheese-makers, and game farms. Put these with a skepticism of high-falutin' New York ways, and you have the makings of the culinary revolution that began in the 1970s. Creative chefs are drawn to the area because of the year-round availability of superior produce and the relative sophistication of native palates and tastes, along with diners' senses of humor and commitment to a casual brand of elegance.

There's a restaurant to suit any occasion, appetite, or budget. There's also likely to be a very good, even great place to dine within walking distance of anywhere you might be. San Francisco is known, after all, as the "walking city." A brisk walk through the cool tang of a San Francisco fog is one of the best appetizers the city has to offer. And it's free.

Tourist Places

In the restaurant profiles that make up this section, you may notice that a few well-known or highly visible restaurants are missing. This is not an oversight. The following restaurants may come to your attention, but in our opinion they're not as worthwhile as other comparable options.

Sinbad's   *Seafood*   Pier 2, Embarcadero Way; (415) 781-2555

Scoma's   *Seafood*   Pier 47, Fisherman's Wharf; (415) 771-4383
588 Bridgeway, Sausalito; (415) 332-9551

Cliff House   *Italian/American/Seafood*   1090 Point Lobos; (415) 386-3330

Empress of China   *Pan Chinese*   838 Grant Avenue; (415) 434-1345

Lori's   *"Fabulous 50s Diner"*   500 Sutter Street; (415) 981-1950
149 Powell Street; (415) 677-9999
336 Mason Street; (415) 392-8646

The Restaurants

Our Favorite San Francisco Restaurants

We have developed detailed profiles for the best and most interesting restaurants (in our opinion) in town. Each profile features an easily scanned heading that allows you, in just a second, to check out the restaurant's name, cuisine, star rating, cost, quality rating, and value rating.

Cuisine   This is actually less straightforward than it sounds. A couple of years ago, for example, "pan-Asian" restaurants were generally serving what was then generally described as "fusion" food—Asian ingredients with European techniques, or vice versa. Since then, there has been a pan-Asian explosion in the area, but nearly all specialize in what would be street food back home: noodles, skewers, dumplings, and soups. Once-general categories have become subdivided—French into bistro fare and even Provençal; "new continental" into regional American and "eclectic"—while others have broadened and fused: Middle Eastern and Provençal into Mediterranean, Spanish and South American into nuevo Latino, and so on. In these cases, we have generally used the broader terms (i.e., "French"), but sometimes added a parenthetical phrase to give a clearer idea of the fare. Again, though, experimentation and "fusion" is growing more common, so don't hold us, or the chefs, to a strict style.

Overall Rating   The overall rating encompasses the entire dining experience, including style, service, and ambience in addition to the taste, presentation, and quality of the food. Five stars is the highest rating possible and connotes the best of everything. Four-star restaurants are exceptional and three-star restaurants are well above average. Two-star restaurants are good. One star is used to indicate an average restaurant that demonstrates an unusual capability in some area of specialization—for example, an otherwise unmemorable place that has great barbecue chicken.

Cost   The expense description provides a comparative sense of how much a complete meal will cost. A complete meal for our purposes consists of an entree with vegetable or side dish and choice of soup or salad. Appetizers, desserts, drinks, and tips are excluded.

Inexpensive	$14 and less per person
Moderate	$15–25 per person
Expensive	$26–40 per person
Very Expensive	Over $40 per person

Quality Rating   The food quality is rated on a scale of ★–★★★★★, with ★★★★★ being the best rating attainable. It is based expressly on the taste, freshness of ingredients, preparation, presentation, and creativity of food served. There is no consideration of price. If you are a person who wants the best food available, and cost is not an issue, you need look no further than the quality ratings.

Value Rating   If, on the other hand, you are looking for both quality and value, then you should check the value rating. The value ratings are defined as follows:

★★★★★	Exceptional value, a real bargain
★★★★	Good value
★★★	Fair value, you get exactly what you pay for
★★	Somewhat overpriced
★	Significantly overpriced

Payment   We've listed the type of payment accepted at each restaurant using the following code: AMEX equals American Express (Optima), CB equals Carte Blanche, D equals Discover, DC equals Diners Club, MC equals MasterCard, and VISA is self-explanatory.

Who's Included   Restaurants in San Francisco open and close at an alarming rate. So, for the most part, we have have tried to confine our list to establishments with a proven track record over a fairly long period of time. The exceptions here are the newer offspring of the demi-gods of the culinary world—these places are destined to last, at least until our next update. Newer or changed establishments that demonstrate staying power and consistency will be profiled in subsequent editions. Also, the list is highly selective. Noninclusion of a particular place does not necessarily indicate that the restaurant is not good, but only that it was not ranked among the best in its genre. Detailed profiles of individual restaurants follow in alphabetical order at the end of this chapter.

SAN FRANCISCO RESTAURANTS BY ZONE

Name	Cuisine	Overall Rating
Zone 1: Chinatown		
The Carnelian Room	New American	★★★★
Palio D'Asti	Italian	★★★★
Sam Who	Chinese	★½
Yuet Lee	Chinese	★★½
Zone 2: Civic Center		
Cafe Majestic	Californian	★★★½
House of Prime Rib	American	★★★½
Max's Opera Cafe	Deli/Barbecue	★½
Millennium	Vegetarian	★★★½
Momi Toby's Revolution Cafe	Eclectic	★★
Perlot	French	★★½
Ruth's Chris Steak House	Steak House	★★½
Swan Oyster Depot	Seafood	★★
Tommy's Joynt	American	★★
Zone 3: Union Square		
Asia de Cuba	Chino-Latino	★★★★
B-44	Spanish	★★★
Cafe de la Presse	French Basque	★★★
Campton Place	French	★★★★★
Compass Rose	Bar and Grill	★★★★
E&O Trading Company	Southeast Asian	★★★
Farallon	Mediterranean/Seafood	★★★★★

SAN FRANCISCO RESTAURANTS BY ZONE *(continued)*

Name	Cuisine	Overall Rating
Zone 3: Union Square *(continued)*		
First Crush	Californian	★★★
Fleur de Lys	French	★★★★
Grand Café	Mediterranean	★★★½
John's Grill	Steak House	★★★
Kuleto's	Californian/Italian	★★★½
Le Colonial	French/Vietnamese	★★★
Lefty O'Doul's	Hof Brau	★★½
Masa's	French	★★★★★
Original Joe's	American/Italian	★★
Pacific Restaurant	Californian	★★★★
Plouf	French	★★
Ponzu	Contemporary Asian	★★★★½
Scala's Bistro	Italian/French	★★★½
Zone 4: Financial District		
MC²	Californian/French	★★★
Tadich Grill	American	★★★
Tommy Toy's	Chinese	★★★½
The Waterfront Upstairs	Californian/French	★★★★½
Yank Sing	Chinese	★★
Zone 5: Marina		
Ana Mandara	Vietnamese	★★★★
Baker Street Bistro	French	★★½
The Brazen Head	Continental	★★★
The Buena Vista Cafe	American	★
Gary Danko	Modern Classic	★★★★
Greens	Vegetarian	★★★★
Izzy's Steak and Chop House	Steak House	★★★
Perry's	American	★★
Zarzuela	Spanish	★★★
Zone 6: North Beach		
A. Sabella's Restaurant	Italian	★★★
Cafe Pescatore	Italian/Seafood	★★★
Calzones	Italian	★★
Enrico's	Californian/Mediterranean	★★
Fior D'Italia	Italian	★★★½
Fog City Diner	American	★★★
Helmland	Afghan	★★★
Kokkari Estiatorio	Greek	★★★
MacArthur Park	American	★★★

SAN FRANCISCO RESTAURANTS BY ZONE (continued)

Name	Cuisine	Overall Rating
Zone 6: North Beach (continued)		
Moose's	Californian	★★★★
Pastis	West Coast Basque	★★★
Red's Java House	Dive	★
The Stinking Rose	Italian	★★★
Trattoria Pinocchio	Italian	★★★½
Zone 7: SoMa/Mission		
Basque	Spanish	★★★
Bistro Clovis	French	★★
Bizou	Mediterranean	★★★½
Boulevard	American/French	★★★½
The Cosmopolitan Cafe	New American	★★★
El Nuevo Fruitlandia	Puerto Rican	★★½
Fringale	French	★★★★
Hamburger Mary's	American	★½
Harpoon Loui's	Bar and Grill	★★
Hawthorne Lane	Californian	★★★★
Hung Yen	Vietnamese	★★½
Johnfrank	New American	★★★
LiveFire	Eclectic	★★★
Lulu	French	★★★½
Luna Park Kitchen and Cocktails	American	★★
Momo's	Californian	★★
Paragon	New American	★★
Red Herring	Seafood	★★½
Shanghai 1930	Chinese	★★★
Sheraton Palace Garden Court	New American	★★★★
South Park Cafe	French	★★★
Thirstybear	Spanish	★★★
Ti Couz	Crêperie	★★
Town's End Restaurant and Bakery	New American	★★★
Tu Lan	Vietnamese	★½
Watergate	French/Asian	★★★★
Zuni Cafe and Grill	Italian	★★★
Zone 8: Richmond/Sunset		
Beach Chalet	American	★★★½
Casa Aguila	Mexican	★★½
Clement Street Bar and Grill	New American	★★
Clementine	French	★★★★
Dusit	Thai	★★½
The Ganges	Vegetarian	★★★

SAN FRANCISCO RESTAURANTS BY ZONE (continued)

Name	Cuisine	Overall Rating
Zone 8: Richmond/Sunset (continued)		
Pat O'Shea's Mad Hatter	Bar and Grill	★★
PJ's Oyster Bed	Seafood	★★
Strait's Cafe	Singaporean	★★★★
Than Long	Vietnamese	★★★
Zone 9: Tiburon/Sausalito		
Ondine	Californian	★★★★
Zone 12: Berkeley		
Santa Fe Bar and Grill	Southwest	★★★

THE BEST SAN FRANCISCO RESTAURANTS

Type and Name	Overall Rating	Cost	Quality Rating	Value Rating	Zone
Afghan					
Helmland	★★★	Inexp	★★★★	★★★★★	6
American					
Beach Chalet	★★★½	Mod	★★★★	★★★★	8
Boulevard	★★★½	Exp	★★★★	★★★★	7
House of Prime Rib	★★★½	Exp	★★★★	★★★★	2
MacArthur Park	★★★	Mod	★★★★½	★★★★	6
Fog City Diner	★★★	Mod	★★★★	★★★★	6
Tadich Grill	★★★	Mod	★★★★	★★★★★	4
Luna Park Kitchen	★★	Mod	★★★½	★★★★	7
Original Joe's	★★	Inexp	★★★½	★★★★	3
Perry's	★★	Inexp	★★★½	★★★★	5
Tommy's Joynt	★★	Inexp	★★★½	★★★★★	2
Hamburger Mary's	★½	Inexp	★★★	★★★	7
The Buena Vista Cafe	★	Inexp	★★★½	★★★	5
Bar and Grill					
Compass Rose	★★★★	Exp	★★★★★	★★★★	3
Harpoon Loui's	★★	Inexp	★★★½	★★★★	7
Pat O'Shea's Mad Hatter	★★	Inexp	★★★½	★★★★★	8
Californian					
Waterfront Upstairs	★★★★½	Exp	★★★★★	★★★★★	4
Moose's	★★★★	Mod	★★★★★	★★★★★	6
Ondine	★★★★	Exp	★★★★½	★★★★★	9
Pacific Restaurant	★★★★	Exp	★★★★½	★★★★	3

THE BEST SAN FRANCISCO RESTAURANTS (continued)

Type and Name	Overall Rating	Cost	Quality Rating	Value Rating	Zone
Californian (continued)					
Hawthorne Lane	★★★★	Exp	★★★½	★★★★	7
Cafe Majestic	★★★½	Exp	★★★★	★★★★	2
Kuleto's	★★★½	Mod	★★★★	★★★★	3
Enrico's	★★★	Mod	★★★★	★★★★	6
First Crush	★★★	Mod	★★★½	★★★★	3
MC²	★★★	Mod	★★★½	★★★★	4
Momo's	★★	Exp	★★★½	★★★	7
Chinese					
Tommy Toy's	★★★½	Mod	★★★★	★★★★	4
Shanghai 1930	★★★	Exp	★★★½	★★★★	4
Yuet Lee	★★½	Inexp/Mod	★★★½	★★★★★	1
Yank Sing	★★	Inexp	★★★½	★★★★	4
Sam Who	★½	Inexp	★★★	★★★★	1
Chino-Latino					
Asia de Cuba	★★★★	Exp	★★★★½	★★★★★	3
Contemporary Asian					
Ponzu	★★★★½	Mod/Exp	★★★★★	★★★★★	3
Continental					
The Brazen Head	★★★	Mod	★★★½	★★★★★	5
Crêperie					
Ti Couz	★★★	Inexp	★★★	★★★★	7
Deli/Barbecue					
Max's Opera Cafe	★½	Mod	★★★½	★★★★	2
Dive					
Red's Java House	★	Inexp	★★★	★★★★★	7
Eclectic					
LiveFire	★★★	Mod	★★★★	★★★★	7
Momi Toby's Revolution Cafe	★★	Inexp	★★★½	★★★	2
French					
Campton Place	★★★★★	Exp	★★★★★	★★★★★	3
Masa's	★★★★★	Exp	★★★★★	★★★★★	3
Clementine	★★★★	Exp	★★★★★	★★★★	8
Fleur de Lys	★★★★	Exp	★★★★★	★★★★	4
Fringale	★★★★	Mod	★★★★★	★★★★★	7
Watergate	★★★★	Mod	★★★★½	★★★★★	7
Lulu	★★★½	Mod	★★★★	★★★★	7

THE BEST SAN FRANCISCO RESTAURANTS (continued)

Type and Name	Overall Rating	Cost	Quality Rating	Value Rating	Zone
French (continued)					
Cafe de la Presse	★★★	Mod	★★★★	★★★★	3
South Park Cafe	★★★	Mod	★★★★	★★★★★	7
Perlot	★★½	Exp	★★★★	★★★	2
Baker Street Bistro	★★½	Inexp/Mod	★★★½	★★★★★	5
Bistro Clovis	★★	Mod	★★★½	★★★★	7
Plouf	★★	Mod	★★★	★★★	3
French/Vietnamese					
Le Colonial	★★★	Exp	★★★★	★★★	3
Greek					
Kokkari Estiatorio	★★★	Exp	★★★★½	★★★★	6
Hof Brau					
Lefty O'Doul's	★★½	Inexp	★★★½	★★★★	3
Italian					
Palio D'Asti	★★★★	Exp	★★★★★	★★★★★	4
Fior D'Italia	★★★½	Mod	★★★★	★★★★★	6
Scala's Bistro	★★★½	Exp	★★★★	★★★★	3
Trattoria Pinocchio	★★★	Mod	★★★★½	★★★★★	6
A. Sabella's Restaurant	★★★	Mod/Exp	★★★★	★★★★	5
Cafe Pescatore	★★★	Mod	★★★½	★★★★	5
Zuni Cafe and Grill	★★★	Mod	★★★★	★★★★	7
The Stinking Rose	★★★	Mod	★★★½	★★★★	6
Calzones	★★	Mod	★★½	★★★	6
Mediterranean					
Farallon	★★★★★	Exp	★★★★★	★★★★★	3
Grand Café	★★★½	Exp	★★★★½	★★★★	3
Bizou	★★★½	Mod	★★★★	★★★★	5
Mexican/Southwestern					
Santa Fe Bar and Grill	★★★	Mod	★★★★½	★★★★★	12
Casa Aguila	★★½	Mod	★★★½	★★★★	8
Modern Classic					
Gary Danko	★★★★	Exp	★★★★★	★★★★★	5
New American					
The Dining Room at the Ritz-Carlton	★★★★★	Exp	★★★★★	★★★★	3
The Carnelian Room	★★★★	Exp	★★★★½	★★★★	4
Sheraton Palace Garden Court	★★★★	Exp	★★★★½	★★★	4
Johnfrank	★★★	Mod	★★★★	★★★★	7

THE BEST SAN FRANCISCO RESTAURANTS (continued)

Type and Name	Overall Rating	Cost	Quality Rating	Value Rating	Zone
New American (continued)					
Town's End Restaurant	★★★	Mod	★★★★	★★★★	7
Cosmopolitan Cafe	★★★	Mod/Exp	★★★½	★★★★	7
Clement Street Grill	★★	Mod	★★★½	★★★	8
Paragon	★★	Mod	★★★½	★★★	7
Puerto Rican					
El Nuevo Fruitlandia	★★½	Inexp	★★★½	★★★★	7
Seafood					
PJ's Oyster Bed	★★★	Mod	★★★★	★★★★	8
Red Herring	★★½	Mod	★★★½	★★★	7
Swan Oyster Depot	★★	Inexp	★★★½	★★★★★	2
Singaporean					
Strait's Cafe	★★★★	Mod	★★★★½	★★★★★	8
Southeast Asian					
E&O Trading Company	★★★	Exp	★★★★	★★★★	3
Spanish					
B-44	★★★	Mod	★★★★	★★★★	3
Basque	★★★	Mod	★★★★	★★★★	7
Zarzuela	★★★	Mod	★★★★	★★★★★	5
Thirstybear	★★★	Mod	★★★½	★★★★	7
Steak House					
Izzy's Steak and Chop House	★★★	Mod	★★★★	★★★★★	5
John's Grill	★★★	Mod	★★★½	★★★★★	3
Ruth's Chris Steak	★★½	Mod	★★★½	★★★★	2
Thai					
Dusit	★★½	Inexp	★★★½	★★★★	7
Vegetarian					
Greens	★★★★	Mod	★★★★	★★★★	5
Millennium	★★★½	Mod	★★★★½	★★★★	2
The Ganges	★★★	Inexp	★★★½	★★★★★	8
Vietnamese					
Ana Mandara	★★★★	Mod/Exp	★★★★½	★★★★	5
Than Long	★★★	Inexp/Mod	★★★★	★★★★	8
Hung Yen	★★½	Inexp	★★★	★★★★	7
Tu Lan	★½	Inexp	★★★	★★★★★	7
West Coast Basque					
Pastis	★★★	Mod	★★★★	★★★★	4

More Recommendations

The Best Bagels
Marin Bagel Company   1560 Fourth Street, San Rafael   (415) 457-8127
Noah's New York Bagels   Bon Air Center, Greenbrae   (415) 925-9971

The Best Beer Lists
Duke of Edinburgh   10801 North Wolf Road, Cupertino   (408) 446-3853
Mayflower Inne   1533 Fourth Street, San Rafael   (415) 456-1011
The Pelican Inn   10 Pacific Way, Muir Beach   (415) 383-6000
Tommy's Joynt   1101 Geary Street, San Francisco   (415) 775-4216

The Best Burgers
Bubba's   566 San Anselmo Avenue, San Anselmo   (415) 459-6862
Flippers   482 Hayes Street, San Francisco   (415) 552-8880
The Golden Nugget   2200 Fourth Street, San Rafael   (415) 456-9066
Harpoon Louie's   55 Stevenson Street, San Francisco   (415) 543-3540
Kirk's   1330 Sunnyvale-Saratoga Road, Cupertino   (408) 446-2988
Pat O'Shea's Mad Hatter   3848 Geary Boulevard, San Francisco   (415) 752-3148
Perry's   1944 Union Street, San Francisco   (415) 922-9022
Rockridge Cafe   5492 College Avenue, Oakland   (510) 653-1567

The Best Business Dining
Bizou   598 Fourth Street, San Francisco   (415) 543-2222
California Cafe   The Village Mall, Corte Madera   (415) 924-2233
The Carnelian Room   555 California, 52nd floor, San Francisco   (415) 433-7500
The Duck Club   100 El Camino Real, Menlo Park   (650) 322-1234
Joe LoCoco's   300 Drakes Landing Road, Greenbrae   (415) 925-0808
Rue de Main   22622 Main Street, Hayward   (510) 537-0812
Tadich Grill   240 California, San Francisco   (415) 391-1849

The Best Coffee
The Dipsea Cafe   200 Shoreline Highway, Mill Valley   (415) 381-0298

The Best Desserts
The Campton Place   340 Stockton Street, San Francisco   (415) 781-5555
Masa's   648 Bush Street, San Francisco   (415) 989-7154

The Best Dining and Dancing
Harry Denton's   450 Powell Street, San Francisco   (415) 395-8595
Horizons   558 Bridgeway, Sausalito   (415) 331-3232

The Best Martinis
The Buckeye   15 Shoreline Highway, Mill Valley   (415) 331-2600
Compass Rose   335 Powell Street, St. Francis Hotel, San Francisco   (415) 774-0167
House of Prime Rib   1906 Van Ness, San Francisco   (415) 885-4605
No Name Bar   757 Bridgeway, Sausalito   (415) 332-1392
Stars   555 Golden Gate Avenue, San Francisco   (415) 861-7827

The Best Oyster Bars

LuLu   816 Folsom Street, San Francisco   (415) 495-5775
PJ's Oyster Bed   737 Irving Street, San Francisco   (415) 566-7775
Swan Oyster Depot   1517 Polk Street, San Francisco   (415) 673-1101

The Best Pizza

Benissimo Ristorante   18 Tamalpais Drive, Corte Madera   (415) 927-2316
Frankie Johnnie & Luigi Too   939 West El Camino Real, Mountain View
  (650) 967-5384
LoCoco's Pizzeria   638 San Anselmo Avenue, San Anselmo   (415) 453-1238
Milano Pizza   1 Blackfield Drive, Tiburon   (415) 388-9100
Mulberry Street Pizza   101 Smith Ranch Road, San Rafael   (415) 472-7272
Salute   706 Third Street, San Rafael   (415) 453-7596

The Best Seafood

The Fish Market   3150 El Camino Real, Palo Alto   (650) 493-9188
Rooney's   38 Main Street, Tiburon   (415) 435-1911
Sam's Anchor Cafe   27 Main Street, Tiburon   (415) 435-4527
Tadich Grill   240 California, San Francisco   (415) 391-1849

The Best Sunday Brunches

The Buckeye   15 Shoreline Highway, Mill Valley   (415) 331-2600
California Cafe   The Village Mall, Corte Madera   (415) 924-2233
Mikayla at the Casa Madrona   801 Bridgeway, Sausalito   (415) 332-0502
North Sea Village   300 Turney Street, Sausalito   (415) 331-3300
Sheraton Palace Garden Court   2 New Montgomery Street,
  San Francisco   (415) 512-1111
The Station House   11180 Shoreline Highway, Point Reyes Station
  (415) 663-1515

The Best Sushi Bars

Robata Grill   591 Redwood Highway, Mill Valley   (415) 381-8400
Samurai   2633 Bridgeway, Sausalito   (415) 332-8245
Yoshi's   510 Embarcadero West, Oakland   (510) 238-9200

The Best Wee Hours Service

Marin Joe's   1585 Casa Buena Drive, Corte Madera   (415) 924-2081
Max's Opera Cafe   601 Van Ness, San Francisco   (415) 771-7300
Sam Woh   813 Washington Street, San Francisco   (415) 982-0596
Yuet Lee   1300 Stockton Street, San Francisco   (415) 982-6020

The Best Wine Bars

El Paseo   17 Throckmorton Avenue, Mill Valley   (415) 388-0741
Hayes and Vine   377 Hayes Street, San Francisco   (415) 626-5301
Manka's Inverness Lodge   30 Calendar Way at Argyle, Inverness   (415) 669-1034
The Mountain Home Inn   810 Panoramic Highway, Mill Valley   (415) 381-9000
Rue de Main   22622 Main Street, Hayward   (510) 537-0812

Restaurant Profiles

A. SABELLA'S RESTAURANT   ★★★

ITALIAN | MODERATE/EXPENSIVE | QUALITY ★★★★½ | VALUE ★★★★½ | ZONE 6

2766 Taylor Street at Jefferson; 3rd Floor (private elevator); (415) 771-6775;
www.asabella.com

Reservations Recommended **When to go** Lunch, dinner **Entrée range** $23–$45
Payment All major credit cards **Service rating** ★★★ **Friendliness rating**
★★★★ **Parking** Street and 2-hour validated parking at 350 Beach Street **Bar** Full
Wine selection Extensive and excellent **Dress** Casual, business **Disabled access**
Yes **Customers** Tourists, locals

Open Daily, 11 a.m.–10:30 p.m.

Setting & atmosphere The Fisherman's Wharf area often equates "tourist trap"
today, and many visitors and locals try to avoid it. There still sits, however, between the
tawdry shops and weird museums, the true wharf of a working fleet and fine seafood
restaurants. A. Sabella's, 110 years old, is one those treasures. A third-floor location lifts
the hungry traveler above the tourist mania and the floor plan, open and unobstructed,
offers each table a spectacular view of the bay and Golden Gate Bridge through large
curved windows. Plan a sunset dinner or, as it often happens in SF, a view of the famous
fog rolling through the Gate. A cozy bar opens to the left of the dining room, offering
an alternate vista of San Francisco's steep hills.

House specialities Fresh seafood prepared and presented so that the flavors of the
sea are brought out to their best. The seasonally changing menu includes: a variety of
Dungeness classics including crab Louie and crab cake; mixed seafood risotto; capellini
with rock shrimp, fish and mussels; sautéed petrale; steamed Maine Lobster; Monterey
Bay red abalone. Three huge saltwater tanks for live Dungeness crab, abalone, and
Maine lobster are maintained year round guaranteeing freshness and availability.

Other recommendations Pasta, meats, desserts; orecchiette with artichoke, shiitake, and tomato; roasted rack of lamb; the classic chocolate profiteroles. A child-
friendly menu for those ages 12 and under is also available.

Summary & comments Antone and Lauren Sabella carry on their family's tradition
of offering to their guests warm Sicilian hospitality combined with the freshest delicacies of the sea. Brave the carny atmosphere of the waterfront and you'll find that at A.
Sabella's the old wharf is alive and well.

ANA MANDARA   ★★★★

MODERN VIETNAMESE | MODERATE/EXPENSIVE | QUALITY ★★★★½ | VALUE ★★★★½
| ZONE 5

891 Beach Street, San Francisco; (415) 771-6800; www.anamandara.com

Reservations Recommended **When to go** Any time **Entrée range** $14–$29 **Payment** All major credit cards **Service rating** ★★★★ **Friendliness rating** ★★★★

Parking Valet parking or 1.5 hours free at Ghirardelli Square **Bar** Full service **Wine selection** Excellent **Dress** Casually elegant **Disabled access** Yes **Customers** Locals, tourists, and celebs

Lunch Monday–Friday, 11:30 a.m.–2 p.m.

Dinner Sunday–Thursday, 5:30–9:45 p.m.; Friday–Saturday, 5:30–10:45 p.m.

Setting & atmosphere Translate Ana Mandara and you get "beautiful refuge," which aptly describes the setting. Part owner Don Johnson of "Nash Bridges" fame got a Feng Shui master to advise on the entrance as well as areas that would be ideal for water and sound. The layout resembles a colonial plantation: a garden, a courtyard, the house, and balcony. Lots of little nooks and subtle lighting make this a very romantic place. Rare Southeast Asian artifacts, antiques, and intricate carvings grace the walls.

House specialties Khai Duong, the Cordon Bleu–educated chef has done a wonderful job combining dishes inspired by his native village of Nha Trang along with his knowledge of French and California cookery. The Vietnamese steamed crêpe with chicken and shrimp stands out. The lobster ravioli is fusion at its best. For a delicious array of subtle flavors, and a playful sense of presentation, try the ceviche of striped bass. For entrées, basa is king. The freshwater fish is flown in daily from Vietnam. The seared lobster with lobster-roe cognac sauce is a favorite as well as the beef tenderloin with sweet onions and peppercress. The mango soup might be the most exciting dessert in town.

Other recommendations Be sure to walk around. The black-and-white photographs that you see near the restrooms are the work of a famous Vietnamese photographer, Long Thanh. Also, check out the Cham Bar upstairs, a comfy cocktail lounge with a Bosendorfer piano. The full menu is available. Smoking is allowed on a patio area adjacent the bar.

Summary & comments From the traditional to the colonial, Ana Mandara reflects the rich cultural heritage of Vietnam. But it doesn't stop there. Chef Khai says, "I am on a mission to take Vietnamese cuisine to the next level." And that he does.

ASIA DE CUBA ★★★★

CHINO-LATINO | EXPENSIVE | QUALITY ★★★★½ | VALUE ★★★★★ | ZONE 3

Cliff Hotel, 495 Geary Boulevard; (415) 929-2300;
www.clifthotel.com/new_page_1.htm

Reservations Recommended **When to go** All day and night **Entrée range** $22–$56 **Payment** All major credit cards **Service rating** ★★★★ **Friendliness rating** ★★★ **Parking** Valet **Bar** Full service **Wine selection** Excellent **Dress** Casually elegant **Disabled access** Yes **Customers** Local swells and wide-eyed tourists

Breakfast Sunday–Monday, 6:30 a.m.–11 a.m.

Lunch Sunday–Monday, 11:30 a.m.–2:30 p.m.

Dinner Sunday–Monday, 5:30 a.m.–11:30 p.m.

Setting & atmosphere Something San Francisco does best: In-your-face elegance backed up by unimpeachable quality and imbued with frontier egalitarianism. You can come here in a tux or sleek strapless gown; you can come here in a sweater or sport coat. It's dark and velvety and trimmed in redwood and held up by huge columns. Plush booths occupy the corners, tables are lined up by the walls, and a T-shaped bar in the center of the room is good for eating or just drinking.

House specialties The cuisine is based on the Chino-Latino cookery of Chinese restaurants in pre-Castro Havana. Many Chinese emigrated to Miami where they continued to prepare dishes that were recognizably of the Chinese school, yet doused with strictly local ingredients and cooking practices that give the finished product a unique and delicious character. Appetizers include Tunapica, a spicy tartare with currants and almonds soy-lime vinaigrette; oxtail spring rolls; lobster potstickers; and crab cakes with shiitake mushrooms. Signature entrées include coriander-encrusted flat-iron steak with bonito mash; Chino-Latino Peking duck; Hunan whole crispy fish.

Other recommendations Entrées are huge and meant to be shared family style. But the side dishes are just as interesting and could be made into meals. Try stir-fried coconut rice, plantain fried rice, or black-bean croquettes.

Summary & comments You might start with a drink in the adjacent Redwood Room bar. Formerly it was a sedate place, but a renovation and the opening of Asia de Cuba have made it a must-have-a-drink place for tourists and locals alike. At any rate, come here hungry and in no hurry. This is a superb place for lingering and malingering.

B-44 ★★★

SPANISH CATALONIAN | MODERATE | QUALITY ★★★★ | VALUE ★★★★ | ZONE 3

44 Belden Lane; (415) 986-6287

Reservations Recommended **When to go** Any time **Entrée range** $15–$20 **Payment** All major credit cards **Service rating** ★★★ **Friendliness rating** ★★★★ **Parking** Street **Bar** Full service **Wine selection** Excellent **Dress** Casual **Disabled access** Yes **Customers** Local bohemians and Europeans

Lunch Monday–Friday, 11:30 a.m.–2:30 p.m.

Dinner Monday–Saturday, 5:30 p.m.–midnight

Setting & atmosphere If it weren't for the fog, you might think you were in Barcelona. Most of the staff are Spanish; the food and wine are Iberian; the television in the restroom plays videos of Spanish scenes. Only the weather and the well made martinis at the full-service bar proclaim that you're in The City.

House specialties Arroz negra is a signature dish of Catalonia and of this restaurant. It's like paella, a rice casserole, but flavored and dyed with the ink of squids. Now don't turn the page! This stuff is music in your mouth, a common dish in Spain, and you should try it. If that doesn't float your boat try lamb chops in a sauce based on aged sherry vinegar; roasted monkfish with clams and fingerling potatoes; or the dish of grilled veggies known as "escalivada." Yum!

Other recommendations Creamy Spanish desserts such as crema catalana, and lovely things made with chocolate by the people who brought chocolate from the Old World to the New.

Summary & comments Chef Daniel Olivella has spent his adult life pleasing the crowd, both as a chef and as a jazz musician. His current gig is bringing the genuine Spanish article to San Francisco. No cloying sangria, no bland, overcooked paella, and no fake Spanish ham. Nothing but the real thing. Including the wine list with a good selection of sherry and manzanilla.

BAKER STREET BISTRO   ★★½

FRENCH | INEXPENSIVE/MODERATE | QUALITY ★★★½ | VALUE ★★★★★ | ZONE 5

2953 Baker Street; (415) 931-1475

Reservations Recommended; required on weekends **When to go** Weekdays and nights **Entrée range** Lunch, $4.50–$7; dinner, $9–$14.50 **Payment** V, MC, AMEX **Service rating** ★★ **Friendliness rating** ★★★ **Parking** Street **Bar** Beer, wine **Wine selection** Limited but good **Dress** Casual, informal **Disabled access** Good but cramped **Customers** Locals, businesspeople, tourists

Breakfast Tuesday–Saturday, 7 a.m.–2 p.m.

Brunch Saturday and Sunday, 10 a.m.–2 p.m.

Lunch Tuesday–Sunday, 10 a.m.–4 p.m.

Dinner Tuesday–Saturday, 5:30–10:30 p.m.

Setting & atmosphere Bewitchingly minuscule French café and bistro occupying two small rooms with yellow walls and an open kitchen on a quiet, tree-lined street.

House specialties Duck liver pâté; escargots forestière; mousseline of scallops; lamb stew printanier; blanquette de veau; rabbit in mustard sauce.

Other recommendations Nightly specials; for lunch, salade niçoise; baguette sandwiches with cornichons.

Summary & comments Baker Street Bistro would not be extraordinary on the boulevards of Paris, but it is in San Francisco, primarily for its rock-bottom pricing sauced with generous dollops of Gaelic charm. The kitchen is tiny, which makes for slow service; the food is not of a quality impressive enough to write to France about, but it is tasty and attractively served, and the portions are adequate. The daytime café is tres gentil for coffee and a breakfast pastry, or a sandwich, or salad lunch.

BASQUE   ★★★

SPANISH/BASQUE | MODERATE | QUALITY ★★★★ | VALUE ★★★★½ | ZONE 7

398 7th Street; (415) 581-0550

Reservations Accepted **When to go** Any time **Entrée range** $8–$16 **Payment** All major credit cards **Service rating** ★★★ **Friendliness rating** ★★★ **Parking** Street **Bar** Full service **Wine selection** Excellent **Dress** Casual **Disabled access** Yes **Customers** The curious and adventurous

Lunch Monday–Friday, 11:30 a.m.–2 p.m.

Dinner Sunday–Thursday, 5–10 p.m.; Friday–Saturday, 5–11 p.m.

Setting & atmosphere An engaging mix of wood paneling and ceramic floor tiles. It's deep, dark, warm, and cave-like with comfy booths and cosy table arrangements. Soft recorded music plays in the background, yet you still find yourself looking for that strolling guitarist. Contemporary artwork graces the walls, and the creative lighting is seductive. It's a fine refuge from the concrete jungle.

House specialties Mariscos al pil pil is a stunning dish of sizzling shellfish presented as delicious visual art. It looks like a piece of Japanese sculpture and tastes like the highest expression of Basque cuisine. Try the old Spanish regulars like patatas bravas (fried potatoes with aioli and paprika sauce), Pimientos rellenos (red capsicums stuffed with house-cured salt cod), and cordero à la moruna (braised lamb shank with cinnamon and spicy sausage).

Other recommendations Take advantage of the list of sherries and manzanillas, as well as the largely Spanish list of table wines. Tapas at the full bar change frequently with what is available, but they are always good and make an excellent snack or appetizer.

Summary & comments Chef Barney Brown is a landmark, creator of other famous San Francisco restaurants. Wherever he goes, diners tend to follow. While the neighborhood here is rather plain looking and the view is of a freeway on-ramp, Barney makes it worthwhile to come here for dinner. So come.

BEACH CHALET ★★★½

AMERICAN BISTRO AND BREWPUB | MODERATE | QUALITY ★★★★ | VALUE ★★★★½ | ZONE 8

1000 Great Highway; (415) 386-8439; www.beachchalet.com

Reservations Recommended **When to go** Sundown **Entrée range** $15.95–$21.95 **Payment** V, MC **Service rating** ★★★ **Friendliness rating** ★★★ **Parking** Free lot **Bar** Full service **Wine selection** Fair **Dress** Casual **Disabled access** Yes **Customers** Locals and tourists in the know

Breakfast Monday–Friday, 8–11 a.m.; Saturday–Sunday, 8 a.m.–2 p.m.

Lunch Monday–Friday, 11 a.m.–5 p.m.; Saturday–Sunday, 10 a.m.–5 p.m.

Dinner Monday–Friday, 5–10 p.m.; Saturday–Sunday, 5–11 p.m.

Setting & atmosphere Built in 1925 as a tea house, the large, historic building sits hard by Ocean Beach at the western end of Golden Gate Park. In the 1930s WPA artists executed a series of murals depicting life in The City, and they are the first thing you'll see upon entering the ground floor. Upstairs it's big, boisterous, and beery—a bubble and hubbub as people enjoy the food, drink, each other and the stunning view of the Pacific Ocean at sunset.

House specialties For breakfast try smoked salmon Benedict or buttermilk pancakes. For lunch you'll see soup, salad, sandwiches, and entrées like rainbow trout, fish tacos, and roast chicken. Dinner features a catch of the day, New York steak, pork loin with fig compote, grilled vegetables, and pasta. A special children's menu is available for $5.50.

Other recommendations The beers and ales. Nearly a dozen house brews from light to stout. You can also have a tour of the brewery if you ask. There is also a decent, though short, wine list featuring California vintages, as well as a full bar.

Summary & comments There are cozy corners for couples, plenty of space for families, and areas that can be screened off for private parties. This is a good place for a business lunch or dinner. The staff are well versed in the house beers and able to offer sound advice on matching them with food

BISTRO CLOVIS ★★

FRENCH | MODERATE | QUALITY ★★★½ | VALUE ★★★★ | ZONE 7

1596 Market Street; (415) 864-0231

Reservations Accepted **When to go** Anytime **Entrée range** $12.50–$19 **Payment** V, MC **Service rating** ★★★ **Friendliness rating** ★★★ **Parking** Street **Bar** Beer, wine **Wine selection** Good **Dress** Casual **Disabled access** Yes **Customers** Locals, businesspeople

Lunch Monday–Friday, 11:30 a.m.–2:15 p.m.

Dinner Sunday–Thursday, 5:30–10 p.m.; Friday and Saturday 5:30–11 p.m.

House specialties A large blackboard displays a wide variety of daily bistro fare. Hot potato salad with herring; lamb salad with sun-dried tomatoes; smoked salmon in white wine sauce; jumbo prawns with avocado and whatever is fresh in the market that day.

Other recommendations Beef bourguignonne, veal stew, and a delightful range of appetizers and desserts.

Summary & comments Traditional, simply prepared, well-presented French bistro food. Come here for dinner after work; it's accessible from much of the city. Relax, enjoy a glass of good wine, and dine in peace.

BIZOU ★★★½

MEDITERRANEAN | MODERATE | QUALITY ★★★★ | VALUE ★★★★ | ZONE 7

598 Fourth Street, (415) 543-2222

Reservations Recommended **When to go** Anytime **Entrée range** Lunch, $8.75–$14.50; dinner, $16–$25 **Payment** V, MC, AMEX **Service rating** ★★★★ **Friendliness rating** ★★★★ **Parking** Street **Bar** Full **Wine selection** Limited but good **Dress** Casual **Disabled access** Good **Customers** Locals, businesspeople, tourists

Lunch Monday–Friday, 11:30 a.m.–2:30 p.m.

Dinner Monday–Thursday, 5:30–10 p.m.; Friday and Saturday, 5:30–10:30 p.m.; Sunday, closed

Setting & atmosphere Simple, rustic, but warm and inviting small bistro with quiet, exceedingly friendly, efficient service.

House specialties Crisp Italian flat breads and pizzas; baked brandade of local cod; buckwheat ravioli with butternut squash; braised beef cheeks with watercress and horseradish; rosemary-braised lamb shank with creamy polenta; curried vegetable tagine; tomatoes with fresh anchovies in a sherry vinaigrette; Catalan sizzling shrimp.

Other recommendations: Delightfully presented traditional desserts, varying with the seasons. Summer berry pudding; bittersweet chocolate vacherin in crème anglaise.

Summary & comments Jewel-box bistros have sprung up like wildflowers in this formerly industrial area of San Francisco. Attentive, efficient service—along with a quiet atmosphere and some rock-solid creativity and know-how in the kitchen—sets this one apart. Bizou's chef Loretta Keller provides a panoply of sturdy, unaffected cuisine from the provinces of France, Italy, and Spain.

BOULEVARD ★★★½

AMERICAN/FRENCH | EXPENSIVE | QUALITY ★★★★ | VALUE ★★★★½ | ZONE 7

1 Mission Street; (415) 543-6084; www.boulevardrestaurant.com

Reservations Recommended **When to go** Anytime **Entrée range** $24–$32 **Payment** V, MC, AMEX, DC, D, CB **Service rating** ★★★ **Friendliness rating** ★★★ **Parking** Valet, metered street **Bar** Full service, fresh squeezed juices **Wine selection** Extensive **Dress** Fashionable/Business **Disabled access** Adequate (*Note:* elevator to restrooms) **Customers** Business and well-heeled young clientele, tourists and families

Lunch Monday–Friday, 11:30 a.m.–2 p.m.

Dinner Sunday–Wednesday, 5:30–10 p.m., Thursday–Saturday, 5:30–10:30 p.m.

Setting & atmosphere Dramatic, dark, Belle-epoque interior. Velvet curtains, artisan ironwork, and art nouveau light fixtures of hand-blown glass recall the French style of the Audiffred Building in which the restaurant is housed. Striking details include a domed roof of pale bricks and a peacock mosaic design on the floor of the bar.

House specialties Chef Nancy Oakes takes care in searching out the best ingredients for seasonal appetizers such as Heirloom Tomato Salad as well as perennial favorites like her Maine Crab Cakes with red pepper coulis and house tartar sauce. Entrées include several seafood options and a variety of meats. The main dishes always have innovative flavorings from vegetables and spices, but are not laden with sauce. The dessert menu changes seasonally and often features fruit and cream pies. Be sure to try the strawberry shortcake when available.

Other recommendations The wine list is impressive and the wait staff well informed so don't hesitate to try a suggested glass to pair with your dish. You won't feel rushed here so consider enjoying a drink from the excellent bar as you peruse the ample menu, and don't forget to save room for the fresh desserts, especially house sorbets and ice creams.

Summary & comments The experience of eating in this bustling restaurant is surprisingly relaxed. You can gaze out of large windows onto the Embarcadero and the Bay Bridge. The open kitchen also gives an entertaining view of the cooks working the grill and wood-fired oven. The feel here is at once cosmopolitan and comfortable as the crew goes about their work with professionalism and friendliness. To top it all off, the food is wonderful.

THE BRAZEN HEAD ★★★

CONTINENTAL | MODERATE | QUALITY ★★★½ | VALUE ★★★★★ | ZONE 5

3166 Buchanan at Greenwich Avenue, (415) 921-7600

Reservations Not accepted **When to go** Before 8 p.m. and after 10 p.m. **Entrée range** $11.95–$16.95 **Payment** No credit cards; ATM nearby **Service rating** ★★ **Friendliness rating** ★★★ **Parking** Street **Bar** Full service **Wine selection** Good

Dress Casual **Disabled access** None **Customers** Locals, other restaurant workers, writers

Dinner Daily, 5 p.m.–1 a.m.

Setting & atmosphere Except for the lack of trophy animal heads, this place has the look and feel of a rich, cozy, European hunting lodge. All is deep and dark; polished hardwood and brass trim. Antique etchings and photographs cover the walls. A loyal patronage returns regularly, and one sometimes gets the feeling of being in the television bar Cheers. No credit cards or checks are accepted, but there is an ATM next to the rest rooms.

House specialties Meat! (And fish.) As befits the hunting lodge atmosphere, grills and roasts of lamb, beef, and pork. Also pan-fried trout, sautéed prawns, chicken, burgers, and a daily pasta dish. All entrées include vegetable of the day and potato or rice. Pepper steak is the chef's signature dish.

Other recommendations A good selection of salads and appetizers such as crab cakes, oysters, and roasted garlic; mixed greens, shrimp, and Caesar salads.

Summary & comments Situated on a street corner not far from the Golden Gate Bridge. The cheery lights of this place beckon through the San Francisco fog like a warm cabin in a cold woods. There is often a wait for a table, but you can join the locals and regulars at the bar for a convivial drink.

THE BUENA VISTA CAFÉ ★

AMERICAN DINER | INEXPENSIVE | QUALITY ★★★½ | VALUE ★★★ | ZONE 5

2765 Hyde Street (at Beach); (415) 474-5044

Reservations Not accepted **When to go** Anytime **Entrée range** $8.95–$15.95
Payment V, MC, AMEX, DC **Service** ★ **Friendliness** ★★ **Parking** Lot and metered street **Bar** Full **Wine list** Limited **Dress** Sporty **Disabled access** None **Customers** Tourists

Breakfast Daily, from 9 a.m., Saturday and Sunday, from 8 a.m.

Lunch Daily, 11 a.m.–9:30 p.m.

Dinner Daily, 11 a.m.–9:30 p.m. (Bar open till 2 a.m. weekdays, 2:30 a.m. weekends). *Note:* No distinction between lunch and dinner menu

Setting & atmosphere The Buena Vista is more than 100 years old and is situated across the street from The Cannery and the Hyde and Powell cable car turnaround. Communal tables of chunky brown wood and yellowing walls don't deter hoards of tourists who enjoy lively rounds of drinking at the bar and the excellent views of Alcatraz Island, the Golden Gate Bridge, and the bay.

House specialties Tourists flock to the Buena Vista not only to visit one of the oldest restaurants in San Francisco, but also to experience "the best Irish coffee in the world." According to the restaurant's lore, the boozy beverage was perfected by onetime owner Jack Koeppler and travel writer Stanton Deleplane in 1952. The Irish coffee is indeed delicious and takes the edge off the sore feet and cold fingers of tourists who have spent the day hiking through the fog. San Francisco's misty landscape it at its most romantic after a generous shot of Irish Whiskey.

Other recommendations Souvenirs are on the menu here and The Buena Vista gift shop sells everything from cocktail napkins to fleece vests emblazoned with the restaurant's logo. The food is standard pub fare with offerings like cheddar burgers and club sandwiches and nightly specials such as corned beef and cabbage. Chicken tenders and grilled cheese are available on the children's menu. Breakfast is served all day long. At day's end, The Buena Vista is the ideal place for a nightcap, and since it is open late you can go there after the theatre or even after a night of clubbing; but keep in mind the kitchen closes at 9:30 p.m.

Summary & comments The Buena Vista seems to bask in the memory of its own good old days but the bustling crowds of today are convivial. A trip to San Francisco is truly complete after an historic gaze at the bay and an Irish coffee here.

CAFE DE LA PRESSE ★★★

FRENCH/BASQUE | MODERATE | QUALITY ★★★★ | VALUE ★★★★½ | ZONE 3

352 Grant Avenue; (415) 249-0900

Reservations Accepted **When to go** Any time **Entrée range** $10–$16 **Payment** All major credit cards **Service rating** ★★★ **Friendliness rating** ★★★ **Parking** Street **Bar** Full service **Wine selection** Excellent **Dress** Business casual **Disabled access** Yes **Customers** Local suits and downtown tourists

Open Monday–Sunday, 11 a.m.–11 p.m.

Setting & atmosphere It looks like it was designed and built in Paris and then shipped entire to San Francisco. Billed as "a European accent on the plate and in the air," it's a quiet haven popular with stock broker types, and you can often tell how the market is doing just by their composure. The wall of windows gives you a good view of the street and all its passers by. Dark wood is warm and comforting, and the enlarged, framed European magazine covers gracing the walls give it just a bit of whimsy.

House specialties Chef Palomes is a native of the French Basque country, and he brings his traditions to the table. Croque Monsieur is good for lunch; duck confit is great for dinner; and veal Marengo any time. Anything from the sea is good when cooked by the Basques. Palomes specializes in charcuterie, so the house made pates and sausages are always recommendable.

Other recommendations A damn fine burger and fries. Croissant pudding.

Summary & comments The staff is very knowledgeable about both food and wine and you can rely on their advice. And be advised that, true to Basque style, not only is the food delicious but the portions are large and on the heavy side. If you don't want to carry away a doggie bag, you might consider sharing a single entrée.

CAFE PESCATORE ★★★

ITALIAN/SEAFOOD | MODERATE | QUALITY ★★★½ | VALUE ★★★★ | ZONE 6

2455 Mason Street; (415) 561-1111

Reservations Accepted **When to go** Sundown **Entrée range** $13.95–$16.50 **Payment** All major credit cards **Service rating** ★★★ **Friendliness rating** ★★★

Parking Street **Bar** Full service **Wine selection** Good **Dress** Casual **Disabled access** Yes **Customers** Tourists and neighborhood regulars

Open Monday–Thursday, 7 a.m.–10 p.m. (closed 10:30–11:30 a.m.); Friday, 7 a.m.–11 p.m. (closed 10:30–11:30 a.m.); Saturday, 7 a.m.–11 p.m.; Sunday, 7 a.m.–5 p.m.

Setting & atmosphere There are a lot of places in the Fisherman's Wharf area that appeal to the casual tourist who might not give due consideration to dining. But Pescatore is not among them. Step in and you can tell immediately that the feel is old San Francisco. Creamy walls, wood trim, tile floors, and moulding at the ceiling, as well as a full bar in the center of the room all speak "The City" in unambiguous terms. Call it "wharf bistro" decor with old timey pix, models of boats hanging from the ceiling and all warmly lit. It's a comfort station in the fog.

House specialties All the usual suspects in an old fisherman's eatery. You can start with classic clam chowder, or roasted tomato soup. Salads and antipasti, even pizza and bruschetta. Move on to linguini con vongole; crab-stuffed ravioli; oven-roasted sea bass. For the meat eater, order a grilled rib eye or a seared chicken breast with marsala sauce.

Other recommendations Cioppino is The City's signature dish and purists say that it can only be made with the local Dungeness crab. But here they violate the rule and make it year round from Alaskan king crab.

Summary & comments This is also a good place to drink—not to party and dance and get wild and loud—but to drink calmly, coolly, leisurely, as you gaze out the large picture windows. So it is fitting that the house offers a wide range of wines, liquors, and cordials. Enjoy a grappa, a single malt scotch, or even a special espresso drink as you watch through the windows as the local folk negotiate the gathering fog.

CALZONES ★★

ITALIAN | MODERATE | QUALITY ★★½ | VALUE ★★★ | ZONE 6

430 Columbus Avenue; (415) 397-3600; www.calzonesf.com

Reservations Accepted **When to go** Anytime **Entrée range** $11.95–19.95 **Payment** All major credit cards **Service rating** ★★★★ **Friendliness rating** ★★★ **Parking** Street, nearby lots **Bar** Full service **Wine selection** Limited, with a $7 corkage fee **Dress** Informal **Disabled access** Yes **Customers** Locals, tourists

Open Daily, 11–1 a.m.

Setting & atmosphere Cool old North Beach 1960's decor: black tiled walls, lots of brightly colored glass bottles; Italian cheeses, salamis, garlic hanging everywhere; chandeliers. Seating indoors and out, at one of the cute little mosaic tables. A bustling little place with a great location in the heart of North Beach supported by a friendly and attentive staff. Small wood-fired brick oven faces the main dining area.

House specialties Naturally there is lasagna, Gnocchi Genovese, ravioli, also many pasta dishes, pizza, roasted chicken, seared lamb loin, and filet mignon.

Other recommendations Blue cheese jalapeño polenta cakes served with a spicy dipping sauce could be a meal unto themselves, excellent table bread and desserts, weekend brunch.

Summary & comments You'll love the wide windows where you can watch the whole world parade by. The food is served on unusually shaped long oblong platters, and that makes it a little difficult to balance everything on a small round table. Portions were more than ample, but the quality is uneven. The vegetable infused patate puree served as a side dish with the entrées is bland. And the gumbo tastes more like minestrone with some seafood thrown in. Better to stick with the delicious appetizers and then splurge on the flourless Chocolate Decadence. And watch the action on Columbus.

THE CAMPTON PLACE ★★★★★

COUNTRY FRENCH | EXPENSIVE | QUALITY ★★★★★ | VALUE ★★★★★ | ZONE 3

340 Stockton Street, 1st Floor; (415) 781-5555; www.camptonplace.com

Reservations Recommended **When to go** Anytime **Entrée range** $29–$40 **Payment** All major credit cards **Service rating** ★★★★★ **Friendliness rating** ★★★★ **Parking** Valet, $8 **Bar** Full service Wine selection Excellent **Dress** Wear a tie; dressy **Disabled access** Yes **Customers** Businesspeople, tourists, the demanding

Breakfast Monday–Friday, 7–10:30 a.m.; Saturday, 8–10 a.m.

Brunch Sunday, 11 a.m.–2 p.m.

Lunch Monday–Friday, 11:30 a.m.–2 p.m.; Saturday, noon–2 p.m.

Dinner Monday–Thursday, 5:30–10 p.m.; Friday and Saturday, 5:30–10:30 p.m.; Sunday, 5:30–9:30 p.m.

Setting & atmosphere Formal but friendly. Tieless men won't be turned away, but they'll wish they'd worn a tie. Decor is modern, clean, and spare compared to most luxurious establishments. Lots of flowers. An elegant setting for a breakfast of corned beef hash and poached eggs.

House specialties Breakfast is famous here. All of the traditional favorites, including corn muffins that are light as a cloud. Duck ravioli with summer vegetable; lobster Napoleon with crisp potatoes; roasted meats, well seasoned and juicy; variety of terrines; veal rack with pasta.

Other recommendations Desserts, especially the pear tart.

Summary & comments In the hotel of the same name. This is a temple to the muse of American cooking in a city famous for its foreign culinary establishments. Excellent American fare prepared to the most rigorous European standards, without the emphasis on fancy sauces. Mark Twain would have written glowingly of it. It's expensive, right down to the drinks in the bar, but nothing's overpriced. Quality is king, and you get what you pay for.

THE CARNELIAN ROOM ★★★★

NEW AMERICAN | EXPENSIVE | QUALITY ★★★★½ | VALUE ★★★★ | ZONE 1

555 California Street; (415) 433-7500; www.carnelianroom.com

Reservations Recommended **When to go** Sunset, brunch, or any other time **Entrée range** Sunday champagne brunch, $30; prix-fixe dinner, $39; entrées, $19–$46

Payment All major credit cards **Service rating** ★★★½ **Friendliness rating** ★★½ **Parking** Pay lots and garages; street **Bar** Full service **Wine selection** Excellent **Dress** Casual, dressy **Disabled access** Good **Customers** Tourists, businesspeople, locals

Brunch Sunday, 10 a.m.–2 p.m.

Dinner Daily, 6–9:30 p.m.

Setting & atmosphere High above the city on the 52nd floor of the Bank of America Building, the Carnelian Room is a private banker's club by day, and it looks it, with high ceilings, dark wood paneling, soft carpet, and upholstered chairs. But the main decorations are breathtaking wraparound views of San Francisco, the bay, the fog, and the hills beyond. The main dining room is the most formal; there's a lounge with equally stunning views and limited food service.

House specialties Pâté of Sonoma foie gras; Dungeness crab cake with French green bean salad; fresh dill-cured salmon; escargots in phyllo; tableside Caesar salad; twice-roasted duck breast; roasted rack of lamb gremolata; braised sea scallops with Swiss chard; live Maine lobster.

Other recommendations Prix-fixe, three-course dinner; Grand Marnier soufflé with crème anglaise.

Summary & comments Restaurant trends may come and go, but nothing quite equals the glamour of an expensive dinner high in the sky, with a view of the surrounding world twinkling below through an evanescent veil of fog. The Bank of America's high-speed elevator has an unnerving rumble as it zooms to the top, but in the bar and dining room luxury and peace prevail. Service is impeccable if a bit stiff, and the food is fine, though not wildly adventuresome. The prices are, of course, a bit steep. Appetizers and drinks, or coffee and desserts in the more intimate lounge, are an excellent way to enjoy the amenities for less money.

Honors & awards *Wine Spectator* Grand Award since 1982.

CASA AGUILA ★★★

MEXICAN | MODERATE | QUALITY ★★★½ | VALUE ★★★★ | ZONE 8

1240 Noriega Street; (415) 661-5593

Reservations Accepted **When to go** Anytime **Entrée range** $10–$16 **Payment** V, MC, AMEX **Service rating** ★★ **Friendliness rating** ★★★ **Parking** Street **Bar** Beer, wine **Wine selection** House **Dress** Casual **Disabled access** Yes **Customers** Locals

Lunch Tuesday–Sunday, noon–3:30 p.m.

Dinner Tuesday–Sunday, 5–10 p.m.

Setting & atmosphere Bright and colorful. Orderly and well kept. Paper fruits, vegetables, and cacti hang from the walls.

House specialties All of the usual suspects in a Mexican restaurant: tacos, burritos, enchiladas. But there's more: moles sweetened with raisins and dates; ceviche with crisp veggies; carne erlinda; puerco adobado marinated in citrus and garlic and broiled, served with vegetables and rice; roast beef.

Other recommendations Serious seafood, mostly grilled and basted with citrus and cilantro.

Summary & comments One of the most memorable things about Casa Aguila is the presentation. Dishes are sculpted rather than arranged on a hot plate as in most Mexican restaurants. The shapes, colors, and textures of the food are contrasted to bring out their pleasing qualities. Great attention to detail.

CLEMENTINE ★★★★

FRENCH | EXPENSIVE | QUALITY ★★★★½ | VALUE ★★★★ | ZONE 8

126 Clement Street (between 2nd and 3rd Avenues); (415) 387-0408

Reservations Accepted **When to go** Anytime **Entrée range** $14.80–$17.95 **Payment** V, MC **Service rating** ★★★ **Friendliness Rating** ★★★ **Parking** Street and free validated **Bar** Full **Wine selections** Mostly French **Dress** Casual chic **Disabled access** Good **Customers** Neighborhood dwellers, French expatriates

Dinner Tuesday–Thursday, Sunday, 5:30–10 p.m.; Friday–Saturday, 5:30–10:30 p.m.

Setting & atmosphere Clementine is a relaxed neighborhood spot. The dining room looks as if it were imported from a little French town. Peach walls are hung with oil paintings and copper pans. Mirrors and soft lighting create a spacious yet cozy effect. Even when the restaurant gets busy, you feel a sense of privacy.

House specialties The menu continues the authentic French approach. Appetizers include a salad of magret de cannard (smoked duck breast), seared foie gras with a port reduction sauce, and escargots. A fresh pea soup garnished simply with fresh chives is delicious. Main dishes, such as rack of lamb with gratin Dauphinois (scalloped potatoes), are well-executed. Coquille Saint-Jacques (scallops) are perfectly cooked and paired with savoy cabbage braised in mussel juice for a light, interesting dish. Confit of duck, quail, and a veal chop are among the typical French offerings.

Other recommendations This is one of the few places in town where you can find traditional French desserts such as ile flottante (meringue) or a colonel (sorbet and vodka). The pain perdu (French toast) in caramel sauce served with hazelnut ice cream is heavenly. You may also finish your meal with a cheese plate. The predominantly French wine list is not long, but reflects interesting selections. The restaurant's wine buyer favors lesser-known wines as a way of getting higher quality at a lower cost.

Summary & comments Clementine is a small neighborhood restaurant with food the caliber of a downtown hot spot. Service is attentive and the overall experience pleasant. This is a good place to keep in mind for smaller parties who like to talk and enjoy a leisurely meal.

CLEMENT STREET BAR AND GRILL ★★

NEW AMERICAN | MODERATE | QUALITY ★★★½ | VALUE ★★★★ | ZONE 8

708 Clement Street; (415) 386-2200

Reservations Recommended **When to go** Anytime **Entrée range** Brunch and lunch, $7–$12; dinner, $10–$17 **Payment** All major credit cards **Service rating**

★★★ **Friendliness rating** ★★★½ **Parking** Street, metered during the day **Bar** Full
Wine selection Fair **Dress** Casual **Disabled access** Good **Customers** Locals,
businesspeople

Brunch Saturday and Sunday, 10:30 a.m.–3 p.m.

Lunch Tuesday–Saturday, 11:30 a.m.–3 p.m.

Dinner Tuesday–Thursday, 5:30–10 p.m.; Friday and Saturday, 5–10:30 p.m.; Sunday,
4:30–9:30 p.m.; Monday, closed

Setting & atmosphere From the entrance, Clement Street Bar and Grill seems dim,
narrow, and dominated by the bar, but there's a roomy rear dining area with an impressive brick fireplace and a ship's cabin atmosphere. It's simply furnished with dark carpet,
varnished plywood benches, and captain's chairs, but the cut-glass candles and white
tablecloths add a touch of ceremony; coat hooks at the entry lend a genial neighborhood mood. No smoking is allowed despite the barroom atmosphere.

House specialties Daily specials may include roasted garlic with crostini; roasted red
pepper filled with three cheeses, herbs, and pine nuts over spinach salad; wild mushroom tortellini; grilled fish specials; veal scaloppine with wild mushrooms. Vegetarian
offerings include grilled portobello mushroom with warm spinach and hazelnuts; grilled
and roasted vegetables; wild mushroom tortellini with roma tomatoes, garlic, herbs, and
white wine.

Other recommendations Salads, sandwiches, and burgers.

Summary & comments This is a sociable place, the sort of comfortable neighborhood restaurant one might head for when friends drop by unexpectedly. The service
combines admirable professionalism with a nice lack of pretense. The regular menu
offers standards such as steaks, burgers, and a few pastas, but daily special appetizers
and entrées are more interesting, generally decent, and often quite good.

COMPASS ROSE   ★★★★

BAR & GRILL | EXPENSIVE | QUALITY ★★★★★ | VALUE ★★★★½ | ZONE 3

335 Powell Street in the Saint Francis Hotel; (415) 774-0167

Reservations Not accepted **When to go** Tea time **Entrée range** $10–$20 **Payment** All major credit cards **Service rating** ★★★ **Friendliness rating** ★★★
Parking Street, garage **Bar** Full service **Wine selection** Limited but good **Dress**
Business **Disabled access** Yes **Customers** Businesspeople, travelers, correspondents,
and spies

Open Daily, 11:30 a.m.–2:30 p.m.; high tea, 3–5 p.m.

Setting & atmosphere Art deco. Large, spacious lounge comfortably appointed
with couches and easy chairs arranged around decorative coffee tables. Long, polished
bar immediately adjacent to the hotel lobby.

House specialties Caviar, smoked salmon, finger sandwiches—all served with elegance and aplomb.

Other recommendations High tea in the afternoon.

Summary & comments Step in and enter the 1930s. Talk discreetly with private eyes, mysterious ladies, and intriguing gentlemen while the trio plays Gershwin. Indulge your fantasies. This place is rich; better if you are, too.

THE COSMOPOLITAN CAFE   ★★★

NEW AMERICAN | MODERATE/EXPENSIVE | QUALITY ★★★ | VALUE ★★★★ | ZONE 7

121 Spear Street; (415) 543-4001

Reservations Recommended **When to go** Anytime **Entrée range** $15–$24 **Payment** V, MC, AMEX, DC **Service rating** ★★½ **Friendliness rating** ★★★ **Parking** Valet at dinner, lot, metered street **Bar** Full **Wine selection** Good **Dress** Business casual **Disabled access** Good **Customers** Business people, tourists

Lunch/Dinner Monday–Friday, 11:15 a.m.–10:30 p.m.

Weekend Dinner Saturday and Sunday, 5:30–10:30 p.m.

Setting & atmosphere The Cosmopolitan Cafe has two large bars, one upstairs with a television for watching sports and a separate menu of appetizers and one below in the main dining room. Lots of dark wood paneling, trendy light fixtures, patterned carpet, and huge portrait of a couple's embrace give the restaurant a young, if somewhat generic feel. Booths and oversized chairs keep diners comfortable.

House specialties Chef Steven Levine creates "inspiration trio" appetizers and dessert plates in which he uses one ingredient in three different ways. These allow ingredients in season to shine and make beautiful presentations. Look out for Manila clams and creative soups on the appetizer menu. High quality meats such as Liberty duck breast and Niman Ranch pork chop form the basis for large entrées. Seafood is paired with vegetables in season. Similarly, desserts show off seasonal fruit and are charming. A plate of baked-to-order chocolate-chunk cookies comes out with an adorable mini-milkshake.

Other recommendations A diversity of ingredients come together here to make California and New American dishes. Crusts of falafel and semolina replace plain breading. Chilies, soybeans, and arugula-walnut pesto give standard preparations a new twist. The breadth of the menu here is surprisingly wide. It is easy to overload your palate with too many flavors, so order carefully. Look out for some quality California wine choices.

Summary & comments Part sports bar and after-work hangout for young professionals, part California comfort food spot with a complex menu, The Cosmopolitan Cafe is doing a lot all at once. The Levines, a husband and wife team, and their friendly staff aim to please, but some very nice details, such as top-quality ingredients, a selection of artisan cheeses, and fine wine miss their due attention amid all the bustle. Still a fine place to keep in mind for good food in a casual setting.

DUSIT ★★½

THAI | INEXPENSIVE | QUALITY ★★★½ | VALUE ★★★★ | ZONE 8

3221 Mission Street; (415) 826-4639

Reservations Accepted **When to go** Anytime **Entrée range** $6–$12 **Payment** All major credit cards **Service rating** ★★½ **Friendliness rating** ★★ **Parking** Street **Bar** Beer, wine **Wine selection** House **Dress** Casual **Disabled access** Limited **Customers** Locals

Lunch Monday and Wednesday–Friday, 11 a.m.–2:30 p.m.; closed Tuesday

Dinner Daily, 5–10 p.m.; closed Tuesday

Setting & atmosphere A small place in an ordinary neighborhood. Nothing remarkable to look at, but it's clean and well lit, and it has just a touch of class. This is a temple of Thai cuisine, and the votaries of this muse are happily at work pleasing anyone who walks in.

House specialties Most of the items you would expect on a Thai menu, but better than usual, especially considering the price. Orchid duck boned and sautéed with ginger, mushrooms, tomatoes, pineapple, and onions; garlic prawn with black pepper and veggies; sautéed squid with bamboo, chile, and basil; chicken salad with sweet-spicy dressing.

Other recommendations Good fried noodles. Vegetarian dinners.

Summary & comments Lunchtime prices are somewhat lower, although the food is just as good and plentiful. But even at dinner it's downright cheap. For quality and quantity, this place is at the top of the list. It's worth a trip across town to dine well at low prices in a pleasant, undemanding environment.

E&O TRADING COMPANY ★★★

SOUTH EAST ASIAN | EXPENSIVE QUALITY ★★★★ | VALUE ★★★★½ | ZONE 3

314 Sutter Street; (415) 693-9136; www.eotrading.com

Reservations Highly recommended **When to go** Weeknights **Entrée range** $8–$30 **Payment** All major credit cards **Service rating** ★★★ **Friendliness rating** ★★ **Parking** Valet after 6 p.m. or Sutter Stockton Garage next door **Bar** Full service **Wine selection** Good **Dress** Casual to business **Disabled access** Yes **Customers** After-work crowd, tourists

Open Monday–Thursday, 11:30 a.m.–10 p.m.; Friday and Saturday, 11:30 a.m.–11 p.m.; Sunday, 5–9:30 p.m.

Setting & atmosphere Bustling energy comes in from Union Square like the tradewinds halting right at the foot of the 35-foot Dragon Bar. Following an age old love story of Theodore Bailey and his escapades the three story craft brewery and pan Asian grill was designed for the downstairs to give the feel of a trading post and the mezzanine to be the meeting house of refined merchants. And that it does with its framed botanical pictures on ivory walls with palm leaf fans.

House specialties Signature Indonesian corn fritters with chile soy dipping sauce; ginger mushroom tower with marinated portobello mushrooms with ginger and sweet soy dipping sauce; Thai crab cakes with lemongrass, chilies, sweet red onions, and red curry dipping sauce; Thai shrimp with pineapple and cashew served open face in a half pineapple; Malaysian shrimp noodle with prawns, red curry paste, carrots, celery, baby corn, bamboo shoots, water chestnuts, and coconut milk served over a crispy noodle cake.

Other recommendations Indo peanut chicken satay marinated in sweet soy, garlic, and spices; ahi tartare mixed with lemongrass, chiles, cilantro, green onion, and sesame oil; papaya avocado with Asian greens, mint, Thai basil, and sweet hot vinaigrette; Choosing whether or not to have beer or wine with dinner might be a toughie. The beers are excellent and crafted inhouse with seasonal selections. The wines are also good and the waitstaff is exceptionally knowledgeable and adept to making suggestions that compliment your meal. You wouldn't be kicked out for opting for both.

Entertainment & amenities Live jazz and blues on Friday, Saturday, and Sunday. Full Moon Parties and Friday Trading Club offers drink specials, munchies and music.

Summary & comments The menu is a combination of Asian cuisines inspired by Indonesia, Vietnam, Thailand, Malaysia, and East India. To make the most of the experience, have fun ordering a table full of small plates, salads, and satays. Whether upstairs or downstairs, this is a great place to people-watch and feel yourself get sucked into the decor and transported overseas. The plate presentations are equally as imaginative and impressive as the interior designed by Paul Ma.

EL NUEVO FRUITLANDIA ★★½

PUERTO RICAN/CUBAN | INEXPENSIVE | QUALITY ★★★½ | VALUE ★★★★ | ZONE 7

3077 24th Street; (415) 648-2958

Reservations Recommended on weekends **When to go** Anytime **Entrée range** $12–$16 **Payment** V, MC **Service rating** ★★★ **Friendliness rating** ★★★ **Parking** Street **Bar** Beer, wine **Wine selection** House **Dress** Casual **Disabled access** Yes **Customers** Locals

Open Tuesday–Friday, 11:30 a.m.–3 p.m. and 5–9 p.m.; Saturday and Sunday, noon–10 p.m.

Setting & atmosphere Unadorned, uncomplicated, unpretentious, and small. But it's friendly and comfortable, and the staff will treat you well.

House specialties Roast pork with rice and yucca; a variety of plantains; chicken in green sauce; shredded beef with peppers; Puerto Rican dumplings; shrimp in garlic sauce.

Other recommendations Batidos de frutas, thick fruit shakes, or smoothies.

Summary & comments This a good place for a lunch that will stay with you the rest of the day and into the evening. If you're planning nocturnal activities and won't be able to sit down to a leisurely dinner, fortify yourself here first. Que rico!

ENRICO'S   ★★★

CALIFORNIAN/MEDITERRANEAN | MODERATE | QUALITY ★★★★ | VALUE ★★★★ |
ZONE 6

---

504 Broadway; (415) 982-6223

Reservations Accepted **When to go** Anytime **Entrée range** $14–$26 **Payment** All major credit cards **Service rating** ★★★ **Friendliness rating** ★★ **Parking** Valet, $10 **Bar** Full service **Wine selection** Very good **Dress** Casual, business **Disabled access** Yes **Customers** Eclectic

Open Sunday–Thursday, 11:30 a.m.–11:30 p.m.; Friday and Saturday, 11:30–12:30 a.m.

Setting & atmosphere A social gathering place as much as an eatery. Booths line the walls; woodwork and plants throughout. One of the more popular bars in North Beach. Between the entry and the sidewalk is an outdoor dining and lounge area. Excellent for people-watching.

House specialties Pizza, pasta, grilled seafood, and steak; casseroles and stews; Spanish-style paella; duck breast gumbo; market steak with white truffle oil.

Other recommendations Pizza with wild mushrooms.

Summary & comments A San Francisco landmark and tradition. Many local writers have used it as their writing studio or general hangout. The young man or woman studiously scribbling away while quaffing black coffee may be someone whose work you'll be reading soon. Enrico's devotees will argue to the death that Irish coffee was invented here. Every night patrons ensconce themselves in the outdoor lounge and fend off the San Francisco fog with this warm and cheering draught. Who cares where it was invented? This is the place to drink it.

FARALLON   ★★★★★

MEDITERRANEAN SEAFOOD | EXPENSIVE | QUALITY ★★★★★ | VALUE ★★★★★ |
ZONE 3

---

450 Post Street off Union Square; (415) 956-6969; www.farallonrestaurant.com

Reservations As far in advance as possible **When to go** Lunch and dinner **Entrée range** $28–$33 **Payment** All major credit cards **Service rating** ★★★★ **Friendliness rating** ★★★★ **Parking** Street or various lots close by **Bar** Full bar **Wine selection** Excellent **Dress** Business, dressy **Disabled access** Yes **Customers** Local, tourist, business

Lunch Tuesday–Saturday, 11:30–2:30 a.m.

Dinner Monday–Wednesday, 5:30–10:30 p.m.; Thursday–Saturday, 5:30–11 p.m.; Sunday, 5–10 p.m.

Setting & atmosphere A total sensory experience. Farallon's decor is an imaginative seascape done with fine art and whimsy. The entrance and bar area are a kelp and seaweed forest of stylized bronze plants wrapped around glowing light columns that rise to the ceiling. Multicolored blown glass jelly fish lamps hang at various levels quietly lighting the sand colored walls. A bronze seaweed staircase curves up to an intimate balcony overlooking the entrance area. The restaurant swirls like the tide out toward the main dinning area, passing a recessed bar overhung with suggestions of fossilized whale bones, flowing by a scooped-out section of rounded booths and whorled columns. The mosaic floor continues to rise gently to the central dining room, a place reminiscent of some ancient sea cave. It's dominated by a curved mosaic ceiling and the huge, fantastical sea anemone lamps hanging from it. Diners are seated in deep, comfortable booths or rounded tables all dressed in snowy napery and elegant table settings. Dinner here needs to be long and slow!

House specialities Seafood superbly cooked and imaginatively presented. Try iced shellfish indulgence: a dish full of surprises and meant to be shared; yellowfin tuna and halibut tartare; seared giant Sea of Cortez scallop and Hudson Valley foie gras; Silverado sweet corn risotto with fried Florida rock shrimp; roasted Massachusetts wild striped bass; seared prawn-stuffed Atlantic skate wing.

Other recommendations The chef's Coastal Cuisine Dinner: an opulent four-course food and wine pairing at $90 per person. The meat dishes: grilled green peppercorn-crusted pork chop and grilled Sonoma rabbit. Every dessert, especially the frozen Tahitian vanilla parfait with oven-roasted peaches and ruby peach coulis.

Summary & comments Farallon is a very popular place. Come early, before the appreciative crowds sweep in to savor the incredible decor, fine food, and superb service.

FIOR D'ITALIA ★★★½

ITALIAN | MODERATE | QUALITY ★★★★ | VALUE ★★★★★ | ZONE 6

601 Union Street; (415) 986-1886; www.fior.com

Reservations Accepted **When to go** Anytime **Entrée range** $12.75–$22.95 **Payment** V, MC, AMEX, DC, D **Service rating** ★★★ **Friendliness rating** ★★ **Parking** Valet, $6–$9 **Bar** Full service **Wine selection** Very good **Dress** Business casual **Disabled access** Good **Customers** Locals, tourists

Open Daily, 11:30 a.m.–10:30 p.m.

Setting & atmosphere Old North Beach. Spacious and well lit; starched napery; big leather booths and roomy tables. The bar is old wood, and the walls are hung with memorabilia. Quiet or boisterous, depending on the crowd. Situated at the corner of Union and Stockton Streets, the restaurant opens onto Washington Park, where it makes a beacon to the hungry on foggy nights.

House specialties Lengthy list of Italian classics. Hot and cold antipasto; pasta, riso, and polenta; veal, chicken, beef, and fish. A separate and lengthy dessert menu features fresh fruit preparations.

Other recommendations A long list of single-malt scotches and grappas.

Summary & comments Established in 1886, this is the oldest Italian restaurant in the country. Originally where Enrico's is today, it moved to its present location in 1952. The restaurant has survived 111 years of the city's earthquakes and social upheavals, and a sedate, unflappable quality has sunk into the place, as if it knows it will be here when you are not. This breeds a justifiable confidence and a reluctance to rush.

FIRST CRUSH ★★★

CALIFORNIAN | MODERATE | QUALITY ★★★★ | VALUE ★★★★½ | ZONE 3

101 Cyril Magnin Street; (415) 982-7874; www.firstcrush.com

Reservations Accepted **When to go** Any time **Entrée range** $7.50–$24 **Payment** All major credit cards **Service rating** ★★★ **Friendliness rating** ★★★ **Parking** Street **Bar** Full service **Wine selection** Huge **Dress** Business casual **Disabled access** Yes **Customers** 20–30 something locals

Open Monday–Sunday, 5–11 p.m.

Setting & atmosphere Situated on a corner with lots of picture windows this place offers a splendid view of San Francisco walking by. The L-shaped dining room has what appear to be church pews (cushioned) running along the walls, and comfy booths in the corners. Despite the windows on the world of San Francisco, it maintains a cozy cave-like atmosphere.

House specialties Reflecting the tapas trend, First Crush offers about 20 "small dishes" that are super for sharing as appetizers, or for constructing a complete dinner of 6–8 courses. The menu is categorized by source. "From the garden" includes egg-plant and potato terrine, and baked white beans. "From the sea" offers curried shrimp succotash, and pistachio-encrusted oysters. "From the land" provides such things as pork loin with sauce valpolicella, and foie gras sandwich with fig jam. "From the pasture" you can order superb cheeses.

Other recommendations There are also about ten full-size entrées available every night.

Summary & comments So many selections from the menu, and 325 (!) from the wine list make it almost a daunting task to dine here. But come in, sit down, close your eyes and just point to places on the menu. You can't go wrong.

FLEUR DE LYS ★★★★

FRENCH | EXPENSIVE | QUALITY ★★★★½ | VALUE ★★★★½ | ZONE 3

777 Sutter Street; (415) 673-7779

Reservations Accepted **When to go** Anytime **Entrée range** $30–$38 **Payment** All major credit cards **Service rating** ★★★★ **Friendliness rating** ★★★★ **Parking** Valet, $10 **Bar** Full service **Wine selection** Excellent **Dress** Dressy **Disabled access** Yes **Customers** Locals, tourists

Dinner Monday–Thursday, 6–9 p.m.; Friday and Saturday, 5:30–9:30 p.m.; Sunday, closed

Setting & atmosphere The interior, designed to resemble the inside of a silken tent, recalls a movie set for the story of a sheik or a medieval joust. Lots of mirrors and cubby holes; very busy. But it's never too much. It's exotic, colorful, entertaining, yet not distracting.

House specialties Many seafood selections: broiled bass fillet with bits of lobster wrapped in spinach and served with a sauce of beets and chives; salmon with horseradish; lobster salmi; salmon with golden caviar and chives. Also, roast lamb chops; veal with onion rings (really good onion rings); duck in spinach leaves with a juniper and pancetta sauce. A reasonably priced wine list, considering the venue.

Other recommendations The Menu Gourmand, offering a fixed selection of appetizer, fish, entrée, and desert; or the larger Menu Prestige. Both help contain costs in an expensive restaurant.

Summary & comments One of the best, most fun restaurants in town. The service is attentive and formal, yet, like the decor, it's never too much. The food presentations are always pleasing, showcasing the natural colors and textures of the food; nothing is too sculpted or contrived.

Honors & awards *Esquire* Restaurant of the Year, 1987.

FOG CITY DINER ★★★

AMERICAN | MODERATE | QUALITY ★★★★ | VALUE ★★★★½ | ZONE 6

1300 Battery Street; (415) 982-2000; www.fogcitydiner.cc

Reservations Recommended **When to go** Off hours if possible **Entrée range** $8–$20 **Payment** All major credit cards **Service rating** ★★★ **Friendliness rating** ★★★ **Parking** Street **Bar** Full Service **Wine Selection** Good **Dress** Casual **Disabled access** Yes **Customers** Local, tourist

Lunch/Dinner Sunday–Thursday, 11:30 a.m.–11 p.m.; Friday and Saturday, 11:30 a.m.–midnight

Setting & atmosphere The Fog City experience starts from a block away. The streamliner-styled café, ablaze with neon, shimmers through the fog like the ghost of a lost dining car. An art deco interior, dark wood paneling, comfy leather booths with etched class dividers, and low lighting provide the relaxed atmosphere necessary for comfort food dining. About the booths and tables are brass name plaques of regulars past and present who have graced Fog City over its 16 year history.

House specialties "There is nothing so American as the diner," states Fog City's menu, and there's never been quite a diner like this one. Yes, you can find your shakes, burgers, and fries, but the hungry diner just in from wandering The City can also choose from The Large Plates: dungeness crab cioppino with prawns and local fish; grilled Sezchuan pork chop with apple-peppercorn chutney and garlic mashed potatoes; macaroni and gouda cheese with Hobb's ham and English peas. If portion size is important, look to The Small Plates: crab cakes with sherry-cayenne mayonnaise; seared sirloin capriccio with bay artichokes and truffle aioli; ahi tuna carpaccio with wasabi cream and daikon sprouts. A specialty of the house is the combination bread plate: jalapeno corn sticks, sourdough loaf with leek and basil butter, toasty piccolo bread with asiago and sundried tomato butter. Coupled with a glass of wine it's a hardy snack, indeed.

Other recommendations The raw oyster bar and the oatmeal and summer fruit crisp ala mode.

Summary & comments The generous booth size offers diners a chance to get together with friends or family for the pleasure of great comfort food and time together. It's a popular place so make reservations or come at off hours.

FRINGALE ★★★★

FRENCH | MODERATE | QUALITY ★★★★½ | VALUE ★★★★★ | ZONE 7

570 Fourth Street; (415) 543-0573

Reservations Recommended **When to go** Lunch and Dinner **Entrée range**
$15–$23 **Payment** All major credit cards **Service rating** 4 **Friendliness rating** 4
Parking street **Bar** full bar **Wine selection** Limited but good **Disabled access** Yes
Customers Local, business, tourist

Lunch Monday–Friday, 11:30 a.m.–2:30 p.m.

Dinner Monday–Saturday, 5:30–10:30 p.m.

Setting & atmosphere After ten years, Fringale has settled comfortably into this corner of SoMa creating the warm ambience of a southern French bistro, a respite from the
frenetic energy of Fourth Street. Chefs Gerald Hirigoyen and Allen Vitti, together with
their superb staff, provide a convivial, relaxed atmosphere that has succeeded in building
up a cadre of regulars, one of whom often shares his wine with fellow diners.

House specialties Modern interpretations drawn from the rich culinary history of
French-Basque fare: sea scallop and potato "purse" with cucumber and mint salad;
sautéed prosciutto and sheep's milk cheese terrine; steamed mussels with marinated
chopped tomatoes and coriander; New York Angus steak with red-wine butter and
pomme frites; marinated, roast rack of lamb with potato gratin.

Other recommendations Pork tenderloin confit with cabbage, onion, and apple
marmalade; all desserts, but especially the sorbet du jour, an intense palate cleanser, and
the exquisite Biarritz "Rocher au Chocolat."

Summary & comments Embraced by the friendliest of staffs, surrounded by decor
both casual and elegant, and comfortably seated, the diner gradually relaxes into the
bistro mood. Chefs Hirigoyan and Vitti have created a taste of the south of France here
in the south of Market.

THE GANGES ★★★

VEGETARIAN INDIAN | INEXPENSIVE | QUALITY ★★★½ | VALUE ★★★★★ | ZONE 8

775 Frederick Street; (415) 661-7290; www.gangesrestaurant.micronpcweb.com

Reservations Recommended on weekends **When to go** Anytime **Entrée range** 3-
course dinner, $11.50–$17.50 à la carte, $10 **Payment** V, MC **Service rating** ★★★½
Friendliness rating ★★★★ **Parking** Street **Bar** Beer, wine **Wine selection** House
Dress Casual **Disabled access** Limited **Customers** Locals, businesspeople

Dinner Tuesday–Saturday, 5:30–10 p.m.; Sunday, 5–10 p.m.; Monday, closed

Setting & atmosphere Like an island of sanity in a chaotic world, the Ganges's aus-
tere setting, further becalmed on weekends by live Indian classical music on the red-
curtained stage at the front of the room, is a surprise package. Even at peak hours, this
is a restful spot.

House specialties Light, nongreasy vegetarian Indian cooking, including ground lentil
dababs; green chile fritters; steamed savory garbanzo dumplings; curries, including

homemade cheese cooked with peas; garbanzo beans with onions, mushrooms, and spices; baby potatoes stuffed with fresh spices; eggplant with onions and spices; stuffed zucchini; and cauliflower with potatoes and onions.

Other recommendations   Mango lassi, a mango and yogurt drink; sheera pudding, shreekhand yogurt and sour cream dessert with rose water and saffron.

Summary & comments   With the delicacy of its cooking and the economy of its dinners, The Ganges puts most Indian restaurants to shame. Throw in the vegetarian menu, helpful staff, and gentle atmosphere, and you have a real alternative to busy city dining. The Ganges, like the jewel hidden in the lotus blossom, is a rare find.

GARY DANKO   ★★★★★

MODERN CLASSIC | EXPENSIVE | QUALITY ★★★★½ | VALUE ★★★★★ | ZONE 5

800 North Point Street (at Hyde); (415) 749-2060; www.garydanko.com

Reservations Strongly recommended **When to go** Dinner **Entrée range** Tasting menus from $55–$74 **Payment** V, MC, AMEX, DC, D **Service rating** ★★★★ **Friendliness rating** ★★★★ **Parking** Valet ($10), metered street **Bar** Full **Wine selection** Outstanding **Dress** Elegant attire requested **Disabled access** Good **Customers** Well-heeled locals and visitors

Lunch   By private booking for parties of 30 to 35 guests

Dinner   Sunday–Wednesday, 5:30–9:30 p.m.; Thursday–Saturday, 5:30–10 p.m.

Bar hours   Daily, 5 p.m.–midnight

Setting & atmosphere   Fresh flowers, soft wood, and beautiful paintings combine in two peacefully elegant dining rooms. The arrangement of luxurious chairs and banquettes make each table feel like a private paradise while at the same time allowing diners to see one another and share in the exquisite tableside service. Two cheese carts fill the air with their rich aroma. Cherries flambe, among other dishes, are finished before your eyes.

House specialties   Chef Danko has organized his menu into five courses based on a traditional continental meal: appetizers, fish, meat, cheese, and desserts. Diners may choose from three to five courses and portions are adjusted accordingly. In addition, a seasonal tasting menu (five courses) with recommended wines is available. Only the best ingredients are used here, so every preparation is special. Game birds such as pheasant and quail are regularly on the menu. International themes are woven into dishes such as Moroccan spiced squab and shellfish with Thai red curry and jasmine rice. The pastry department turns out precise, beautiful desserts, taking dark chocolate, real vanilla beans, fresh cream, and ripe fruit to the highest heights.

Other recommendations   A mouth-watering salad of lobster, artichoke, fennel, and roasted tomatoes. Loin of lamb cooked to succulent perfection and served with a simple vegetable tian. The wine list is an extraordinary collection of treasures. A good number of wines are available by the half and whole glass—a great feature for pairing with multiple courses.

Summary & comments   The truly professional staff will make you feel like the center of the world. It is worth asking your waiter questions and seeking guidance when ordering. The sommelier is also available to pair wines with your food.

GRAND CAFE ★★★½

MEDITERRANEAN | EXPENSIVE | QUALITY ★★★★½ | VALUE ★★★★ | ZONE 3

501 Geary Street; (415) 397-3600; www.grandcafe.net

Reservations Accepted **When to go** Anytime **Entrée range** $14–$25 **Payment** All major credit cards **Service rating** ★★★★ **Friendliness rating** ★★★ **Parking** Street, nearby parking lots **Bar** Full **Wine selection** Extensive **Dress** Evening casual **Disabled access** Yes **Customers** Locals, tourists

Breakfast Monday–Friday, 7–10:30 a.m.; Saturday, 6–10:30 a.m.

Brunch Sunday, 9 a.m.–2:30 p.m.

Lunch Monday–Saturday, 11:30 a.m.–2:30 p.m.

Dinner Sunday–Thursday, 5:30–10 p.m.; Friday and Saturday, 5:30–11 p.m.

Setting & atmosphere Originally a hotel ballroom, and a very elegant one. Everything is marble, brasswork, and wood. Huge columns support the high chandelier ceiling. There is always a lot of hubbub and goings on here. Tourists gawk at the splendor, regulars table hop, everybody eats and drinks well.

House specialties It's a Mediterannean inspired menu with a good balance of meat, fish, and fowl. For lunch start with vichyssoise, confit of duck and arugula salad, or heirloom tomato salad. Grillades and rotis include oven roasted pork chop on lentilles du puy, vegetable cassoulet, croque monsieur on housebaked sour cream bread. For dinner consider a starter of Prince Edward Island mussels steamed in white wine, Hudson Valley foie gras steak or limestone lettuce salad, grilled asparagus and red potatoes. Follow with grilled sundried tomato ahi tuna, black peppercorn-crusted Sonoma duck breast, or pan seared slmon on potato galette. Selections change seasonally, so be prepared to dine according to Mother Nature, not to what's coming in from Chile.

Other recommendations Side dishes can make a meal. Mashed potatoes, sautéed summer beans with garlic pommes frites, grilled asparagus.

Summary & comments This is a good place to dress up. It's very fancy without being snooty. It opens with a large and comfy cocktail lounge, but it's a very popular watering hole and sometimes simply impossible to find space. Have a drink at your table. Being a block from the Geary Theater this is a good place before or after a show.

GREENS ★★★★

VEGETARIAN | MODERATE | QUALITY ★★★★ | VALUE ★★★★ | ZONE 5

Building A Fort Mason (Marina Boulevard and Buchanan); (415) 771-6222; www.greensrestaurant.com

Reservations Required **When to go** Lunch **Entrée range** $14–$19 **Payment** V, MC, D **Service rating** ★★★ **Friendliness rating** ★★★ **Parking** Lot **Bar** Beer, wine **Wine selection** Very good **Dress** Casual **Disabled access** Yes **Customers** All walks of life

Brunch Sunday, 10 a.m.–2 p.m.

Lunch Tuesday–Friday, 11:30 a.m.–2 p.m.; Saturday, 11:30–2:30 p.m.

Dinner Monday–Saturday, 5:30–9:30 p.m. (Saturday, prix fixe only, $45); late evening desserts, Monday–Saturday, 9:30–11 p.m.

Setting & atmosphere Full view of the Golden Gate Bridge bordered by the southern promontories of Marin County. Large and airy; the restaurant was formerly an enclosed pier. Polished wood floors, lovely paintings on the walls, and comfortable lounging area. Serene atmosphere.

House specialties Mesquite grilled winter vegetables; salad of watercress and escarole, sierra beauty apples, and walnuts tossed with walnut vinaigrette; cubed winter squash baked in parchment with fresh thyme and garlic.

Other recommendations Chocolate sabayon cake crème chantilly.

Summary & comments No health food, no hippie food, no orange and parsley garnish, but the finest in vegetarian cuisine. This is not a PC restaurant, no one is on a crusade here. Its reason for being is the best of dining without meat. When it opened 20 years ago this was the only restaurant of its kind. Some people are saying that it's not keeping up with the new competition. It's still good though not quite great. And it still has what is arguably the best Sunday brunch in town.

HAMBURGER MARY'S ★½

AMERICAN | INEXPENSIVE | QUALITY ★★★ | VALUE ★★★ | ZONE 7

1582 Folsom Street;(415) 626-5767 or 626-1985; www.hamburgermary.com

Reservations Accepted **When to go** Anytime **Entrée range** Breakfast, $3.50–$9.25; lunch or dinner, $6.50–$10.50 **Payment** All major credit cards **Service rating** ★★★ **Friendliness rating** ★★★½ **Parking** Street **Bar** Full service **Wine selection** House, some others **Dress** Casual **Disabled access** Good **Customers** Locals, tourists, businesspeople

Open Tuesday–Thursday, 11:30–1 a.m.; Friday, 11:30–2 a.m.; Saturday, 10–2 a.m.; Sunday, 10–1 a.m.; Monday, closed; specials available after 5 p.m.

Setting & atmosphere Like the lair of a demented antique dealer: baby bottles and broken chandeliers; handpainted mirrors and headless mannequins; chromium starbursts and a life-sized cardboard Elvis; road signs, street signs, soda-pop posters, and sheet music; stained-glass windows and junkshop furniture. All jumbled together and set to driving rock and roll. There's a breakfast counter in front, a barroom to the rear, and a separate (you should pardon the expression) dining area in the corner.

House specialties Breakfast all day. Burgers with mushrooms, chile, bacon, bleu cheese, and/or avocado, served on whole-wheat toast.

Other recommendations Vegetarian burgers, soups, and sandwiches; salads; club, BLT, or crab-salad sandwich. Chipped beef on toast.

Summary & comments The sign at the door reads, "Seat yourself at any available table." Doing so in this 1970s relic is like wandering through the fun house: you have no idea what may appear around the next corner. The food at Hamburger Mary's is unremarkable, though. You can find better burgers with fresher accompaniments in most restaurants around town. Perhaps the best reason to go to Mary's is to eat breakfast anytime in an atmosphere that suggests you're still dreaming.

HARPOON LOUI'S ★★

BAR AND GRILL | INEXPENSIVE | QUALITY ★★★½ | VALUE ★★★★ | ZONE 7

55 Stevenson Street; (415) 543-3540

Reservations Accepted **When to go** Lunch **Entrée range** $6–$10 **Payment** V, MC, AMEX, D **Service rating:** ★★ **Friendliness rating** ★★★★ **Parking** Street **Bar** Full service **Wine selection** House **Dress** Casual **Disabled access** Yes **Customers** Locals, businesspeople

Lunch Monday and Tuesday, 11 a.m.–3 p.m.; Wednesday–Friday, 11 a.m.–7:30 p.m.; Saturday and Sunday, closed

Setting & atmosphere A neighborhood tavern in an old brick building. Old photos of old stars and local sports figures and a big oil painting of a leggy nude cover the walls. Pretty much a male hangout, but ladies are welcome.

House specialties Hamburgers and big schooners of draught beer; fried fish of the day; pasta; salads. The menu changes daily, but you can get on the mailing list and learn of advance changes if you want to be a regular. Everything is cooked to order.

Other recommendations The Blue Plate Special. Free hot dogs at happy hour.

Summary & comments Harpoon Loui's is a neighborhood place that considers itself part of the community. After the Loma Prieta earthquake of 1989, Loui's fed locals on the street. Service can be slow, so don't go when you're pressed for time.

HAWTHORNE LANE ★★★★

CALIFORNIAN | EXPENSIVE | QUALITY ★★★½ | VALUE ★★★★ | ZONE 7

22 Hawthorne Street; (415) 777-9779; www.hawthornelane.com

Reservations Recommended **When to go** Any time **Entrée range** $13–$34 **Payment** All major credit cards **Service rating** ★★★★ **Friendliness rating** ★★★ **Parking** Street **Bar** Full service **Wine selection** Excellent **Dress** Business **Disabled access** Yes **Customers** Demanding locals with cash

Open Monday–Thursday, noon–1:30 p.m. and 5:30–10 p.m.; Friday, noon–1:30 p.m. and 5:30–10:30 p.m.; Saturday, 5:30–10:30 p.m.; Sunday, 5:30–10 p.m.; closed on some holidays

Setting & atmosphere This is arguably one of the most gorgeous restaurants in The City. It's like dining in a museum of fine art. The layout is sleek and modern with clean lines, lots of warm wood, huge floral arrangements, and soft, comfy booths that you can sink into and not want to leave. Beautiful paintings grace the walls, and even the dishes are works of art. It enriches the experience if you contemplate them before eating from them.

House specialties Start with house breads, a basket of which will be delivered to your table upon arrival. They are varied and delicious, pretty and whimsical, and the scent of the sweet butter is seductive. And that's just the bread and butter! Signature dishes include duck roasted in a Chinese inspired–style with green onion buns and a blood orange sauce. Rack of veal is magic in port wine sauce; Sonoma lamb in lavender honey sauce, and pan roasted monk fish are there for your pleasure.

Other recommendations The menu changes with the seasons, and chef Briget Batson was raised on a farm so she is keenly attuned to vegetables and fruits at their times of harvest. Watch especially for seasonal soups and salads. She is especially fond of peas and other legumes, and she will seduce you with them.

Summary & comments In keeping with the decor, the dishes at Hawthorn Lane are beautiful to look at. This is truly food as art. And while the menu is very diverse, it is not confused. Everything fits nicely together. Never worry that one dish will conflict with another. Order what you will and feel free to share with your table mates. You'll all be enriched.

HELMLAND ★★★

AFGHAN | INEXPENSIVE | QUALITY ★★★★ | VALUE ★★★★★ | ZONE 6

430 Broadway; (415) 362-0641

Reservations Accepted **When to go** Anytime **Entrée range** $9.95–$15.95 **Payment** V, MC, AMEX **Service rating** ★★★★ **Friendliness rating** ★★★ **Parking** 468 Broadway; valet $6 on weekdays and $10 on weekends **Bar** Full service **Wine selection** Fair **Dress** Casual **Disabled access** Yes **Customers** Locals, businesspeople, tourists

Dinner Sunday–Thursday, 5:30–10 p.m.; Friday and Saturday, 5:30–11 p.m.

Setting & atmosphere Named for a river in Afghanistan. Rooms are decorated in classical Persian simplicity, and the tables are set with Western, though not stuffy, formality. Beautiful Persian rugs everywhere; walls are hung with Afghan portraits. Afghan strings and flutes play softly in the background.

House specialties Afghan food is heavily influenced by neighbors India and Persia. It's based on flat breads and rice, fresh vegetables, and lamb and chicken cooked in mild spice mixtures. Tomatoes or yogurt are common bases for sauces. Dishes include rack of lamb with Persian spices; chicken sautéed with yellow split peas; potatoes and garbanzo beans in vinaigrette with cilantro; meat pies flavored with onion; leek-filled ravioli.

Other recommendations A good number of meatless dishes and salads.

Summary & comments This is a good family restaurant, and as such it's a bellwether for the changing neighborhood, which was once the heart of the city's topless district. The low prices and the generous portions make this one of the best restaurant deals in town. And it's the only Afghan restaurant in town. You'll find it crowded on weekends.

HOUSE OF PRIME RIB ★★★½

AMERICAN | EXPENSIVE | QUALITY ★★★★ | VALUE ★★★★½ | ZONE 2

1906 Van Ness Avenue; (415) 885-4605

Reservations Strongly advised **When to go** Dinner only **Entrée range** $22.95–$26.95 **Payment** V, MC, AMEX **Service rating** ★★★ **Friendliness rating** ★★★½

Parking Valet, $6 **Bar** Full service **Wine selection** Good **Dress** Business, dressy **Disabled access** Yes **Customers** Locals, businesspeople, tourists

Dinner Monday–Thursday, 5:30–10 p.m.; Friday, 5–10 p.m.; Saturday, 4:30–10 p.m.; Sunday, 4–10 p.m.

Setting & atmosphere Plush. Large, comfortable rooms with booths and alcoves; tables set with heavy napery. A mirrored bar with hardwood floor and fireplace in the lounge. Wall adorned with murals and heavy draperies.

House specialties Prime rib, of course. You can have it thick cut or "English cut"— several thinner slices that some people say brings out more flavor. The jury is out on this, but either taste is accommodated here. Baked or mashed potato; creamed spinach; generous tossed salad.

Other recommendations Fresh catch of the day for the occasional patron who prefers not to have red meat.

Summary & comments One of the older restaurants in town and a temple to red meat. It would be hard to find more civilized surroundings for indulging in that most primitive of appetites. The meat is wheeled to your table on a silver steam cart, and the great haunch is displayed to you in all its glory. "Thick cut, madam? English cut, sir?" It can make you proud to be a carnivore.

HUNG YEN   ★★½

VIETNAMESE | INEXPENSIVE | QUALITY ★★★★ | VALUE ★★★★½ | ZONE 7

3100 18th Street; (415) 621-8531

Reservations Recommended **When to go** Lunch **Entrée range** $6–$14 **Payment** Cash **Service rating** ★★ **Friendliness rating** ★★ **Parking** Lot **Bar** Beer, wine **Wine selection** House **Dress** Casual **Disabled access** Limited **Customers** Locals

Open Monday–Saturday, 10 a.m.–9 p.m.; Sunday, closed

Setting & atmosphere You can tell that it used to be a Mexican restaurant, but don't let it distract you. At the corner of Harrison Street and across from the PG&E, this is an ideal place to meet for a fine Vietnamese lunch.

House specialties Hung Yen is best know for its spicy beef noodle soup: a broth scented with lemon grass and chiles, beef sliced so thin that it cooks in the broth, noodles, onions, and fresh mint or basil. At $6, it's one of the best lunch bargains you'll find in the city.

Other recommendations A full range of Vietnamese fare: fried noodle or rice dishes; combination plates; excellent vegetarian dishes. Soups and stir-fries are the most common preparations. Deep-fried imperial rolls; lemon beef salad; prawn curry; fried pineapple.

Summary & comments According to the extensive menu, "Hung Yen does party. Up to sixty people." It also lists "ten dishes to die for." In good weather diners often avail themselves of the covered patio (which has even more Mexican ambience than the interior). Despite the confused decor, if you can concentrate on the dishes in front of you, you might think you're in Saigon.

IZZY'S STEAK AND CHOP HOUSE ★★★

STEAK HOUSE | MODERATE | QUALITY ★★★★ | VALUE ★★★★★ | ZONE 5

3345 Steiner Street; (415) 563-0487

Reservations Accepted **When to go** Anytime **Entrée range** $14.95–$24.95 **Payment** All major credit cards **Service rating** ★★★ **Friendliness rating** ★★★ **Parking** Street **Bar** Full service **Wine selection** Good **Dress** Casual **Disabled access** Yes **Customers** Locals, businesspeople, tourists

Dinner Monday–Saturday, 5:30–10 p.m.; Sunday, 5–10 p.m.

Setting & atmosphere A modernized version of an old-time steak house. Sometimes fills to overflowing with locals who come for beef, booze, and merriment. You'll see a lot of back slapping, glad handing, laughing, and carrying on here. In the bar, where patrons are in no particular hurry, the generations mix as the big drinks flow.

House specialties Aged Black Angus beef served in he-man portions: New York steak; pepper steak; Cajun-style blackened steak; untampered with, unalloyed steak.

Other recommendations Creamed spinach. Huge and tasty desserts.

Summary & comments Many of the patrons are regulars who live in the neighborhood and know each other. When they meet here it's party time. Don't come for quiet, and don't come overdressed. Come hungry and happy. On Fridays and Saturdays they can't accommodate parties of more than eight.

JOHNFRANK ★★★

NEW AMERICAN | MODERATE | QUALITY ★★★★ | VALUE ★★★★½ | ZONE 7

2100 Market Street, (415) 503-0333; www.johnfrankrestaurant.com

Reservations Suggested **When to go** Dinner or brunch **Entrée range** $18–$26 **Payment** V, MC, AMEX **Service** ★★★ **Friendliness** ★★★½ **Parking** Valet ($8), metered street **Bar** Full service **Wine selection** Ample **Dress** Castro Chic **Disabled access** Good **Customers** Neighborhood dwellers (many gay and lesbian couples), some visitors

Brunch Sunday, 11 a.m.–2 p.m.

Dinner Monday–Thursday, 6–10 p.m.; Friday–Saturday, 6–11 p.m.; Sunday, 6–9 p.m.

Setting & atmosphere The brown wooden exterior of this restaurant dominates one of the Castro's busiest intersections; but the minimalist interior has an airy, sleek feel. Huge windows look out onto the street, which makes for great people watching and also fills the restaurant with natural light. Bamboo, orchids, and details in cream and black create an Asiatic effect that is at once classic and modern.

House specialties Go for the grilled here, where skilled cooks fire up perfect orders of pork chops and tuna steaks. The food is tender and juicy, never overcooked. Appetizers change with the seasons and include produce from small organic farms. Dandelion greens, frisee, and chicory are paired with roasted crimini mushrooms. The flavor of the lentil soup reflects a carefully made stock and fresh ingredients. At the same time, Johnfrank doesn't starve the veggie challenged; plates of carpaccio, mussels, and rich gnocchi more than satisfy anyone's taste.

Other recommendations The wine list is organized by grape variety and many of the international wines are offered by the glass and the servings are generous. The beautiful dark wood bar is an ideal place to meet for happy hour or weekend drinks and offers a separate menu of snacks such as tempura-fried butternut squash.

Summary & comments Johnfrank is an elegant restaurant with a neighborhood feel. It is the perfect place for a romantic meal and the staff is friendly and upbeat. The Castro location, the design of the dining room, and the hip management and clientele make the restaurant a wonderful part of the San Francisco community.

JOHN'S GRILL ★★★

STEAK HOUSE | MODERATE | QUALITY ★★★½ | VALUE ★★★★★ | ZONE 3

63 Ellis Street, (415) 986-DASH (0069); www.johnsgrill.com

Reservations Accepted **When to go** Anytime **Entrée range** $16.95–$43.95 **Payment** V, MC, AMEX, DC, D **Service rating** ★★★ **Friendliness rating** ★★★ **Parking** Street, lot **Bar** Full service **Wine selection** Good **Dress** Casual, Business **Disabled access** No **Customers** Locals, businesspeople, tourists

Open Monday–Saturday, 11 a.m.–10 p.m.; Sunday, 5–10 p.m.

Setting & atmosphere Dark wood and brass trim; the 1930s at their best. You're transported to another (many would say better) San Francisco. Sepia photographs of celebs and local potentates cover the west wall. Deep and narrow with booths and small tables; the general feeling is one of cozy intimacy.

House specialties Steaks, chops, and seafood. Dungeness crab cakes (a must at any historic place in the city); fried oysters; sand dabs; Sam Spade's lamb chops; pork chops with apple sauce; a giant porterhouse steak; broiled calf livers; chicken Jerusalem.

Other recommendations Variety of salads; clam chowder; oysters Wellington.

Summary & comments "Spade went to John's Grill, asked the waiter to hurry his order of chops, baked potato, sliced tomatoes . . . and was smoking a cigarette with his coffee when . . . ." Open since 1908, this landmark restaurant was the setting for Dashiell Hammett's novel *The Maltese Falcon.* To dine or drink martinis here is to imbibe the history and literature of the city.

KOKKARI ESTIATORIO ★★★

GREEK | EXPENSIVE | QUALITY ★★★★½ | VALUE ★★★★ | ZONE 6

200 Jackson Street (at Front); (415) 981-0983; www.kokkari.com

Reservations Recommended **When to go** Anytime **Entrée range** $16.50–$32.95 **Payment** V, MC, AMEX, DC, D **Service rating** ★★★ **Friendliness rating** ★★★ **Parking** Valet at dinner, metered street, lots **Bar** Full service **Wine selection** Extensive **Dress** Fashionable, business, or semi-formal attire **Disabled access** Reasonable (elevator to restrooms) **Customers** Well-heeled crowd of locals and tourists

Lunch Monday–Friday, 11:30 a.m.–2:30 p.m.; bar menu, 2:30–5:30 p.m.

Dinner Monday–Thursday, 5:30–10 p.m.; Saturday, 5–11 p.m.

Setting & atmosphere Kokkari has a dramatic setting with a number of unique details such as huge wood-shuttered windows and an enormous fireplace. Everything, from the chairs to the water glasses, is oversized. The dark and elegant space envelopes and transports you to a far off place more elegant than Athens.

House specialties Traditional Greek dishes are put in their best light through thoughtful preparation and good ingredients. Lamb shanks and chops brought in from a Texas ranch have diners raving. Seafood offerings such as flash fried smelt and a whole grilled striped bass are simply but beautifully prepared. A plateful of Greek spreads makes a mouth watering appetizer with tzatziki so rich that it is hard to believe it was made with yogurt alone; and don't forget the hot grilled pita bread. Everything at Kokkari is perfectly fresh.

Other recommendations You can't go wrong when ordering at this restaurant so don't be afraid to try something different. The chefs at Kokkari have respect for tradition but also know how to innovate. A bowl of risotto with herbed feta and fava beans uses Greek staples in the style of California cuisine. A roasted quail with poached figs and quail jus demonstrates similar inspiration. Desserts such as yogurt sorbet and tangerine-mint granita lift up the palate at the end of a long meal. Details such as crispy tuile never miss a note.

Summary & comments Kokkari has a grand and lavish feel befitting a special occasion. Two separate rooms are available for private events and the main dining rooms, while not packed, feel somehow communal. The perfect setting for a clan-like family celebration. The food here is fit for kings but retains its connection to the earth. A truly outstanding dining experience.

KULETO'S ★★★½

CALIFORNIAN/ITALIAN | MODERATE | QUALITY ★★★★ | VALUE ★★★★ | ZONE 3

221 Powell Street, (415) 397-7720; www.kimptongroup.com/kuleto_s.html

Reservations Recommended **When to go** Any time **Entrée range** $10–$25 **Payment** All major credit cards **Service rating** ★★★ **Friendliness rating** ★★★★ **Parking** Street **Bar** Full service **Wine selection** Good **Dress** Smart/casual **Disabled access** Yes **Customers** Tourists and local regulars

Open Monday–Sunday, 7 a.m.–11 p.m.

Setting & atmosphere Enter through the adjacent wine bar with its hardwood floor, marble table tops and friendly staff. Here in a corner of the lobby of the elegant Villa Florence hotel ask for the advice of the bar staff on how to begin your wine and dine experience. After a glass of something sparkling, amble over to the main restaurant. High vaulted ceilings, Italian marble floors, wrought iron and copper railings backed by dark wood and warm lighting provide a gleeful combination of old San Francisco elegance and Italian verve and vitality.

House specialties Contemporary Italian cuisine with a concentration on fresh Californian ingredients. Excellent house-made pastas, traditional Italian salads with balsamic vinegar, mesquite grilled fresh fish, and flavorful meats. All baked goods, pastries, and desserts are prepared daily in-house.

Other recommendations Desserts are outstanding. Crisp cannoli pastry shells filled with mascarpone cream and toasted pistachios; warm peach-and-blackberry cobbler with house-made vanilla gelato; lime-champagne zabaglione with fresh seasonal berries; tiramisu, espresso, and rum-soaked ladyfinders with mascarpone cream.

Summary & comments This is a warm and festive place, always full of happy, convivial people looking for a good meal and a good time. Tourists and locals alike find their way here, and they usually find their way back.

LE COLONIAL ★★½

FRENCH/VIETNAMESE | EXPENSIVE | QUALITY ★★★★ | VALUE ★★★ | ZONE 3

20 Cosmo Place (between Taylor and Jones, Sutter and Post); (415) 931-3600; www.lecolonialsf.com

Reservations Recommended **When to go** Any time **Entrée range** $12–$32 **Payment** All major credit cards **Service rating** ★★★★ **Friendliness rating** ★★★★ **Parking** Valet parking, $4 for first hour, $2 each 30 minutes thereafter **Bar** Full service **Wine selection** Very good **Dress** Casually elegant, no athletic wear **Disabled access** Yes **Customers** Trendy locals in the know

Dinner Sunday–Thursday, 5:30–9:30 p.m.; Friday–Saturday, 5:30–11 p.m.

Setting & atmosphere Rattan couches and chairs, wooden shutters, ceiling fans, and palm fronds transport you back to a bygone time of colonial enterprise. This 1920s-themed two-tiered French-Vietnamese restaurant certainly does more than serve fine food; between the tropical decor and savory tastes you might well forget you're in San Francisco. Downstairs is the more formal dining area. Upstairs, hipsters enjoy the trendy watering hole where jazz can be heard on Friday and Saturday nights starting at 10 p.m..

House specialties Most dishes, particularly the appetizers, are for sharing. The crispy spring rolls with shrimp, pork, and chili fish sauce come highly recommended. Many enjoy the mini crab cakes and so should you. They're served with a wonderfully harmonized chili-lime sauce. Dinner entrées: steamed sea bass wrapped in a banana leaf with shiitake mushrooms, ginger, and scallions is a favorite. The Maine lobster is also popular.

Other recommendations There's a fine selection of Scotch and lots of tropical concoctions. Smoke on the patio downstairs or upstairs on the outdoor verandah. Other civil establishments in The City only offer the sidewalk.

Summary & comments Le Colonial is good place to relax and take in the social scene of San Francisco. There is plenty to contemplate: Asian-inspired dishes prepared with local ingredients; an urban and cosmopolitan crowd. The sounds of many languages and the teasing aroma of a varied cuisine. Period photographs from Vietnam grace the walls. The Orient, Europe, and California meet here for a gracious time.

LEFTY O'DOUL'S ★★½

HOFBRAU | INEXPENSIVE | QUALITY ★★★½ | VALUE ★★★★ | ZONE 3

333 Geary Boulevard, (415) 982-8900

Reservations Not accepted **When to go** Anytime **Entrée range** $5–$10 **Payment** V, MC **Service rating:** ★★ **Friendliness rating** ★★★ **Parking** Street **Bar** Full ser-

vice **Wine selection** House **Dress** Casual **Disabled access** Limited **Customers**
Locals, businesspeople

Open Daily, 7–2 a.m. Breakfast is served weekdays 7–11 a.m. and Saturday and Sunday
until 1 p.m.

Setting & atmosphere A rather gritty sports bar with a steam table and a baby grand
piano. Directly across the street from the elegant Compass Rose in the Saint Francis
Hotel, Lefty's seems to have been put there deliberately to add counterpoint to the high-
toned hostelry and its expensive watering hole.

House specialties All the usual roasts: beef, turkey, ham. Dinner plates, hot open-
faced sandwiches. Polish sausage, lasagna, soup, salad, and daily specials. Omelettes and
pancakes for breakfast.

Summary & comments Named for the baseball player, this is a neighborhood institution full of regulars and hungry shoppers. It's big and cavernous, yet it maintains an air
of cozy familiarity. It's also considered neutral ground by warring factions. When the San
Francisco 49ers won their first Super Bowl there was pandemonium in the streets and
a huge police presence. The celebrations went on long into the night, exhausting cops,
revelers, and paddy-wagon drivers. Between skirmishes, both sides could be seen recu-
perating at adjacent tables in Lefty's.

LIVEFIRE ★★★

ECLECTIC | MODERATE | QUALITY ★★★★ | VALUE ★★★★ | ZONE 7

100 Brannan Street, (415) 227-0777; www.livefiresf.com

Reservations Recommended **When to go** Any time **Entrée range** $11.50–$25.95
Payment All major credit cards **Service rating** ★★★ **Friendliness rating** ★★
Parking Street **Bar** Full service **Wine selection** Good **Dress** Casual **Disabled
access** Yes **Customers** Locals in the know

Open Monday–Sunday, 5–11 p.m.

Setting & atmosphere A popular watering hole as well as a trendy restaurant. The
full bar is walled by glass and provides a stunning view of the San Francisco Bay all the
way to Oakland and the hills beyond. The ultra modern design of the dining room is
conducive to table hopping and schmoozing, so come and schmooze. And contemplate
a menu that is unique, unexpected, and delightful.

House specialties Do not leave this place without tasting Fred's Famous French
Nachos. Fresh, house made, big, fat potato chips piled with Danish blue cheese and
dressed with pesto. Comfort food deluxe. Try barbequed oysters with sweet onion jam;
grilled asparagus with romesco sauce; a range of pizza, pasta, and risotto; wood grills and
oven fired plates such as salmon with steamed potatoes, striped bass with tomato confit, marinated crispy duck with caramelized carrots, a salade Nicoise with grilled ahi tuna.

Other recommendations Side dishes are good enough that you could make a meal
of four of them. Try herb dumplings, roast potatoes and garlic, garlic mashies, sautéed
broccoli rabe. And for dessert a hot fudge sundae.

Summary & comments With all the glass surrounding you, this is a great place to
come at sunset, even if only for a drink. But you'll be cheating yourself if you don't stay
for dinner.

LULU ★★★½

RUSTIC FRENCH/PROVENCALE | MODERATE | QUALITY ★★★★ | VALUE ★★★★½ |
ZONE 7

816 Folsom Street, (415) 495-5775; www.restaurantlulu.com

Reservations Recommended **When to go** Anytime **Entrée range** $10.95–$22.95
Payment V, MC, AMEX, DC **Service rating** ★★★ **Friendliness rating** ★★★
Parking Valet, $10 **Bar** Full service **Wine selection** Extensive **Dress** Fashionably
casual **Disabled access** Good **Customers** Locals, businesspeople, some tourists

Open Monday–Thursday, 11:30 a.m.–10:30 p.m.; Friday and Saturday, 11:30 a.m.–
11:30 p.m.

Setting & atmosphere Towering ceilings, skylights, statuesque floral arrangements
all add to the wide open feeling of space within this environment. The muted tones of
the walls are offset by a vibrant wall mural, which complements the bustling and festive
ambience of this place. Family style dining: massive portions served on gorgeous blue
and yellow crockery just perfect for sharing.

House specialties Changing seasonal menu, nightly rotisserie specials. Predominantly
Mediterranean influenced dishes: delicious Fritto Misto with aïoli and parmesan; goat
cheese with calamata olives; a very dramatic serving of iron skillet roasted mussels;
incredibly moist pork loin with fennel; fresh salmon with fava beans, corn, leeks and
basil broth. The vegetable side dishes are not to be missed. The olive oil mashed potatoes and piquant broccoli rabe both particular standouts.

Other recommendations The restaurant is making an effort to put more of an
emphasis on wine here, now pouring over 70 different wines by the glass as well as
ample choices for dessert. But the bar itself is also worth note, serving a martini prepared perfectly to instructions as well as an interesting liqueur-laced machiotto.

Summary & comments It's great to see that the nature of service has improved
radically since previous visits. The noise level is a bit daunting at first, but the knowlegable and helpful staff put one almost immediately at ease. Lulu is a class act from start
to finish.

LUNA PARK KITCHEN AND COCKTAILS ★★

AMERICAN | MODERATE | QUALITY ★★★½ | VALUE ★★★★ | ZONE 7

694 Valencia Street, (415) 553-8584; www.lunaparksf.com

Reservations Recommended **When to go** Lunch and dinner **Entrée range**
$12.75–$13.95 **Payment** V, MC, AMEX, DC **Service rating** ★★★ **Friendliness
rating** ★★★ **Bar** Full **Wine selection** Good **Dress** Very casual **Disabled access**
Good **Customers** Local

Open Lunch Monday–Friday, 11:30 a.m.–2:30 p.m.

Dinner Monday–Thursday, 5:30–10:30 p.m.; Friday–Saturday, 5:30–11:30 p.m.; Sunday,
5:30–10 p.m.

Setting & atmosphere The Mission District has long been known for down to Earth restaurants with reasonable prices, and Luna carries on the tradition. A small storefront entrance opens onto an airy rectangular space made cool and inviting by its dark maroon walls. Deep booths line the walls and surround a small central dining area while colorful crystal chandeliers run the length of the room. The open kitchen bustles with activity and emanates warmth and good smells. A bar extends along one side providing the neighborhood with a pleasant gathering place.

House specialities Comfort food with patrician taste is what Luna is all about: marinated Hawaiian tuna "Poke" with fried wonton chips; Chef Joe Jack's tomato stack with heirloom tomatoes and fresh mozzarella; braised pork cutlet stuffed with mushrooms and Gruyere cheese combined with mashed potatoes, string beans, and apple-cranberry sauce; slowly simmered beef brisket, carrots, turnips, leeks, and potato in broth.

Other recommendations Desserts made to cure the blues, especially: bananas Foster with banana ice cream; s'mores you make at the table: molten marshmallow and bittersweet chocolate served with house graham cookies.

Summary & comments Since Luna is a popular spot noise can be a big problem. Come early to avoid it or be ready to jump into the bedlam. Management is presently looking into sound abatement devices.

MACARTHUR PARK ★★★

AMERICAN | MODERATE | QUALITY ★★★★½ | VALUE ★★★★ | ZONE 6

607 Front Street, (415) 398-5700

Reservations Recommended **When to go** Anytime **Entrée range** $11.95–$27.50
Payment All major credit cards. **Service rating** ★★★ **Friendliness rating** ★★
Parking Valet , street, nearby private garages **Bar** Full service **Wine selection** Good
Dress Casual **Disabled access** Good **Customers** Locals, businesspeople

Open Monday–Thursday, 11:30 a.m.–10:30 p.m.; Friday, 11:30 a.m.–11 p.m.; Saturday, 5–11 p.m.; Sunday, 4:30–10 p.m.

Setting & atmosphere Upscale brick and timber loft-like setting with modern Americana art. In the heart of Jackson Square and just down the street from Levi's Plaza, this 25-year-old restaurant has made its home from an old Barbary Coast warehouse built in the early 1900s. There are two upfront bar sections, two dining areas and an outside patio.

House specialties Upscale barbecue and American comfort food. House-smoked salmon cured over alder chips and presented with special mustards and walnut toast; griddled corn and crab cakes with Maryland-style tartar sauce; dry aged New York steak with onion strings and spinach; famous baby back ribs with cole slaw and garlic mashed potatoes; grilled calves liver with garlic mashed potatoes, caramelized onions, and smoked bacon; signature tamarind flavored barbecue sauce.

Other recommendations Great bar and wine list featuring microbrew beers on tap, American whiskey and a good wine list showcasing Zinfandel. One of the best happy hours in town offering free chicken wings, fries, chips and dip, veggies, super guacamole, rice and beans and more. Tap Tuesday is exceptionally popular for its beer deals.

Summary & comments Experienced chef Melissa Miller is masterful at balancing a classic menu with a regular crowd. If everyone but one person in your party wants barbecue have no fear, there are many menu options for all. This is the kind of place you come to when you want homestyle cooking but don't want to do it yourself. After work, or in between shopping, eat in or take home with their great take-out menu. Delivery is available through Waiters on Wheels or Dine-One-One, and excellent for football season.

MASA'S ★★★★★

FRENCH | EXPENSIVE | QUALITY ★★★★★ | VALUE ★★★★★ | ZONE 3

648 Bush Street, (415) 989-7154

Reservations Required **When to go** Anytime **Entrée range** $15 and up; prix fixe, $60–$105 **Payment** Major credit cards **Service rating** ★★★★★ **Friendliness rating** ★★★★ **Parking** Valet, $11 **Bar** Full service **Wine selection** Excellent **Dress** Formal **Disabled access** Yes **Customers** Locals, tourists

Dinner Tuesday–Saturday, 5:30–9:30 p.m.; Sunday and Monday, closed

Setting & atmosphere It ain't cheap, and it don't look it. But it's never intimidating. How a place can be so grand and yet not be stuffy, pretentious, or snobby is hard to fathom, but there you have it. The staff are not concerned with impressing or looking down at their patrons, but with seeing that they get the superb gastronomic experience they pay so dearly for.

House specialties A unique blend of French and California turned out in an elegant fashion that no other restaurant could imitate even if it tried. It's the result of the Japanese founder's 30 years in French kitchens, honing his style and making his mark. The rather short menu may begin with seafood sausage in beurre blanc or house-made foie gras with spinach. Entrées include roasted partridge with cabbage and thyme; veal or beef with marrow and truffles; grilled fish with caviar or herb confit; grilled lobster with quenelles.

Other recommendations Desserts are worth the trip if you have a sweet tooth. Pineapple in dark caramel sauce; frozen mousses with crushed filberts.

Summary & comments This is often said to be a New York restaurant located in San Francisco. That might be saying a little too much for New York. It is without a doubt one of the best restaurants in the city and, indeed, in the state. It could also be the most expensive, especially if you have wine with your meal. And the corkage fee is $30! But if you're swimming in money or content to eat humble fare for a week or two after, it's worth a blow-out splurge.

MAX'S OPERA CAFÉ ★½

DELI/BARBECUE | MODERATE | QUALITY ★★★½ | VALUE ★★★★ | ZONE 2

601 Van Ness Avenue, (415) 771-7300

Reservations Not accepted **When to go** Before or after the show **Entrée range** $12–$25 **Payment** Major credit cards **Service rating** ★★½ **Friendliness rating** ★★★ **Parking** Street **Bar** Full service **Wine selection** Limited but good **Dress**

Casual to dressy **Disabled access** Yes **Customers** Theatergoers, tourists, locals

Open Monday, 11:30 a.m.–10 p.m.; Tuesday–Thursday and Sunday, 11:30 a.m.–11 p.m.; Friday, 11:30 a.m.–2 p.m.; Saturday, 11:30–1 a.m.

Setting & atmosphere New York deli cum piano bar and cocktail lounge with barbecue on the side. Spacious and well-lit, with high ceilings and a large window onto the streets and city hall. Though it's a broad space, it has lots of nooks, booths, and intimate corners.

House specialties Big deli sandwiches; barbecue with unique sauces, some with subtle hints of Asian spices; pasta with wild mushrooms; pastrami and corned beef (ask for it easy on the lean). Take-out orders are available.

Other recommendations Desserts and salads.

Summary & comments Located near the War Memorial Opera House, Herbst Theater, and Davies Symphony Hall, this is an ideal spot for a pretheater dinner. Service is generally quick and efficient with no fluff or folderol; they know you've got tickets to the show. Parking can actually be had on the street now and then.

MC²   ★★★

FRENCH/CALIFORNIAN | MODERATE | QUALITY ★★★½ | VALUE ★★★★½ | ZONE 4

470 Pacific Avenue, (415) 956-0666; www.mc2restaurant.com

Reservations Accepted **When to go** Anytime **Entrée range** $18–$29 **Payment** V, MC, AMEX, DC **Service rating** ★★ **Friendliness rating** ★★½ **Parking** Valet (for dinner), street, and nearby lots **Bar** Full **Wine selection** Varied, though not extensive **Dress** Business to dress casual **Disabled access** Yes **Customers** Locals, tourists, creatives from nearby ad agencies

Lunch Monday–Friday, 11:30 a.m.–2 p.m.

Dinner Monday–Thursday, 5:30–9:30 p.m.; Friday and Saturday, 5:30–10:30 p.m.

Setting & atmosphere A techno-modern, industrial chic design that gathers warmth and light from exposed brick and front wall of glass that looks onto quaint tree-lined Pacific Avenue. Open seating in the main room is spacious and all tables feel private. Small groups may enjoy dining in an unusual, stand-alone, circular banquette done in French blue.

House specialties The menu changes four times a year to reflect the freshest offerings. Though self-styled as contemporary French with California influence, executive chef Yoshi Kojima's Japanese roots are very apparent in the light hand passed over all the dishes. The grilled Maine lobster with foie gras, asparagus, fennel confit, and basilorange lobster sauce combines just about every taste and texture one could ask for in a single dish. Not always on the menu but worth asking for is the squid ink pasta with sunflower sprouts and calamari in saffron sauce. You'll recognize a Japanese sensibility at work in the perfect hint of salt that comes from the sprig of celery leaf.

Other recommendations All the fish and seafood dishes are excellent. The pan roasted duck with pea sprouts comes with slices of kumquat that add a bright, astringent zip with the sprouts providing a surprisingly deep walnut flavor. Together, they bring out the entire range of the duck's warm flavors.

Summary & comments Despite some national notices MC^2 has never attracted the crowd that its food deserves. After a flamboyant start three years ago, it's looking a bit shop-worn but the food remains as crisp and fresh as ever. The huge windows make this a perfect spot for a cool, foggy day in San Francisco. A quiet place where it's easy to spend a long evening savoring outstanding food and good conversation.

MILLENNIUM ★★★½

VEGETARIAN/VEGAN | MODERATE | QUALITY ★★★★½ | VALUE ★★★★½ | ZONE 2

246 McAllister Street, (415) 487-9800; www.millenniumrestaurant.com

Reservations Recommended **When to go** Dinner **Entrée range** $10.75–$18.95 **Payment** V, MC, AMEX **Service rating** ★★★ **Friendliness rating** ★★★½ **Parking** Street **Bar** Beer, Wine **Wine selection** Well chosen **Dress** Casual **Disabled access** Yes **Customers** Locals

Dinner Daily, 5–9:30 p.m.

Setting & atmosphere In the ground floor and basement of the restored Abigail Hotel. Softly lit and cozy throughout, with touches of modern art. Best seat in the house is downstairs at the far end, with a picture window looking onto a tiny Japanese-style garden.

House specialties Some of the best vegan dining to be had anywhere. The dedicated carnivore can feast sumptuously at Millennium and not even realize that he's just had a meatless, dairyless meal. A vegan diet would be a lot more popular if all the cooks came from here. The signature dish is a plantain torte; a sweet and spicy mixture of plantain is spread between layers of fresh tortilla and served over a tomato and papaya salsa. No words do it justice. It's not too sweet or spicy, and it doesn't taste Mexican despite the tortillas. If you eat nothing else in San Francisco besides the famous sourdough bread, eat this.

Other recommendations Fresh fig and Asian pear salad; smoked portobello mushroom; morel risotto; roasted sweet onion stuffed with black bean chile.

Summary & comments An eclectic menu informed by classic cooking techniques makes Millennium one of San Francisco's treasures. Executive chef Eric Tucker makes no compromise in the pursuit of the gourmet dining experience. He labors to extract the last measure of value and character from all of the foods at his disposal, making even the simplest root or leafy green come alive on your palate. The dishes are vibrant with flavor, aroma, and varying textures and colors. A feast for all the senses.

MOMI TOBY'S REVOLUTION CAFÉ ★★

ECLECTIC | INEXPENSIVE | QUALITY ★★★½ | VALUE ★★★★ | ZONE 2

528 Laguna Street, (415) 626-1508

Reservations Not accepted **When to go** Anytime **Entrée range** $4.25–$6.95 **Payment** Cash **Service rating** ★★ **Friendliness rating** ★★★ **Parking** Street **Bar** Beer, wine **Wine selection** House **Dress** Casual **Disabled access** No **Customers** Neighborhood

Open Monday–Friday, 7:30 a.m.–10 p.m.; Saturday and Sunday, 8 a.m.–10 p.m.

Setting & atmosphere This renovation of a 100-year-old bakery is reminiscent of a Berlin café, right down to the lamps and the bar. Dark paneled walls and hardwood floors abound and create a comfortable atmosphere for long conversations over coffee, lunch, or dinner.

House specialties Along with the usual coffee-shop fare try enchilada pie; meatless pesto lasagna; taqueria-style burritos; Caesar salad. It seems at first glance that this is a menu that can't make up its mind, but it all hangs together nicely.

Summary & comments This is not just a restaurant, it's a local hangout. The regulars are very regular, and people come often just to relax, linger over coffee, meet friends, and feel at home.

MOMO'S ★★

CALIFORNIAN | EXPENSIVE | QUALITY ★★★½ | VALUE ★★★½ | ZONE 7

760 Second Street; (415) 227-8660; www.eatatmomos.com

Reservations Recommended **When to go** Anytime **Entrée range** $16–$35 **Payment** All major credit cards **Service rating** ★★ **Friendliness rating** ★★ **Parking** Valet and street **Bar** Full service **Wine selection** Good **Dress** Business **Disabled access** Yes **Customers** South Beach residents, off work dot-commers

Lunch Sunday–Friday, 11:30 a.m.–4 p.m; Saturday, 11 a.m.–3 p.m.

Dinner Sunday–Thursday, 5–10 p.m.; Friday and Saturday, 5–11 p.m.

Setting & atmosphere Location. Location. Location. Directly across from the new Giants Ball park, it will be impossible for this trendy hot spot not to get any hotter. That is if it can blend the baseball crowd with those turning the outdoor patio into a kennel for cellphone junkies. Inside an elegant wood lined bar and dining room on the verge of but not quite being considered upscale. Main and private rooms have a cozy table arrangement similar to that of an Italian family style restaurant. Great for dates and eavesdropping but not for privacy. The walls are lined with nostalgic period San Francisco black and white photos and bright baseball enthusiast oil paintings.

House specialties Spicy seared rare ahi, and we mean spicy, bring kleenex; salmon corn salad; ostrich fillet served with soba noodles with tangerine hoisin glaze; wood oven roasted Thai snapper stuffed with fennel, lemon, and herbs.

Other recommendations Heirloom tomatoes with goat-cheese crostini; crispy onion rings; double cut pork chop over garlic mashed potatoes with a dried sherry and apricot port sage sauce.

Summary & comments This is a hip and happening after-work spot. The bar and heated patio are routinely packed. It's going to be very interesting to see how the restaurant develops as the rest of the neighborhood does. So far, it seems like they're trying too hard to be more than they need to be.

MOOSE'S ★★★★

CALIFORNIAN | MODERATE | QUALITY ★★★★½ | VALUE ★★★★½ | ZONE 6

1652 Stockton Street, (415) 989-7800; www.mooses.com

Reservations Accepted **When to go** After the theater **Entrée range** $11–$29 **Payment** All major credit cards **Service rating** ★★★★ **Friendliness rating** ★★★★ **Parking** Street, valet $6–$9 **Bar** Full service **Wine selection** Excellent **Dress** Business **Disabled access** Good **Customers** Locals, tourists

Brunch Sunday, 10 a.m.–2:30 p.m.

Lunch Thursday, Friday, and Saturday, 11:30 a.m.–2:30 p.m.

Dinner Sunday–Thursday, 5–10 p.m.; Friday and Saturday, 5:30–11 p.m.

Setting & atmosphere Classic San Francisco egalitarian elegance. A fancy festive atmosphere and a staff that performs with aplomb. They are knowlegable but unpretentious, helpful but not obsequious. Even the sommelier is a regular guy, and he aims to please. You know you're in a place dedicated to the enjoyment of a good dinner when you see table tents with the polite request to turn off your cell phone, please.

House specialties A hard-to-pigeonhole mix of Italian, French, and California. Pizza, pasta, and Caesar salad; lamb chops and roasted chicken; smoked meats and crab cakes; mashed potatoes and gravy. It changes seasonally, and when the Dungeness crabs are running this is the best place in town for San Francisco's signature dish: cioppino (cho PEEN oh).

Other recommendations Organic garden greens are regularly served, as is prosciutto with mission figs. House smoked pork loin is always worth trying. And vegetarian selections are always good.

Entertainment & amenities String duets or trios often play in the entryway; nightly jazz.

Summary & comments The warmth and conviviality of Moose's is the most sure antidote to a night of San Francisco's fog. String duets or trios often play in the entryway, sometimes classical, sometimes jazz. Every dish is prepared with the utmost love and care and professionalism. In the open kitchen, where skillful hands are the most valuable tools in the shop, you can watch superior workers practicing their art. The wine list is impressive and contains many unique or hard-to-find wines.

ONDINE ★★★★

CALIFORNIAN | EXPENSIVE | QUALITY ★★★★½ | VALUE ★★★★★ | ZONE 9

558 Bridgeway, Sausalito; (415) 331-1133

Reservations Recommended **When to go** Sunset **Entrée range** $28–$34 **Payment** All major credit cards **Service rating** ★★★★ **Friendliness rating** ★★★ **Parking** Valet $4 hourly or street **Bar** Full bar **Wine selection** Excellent **Dress** Evening casual **Disabled access** Yes **Customers** Local, tourist

Sunday brunch 10 a.m.–2 p.m.

Dinner Monday–Sunday, 5–11 p.m.

Setting & atmosphere Through its large wrap-around windows, Ondine has a rare, spectacular view of the bay and San Francisco skyline. No decor could ever compete with that, and wisely, the owners haven't tried. The curving, wooden sculpture spiraling along the ceiling, suggests the inside of a seashell while the warm mauves and rusts of the walls and carpet promote a peaceful atmosphere. Lighting is muted, enhancing the spectacle that is San Francisco at night.

House specialties Chef John Caputo has crafted a menu that celebrates California in all its diversity, especially in seafood. Each course is a medley of visual beauty, aromas, and textures that are pleasing to eye and palate. Start with Peekytoe crab salad, just because it sounds so whimsical. Or go with a stolid corn and crayfish chowder, or a dozen oysters, or if you're flush have the caviar service. The entrée list is rather short but everything is superb. Orange- and cumin-marinated rabbit loin; rack of lamb with fig-cardamom essence; swordfish with black pepper crust and pinot noir glaze.

Other recommendations Desserts are sugary flights of fancy. Or if you have no sweet tooth, try a cheese platter of domestics and imports.

Summary & comments It is said that a restaurant with such a stupendous view of the city doesn't need to depend on a high quality of service and food for success. Ondine, gratefully, does not subscribe to this theory. Each item on the menu is fresh, amazingly beautiful in presentation—a complex blend of interesting flavors and textures served in a timely manner by a knowledgeable wait person.

ORIGINAL JOE'S   ★★

AMERICAN/ITALIAN | INEXPENSIVE | QUALITY ★★★½ | VALUE ★★★★ | ZONE 3

144 Taylor Street, (415) 775-4877

Reservations Recommended **When to go** Anytime **Entrée range** $7.95–$25 **Payment** All major credit cards **Service rating** ★★ **Friendliness rating** ★★★ **Parking** Lot **Bar** Full service **Wine selection** Fair **Dress** Casual **Disabled access** Yes **Customers** Locals, tourists, regulars

Open Daily, 10:30 a.m.–midnight

Setting & atmosphere This is the original Original Joe's. It's one of the oldest places in the neighborhood, and many will say it looks like it. Most of the staff seem to date from the same year. The menu, decor, and patrons never seem to change either. Red plastic booths and a long bar and counter overlooking the kitchen; low lights and some plants. A certain inconsistency prevails, perhaps borne of old familiarity.

House specialties Italian meat and potatoes. Joe's buys whole sides of beef and then ages and cuts them in-house. From these come the monster steaks and hamburgers that the regulars eat in quantity. Also, overcooked pasta with superior sauce; thick-cut french fries; corned beef and cabbage; prime rib.

Summary & comments The neighborhood has gone down in recent years, so you should park in the lot or nearby on the street. Unlike the OJ's in San Jose, the bar here serves up a hefty drink in a convivial atmosphere.

PACIFIC ★★★★

CONTEMPORARY CALIFORNIA CUISINE | EXPENSIVE | QUALITY ★★★★½ | VALUE ★★★★½ | ZONE 3

500 Post Street; third floor of the Pan Pacific Hotel, (415) 929-2087

Reservations Recommended **When to go** Any time **Entrée range** $15–$36 **Payment** All major credit cards, personal checks **Service rating** ★★★★ **Friendliness rating** ★★★★ **Parking** Valet parking **Bar** Full service **Wine selection** Very good **Dress** Casual **Disabled access** Yes **Customers** Tourists and local regulars

Breakfast Monday–Friday, 6:30–11 a.m.; Saturday and Sunday, 7–10 a.m.

Brunch Saturday and Sunday, 10 a.m.–2 p.m.

Lunch Monday–Friday, 11:30 a.m.–2:30 p.m.

Dinner Sunday–Thursday, 5:30–9:30 p.m.; Friday–Saturday, 5:30–10 p.m.

Setting & atmosphere This is not a place to people watch but a place to dine in splendid isolation. Take a lover here on a special evening, or take a table or two with friends and relish the great food and quiet setting. A spacious outlay of tables contributes to a sense of calm. You certainly don't feel like you're in a hotel. The dining area is graciously tiered and divided from the courtyard with low glass walls and four trees. There's a roaring fireplace, a fine antidote to a foggy evening. Four larger-than-life bronze figures by Elbert Weinberg pose gracefully around a fountain. First glance: the spirit of Matisse's painting *Dance* has taken flight from the canvas.

House specialties The menu showcases a sumptuous collection of dishes from the Pacific Rim. For starters try the oysters with cucumber mignonette or the ahi variation with ginger dressing and big island hearts of palm. Try the wild striped bass with chanterelles, caramelized garlic, fingerling potatoes, and the seared diver scallops with white corn, huitlacoche fritter, and summer truffle sauce. The crème brûlée is the most popular dessert but the roasted banana cream pie with rum anglaise is a close second.

Other recommendations The Pacific caters to the theater going crowd so it's not surprising to find an excellent selection of wine by the glass and a delicious selection of appetizers. A five-course tasting menu is available. You have the option of a paired beverage for each course, a choice of appetizers as well as entrées. Here, you can play with all sorts of tasty delights and indulge in Chef Canavan's culinary predilection: "My favorite customers are those who come and say, 'Just give me five courses.'"

Summary & comments The Pacific is one of the area's top culinary destination points and definitely the hardest working hotel restaurant in town. The menu is comprised of seasonally inspired dishes. Seafood is their specialty. Live entertainment Friday and Saturday from 5:30 to 9:30 p.m.

Honors & awards AAA Four Diamond Award for exceptional cuisine and service in a fine dining establishment.

PALIO D'ASTI ★★★★

ITALIAN | EXPENSIVE | QUALITY ★★★★★ | VALUE ★★★★★ | ZONE 1

640 Sacramento; (415) 395-9800 / (415) 362-6002; www.paliodasti.com

Reservations Recommended **When to go** Lunch, dinner **Entrée range** $13.25–$24 **Payment** V, MC, AMEX, D **Service rating** ★★★★ **Friendliness rating** ★★★★ **Parking** Street **Bar** Wine bar and full bar **Wine selection** Excellent and extensive **Dress** Casual, business **Disabled access** Yes **Customers** Local, business

Lunch Monday–Friday, 11:30 a.m., with the last seating at 2:30 p.m.; Enoteca della Douja: Monday–Friday, from 5 p.m.

Dinner Monday–Friday, 5:30 p.m. ,with the last seating at 9 p.m.

Setting & atmosphere Rough concrete pillars, set at odd angles in the spacious dining room of this 1905 building, disappear into the lofty ceiling leaving the impression that one has entered the streets of medieval Italy. Brilliant banners in the colors and designs of the Palio, the ancient bareback horse race celebrating the harvest season in Italy, are suspended overhead. Vast gray reaches of wall are softened by sound absorbing cloth panels, a dropped ceiling, and warmed by the extensive use of dark woods and glowing brass fixtures. Comfortable banquettes and strategically placed tables round off this pleasant ambience. The glass enclosed kitchen provides patrons with an intriguing view of kitchen activities.

House specialities Italian, specializing in the Piedmonte and Toscana regions of Italy. The restaurant has always been known for wonderful house pastas and risottos using the freshest and most authentic Italian products. The menu changes often providing the diner with such delicacies as: thinly sliced Parma ham with seasonal melon, and Parmigiana crisps; house almond-and-fontina filled ravioli in broth with spinach and white truffle oil; house cuttlefish-ink pasta with squid, conch, and summer squash; sautéed milk-fed veal and buckwheat polenta with a sauté of blue point oysters, smoked veal bacon, and house-pickled peppers.

Other recommendations The wine bar at the front of the restaurant, Enoteca della Douja, named after the famous wine competition that takes place in Asti each September. Here, 30 wines, mostly Italian, are available by the glass or by the 2½-ounce taste. During the week it is also an "enoteca," or place where people can meet to share small plates of regional dishes.

Summary and comments Palio d'Asti is a true ristorante Piemontese known for its great pastas, risotto, and freshest and most authentic Italian products. Its new wine bar, Enoteca della Douja, is one of the City's foremost gathering places for savvy foodies and society folks.

PARAGON ★★

NEW AMERICAN | MODERATE | QUALITY ★★★½ | VALUE ★★★ | ZONE 7

701 Second Street (at Townsend); (415) 537-9020; www.paragonrestaurant.com

Reservations Recommended (especially for pre-game meals) **When to go** Anytime **Entrée range** $10–$23 **Payment** V, MC, AMEX, D **Service rating** ★★½ **Friendliness rating** ★★★ **Parking** Complimentary with validation at lunch, street **Bar** Full **Wine selection** Small, California focus **Dress** Casual **Disabled access** Good **Customers** Game goers headed to Pac Bell Park, young business types

Lunch Monday–Friday, 11:30 a.m.–2:30 p.m.

Dinner Monday–Thursday, 5:30–10 p.m.; Friday and Saturday, 5:30–11 p.m.

Setting & atmosphere Located just a block away from Pac Bell Park, Paragon is a lively young spot. High ceilings, chrome, and mirrors create an industrial chic ambience. A large cherry wood bar is the heart of this large restaurant. A partially open kitchen and a private room can be found towards the back of the house. Jazz plays over the din of conversation that the acoustics of the space encourage.

House specialties French brasserie meets American pub in this restaurant where duck confit with lentils might share the table with a gourmet bacon cheeseburger. Dishes often include seasonal and Mediterranean accents as well. Pastas such as saffron fettuccine with goat cheese or capellini with fresh vegetables and herbs are available for vegetarians, but most of the menu focuses on meats and shellfish. Big entrées like grilled double-cut pork chop and roasted lamb sirloin are sure to tide you over through every inning of the baseball game.

Other recommendations Paragon could be described as a drinker's restaurant with a food lover's taste. The bar boasts more than 50 varieties of vodka, and 18 wines, mostly California vintages, are available by the glass. In addition to French aperitifs including Lillet, Paragon offers classic American cocktails and a menu of house specialty drinks. All of these drinks pair nicely with rich appetizers such as wild mushroom tart and buttery mussels.

Summary & comments Paragon's proximity to Pac Bell Park makes its pace unique. On game nights, huge crowds have come and gone from the restaurant by 7 p.m. The atmosphere transforms from clamorous to calm and you find yourself enjoying a quiet dinner spot.

PASTIS ★★★

WEST COAST BASQUE | MODERATE | QUALITY ★★★★ | VALUE ★★★★ | ZONE 6

1015 Battery Street; (415) 391-2555

Reservations Recommended **When to go** Lunch, dinner **Entrée range** $12.75–$22 **Payment** All major credit cards **Service rating** ★★★ **Friendliness rating** ★★★ **Parking** Street **Bar** Full bar **Wine selection** Extensive, excellent **Dress** Casual, business **Disabled access** Yes **Customers** Local, business

Lunch Monday–Friday, 11:30–3 p.m.

Dinner Monday–Saturday, 5:30–10 p.m.

Setting & atmosphere Entering Pastis from the brick and steel of the Battery Street warehouse area is a comforting experience. Reminiscent of the Basque men's dining clubs of San Sebastian, you're surrounded by warm wood paneling, low, exposed beamed ceiling, soft lighting and a sense of conviviality. The bar runs the length of the main dining area; its mirrored back wall adding depth to this small bistro. The bar gives those waiting a chance to observe and lust after the hardy and innovative Basque cuisine on its way to table.

House specialities Basque in essence. The menu changes regularly, taking advantage of the seasons. On any given night you might find a superb cherry tomato tartlet with basil and balsamic vinegar; Maine crab and piquillo pepper salad with mango and fresh herbs; piperade with poached egg and Serrano ham; duck confit with fried garlic potatoes; marinated roasted rack of lamb with garlic jus and potato gratin.

Other recommendations The asparagus spears with basil; all desserts, but especially the rich almond delight of gateau Basque and the delicate turron parfait with roasted almonds.

Summary & comments Basque food is hardy and savory and needs time to be enjoyed thoroughly. Pastis brings you this experience but not quite at peak hours. It is a San Francisco favorite and can be very crowded. To take advantage of the friendly and knowledgeable staff and fully enjoy the delicious food, go early or at off hours.

PAT O'SHEA'S MAD HATTER   ★★

BAR AND GRILL | INEXPENSIVE | QUALITY ★★★½ | VALUE ★★★★★ | ZONE 8

3848 Geary Boulevard, (415) 752-3148; www.patosheas.com

Reservations Large parties only **When to go** Anytime **Entrée range** $8–$14 **Payment** All major credit cards **Service rating** ★★ **Friendliness rating** ★★★ **Parking** Small lot, street **Bar** Full service **Wine selection** House **Dress** Casual **Disabled access** Yes **Customers** Locals, tourists

Brunch Saturday and Sunday, 10:30 a.m.–3 p.m.

Lunch Monday–Friday, 10 a.m.–3 p.m.

Dinner Daily, 3–10 p.m.

Setting & atmosphere A sports bar since 1937; its motto has always been, "We cheat tourists and drunks!" This is a proper bar with proper television sets showing proper games to proper sports fans drinking proper drinks. You won't find ferns or silk wall hangings among the wooden floors and pictures of sports greats. The place just happens to serve great food.

House specialties The cook is a proper chef from proper restaurants who decided he would have more fun in a bar. He produces a limited but faultless selection that leans heavily on meat and potatoes. Two-third pound burgers; carrot soup; grilled swordfish or other catch of the day; pasta with whatever is on hand; simple but excellent salads. Altogether superb pub grub. Good selection of beers and cocktails that raise mixology to the status of art.

Summary & comments Since before World War II, serious sports people have been coming here and making it their office away from the office. Sportswriters are especially in evidence and are hailed by name by the staff. You'll see every kind of person come through here to watch a game, have a drink, hold forth in Western fashion at the bar, and tell tall tales. It's a Cheers with food.

PERLOT   ★★½

NEW FRENCH | EXPENSIVE | QUALITY ★★★★½ | VALUE ★★★½ | ZONE 2

Hotel Majestic, 1500 Sutter Street (at Gough); (415) 776-6400; www.hotelmajestic.net/restaurant.html

Reservations Accepted **When to go** Dinner, brunch, or breakfast **Entrée range** $23–$32 **Payment** V, MC, AMEX, DC, D **Service** ★★★½ **Friendliness** ★★★ **Parking** Valet ($8) and street **Bar** Full **Wine selection** California only **Dress** Comfortably fancy **Disabled access** Good **Customers** Hotel guests, some city dwellers

Breakfast Daily 7–10:30 a.m.

Brunch Sunday 10:30 a.m.–2:30 p.m.

Dinner Wednesday–Saturday 5:30–9:30 p.m.

Setting & atmosphere The feeling in the dining room at Perlot is one of classic elegance and hushed romance. The name of the restaurant is taken from an old-fashioned French word for Oyster. Plush and spacious, the restaurant really is a treasure in the Majestic Hotel. The space was recently re-designed in soft yellows and greens. Noise absorbing wall panels keep the mood private while lofty floral arraignments, comfortable stuffed chairs, and beautiful glass wine cabinets make you feel positively royal.

House specialties Chef Geoffrey Blythe enjoys giving traditional continental preparations a fresh twist as in his pot-au-feu made with Sonoma Valley Duck or "free form" cassoulet of lobster, sweetbreads, and root vegetables. An ambitious appetizer combination of Spring Lady peaches and herbed ricotta on toast with a touch of purple basil. Seasonal tasting menus show off ingredients such as heirloom tomatoes, mission figs, and morel mushrooms. A chef's tasting menu in six courses is also available.

Other recommendations Perlot serves strictly California wines, many of which are outstanding, but also look out for European selections in ports, sherries, and champagne. Distinctive cheeses and desserts are worth saving room for here. Artisan cheeses bring an earthy quality to this fancy restaurant. Offerings include Sally Jackson's sheep's milk and Cowgirl Creamery's "Mt. Tam." Pastry chefs trained at the Ritz-Carleton Dining Room and Citizen Cake whip up excellent ice creams and sorbets. They also reflect the innovation of Chef Blythe in desserts such as lemon-basil crème brûlée and cucumber gelee.

Summary & comments Perlot is a newcomer that proves a nice antidote to the trendy hot spots that have mushroomed around town in recent years. Its elegance is timeless and the chef pampers his guests with an amuse-bouche before a meal or a petit-four to finish.

PERRY'S ★★

AMERICAN | INEXPENSIVE | QUALITY ★★★½ | VALUE ★★★★½ | ZONE 5

1944 Union Street, (415) 922-9022

Reservations Accepted **When to go** Anytime **Entrée range** $11.95–$24.95 **Payment** All major credit cards **Service rating** ★★★ **Friendliness rating** ★★★ **Parking** Street **Bar** Full service **Wine selection** Fair **Dress** Casual **Disabled access** Yes **Customers** Locals, businesspeople, singles

Open Sunday–Thursday, 9 a.m.–11 p.m.; Friday and Saturday, 9 a.m.–midnight

Brunch Saturday and Sunday, 9 a.m.–3 p.m.

Setting & atmosphere Sports bar, singles meeting place, business rendezvous, bar and grill; a pleasant American bistro. Congenial long bar surrounded by checker-clothed tables on a bare wood floor. Wide windows overlook fashionable Union Street, and the back has a pleasant patio for quieter dining.

House specialties Burgers; shoestring fries; one of the few places in town serving sautéed calf livers with bacon and onions; grilled double chicken breast; New York steak; linguine with clams.

Other recommendations Apple Brown Betty.

Summary & comments This bar has always been a great place to meet friends or strangers. Go for a cocktail before or a cordial after dinner, or a late snack after dancing.

PJ'S OYSTER BED ★★★

SEAFOOD | MODERATE | QUALITY ★★★★ | VALUE ★★★★ | ZONE 8

737 Irving Street, (415) 566-7775

Reservations Recommended **When to go** Anytime **Entrée range** $14.95–$26
Payment All major credit cards **Service rating** ★★★ **Friendliness rating** ★★★½
Parking Street **Bar** Beer, wine **Wine selection** Adequate **Dress** Casual **Disabled
access** Yes **Customers** Locals, tourists

Lunch Daily, 11:30 a.m.–3 p.m.

Dinner Sunday–Thursday, 5–10 p.m.; Friday and Saturday, 5–11 p.m.

Setting & atmosphere Casual, comfortable atmosphere; always intriguing counter seating and table service.

House specialties Wide selection of oyster dishes and many Cajun specialities. New Orleans–style gumbo.

Other recommendations Try the alligator. It's good.

Summary & comments With its "distinctive" weather this has always been a hot-bowl-of-soup kind of town, and PJ's clam chowder fits the bill for a respite from those chilling winds and damp fogs.

Honors & awards Voted Best Seafood Restaurant 1994 by the *Bay Guardian*.

PLOUF ★★

FRENCH | MODERATE | QUALITY ★★★ | VALUE ★★★ | ZONE 3

40 Belden Place (between Bush and Pine); (415) 986-6491; www.plouf.com

Reservations Accepted **When to go** Anytime **Entrée range** $14–$24 **Payment** V,
MC, AMEX **Service rating** ★★ **Friendliness rating** ★★ **Parking** Metered street,
neighborhood lots **Bar** Full **Wine selection** Extensive; $12 corkage fee **Dress** Casual
Disabled access Good **Customers** Young clientele, business people

Lunch Monday–Friday 11:30 a.m.–3 p.m.

Dinner Monday–Wednesday 5:30–10 p.m., Thursday–Saturday 5:30–11 p.m.

Setting & atmosphere Plouf has an oceanic theme. Huge trophy fish hang from the walls and the old-fashioned white tile floor and high pressed-tin ceiling with skylights give the restaurant a spacious feel. Café-style tables are somewhat close together but the folding chairs are more comfortable than they appear. The mood here is bustling and young, as friendly staff maneuver hot crocks of mussels amid the crowd. A functional fireplace adds a cozy touch on cold nights, and when it is warm enough the outdoor patio fills up like a Parisian café.

House specialties Mussels, mussels, and more mussels. Any diner who has traveled in France will appreciate the authenticity of the menu. Moulles Mariniere, Provencal, and Bretonne recall the offerings of every French mussel bistro. The seafood doesn't stop with the mussels though. Plouf features several fish entrées daily and also has oysters on the half shell, calamari, prawns, and scallops on the appetizer menu. If anyone in your party is averse to seafood they can still enjoy some French fare in the form of a leek tart with Roquefort cheese or classic dinners such as duck confit and steak frites.

Other recommendations The offerings from the bar are impressive. In addition to the large wine list, aperitifs, champagne, and after dinner liqueurs bring the European drinking sensibility to the American table. Why not enjoy a relaxed drink before you even order?

Summary & comments Plouf is a good spot to know about if you are working or shopping downtown and need a place to eat or have a drink. The weekday lunch is a good value. The French staff is upbeat and hard-working and the Belden Place location, adjacent to Cafe Bastille and a few other casual but trendy eateries that also occupy sidewalk space, gives Plouf a distinctly European feel.

PONZU ★★★★½

CONTEMPORARY ASIAN | MODERATE/EXPENSIVE | QUALITY ★★★★½ | VALUE ★★★★★ | ZONE 3

401 Taylor Street, (415) 775-7979; www.kimptongroup.com/ponzu.htm

Reservations Recommended **When to go** Anytime **Entrée range** $13–$22 **Payment** All major credit cards **Service rating** ★★★★ **Friendliness rating** ★★★★ **Parking** Validated parking **Bar** Full service **Wine selection** Very Good **Dress** Casually elegant, no athletic wear **Disabled access** Yes **Customers** Locals in the know

Breakfast Monday–Friday, 7–10 a.m.; Continental, Saturday–Sunday, 8–11 a.m.

Dinner Sunday–Thursday, 5–10 p.m.; Friday–Saturday, 5–11 p.m.

Bar Hours Daily, 4:30 p.m.–midnight; (beverages only until 5 p.m.)

Setting & atmosphere Hip and edgy decor softened with a wonderful touch of feng shui: low undulated walls, artful light fixtures, a circular ceiling pattern repeated on the floor, lots of curves, and soft velvet-covered seats. Festive and youthful atmosphere, particularly after the middle of the week. Lots of space and plenty of romantic nooks for an evening with someone special.

House specialties Traditional Asian techniques and cooking styles combined with local ingredients cannot be done better. The menu consists of meticulously crafted Thai, Malaysian, Japanese, Chinese, Korean, and Vietnamese dishes. But this is not fusion food. Nothing is muddled together. For starters try the Bangkok melon salad with lime leaf, crispy shallots, and Thai basil as well as the garlic-fried roti bread with mango chutney and garam masala. Among the entrées, the sour orange-curry sea bass with green papaya and crispy shallots; and the stir-fried scallops and duck with spicy black-bean greens are extraordinary.

Other recommendations Ponzu has happy hours twice nightly from 5 to 7 p.m. and again from 10 p.m. to midnight. Lots of theater going folks can be found here and the actors hang out during the second happy hour. Lots of wonderful finger food to share. Try the specialty cocktails. They're served with swizzle sticks, umbrellas, and other playful garnishes and are as exotic as their names suggest: Buddha's Passion, Spiritual Sparkler.

Summary & comments This is one of the best deals in town, a great bang for your buck. There's a seasonal twist to the menu but it basically stays the same. The mood shifts over the course of the evening. The darker, the sexier, and so it goes as the evening wears on. It's best to valet park. The neighborhood, though vastly improved, is still a little raw. The restrooms may be the coolest in the City.

RED HERRING ★★½

FUSION SEAFOOD | MODERATE | QUALITY ★★★½ | VALUE ★★★ | ZONE 7

55 Steuart Street (between Mission and Howard); (415) 495-6500; www.redherringrestaurant.com

Reservations Accepted **When to go** Anytime **Entrée range** $14.95-$29.25 **Payment** V, MC, AMEX, DC, D **Service rating** ★★½ **Friendliness rating** ★★★ **Parking** Valet (except Sunday), metered street **Bar** Full **Wine selection** Wide **Dress** Business casual **Disabled access** Good **Customers** Tourists, businesspeople

Lunch Monday–Friday, 11:30 a.m.–3 p.m.

Dinner Monday–Saturday, 5:30–10:30 p.m.; Sunday, 5–9:30 p.m.

Setting & atmosphere A lovely, peaceful view of the Embarcadero and San Francisco Bay is this seafood restaurant's greatest asset. Inside, the long narrow space is filled with a small dining room of tables with bay views, a raw bar, booths in the center, and dark sports bar at the entrance. The restaurant is accessed through the Hotel Griffon lobby where couches and soft lamps accommodate waiting parties and cellphone users. The feel here is masculine and it is well suited to business meals.

House specialties A full raw bar offers a nice way to start your meal. Selections include littleneck clams and ceviche. A signature appetizer, baby lobster and mango cones are rich with avocado; the crispy shell and tobiko caviar provide a nice contrast to the soft filling. Tuna tartar is another tasty starter here. The dinner menu is separated into Asian, Latin, and American sections. Standouts are the shellfish preparations such as "angry" soft-shell crabs with Hong Kong fried rice. Beware of overcooked fish though, and be sure to ask for yours rare.

Other recommendations Red Herring is a great spot for drinks. An impressive selection of vodkas and an international wine selection give the bar a nice depth. The raw bar and appetizers marry well with the drink selections and you might even fill up on these and just want a bowl of chowder or a salad for dinner.

Summary & comments Service is professional and friendly here making it a valuable place to know about for professional meetings. With the view of the bay and the multi-cultural seafood menu, the feeling at Red Herring is very San Francisco.

RED'S JAVA HOUSE ★

DIVE | INEXPENSIVE | QUALITY ★★★ | VALUE ★★★★★ | ZONE 6

Pier 30, No phone

Reservations No way **When to go** Daytime **Entrée range** $2.70–$4.65 **Payment** Cash **Service rating** ★ **Friendliness rating** ★ **Parking** Street **Bar** Beer **Wine selection** None **Dress** Work clothes **Disabled access** No **Customers** Locals, workers

Open Daily, 6 a.m.–5 p.m. or at the staff's discretion

Setting & atmosphere The chief attraction here is the view. In front you can see the East Bay and the Bay Bridge. Behind you is the bulk of the city. Red's 40-year history is documented in scores of black and white photos of people and patrons from the waterfront. All else is tacky and dirty.

House specialties Double burgers; double hot dogs; deviled-egg sandwiches.

Other recommendations What many will argue is a great cup of coffee.

Summary & comments A historical gathering place for working people during the glory days of the San Francisco waterfront. Down to your last dollar? Eat here.

RUTH'S CHRIS STEAK HOUSE ★★½

STEAK HOUSE | MODERATE | QUALITY ★★★½ | VALUE ★★★★ | ZONE 2

1700 California Street, (415) 673-0557; www.ruthschris.com

Reservations Strongly advised **When to go** Anytime **Entrée range** $17–$29.95 (á la carte) **Payment** All major credit cards **Service rating** ★★★ **Friendliness rating** ★★★ **Parking** Street **Bar** Full service **Wine selection** Good **Dress** Casual **Disabled access** Yes **Customers** Locals, tourists

Dinner Sunday–Thursday, 5–10 p.m.; Friday and Saturday, 5–10:30 p.m.

Setting & atmosphere A proper-looking steak house in the best tradition. The dark wood suggests a cattle ranch, and the well-set, clean tables tell you you're in a place of serious eating. Any doubts are dispelled by the black-and-white-clad waiters, who look like real pros.

House specialties Serious steak. It's all from the Midwest, where beef is something more than mere food. Corn-fed, aged USDA prime is what you'll get here. It makes up the top 2% of market beef; you'll taste the difference.

Other recommendations Barbecued shrimp; pork chops; salmon; chicken; shellfish. Creamed spinach; potatoes au gratin; shoestring potatoes.

Summary & comments The menu defines what rare means—as well as the other grades of doneness—and the cooks are good about it. You'll get what you order. Portions are big and may look daunting, but they're so good that they seem to disappear.

SAM WOH ★½

CHINESE | INEXPENSIVE | QUALITY ★★★ | VALUE ★★★★ | ZONE 1

815 Washington Street, (415) 982-0596

Reservations Not accepted **When to go** Lunch **Entrée range** $4–$8 **Payment** Cash **Service rating** ★ **Friendliness rating** ★ **Parking** Street **Bar** None **Wine selection** None **Dress** Casual **Disabled access** Adequate **Customers** Locals, businesspeople

Open Monday–Saturday, 11–3 a.m. Closed Sunday.

Setting & atmosphere Hole-the-wall rabbit warren. Three floors of deep, narrow rooms with a definite cramped feeling, especially during the lunchtime squeeze. Even when you're alone in the place you feel the need for elbow room. And the decor? There is no decor.

House specialties All the usual suspects in a Chinese restaurant. Chow mein with a variety of additions; crisp fried noodles; sautéed shellfish; won ton soup; fried rice.

Other recommendations More of the same.

Summary & comments The motto hangs from the wall: "No credit card, no fortune cookie, just damn good food!" It's not quite a dive, but almost. And it's one of the most popular places in the neighborhood. Of its kind, it might be the most popular place in town. The staff are singularly intolerant, demanding, disputatious, and sometimes downright rude. "You! Move over. Somebody else gotta sit down, too." That's how you get seated when it's very crowded, as it is daily at noon. Lingering too long after lunch? "You! Whatsamatta you? People waiting. You go!" Somehow it's not insulting. Somehow that's just the way they say howdy. There is no wine or beer, but the package store just across the street will sell you a cold one or a bottle of jug wine and wrap it a brown paper bag for you to take into the restaurant. They know the drill, and they're quick about it. You hungry now? You go!

SANTA FE BAR AND GRILL   ★★★

SOUTHWEST | MODERATE | QUALITY ★★★★½ | VALUE ★★★★½ | ZONE 12

1310 University Avenue, Berkeley; (510) 841-4740

Reservations Accepted **When to go** Anytime **Entrée range** $13.95–$16.95 **Payment** V, MC, AMEX **Service rating** ★★½ **Friendliness rating** ★★½ **Parking** Free lot **Bar** Full service **Wine selection** Good **Dress** Business **Disabled access** Good **Customers** Local, business

Lunch Monday–Friday, 11:30 a.m.–3 p.m.

Dinner Sunday–Thursday, 5–10 p.m.; Friday and Saturday, 5–11 p.m.

Setting & atmosphere The reconstructed historic Santa Fe railway station. Spanish mission style interior and exterior, but stripped down to its architectural essence. Clean lines, no fluff or red tiles, white washed walls in and out. Simple elegance in the unique Southwestern style. The garden greens and herbs are impeccably fresh since they are grown in the restaurant's own garden right behind the building. An expert gardener is employed full time to tend and harvest the crops. Taste the difference.

House specialties Smoked meats, fish and poultry; corn, beans and rice. Southwestern specialties done to perfection, as well as a good selection of pastas and pizzas. The wood-smoked pork chop is two inches thick and it's moist and worth a trip across the bay. If that doesn't float your boat, try the Petaluma duck with basmati rice.

Other recommendations Ceviche of shellfish, black bean soup, clam chowder with saffron.

Entertainment & amenities Live pianists, usually on weekends, but sometimes mid-week. They often play the music of a chosen decade and dress accordingly.

Summary & comments This place became famous originally under Jeremia Tower. Though he is gone to other pastures, Chef Barbara Bargiel is keeping it a regular stopping place for East Bay locals. Easy access from the freeway on one side and the hills from the other doesn't hurt. Being near the Berkeley Rep makes it a good spot for after theater dining. It is also the only place in the East Bay that one could describe as elegant. Though not imposingly so. You'll feel at home in a tie or shirtsleeves.

SCALA'S BISTRO ★★★½

ITALIAN/FRENCH | EXPENSIVE | QUALITY ★★★★ | VALUE ★★★★ | ZONE 3

432 Powell Street, (415) 395-8555; www.scalasbistro.com

Reservations Accepted **When to go** Anytime **Entrée range** $11–$29.50 **Payment** All major credit cards **Service rating** ★★★★ **Friendliness rating** ★★★ **Parking** Street, nearby lots; valet $11 **Bar** Full service **Wine selection** Extensive **Dress** Evening casual **Disabled access** yes **Customers** Locals, tourists

Breakfast Monday–Friday, 7–10:30 a.m.; Saturday and Sunday, 8–10:30 a.m.

Lunch Daily, 11 a.m.–4 p.m.

Dinner Daily, 5:15 p.m.–midnight

Setting & atmosphere Located in the historic Sir Francis Drake hotel. Walking into this place feels like walking into an older, more colorful and vibrant San Francisco. It's very much alive. Rows of wood and leather booths sit beneath mural-painted walls, and large windows give a sweeping view of the street and all its pageant flowing by.

House specialties A mix of regional Italian, country French and California. The menu changes often, but grilled double cut porkchop with fingerling potatoes, artichokes and roasted garlic is a signature dish and can be counted on, as is seared salmon filet with buttermilk mashed potatoes. For pasta the best is tagliatelle with roasted mushrooms.

SHANGHAI 1930 ★★★

CHINESE | EXPENSIVE | QUALITY ★★★★ | VALUE ★★★★ | ZONE 7

133 Steuart Street; (415) 896-5600

Reservations Accepted **When to go** Anytime **Entrée range** $9–$25 **Payment** All major credit cards **Service rating** ★★★ **Friendliness rating** ★★★ **Parking** Valet $10, street **Bar** Full service **Wine selection** Varied, with many California wines **Dress** Business **Disabled access** No **Customers** Locals, tourists

Lunch Monday–Friday, 11:30 a.m.–2:30 p.m.

Dinner Monday–Thursday, 5:30–10 p.m., Friday and Saturday, 5:30—11 p.m. Closed Sunday. Live jazz Friday and Saturday evenings.

Setting & atmosphere Another theme restaurant from SF restaurateur George Chin, this one evoking the glamorous, indulgent, and romantic Shanghai of the 1930s. The gorgeous blue art deco–style bar evokes the feel of an elegant opium den and has been used as a set for the television series "Nash Bridges." Comfortable booths line both sides of the main room and a large room at the rear is available for groups.

House specialities Owner Chin has completely revised his already highly successful menu into four sections. "Signature selections" cover the popular mainstays that are unlikely to threaten yet still include a creative twist, such as fish on a vine, a fillet of whole fish shaped to resemble a cluster of grapes. The traditional favorites selections go a bit more authentic with cuttlefish and "ants climbing a tree" (a puffed rice noodle tree with chili infused sauce). "Connoisseur classics" and "exotic adventures" offer even more unusual ingredients and will appeal to those who either know their Chinese dishes well or are willing to order ahead for dishes such as the slow cooked Beggar's Chicken.

Other recommendations Go for contrasts and the unusual. The eel crisp and the Yiubao prawns eaten with shells on. Don't let these dishes get cool before starting.

Summary & comments Out of town guests searching for a taste of the elegance they've seen in Zhiang Ximou movies will feel as though they have arrived on the set as they descend the stairs into this subterranean restaurant. The atmosphere could only be improved if everyone wore white smoking jackets or slinky satin dresses.

dupe entries; needs to be sorted

SHERATON PALACE GARDEN COURT ★★★★

NEW AMERICAN | EXPENSIVE | QUALITY ★★★★½ | VALUE ★★½ | ZONE 7

Market Street at New Montgomery Street #2, (415) 512-1111

Reservations Recommended **When to go** Anytime **Entrée range** Breakfast buffet, $23; Sunday brunch, $45; lunch, $14.50–$17.75; dinner, $21–$32 **Payment** All major credit cards **Service rating** ★★½ **Friendliness rating** ★★½ **Parking** Hotel garage **Bar** Full service **Wine selection** Excellent **Dress** Informal, dressy **Disabled access** Good **Customers** Tourists, businesspeople, locals

Breakfast Monday–Saturday, 6:30–10 a.m.; Sunday, 6:30–11 a.m.

Brunch Sunday, 11:30 a.m.–1:30 p.m.

Lunch Monday–Saturday, 11:30 a.m.–2 p.m.

Dinner Wednesday–Saturday, 6–10 p.m.

Setting & atmosphere The Sheraton Garden Court may be the most gorgeously Rococo room in San Francisco, with its 40-foot atrium ceiling and copious lead crystal chandeliers dwarfing the baby grand. The room is softly carpeted, with plush sofas in the lounge. This is as grand as it gets.

House specialties Breakfast or Sunday brunch buffet; Japanese breakfast; warm lobster salad or potato-wrapped lobster; venison scaloppine with red lentils; pan-roasted boneless quail; organic chicken with buckwheat polenta and chanterelles; rare muscovy duck breast with sun-dried plum sauce.

Other recommendations Filet mignon; John Dory with wild mushroom ragoût; herb-encrusted monkfish with fingerling potatoes.

Summary & comments Opulent, plush, hushed, and halcyon; if you've recently won the lottery, the Garden Court's grandeur will no doubt satisfy your need to pamper yourself. You're definitely paying for the atmosphere and deferential service; the food, while meticulously prepared and admirably presented, is among the highest priced in the city and can be equaled in quality elsewhere for considerably less. Best bet: stop in for a drink on the way to somewhere else. The afternoon teas, topping off with a champagne tea for $22.95, are a luxurious treat.

SOUTH PARK CAFÉ   ★★★

FRENCH | MODERATE | QUALITY ★★★★ | VALUE ★★★★★ | ZONE 7

108 South Park Boulevard, (415) 495-7275

Reservations Recommended **When to go** Anytime **Entrée range** Lunch, $8.50–$15; dinner, $12.50–$19.50 **Payment** All major credit cards **Service rating** ★★★½ **Friendliness rating** ★★★½ **Parking** Street **Bar** Full service **Wine selection** Limited but good **Dress** Casual, informal **Disabled access** Good **Customers** Locals, businesspeople, tourists

Breakfast Monday–Friday, 8–11:30 a.m. for pastries and coffee

Lunch Monday–Friday, 11:30 a.m.–2:30 p.m.

Dinner Monday–Saturday, 6–10 p.m.

Setting & atmosphere South Park Cafe's enchanting location on historic South Park Boulevard creates a pared-down neighborhood bistro ambience: affable clamor and bustle with relatively bright lighting. It's a very romantic street but not a romantic restaurant.

House specialties Dinners include grilled duck breast with wild honey and spices; boudin noir with sautéed apples; steamed mussels with saffron cream; roast rabbit with lemon confit.

Other recommendations Nightly specials, including desserts: apple cake with geranium ice cream and Calvados crème anglaise.

Summary & comments South Park's minimalist approach arrived as a forerunner antidote to the more flamboyant and expensive dinner houses of the 1980s. Heralding the gentrification of quaint South Park Boulevard, the original affluent section of old San Francisco then down at the heels in an industrial neighborhood, South Park offered a small, well-executed bistro menu served in a simple setting for shockingly low prices. Others have followed, spiffing up the neighborhood and spawning a whole movement.

THE STINKING ROSE   ★★★

ITALIAN | MODERATE | QUALITY ★★★½ | VALUE ★★★★ | ZONE 6

325 Columbus Avenue, (415) 781-7673; www.thestinkningrose.com

Reservations Recommended **When to go** Anytime **Entrée range** $9.95–$32.95 **Payment** All major credit cards **Service rating** ★★★ **Friendliness rating** ★★ **Parking** Street **Bar** Full service **Wine selection** Short but good **Dress** Casual **Disabled access** Yes **Customers** Locals, tourists

Open Daily, 11 a.m.–midnight

Setting & atmosphere The main room is a mix of murals, a Rube Goldberg garlic factory, and toy trains. Garlic braids hang from the ceiling, photos of celebrities smile from the walls, and understatement is nowhere in sight. A recently added second room is strewn with plain wooden tables and festooned with straw-wrapped Chianti fiasci. All is exuberant without being overpowering, rather like the aroma of cooked garlic.

House specialties "Garlic seasoned with food." The mostly Italian menu is comprised of well-made pastas and seafood laden with garlic. The garlic is usually cooked long and slow to mellow it, so you won't step out of here a bane to vampires, but people will know where you've been. Weekly specials include meat loaf with garlic mashed potatoes, paella, and salt cod.

Other recommendations Forty-clove chicken, pork chops with sweet garlic relish and apples, braised rabbit, vegetarian dishes. Specially marked items can be made without the pungent lily on request.

Summary & comments 1.5 tons of garlic and 12,000 mints a month! This is a fun place, one that takes itself not too seriously but not too lightly either. It's dedicated to gustatory enjoyment. The bar is a popular place to meet. Regulars will often come in just for a drink and a deep breath or two. At Candlestick Park you can buy the Stinking Rose's 40-clove chicken sandwich.

STRAITS CAFE ★★★★

SINGAPOREAN | MODERATE | QUALITY ★★★★½ | VALUE ★★★★★ | ZONE 8

3300 Geary Boulevard, (415) 668-1783; www.straitscafe.com

Reservations Accepted **When to go** Any time **Entrée range** $9.50–18 **Payment** All major credit cards **Service rating** ★★★★ **Friendliness rating** ★★★★ **Parking** No valet parking **Bar** Full service **Wine selection** Limited **Dress** Casual **Disabled access** Yes **Customers** Trendy locals

Lunch Sunday–Thursday, 11 a.m.–2:30 p.m.; Friday–Saturday, 11 a.m.–4 p.m.

Dinner Sunday–Thursday, 6–10 p.m.; Friday–Saturday, 5–11 p.m.

Setting & atmosphere Chris Yeo, owner/chef has worked magic in the smallest of spaces. The playful decor evokes a Singaporean street scene with pastel-colored facades, balconies, shutters, even clotheslines. Subtle lighting. Busy with people of every ethnicity.

House specialties Singaporean cookery blends the best of Indonesian, Chinese, Malay, Indian, and Nonya cuisines. (The latter a result of the marriages between Chinese men and Malay women generations ago.) Dishes are designed to be shared. Start with the roti prata, a grilled Indian bread served with a subtle curry dipping sauce. Another house specialty is the wok-roasted mussel with cracked pepper, and garlic; and the ahi tuna with mixed greens, pickled ginger, peanuts, and shallots tossed in ginger-plum dressing and topped with crispy taro root.

Other recommendations Phillip, the bartender, specializes in a long list of tropical concoctions and a variety of infused drinks: pineapple, mango, ginger, and apple. The recommended Navarro white wine admirably complements many of the dishes on the menu.

Summary & comments A great place for superbly tasty, beautifully presented food in an intimate setting. This is still a neighborhood restaurant: affordable, cozy, and filled with regulars. Straits Cafe is San Francisco's first, and only, authentic Singaporean restaurant. Soon, Chris plans to open another Straits Cafe downtown.

SWAN OYSTER DEPOT ★★

OYSTER BAR | INEXPENSIVE | QUALITY ★★★½ | VALUE ★★★★★ | ZONE 2

1517 Polk Street, (415) 673-1101

Reservations Not accepted **When to go** Lunch **Entrée range** $13–$32 **Payment** Cash **Service rating** ★★★ **Friendliness rating** ★★★ **Parking** Street **Bar** Beer, wine **Wine selection** House **Dress** Casual **Disabled access** No **Customers** Locals

Open Monday–Saturday, 8 a.m.–5:30 p.m.

Setting & atmosphere Really a fishmonger's, this little gem boasts a long marble bar where you sit on ancient stools feasting on the freshest seafood in town. It's an old-time San Francisco neighborhood joint.

House specialties Raw oysters; shellfish cocktails; seafood salads.

Other recommendations New England clam chowder with sourdough bread.

Summary & comments Friendly family members of this Polk Street business entertain you with continuous conversation while they shuck, peel, and crack your order of shellfish. One of the few places in town that still serves old-fashioned oyster crackers.

TADICH GRILL ★★★

AMERICAN | MODERATE | QUALITY ★★★★ | VALUE ★★★★★ | ZONE 4

240 California Street, (415) 391-1849

Reservations Not accepted **When to go** Anytime **Entrée range** $12–$20 **Payment** V, MC **Service rating** ★★★ **Friendliness rating** ★★½ **Parking** Street **Bar** Full service **Wine selection** Good **Dress** Casual, business **Disabled access** Yes **Customers** Locals, businesspeople, tourists, daytrippers

Open Monday–Friday, 11 a.m.–9 p.m.; Saturday, 11:30 a.m.–9 p.m.

Setting & atmosphere The oldest restaurant in the city; 150 proud years in the same location. It's brightly lit, but the heavily draped tables and curtained booths give a warm ambience (if you're lucky enough to get a table or booth). Otherwise, a seat at the long marble counter affords delightful glimpses into the open kitchen.

House specialties Seafood. Or anything else you want grilled. Tadich is a place for plain cooking, no fancy sauces or tarted-up presentations. Straightforward and honest Yankee fare.

Other recommendations Good bar to help you through the long wait for seating.

Summary & comments A culinary, cultural treasure. Quite possibly built over the sunken ships of the gold rush. Step into Tadich and partake of the city's rich gastronomic history.

THAN LONG ★★★

VIETNAMESE | INEXPENSIVE/MODERATE | QUALITY ★★★★ | VALUE ★★★★ | ZONE 8

4101 Judah Street at 46th Avenue, (415) 665-1146

Reservations Recommended on weekends **When to go** Weeknights **Entrée range** $8.95–$26 **Payment** All major credit cards **Service rating** ★★★ **Friendliness rating** ★★★★ **Parking** Street, valet **Bar** Beer, wine **Wine selection** House **Dress** Casual, informal **Disabled access** Good **Customers** Locals, businesspeople, tourists

Dinner Tuesday–Thursday and Sunday, 4:30–10 p.m.; Friday and Saturday, 4:30–11 p.m.; closed Monday

Setting & atmosphere Operated by the An family for more than 20 years, Thanh Long has recently renovated its dining room in shades of muted green, with one wall papered with tropical flowers. Not that anyone really notices; the food's the star here. Thanh Long is close to the beach and a neighborhood favorite, so it can get crowded on warm weather weekends.

House specialties Whole roasted crab with garlic and lemon butter or sweet-and-sour sauce; soft rice-paper shrimp rolls; crab cheese puffs; butterfly prawns in pastry; Saigon beef broiled paper-thin around green onions; squid stuffed with pork and mushrooms; lemon-grass chicken; broiled red snapper.

Summary & comments Thanh Long's soft, green ambience provides a cool backdrop for the vibrant, flame-colored platters of whole crabs emerging from the kitchen. Crab is the main event here, and everyone orders it in one form or another; some say it's the best to be had in a town famous for its crab purveyors. The shrimp rolls are also excellent, as is the grilled pork, beef, and squid. Thanh Long is a good dinner stop after a day at the beach, but make reservations in advance to avoid a wait.

THIRSTYBEAR ★★★

SPANISH | MODERATE | QUALITY ★★★½ | VALUE ★★★★ | ZONE 7

661 Howard Street, (415) 974-0905; www.thirstybear.com

Reservations Recommended **When to go** Anytime **Entrée range** Tapas, $3.50–$7.50; entrées $14–$18 **Payment** All major credit cards **Service rating** ★★★★ **Friendliness rating** ★★★ **Parking** Self parking at the Moscone Parking Garage on 3rd **Bar** Full service but specialized in-house brewed beers **Wine selection** Good **Dress** Casual **Disabled access** Good **Customers** Businesspeople and late–20–30 somethings

Lunch Monday–Friday, 11:30 a.m.–2:30 p.m.; Saturday, noon–3 p.m.

Dinner Monday–Thursday, 5:30–10:30 p.m.; Friday–Saturday, 5:30 p.m.–midnight; Sunday, 5–10 p.m.

Setting & atmosphere High energy bounces off the walls and lofty timber-beamed ceilings in this brewpub cum Spanish cookery. The modern wall art and showcased stainless steel brewery equipment is balanced by the weathered brick walls typical of SoMa buildings. If the noise level in the frontal bar area can make it hard to hear conversations, venture upstairs where there are pool tables and often banquets. Let the desserts overwhelm you instead of the crowd.

House specialties Dessert: Madonna's bra—two upside-down pointed chocolate sugar cones covering rich chocolate mousse and surrounded by fresh whipping cream. Torrada-toasted peanut bread rubbed with tomato and garlic and house cured salmon; seared Ahi Tuna with watercress and pimento mustard sauce; Setas á la plancha-mixed mushrooms á la plancha; Gambas al Pil-Pil-sautéed shrimp with garlic and white wine; Paella Valenciana prepared in a cazuela with squid, shrimp and mussels and named after the town in Spain where paella originated.

Other recommendations It's easy to fill up on a mixture of cold and hot tapas but leave room for Tony's amazing entrées. Brochetas al Adobo-Escolar and shrimp in lemon marinade with artichokes and saffron aïoli; Chuletillas á la Brasa—grilled lamb chops, roasted peppers and garlic potatoes. Try the seasonal beers in addition to the favorite standbys like the IPA.

Entertainment & amenities Upstairs available for banquets and parties.

Summary & comments More than just an after work hangout for good beer and gossip, ThirstyBear is a fantastic place to bring out of town visitors to dinner. It's popularity seems to be focused on the beer and tapas, while true kudos should be shifted to chef Tony Miller and his continuous dedication to preserving the flavors of Spain. Each new waiter trains for three days with Tony learning the details of the menu plate by plate. In addition, Tony returns to Spain at least once a year to study the cuisine and expand the menus.

TI COUZ ★★

CRÊPERIE | INEXPENSIVE | QUALITY ★★★ | VALUE ★★★★ | ZONE 7

3108 16th Street, (415) 252-7373

Reservations Not accepted **When to go** Before or after a movie **Entrée range** $5–$12 **Payment** All major credit cards **Service rating** ★★ **Friendliness rating** ★★★ **Parking** Street **Bar** Full bar **Wine selection** Adequate **Dress** Casual **Disabled access** Yes **Customers** Locals, moviegoers

Open Monday–Wednesday, 11 a.m.–11 p.m.; Thursday and Friday, 11 a. m.–midnight; Saturday, 10 a.m.–midnight; Sunday, 10 a.m.–11 p.m.

Setting & atmosphere Clean, bright, polished blue and white. Simple decor befitting the simple yet good fare. Located across from the Roxie Theater, it's often peopled by a boisterous and friendly mob of film fans and bookstore denizens.

House specialties Crêpes, crêpes, and more crêpes. Crêpes of every description and possible filling. Sweet crêpes, savory crêpes, plain and fancy crêpes. Fillings include seasonal fruits and butter or chocolate; mushrooms with sauce; seafood with sauce; cheese and crème fraîche.

Other recommendations A pretty good selection of beers.

Summary & comments It's quick and good, and the surroundings are undemanding of the discriminating diner. And that's meant in the nicest way. You don't have to put on the dog or your best clothes to have a good feed here.

TOMMY TOY'S ★★★½

CHINESE | MODERATE | QUALITY ★★★★ | VALUE ★★★★½ | ZONE 4

655 Montgomery Street, (415) 397-4888; www.tommytoys.com

Reservations Recommended **When to go** Anytime **Entrée range** $9–$25.95 **Payment** All major credit cards **Service rating** ★★★★ **Friendliness rating** ★★★ **Parking** Street **Bar** Full service **Wine selection** Good **Dress** Business; jacket and tie required for dinner **Disabled access** Yes **Customers** Locals, tourists

Lunch Monday–Friday, 11:30 a.m.–2:30 p.m.

Dinner Daily, 6–9:30 p.m.

Setting & atmosphere The pedestrian entrance to Tommy's belies the magnificent setting that awaits the patron inside. The decor was fashioned after the 19th century sitting room of the Empress Dowager and is a tapestry of etched glass panels, carved wooden arch ways , silvered mirrors, silk draperies, and ancient Chinese artifacts.

House specialties According to Toy there are only two great cuisines: Chinese and French. His chef prepares dishes that combine the best features of both traditions: minced squab imperial served in lettuce cups, seafood bisque chinoise with yellow chives, pan fried fresh foie gras with sliced pear and watercress in sweet picked ginger sauce, Maine lobster dismembered and prepared with spices, then reassembled on the plate.

Other recommendations Reading the menu is its own special delight presenting unusual but delicious combinations; smoked black cod with camphorwood and tea leaves served with chives, string beans and wood ear mushrooms; vanilla prawns with fresh melon and raisins; and deep fried tenderloin of pork with Chinese fruits in cassia nectar.

Summary & comments Prix fixe dinners are offered averaging about $57.50 per person depending on the season and selections, or order á la carte. It's best to put yourself in the very capable hands of the gracious and knowledgeable staff for your dinning selections. They know all the items on the menu, what goes best with what and can prepare a fine evening of culinary delights for you and your guests. Do start the evening at Tommy's intimate and cozy bar. Just sitting in its tranquil atmosphere melts the day's tensions away.

TOMMY'S JOYNT ★★

AMERICAN | INEXPENSIVE | QUALITY ★★★½ | VALUE ★★★★★ | ZONE 2

1101 Geary Boulevard, (415) 775-4216

Reservations Not accepted **When to go** Anytime **Entrée range** $6.50–$10 **Payment** Cash **Service rating** ★★ **Friendliness rating** ★★ **Parking** Lot **Bar** Full service **Wine selection** Fair **Dress** Casual **Disabled access** Poor **Customers** Everybody

Open Daily, 11 a.m.–1:45 a.m.

Setting & atmosphere Crowded, noisy, crazy place with everything conceivable on the walls and ceiling. If you've ever lost anything, you might well find it here.

House specialties Hof brau and deli; you can also find what roams on the range: genuine buffalo stew and, as an added treat, buffalo chile. Also famous for their pastrami and corned beef. The Irish come here on St. Patrick's day.

Other recommendations Cheesecake, innumerable beers.

Entertainment & amenities The decor.

Summary & comments This is one of the older places in the city to survive the earthquake of 1906. Don't come here to relax—come for the beer, buffalo, and fun.

TOWN'S END RESTAURANT AND BAKERY ★★★

NEW AMERICAN | MODERATE | QUALITY ★★★★ | VALUE ★★★★½ | ZONE 7

2 Townsend Street, Building 4, (415) 512-0749

Reservations Recommended **When to go** Anytime **Entrée range** Breakfast or brunch, $5–$10; lunch, $10–$14; dinner, $12–$20 **Payment** V, MC, AMEX **Service rating** ★★★ **Friendliness rating** ★★★½ **Parking** Street, metered during day **Bar** Beer, wine **Wine selection** Limited but good **Dress** Casual, informal **Disabled access** Good **Customers** Locals, businesspeople, tourists

Breakfast Tuesday–Friday, 7:30–11 a.m.

Brunch Saturday and Sunday, 8 a.m.–2:30 p.m.

Lunch Tuesday–Friday, 11:30 a.m.–2:30 p.m.

Dinner Tuesday–Thursday, 5–9 p.m.; Friday and Saturday, 5–10 p.m.

Setting & atmosphere Located at the breezy vanguard of the tony South Beach Marina Apartments on the Embarcadero south of the Bay Bridge, Town's End doesn't exactly command a view, but it feels as if it does, with its azure trompe l'oeil mural, glass walls, and the bridge twinkling in the distance to the north. The long, narrow dining area has an airy feel, an open kitchen, and a Zen approach to flower arrangement.

House specialties Baskets of house-baked breads; homemade pastas, and house-smoked red trout and salmon. Niçoise salad; grilled salmon with corn and tomatillo relish; curried lamb stew with pecan-currant couscous; grilled chicken marinated in garlic, lemon, and lime with organic greens, pears, Roquefort, and walnuts. Lemon meringue pie with raspberry sauce; white chocolate Napoleon; raspberry brown butter tartlet.

Other recommendations Brunch: fritatta scamorza with smoked mozzarella; wild mushrooms, sun-dried tomatoes and fresh herbs; Dungeness crab cakes with red peppers and green onions; Swedish oatmeal pancakes with pears and almonds.

Summary & comments Town's End is another SoMa venue with moderate prices and a tasty, freshly prepared menu. The fresh breads, pastries, and pastas are outstanding, but the salads and grilled offerings are good, too. Town's End's sauces are its major failing; they frequently do not equal the expertise of the pastas. Still, the unusual waterfront location, with neighboring gardens and parks, offers an idyll away from but still within the boundaries of city life. All wines on the small list are offered by the glass. The bakery section, with a few small tables, is open all day for coffee and pastry.

TRATTORIA PINOCCHIO ★★★

ITALIAN | MODERATE | QUALITY ★★★★½ | VALUE ★★★★★ | ZONE 6

401 Columbus Avenue; (415) 392-1472; www.trattoriapinocchio.com

Reservations Accepted **When to go** Any time **Entrée range** $8.95–18.95 **Payment** All major credit cards **Service rating** ★★★★ **Friendliness rating** ★★★★ **Parking** No valet **Bar** Full service **Wine selection** Limited but good **Dress** Casual **Disabled access** Yes

Lunch Daily, 11:30 a.m.–4 p.m.

Dinner Sunday–Thursday, 4–11 p.m.; Friday and Saturday, until 1 a.m.

Setting & atmosphere Traditionally a trattoria is a notch below a ristorante in decor. Not so here. A sleek marble bar runs nearly the length of the restaurant. And a marble counter wraps around the open kitchen affording views of the skilled staff. But there's still the la familia feel to the place, as if everyone knows everyone. Almost all the staff is Italian, very professional, and friendly.

House specialties "Tomatoes, basil, and garlic, that's Italian, it's very simple," explains Elena Fabbri, the Tuscan-born chef of Pinocchio. The portobello is her signature dish. The mare caldo: steamed calamari, shrimp, clams, mussels with olive oil is also a favorite as is the carpaccio prepared the traditional way: hand cut and pounded into paper-thin slices. Recommended entrées: Cacciucco (kah-choo-ko) a seafood stew of clams, mussels, prawns, fresh fish, calamari, and tomatoes. Mare misto or fresh fish, prawns, and calamari quickly seared with a touch of olive oil. And perhaps the only dish with a sauce, the delicious grilled filet mignon, whole peppercorns, demi-glace sauce served with grilled asparagus and ciabatta bread. The bread absorbs the tasty flavors and the dish goes very well with a wonderful red wine: Montepulciano d'Abruzzo.

Other recommendations Pizza. There is no dessert menu. Such specialties are prepared daily so be sure to ask.

Summary & comments If you're on a walkabout, this is great place for a respite. The windows stretch from floor to ceiling and provide a great opportunity to sit and soak up the ambience of North Beach. There are also plenty of outdoor tables, all heated for the inevitable chilly evening.

TU LAN ★½

VIETNAMESE | INEXPENSIVE | QUALITY ★★★ | VALUE ★★★★★ | ZONE 7

8 Sixth Street, (415) 626-0927

Reservations Not accepted **When to go** Anytime **Entrée range** $4–$12 **Payment** Cash **Service rating** ★★ **Friendliness rating** ★★ **Parking** Street **Bar** Beer, wine **Wine selection** House **Dress** Casual **Disabled access** No **Customers** Locals, businesspeople

Open Monday–Saturday, 11 a.m.–9:30 p.m.; Sunday, closed

Setting & atmosphere A scruffy, old, downtown diner with no friends. Old wooden floors, a long Formica counter, and rickety wooden tables and chairs, none which have four legs of the same length.

House specialties Some really outstanding Vietnamese fare considering the price. Hot and spicy soup dotted with pineapple bits; pounded shrimp wrapped on sugarcane sticks and broiled; spring rolls; imperial rolls; ginger fish or chicken; pork shish kebab; lemon beef salad.

Other recommendations Curry potatoes.

Summary & comments You can't miss Tu Lan. It's the tacky place on the corner with all the newspaper and magazine reviews taped on the window. There is only one reason to come here: to get what is, for the money, one of the best Vietnamese meals you can find outside of Saigon. It's located in what has been for a long time a tough and seedy neighborhood. The local denizens will likely be hanging out along your route, but if you walk by quickly they won't bite.

THE WATERFRONT UPSTAIRS ★★★★½

CALIFORNIA CUISINE/FRENCH ACCENTS | EXPENSIVE | QUALITY ★★★★★ | VALUE ★★★★★ | ZONE 4

Pier 7 on Embarcadero, (415) 391-2696

Reservations Recommended **When to go** Any time **Entrée range** $27–33 **Payment** All major credit cards **Service rating** ★★★★ **Friendliness rating** ★★★★ **Parking** Free valet parking **Bar** Full service **Wine selection** Very good **Dress** Downstairs, casual; upstairs, casually elegant/formal **Disabled access** Yes **Customers** Wide-eyed tourists and local swells

Waterfront Cafe hours Daily, 11:30 a.m.–4 p.m. (downstairs), 5:30 –10:30 p.m.; Sunday, 10 a.m.–4:30 p.m.

Waterfront Restaurant hours Daily, 5:30 –10 p.m. (upstairs)

Setting & atmosphere There are two unique dining experiences at the Waterfront. Downstairs the setting is spacious and comfortable. Gently swirling ceiling fans, soothing music, and a view over the bay. Upstairs the decor is far more elegant, spacious, and romantic. Any table provides some of the best views in town, particularly of the pearly lights stretched along the Bay Bridge.

House specialties (upstairs) Upstairs, Executive Chef Andrew Shimer delights in "things that don't ordinarily go together." Such combinations make for a palatable adventure. In the starter category, the pan seared foie gras is served up with brandy sauce, pain perdue, and caramelized white peaches. Likewise, the ahi tuna tartare comes in layers with white truffle, black radish, cucumber, mint, and the scrumptious addition of mangos. The entrées are equally exciting. Grilled Australian organic tenderloin beef with morel mushrooms, herb roasted potatoes, rapini, horseradish crème fraîche, and a braised oxtail-roasted shallot daube. Other favorites: the pan-roasted local halibut and the Australian rack of lamb.

Other recommendations The menu changes by the season. Freshness is key and so is texture. The Waterfront is best known for fresh seafood. Ask the very helpful staff for recommendations.

Summary & comments There's something for everyone as well as every occasion here. It's the best place in town for an on-the-water brunch (weekends downstairs). The elegant dining room, and the dishes described above, are upstairs, but downstairs you can have a beer at the bar and count the passing freighters or enjoy a more casual, though excellent, meal either inside or outside. For an early evening cocktail, there is also a wonderful outdoor area, shielded from the wind by glass.

Honors & awards Winner of Zagat Survey Certificate of Distinction; winner of Goyot Survey Certificate of Distinction

WATERGATE ★★★★

FRENCH/ASIAN | MODERATE | QUALITY ★★★★½ | VALUE ★★★★★ | ZONE 7

1152 Valencia at 22nd, (415) 648-6000

Reservations Accepted **When to go** Anytime **Entrée range** Prix fixe menu $25–$35 **Payment** All major credit cards **Service rating** ★★★ **Friendliness rating** ★★★ **Parking** Street **Bar** Beer, wine **Wine selection** Excellent **Dress** Casual **Disabled access** Yes **Customers** Locals, tourists

Dinner Sunday–Thursday, 5:30–10 p.m.; Friday and Saturday, 5:30 p.m.–11 p.m.

Setting and atmosphere Elegant dark wood wainscoting contrasting with creamy walls. Wide open windows opening out into the warm Mission evening. Gorgeous framed mirrors and geometric, semi-cubist mosaics on the wall give this place an air of the 1920s. Beautiful brocade chairs, linen tablecloths.

House specialties Interesting pairings of traditional French sauces with many unusual Asian ingredients; unusual salads; wonderful soft-shell crab, daikon & tomato salad, hazelnuts, mustard sauce; sautéed foie gras, grapes, verjuice sauce; black mission figs filled with brie cheese, prosciutto, veal sauce; Salmon carpaccio, avocado salad, tobikko, basil oil. Seasonal menu changes daily.

Other recommendations The desserts are lovely (especially the Napoleons); definitely sample one of the many after dinner teas served in charming one-of-a-kind purple clay teapots.

Summary & comments A wonderfully refined and understated place without the snootiness associated with an establishment of this caliber. The presentation and colors of the prepared dishes is exceptional, as well the as freshness of the ingredients. Wonderfully unique cuisine in an unexpected environment: directly in the heart of burrito heaven: the Mission.

YANK SING ★★

CHINESE | INEXPENSIVE | QUALITY ★★★½ | VALUE ★★★★ | ZONE 4

101 Spear (located at One Rincon Center); (415) 957-9300; www.yanksing.com

Reservations Accepted **When to go** Lunch **Entrée range** $4–$8 (à la carte) **Payment** All major credit cards **Service rating** ★★½ **Friendliness rating** ★★ **Parking** Street **Bar** Beer, wine **Wine selection** House **Dress** Casual **Disabled access** Yes **Customers** Locals, businesspeople

Open Monday–Friday, 11 a.m.–3 p.m.; Saturday and Sunday, 10 a.m.–4 p.m.

Setting & atmosphere A modernly furnished restaurant; white tablecloths and impeccable service make it a step above the usual dim sum house. A class act for simple fare.

House specialties Dim sum and yet more dim sum constantly issuing forth fresh from the kitchen. Choose barbecued pork buns; shrimp moons; and silver wrapped chicken wheeled out on trolleys.

Other recommendations Small portions of Peking duck. A wide variety of vegetarian dim sum, including pea leaves; sautéed eggplant and mustard greens. Chrysanthemum blossom tea.

Summary & comments Selections are cooked with less fat than usual. Yuppies love it here; they can stuff themselves without having to spend any extra time at the gym.

YUET LEE ★★½

CHINESE | INEXPENSIVE/MODERATE | QUALITY ★★★½ | VALUE ★★★★★ | ZONE 1

1300 Stockton Street, (415) 982-6020

Reservations Not accepted **When to go** Anytime **Entrée range** $4–$11 **Payment** Cash only **Service rating** ★★★ **Friendliness rating** ★★★ **Parking** Street, public pay lots **Bar** Beer, wine **Wine selection** House **Dress** Casual **Disabled access** Good **Customers** Locals, businesspeople, tourists

Open Wednesday–Monday, 11–3 a.m.

Setting & atmosphere Nondescript, clangorous, Formica-tabled seafood and noodle shop on a busy corner in north Chinatown; fresh seafood tanks, chartreuse-framed windows, and an open kitchen with flying cleavers.

House specialties Fresh seafood specialties: seasonal lobster; pepper and salt prawns; crab with ginger and onion; fresh boiled geoduck or razor clams; steelhead fillet with greens; sautéed fresh and dried squid. Clay pots: salted fish with diced chicken and bean cake; roast pork, bean cake, and shrimp sauce; oyster and roast pork with ginger and onion. Roast squab; braised chicken with abalone; fresh New Zealand mussels with black bean sauce; steamed live rock cod with ham and shredded black mushrooms. Also, a vast assortment of noodles and noodle soups: wontons and dumplings; braised noodles with beef stew; Amoy- or Singapore-style rice sticks.

Other recommendations Rice soups or plates; roast duck.

Summary & comments There are basically two kinds of people in the world: those who believe salvation can be found in a bowl of Chinese noodles and those who do not. If you are among the former, you will not care about Yuet Lee's fluorescent lighting, linoleum floors, and slam-bang service. You will forsake soft music and cloth napkins and candlelight. You will know that each vessel of glistening dumplings swimming in broth perfumed by star anise and ginger and scattered with emerald scallions contains all the mysteries of the universe. You will want to taste every item on the menu; stay until closing time at 3 a.m. just to watch the fragrant platters come steaming from the kitchen, yea, verily, to become one with the noodles and the fish.

ZARZUELA ★★★

SPANISH | MODERATE | QUALITY ★★★★ | VALUE ★★★★★ | ZONE 5

2000 Hyde Street, (415) 346-0800

Reservations Not accepted **When to go** Anytime **Entrée range** Tapas, $2.75–$7.25; entrées, $10.50–$15.95 **Payment** V, MC **Service rating** ★★★★ **Friendliness rating** ★★★★ **Parking** Street **Bar** Beer, wine **Wine selection** Limited but good **Dress** Casual **Disabled access** Good **Customers** Locals, tourists

Dinner Tuesday–Thursday, 5:30–10 p.m.; Friday and Saturday, 5:30–10:30 p.m.

Setting & atmosphere Disarming warmth beckons as piquant aromas of garlic and seafood waft over the sidewalk. Modest appointment inside; tawny walls and tile floors, beamed ceilings and arched windows, hand-painted dishes on the walls, and the music of soft guitars. The nuances of Spanish culture and charm softly beguile.

House specialties Thirty-eight types of tapas. Mussels or clams with white wine and garlic; grilled shrimp; poached octopus with potatoes and paprika; snails baked on croutons; grilled scallops and chard with red pepper sauce; Spanish sausage with wine; cold roast veal with olives; grilled vegetables; rolled eggplant with goat cheese. Entrées include Zarzuela, a Catalan seafood stew; pork tenderloin in raisin and pine nut sauce; paella; loin of lamb in thyme and red wine.

Other recommendations Sangria; gazpacho; romaine salad with roasted garlic; caramel flan; Alicante Muscatel dessert wine.

Summary & comments Oranges and olives, garlic and olives, red wine and sherries; Spanish cuisine presents a provocative departure from French and Italian in its colorful little tapas plates and the substantial offerings issuing forth from Zarzuela's kitchen. Dishes are as refined as they are close to the earth. Prices are as soothing as the ambience, and a small group of diners can sample a wide assortment of dishes without having to run to the ATM. Darkly sweet and spicy Sangria is poured into large goblets. Zarzuela is a quintessential neighborhood restaurant: low key, low priced, and welcoming.

ZUNI CAFÉ AND GRILL ★★★

ITALIAN | MODERATE | QUALITY ★★★★ | VALUE ★★★★½ | ZONE 7

1658 Market Street, (415) 552-2522

Reservations Accepted **When to go** Anytime **Entrée range** $17–$22 **Payment** V, MC, AMEX **Service rating** ★★★ **Friendliness rating** ★★★ **Parking** Street **Bar** Full service **Wine selection** Superior **Dress** Casual, business **Disabled access** Yes **Customers** Locals, businesspeople, tourists

Open Tuesday–Saturday, 11:30 a.m.–midnight; Sunday, 11 a.m.–11 p.m.

Setting & atmosphere Lots of bustle. A happy and exuberant place full of people coming and going, eating and enjoying at all hours of the day and into the night. There's a long copper bar just right for bellying up and holding forth to all who will listen and an excellent view of busy Market Street.

House specialties The menu changes daily, and only the best stuff is purchased for Zuni. Rib-eye steak; roast chicken; grilled tuna; braised cod; pasta dishes; any soup; vegetable fritters.

Other recommendations Regularly available hamburgers and pizza.

Summary & comments This place concentrates on perfecting the simple. The kitchen team will mine a single ingredient or recipe for the most it can give while still retaining its essential character. An example is the use of Meyer lemons. They are grown almost exclusively in the backyards of East Bay homes and are sweeter and more aromatic than other lemons. The Meyer is to lemons what the truffle is to mushrooms.

Part Eight

Entertainment and Nightlife

Performing Arts

While San Francisco has to fight off a reputation for provincialism when it comes to the arts, it's the only city on the West Coast to boast its own professional symphony, ballet, and opera companies. They benefit from the thriving support of the city's upper crust, who wine and dine their way through glittering fund-raisers. Other hallmarks of the San Francisco cultural milieu include free summer music concerts and a burgeoning theater scene.

Classical Music

Louise M. Davies Symphony Hall (201 Van Ness Avenue at Hayes Street; (415) 864-6000) is the permanent home of the **San Francisco Symphony.** Conductor Michael Tilson Thomas and many of the world's best-known soloists and guest conductors offer a year-round season of classical music, as well as occasional performances by offbeat musical and touring groups. Ticket prices vary by concert, but the least expensive seats are generally around $30. Call about the availability of standby tickets on the day of a concert; they sometimes cost less than $30; visit www.sfsymphony.org.

A night at the opera in San Francisco is no small affair. The newly renovated **War Memorial Opera House** in the Civic Center District is an opulent venue for the **San Francisco Opera Association,** which has been getting rave reviews since the building opened in 1932. Rated the best of the city's top cultural trio (symphony, opera, ballet), the San Francisco Opera consistently wins critical acclaim for operatic warhorses as well as obscure Russian opuses that other companies prefer not to tackle.

With its considerable international weight, the San Francisco Opera pulls in heavy hitters such as Placido Domingo, Marilyn Horne, Joan Sutherland, and others. The three-month main season starts at the end of September, and opening night is one of the main social events on the West Coast. Tickets start at more than $50, but standing room costs considerably less. For ticket and schedule information, call (415) 864-3330; or visit www.sfopera.org

Ballet

The **San Francisco Ballet** also calls the War Memorial Opera House home. The oldest and third-largest ballet company in the United States has a four-month season lasting from February to May. The San Francisco Ballet was the first company in the country to perform "The Nutcracker" as a Christmas event (and still does each December) and offers consistently excellent productions of full-length neoclassical and contemporary ballets. Tickets range from $9 to $25. For ticket and schedule information, call (415) 865-2000; or visit www.sfballet.org.

Summer Classical Music Festivals

The **Stern Grove Midsummer Music Festival** is the nation's oldest (since 1938) free summer music festival. The festival presents ten outdoor concerts on Sunday afternoons from June through August at the sylvan **Sigmund Stern Grove** in San Francisco. Performances include the San Francisco Ballet, Symphony, and Opera, as well as a diverse mix of blues, jazz, popular, and world music. Come early with a blanket to this magnificent, eucalyptus-lined grove. For schedule information, call (415) 252-6252; or visit www.sterngrove.org.

Midsummer Mozart presents a summer season of the works of Mozart in many venues around the Bay Area. The **Festival Orchestra** is conducted by George Cleve and features well-known soloists. Chamber concerts are presented on the first Saturday of the month during the year at the Legion of Honor. Tickets range from $20 to $40. For schedule and ticket information, call (415) 292-9620; or visit www.Midsummer Mozart.org.

Theater

The majority of San Francisco's theaters congregate downtown around the Theater District, just west of Union Square. The **American Conservatory Theater** (ACT) is the Bay Area's leading theater group, offering celebrated classics and new works on the stage of the recently restored **Geary Theater** (450 Geary Boulevard at Taylor Street). Celebrated thespians to appear in ACT productions include Olympia Dukakis, John Turturro, and Jean Stapleton. The season runs from September through July, and tickets range from $11 to $61. For more information, call the box office at (415) 749-2ACT; or visit www.act.sfbay.org.

Three downtown theaters concentrate on Broadway productions; call (415) 551-2000 for schedule and ticket information; or visit www.bestof broadway-sf.com. The **Curran Theatre** (445 Geary Boulevard at Taylor Street) tackles the bigger shows, such as Andrew Lloyd Webber's *The Phantom of the Opera* under the direction of its original London production team; the open-ended run began in 1993. The recently restored **Golden Gate Theatre** (1 Taylor Street at Market Street) is the city's most elegant theater. The **Orpheum Theatre** (1192 Market at Eighth Street) focuses on cabaret and song-and-dance performances.

After the ACT, **The Magic Theatre** in Fort Mason is the city's busiest and largest company—and consistently rated the most exciting. The company specializes in the works of contemporary playwrights and emerging talent; Sam Shepard traditionally premieres his new plays here. For schedule and ticket information, call (415) 441-8822; or visit www.magictheatre.org.

In the heart of San Francisco, the **Center for the Arts at Yerba Buena Gardens** presents art and art education in an attractive venue. Attractions include award-winning theater groups, film and video presentations, and free outdoor events. The center is located at 701 Mission Street across from the Moscone Convention Center in SoMa. For ticket information, call (415) 978-ARTS; or visit www.yerbabuenaarts.org.

Ticket Agencies

Mr. Ticket (2065 Van Ness Avenue) is the Bay Area's largest ticket agency offering premium seating for sports, concerts, and theater at market prices. Major credit cards are accepted, and delivery is available. For more information, call (800) 424-7328 outside the (415) and (510) area codes, and (415) 775-3031 from San Francisco; or visit their website at www.mrticket.com.

Tickets.com offers tickets for theater, sports, concerts, and other Bay Area events through their website. A service charge is added to the ticket price.

TIX Bay Area sells half-price, day-of-performance tickets for selected theater, dance, and music events (cash only), as well as full-price, advance-sale tickets for local performing events (by credit card). A service charge is added to ticket prices. TIX is located in the Union Square garage (Geary Street entrance). Call (415) 433-7827 for information; or visit www.theatrebayarea.org/tix2.html.

San Francisco Nightlife

You've just landed in one of the best nightlife cities in the Western world. Do you want to dance? Free form, rhumba, tango, or swing? Dressed in formal, leather, or naked (well, almost)? Do you want to drink micro-brews with local Bohemians, shoot darts with the Irish, sing off-key with tourists, or prowl a singles meat market where hormones are as thick as San Francisco fog? Do you want fancy, not so fancy, or downright dirty? Straight, gay, bi, all of the above, or just confused? San Francisco opens its Golden Gate to you.

Any style, taste, gender, or orientation can be found here, but one of the most important trends in San Francisco nightlife and culture is the "retro" scene. Choose your decade: 1940s big-band elegance, 1950s swing, even 1960s groove (1970s disco rarely rears its blow-dried head). Take a trip to a vintage clothing store or just come as you are. Step into a retro club and through the portals of time. The bouncer is dressed in a zoot suit or bears a faint resemblance to Elvis. The bartender is shaking martinis, there's a cigarette girl making her rounds, the dance floor is full of jitterbugs, and the only way you can tell that the girl in the 1940s hairdo and the poodle skirt isn't Rosie the Riveter is by the ring in her nose. Retro does not preclude piercings and tattoos.

A related aspect of this scene, permeating all nightlife culture, is the return of "cocktail nation." Skillful mixologists are now almost as highly regarded as the DJs who mix the music. Gone, mercifully, are the days when a club-hopper ordered just a glass of white wine or some crazy brain-food drink, or a slam-dunk to a cheap drunk. The martini in classic form and many variations, along with its cousin the Cosmopolitan, are among the most popular drinks.

Along with this return to Happy Days is a sense of elegance and a restoration of polite behavior. In a retro club, and even in a not-so-retro club, it is not considered chic, progressive, or relevant to talk with a loud or foul mouth, energetically condemn the establishment, or dress like a slob to show one's lemming-like individualism. San Francisco, always a more civilized place than most, is these days even more civilized.

The city is also one of the most important musical centers of the nation. All kinds of jazz, rock, punk, acid, and even orchestral music have been incubated here. The only thing you won't find here is country/western music. You'll have to head south to San Jose for line dancing and cowboy hats. The lack of country music notwithstanding, virtually every neighborhood in the city has a variety of music venues. They're so common and plentiful that they're taken for granted.

Some practical considerations: Most of the clubs listed are located in a contiguous swath running from North Beach (quaint, excellent views, less fog) through the Union Square area (uptown, elegant) to the SoMa and Mission Districts (leading edge, alternative). And since San Francisco is a small city, clubs are not far apart. If you don't find one to be your cup of tea, just check out its neighbors. In North Beach all you have to do is walk along Broadway, peering down the side streets as you go. At Union Square just stand on a corner and point yourself in any direction. In the SoMa and Mission Districts the greatest concentration of clubs is on Folsom Street, between Seventh and Eleventh Streets. It's a good idea to go by foot or taxi. Driving under the influence is a serious offense here, and the cops will frequently set up drunk-driver checks on the main streets.

A good way to see the city by night without having to drive is to travel with **3 Babes & a Bus.** Every Saturday and sometimes on Friday, for $35 Rishi, CC, and Jaz will load you and yours onto a party bus with a highly mixed and totally unpredictable crowd of revelers and take you on a nocturnal tour of the city, stopping at three or four of the more popular clubs. You won't have to pay cover charges, you get priority admittance and one free drink, and you leave the driving and often impossible parking to them. This is also a good way to meet other revelers. Gentlemen should be advised that bachelorette parties are frequent patrons of the 3 Babes. In fact, women usually make up the majority of patrons. You must be 21 with a valid ID, and jeans and tennis shoes are a no-no. Pickup is at Union Square at 9 p.m. with drop-off around 1:30 a.m. (call (800) 414-0158 or visit www.threebabes.com).

Another kind of moveable feast is **Mr. Rick's Martini Club.** If you like vintage clothing, a touch of elegance, swing and ballroom dancing, and convivial dining with like-minded people this is for you. Martini Club events happen at a different location every month or so. Cover charge is about $30 per person and includes the martini of your choice. The fixed-price dinner also usually runs about $25. The best big bands and swing ensembles play these gigs, and some very fine dancers and eager beginners fill the floor. Get the schedule from Laurie Gordon at (415) 566-2545; or check out the website at martinimusic.com/clubdex.htm.

Up-to-the-minute club information is listed in the *San Francisco Guardian* and *San Francisco Weekly,* free weekly newspapers available at any newsstand. The Sunday edition of the *San Francisco Examiner* provides the "pink section" that lists nearly every entertainment happening in town.

In 1999, California's anti-smoking ordinance took effect. It is now illegal to smoke in any restaurant, and in any bar not owner-operated. Most Californians are nonsmokers and support the law. And if you call a bar and ask if they are in comportment with the law they will likely say "yes." The truth, however, is often a bit more, shall we say, smoky. A few establishments are in open defiance and have become havens for smokers. And some have been heavily fined for it. You will know which ones they are immediately you enter them. And it's easy to tell which ones are in conformity, as they will have a small crowd of patrons standing outside lighting up. The smoking map changes from time to time, but as of this writing there are no scofflaws in this book.

Ever since the gold rush of 1849, San Francisco has been a city of revels. Many locals live for it. Some make it an art form. People from Los Angeles and Seattle fly in for it. And now you're in the middle of it. Tip a dollar per drink, pace yourself, and don't forget your trench coat.

SAN FRANCISCO NIGHTCLUBS BY ZONE

Name	Description
Zone 1—Chinatown	
Li Po	Bar
Tonga Room	Tropical island bar
Top O' the Mark	Rooftop lounge and dance floor
Zone 2—Civic Center	
Fillmore	Rock and roll ballroom
Great American Music Hall	Rock concert hall
Noc Noc	Cave bar
Zone 3—Union Square	
Biscuits & Blues	Blues supper club
Blue Lamp	Smoky old blues bar
Gold Dust Lounge	Barbary Coast saloon
Harry Denton's Starlight Room	Rooftop dance club
The Plush Room	Cabaret and cocktail lounge
The Red Room	Retro cocktail lounge
Zone 4—Financial District	
Martunis	Cocktail lounge as art
Occidental Grill	Saloon and restaurant
Zone 6—North Beach	
Bimbo's 365 Club	Classic big-band nightclub
Pier 23	Jazz bar and restaurant
Savoy Tivoli	Meat-market nightclub
Tosca's	Opera bar
Zone 7— SoMa/Mission	
Bruno's	Jazz bar
Cafe du Nord	Dance club
Cafe Istanbul	Middle Eastern coffee house
Cat Club	"Bondage-a-Go-Go"
Gold Club	High-class strip club, bar, and restaurant
Harvey's	Gay bar
Julie's Supper Club	Eclectic supper club

SAN FRANCISCO NIGHTCLUBS BY ZONE

Name	Description
Zone 7— SoMa/Mission (continued)	
Make-Out Room	Neo-Bohemian hipster bar
The Café	Gay and lesbian club
The Elbo Room	Neighborhood pub cum dance club
Zone 8— Richmond/Sunset	
Club Deluxe	Retro hot spot
Plough and the Stars	Irish pub

BIMBO'S 365 CLUB

CLASSIC BIG-BAND NIGHTCLUB

Who Goes There Very mixed crowd

1025 Columbus Avenue; (415) 474-0365; www.bimbos365club.com
Zone 6 North Beach

Cover Varies according to show **Minimum** Two drinks **Mixed drinks** $4.50 and up
Wine $4–$8 **Beer** $3–$4 **Dress** Varies **Food available** None

Hours Shows usually begin at 8 p.m., with doors open 1 hour before

What goes on A wide range of musical entertainment from lounge to jazz to rock
and soul. The big draws these days are retro nights, when guys and dolls wear zoot
suits, circle skirts, tuxedos, and full-length gowns. The Preservation Hall Jazz Orchestra
or Mr. Rick's martini band might play after Work That Skirt gives free dance lessons. Tap
and bubble dancers often round out the program.

Setting & atmosphere Beautifully restored, 1940s-style nightclub with a large stage
and dance floor, roving photographer and cigarette girl, and the famous Dolphina, the
nude lady in a giant fish bowl. Put on your black and white and step into another, better
time.

If you go Call for information and reservations.

BISCUITS & BLUES

BLUES SUPPER CLUB

Who Goes There Eclectic crowd of blues lovers

550 Geary Street; (415) 292-2583; www.biscuitandblue.citysearch.com
Zone 3 Union Square

Cover $5–$30 (varies by artist) **Minimum** None **Mixed drinks** $3.50–$8 **Wine**
Bottles, $14–$28; $6–$8 by the glass **Beer** $3.50–4.75 **Dress** Casual **Food available**
Full menu

Hours Monday–Friday, 5 p.m.–12:30 a.m.; Saturday and Sunday, 6 p.m.–12:30 a.m.

What goes on Dedication to the preservation of the blues. All manner of people with a liking for the blues come to eat southern country cooking and listen raptly and politely to some great and some not-so-great practitioners of this uniquely American musical form. In recent months other musical forms have been featured as well: rockabilly, funk, and swing are among the more popular. Call for the current acts.

Setting & atmosphere The club is located in the type of basement venue that was first a necessity, then a statement, and now the norm for jazz, blues, and other nonmainstream types of music clubs. It's close/cramped/intimate, with some splashes of modern art, and candles on tables arranged horseshoe shape around the stage and small dance floor. Movie actor Danny Glover is a part owner and his culinary background is reflected in a menu featuring fried chicken and biscuits (quite good), hush puppies (not quite so good), deep fried dill pickles (you be the judge), and black-eyed peas. Some good beers, a short wine list, and a fine collection of single-malt scotch.

If you go The kitchen can be glacially slow until food service stops at about 10 p.m. People start dancing at about the same time.

BLUE LAMP

SMOKY OLD BLUES BAR

Who Goes There Neighborhood regulars, European budget travelers, all ages, ethnic

561 Geary Street; (415) 885-1464; www.bluelamp.com   Zone 3 Union Square

Cover Friday and Saturday, $5 **Minimum** None **Mixed drinks** $3–$6 **Wine** $3.50 **Beer** $2.75–$3.50 **Dress** Casual; anything goes in the Tenderloin **Specials** Blue Lamp Ale on draft, $3 **Food available** None

Hours Daily, 11–2 a.m.

What goes on Local blues, rock, and acoustic bands starting at 10 p.m. Amateur musicians take turns jamming the blues on Sundays after 9 p.m. Just belly up to the bar and let them serve you a cold one. One pool table is open, and a working jukebox plays while you're waiting for the band to set up.

Setting & atmosphere You don't have to squint too hard to see Scarlett O'Hara's Tara grown old. Dimly lit chandeliers hide the age on the antique burgundy curtain-cum-wallpaper decor. The fireplace is empty, and sports plays on televisions at both ends of the bar.

If you go Know that there ain't a whole lot of women. Men, you won't find your future bride here. Women, Mr. Right Now is here for the taking if you can get him to leave the pool table.

BRUNO'S

JAZZ BAR

Who Goes There Glamorous Bohemians

2389 Mission Street; (415) 648-7701; www.brunoslive.com   Zone 7 SoMa/Mission

Cover $5–$10 **Minimum** None **Mixed drinks** $4 and up **Wine** $6–$11 **Beer** $3.50 **Dress** Evening casual **Food available** Bar menu

Hours Daily, 7 p.m.–2 a.m.

What goes on Live music every night from gospel to Latin to smoky blues and cool jazz. People hiding out or snuggling in the big booths in the dark depths of the long, narrow main room. Perfectly coiffed and made-up women displaying themselves with studied nonchalance. The proclaiming of "cocktail nation" with every perfect martini or Cosmopolitan shaken.

Setting & atmosphere Nightclub chic done with restraint. Artistically and subtly lit with black, red, and green. Paneled in wood and appointed with red leather, it's just glamorous and stylish enough. It makes you want to stay. You'll feel hip but not tragically so.

If you go Go on a slow night. On weekends this place is too popular for its own good.

THE CAFE

GAY AND LESBIAN

Who Goes There Women seeking women, men seeking men

2367 Market Street at Castro Street; (415) 861-3846   Zone 7 SoMa/Mission

Cover None **Minimum** None **Mixed drinks** $3.50 **Wine** $2.50–$4.75 **Beer** $1.25–$3 **Dress** Everything from jeans to drag **Food available** None

Hours Daily, noon–2 a.m.

What goes on The question is, what doesn't go on? Originally set up by women to be one of the premier lesbian social centers, The Cafe has become extremely popular among gay male fun-seekers. Mostly a dance house for high-energy techno music, but there's a pool table for variety.

Setting & atmosphere A dark, neon-lit, coed dance club that overlooks the Castro. It's hot and hopping in here, but there's an outdoor balcony where you can take a breather. Don't bother coming if you don't want to be checked out; this is definitely a spot where you'll be hit on, unless you're obviously straight. The drinks are cheap and the staff is friendly.

If you go You better not care about second-hand smoke, or PDA (public displays of affection) for that matter. On weekends it's nearly impossible to get in, so start early. And don't worry about taking the time to go to the bank; there's an ATM in the back by the bar.

CAFE DU NORD

DANCE CLUB

Who Goes There 20- to 30-something hipsters, swing enthusiasts

2170 Market Street; (415) 861-5016; www.cafedunord.com   Zone 7 SoMa/Mission

Cover $3, and sometimes more for bigger venues; no cover before 8 p.m. **Minimum** None **Mixed drinks** $4–$9 **Wine** $3.50–$6.50 **Beer** $3.75–$4.50 **Dress** Dress to impress; 1920s–1960s retro **Specials** Happy hour, daily, 4–7:30 p.m.; martinis and Manhattans, $2.50; well drinks, draft, wine, $3 **Food available** American continental with European flair; Thursday–Saturday, 6:30–11 p.m. Entrées, $13.50–$16.

Hours Sunday–Tuesday, 6 p.m.–2 a.m.; Thursday–Saturday, 4 p.m.–2 a.m.; dinner served Wednesday–Saturday, 6:30–11 p.m.

What goes on Tuesday nights usually feature live jazz, while Saturdays often show-case a live rock band. Some nights have DJs instead of live bands and are aimed at the Gen-Xers, with the crowd leaning to the gothic younger side. Check out the club's website for updated show schedules.

Setting & atmosphere If you get past the weekend line, you'll walk downstairs to this basement cabaret that used to be a 1920s speakeasy. There are oil paintings along-side black-and-white photos dimly lit by converted gaslamps. Experienced swing and salsa dancers inspire you to take lessons. If the scene is too fast for you, escape back past the bar to cuddle up with a love interest on an antique couch. The polished hard-wood floors and trim compliment the well-dressed hipsters and specialty liquors. If you're not here on a date, it's quite possible you could leave with one.

If you go The place doesn't start jumpin' until around 10 p.m., so if you're not into big bands or scary 1980s DJ music, come early for a pint or a whiskey and cuddle up on a couch with your honey at one of the most seductive lounges in town.

CAFE ISTANBUL

MIDDLE EASTERN COFFEE HOUSE

Who Goes There The quiet, the tired, the bleary-eyed club-hopper

525 Valencia Street; (415) 863-8854; www.amiraistanbul.com   Zone 7 SoMa/Mission

Cover None **Minimum** None **Mixed drinks** None **Wine** $3.50 **Beer** $3.50 **Dress** Casual **Specials** Middle Eastern music **Food available** Sandwiches, salads, soups, Turkish and Greek snacks and desserts

Hours Sunday–Thursday, noon–midnight; Friday and Saturday, noon–1 a.m.

What goes on A recovery room in the night scene of the Mission District. A chance to decompress with a delicious cup of rich, black, steamy Turkish coffee and a bite to eat. People come here to wind down after an evening's revels or just to catch their breath in the midst of an all-nighter.

Setting & atmosphere Arabian Nights setting; a golden glow in the foggy San Francisco evening. Low tables, stools, throw pillows, brass artifacts, and the smell of coffee and rosewater.

If you go On belly dancing nights you'll need reservations after 8:30 p.m.

CAT CLUB

"BONDAGE-A-GO-GO"

Who Goes There Just about everyone

1190 Folsom Street; (415) 646-1190   Zone 7 SoMa/Mission

Cover $7–$10 **Minimum** None **Mixed drinks** $5–$8 **Wine** $4–$6 **Beer** $2–$5 **Dress** Whatever suits your fancy **Food** None

Hours 9 p.m.–3 a.m.; bondage party Wednesday night

What goes on As if you didn't know! This greatly diminished weekly club has come down a little in the underworld, from the once spacious surroundings of the Trocadero now to the cramped Cat Club. Two dance floors to travel between, one playing gothic/industrial/trance and the other more metal-flavored, head banger rock and roll. Whatever fuels your particular fantasy, right?

Setting and atmosphere OK, so it's not Berlin in the 1920s, but it still has that unique South of Market flavor. Get here early and you may be able to see demonstrations of all kinds of interesting tools and techniques on live human bodies. Does this pique your curiosity? Then try being a volunteer. Lots of eye candy for those more of the voyeuristic persuasion; plenty of costumes, lingerie, latex wear, and leather. And then there are always the professional (and amateur) dancers doing tabletop and mirror displays. This place gets packed but remains fairly friendly. Just admire respectfully.

If you go The door charge is less if you're wearing fetish or club gear!

CLUB DELUXE

RETRO HOT SPOT

Who Goes There Gen-X retro hipsters, Haight Street locals

1509–1511 Haight Street; (415) 552-6949; www.clubdeluxe.com
Zone 8 Richmond/Sunset

Cover Varies **Minimum** None **Mixed drinks** $3.50–$8 **Wine** $3–$5 **Beer** $3–$5 **Dress** Vintage **Food available** None

Hours Monday–Friday, 4 p.m.–2 a.m.; Saturday and Sunday, 3 p.m.–2 a.m.

What goes on Sipping cocktails, lounging like a lizard, and looking cool. This is the place to show off your latest find from Buffalo Exchange just down the street.

Setting & atmosphere A step back from the 1960s world of Haight-Ashbury to the hip, art deco 1940s. Smooth leather booths and slick Formica tables accessorize the suspenders, skirts, suits, and 'dos of the impressively retro and ultimate retro crowd. Quality local jazz and swing bands play Wednesday through Sunday after 9 p.m. ATM inside, cover Friday, Saturday, and Sunday.

If you go Known among locals to have the best Bloody Mary in town. Parking, like everything else, can sometimes be crazy on Haight Street. Try a few blocks up from the strip or take the 6, 7, 33, or 43 Muni bus.

THE ELBO ROOM

NEIGHBORHOOD PUB CUM DANCE CLUB

Who Goes There Local Bohemians

647 Valencia Street; (415) 552-7788; www.elbo.com Zone 7 SoMa/Mission

Cover $5–$7 **Minimum** None **Mixed drinks** $4 **Wine** $4–$8 **Beer** $3.50 and up **Dress** Casual **Specials** Drink specials nightly **Food available** None

Hours Daily, 5 p.m.–2 a.m.

What goes on In the large bar downstairs, neighborhood regulars drink beer, shoot pool, and schmooze. One expects to see Archie Bunker in his younger days. Upstairs, soul funk and Latin musicians play for a very discriminating crowd of music aficionados and polished dancers (beginners are welcome, too). On nights with no live music, talented DJs work the sounds.

Setting & atmosphere Look at it with one eye and you'd call it "working class." Look at it with the other eye and you might call it "Bohemian." Either way it's unpretentious, and unventilated as well. People here don't mind sweating.

If you go Don't go tired or hungry.

FILLMORE

ROCK AND ROLL BALLROOM

Who Goes There Those looking to see a great band or needing a nostalgia fix

1805 Geary Boulevard (at Fillmore Street); (415) 346-6000; www.thefillmore.com
Zone 2 Civic Center

Cover $9 and up **Minimum** None **Mixed drinks** $3.75–$6.75 **Wine** $3.75–$5.25 **Beer** $3.50–$4.75 **Dress** Varies **Food available** American cuisine upstairs amid a selection of infamous vintage psychedelic concert posters

Hours Doors usually open at 7 or 8 p.m.; show starts an hour later

What goes on "Return to the sixties" parties, big-name and on-the-rise rock concerts, formal sit-down dinners. This rock-and-roll landmark continues to put out the San Francisco sound that made it famous in the 1960s.

Setting & atmosphere Distinct San Francisco soul still lives and breathes direct from the Fillmore. The place that birthed the Grateful Dead, Janis Joplin, and Santana still gives the leg up to climbing, young, quality bands. This hall features the largest collection of historic concert posters on view in the world. It has a spacious feel to it, and there's plenty of ground floor for getting a good view. A few tables and chairs are in the balconies off to the sides.

If you go You can always find a listing of upcoming events in the Sunday "pink pages." Tickets are on sale at Tickets.com (subject to a service charge) and on show nights 7:30–10 p.m. Advance tickets are on sale at the Fillmore box office Sunday, 10 a.m.–4 p.m. only, with a limit of six tickets per person. The hall is available to rent for parties or events and holds 1,250.

GOLD CLUB

HIGH-CLASS STRIP CLUB, BAR, AND RESTAURANT

Who Goes There Mixed male crowd

650 Howard Street; (415) 536-0300; www.goldclubsf.com   Zone 7 SoMa/Mission

Cover $20 after 7 p.m. **Minimum** None **Mixed drinks** $8 **Wine** $8 and up **Beer** $6 **Dress** Casual to dressy **Specials** Happy hour weekdays, 3–7 p.m. **Food available** Full menu of steak, chicken, fish; adequate but nothing fancy

Hours Monday–Friday, 11:30–3 a.m.; Saturday and Sunday, 6 p.m.–2 a.m.

What goes on Males from all stations in life and all ages over 21 come here to eat red meat, drink whiskey, smoke cigars, and howl at the moon.

Setting & atmosphere Formerly a modern dance venue with DJ, light show, and full bar. Two floors surround a central stage backed by a mirror and fronted by a fireman's pole; some of the best-looking nearly naked ladies in town perform (topless only). Those women not dancing at the moment are available for "table dances," in which they come to your table and get close, but (usually) leave a millimeter or so of space between you and her. Cost, $10 and up.

If you go You'll never feel sleazy or tawdry in a place like the Gold Club. The upper floor is known as the VIP Lounge and has an extra cover of $10. The women are mostly intelligent and articulate. Check the prices on the wine list carefully; they are high.

GOLD DUST LOUNGE

BARBARY COAST SALOON

Who Goes There Mixed crowd of tourists and local regulars

247 Powell Street; (415) 397-1695   Zone 3 Union Square

Cover None **Minimum** None **Mixed drinks** $3.50 **Wine** $3–$5 **Beer** $3–$5 **Dress** Anything goes **Specials** None **Food available** None

Hours Daily 6–2 a.m.

What goes on Live Dixieland jazz in a bawdy and gaudy San Francisco classic saloon est. 1933. As the place is centrally located and the sound of its rollicking good times spills onto the street, tourists from all over the world and the USA find themselves in here. There's no room to dance, but people do it anyway.

Setting & atmosphere Like a lot of older joints in the City, it's deep and narrow and often tightly packed so it's hard not to get friendly with the people next to you. A lot of rich wood, brass and gilt, and paintings of early twentieth-century nymphs and satyrs cavorting in what were once considered risque postures. This is the San Francisco of old-movies fame.

If you go Brush up on your foreign-language skills; you may have a chance to use them. And be prepared to sing along with the band.

GREAT AMERICAN MUSIC HALL

ROCK CONCERT HALL

Who Goes There Music enthusiasts of all types

859 O'Farrell Street (at Polk and Larkin); (415) 885-0750; www.musichallsf.com Zone 2 Civic Center

Cover $5 and up **Minimum** None **Mixed drinks** $3–$4 **Wine** $3–$5 **Beer** $2.75–$3.50 **Dress** Casual to impressive **Food available** Assorted appetizers, finger food

Hours Vary

What goes on A variety of nationally or internationally recognized music shows ranging from local bands on their way up, to Latin ensembles, folk, country, and even jazz. Occasionally San Francisco radio stations sponsor select bands or events where you can get free stuff.

Setting & atmosphere The fact that this turn-of-the-century bordello theater has been preserved is one of the things that makes San Francisco so special. Although the place can get a bit smoky, the gold rococo balcony, wood floors, high fresco ceiling, and marble columns make it a timeless classic. For your favorite bands, come early and scream away Beatlemania-style up front by the stage.

If you go The hall is available to rent for events and parties of up to 600. Be on the lookout for a touch of the dangerous and the lewd; next door is the famous Mitchell Brothers' O'Farrell Theater, described by Hunter S. Thompson as "the Carnegie Hall of public sex in America."

HARRY DENTON'S STARLIGHT ROOM

ROOFTOP DANCE CLUB

Who Goes There A well-dressed mixed crowd

450 Powell Street; (415) 395-8595; www.harrydenton.com   Zone 3 Union Square

Cover $5–$10 **Minimum** None **Mixed drinks** $4.50 and up **Wine** $5.75–$10 **Beer** $4–$5 **Dress** Dressy **Specials** Happy hour, Monday–Friday, 5–8 p.m. **Food available** Hors d'oeuvres, raw bar

Hours Daily, 4:30 p.m.–2 a.m.

What goes on Party, party, party! Dance to a wide variety of music, heavy on rock and retro. Cocktail culture asserts itself in style. Socialites, yuppies, tourists, other club owners, the odd Bohemian stuffed into a jacket and tie, and Harry Denton himself (no dancing on the bar unless accompanied by Harry) are drawn to the Starlight Room like moths to a flame; they all party and dance to the Starlight Orchestra's repertoire, which runs the gamut from the 1940s to the 1990s.

Setting & atmosphere Exuberantly elegant decor and staff on the top floor of the Sir Francis Drake hotel. At the bar, the sound of the cocktail shaker never stops. Through the big picture windows the stars twinkle, and overhead, yes, that's you looking into the mirrored ceiling. The atmosphere is thick and heady, the crowd is at capacity, and there is so much energy that it will be a long time before you sleep again.

If you go Go early or late, unless you're a party animal. Make sure you have a supply of one- and five-dollar bills for tipping the waiters and bartenders and the coat-check girl. Call for information on entertainment and private parties. Reservations are necessary.

HARVEY'S

GAY BAR

Who Goes There Locals, gay pilgrims, and straight looky-loos

500 Castro Street; (415) 431-4278   Zone 7 SoMa/Mission

Cover None **Minimum** None **Mixed drinks** $3.50 and up **Wine** $6.25–$8 **Beer** $3.50 **Dress** Casual **Food available** Appetizers, burgers, salads, chicken dishes

Hours Monday–Friday, 11 a.m.–midnight; Saturday and Sunday, 9–2 a.m.

What goes on A hard core of locals using it as their neighborhood pub and tourists of any persuasion who come to pay homage or gawk. Named after Harvey Milk, the assassinated gay city supervisor, this was once a place where members of the local gay community came to relax and take pride. Now many locals are embarrassed by its notoriety.

Setting & atmosphere Like a Hard Rock Cafe with a gay theme. Lots of media and sports memorabilia tacked to the walls. Despite the fact that most of the patrons are gay men and the bartenders are lesbians, the place is oddly "normal" looking and there are no wild goings on. It's just a neighborhood good-time bar. A gay "Cheers." Sundays occasionally feature drag shows.

If you go Be cool.

JULIE'S SUPPER CLUB

ECLECTIC SUPPER CLUB

Who Goes There Well-dressed 20- to 30-somethings

1123 Folsom Street; (415) 861-0707   Zone 7 SoMa/Mission

Cover None **Minimum** None **Mixed drinks** $4.25–$4.75 **Wine** $6–$7 **Beer** $3.75 and up **Dress** Evening casual **Food available** Full menu

Hours Monday–Saturday, 5:30 p.m.–2 a.m.; Sunday, closed

What goes on The dancing-est nondance club in town. Recorded jazz, blues, and R&B keep the atmosphere charged with dance fever even though there's no dance floor. Diners usually remain seated, but people at the bar will carve out any space they can to boogie. It can get crowded and loud; that's how they like it.

Setting & atmosphere Happy Days meets the Jetsons. A 1950s vision of space-age decor. Mint green, mouthwash blue, and splashes of neon punctuated with a curvy bar and black-and-white photos of 1950s celebrities. Yeah, it's weird. But it's good weird.

If you go Call ahead for dinner reservations. This is a fun and friendly place, although it can get intense. If it gets to be too much, there are many respites nearby. Julie's is at the foot of a T intersection formed by Folsom and 11th Streets; you'll find the greatest concentration of clubs in the SoMa area right here. Just start walking west.

LI PO

BAR

Who Goes There Locals in the know and accidental tourists

916 Grant Avenue; (415) 982-0072   Zone 1 Chinatown

Cover None **Minimum** None **Mixed drinks** $3.50 **Wine** $4 **Beer** $2.50–$3 **Dress** Casual **Specials** Li Po Special Snifter, $6 **Food available** None

Hours Daily, 2 p.m.–2 a.m.

What goes on Drinking in the dark. Pinball on a "Creature of the Black Lagoon" machine. Low conversations in the nooks and crannies of an ancient labyrinthine structure. A few Chinese-speaking Chinese and a lot of hip white folks from North Beach speaking English. A good place for spies to meet.

Setting & atmosphere Dark and cavernous. Like a subterranean Chinese shrine to money and Miller Genuine Draft. The main room is dominated by a Chinese deity and currency from around the world tacked to the wall. Chinese lanterns and brewing-company neon leap out at you. If you've ever been a sailor in old Hong Kong, you'll feel nostalgic. If you've seen the movie Suzy Wong, you'll feel like you just stepped onto the set. It's a cliché with drinks.

If you go It's so garish and in such bad taste that it will charm you from the moment you enter.

MAKE-OUT ROOM

NEO-BOHEMIAN HIPSTER BAR

Who Goes There Gen-Xers looking for alternatives

3225 22nd Street (near Mission Street); (415) 647-2888; www.makeoutroom.com
Zone 7 SoMa/Mission

Cover $5–$7 **Minimum** None **Mixed drinks** $4.50 and up **Wine** $3.50–$8 **Beer** $3.75 and up **Dress** Casual **Food available** None, but you can bring it in.

Hours Daily, 6 p.m.–2 a.m.

What goes on Nightly entertainment. The main attraction is escaping from the usual smoke-filled, shoulder-to-shoulder, ear-shattering trauma that is the delight of so many club-hoppers. You can hear the music, but you can hear the conversation, too. You can shoot pool and you won't get a cue in the gut when you turn around. You can enjoy a microbrew or a cocktail at the bar or a booth or table and feel that you're in a happening place, but it won't overwhelm.

Setting & atmosphere This place is cavernous. It looks almost like a high-school gym decorated for a dance. The big space, high ceiling, and darkness sprinkled with colored lights feel outdoorsy, especially when the doors are open and the fog rolls in.

If you go Be cool. Relax. Enjoy. Pssst: people don't really make out here.

MARTUNIS

COCKTAIL LOUNGE AS ART

Who Goes There Mixed crowd of gay and straight

4 Valencia Street; (415) 241-0205   Zone 7 SoMa/Mission

Cover None **Minimum** None **Mixed drinks** $6 **Wine** $5–$8 **Beer** $3.50–$4.75 **Dress** Evening casual **Food available** None

Hours Daily, 4 p.m.–2 a.m.

What goes on A variety of cool jazz and other lounge music accompanied by the cheerful clinking of cocktail glasses. Music might be a trio or just a singer at the copper-topped piano bar. Classic cocktails and new inventions are served up large, with a smile. If you sit at the piano, you might be asked to sing.

Setting & atmosphere It might have been called the Black Room, a Yin to the Red Room's Yang. It's dark in here. And the heavy drapes, thick carpet, and indirect lighting make it more so. Even when you come in at night, you have to let your eyes adjust. But it gives you the sense of being far away in some cozy, friendly getaway where all the strangers are just friends you haven't met.

If you go Don't go on an empty stomach. The drinks are huge, and you'll be bombed before you know it.

NOC NOC

CAVE BAR

Who Goes There Gen-Xers, 30-something locals

557 Haight Street (at Fillmore and Steiner Streets); (415) 861-5811
Zone 2 Civic Center

Cover None **Minimum** None **Mixed drinks** None **Wine** $3.25 and up **Beer** $3.25–$4.75 **Dress** Casual, alternative **Specials** Sake: $3, small; $5, large; happy hour on weekdays, 5–7 p.m. Monday features a Tarot reader, 7–10 p.m. ($3 donation). **Food available** Bar snacks

Hours Daily, 5 p.m.–2 a.m.

What goes on Whether starting off the night or closing it down, Gen-Xers come here to be mellow and avoid those who care to see and be seen. Perfect post-date spot for the tragically hip and alternative.

Setting & atmosphere The Stone Age meets Road Warrior. A small cave den littered with hieroglyphics, metal levers, bombs, and airplane wings. Scattered large throw pillows and pit booths are great for intimate chatting. A cozy escape from the harried lower Haight scene.

If you go Great locations for a crawl. The Toronado, known by beer connoisseurs for its wide selection on draft and bottled, is just a few doors down. Also a stone's throw away are the British hangout Mad Dog in the Fog, Midtown, and Nickie's BBQ. Note that these bars specialize in beer; you'll have to go elsewhere if you want a decent cocktail. The ATM inside is an added bonus.

OCCIDENTAL GRILL

SALOON AND RESTAURANT

Who Goes There Financial District suits, locals, 30-somethings

453 Pine Street; (415) 834-0484   Zone 4 Financial District

Cover None **Minimum** None **Mixed drinks** $5 and up **Wine** $4.50–$15, by the glass **Beer** $4.25 **Dress** Casual **Specials** Martinis **Food available** Full menu of meat-and-potatoes fare, elegantly done

Hours Monday–Friday, 11:30 a.m.–11 p.m.

What goes on The original building came down in the 1906 earthquake, but this is the site of the birthplace of the martini. First concocted by "Professor" Jerry Thomas and served to his "patients" at the Occidental, it is still being poured, at a rate of over 100 a day, in a form little changed since 1863.

Setting & atmosphere Brick walls, rich wood, and long brass rail in the bar. Starched white tablecloths and booths with padded seats in the restaurant. 1920s and 1930s crooners on the sound system, including Satchmo, der Bingle, Rudy Valley, and Lena Horne. As is common in the city, it's high class without being snooty. In the spirit of frontier egalitarianism, it's what's in your pocket, not your pedigree.

If you go Be prepared for well-dressed men and women stepping outside for fat cigars in the designated area and talking shop. On the plus side, when bothersome sellers of flowers, drugs, illegal weapons, or souvenirs wander in, they are quickly ushered out with the stern admonition, "It's against our regulations!"

PIER 23

JAZZ BAR/RESTAURANT

Who Goes There Locals, sailors, and jazz aficionados

Pier 23, between Green Street and Battery Street; (415) 362-5125
Zone 6 North Beach

Cover $5, Friday–Sunday **Minimum** None **Mixed drinks** $4.50 **Wine** $3.50–$8
Beer $3.50–$4.75 **Dress** Casual **Food available** Meat and potatoes, seafood

Hours Monday–Saturday, 11:30–2 a.m.; Sunday, 11:30 a.m.–11 p.m.

What goes on In the afternoons you can sit at the beaten copper bar, drink, and watch the parade of watercraft on the bay. In the evenings, dine and listen to popular local jazz bands of all kinds.

Setting & atmosphere An airy waterfront version of a smoky, late-night jazz basement. It's an old-time dockside café with a concrete floor; the pier in the back serves as a patio and a place for the fireboats to tie up. A cheery place with lots of regulars.

If you go The bands play inside, where there's limited seating for dinner, so many dine outside on the pier and listen to the music being piped out. If you do this, remember the highly changeable San Francisco weather and bring a coat.

PLOUGH AND THE STARS

IRISH PUB

Who Goes There Irish gents and lasses, Richmond-area locals

116 Clement Street, between Second and Third; (415) 751-1122
Zone 8 Richmond/Sunset

Cover $4 on weekends **Minimum** None **Mixed drinks** $3.50–$3.75 **Wine**
$3.50–$5 **Beer** $3.50–$4 **Dress** Casual **Specials** Happy hour, weekdays, 4–7 p.m.
Food available Cheese and crackers during Friday happy hour

Hours Monday, 4 p.m.–2 a.m.; Tuesday–Thursday, 2 p.m.–2 a.m.; Friday–Sunday, noon–
2 a.m.

What goes on Home of traditional Irish music in the Bay Area; good local bands play nightly after 9:30 p.m. Pool, darts, and chewing the fat with the regulars.

Setting & atmosphere Accents are thick, and so is the Guinness. No one comes here just once, so make yourself comfortable at the long wooden tables or pull up a stool and chat with the regulars at the bar. It's easy to forget you're in San Francisco, not Ireland, amid the acoustic ballads beneath the Irish Republic flag. It's sometimes hard to have an intimate conversation when everyone is clapping their hands to the music.

If you go Feel free to do the Irish crawl. Though Plough and the Stars is known among locals to have the best Guinness in town, there's a plethora of Irish hangouts just a jig away, including the Bitter End, Ireland 32s, Pat O'Shea's, and the Front Room.

THE PLUSH ROOM

CABARET AND COCKTAIL LOUNGE

Who Goes There Older gay men, tourists, some locals

940 Sutter Street (between Levenworth and Hyde) in the York Hotel; (415) 885-2800; www.plushroom.com   Zone 3 Union Square

Cover $20–$35, for shows **Minimum** 2 drinks **Mixed drinks** $6.50–$10.50 **Wine** $6.50–$7.50 **Beer** $4.50 **Dress** Gussied-up, rhinestones and silk **Specials** Changing jazz and cabaret performances **Food** None

Hours Monday–Saturday, 5 p.m.-2 a.m.

What goes on Lounge acts. Sultry cabaret singers and jazz music. Old time talents include Rita Moreno and Paula West.

Setting and atmosphere A San Francisco nightlife tradition lives on in the Plush Room of the York Hotel. The stained glass ceiling from the early 1900s reinforces the old-fashioned style. Reams of red velour and generic hotel carpeting and furniture sound a note of tacky schmaltz, but it somehow makes the place feel more authentic. Fresh flowers atop the baby grand add a touch of genuine elegance, and when the lights go down and the star glimmers before you, you're transported to a world of splendor.

If you go Love a cabaret. Service can be slow and drinks weak, but if you appreciate the tawdry antics and true skill involved in a lounge act, this is the spot for you.

THE RED ROOM

RETRO COCKTAIL LOUNGE

Who Goes There Hipsters in their 20s and 30s

827 Sutter Street; (415) 346-7666   Zone 3 Union Square

Cover None **Minimum** None **Mixed drinks** $4–$7 **Wine** $6–$8 **Beer** $3.50–$4.75 **Dress** Dressy **Food available** None

Hours Daily, 5 p.m.–2 a.m.

What goes on A 1950s lounge lizard meets Details magazine. Young yuppies who are too cool to cop to the term come to this oh-so-hip location to advance the cause of cocktail culture. Aside from the decor, nothing distracts the patrons from themselves and their long-stemmed glasses.

Setting & atmosphere Red. Crimson. Vermillion. Sanguine. Longer wavelengths of the visible light spectrum. It's red, by God, red! The ceiling, the floor, the wallpaper, the drapes. Even the lights are red, though you should read nothing into that. The place is small and smoky, with a horseshoe bar commanded by an Amazon and her assistant; they slosh out a variety of martinis into cocktail glasses the size of bull horns.

If you go Go early. The terminally hip tend to crowd this place so much in the evening that a doorman has to ask guests to form a line; they're allowed in only after a reverential wait. But don't let this deter you. Before the hordes of hip descend, it's a great place for a predinner cocktail. All that red is somehow soothing when accompanied by a well-made martini.

SAVOY TIVOLI

MEAT-MARKET NIGHTCLUB

Who Goes There The young and the restless

1434 Grant Avenue (Green and Union Streets); (415) 362-7023;
www.savoy-tivoli.netfirms.com   Zone 6 North Beach

Cover None **Minimum** None **Mixed drinks** $4.50–$7 **Wine** $5.50 and up **Beer** $3.50–$4.75 **Dress** Casual seductive **Food available** Wonderful North Beach Italian cuisine all over the neighborhood. Management allows you to bring in any food, but no drinks.

Hours Monday–Saturday, 5 p.m.–2 a.m.; Sunday, closed

What goes on A neighborhood party for those on the make. For those who can concentrate, there are three pool tables.

Setting & atmosphere Every bit of this large North Beach bar is packed on weekends. The overflow hangs out of the wall-sized open windows in the heated patio facing the street. Partygoers are mostly in their 20s, and they're ready for some serious action. The jukebox is enough to keep this popular bar rocking.

If you go Get ready to be checked out. This is a desperate singles haven and a fun place despite its meat-market reputation. It's surrounded by great eateries and other bars. Conveniently located; a perfect stop after a nice dinner when entertaining out-of-towners.

TONGA ROOM

TROPICAL ISLAND BAR

Who Goes There Nob Hill locals, tourists, and happy hour crowd

950 Mason Street in the Fairtmont Hotel; (415) 772-5278; www.tongaroom.com
Zone 1 Chinatown

Cover $4 after 8 p.m. **Minimum** 2 drinks **Mixed drinks** Tropical cocktail specials $8.50–$25 **Wine** $6 and up **Beer** $4 and up **Dress** Evening casual to dressy **Specials** Live music; happy hour, weekdays 5–7 p.m. **Food available** Yes

Hours Sunday–Thursday, 5 p.m.–midnight; Friday and Saturday, 5 p.m.–1 a.m.

What goes on A wide mix of people come to drink the island cocktails and swoon to their sweatheart beneath straw huts and palm trees, but most just drink their drinks and wait for the periodic man-made thunderstorms.

Setting & atmosphere A tropical island oasis in the Fairtmont Hotel atop Nob Hill. Watch a live band on a moated island while sipping an umbrella-clad drink from a coconut. The South Seas decor is more of an upscale tiki lounge than a seaman's dive.

If you go Don't miss the $6 all-you-can-eat weekday buffet from 5 to 7 p.m (with a one drink minimum). It's easy to make a meal out of potstickers, barbeque spareribs, terriyaki drumsticks, veggies and dip, a cheese plate, egg rolls, and more. Watch out for the Scorpion. It's the most expensive drink on the menu for a reason.

TOP O'THE MARK

ROOFTOP LOUNGE AND DANCE FLOOR

Who Goes There Well-dressed 30s and up, tourists, and regulars

999 California Street, 19th floor; (415) 616-6916;
http://hotels.san-francisco.interconti.com/dining/di01a.html   Zone 1 Chinatown

Cover Weeknights, $8; weekends, $10 **Minimum** None **Mixed drinks** $7 and up
Wine $6 and up **Beer** $5 and up **Dress** Smart casual to dressy **Specials** The view at
sunset **Food available** Finger foods, elegant hors d'oeuvres, 3-course prix fixe on
Thursday, Friday, and Saturday, $39

Hours Opens daily at 3 p.m.

What goes on Dancing, romancing, schmoozing, and boozing. Musical offerings
include in-house pianists, cool jazz combos, and retro groups. People come here for
swing and ballroom dancing, sunset cocktails, business talks, romantic assignations, and
conspiracies.

Setting & atmosphere Understated elegance on the most romantic rooftop in
town, on top of the Mark Hopkins hotel, on top of Nob Hill. The elevated dance floor
is in the center of the room and surrounded by plush seating along the huge windows
that give a near 360° view of the city. Despite the price and the sophistication, it's never
intimidating, always welcoming, almost homey.

If you go Valet parking is $21. Take a taxi or the California line cable car and get off
right at the Mark. No minors are allowed after 8:30 p.m.

TOSCA'S

OPERA BAR

Who Goes There Mostly locals, 30-something and up

242 Columbus Avenue; (415) 391-1244   Zone 6 North Beach

Cover None **Minimum** None **Mixed drinks** $3.50–$3.75 **Wine** $4–$6 **Beer**
$2.50–$3.50 **Dress** Come as you are **Specials** Irish coffee, house cappucino **Food
available** None

Hours 5 p.m.–2 a.m.

What goes on Conversation and playing the jukebox. It's the only one in town with
selections only from the world of opera. A lot of locals, including a few celebs, camp out
here. In the back is an invitation-only pool room said to be a fave of Sam Shepard and
Francis Ford Coppola.

Setting & atmosphere A big place for a bar. All wood with red upholstered booths
and a long bar on which sit dozens of Irish coffee glasses already charged with whiskey,
sugar, and cream, waiting to be filled with hot coffee.

If you go Afternoon to early evening is best, especially when the fog rolls in. At night
the thunderous base notes of the disco in the basement can be felt through the floor.

Part Nine

Shopping in San Francisco

In the gold-rush days of miners, soldiers, sailors, and scoundrels, folks used to come into the city of San Francisco to shop. The city has long since been eclipsed by Los Angeles as a West Coast center of consumer excess, but it still has unmatched treasures. It's still a frontier town, although today the frontiers are different; multimedia and technology, global commerce, and artistic innovation are some of the new territories.

There's been a new gold rush, of course: computers, multimedia, and e-commerce have made San Francisco and nearby Silicon Valley one of the most expensive places to live—and shop—in the country. Since the dot bomb, the tech rush has simmered down, but, undeniably, new money has been created—very new money. The infusion of money and youth (and moneyed youth) has ratcheted up the quality of the shopping (they gotta spend it somewhere)—and the prices along with it.

Rest assured that San Francisco's merchants still know how to separate fools from their gold. Shopping here is about more than getting the goods; it's about the neighborhood. And shopping in these distinct neighborhoods (they even have their own "microclimates") is a good way to glimpse the city's kaleidoscope of cultures.

Real San Franciscans wouldn't be caught dead in a mall or a superstore for something they can find at a neighborhood place for less. In a city that loves its neighborhoods, supporting small businesses and local artists and craftspeople who sell their wares is a matter of civic pride, a way of voting with the wallet, a mix of economic necessity, political conscientiousness, and style. It's a way of saying, "I like where I live, and I want this place to stay as individualistic and eccentric as I am." The locals don't say "I'm going shopping." (How suburban!) They say, "I'm going to the Haight (or the Castro or Cow Hollow or the Mission)." They have a thing for shops with personality. The neighborhoods here are notorious for banning chains from their enclaves and supporting

333

mom-and-pop operations (even if the mom and pop in question are a pair of 20-something, mom-and-mom entrepreneurs).

If you time your visit right, you can catch some of the best shopping values (and best people-watching) at the annual spring and summer street fairs thrown by the city's major neighborhoods. The biggies are the Union Street fair (late May) and the Haight, Castro, and Folsom Street fairs (September and October).

Here's a look at San Francisco shopping, with an eye on the specialties (and peculiarities) of the Bay Area—its fixations on food, wine, recycled and earth-friendly merchandise, and, of course, sex, drugs, and rock and roll. This is the birthplace of such stylish hometown enterprises as Levi Strauss, Gap, Banana Republic, Old Navy, Esprit, Williams-Sonoma, and Bebe. It's also the hothouse of trends; the continuing craze for tattooing and piercing was born here.

Those hunting for bargains might pick up Sally Socolich's definitive *Bargain Hunting in the Bay Area* (published by Chronicle Books), which maps out discount shopping in the city and surrounding areas. If you want some shopping guidance, consider a shopping tour such as **Shopper Stopper Shopping Tours** (phone (707) 829-1597). You might also check online at the San Francisco websites—**CitySearch San Francisco** (www.citysearch7.com) and the somewhat more hip **www.sfstation. com**—both of which are continually updated with up-to-the-minute information on new shops or new tours on offer.

Combined with a stop at one of the area's almost ridiculously plentiful cafés, window-shopping is as satisfying as shelling out the cash. When you go home (if you do), you can take back something more than a loaf of airport gift-shop sourdough, a Hard Rock Café T-shirt, and a case of Rice-A-Roni.

Top Shopping 'Hoods

Union Square: Zone 3

While the word epicenter should not be thrown around too casually in this town, Union Square is indeed the epicenter of shopping. While not exactly a neighborhood, Union Square, is the closest the city comes to a downtown, at least in terms of shopping. There's an enormous underground public parking lot beneath the 2.6-acre green park at the center of the square; the park above is peopled with chess players, street artists and musicians, street characters, and bustling shoppers from around the world.

Framing this colorful square are the main shopping streets (Stockton Street, Powell Street, Geary Boulevard, and Post Street) and the city's densest concentration of major department stores, tony boutiques, restaurants and cafés, big hotels, and corner flower stands.

Moving clockwise from the Saint Francis Hotel on Powell Street, you'll find the following: **Disney Store** (400 Post Street at Powell Street; (415) 391-6866), **Borders Books and Music** (400 Post Street; (415) 399-1633), **Saks Fifth Avenue** (384 Post Street; (415) 986-4300), **Tiffany** (350 Post Street at Union Square; (415) 781-7000), and **Neiman Marcus** (150 Stockton Street at Geary Boulevard; (415) 362-3900), which each year sends the city's most spectacular Christmas tree soaring to the top of its stained-glass dome. Who says New York's windows are the only ones to see? A megalithic **Macy's** (170 O'Farrell Street at Stockton Street; (415) 397-3333), which took over the building vacated by the sadly folded San Francisco institution I. Magnin & Co., recently underwent a handsome renovation. Sprawling over three city blocks, it includes a new **Wolfgang Puck Express,** where you can nosh on made-to-order pastas, salads, entrées, and sushi; **Boudin's Bakery,** where you can get clam chowder in a sourdough bread bowl; and fresh-squeezed smoothies and soups at **Jamba Juice.** The massive, three-story **FAO Schwarz** (48 Stockton Street at O'Farrell Street; (415) 394-8700) has a Barbie boutique the size of most other department stores' women's clothing sections, and its candy department, with a Jelly Belly district, is a wonder of the world.

During the computer boom the Union Square district saw a burst of new growth, including Sony's state-of-the-art **Metreon Center** (101 Fourth Street at Mission Street; (415) 369-6000), a sleek, high-style, high-tech shopping and entertainment complex, which landed upon downtown like the Retail Mothership.

Like elsewhere in the country, chain stores are moving into San Francisco, robbing the Union Square shopping zone of some of its legendary exclusivity. The square has been recently colonized by the theme park–like megastores, the shopping equivalents of Planet Hollywood and Hard Rock Cafe. The newest is the **Levi's Superstore** (300 Post Street at Stockton Street; (415) 501-0100) a four-story retail entertainment hybrid which features clothing-customization services such as 3D body scanning, laser etching, hand painting, fabric ornamentation and embroidery, and **Shrink-to-Fit**—a 40-minute shrink-your-jeans-while-you-wear-them hot tub experience; other Union Square superstores include **Niketown** (278 Post Street; (415) 392-6453), **Disney Store,** and **Virgin Records** (2 Stockton Street at Market Street; (415) 397-4525). The newest twist on the megastore is the in-store DJ—everyone's got one now, including **Levi's, Virgin,** and **Diesel** (101 Post Street at Kearny Street; (415) 982-7077), where you can shop the four-story oasis of uncasually priced casual gear and denim while grinding your teeth and snapping your fingers to the tweakiest techno in town. The sweetest-smelling superstore has to be **Sephora** (1 Stockton at Market Street; (415) 392-1545), a French cosmetics superstore featuring every imaginable cologne, bath, and beauty product from conservative to cutting edge. It sure stinks pretty in here!

The dozens of tony boutiques on the side streets offer shopping with an international feel and "if you have to ask . . ." prices: **Celine of Paris** (233 Geary Street at Stockton; (415) 397-1140), **Gucci** (200 Stockton Street; (415) 392-2808), **Hermes** (212 Stockton Street; (415) 391-7200), **Louis Vuitton** (233 Geary Street; (415) 391-6200), **Alfred Dunhill of London** (250 Post Street between Grant and Stockton Streets; (415) 781-3368), and **Cartier** (231 Post Street between Grant and Stockton Streets; (415) 397-3180).

Tangential to the square is Maiden Lane, a narrow, car-free alley that once housed ladies of the evening. Now the quaint street features pricey shops and restaurants, including a three-floor **Chanel** (155 Maiden Lane between Grant and Stockton Streets; (415) 981-1550), the Paris-based **Christofle Silversmiths** (140 Grant Avenue at Post Street; (415) 399-1931), and an outpost of Seattle's **Sur La Table** (77 Maiden Lane between Grant and Kearny Streets; (415) 732-7900), a gourmet kitchenware boutique. If you can afford to browse on Maiden Lane, nearby you'll find the equally elegant and snooty **Emporio Armani Boutique** (1 Grant Street between Market and O'Farrell Streets; (415) 677-9400), in the 1911 Security Pacific Bank building (where you can get a designer snack in the oh-so-Italian Armani café and be seen noshing at its outdoor tables).

Also in the Union Square area are a handful of San Francisco–based stores, including 150-year-old **Shreve & Co. Jewelers** (200 Post Street at Grant Street; (415) 421-2600) and the equally venerable **Gumps** (135 Post Street between Kearny and Grant Streets; (415) 982-1616), one of the world's most beautiful and unusual department stores. Gumps features china, crystal, Asian art treasures, antiques, and one-of-a-kind objects and furniture.

These old-timers are balanced out by fresh-faced young merchandisers near Union Square like fun and funky **Urban Outfitters** (80 Powell Street; (415) 989-1515), the **Williams-Sonoma** flagship store (150 Post Street between Kearny and Grant Streets; (415) 362-6904), **Crate & Barrel** (55 Stockton Street at O'Farrell; (415) 986-4000), and the vast khaki-and-cream expanses of the **Banana Republic** flagship store (256 Grant Street at Sutter Street; (415) 788-3087).

San Francisco–based **Gap** boasts a sleek, stark, three-story flagship store at Union Square, which also houses siblings **Gap Kids** and **Baby Gap** (890 Market Street at Powell Street; (415) 788-5909) right next to the tourist-choked cable-car turnaround on Market Street. And it's wired; you can mix and match clothing components ("you want a belt with that?") on a computer screen while lounging on a sofa. Across the street is the even more recently-opened three-story flagship store of Gap's kid-sister store **Old Navy** (Market Street at 4th Street; (415) 344-0375), which features a good, low-cost café called Torpedo Joe's (to go with the good, low-cost shopping experience).

Across Market Street from the cable-car turnaround is the **San Francisco Shopping Centre** (865 Market Street at Fifth; (415) 495-5656; www.sanfranciscocentre.com), a multilevel enclosed urban mall anchored by **Nordstrom** (phone (415) 243-8500) with its five-floor spiral escalator, and a "mall-esque" array of shops including **Abercrombie & Fitch** (call (415) 284-9276) and its competitive clone **American Eagle Outfitters** (phone (415) 543-4550) and **The Body Shop** (call (415) 281-3760).

Pacific Heights/Cow Hollow/Marina: Zone 5

The city's second-largest upscale shopping zone covers three linked neighborhoods: the five blocks of Fillmore Street between Geary Boulevard and Jackson Street, the six-block stretch of Union Street from Gough to Steiner Streets (also known as Cow Hollow because it evolved from grazing pasture to browsing nirvana), and the seven blocks of Chestnut Street known as the Marina District.

The beautifully preserved Victorian and Edwardian homes of Union Street, many of which survived the 1906 earthquake, now house hip, upscale, yuppie boutiques and cafés and offer some of the city's best window-shopping (just be careful not to get run over by a baby stroller pushed by one of the area's fast-moving power moms). Fillmore has evolved from a run-down area into a gauntlet of chic boutiques and restaurants. And the Marina is another warren of cute shops catering to the moneyed—its main drag is Chestnut Street.

Chinatown: Zone 1

More car chases are filmed in Chinatown than in any other neighborhood of this cinematic city. A visit to this famous, fascinating district—home to more than 200,000 Chinese Americans (the Chinese community is second in size only to New York's Chinatown)—begins at the large, ornate gateway at the intersection of Grant and Bush Streets, just above Union Square. Don't even think of driving in Chinatown. You'd miss all the sights, sounds, tastes, and smells of the bustling streets, where you'll encounter otherworldly vegetables, live animals, exotic spices, herbs, ivory, jade, pearls, and other prizes amid the Oriental kitsch. Shops like **Dragon House** (455 Grant Avenue; (415) 421-3693) and the **China Trade Center** (838 Grant Street between Clay and Washington Streets; (415) 837-1509), which is a three-floor mini-mall, encapsulate the best of Chinatown and minimize the jostling. But half the adventure is getting lost in this intriguing world and discovering a few treasures among the trinkets.

Bordering Chinatown is the formerly Italian neighborhood known as North Beach, the main stomping grounds of the Beat poets and artists who made **City Lights Bookstore** (261 Columbus Avenue at Broadway; (415) 362-8193) and **Caffe Trieste** their home. You'll find hours of browsing potential on the streets bordering Washington Square Park, and the plentiful Italian cafés and pastry shops alone are a shopping experience.

Japantown: Zone 8

Sunday is the busiest shopping day in Japantown, and the five-acre enclosed mall **Japan Center** (1625 Post Street; (415) 922-6776) is its heart. The shops and boutiques contain everything from antique kimonos and scrolls to ultramodern furniture and electronics. Favorite shops for Westerners are **Kinokinuya Stationery and Gifts** (1581 Webster Street at Post Street; (415) 567-8901) with its fascinating array of intricate notecards and writing implements, and **Kinokinuya Book Store** (1581 Webster Street at Post Street; (415) 567-7625), which has a vast assortment of books and magazines in Japanese and English. The complex also includes the **AMC Kabuki 8 Cinemas** (1881 Post Street; (415) 931-9800) and the recently renovated **Kabuki Springs and Spa** (1750 Geary Boulevard; (415) 922-6002), Japanese spa where you can steam, soak, and sigh away a hard day's shop.

Hayes Valley: Zone 7

Colonel Thomas Hayes probably wouldn't recognize the urban "valley" that bears his name. It's more like the Valley of the Interior Decorators: distressed-furniture boutiques, art-deco specialty shops, and other retro-contemporary brokers line this relatively small shopping district between the Castro and Civic Center, along with dozens of tiny boutiques that look like settings for photo shoots for Wallpaper magazine. Good bets include **Red Desert** (1632 Market at Gough; (415) 552-2800), a remarkable retail collection of cacti (a perfect gift for brown thumbs); **Wishbone** (601 Irving at 7th Avenue; (415) 242-5540), an eccentric tchochke shop; and the San Francisco franchise of the **Psychic Eye Book Shops** new age megastore chain (301 Fell at Hayes; (415) 863-9997).

The Haight: Zone 8

Hip and hippie—that's the essence of the Haight today. To many visitors and residents, the time warp known as Haight Street is still synonymous with hippies. Even though the famous corner of Haight and Ashbury Streets is now bounded by a **Ben & Jerry's** and a **Gap,** and even though music and fashion have passed through punk and techno, the Haight has managed to hang onto its 1960s reputation. A mishmash of head shops, secondhand stores, record and book shops, and the city's most alternative shopping experiences line Haight Street from Masonic to Stanyan Streets.

Although the novelty of flower power has faded, today's progressive subcultures add a changing style to the Haight. You'll still find clusters of head shops, packs of grungy panhandling teens, and other historical artifacts like the Red Vic Theater, Haight-Ashbury Free Clinic, and **Bound Together Anarchist Bookstore** (1369 Haight Street between Central and Masonic Streets; (415) 431-8355), but now the Haight offers a fusion of old and new.

Some of the street's colorful landmarks include **Pipe Dreams** (1376 Haight Street between Central and Masonic Streets; (415) 431-3553), a venerable head shop with the usual drug accoutrements and jewelry, T-shirts, and maybe even a blacklight poster or two; **Planet Weavers** (1573 Haight Street at Clayton Street; (415) 864-4415), a Toys 'R Us for fans of new age, world music, and multiculturalism in general, filled with candles, drums, and fountains; and **Bound Together,** the truly anarchist bookstore previously mentioned.

South of Market: Zone 7

Otherwise known as SoMa, the sprawling, industrial warehouse–filled South of Market area, with clusters of outlet and discount stores, is a focal point for bargain hunters. An enormous **Costco** (450 10th Street; (415) 626-4288), dominates an entire city block; other discount stores include **Tower Records Outlet, Bed Bath & Beyond, Trader Joe's, Yerba Buena Square,** and **Burlington Coat Factory.** Because the nightclub scene also thrives in SoMa, there's a host of leather and fetish stores and other purveyors of "underground" attire and accessories, including **Stormy Leather** (1158 Howard Street; (415) 626-1672).

The Castro: Zone 7

In the sunny, predominantly gay and lesbian neighborhood known as the Castro, you never know what you'll see. A controversy recently erupted over a bookstore's window display, which featured an anatomically correct porn star; many other gift stores, including the aptly-named and in-your-face erotic art shop Erotic Art, continue to make window-shopping in the Castro an eye-popping, NC-17, at-your-own-risk experience.

A self-sufficient village, the Castro has become the equivalent of an island resort overrun with pricey boutiques offering gifts, trendy clothing, coffee, burritos, more coffee, more burritos, and fruit juice. Don't-miss shops include the neoclassic **Cliff's Variety** hardware store (479 Castro at 18th Street; (415) 431-5365), sort of Mayberry R.F.D. circa 2021, **RoCo-coa Faerie Queene Chocolates** (415 Castro at 17th Street; (415) 252-5814), a phantasmagorical candy store like no other, and **Under One Roof** (549 Castro Street at 19th Street; (415) 503-2300), a lovely, imaginative upscale gift boutique staffed entirely by volunteers—all profits are divided among more than 50 AIDS organizations in the area.

Berkeley: Zone 12

In the Republic of Berkeley there is one street that maintains a pretty good balance between indie and mainstream. **Fourth Street** manages to appeal to the newfound yuppiness of the surrounding neighborhood while keeping in tune with the hippie vibe that has marked Berkeley as the brainchild of creative innovation. Whether you are looking for a gift for someone else or looking to indulge yourself you can find almost anything here—from **Gardener's Eden** (phone (510) 889-9105) at the southern end of the strip to a **Crate & Barrel Outlet** (phone (510) 528-5500) on the other end. It's niche shopping at its best. You can walk away with hard-to-find CDs or books from **Hear Music** (phone (510) 559-9500) or **Cody's Books** which has two locations; one on Fourth street (phone (510) 559-9500) and the other on Telegraph Avenue (phone (510) 845-7852). There are plenty of shoe stores and hipster Euro-style boutiques also. How 'bout walking away with some garbage? **Urban Ore** on nearby Sixth street (phone (510) 559-4454) sells for reuse over 3,500 tons of "garbage" retrieved from the Berkeley garbage pits. As you would expect from Berkeley, even the stores do their share in maintaining a balanced environment. One-of-a-kind finds are what lure Berkeleyites—the home remodeler, the collector, the musician, etc. ... here year after year. Berkeley is also where you will find one of the most beautiful grocery stores ever. **Berkeley Bowl** (2020 Oregon Street; (510) 843-6929) boasts the largest produce (mostly organic) section in all of Northern California. Come to select food or come to take pictures! Its international section is a one-stop shop for everything—wasabi, pickled ginger, and seaweed paper!

If it's a lazy sunny afternoon and you've hit Fourth street, another shopping enclave is Telegraph Avenue, which runs directly toward the Berkeley campus. As you can imagine, it is packed with college rats, but the stores and sidewalk vendors are worth a browse. Through all the tie-dye and hippie craftsmanship on sale on the streets, you will discover unique book and music stores, shoe stores, pastry shops, and, if you are lucky, a group of singing Hare Krishnas. If you can brave the parking challenges, you will be excited by the unique shopping opportunities here. It's a day well spent!

The Malls

Despite what you may have seen in movies like *Clueless* and *Valley Girl,* malls no longer define the California shopping experience (and anyway, that was Southern California!). The Bay Area is almost actively anti-mall, and neighborhood shopping is de rigueur. But if you must mall it, there are several not unattractive options.

The latest un-mall is Sony Corporation's retail and entertainment megaplex called **Metreon** (101 Fourth Street at Mission Street; (415) 369-6000; www.metreon.com), which architects and shoppers alike are hailing as the wave of the future. Featuring 14 state-of-the-art movie theaters and an 8-story IMAX auditorium, plus a high-tech game arcade and restaurants that go way beyond the term "food court," the shops include **Sony Style, Hear Music, Discovery Channel Store,** plus the ubiquitous **Starbucks.**

Built in 1988 to house Nordstrom, the downtown **San Francisco Shopping Centre** (865 Market Street at Fifth Street; (415) 495-5656; www.sanfranciscocentre.com) boasts over 100 different merchants, including **Kenneth Cole, J. Crew, Ann Taylor, Abercrombie & Fitch, Hold Everything,** and **Victoria's Secret.** Shoppers wind their way up curved escalators designed by Mitsubishi through four floors of shops; connection to the Powell Street BART and Muni terminal makes getting there easy.

Too fancy to be called a mall, the seriously stylin' **Crocker Galleria** (50 Post Street at Kearny Street; (415) 393-1505; www.shopatgalleria .com) in the heart of the downtown Financial District was fashioned after the Galleria Vittorio Emanuele in Milan. The galleria offers 50 shops, restaurants, and services, including **Versace** and **Nicole Miller** boutiques and a charming rooftop park. Parking is free on Saturday with a $10 purchase (which, in a place that sells $50 undershirts, should take about 10 seconds).

By the waterfront is the monumental **Embarcadero Center** (Clay Street between Battery Street and Justin Herman Plaza; (415) 772-0500; www.embarcaderocenter.com), a complex of four office towers housing two levels of restaurants, movie theaters, and shops, including **The Limited, Ann Taylor, Banana Republic, Gap, Crabtree and Evelyn, Pottery Barn,** and **Sam Goody**, plus a few interesting local boutiques like **Essentiel Elements,** an aromatherapy bath and skin-care shop, and **Earthsake,** which offers exquisite eco-friendly objects for the home.

The **Stanford Shopping Center** (180 El Camino Real, Palo Alto; (650) 617-8585; www.stanfordshop.com), which is owned by Stanford University, offers the most concentrated upscale retail experience in the area, with **Bloomingdale's, Neiman Marcus, Macy's, Nordstrom, Tiffany, Smith & Hawken,** and **Crate & Barrel.** San Francisco's only genuine enclosed mall in the city limits is **Stonestown Galleria** (3251 20th Avenue at Winston Street; (415) 759-2626; www.stonestown galleria.com) in the outer Sunset District. The mall includes a substantial 120 shops anchored by **Nordstrom, Macy's, Pottery Barn, Eddie Bauer,** and **Williams-Sonoma.**

Outlets

The SoMa District is full of big game for bargain hunters, and you can find particularly good sport at the **Esprit Outlet Store** (499 Illinois Street; (415) 957-2540), with discounts of up to 70% off Esprit clothes for women, teens, and kids; and **Yerba Buena Square,** an urban outlet mall (899 Howard Street at Fifth; (415) 543-1275) anchored by a **Burlington Coat Factory Warehouse** and **The Shoe Pavilion.** Not so far away is the **Six Sixty Factory Outlet Center** (660 Third Street at Townsend Street; (415) 553-8390) with bargains on many name brands. The **Gunne Sax** or **Jessica McClintock Outlet** in South San Francisco (494 Forbes Boulevard; (415) 495-3326) has been outfitting girls in prom dresses since the early 1980s. Dresses normally over $100 may be discounted to as little as $30 here. Moms can sigh in relief. Have you checked the price of Gore-Tex lately? Nothing is more pricey than a Gore-Tex down parka from The North Face—unless you check out the deals at **The North Face Outlet** (1325 Howard Street; (415) 626-6444.) Outdoor gear here at pretty good prices, although don't expect their high-end line. Although there is no shortage of Tower Record stores in your hometown probably, you may find better prices at the **Tower Records Outlet** (660 3rd Street; (415) 957-9660), which is the clearing-house for their music empire. You'll find mostly old stock CDs, cassettes, videos, DVDs, and books. New releases are hard to come by here.

Specialty Shops

Alternative Shopping

San Francisco specializes in eccentrics and subcultures (this is, after all, a city with a church—St. John Coltrane African Orthodox Church—devoted to jazz music), so shoppers can always expect the unexpected. Along with tattooing, body-piercing has become hot stuff (some say the craze began here), and body modification is one souvenir that keeps on giving. If you decide to get a new perforation while you're here, you might as well get something cool to put in it. For body jewelry and other accessories, visit **Anubis Warpus** (1525 Haight Street at Ashbury; (415) 431-2218) and **Body Manipulations** (3234 16th Street between Guerrero and Dolores Streets; (415) 621-0408).

The Beats go on, and so do the hippies, at least in the memories and imaginations of most visitors. For Beat memorabilia, **City Lights Bookstore** (261 Columbus Avenue at Broadway; (415) 362-8193) in North Beach is un-Beat-able; a window-shopping stroll through the Haight District will turn up all sorts of flashbacks, from head shops to vintage rock-concert poster peddlers.

Hip shoppers and grown-up kids find themselves kitschy-cooing over **Uncle Mame's** (2241 Market Street near Noe Street; (415) 626-1953), whose larger-than-life proprietor provides a loving home for misfit toys and all-but-forgotten fads—everything you weren't allowed to have as a kid. And kid-aged kids love the **Sanrio** flagship store (39 Stockton Street near Market Street; (415) 981-5568) in Union Square, with two candy-colored floors of Hello Kitty and her cloyingly cute chums. **Wig Factory** (3143 Mission Street between Army and Precita Streets; (415) 282-4939) displays the city's most outlandish collection of wigs (and in San Francisco, that's really saying something).

More silliness: **House of Magic** (2025 Chestnut Street at Fillmore Street; (415) 346-2218) is an old-fashioned all-purpose magic supply store with the usual unusual array of gag gifts and gadgets. **Gamescape** (333 Divisadero Street at Oak Street; (415) 621-4263) specializes in games for all ages, ranging from casual board games and puzzles, to fantasy and strategy games, to computer games. They also sell used games.

For shopping of an X-Files bent, check out **Psychic Eye** (301 Fell Street at Gough Street; (415) 863-9997), a vast new-age superstore overstuffed with crystals and candles, sculptures and spell books, and the city's largest selections of tarot cards and psychics to read them for you. **Botanica Yoruba** (998 Valencia Street; (415) 826-4967) offers candles, potions, herbs, and incantations for every need or desire—sort of a "Pagans 'R Us." Gothic Central in the Haight is **Gargoyles** (1324 Haight Street at Central Avenue; (415) 552-4274), featuring a storeful of baleful ghoulies, plus other accessories for this spooky, spectral, tragically-chic lifestyle. One of the most unusual and off-the-beaten-path shops in town, **Paxton Gate** (824 Valencia Street; (415) 824-1872) may be the world's most bizarre gardening store, as evidenced by its displays of eerie air plants, mounted bugs and butterflies, and stuffed and costumed mice.

Amid the usual bazaars and holiday sales, there's an annual crafts fair for people who loathe Christmas; **Naughty Santa's Bizarre Bazaar** is presented by Space Cowgirls/Sounds Good! in early December and features gifts by more than 50 fringe artisans at the **SOMAR Gallery** (934 Brannan Street).

Extreme Sports

San Francisco has hosted the X-games and that's no coincidence. The city is full of adrenaline-inducing jumps, trails, surf, rock, and slopes. No place is proper gear more mandatory than this playground of a city.

Despite appearances, it ain't cheap being a skatepunk. What with the skater duds, shoes, customized boards, wheels, and magazines, you gotta keep up. At **DLX** (1831 Market Street at Octavia Street; (415) 626-5588) they've got it all. Same goes for snowboarding, another accessory-intensive sport: **SFO** (618 Shrader Street at Haight Street; (415) 386-1666) is the sweet spot for boots, boards, and bundle-up wear. Gear-head heaven for any sport is located in either **Sports Basement** (1301 Sixth Street; (415) 437-0100); or **Lombardi Sports** (1600 Jackson Street; (888) 456-6223). Both places offer helpful and knowledgeable service, and floors are divided by activity. For rock climbing you can visit either of the multi-purpose stores mentioned above or head to **Mission Cliffs** (2295 Harrison Street at 19th street; (415) 550-0515). They have all the necessary gear including helmets, harnesses, climbing shoes, ropes, biners, etc.

Antiques

San Franciscans are in love with history, and the antique stores are stocked with everything from ultra-pricey traditional pieces and 1950s kitschware to last month's fads.

In the area once known as the Barbary Coast, Jackson Square, San Francisco's first designated historic district (it was the only group of downtown buildings to survive the 1906 earthquake and fire), has fittingly become the city's official antique district. Bounded by Jackson, Washington, Montgomery, and Sansome Streets, the square, which showcases its pieces like small museums, houses about two dozen dealers, such as **Dillingham and Company** (431 Jackson Street between Sansome and Montgomery Streets; (415) 989-8777) with seventeenth-, eighteenth-, and nineteenth-century English antiques; **Argentum—The Leopard's Head** (414 Jackson Street near Sansome Street; (415) 296-7757) with eighteenth- and nineteenth-century continental furniture; and **Daniel Stein Antiques** for traditional English and American furniture (458 Jackson Street near Balance Street; (415) 956-5620).

Market Street near the Civic Center has evolved into an unofficial antiques district. **Grand Central Station Antiques** (1632 Market Street #A between Franklin and Gough Streets; (415) 252-8155) is like a classic jumble sale, with two floors of fun finds. Next door, at **Beaver Bros. Antiques** (1637 Market Street between Franklin and Gough Streets; (415) 863-4344), you can rent the merchandise; the two-floor shop is the city's biggest prop-rental outfit, supplying furniture and colorful clutter for movie and TV sets.

Perhaps the most pleasurable antique shopping is on Russian Hill at spots like **Russian Hill Antiques** (2200 Polk Street at Vallejo Street; (415) 441-5561) and **J. Goldsmith Antiques** (1924 Polk Street between Jackson and Pacific Streets; (415) 771-4055), specializing in early American furniture, collectibles, and toys. If early American seems a bit too drab for your taste, head to **Trout Farm—Retrospect Fine Furniture** (1649 Market Street; (415) 863-7414). It's all about retro here—from the 1940s, 1950s, and 1960s. And right next door in their best Miami South Beach fashion, **Decodence** (1684 Market Street, between Gough and Franklin Streets; (415) 553-4525) is bulging art deco at the seams.

Bargains/Thrift

Although shopping in San Francisco may not be the way of life or contact sport it is in Los Angeles or New York, the locals are nevertheless competitive about what they get. And how they get it. If you compliment a San Franciscan about his new computer bag or her little black dress, be prepared to hear the tale of how cheap it was at a thrift store (or at a sidewalk sale). The more obscure the source and the lower the price, the better. Never underestimate the talent it takes to emerge from **Community Thrift** with something cheap that you'll actually use or wear! In San Francisco, people try on and toss off new personas the way other folks change underwear. Previously owned and recycled everything—from clothes to records to kitchenware—is big business. Nostalgia cycles seem to speed up in this town and Bohemian, artist-friendly neighborhoods like the Haight and the upper Mission have particularly high concentrations of vintage and thrift stores, but you can go on a bargain bender even in snooty Pacific Heights.

American Rag (1305 Van Ness Avenue at Sutter Street; (415) 441-0537) has the largest and trendiest selection of retro rags in town, but the prices don't really qualify as thrift. Gargoyles guard the carnival-like exterior of the Haight's **Wasteland** (1660 Haight Street at Clayton Street; (415) 863-3150), and if you can bear the famously loud and obnoxious music, you'll be rewarded with great finds. **Community Thrift** is a veritable secondhand department store (623 Valencia Street; (415) 861-4910) where you can specify which of more than 30 charities you want your purchase to benefit. Other old faithfuls include **Crossroads Trading Co.** (1901 Fillmore Street; (415) 775-8885; or 2231 Market Street near 16th Street; (415) 626-8989) and **Buffalo Exchange** (1555 Haight Street between Clayton and Ashbury Streets; (415) 431-7733; 1800 Polk Street at Washington Street; (415) 346-5726). The enormous **Goodwill** store (1580 Mission Street at South Van Ness Avenue; (415) 575-2240) is as brightly lit as any grocery store, and it's always chock-full of new and old trash and treasure.

For a highbrow rummage-sale experience, try the Pacific Heights version. Rich folks unload their castoffs at the **Next-to-New Shop** (2226 Fillmore Street between Sacramento and Clay Streets; (415) 567-1628), which gets its goods from the Junior League of San Francisco, and at **Repeat Performance Thrift Shop** (2436 Fillmore Street between Jackson and Washington Streets; (415) 563-3123), which benefits the San Francisco Symphony.

Secondhand shopping isn't confined to clothing. The trend for recycled merchandise extends to books, CDs, records, and even cookware. **Cookin'** (339 Divisadero Street near Haight Street; (415) 861-1854) is like your grandmother's attic, filled with classic kitchen gadgets, dishware, cookbooks, and anything else the gourmet in you might desire.

Near the holidays, in early November and May before Mother's Day, the merchants of the **Gift Center** (888 Brannan Street at Eighth; (415) 861-7733) offer their samples and overstock on four levels of the building. It's like the world's biggest garage sale; there's something for everyone, and you can have a nice lunch or a drink at the **Pavilion Café and Deli,** which also houses the popular **Peet's Coffee** (call (415) 552-8555).

Books and Magazines

Since many come to San Francisco to be writers, artists, and musicians (or just to be near them), the city has an unusually well-read population and plenty of well-stocked and personable bookstores. The big guys are here, of course—including **Borders Books & Music** (400 Post Street at Powell Street; (415) 399-0522), a superstore with four stories of books, music, and videos, and **B&N** (well, if we have to spell it out for you— **Barnes and Noble**) at 2552 Taylor Street; (415) 292-6762.

But as is the case with other shoppers in San Francisco, book enthusiasts are loyal to their neighborhood booksellers. One of the city's favorite bookstores, **A Clean Well-Lighted Place for Books** (Opera Plaza, 601 Van Ness Avenue at Golden Gate; (415) 441-6670), offers frequent readings, book signings, and bountiful sale and remainder tables. You'll find (or stumble over) more than a million used books, records, and magazines in the overstuffed **McDonald's Bookshop** (48 Turk Street near Market Street; (415) 673-2235), affectionately known as "A Dirty, Poorly Lit Place for Books." **A Different Light** is a remarkably well-stocked gay and lesbian bookstore that functions as a de facto community center (489 Castro Street at Eighteenth; (415) 431-0891). Beat headquarters and the publishing home and hangout of Jack Kerouac and Allen Ginsberg, **City Lights Booksellers & Publishers** (261 Columbus Avenue between Pacific Street and Broadway; (415) 362-8193) is probably San Francisco's best-known bookstore. You still may find founder-poet Lawrence Ferlinghetti hanging around; he'll pose for pictures if it's a good day.

Magazine lovers should check in at **Harold's International Newsstand** (454 Geary Boulevard between Mason and Taylor Streets; (415) 441-2665). **Naked Eye News and Video** (533 Haight Street; (415) 864-2985) specializes in culture rags and 'zines—the more obscure, the better. **The Magazine** (920 Larkin Street; (415) 441-7737) is one of many strangely wonderful shops in town; it's where all those old magazines you threw away wind up, and its obsessively catalogued gay and straight porn section is a miracle of modern library science. Or something.

For the best used bookstore, it's a tie between Russian Hill's **Acorn Books** (1436 Polk Street at California Street; (415) 563-1736) and Richmond's bewildering, maze-like **Green Apple Books** (506 Clement Street at Sixth; (415) 387-2272). Bookstores cater to almost every specialized taste. Find books from an African-American perspective at **Marcus Books** (1712 Fillmore Street; (415) 346-4222). **William Stout Architectural Books** (804 Montgomery Street at Jackson Street; (415) 391-6757) is one of the best of its kind in the country. **Fields Book Store** (1419 Polk Street between Pine and California Streets; (415) 673-2027) seriously specializes in spiritual and new age books. **The Limelight** (1803 Market Street; (415) 864-2265) is stocked with books on film, TV, acting, and its main attraction, unbound sometimes yet to be published screenplays. For fun, head to the **Government Printing Office Bookstore** (303 2nd Street; (415) 512-2770). If this bookstore confirms your theory that there is a micro-bug in your eyeglasses, head next to **Socialist Action Bookstore** (3425 Cesar Chavez Street at Valencia; (415) 821-0459), where you can catch up on everything anarchy, plots to overthrow the government, and books by such renegades as Che Guevara and Malcolm X. Travelers can map out their lives at **Rand McNally Map & Travel Store** (595 Market Street; (415) 777-3131) and the charming little **Get Lost Travel Books Maps & Gear** (1825 Market Street at Pearl Street; (415) 437-0529).

Clothing

San Franciscans take pride in defining themselves by what they are not—as in, not L.A. and not N.Y. A (sometimes ostentatious) lack of ostentation defines Northern California style. Sure, San Francisco may be less image conscious and clothes crazy than, say, Los Angeles; but as low key and (sophisticatedly, sensibly) dressed down as San Franciscans are, they like to look good. Fortunately, there are plenty of places to dress up (or down).

For women, **Union Square** is the hot spot for shopping, offering all the famous fashion names in boutiques and department stores. Union Street, in its ten-block shopping area, has more than 40 clothing boutiques, from trendy to traditional, including San Francisco–based **Bebe** (2095 Union Street; (415) 563-2323), which has classic-to-trashy suiting for the chic and slim contemporary woman, and **Girlfriends** (1824 Union Street; (415) 673-9544), whose distinctive logo items have become coveted souvenirs. For the unpredictable San Francisco weather, layering is essential. Stop at **House of Cashmere** (2764 Octavia Street near Union Street; (415) 441-6925) and **Three Bags Full** (2181 Union Street at Fillmore; (415) 567-5753) for hand-knit sweaters and sportswear. At **Carol Doda's Champagne and Lace** (1850 Union Street; (415) 776-6900) in a picturesque Union Street alley, San Francisco's famous former stripper sells lingerie and bodywear for women of every size.

Canyon Beachwear (1728 Union Street; (415) 885-5070) is San Francisco's only women's specialty swimwear shop.

Behind the Post Office (1510 Haight Street; (415) 861-2507) is known for its shabby-chic style made by top local designers. You won't have the problem of duplicates at a party if you shop at this store. Sizes run small so you gotta like them tight-fitted. If you want to sport true 1940s patterns with todays chic infused in the fabric, check out **Manifesto** (514 Octavia Street; (415) 431-4778). The two owner/designers make their own designs on the premises, which also serves as their studio. Combining the appeal of those sit-and-gossip hair salons—the owner of **Brown Eyed Girl** (2999 Washington Street; (415) 409-0214) opened her boutique in a quaint Victorian home to welcome women inside not just for shopping but for an intimate getaway. Shopping as an experience! You can find evening dresses to just the right everyday purse here. Europe meets Asia for a trendy funk infusion at **Ab Fits** (1519 Grant Avenue; (415) 982-5726). Service is excellent here especially when it comes to finding the proper fit in jeans, which is the lure for many jeans seekers. Whether you are going to trendy night spots or looking for a chic outfit to teach the third grade, a city favorite amongst females is **Ambiance** with two locations: one on 1458 Haight Street (phone (415) 552-509) and the other on Union Street (phone (415) 923-9797). The store on Union Street is said to be the friendliest around.

After loading your arms down in clothing purchases, **Shine** (808 Sutter Street; (415) 409-0991) is one of the best places to accessorize. This Tenderloin/Nob Hill boutique carries one-of-a-kind shoes, bags, and jewelry. You can find velvet bags by local designer Mona Milkface to shoes by New York's funky Cynthia Rowley.

Look sharp, men. San Francisco's snazzy Mayor Willie Brown is friendly with the equally dandyish proprietor of **Wilkes Bashford** (375 Sutter Street between Grant and Stockton Streets; (415) 986-4380), who keeps Brown in fedoras and tailored suits in an opulent atmosphere; Don Johnson shops here, too. For more traditional men's clothing, **Cable Car Clothiers** (441 Sutter Street near Stockton Street; (415) 397-4740) at Union Square is a good bet for the jacket-and-tie set. On the other side of the couture coin, the new **Saks Fifth Avenue Men's Store** (384 Powell and Post Streets; (415) 986-4300) stocks gear by Versace, Gaultier, and Dolce & Gabbana, and San Francisco–based **Billyblue Menswear** (54 Geary Street; (415) 781-2111) creates stylish modern classics. For nightlifers, **Daljeets** (541 Valencia Street between 16th and 17th Streets; (415) 626-9000) has off-the-wall clothes for street and club wear, and the clothing and underwear shop **Rolo** (450 Castro Street between 18th and Market Streets; (415) 626-7171; or 2351 Market Street near Castro Street; (415) 431-4545) is so up-to-date it's futuristic.

Shoes

We won't mention the infamous political leader's wife who had enough shoes to probably circle the earth if placed toe-to-heel, but if you can sympathize with her cause and want to go home with some marvelous magic slippers, San Francisco will be a foot-pleaser. Aside from the great selections at top department stores like Macy's or Nordstroms, there are some quaint shoe stores like **Smash Footwear and Accessories** (2030 Chestnut Street; (415) 673-4736) that redefine that little black shoe. For a bit of Marcia Brady in your wardrobe with an urban slant, one of the most popular fashions for feet is this Haight favorite—**Shoe Biz** (1446 Haight Street; (415) 864-0990). The selection will please club kids and even conservative classic dressers with a bit of a funky edge.

Retro Clothing

San Francisco is a nexus of the retro-swing craze, and what with Lindy-hoppin' hotspots like Club Deluxe and others, some people here make living in the past a full-fledged way of life. Vintage clothing is big business, and while these shops are no bargain, you can find the real deal. **Guys and Dolls** (3789 24th Street at Church Street; (415) 285-7174), **RetroFit** (910 Valencia Street at 19th Street; (415) 550-1530), and **Ver Unica** (148 Noe Street at Henry Street; (415) 431-0688) are the first places for fashion-forward people to start looking back.

Creativity and the Decorative Arts

San Francisco is known for its creativity and free spirit. Start beautifying your life with a stop at **FLAX** (1699 Market Street at Valencia Street; (415) 552-2355), a distinctive arts-supply superstore with paints and paper, furniture, lighting, framing, wrapping paper, and unusual jewelry and toys. **Art & Craft Supplies Outlet** (41 14th Street; (415) 431-7122) is a right-brain sort of store—cluttered but creative. It has art, craft, and party supplies at 50% or more off original retail prices, plus some things you never knew you wanted.

You can actually rent a painting (with an option to buy) from the **San Francisco Museum of Modern Art Rental Gallery** (Building A, Fort Mason Center at Buchanan Street and Marina Boulevard; (415) 441-4777). The gallery's goal is to give exposure to new artists, and if you decide the work looks good over your couch, half of the rental fee goes toward the purchase price.

Flowers and Plants

The Bay Area is one of the nation's premier flower-growing areas, and the city is abloom with talented florists like **Fioridella** for the social set (1920 Polk Street; (415) 775-4065) and the Castro's more avant-garde **Ixia**

(2331 Market Street between Noe and Castro Streets; (415) 431-3134). You can make your own arrangements after a visit to the **San Francisco Wholesale Flower Mart** (640 Brannan Street at 6th Street; (415) 392-7944), which fills an entire city block with blooms and branches. Some parts of the market are accessible only to professionals with badges, but several outlets offer fresh and unusual flowers, plants, and paraphernalia at budget prices. One of the best deals in the city is the green-and-white tent that is **Rincon Flowers** (corner of Spear and Mission Streets). Every Friday they run a half-off special—just in time for that dinner, or date, or sprucing up your hotel or home for a weekend alone.

If you want an arrangement to last longer, head to **Silks** (635 Brannan Street between Fifth and Sixth Streets; (415) 777-1354), which specializes in eternal silk flowers. **Coast Wholesale Dry Florist** (149 Morris Street in the Flower Market; (415) 781-3034) is a warehouse with dried versions of nearly every plant on earth. For more exotic specimens, try **Red Desert** (1632 Market Street between Franklin and Gough Streets; (415) 552-2800), an aptly sand-floored shop with a collection of cacti and succulents. The **Palm Broker** (1074 Guerrero Street; (415) 626-7256) specializes in palm trees and variants for that Southern California look.

Food

Perhaps because San Francisco is the home of California cuisine, restaurant dining has become one of the city's most popular participatory sports, and locals watch the trades and power plays of big-name chefs the way they watch their quarterbacks and stock options. Many of the city's foodies, known for their sophisticated tastes and obsession with fresh local ingredients, will tell you they live here because it's so near the source of wonderful produce. And with Napa Valley and Sonoma wine country so close, almost everyone knows something about wine.

A few food specialty stores, including an outpost of Seattle's **Sur La Table** (77 Maiden Lane; (415) 732-7900), can be found in Union Square. In North Beach, you can't go wrong at many of the Italian bakeries and delis; start at the century-old deli **Molinari's** for first courses (373 Columbus Avenue at Vallejo Street; (415) 421-2337). In Chinatown, **The Wok Shop** (718 Grant Street between Sacramento and Clay Streets; (415) 989-3797) specializes in everything you need for cooking Chinese cuisine, including cookbooks, spices, and sauces. And for the perfect end to the meal, **Golden Gate Fortune Cookies** (56 Ross Alley off Jackson Street; (415) 781-3956) makes traditional fortunes, and, um, more modern ones. **Joseph Schmidt Confections** (3489 16th Street; (415) 861-8682) is the city's premier (and quite imaginative) chocolatier, especially famed for its chocolate sculptures. Bring back your souvenirs in chocolate.

Even something as mundane as grocery shopping can provide a California experience at places like **Real Food Company** (2140 Polk Street between Vallejo Street and Broadway; (415) 673-7420); **Whole Foods** (1765 California Street; (415) 674-0500), a gourmet megastore where museum-quality carrots, tomatoes, and peppers are displayed as if this were the Produce Prado; and **Rainbow Grocery Cooperative** (1745 Folsom at Division Street; (415) 863-0621), a crunchier, co-op version of Whole Foods, with pierced, tattooed staffers ringing up your bulk food items. **Trader Joe's** (555 Ninth Street at Bryant Street; (415) 863-1292) has become a favorite for its discount gourmet snacks, health foods, and fresh juices, and a great selection of wines and beers.

Coffee is still the craze in hyper-caffeinated San Francisco, and you can find a café selling java and whole beans on almost every corner. But **Eureka Coffee** (2747 19th Street between Bryant and York Streets; (510) 595-0935) in SoMa sells coffee beans. Only. Roasted fresh on the premises, at up to half the prices you'll pay at Starbucks, et al. And the aroma of fresh-roasted coffee in the blocks around **Graffeo** (735 Columbus near Filbert Street; (415) 986-2420), a beloved hometown roastery and wholesale distributor in North Beach, is one of the signature scents (and tastes) of San Francisco. If you are a java junkie you might want to take in a tour of the best of San Francisco coffee with **Java Walk Coffee Tours.** Led by Elaine Sosa, a coffee socialite of sorts, the tour takes you to the most worthwhile coffee shops in North Beach, Chinatown, and nearby neighborhoods. For information call (415) 673-9255. If you want dessert with your coffee, make a stop at **Mitchell's Ice Cream** (688 San Jose Avenue; (415) 648-2300), unarguably the best ice cream in the city—proven by the lines of tongue lapping wannabes with their number in hand, anxiously waiting. You'll find the traditional flavors like vanilla, chocolate, yeah, yeah, yeah, but it's the unusual flavors that put Mitchell's on the map. Try mango, langka (a tart melon), macapuno (meaty coconut), Chicago Cheesecake, or our favorite Cinnamon Snap. You can pick up pints and enjoy it all week.

Another distinctive San Francisco shopping experience is an early morning visit to one of the weekly farmers' markets. On Wednesday and Sunday at **United Nations Plaza** (Market Street between Grove and Fulton Streets, near the Civic Center), the **Heart of the City Farmers' Market** (1182 Market Street at 8th Street; (415) 558-9455) replaces the panhandlers with dozens of booths featuring fresh-from-the-farm fruits, vegetables, and flowers. And Saturday morning the outdoor **Ferry Plaza Farmers' Market** (in the Embarcadero at the Ferry Building) opens with cooking demonstrations and craftspeople adding to the flavor. Chinatown's open produce markets, which have the feel of exotic farmers' markets, are open every day.

Plump Jack Wines (3201 Fillmore Street at Greenwich Avenue; (415) 346-9870) in the Marina is a companion store to the Getty-owned Plump Jack Café, and it's one of the best places in San Francisco to find impressive and obscure labels. Free delivery is available anywhere in the city. The name says it all—the **Napa Valley Winery Exchange** (415 Taylor Street between Geary Boulevard and O'Farrell Street; (415) 771-2887) is a wine boutique specializing in hard-to-find vintages and labels from nearby Napa. They ship. So does the **Cannery Wine Cellar and Gourmet Market** (in the Cannery, 2801 Leavenworth Street at Jefferson Street; (415) 673-0400), which showcases a hearty array of California labels plus beers and single-malt scotches. Other good spots for California wines are **D&M Liquors** in Pacific Heights (2200 Fillmore Street at Sacramento Street; (415) 346-1325) and Wine Club (953 Harrison Street; (800) 966-7835), which sells wine from jug to connoisseur at just above wholesale prices. The **Wine Club** boasts the largest selection of Burgundy and Bourdeaux wines west of the Mississippi. For spirits of another sort, head to the Financial District for a visit to **John Walker & Co. Liquors** (175 Sutter Street between Montgomery and Kearny Streets; (415) 986-2707), the city's largest specialty and import liquor merchant.

Insider Shops

Cliff's Variety (479 Castro Street between 18th and Market Streets; (415) 431-5365), with its friendly, small-town feeling, everything-but-the-kitchen-sink stock, and outlandish seasonal window displays, has become a Castro institution. If you need a gift but are stumped about what to give, turn the problem over to the staff at **Dandelion** (55 Potrero Avenue at Alameda Street; (415) 436-9500), which celebrates "the home and sharing great things with friends" in 40 mini-departments on two floors. **Quantity Postcards** (1441 Grant Avenue at Green Street; (415) 790-7000) stocks hundreds of postcards from the comfortingly antique to the shockingly modern. Try the North Beach location at 1441 Grant Street between Green and Union Streets (phone (415) 986-8866), which features an earthquake simulator. **See's Candies** is an old-fashioned candy shop—the kind where people behind the counter give you a free sample if you buy something and sometimes even if you don't. Stores are located throughout the city (phone (800) 347-7337).

Real insiders skip Crate & Barrel and Home Depot and go right to the source—the supply stores. If you need a few dozen martini glasses or those cool white china coffee cups, who ya gonna call? **Economy Restaurant Fixtures** (1200 Seventh Street; (415) 626-5611). And if you had a hammer, you wouldn't need **Discount Builders Supply** (695 Mission Street; (415) 621-8514), would you?

And if you need something at any hour, there's a good chance you'll find it (or something that will do until the shops open) at one of the city's all-purpose 24-hour stores, including **Safeway** (2020 Market Street at Church Street; (415) 861-7660) and **Walgreen's** (498 Castro Street at 18th; (415) 861-6276).

Kids

Kids will get a kick out of a visit to the Basic **Brown Bear Factory** (444 De Haro Street at 17th; (415) 626-0781), where they can watch a bear-making demonstration and pick out their own cuddly pal. Pacific Heights and the Marina are the spots for the stroller set; **Dottie Doolittle** (3680 Sacramento Street between Locust and Spruce Streets; (415) 563-3244), **Jonathan-Kaye by Country Living** (3548 Sacramento Street between Laurel and Locust Streets; (415) 563-0773), and **Mudpie** (1694 Gough Street; (415) 771-9262) are just a few of the upscale kidswear boutiques for label-savvy Pacific Heights tots.

As a major metropolis, San Francisco has its **FAO Schwarz** (phone (415) 394-8700) and **Toys 'R Us** (phone (415) 931-8896), of course, but the hometown toybox of choice is **Jeffrey's Toys** downtown (7 Third Street at Market Street; (415) 243-8697), a center for all things Pokémon. Just try to extricate your offspring from the Maurice Sendak-inspired **Where the Wild Things Are** and the first-in-the-world, hands-on **Sony Playstation Store,** both at **Metreon** (150 Fourth Street at Mission; (415) 369-6000).

Museum Shops

San Francisco is rich with museums, and the museum shops are full of take-home treasures. Consider these shops your own ace team of personal shoppers. **The California Historical Society** (678 Mission Street at Fourth; (415) 357-1848) has beautiful graphics of California's parks, including Muir Woods and Alcatraz. There are three museums in Golden Gate Park, each with its own unique shop. **The Academy Store** in the California Academy of Sciences (Golden Gate Park; (415) 750-7330) focuses on science and natural history, with dinosaur models, earth-friendly gifts, and a boutique devoted to the work of *Far Side* cartoonist Gary Larson, who has his own gallery at the museum. Across the courtyard is the **Legion of Honor** (Golden Gate Park; (415) 750-3642), which sells books and objects related to recent shows. The internationally famous **Exploratorium** (3601 Lyon Street next to the Palace of Fine Arts; (415) 561-0390) is an interactive, hands-on science museum, and its gift shop is full of intriguing science kits, games, and puzzles for children of all ages. The **San Francisco Museum of Modern Art** (151 Third

Street; (415) 357-4035) is a San Francisco landmark, and its innovative museum store has racked up high sales.

Music

The birthplace of acid rock, a hotbed of jazz, and a historically culture-craving town full of classical music buffs and operaholics, San Francisco is rich in record stores. There are two **Tower Records** locations (Castro: 2280 Market at Noe Street, (415) 621-0588; Fisherman's Wharf: Columbus Avenue and Bay Street, (415) 885-0500) and a **Tower Records Outlet** (660 Third Street near Brannan Street; (415) 957-9660); these are really fun to shop. The **Virgin Megastore** (2 Stockton Street at Market Street; (415) 397-4525) has three sprawling, noisy floors of CDs, cassettes, videos, CD-ROMs, books, magazines, a café, and its own DJ. It's a good place to listen before you buy, and the import section is tops.

The used records scene is a way of life. The new kid on the old-music block, and instantly the biggest used-records game in town, is **Amoeba** (1855 Haight Street; (415) 831-1200), which recently opened a superstore in a former Haight Street bowling alley. Other places to search for that Holy Grail–like CD or record: **Streetlight** (3979 24th Street between Sanchez and Noe Streets; (415) 282-3550) and **Recycled Records** (1377 Haight Street at Masonic Street; (415) 626-4075). Vinyl lives on at **Grooves** (1797 Market Street at Elgin Park; (415) 436-9933) and **Medium Rare Records** (2310 Market Street near Castro Street; (415) 255-RARE), which specializes in all sorts of campy old platters.

Then there's the new and the next. San Francisco has a thriving dance culture and techno scene, and the hippest kids shop where the local DJs get their discs: **CD Record Rack** (3897 18th Street at Sanchez Street; (415) 552-4990) and **Soundworks** (228 Valencia Street at Clinton Park; (415) 487-3980).

Pleasure Chest: Sexy Shopping

With its (well-deserved) anything-goes reputation, San Francisco is synonymous with sex. Here's where to get your sensual supplies. **Good Vibrations** (1210 Valencia Street between 23rd and 24th; (415) 974-8980) is a friendly, nonfurtive store that's been women-owned and operated for 20 years; it sells sex supplies, books, and videos. Check out the vibrator museum. **Jaguar** (4057 18th Street between Castro and Hartford Streets; (415) 863-4777) carries an eye-popping array of men-on-men erotica and supplies. Often voted "best place to buy drag" in local alternative weeklies, **Piedmont Boutique** (1452 Haight Street; (415) 864-8075) is a glitzy showgirl shop, but most of the showgirls are guys. Piedmont has been dressing strippers and drag queens for 25 years. **Foxy Lady Boutique** (2644 Mission Street between 22nd and 23rd; (415) 285-4980) has wigs, gowns, lingerie, accessories, and shoes and boots up to size 15.

Stormy Leather (1158 Howard Street between Seventh and Eighth; (415) 626-1672) specializes in leather and vinyl fetish wear for women. **A Taste of Leather** (2370 Market Street between 16th and 17th; (415) 552-4500) carries a full range of leatherwear for out on the street and (one hopes) the bedroom. **Leather Etc.** (1201 Folsom Street at Eighth; (415) 864-7558) for men and women has lots of sexy clothes.

Touristarama

If you absolutely must go home with an Alcatraz shot glass, miniature cable car, or "fog dome," all this tourist merchandise and more (mind-bogglingly more) is conveniently concentrated in the boardwalk-like waterfront area known as **Fisherman's Wharf.** Shopping for nonessentials and unnecessary items is plentiful at the wharf's street vendors, as well as at Pier 39. **Ghirardelli Square** (900 North Point; (415) 775-5500), with its clusters of 70 specialty shops surrounding the delightfully old-fashioned **Ghirardelli Chocolate Manufactory and Soda Fountain** (phone (415) 781-2601), and the **Cannery** (2801 Leavenworth Street near Hyde Street; (415) 771-3112) is where you can take a breather from shopping with the live entertainment in the courtyard. One place that stands out is **Golden Gate Bridge Shop** (at the bridge toll plaza on the San Francisco side of the bridge; (415) 923-2331), where you can purchase authentic pieces of cable and rivets from the Golden Gate Bridge. You can also pick up an original Lombard Street brick from the **City Store** in Pier 39. The store is run by homeless and formerly homeless folk in cooperation with a nonprofit organization and the city.

We've Got What You Need: The Bests

The Best Gap   Market and Dolores; Polk and California Streets

Best Shopping Streets   Chestnut Street in the Marina or Union Street in Cow Hollow; upper and lower Fillmore; The Haight

Best Trinket Shop   Golden Gate Bridge Shop (call (415) 923-2331)

Best Place to Buy a Gift "from San Francisco"   Mark Reuben Galleries (900 North Point; (415) 543-5433) and the City Store at Pier 39

Best Shops for the Nieces and Nephews   Exploratorium (at Marina Boulevard and Lyon Street; (415) 561-0390); Gamescape (333 Divisadero Street; (415) 621-4263)

Best Place for Pop Culture   Uncle Mame (2075 Market Street; (415) 626-1953)

Best Purchase to Make Your Trip More Fun   Kite Flite at Pier 39

Best Dressing Room   Saks Fifth Avenue (384 Post Street; (415) 986-9300)

Best Used-Book Store   Green Apple Books (506 Clement Street; (415) 387-2272)

Part Ten

Exercise and Recreation

In San Francisco, simply going from your hotel to your car or out to brunch can be more exercise than most people get in a week. The city is a giant playground equipped with natural jungle gyms—paved hills, zigzagging steps, and giant green spaces expansive enough to fly a kite or heck—even paraglide. Those who live here know what treasures await. And instead of replacing their clutch every month or so they opt to foot it, bike it, climb it, pedal it, and public-transport it, which can require a whole new level of flexibility and balance during those sardined rides. So as the *Unofficial Guide* sets out to do, we want to empower you with the insider scoop—to do as the locals do but with a newcomer perspective!

The Great Indoors

Fitness Centers and Aerobics

The gyms in San Francisco understand the conditioning demanded by the city's fitness freaks. Whether they are training for foot or bike marathons, or the popular Escape from Alcatraz swim, the gyms provide equipment and classes that can get any glute, tri, bi, quad, or calf pumped up. Hours for most gyms are similar—from 5:30 to 6 a.m. to about 8 p.m. A popular place for biker-shorts clad, fitness-sophisticate Marina types is the heart-thumping, music-blaring **Gorilla Sports** (2324 Chestnut Street, (415) 292-8470; 2450 Sutter Street, (415) 474-2699; www.gorillasports.com). The gym's two locations offer a free 3-day trial pass. Another location on Polk Street between Union and Green Streets is due to open in 2002. Their classes are pretty extensive, incorporating yoga, pilates, kickboxing, and traditional aerobics.

Club One, www.clubone.com, has five locations with free weights, Nautilus, aerobic equipment, Jacuzzis, steam rooms, aerobics classes, and certified fitness trainers. Locations are Citicorp Center (1 Sansome

Street; (415) 399-1010), Yerba Buena (350 Third Street; (415) 512-1010), Embarcadero Center (2 Embarcadero Center; (415) 788-1010), and Jackson Square (30 Hotaling Place; (415) 837-1010). The daily rate is $15 with a member; $20 without.

24-Hour Fitness, www.24hourfitness.com, is one of the favorites of locals. Their color-coded machines, depending on which part of the body you want to work, is a convenient way to a self-guided workout. Although some feel that the gyms are too bare bones and a bit grungy, the locations are convenient—seven in all, including 100 California Street (phone (415) 434-5080) and 1200 Van Ness Avenue (phone (415) 776-2200). The daily rate for each facility is $15.

Why not the Y? The **YMCA**s, www.ymcasf.org, in San Francisco are not bleach-smelling, family-infested, cinder-blocked gyms. They are clean and surprisingly effective facilities. The YMCA at the Embarcadero (169 Steuart Street; (415) 957-9622) is a favorite for its huge swimming pool (5-meter, 25 lanes), excellent views, and low-key clientele. Cardio equipment, located in two adjoining rooms, includes 18 treadmills and 14 Netpulse internet-equipped stationary bikes. Keep track of your workouts electronically with the FitLinxx system. The deck on the fifth floor is a hot-spot for sun worshippers also. Daily rate is $15.

At two of the four locations of **Pinnacle Fitness,** www.pinnaclefit ness.com, guests can swim at indoor pools after working out on Cybex weight-training gear or free weights; all locations have steam rooms. The club with a pool is at 1 Post Street (phone (415) 781-6400). Other locations are 345 Spear Street in the Hills Plaza on the Embarcadero (phone (415) 495-1939) and 61 Montgomery Street across from the Sheraton Palace hotel (phone (415) 543-1110). The daily fee is $15.

Hotels for Heavy Sweaters

Are you are the type who lugs around a portable ab roller purchased off some infomercial featuring Suzanne Somers and, while vacationing or attending business in San Francisco, is anxious about keeping the heart-rate and metabolism on schedule? Most of the larger downtown hotels have excellent fitness centers on the premises, including the **Ritz Carlton, the St. Francis,** and the **Nikko.** The Nikko comes with quite an extensive gym and swimming pool which are free if you purchase certain hotel packages. If not, there is a per day use fee of $6. The **Grand Hyatt, Sheraton Palace, Beresford, Diva, Donatello, Juliana, Cartwright,** and the **Hilton Hotels** struck a deal with Pinnacle Fitness Centers allowing guests to work out at any Pinnacle facility for only $10. The **Nob Hill Lambourne** on Pine Street is for the most exercise-obsessed. Stationary bike, treadmill, and rowing machine come in each room, and the hotel offers private in-room yoga sessions. Call (415) 433-2287; www.nobhilllambourne.com.

Mind Body

Yoga

It bends. It stretches. It turns you into a human pretzel. In no place has yoga become a hotter pastime than in San Francisco. Out of the varying disciplines, including easy Iyengar, Kundalini, moderate Sivananda, to more challenging forms such as Ashtanga, San Franciscans' choice is Bikram or Choudhury (Hot Yoga). With the thermostat set to 38º Celsius or more, students are led through 26 postures designed to stretch muscles and tendons in a certain order. The heat warms the muscles, helping them stretch more.

Yoga Haven, with its sunny studio on 3305 Buchanan Street, along Chestnut in the Marina, is one of the most popular places to turn up the yoga heat. It's also one of the cleanest Bikram studios. Unlike other, less-maintained studios, Yoga Haven is well ventilated and thanks to the owners, who sprinkle their floor coverings with baking soda daily, does not offend with sweat-soaked, malodorous carpets. There are men and women showers, and towels are free. Drop-in rate is $10, which is good for a whole week. Call (415) 775-9642; www.yogahavensf.com.

An alternative to melting your muscles is **The Mindful Body,** 2876 California Street. You can learn Ashtanga and Hatha from one of the Bay Area's most popular yogi master, Michael Cooper. The studio also has a therapeutic pool, bodywork offerings, facials, and offers acupuncture. You could turn your visit into an all-day affair. The drop-in rate for non-members is $12 but they offer first-time visitors 50% off, making your first class only $6. Call (415) 931-2639; www.themindfulbody.com.

In July only, yoga combines the best of mind and body with nature. A naturalist and a Hatha yoga instructor host an evening of nature and nurture for the body in Coyote Hills Regional Park. Call (510) 795-9385.

Pilates

No, it doesn't rhyme with gyrates. This increasingly popular mind body workout incorporates the work of Joseph Pilates (pronounced piLAH-tees) to strengthen and lengthen the spine and the "powerhouse," which is your abs, lower back, and butt. It's popular with dancers but effective for anyone from your arthritic mother to your motorcycle riding man. Mat classes are at the heart of the technique but the fun really comes into play when you strap yourself into specially designed machines, such as the Reformer, the Cadillac, the Barrel, or the Chair. At first glance it resembles an S&M torture chamber, with leather stirrups and springs.

The fancy price tag—at over $70 for one-hour private session—makes Pilates popular with upper crust Seacliff or Pacific Heights prima donnas. Group mat classes are cheaper and are offered at many gyms, including Gorilla Sports. **Golden Gate** Pilates (on Pierce between Chestnut and Lombard; (415) 441-6985) offers an excellent small studio with all the necessary equipment. The teachers are top-notch too. They don't offer any mat classes, however. It's best if you are seeking out a one-on-one experience. Nearby, at **Body Kinetics** (2399 Greenwich Street off of Pierce; (415) 931-9922), is a larger pilates studio that offers private sessions as well as mat classes, and you can simply pay a small fee to use the studio's pilates equipment. Inquire with them regarding class schedules.

Spas

Whether you are looking for a back massage, acupuncture, manicures and pedicures, tanning, facials, or even communal baths, San Francisco has plenty of offerings. **Kabuki Springs and Spa** (Japan Center, 1750 Geary Boulevard at Fillmore; (415) 922-6000; www.kabukisprings.com) offers traditional Japanese communal baths. Don't knock it until you've tried it. You can take a cold plunge and then soak in hot baths while you polish your skin with sea salts. Your skin will feel cleansed and buffed. No hanky panky goes on here—although bathing suits are optional, except on Tuesday, when they are enforced. The baths are open for women only on Sunday, Wednesday, and Friday, and to men only on Monday, Thursday, and Saturday. Tuesday is co-ed (thus the bathing suit mandate.) If bathing isn't your forte, the spa also offers 18 different spa treatment rooms, including acupuncture. Appointments are necessary. One neighborhood novelty for the last 20 years or so is Noe Valley's **Elisa's Beauty & Health Spa** (4028 24th Street; (415) 821-6727; www.elisasbeauty.citysearch.com). Elisa's has indoor and outdoor hot tubs and saunas and is pretty laid back— usually you can just show up. Also on offering are wraps of every kind, facials, waxing, and a variety of massages. Specials are run quite often, so be sure to call. One of the best places in the city is the chichi **Spa Radiance Day Spa** (3061 Fillmore Street; (415) 346-6281). If you are prepared to feel like a shrink-wrapped piece of meat and pay big bucks for it, then this is the place. Everything from body wraps to specialized facials is on offer, as well as endermologie—a rub-down treatment for cellulite.

Climbing

If you've ever dreamed of clinging to a wall or ceiling like Spiderman, **Mission Cliffs** (2295 Harrison Street at 19th Street; (415) 550-0515; www.touchstoneclimbing.com), the Bay Area's premier indoor climbing haven, has more square clingage than even the original superhero could handle. With over 14,000 square feet of climbing terrain, and walls exceeding 50 feet high, it is the best preparation if you plan on taking advantage of real rock in nearby climbing haven Yosemite or other national parks. Mission Cliffs is a must-try if you have never climbed, and a perfect way to confront that fear of heights once and for all! The gym also has a complete weight room, locker rooms, showers, and sauna. It's open seven days a week until 10 p.m. You will have to pass a belay test, which will cost you $20, and once certified you can come and climb till your fingers cramp in. For nonmembers, the weekday price after 3 p.m. and on weekends is $20; before 3 p.m. and for kids ages 14 and younger it's $10. You can rent all the necessary gear for $5. If you'd like to see what Mission Cliffs looks like, take a virtual tour at their website.

Dancing

Every Tuesday at **Broadway Studios** (435 Broadway; (415) 291-0333; www.broadwaystudios.com) you can swing the night away with Bay City Boogie. They offer lessons for $15—7 p.m. for beginners, 8 p.m. for intermediate swingers, and no partner is needed. From 9:30 p.m. to midnight you can jam with live music by "The Swing Session," a San Francisco sextet renowned for their jumpin' rhythm, wailing improvisations, and relentless energy. **Emeryville's Allegro Ballroom** (5855 Christie Avenue, Emeryville; (510) 655-2888; www.allegroballroom.com) hosts salsa on Sunday, taught by one charismatic Garry Johnson and Isabelle Rodriguez. There are two afternoon classes, and a party in the evening is included in your $10 fee. If either salsa or Sunday isn't your speed, try Argentinean tango on Tuesday.

Ice Skating and Bowling

The new **Yerba Buena Ice Skating and Bowling Center** provides public skating and bowling—also lessons. The center is located at 750 Folsom Street (phone (415) 777-3727).

Outdoors, Naturally!

Walking: Fun City Rambles

Imagine this. An old Dutch windmill to the right, and as you pass, the trees clear with the lightest of ocean breezes revealing Ocean Beach. Continuing this walk through **Golden Gate Park** you come to Funston, where you can perch yourself on a dizzying cliff that overlooks the crashing waves below. And what is this? Is it a bird, a plane . . . ? It's a hang glider swooping and sailing the wind's current just in front of you over the waves. Just an ordinary walk in San Francisco! Whether you prefer simple rambles or full-blown hikes, there are tons of opportunities in San Francisco. It would be a sin to leave the walking shoes at home.

San Francisco's premier rambling destination is the **Golden Gate Promenade,** a three-and-a-half-mile paved footpath that starts in Fort Mason (just west of Fisherman's Wharf) and ends at the famous bridge of the same name. As the trail follows the shoreline along San Francisco Bay, it passes through Marina Green, the Yacht Harbor, Crissy Field, and the Presidio; it ends at Fort Point (a Civil War–era brick fortress). Along the way are picnic areas, rest rooms, restaurants, beaches, drinking water, fishing piers, quiet stretches of shoreline, and breathtaking views, not to mention excellent photo ops of Alcatraz. To lengthen the walk, hike the Coastal Trail along the Pacific coast to Cliff House. Temperatures can change rapidly along the shoreline, and wind is often strong; bring a jacket or sweater.

Visitors can begin a stroll in South Beach Harbor on the east side of the city facing Oakland. Start at Pier 40 and walk north along the promenade past the new marina, new apartment complexes, and South Beach Park, where artists sometimes set up their easels on the lawn beneath the colossal red-and-silver Mark di Suvero sculpture "Sea Change." It's a place where picnickers and dog-walkers gather to watch the boats. As you walk north, the Bay Bridge soon arches above; curving along the sidewalk for nearly half a mile is a ribbon of glass blocks lit with fiber-optic cable and set in concrete; some of it is raised for use as benches or tables. This public art is a nice place to relax and watch the bay and the parade of joggers, skaters, and strollers.

There are other great places to walk in San Francisco. In the northwest corner of the city, the 1,480-acre Presidio has 11 miles of trails in a variety of landscapes, including coastal bluffs, forested hills, and historic architectural settings (such as the old army buildings on the main post). You can pick up a trail map at the visitor center, open from 9 a.m. to 5 p.m. daily. Golden Gate Park features miles of walking, multipurpose bicycle, and bridle paths. Probably the best place for walkers is Strybing Arboretum near the Japanese Tea Garden. The beauty and tranquility of the many gardens inside the 70-acre arboretum and its manicured lawns are unsurpassed.

Only about 30 minutes outside of the city, another not-to-be-missed walk is through the towering redwoods of **Muir Woods** (phone (415) 388-2596). Paved trails wander through the forest of giant trees, and information signs guide your experience. Located on the south side of Mount Tam, 12 miles north of San Francisco, the park is open daily from 8 a.m. to sunset. It can get crowded on weekends. Admission is $2. (For more information, see Part Six, "Sightseeing, Tours, and Attractions.")

Hiking

The Marin Headlands   Hiking paradise exists just over the Golden Gate Bridge in the **Marin Headlands,** close in distance and time but many moods apart. Within 15 minutes from leaving the city you are in total solitude, with hiking trails of varying difficulty intersecting all around you. A lovely stretch of the California Coastal Trail, a 1,200 mile trail that stretches the entire length of the California Coast (and hugging the Pacific the entire way), travels through the Headlands. You can meet up with it for day-hikes or pack along with the tent and sleeping bag and find shelter for a weekend hike. It's also called the Bay Area Ridge Trail, so don't get confused. The trail is used by hikers, bikers, and horseback riders. The approach is different for each user but all meet up at the trail at a junction called Five Corners. The trailhead for hikers starts shortly after the Golden Gate Bridge.

Mt. Tamalpais is another favorite. Although the hikes are shadowed by the world-class fat-tire trails, there are still top-notch hiking trails for all levels with views and gorgeous scenery. Or if mountains and altitude have you panting for breath already, try hikes along **Muir Beach** or **Stinson Beach.** It is much easier to hike downhill! Stinson stretches beneath steep hills (the ones you would be hiking up if choosing Mt. Tamalpais option) with vistas out to sea. **Olema Valley** is for the more advanced hiker as the trails are long and steep, ascending to ridgetops for breathtaking ocean views. Some trails connect the Valley to **Point Reyes National Seashore,** over 70,000 acres of pristine coast land. Point Reyes has over 147 miles of trails and 4 designated backcountry camping areas. This is a preferred hiking destination because of the diversity of trail levels, well-maintained camp sites, and the almost certain chance of seeing northern fur seals, sea lions, and herds of Tule elk. You can moonlight on the Point during summer months. What better than hiking under a full moon? You can get a naturalist guide for your nocturnal hike by calling Abbotts Lagoon at (415) 663-1200. Muir Woods also hosts evening hikes every full moon. There is nothing more special than to look up at the towering trees illuminated by the moon. No planning necessary. Just come with a flashlight and meet at the Muir Woods Visitor Center at 7 p.m. sharp. For information call (415) 388-2596.

Listing all the trails and hiking opportunities within the Headlands and beyond would need a book of its own. Space is limited here unfortunately. But if the Grizzly Adams in you desires more, there are tons of other hikes in the Headlands and the best resource for trail maps and lodging information is the Golden Gate National Recreation Area, which begins where the Pacific Ocean meets San Francisco Bay. All in all, it is the largest urban national park in the world, a whopping 76,500 acres of land and water that includes 28 miles of wild coastline. You can get information by calling (415) 556-0560; browsing www.nps.gov/goga; or writing Golden Gate National Recreation Area, Fort Mason, Building 201, San Francisco, CA 94123-0022. Inquire about their new hiking property—Phleger Estate.

A few things to remember: the weather varies hourly. Fog and winds are usually at their most fierce closer to the bridge. Bring a fleece, plenty of water, and always wear wool socks for foot ventilation. Depending on the length of your hike, boots or Teva sandals are sufficient.

Only in San Francisco

Step Right Up

In no other city will you find more stairs outside, and in the most innovative and creative city in the country you shouldn't be surprised to find them used as stairways to buns of steel. Here is a breakdown of some of our favorite urban climbs.

The Greenwich Steps (East)

Where Bottom, on Sansome and Greenwich Streets; Top, Telegraph Hill Place at Greenwich Street
Countdown to Heaven or Hell 387 steps

Perched along the precariously steep slopes of Telegraph Hill and set among what seems to resemble gardens in Tuscany, this stairway is chock full of camera-toting tourists gawking at the view. Sights along the climb include the art deco apartment house at 1360 Montgomery Street that was the façade used in the Humphrey Bogart/Lauren Bacall flick, *Dark Passage;* the doggie park on Montgomery Street, and the romantic quaint restaurant Julius' Castle.

Lyon Steps

Where Bottom, Green Street at Lyon; Top, Broadway at Lyon Street
Countdown to Heaven or Hell 291 steps; for the best views, the top 166

A meat market of sorts—and a fashion show. Bring your best work-out duds and don't forget the makeup. Business cards a necessity.

Pemberton Steps

Where Bottom, Clayton Street at Pemberton Place (look for a hidden sign on the right); Top, Pemberton Place and Crown Terrace
Countdown to Heaven or Hell 204 seemingly endless stairs

A very low-key relaxed and shaded atmosphere with daisies and rhododendrons with a view of Mount Diablo in the distance.

Bench Warming

It may not be the most effective for calorie burning or physical recreation, but for many, sitting on a good bench and people-watching is recreation enough. San Francisco has some darn good benches. Consider it a mental exercise to feel the burn of a city and its people in motion. Along the **Marina Green** off of Marina Boulevard, near Crissy Field offers the best benches for watching the city's yuppie set jog, walk Fido, or rollerblade. There are kite flyers, groups of friends playing volleyball, and the obvious perk of views of Alcatraz, the bay, the Headlands, and the Golden Gate Bridge. Nearby, the **Palace of Fine Arts** is also home to some fine benches. Wedding parties are usually dispatched here in droves for photo ops—always a fun sight. And at sunset the Palace lights up and is almost as dramatic as Rockefeller's Christmas Tree. Whether or not you play golf you will appreciate the benches at the thirteenth hole of **Lincoln Park Golf Course,** which you can reach after a beautiful drive through the Presidio. It's one of the most beautiful panoramic vistas of downtown San Francisco anywhere. Across the bridge in **Tiburon,** while you wait for the ferry to Angel Island or for the return trip back to San Francisco, the benches that line the waterfront are great for watching walkers, dogs, boats, rolling fog, and the cityscape on the horizon.

Islands in the Bay

At 4:30 p.m. the last ferry floats out from **Angel Island State Park** smack dab in the middle of San Francisco Bay. Why do you need to know this? Because if you are looking for your own private heaven— Angel Island is just that. No cars to wind gears into your slumbering dreams, just endless hiking trails, camping facilities, and a perch at the top with fine, fine views (as you noticed there is no shortage of fine views in this city.) It's the perfect place for a remote retreat. You never feel totally alone though. The evenings are illuminated by lights from the city and the Golden Gate Bridge, and during day-hikes, it seems as if the entire bay area has its energetic glow wrapped around you. There are nine campsites complete with picnic areas, food lockers, pit toilet, and grills. Reservations are required and cost $14 per night, plus $6.75 reservation fee. The only way to and from the island is by ferry from Pier 43 in San Francisco ($9), Tiburon ($5), or Vallejo ($10). The price includes the state park entrance fee. The boat drops you at Perimeter Trailhead, which takes you around the island on clearly marked and well-maintained trails. Along the trail are opportunities for bike rentals ($12 to $25 per day depending on style of bike), new tram tours ($4 per person), kayak rentals ($20 for 2 hours), and eating at the Cove Café. For recorded information, call (415) 435-1915; or look at www.angelisland.org.

Prisoners once dreamed of "walking." And now the place that barred them from freedom, Alcatraz Island, is an evolving ecological preserve— and a great walking destination. The absence of four-footed predators has made the island a haven for birds, as well as thriving populations of crabs, starfish, and other marine animals living in tide pools. Visitors can see this on the **Agave Trail,** which follows the islands's shoreline. Ferries to Alcatraz leave from Pier 41 at Fisherman's Wharf; make reservations in advance. For information and ticket purchases, call (415) 705-5555. You can also order tickets online at www.telesales.com.

Running

There are enough running opportunities in San Francisco to satisfy the Forrest Gump in all of us. You'll see plenty of runners on the sidewalks downtown. But for visitors who would rather avoid traffic, large crowds, and stoplights, there are plenty of other options. Flat but usually windy, the 3.5-mile **Golden Gate Promenade** offers runners a paved and scenic route for a workout, not to mention a friendly comraderie among other runners; the round trip from Fort Mason to the Golden Gate Bridge is seven miles. Not that you have to stop at the landmark span; you can run across the bridge on its pedestrian walkway to the challenging **Marin Headlands** or continue along the Pacific coast on the **Coastal Trail.** The Coastal Trail is a scenic 9.2 mile run that will lead you through the posh neighborhood of Seacliff, China Beach, Land's End, and the Cliff House near Ocean Beach. If you want a fun side excursion, run up Seacliff Avenue past the mauve house flying the flag with the blue wolf on it—that's where Robin Williams lives.

If the hills of the Headlands seem too challenging for you, after the bridge turn right toward Sausalito—it's about a 9-mile run from Aquatic Park on the Promenade. The run is refreshingly downhill and if you are exhausted you can take the ferry back from Sausalito to Fisherman's Wharf.

Usually less windy, Golden Gate Park has plenty of paved roads and miles of pedestrian, bike, and bridle paths on rolling terrain; the main drag, Kennedy Drive, is closed to traffic on Sundays. On the east side of the city in South Beach, a promenade heads north along the shoreline toward the Bay Bridge; it's a favorite destination for joggers and runners.

Although most folks drive or take a tour bus, a more exhilarating way to get to the summit of **Twin Peaks** and its stupendous view is to run or walk. Routes include the back roads from the University of California Medical Center or either of the two main roads that lead to the top. The best time is early morning when the city is quiet and the air is crisp; just make sure you pick a morning that's not fog-bound.

Road Bicycling and In-Line Skating

In downtown San Francisco, most visitors will want to leave bicycling and in-line skating to bike messengers and street-savvy natives. Yet skinny-tire cyclists and skaters don't need to go far to find some excellent places to spin the cranks or skate the black ice. The **Golden Gate Promenade** starts in Fort Mason (just west of Fisherman's Wharf) and follows the bay shore for three and a half miles to the bridge of the same name (which has a pedestrian and bike lane). The scenery from the bridge is spectacular, but winds are usually strong enough to push you over. Across the bridge in **Marin County** at the end of the Vista Point parking lot is a bike lane that parallels US 101 and then turns off to Alexander Avenue through Sausalito. The Hills on the Marin side of the Bridge run are killer—affectionately called the Rambo run by those who frequent it! Be prepared. Temperatures also increase on this side as well, so hydration is important.

For a more recreational bike run than those in the Headlands and closer to home, **The Presidio** has 14 miles of paved roads, open to cyclists and in-line skaters, that weave through groves of trees and wind past military housing. Because most of the old military post's roads were laid out in horse-and-buggy days, all grades are easy to moderate. **Golden Gate Park** has seven and a half miles of designated designated paved trails for bikes that extend from the tip of the Panhandle through Golden Gate Park to Lake Merced. In addition, some roads (such as Kennedy Drive, the main drag) are closed to car traffic on Sundays; it's heaven for San Francisco in-line skaters.

With its three bicycle lanes, the flat, three-mile sidewalk along **Ocean Beach** (Great Highway) provides a great workout and can be incorporated into a longer tour of the Sunset District. Ride south on the Great Highway for two miles past the San Francisco Zoo to Sloat Boulevard and turn right onto Lake Merced Boulevard; then ride for five miles around the lake and nearby gold course.

For another variation along the Pacific shoreline, ride north along the Great Highway from Lake Merced toward Cliff House. Just before you get there, gear down for a 200-foot ascent. Then veer right onto Point Lobos Avenue and turn right onto 43rd Avenue. Then it's all downhill to Golden Gate Park; enter at Chain of Lakes Drive East, which takes you back to Kennedy Drive. Turn right and continue west to the Great Highway, which takes you back to Lake Merced.

A San Francisco classic for the thin-tire set is a 19-mile loop ride across the Golden Gate Bridge to Sausalito and Tiburon that returns you to San Francisco on a ferry. The ride can start at the parking lot at the south end of the bridge or at Fisherman's Wharf; after the one-and-a-half-mile bridge crossing, descend into Sausalito on Alexander Avenue, ride into Tiburon, and catch the ferry to Fisherman's Wharf. Check with a local bike shop for turn-by-turn directions and a map; it's also a good idea to check the ferry schedule by calling the Red and White Fleet at (800) 229-2784.

Biking Wine Country

One way to avoid drinking and driving but still feel a buzz is to bike it! Napa is way too street-crowded for such an excursion, so instead head to calmer pastures in Sonoma County, specifically the nice, flat, wide Dry

Creek Valley. Healdsburg is the starting point. Leave your car here—a convenient place to return to and eat, or hang in the park. Dry Creek Road starts at Healdsburg Avenue and you can stay on it until you are too tired or too hammered. Wineries line the road and along the turn off at Lambert Bridge Road, which loops you around to West Dry Creek Road for a total trip distance of 14 miles.

For Extreme Eyes Only!

This guide wouldn't be called *Unofficial* if it didn't include the Everest of in-line skating ops. **6 Parnassus Ski Lift,** as it is called, that runs down the Ninth and Tenth Avenue "slopes", was first made famous by intrepid and lunatic skateboarders who first discovered the great hill. The procedure: take the bus at Ninth Avenue and Judah, and don't forget that transfer ticket because it is what gets you up and down the hill over and over for the next two hours. The hill is long, steep, and will have you close to breaking the sound barrier in no time! You don't want to forget the helmet, knee pads, and wrist guards for this run. If you prefer fancy footwork, try **Hubba Hideout,** at Maritime Plaza at Battery Street. Stairs, and handrails, and hills oh my!

Renting Bikes and In-Line Skates

Bike and skate rentals are widely available throughout San Francisco; some shops also provide guided tours. **Bay Bicycle Tours & Rentals** at the Cannery in Fisherman's Wharf (phone (415) 436-0633) rents 21-speed hybrid (city) bikes starting at $5 an hour and $25 a day; helmet, rear rack and bag, lock, maps, tour info, and water bottles are included. They also offer a guided tour for four or more people across the Golden Gate Bridge to Sausalito and a return to San Francisco by ferry for $35.

Blazing Saddles rents computer-equipped bikes for self-guided tours of San Francisco, the Marin Headlands, Muir Woods, and Mount Tamalpais. Mountain bike rentals start at $7 an hour or $28 a day, and they off er even lower rates for multi-day rentals. Also available for rent are road bikes, city bikes, tandems, kids' bikes, and car racks. The shop is located at 1095 Columbus Avenue (at Francisco); call (415) 202-8888; or visit www.blazingsaddles.com. There is also a satellite store at Fisherman's Wharf which makes it convenient to rent and then hop over to Angel Island or Tiburon.

In Golden Gate Park, **Surrey Bikes & Blades** rents in-line skates starting at $7 an hour and bikes at $8 an hour; the shop, located at Stow Lake (closed Wednesdays and rainy days) also rents tandem bikes, electric bikes, and pedal-powered surreys. For more information call (415) 668-6699.

Skates on Haight, half a block from Golden Gate Park in Haight-Ashbury, rents in-line skates for $6 an hour and $24 a day; the price includes head, knee, and wrist protection. The shop is open daily; call (415) 752-8375 for more information.

At Angel Island State Park in San Francisco Bay, **Angel Island Company** rents 21-speed mountain bikes for exploring traffic-free roads and paths on the island. Basic rentals start at $10 an hour or $30 a day and include a helmet. Open daily May through October, and weekends only in November and March; closed December through February. Call (415) 897-0715 for more information on rentals and (800) 229-2784 for ferry schedules from Pier 43 in Fisherman's Wharf.

Mountain Biking

While fat-tire mountain bikes are fine for riding on San Francisco's streets and paved trails, off-road afficionados who prefer the feel of dirt between their knobbies should look farther afield, but not too far. Across the Golden Gate Bridge lies Marin County, where popular myth says mountian biking was invented 20 years ago.

The cradle of mountain biking civilization is reputed to be Mount Tamalpais. It's so popular a destination among fat-tire fanatics that the sport has been banned from single-track trails, and cops armed with radar guns give out tickets to cyclists who exceed 15 miles an hour on the fire roads. The most popular route is the technically easy, but aerobically demanding, Old Railroad Grade to the historic West Point Inn (where incidentally, you can stop over a stack of pancakes) and the East Peak. There are lots of scenic spots along the way, and the reward is a breathtaking (not that you'll have much breath left), 360° view of San Francisco Bay. And, as they say, it's all downhill from here. Once you reach the top there is a snack bar with hot dogs and bagels and cream cheese. (Not advertised, reserved for those in the know, are the frozen fruit bars. Ask for them.) You could even choose to make a weekend out of it and stay overnight at the West Point Inn.

To reach the Old Railroad Grade (an unpaved fire road), load your bike onto your car and take US 101 north across the Bay Bridge to the Tiburon Boulevard/East Blithedale Avenue exit. Then turn left, heading under US 101 and west onto East Blithedale Avenue. Take East Blithedale as it turns into West Blithedale Avenue and go past an intersection with Eldridge Road. About a mile later, Old Railroad Grade branches off to the right over a wooden bridge. Park as close to this bridge as you can. Unload your bike and ride across the bridge.

If you are new to the sport and want to earn bragging rights for having survived fat-tire trails in Cali, try Crystal Springs Reservoir, in the South Bay. The heart barely pumps and the adrenaline stays at a minimum on the flat wooded path that starts at the gate jsut off the Highway 92 West Exit. The path circles the reservoir eventually depositing you at the dam where another trail heading to Skyline Boulevard intersects. Your only obstacles are joggers and trees.

The all-inclusive combo recreational/sightseeing haven is of course Angel Island. Again, take the ferry from Fisherman's Wharf or Tiburon to get there; bikes are permitted on the ferry for free except from Tiburon where they charge you $1. You can also rent one on the island (see above), but rentals are cheaper on the mainland. There are about eight miles of easy, unpaved fire roads to explore, and the scenery is terrific, especially from the upper fire road. Alas, mountain bikes are not permitted on trails on the island and ferry service is limited to weekends in the winter.

Beaches

All you Bay Watch wannabe's the bad news is that it's usually too chilly to put on those teeny-weenie bikinis and lather up on the beach. The Pacific is frigid—just dip your toes in and see—and the unpredictable fog causes lines at most area tanning salons. But just because the Bay Area beaches aren't perfect for sunbathing or swimming doesn't eliminate them altogether. Most are Hollywood-perfect with cliffs breathing down over quiet coves, and each beach creates a unique vibe appreciated by natives and remembered by visitors. To highlight these unique uses and features, we've compiled a rather unofficial survey of what's on offer at the beaches by the bay.

Best Contemplative Currents **Muir Beach** in Marin County off Highway 1 (west of Highway 101—take the Stinson Beach/Mill Valley exit) with its pristine sand and quaint cove surrounded by towering cliffs, is the best beach to bring a copy of *Conversations with God,* or your journal. It's quiet and just an all-around good beach.

Biggest Waves **Ocean Beach** is the best place to watch surfers who come for the picture-perfect pipes. The Great Highway, which runs parallel to Ocean Beach's four miles (the longest beach in the Bay Area), is sometimes closed due to the too-close-for-car-comfort crashing waves. The water is treacherous even when it looks calm so use extreme caution if wading or swimming.

Most Romantic Beach **Drake's Beach** along Point Reyes National Seashore, off Highway 1, with its sheltered beach, towering white cliffs breathing down upon the fine sand is one of the most romantic. The drive to get there is all part of the seduction.

Best Beach to Recreate Scenes from "Beach Blanket Bingo" Even the road getting there—along Highway 1 off of 101 is good for a party. Put the top down on the car and wind over narrow cliff clinging roads down to the lively, friend gathering **Stinson Beach.**

Best Birthday Suit Beach **North Baker Beach** is the most popular naked spot in the city. The sand is clean and the parking lot safe. Temps are chilly though . . . so beware. Also, nudity is not permitted at the south end of the beach. The beach is located at Lincoln Boulevard and

Bowley Street, near 25th Avenue. Honorable mentions include: **Fort Funston,** off of Great Highway north of Skyline Boulevard; **Lands End** on the western edge of the city (popular with gay men), just above Cliff House on the Great Highway.

Best Beach for the Little Ones   The stretch of **China Beach** is small enough to keep an eye on them and all facilities including picnic tables, and restrooms are spotless (would you expect anything less in the Seacliff neighborhood?) You can also walk up Seacliff Avenue past the mauve house flying the flag with the blue wolf on it—that's where Robin Williams lives.

Best Beach for Fido   If you couldn't stomach leaving the dog at the kennel, the beach along **Crissy Field** at the end of the Marina Green is small but it is one huge frolicking playground for the pups. Let 'em loose and sit back and enjoy the wind and kite surfers circle the pillars of the Golden Gate Bridge. (Don't forget the plastic gloves to de-poop the beach of your doggy's droppings).

A Note on Nudity

Many beaches around San Francisco allow nudity, with the interesting caveats that you don't touch anybody and nobody complains. (If you equate nudity with sex, keep in mind that in the Golden Gate National Recreation Area, where many of the nude beaches are located, public sex is a federal offense.) Other negatives to lounging in the buff at San Francisco beaches include cool temperatures, fog, wind, rocky beaches with little or no sand, and gawkers. In addition, many of the beaches are difficult to reach, requiring long walks on narrow, steep paths lined with poison oak.

Sea Kayaking

The currents in the bay are quite tough to maneuver but despite this, kayakers come from all over to slide their sleek craft—a stable, covered boat similar to a canoe but propelled by a double-bladed paddle—into the waters off San Francisco. **Sea Trek Ocean Kayaking Center** offers tours for novices around Angel Island, Sausalito, and Point Reyes. A novice can glide out from Sausolito's Schoonamaker Point marina and join seals, pelicans, and even the occasional whale in Richardson Bay. Rentals for single kayaks: $15 for the first hour and $10 each additional hour; double kayaks are $30 the first hour and $10 each additional hour. Wetsuits, paddle jackets, sprayskirts, paddles, pumps, and paddle floats are included with rentals. Call (415) 488-1000 for more information; or visit www.sea trekkayak.com. To check on tide conditions look up www.tidesonline.nos. noaa.gov before heading out.

Blue Waters Kayaking in Marin County offers instruction, rentals, and tours in Point Reyes and Tomales Bay; no experience is necessary for some tour packages. They offer a half-day morning tour from 10 a.m. to 1 p.m. for $49; $79 for their "Day on the Bay" tour. An all-day introductory kayaking course is $79. Sea kayak rentals start at $30 for 2 hours and $50 for 4 hours. Double kayaks start at $40 for 2 hours and $70 for 4 hours. For reservations and more information, call (415) 669-2600; www.bwkayak.com.

Rock Climbing

If you have already tried the plastic holds of an indoor climbing gym and want to test your skill on real granite there is no better destination than the Bay Area. **Yosemite** is *the* climbing destination and it is only about a three-hour drive away! Closer still is **Red Rock Beach,** south of Stinson Beach off of Highway 1 at mile post 11.43. Mickey's, as locals call it, is a demanding rock with a dazzling ocean view. It's face rises and falls with 55 feet of cracks and crevices. You just may want to look down here—nudists populate the beach below. Because the Pacific pounds below access to most of its face depends on tides. Safety check: the rock isn't appropriate for beginners, and tides control access to most of its face (so check www.tidesonline.nos.noaa.gov before heading up). Skilled climbers only.

Climbers of all levels can head to a more controlled environment at **Mission Cliffs,** the Bay Area's indoor climbing gym (see page 359).

Hang Gliding

With its persistent coastal winds, San Francisco is an excellent place to go hang gliding. The **San Francisco Hang Gliding Center** specializes in tandem hang-gliding flights. You can see some of Northern California's most beautiful terrain while flying with Bodhi Kroll, (510) 528-2300; www.sfhanggliding.com), a pro with an unblemished 14-year safety record. The basic tandem flight is $275 ($325 weekends). Simply call can you can arrange a meeting spot at the alunch—usually Mount Tamalpais. From there you glide to the north end of Stinson Beach. If you'd rather just watch, head for Fort Funston south of Ocean Beach, where hang gliders launch off 200-foot cliffs and soar on coastal breezes. There are benchee atop the cliff that are perfect for observing. Be careful not to enter the launch and landing zone. Pilots are pretty adamant about it.

Sailing

San Francisco Bay, one of the largest and most beautiful harbors in the world, is also a major yachting center—although sailing on the bay is challenging even for the most experienced sailor. Certified skippers can charter anything from day sailors to luxury yachts and sail past all the landmarks that make the bay so famous. Don't know a spinnaker from a jib? You can also learn how to sail while you're on vacation in San Francisco.

Cass' Marina charters day sailors that accommodate up to 6 people, starting at $127 a day on weekdays; each boat is equipped with toilet facilities and life vests. Cruising boats for large daytime outings or overnight charters start at $243 a day; weekend, 5-day, and weekly rates are also available. Cass' offers a full compliment of instructional courses for beginners to advanced sailors. A basic keelboat certification course with 29 hours of instruction is $775; completion qualifies you to bareboat (no crew) charter a cruising sailboat. Private instruction is available for about $284 for 3 hours on weekdays (for 1 or 2 people), and $315 on weekends. Cass' Marina is located at 1702 Bridgeway at Napa Street in Sausalito (across the bay from San Francisco); (415) 332-6789; www.cassmarina.com, for more information.

Also in Sausalito is **Atlantis Yacht Charters,** where you can charter 30-foot and longer yachts. Bareboat charters start at $295 a day for an Ericson 30 that sleeps 4; a Nordic 44 goes for $600 a day midweek and sleeps 7 adults. Skippered charters start at $575 for 4 hours midweek; the price includes captain, yacht, and fuel. For more information, call (800) 65-YACHT; or visit www.yachtcharter.com.

Horseback Riding

San Francisco's only equestrian center used to be Golden Gate Park Stables, located in Golden Gate Park at Kennedy Drive and 36th Avenue. The stables have been closed since September 2001. There are efforts to save the stables and if you feel so inclined to help, visit www.savethestables.com.

Windsurfing and Kitesurfing

Good coastal winds make San Francisco one of the top spots in the country for windsurfing, and the increasingly popular kitesurfing, where riders are lifted out of the water by, yep, you guessed it, one big kite. The premier location in the city is **Crissy Field,** where experienced board sailors frolic on wind and waves. Newcomers can learn the basic skills of this difficult sport in the more gentle environment of Lake Merced and its consistent, gentle breezes. The **San Francisco School of Windsurfing** offers a 3-hour beginner course at the freshwater lake for $100 a person. After land instruction, students work in the water until they become proficient at the skills of sailing in light winds; once certified, they can rent equipment at Lake Merced. For more information, call the school at (415) 753-3235; or look up www.sfwindsurf.com.

Golf

San Francisco has two municipal golf courses that are open to the public. **Golden Gate Park Course** (47th Avenue and Fulton Street; (415) 751-8987) is a small 9-hole course covering 1,357 yards. It is open every day,

6:30 a.m. until dusk. Green fees are $8 during the week and $10 on weekends **Lincoln Park Golf Course** (34th Avenue and Clement Street; (415) 750-4653) offers 18 holes and covers 5,081 yards. The oldest course in the city, it offers beautiful views and fairways—just stop and check out what's in front of you at the 13th hole! It is open every day, 6:30 a.m. until dusk. Green fees are $23 during the week and $27 on weekends and holidays. In Berkeley, the Tilden Park Golf Course (Grizzly Peak Blvd, and Shasta Road (510) 848-7373; www.tildenparkgold. com) offers the best deals in town. It's easy and cheap to get in 18 holes before dark—it's a $20 twilight rate. If you consider yourself more of a morning golfer—how does $15 sound to you?

Tennis

More than 140 tennis courts are operated throughout the city by the San Francisco Recreation and Parks Department. All are available free on a first-come, first-served basis, with the exception of 21 courts in **Golden Gate Park,** where a fee is charged and reservations must be made in advance for weekend play. The courts are locates off Kennedy Drive opposite the Conservatory; individual and group lessons are available.

To make weekend reservations at a court in Golden Gate Park, call (41 5) 753-7101 on the preceding Wednesday evening between 4 and 6 p.m. , the preceding Thursday between 9:15 a.m. and 5 p.m., or the preceding Friday between 9:15 and 11:30 a.m. (Call Wednesday evening to avoid disappointment.) The nonresident court fee is $8 for a 90-minute play period. For more information and the locations of other courts around San Francisco, call the parks department at (415) 753-7100; or visit www.parks.sfgov.org.

Fishing

Deep-sea fishing charter boats leave Fisherman's Wharf daily, depending on weather and season. Catches in the Pacific waters beyond the Golden Gate include salmon, sea bass, halibut, striped bass, bonito, shark, tuna, and albacore. Licenses (required), rods, and tackle are available on board; plan for wind and some rough seas, and bring motion-sickness preventatives and warm clothing. *Miss Farallones,* a 50-foot charter boat, sets out on sportfishing expeditions from Fisherman's Wharf most days and can carry up to 38 passengers. For rates and more information, call (510) 352-5708; www.sfsportfishing.com.

Freshwater fishing is available at **Lake Merced,** south of downtown where Skyline Boulevard meets the Great Highway at the Pacific coast. Large trout and some catfish and bass are stocked in the 360-acre lake, which is open year-round. Anglers must purchase a $9.70 one-day fishing license and pay a $4 access fee. Rowboats are available for rent for $11 an hour. Paddleboats, which can hold up to 4 people, rent for $15 an hour. They no longer rent electric boats. You can also fish from the bank of the lake, which stocks trophy trout of two pounds and more. For more information, call (415) 752-7869.

Nature Viewing

Whale Watching

Each year gray whales embark on one of the longest migrations of any mammal, and the coast near San Francisco is one of the best places to observe these giants during their 6,000-mile journey between their Arctic feeding grounds and Baja, California. The nonprofit **Oceanic Society** offers naturalist-led expeditions year-round to observe the whales and nature cruises to the Farallon Islands, stark granite cliffs 27 miles from the Golden Gate that teem with marine life.

Gray whale cruises depart from San Francisco at 9:30 a.m. on selected dates from December to May and last six hours, returning to the dock at 4 p.m. Rates for adults start at $50; bring your own lunch and beverages. The expedition transports guests under the Golden Gate Bridge and north along the Marin coast to search for gray whales off the Bolinas and Point Reyes areas.

Farallon Islands nature cruises depart at 8:30 a.m. on selected dates from June through November and last eight hours. Rates for adults start at $60; bring your own lunch and beverages. The cruise sails under the Golden Gate Bridge and goes west to the Farallon Islands, where a quarter-million seabirds nest and visible marine mammals include California sea lions, Steller's sea lions, northern elephant seals, harbor seals, and possibly humpback and blue whales. A not so visible resident is the Great White— this is the largest breeding ground in the world for them after all!

All cruises are aboard the *New Superfish,* a 63-foot Coast Guard–certified, fully-insured motor vessel with an open observation deck, indoor salon, and a passenger capacity of 49. Off-street parking is available at the harbor at Fort Mason. Youths ages 15 and under must be accompanied by an adult, and children ages 10 and under aren't permitted on the boat. Reservations are required; call (800) 326-7491 or (415) 474-3385 for a schedule, and make reservations at least two weeks in advance (although it's possible to get aboard at the last minute if there are cancellations). Look up www.oceanic-society.org for more information.

Bring rain gear and warm clothing; the cruises depart rain or shine. Don't forget binoculars, a camera with a telephoto lens, sunscreen, and motion-sickness medicine. More advice: bring crackers to nibble and ginger ale to sip to help avoid queasiness on the cruise. If you are taking seasickness medication be sure to take it before you depart. Once the sickness starts it is too late.

California Sea Lions and Seals

OK, it may not be the most pristine of scenes but the California Sea Lions that bark, clap, and flop over the floating piers at Pier 39 near Fisherman's Wharf are certainly worth a trip. Otherwise, you can usually spot them popping up for air at any point along the bay. **The Marine Mammal Center** in Fort Cronkite near Rodeo Lagoon in the Marin Headlands, (415) 289-7325, is where you can go to see marine biologists nurse ailing and orphaned California sea lions and seals back to health. You can watch pups being bottle-fed, and ask questions about them as well as the whales found in these waters. A great place for the family.

Zebra?

Yes, zebra as well as giraffes, lemurs, several cats, and other exotic game can be found at **Safari West Wildlife Preserve and Tent Camp** (3115 Porter Creek Road, Santa Rosa; (707) 579-2551; safariwest@safari west.com) The sanctuary is one of a few in North America that sets out to protect these endangered species through breeding, education, and research. It is home to over 400 mammals and birds. In fact, two species of bird—the white-naped crane and the Indian hornbill—are currently registered with the international Species Survival Program.

To go on "safari" you will need to make reservation. Tours run at 9 a.m., noon, and 3 p.m. in the summer season, or 10 a.m. and 2 p.m. the remainder of the year. The tours, consisting of both driving and walking portions, last two-and-a-half hours and are guided by a naturalist. Prices for adults are $48, and for children under 14 years, $24. The adventurous can choose to make a weekend out of it and rent one of the tents for $225 per night per couple, two night minimum. If the thought of a wild cat creeping up on you in the middle of the night makes the hairs on your arms stand up, you can stay in the luxurious resort for a whopping $500 per night on weekends and $450 on weekdays. The price includes four adults and a two-night minimum. It's great to do this with a group.

Bird Watching

Point Reyes National Seashore is probably the premier place to bring the binoculars and spot birds like California Quail, Anna's and Allen's, Hummingbirds, Nuttall's Woodpecker, Pacific-slope Flycatcher, Hutton's Vireo, Chestnut-backed Chickadee, Oak Titmouse, Pygmy Nuthatch, Wrentit, and California Towhee. Seabirds such as Red-throated and Pacific Loons, Brown Pelicans are also primary residents of this bird haven. You can head on a self-guided tour if you are an experienced bird peeper, or for tour information call (415) 454-5100. The park service offers a Beginning Birding tour once a month on Sundays, as well as guided tours to the lighthouse on Saturday, Sunday, and Monday at 12:30 p.m. Alcatraz island is also becoming quite a bird sanctuary.

Black-crowned Night Heron are one of many bird species that nest on Alcatraz. For guided tours, call (415) 705-5555.

Spectator Sports

By and large, San Franciscans are sports enthusiasts—not just in participatory activities such as running, biking, and tennis. In fact, Bay Area fans' dedication to their professional sports teams can verge on the obsessive. How much so? Enough that the San Francisco Giants just got a new multimillion dollar stadium. The professional sports scene in the Bay Area includes football, baseball, basketball, and horse racing.

Pro Teams

Baseball

The National League **San Francisco Giants** play home games at the new Pacific Bell Park, located at 24 Willie Mays Plaza in the China Basin area, south of Market Street. The season starts in April and goes through October. Tickets are usually available up until game time., but the seats can be regrettably far from the on-field action. Tickets are available through Tickets.com.

The American League **Oakland Athletics,** the 1989 world champs, play at the sunnier Oakland Coliseum across the bay (take the Hegenberger Road exit off I-880). The stadium seats 50,000 fans and is served by BART's Coliseum station. Tickets to home games are available from the coliseum box office or by phone from Tickets.com.

Football

The **San Francisco 49ers,** five-time Super Bowl champs, play home games at 3Com Park Sundays from August through December. They're best known for their intelligence, speed, and grace. Good luck getting tickets, though. The games sell out early in the season but sometimes select tickets are available; call the box office at (415) 468-2249. If you're willing to pay an inflated price, tickets may be available from ticket agent s before game days and from scalpers at the gate; expect to pay up to $10 0 for a seat. Talk to your hotel concierge or stop by City Box Office (141 Kearny Street; (415) 392-4400). Muni operates special express buses to the park, located about eight miles south of downtown, from Market Street on game days; call (415) 673-6864 for more information.

Also, the Bay Area has two pro football teams again. Across the bay are the 49ers' arch enemy the **Oakland Raiders,** who returned to Oakland from Los Angeles in 1995 after abandoning the city for sunny South ern California 13 years before. Known as blue-collar heroes the team charges country-club prices; expect to pay at least $60 for a ticket. Home games are played at the Oakland Alameda County Coliseum off I-880. For tickets information, call (800) 949-2626.

Basketball

The Bay Area's NBA team is the **Golden State Warriors,** who play in the newly renovated Oakland Coliseum Arena across the bay. The season runs from November through April; most games start at 7:30 p.m. The arena is located at the Hegenberger Road Exit off I-880, south of downtown Oakland. For tickets, go to Tickets.com or www.gs-warriors.com.

If you aren't so interested in spending half your vacation money on courtside tickets consider heading to the San Francisco Bay Area Pro-Am Summer Basketball League. It's free—but the talent is top notch. Top pro and former collegiate players gather in Kezar Pavilion from mid-June through mid-August to stay on top of their game. You can get your hoop thrills at 755 Stanyan Street; www.sanfranciscoproam.com.

Horse Racing

The Bay Area is home to two horse-racing tracks. **Scenic Golden Gate Fields,** located in the East Bay off Gilman Street (off I-80 in Albany, ten miles northeast of San Francisco), features thoroughbred racing from November through January and March through June. For post times and more information, call (510) 559-7300; or visit www.ggfields.com.

The autumn racing closest to San Francisco is at **Bay Meadows,** south of San Francisco in San Mateo (on US 101 at the Hillsdale exit). The thoroughbred and quarter-horse track hosts races Wednesday through Sunday from January through March and September through November. It's one of the oldest, busiest, and most beautiful ovals in California. For more information and post times, call (650) 574-7223; or visit www.baymeadows.com.

Amateur Sports

Local college gridiron action is provided by the **University of California Golden Bears,** who play at Memorial Stadium across the bay in Berkeley. For game times and ticket information, call (800) GO-BEARS; or visit www.calbears.com; tickets are usually available on game day. From November to March the Bears men's basketball squad plays at the new $40 milllion Haas pavilion, which opened on campus in 1999.

The **University of San Francisco Dons** men's basketball team provides on-the-court excitement from November to March at the War Memorial Gymnasium on campus (5300 Golden Gate Avenue). Games start at 7 p.m.; for tickets and schedules, call (415) 422-6USF or visit Tickets.com.

Events for the Outdoor Enthusiast

Contact the Visitors and Conventions Bureau for up-to-date information regarding these events and possible participation. (415) 391-2000; www.sfvisitor.org.

Escape from Alcatraz Triathalon   Amateur and professional athletes make the 1.5-mile swim from Alcatraz Island in the treacherous waters of the bay. The race continues with an 18-mile bike ride out to the Great Highway, through the Golden Gate Park, and concludes with an 8-mile run through the Golden Gate National Recreation Area. The finish is at The Marina Green for the Fitness Festival.

San Francisco Grand Prix   This 125-mile biking race starts and finishes on the Embarcadero at the end of Market Street. From the start/finish lines, the course winds through North Beach, along Fisherman's Wharf and the Marina. Halfway through the ten-mile circuit, the flatlands along the scenic bay give way to the intense climb up Fillmore Street. The event is for professionals only, and many from the Tour-de-France attend. For information check out the website at www.sfgrandprix.com.

Bay to Breakers Foot Race   Not quite for the competitive at heart, although serious runners do compete. Most come dressed in costume or not (clothes optional) and bring everything including the kitchen sink and kegs of beer. Anyone can participate in this annual spring ritual usually held in May.

San Francisco Chronicle **Marathon**   For the big guns who can handle the 26.2 mile course, and even for those who want to participate in half of that in the Split the Distance Marathon, Half Marathon, or 5K Fun Run—all on the same day, usually in July each year. The course takes in the "best of San Francisco," offering a scenic loop. For more information including how to registe,r check out the website at www.chronicle marathon.com; or call (800) 698-8699.

Index